OPTICAL AND ELECTRO-OPTICAL
INFORMATION PROCESSING

OPTICAL AND ELECTRO-OPTICAL
INFORMATION PROCESSING

Edited by

James T. Tippett
David A. Berkowitz
Lewis C. Clapp
Charles J. Koester
Alexander Vanderburgh, Jr.

THE MASSACHUSETTS INSTITUTE OF TECHNOLOGY PRESS

Cambridge, Massachusetts and London, England

Second Printing, November 1968

Library of Congress Catalog Card Number 65-20593
Printed in the United States of America

PREFACE

This volume comprises the Proceedings of the Symposium on Optical and Electro-Optical Information Processing Technology which was held in Boston, Massachusetts, on November 9 and 10, 1964. The meeting was co-sponsored by the Professional Group on Electronic Computers of the Institute of Electrical and Electronics Engineers, Boston Chapter; the New England Section of the Optical Society of America; the Greater Boston Chapter of the Association for Computing Machinery; and the Office of Naval Research. Approximately 800 scientists and engineers attended the symposium. The objectives of the sponsors were to bring together once again research workers in the fields of optics and information processing in order to promote information exchange through the presentation of scientific papers, through the medium of informal discussion, and through the dissemination of recently generated research results by means of the publication of a symposium proceedings. Because of time limitations on the oral presentations the authors were encouraged, in the preconference instructions, to include in their manuscripts any additional pertinent material which they could not present during their session. The manuscripts were submitted at the meeting.

The interest in optics and electro-optics for use in information processing devices, circuits, and systems appears to be constantly increasing. This interest stems from the never-ending search to increase the speed, reliability, capacity, capability, and utility while decreasing the cost of modern computing machines. Thus any contribution that can be obtained by using optics to improve the ability for humans to interact with the processing system, to increase the number of logical functions performed per unit time, and to make the results available in the most usable form will be of great value to the field of information processing, provided these advances can be achieved competitively on an economical basis.

The first of the series of technical meetings co-sponsored by the Office of Naval Research on the use of optics in information sciences was the "Symposium on Optical Character Recognition," held on January 15, 16, and 17, 1962, in Washington, D. C. The second technical meeting of this type was the "Symposium on Optical Processing of Information," held on October 23 and 24, 1962, in Washington, D. C. These proceedings report on the third technical meeting in this series.

This conference was gratifying because of the participation and splendid cooperation given by the three professional societies that co-sponsored the symposium. Important benefits were derived through the participation of all of the organizations involved. These included the interchange of information between groups of varied scientific backgrounds and the establishment of warm personal contacts which should ensure future cooperation and exchange of information between these professional groups.

Many individuals and organizations made significant contributions to this symposium and its proceedings. Without their contributions, it would have been impossible to conduct such a meeting. Sincere appreciation is expressed to each of the following individuals and their organizations.

CONFERENCE COMMITTEE CO-CHAIRMEN

Donald K. Pollock, CHAIRMAN   *Office of Naval Research*
Lewis C. Clapp*   *Bolt Beranek and Newman Inc. (ACM)*
Charles J. Koester   *American Optical Company (OSA)*
Alexander Vanderburgh, Jr.   *M.I.T., Lincoln Laboratory (IEEE)*

PROGRAM COMMITTEE

James T. Tippett, CHAIRMAN   *Department of Defense*
David A. Berkowitz   *The MITRE Corporation*
Lewis C. Clapp*   *Bolt Beranek and Newman Inc.*
Charles J. Koester   *American Optical Company*
Alexander Vanderburgh, Jr.   *M.I.T., Lincoln Laboratory*

ARRANGEMENTS COMMITTEE

John O'Brien, CHAIRMAN   *Itek Corporation*
Robert L. Cushman   *Control Data Corporation*
Louis Sutro   *M.I.T.*
Jay Blum   *System Development Corporation*

TREASURER

Edward R. Santoro   *Bolt Beranek and Newman Inc.*

INFORMATION CENTRAL

Barbara McKinney   *Computer Associates, Inc.*

* Present affiliation: Computer Research Corporation.

REGISTRATION

James T. Tippett   *Department of Defense*

PRESS RELATIONS

Geraldine Carey   *Bolt Beranek and Newman Inc.*
Russell Greenbaum   *Office of Naval Research*

At the Office of Naval Research, the acknowledgment includes all members of the Information Systems Branch, the staff of the Administrative Services Branch, the scientific staff of the ONR Boston Branch Office, and Dr. F. T. Byrne of the Physics Branch. Sincere appreciation is expressed to the Naval Research Laboratory's Technical Information Division which provided announcements, programs, and badges.

At the Department of Defense and several private industrial organizations and educational institutions, the acknowledgment includes the many associates, co-workers, and supervisors of the individuals listed above.

Our appreciation is expressed to the authors of the papers in whose hands rests the ultimate success or failure of the meeting. Our sincere thanks are extended to the session chairman, to the keynote speaker, Dr. John R. Pierce of the Bell Telephone Laboratories, Inc., and Dr. W. V. Smith of Thomas J. Watson Research Center, International Business Machines Corporation, who gave the critique at the end of the symposium. Finally, the committee would like to thank the M.I.T. Press for the cooperation it has given in preparing and publishing this book.

DONALD K. POLLOCK
Office of Naval Research
Conference Committee Chairman

CONTENTS

x   Contents

CHAPTER GUIDE TO SUBJECT CONTENTS

AN OPTICALLY ACCESSED MEMORY USING THE LIPPMANN PROCESS FOR INFORMATION STORAGE *

H. Fleisher, P. Pengelly, J. Reynolds, R. Schools, and G. Sincerbox

Development Laboratory, Data Systems Division
International Business Machines Corporation, Poughkeepsie, New York

Introduction

The standing-wave read-only memory is based on the Lippmann process, originally proposed as a method of color photography. In this process, a panchromatic photographic emulsion is placed in contact with a metallic mirror, historically mercury. Sufficiently coherent light passes normally through the emulsion, reflects from the mirror, and returns through the emulsion. This sets up standing waves with a node at the metallic mirror surface. Developable silver ions form in the regions of the antinodes of the standing wave. On processing, a periodic layer structure of reduced silver is set up. Because of the periodic variation in index of refraction, interference occurs in the reflected light; constructive interference occurs only for the wavelength which originally set up the layers during exposure. Hence the reflected light wavelength is an accurate reproduction of the exposing light wavelength.†

Furthermore, if several anharmonic wavelengths are used to expose the same region of the emulsion, each will set up a separate layer structure, provided the grain size is sufficiently small. Broadband light energy, which now is reflected from the emulsion, will contain all of the original wavelengths. Conceivably n color sources spaced appropriately over the band of sensitivity could provide n information bits, one per color, at each location.

* Work performed under Government Contract No. AF33-657-11589, Aeronautical Systems Division, Wright-Patterson Air Force Base, Ohio.
† This is true except for shrinkage effects that occur during processing.

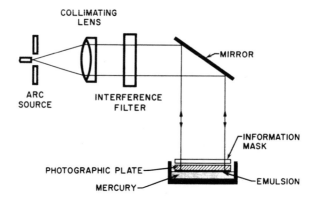

FIG. 1. Setup for making Lippmann exposures.

The reflected light can be detected by a photodetector, i.e., photomulti-pliers. One convenient method involves the use of a dispersive material, such as a grating which spatially separates the wavelengths, allowing each bit to be read in parallel. Another method uses the Bragg effect, which causes the reflected light to shift to shorter wavelengths as the angle of incidence increases. (See Appendix III for a more complete discussion.) With this method, a monochromatic light source, say of violet color, could read out the violet bit at normal incidence and the red bit at the appropriate angle from normal. Hence, a single monochromatic source, such as a laser, could be used to read out all bits. See Fig. 22, Appendix III. Both methods have been demonstrated during the course of this work.

A simple diagram of the exposure device is shown in Fig. 1. A source of light covering the wavelengths of interest is condensed and collimated. The light passes through a filter of narrow enough bandwidth to set up the coherence length sufficient for the thickness of the emulsion. The light is

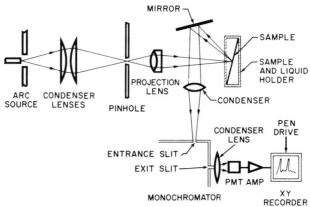

FIG. 2. Experimental readout system.

directed through an "information mask" which exposes an appropriate pattern on the sample.

Once the emulsion is processed, the reflected spectrum is read and recorded. An experimental readout system is shown in Fig. 2. Here, a microscope objective projects a small spot of light onto the sample. The sample is held in a filter cell filled with a fluid which matches the emulsion index of refraction. This minimizes unwanted reflections from the emulsion surfaces. The sample is placed at an angle to the face of the cell so that the light reflected from the cell face and the Lippmann reflection can be separated. The light is directed into a monochromator and photomultiplier tube. The resulting electrical signal is amplified and displayed on an x-y recorder.

Writing/Reading

Exposure

In order that the active memory region have high bit capacity, the signal due to each bit must cover less than $1/m$th of the usable wavelength range, m being the number of bits/cell, in addition to having a reasonably high signal-to-noise ratio. A large number of reflecting planes within the emulsion is required for large signal and small bandwidth on readout. The grain size of the emulsion must also be small so that many separate layer structures (for large values of m) may be recorded.

Ideally, the standing wave during exposure should cover the full thickness of the emulsion. This means that the coherence length of the exposing light must be at least twice the emulsion thickness, and the absorption of the emulsion must not be so large that there is no standing-wave amplitude left at the top surface of the emulsion.

The optimum emulsion thickness t_0 for use with the writing bandwidth $\Delta\lambda_w$ is

$$t_0 = \frac{\lambda_w{}^2}{2n\ \Delta\lambda_w} = \frac{\lambda_w}{2n}\ \frac{\lambda_w}{\Delta\lambda_w}$$

where

$$n = \text{emulsion index of refraction}$$
$$\lambda_w = \text{writing wavelength}$$

The term $\lambda_w{}^2/\Delta\lambda_w$ is the well-known "coherence length" of a light wave train. This distance must, of course, equal twice the emulsion thickness for it to be fully used. The form of the previous expression written on the right shows the relation of the distance between antinodes ($\lambda_w/2n$) and the character of the source ($\lambda_w/\Delta\lambda_w$). See Appendix I for a further discussion of this expression.

This last term also equals the number of possible layers within the emulsion. It is noted in the following that the peak reflected intensity for no absorption is proportional to N^2 (N = number of layers) or $(\lambda_w/\Delta\lambda_w)^2$. We have used filters with a bandwidth of about 5 Å with zirconium and mercury arc sources. These filters provide a coherence length which could fill emulsions of 200μ thickness. This is larger by an order of magnitude than emulsion thicknesses commercially available now. Our standard emulsion is the 15μ 649F Eastman Kodak spectroscopic plate. According to the literature, Lippmann-type emulsions typically have grain sizes around 0.05μ corresponding to $1/10\lambda$ for green light.[1] This would limit the wavelength separation of adjacent signals to about 500 Å. However, we have achieved readout of 50-Å bandwidth lines with separations of 100 Å. This would indicate an average grain size apparently much smaller than 0.05μ, i.e., $<0.01\mu$. This grain size corresponds to a surface resolution of about 10,000 lines per mm, which is well above the published data for the 649F emulsion.

Readout

When light of intensity I_0 is incident on a periodic reflecting structure of N layers, the expression governing the reflected light intensity I is that of the interference term in the diffraction grating, namely,

$$I = I_0 \left(\frac{\sin Nz}{\sin z}\right)^2$$

where z = phase difference between successive rays. It is approximately true in our case because it assumes (1) no absorption within the emulsion, and (2) that the incident intensity is effective throughout the emulsion. In addition, it accounts for no multiple reflections within the layer system. In spite of these restrictions, it has been useful in predicting the readout signal bandwidth.

The bandwidth of the reflected light signal $\Delta\lambda_R$, (i.e., full width at $\frac{1}{2}$ peak intensity level) can be determined from the expression

$$\frac{\sin Nz}{\sin z} = \sqrt{\tfrac{1}{2}}$$

For large N,

$$\Delta\lambda_R \approx \frac{0.9\lambda_R}{N}$$

where λ_R = reflected light wavelength. The readout wavelength need not be the same as the exposing wavelength. This is due to effects of processing which may cause the emulsion to swell or shrink, thereby changing the layer separation. If we represent this change by the shrinking factor

$$k = \frac{t_0}{t}$$

where t = emulsion thickness after processing, then the readout bandwidth is

$$\Delta\lambda_R \approx \frac{0.9\lambda_R{}^2}{2nt} = \frac{0.9\lambda_R{}^2}{2nt_0}k$$

See Appendix II for expanded discussion of this expression. It is shown there that the shrinkage factor is also equal to λ_w/λ_R. Hence the expression can be written

$$\Delta\lambda_R = \frac{0.9\lambda_w{}^2}{2nt_0k}$$

In Fig. 3 is shown the relationship between $\Delta\lambda_R$ and emulsion thickness t_0 for various exposing wavelengths with no shrinkage (i.e., $k = 1$). The

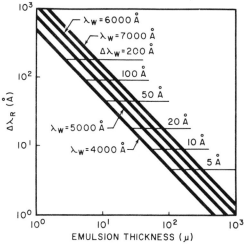

Fig. 3. Readout bandwidth versus emulsion thickness.

decrease in $\Delta\lambda_R$ as t increases is apparent. The relationship between $\Delta\lambda_w$, the writing wavelength bandwidth, and emulsion thickness is also presented in Fig. 3. The optimum thickness is shown by the intersection of the horizontal line corresponding to exposing bandwidth and the slant line corresponding to the wavelength used. The readout bandwidth for emulsions of greater thickness is limited only by the exposing bandwidth. For thinner emulsions, the readout bandwidth is limited by the emulsion thickness.

Using the 5 Å filters to expose the 15μ 649F emulsion, we have achieved, for single colors, bandwidths of about 50 Å at a 1 per cent to 4 per cent reflection intensity. The bandwidth is very close to the theoretically predicted value. In Table 1, a comparison between the theoretical and experimental results is given. For example, at $\lambda_w = 5461$ Å, λ_R is equal to 4450 Å because of shrinkage. The experimentally found readout bandwidth is 45 Å, while the predicted value for this case is 49 Å. As can be seen the agreement is very good. At the bottom of the table is the comparison for various emulsion thicknesses. At the far right is shown the coherence length $\Delta l'$

TABLE 1   COMPARISON OF THEORETICAL AND EXPERIMENTAL RESULTS

λ_w (Å)	λ_R (Å)	$\Delta\lambda_R$ (Å) (theory)	$\Delta\lambda_R$ (Å) (exp)	$\frac{1}{k} = \frac{\lambda_R}{\lambda_w}$
5461	4450	49	45	0.82
5790	4930	57	60	0.85
6104	5120	63	54	0.84
6708	5642	76	80	0.84

$$t_0 = 15\mu,\ \Delta\lambda_w = 5\ \text{Å}$$

t_0 (emulsion thickness)	$\Delta\lambda_w$ (Å)	λ_R (Å)	$\Delta\lambda_R$ (Å) (theory)	$\Delta\lambda_R$ (Å) (exp)	$\frac{\Delta l'}{2}$
2μ	100	5000	410	490	10μ
4μ	100	5380	210	250	10μ
15μ	100	5750	95	140	10μ
15μ	55	4700	52	98	18μ
15μ	5	4450	49	45	200μ

$$\lambda_w = 5461\ \text{Å},\ n = 1.5$$

corresponding to the given $\Delta\lambda_w$. It can be seen that for $t_0 = 2\mu$ and 15μ ($\Delta\lambda_w = 5$ Å), the bandwidth is limited by the emulsion thickness. There is good agreement for these extreme cases. For $t_0 = 15\mu$ and $\Delta\lambda_w = 55$ Å the parameters of emulsion and reflected coherence length are almost matched. For this condition, the results are not in agreement. This indicates that the definition of coherence length is not an exact one and that any "tails"

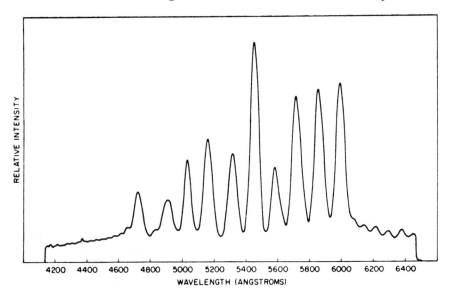

FIG. 4. Readout signal versus wavelength.

on the wave packet are affecting the results in a deleterious way. This result shows the importance of avoiding an exactly "matched" condition.

Ten color exposures were made with bit separations of 150 Å. See Fig. 4. The colors are well resolved but the magnitudes are not all equal. This is due in part to the envelope of the reading light spectrum.

In addition to the 15μ emulsions, we have exposed some special 26μ thick emulsions from Eastman Kodak. While the density of the thinner emulsion is about 0.3 (50 per cent transmission), that of the thicker is 0.48 (33 per cent transmission). The bandwidth of reflected light for the thicker emulsion was larger than that of the 15μ (single color). This would indicate that absorption is preventing the setting up of the standing wave through the full thickness of the emulsion. In fact, it appears that it is preventing the establishment of the equivalent number of layers, as in the thin emulsion.

Parameter Interrelationships

The exposed region for the ten-color shot shown in Fig. 4 was large (greater than 3 mm squared). One of the most important studies we are making is the effect on the parameter interrelationship (relative exposure, number of colors, sequence) as the exposed region is decreased to the proposed working spot size (20μ). The smallest exposed region observed to date has been the line groups on the USAF 1951 resolution chart ranging from 50 to 100 lines/mm. See Fig. 5. This corresponds to 0.0004 to 0.0008

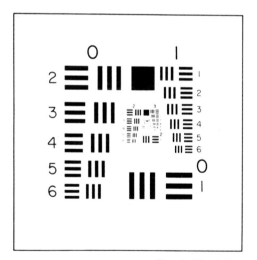

LINE WIDTH GROUP	RESOLVING POWER RANGE	
0	1.00 –	1.78 l/mm
1	2.00 –	3.56 l/mm
2	4.00 –	7.13 l/mm
3	8.00 –	14.30 l/mm
4	16.00 –	28.50 l/mm
5	32.00 –	57.00 l/mm
6	64.00 –	114.00 l/mm
7	128.00 –	228.00 l/mm

FIG. 5. Resolution chart.

in./line which are the equivalent of 10μ to 20μ spot diameters. The observation consisted of a visual check of the reflected color from the spots and a check on the Bragg effect.

Beam Convergence

An idealized requirement of the exposing (and readout) light beam is that it be highly collimated. In practice, of course, this condition cannot be completely met. Many factors enter, but the ultimate limit is that of diffraction. A derivation shows that the minimum beam diameter b_m for parallel light is

$$b_m = 2\sqrt{l\lambda}$$

where

$$\lambda = \text{light wavelength}$$
$$l = \text{beam length or throw}$$

If we take $\lambda = 5000$ Å and a throw of about 6 in. as being reasonable,

$$b_m = 0.02 \text{ in.}$$

In practice, however, the minimum diameter of a collimated beam might exceed 0.030 in. This would limit the surface cell density to 1000 cells/in².

The foregoing result indicates the need for a convergent beam. An idea of the improvement which can be had is shown from the following example. For a beam with a shallow convergence of $f/20$, the Rayleigh criterion indicates a spot separation of about 0.0005 in., which is a 40 times improvement. The convergence angle corresponding to $f/20$ is 2°.

The effect of beam convergence on the Lippmann standing wave during exposure is to spread the antinode region over the range

$$\Delta\lambda = \lambda_0 - \lambda_0 \cos\theta' = \lambda_0(1 - \cos\theta')$$

where

$$\lambda_0 = \text{exposing wavelength}$$
$$\theta' = \sin^{-1} \text{ N.A. within the emulsion}$$

This range on λ could limit the wavelength packing or the number of bits recorded within the wavelength range per bit location. For example, if $\theta = 2°$, $\lambda_0(1 - \cos\theta') = 0.00025\lambda_0 \sim 1$ Å. At bandwidths of 50 Å this effect should be negligible. However, if $\theta = 10°$, $\lambda_0(1 - \cos\theta') = 0.006 (5000) = 30$ Å.

During readout, the effect of beam convergence again spreads the bandwidth to the same extent as on exposure, i.e., by the $\Delta\lambda = \lambda_0(1 - \cos\theta')$ factor. If readout by the Bragg effect is included, this factor can be generalized to $\Delta\lambda = \lambda_0(\cos\theta' - \cos\theta_0')$. Since $\cos\theta$ increases more rapidly as θ increases from zero, this factor becomes more important and $\Delta\lambda$ increases much faster as θ increases. As shown in Fig. 6, a graph of this function indicates that if $\Delta\lambda$ is to be kept below 50 Å due to convergence spread alone, with a 2° convergence, the Bragg angle is limited to about 10° from the normal.

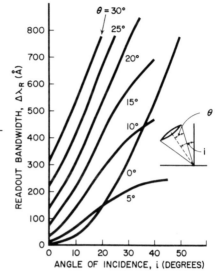

FIG. 6. Readout bandwidth versus angle of incidence.

Process Technology

Optimization of the readout characteristics of the standing-wave memory is controlled by proper choice and matching of both exposure and processing. Whereas only a few variables such as spectral sensitivity, grain size, time, and intensity are present in the production of the latent image, the processing of this image introduces several variables, including type, temperature, time, pH, and concentration of the various solutions. These variables are dependent on one another and must be thoroughly understood and controlled for proper optimization and reproducibility of results. The present investigational procedure has been to adopt a standard process and to make systematic variations in the parameters.

Basic Process

The process originally used was recommended by Eastman Kodak for their high-resolution plates. This process consists of:

1. Develop in Kodak D-19 developer for 5 min at 68 °F with continuous agitation.
2. Rinse in Kodak Stop Bath SB-5 for 30 sec at 65 to 70 °F with agitation.
3. Fix in Kodak Fixing Bath F-5 for 5 to 10 min at 65 to 70 °F with frequent agitation.
4. Wash for 20 to 30 min in running water at 65 to 70 °F.

In addition to the preceding, a bleaching step has been added to increase the transparency of the image. (The importance of this addition will be discussed later.)

5. Bleach in mercuric chloride solution for 30 sec at 65 to 70 °F.

6. Wash for 10 min in running water 65 to 70 °F.

7. Dry in dust-free area.

Using this process, the following observations and investigations have been made.

Development

Two major requirements exist for the development stage of the process. First, the developer must act uniformly throughout the depth of the emulsion to produce as many silver planes as possible. It is desirable that all of the planes be formed as identical to each other as possible. Next, the developer must be of the fine-grain, high-contrast class that will produce distinct, separate planes and not large masses of silver that might result in irregular or possibly overlapping planes.

The former requirement is of course a function of the thickness of the emulsion being used. For a very thick emulsion it is reasonable to expect that the developer will act on the outside surface to such a degree as to impede further penetration of developer into the underlying regions. If the developing times are correspondingly increased to allow full development of these underlying layers, then the surface will become greatly overdeveloped. This may be to such an extent as to completely destroy the near-surface planar structure in addition to preventing the reading light from reaching the lower lying planes. A subsequent broadening of reflection bandwidths and reduction of bit resolution and intensity would be expected. For thick emulsions, however, it is possible to employ a technique similar to that used in the processing of nuclear emulsions. This involves precooling of the developer to a temperature that renders it nearly inactive (approx. 5 °C for Amidol developer). The emulsion to be processed is brought to the same temperature by placing it in a room-temperature water bath and reducing the water temperature slowly to the same temperature as the developer. If the plate is now placed in the developer, the solution will penetrate into the emulsion with little or no developing action. The bath temperature is now elevated to allow the developer to act. Similar temperature variation is also employed in subsequent steps of the process to allow their full penetration and action.

This low-temperature process has provided excellent results for nuclear emulsions[2] and is expected to be of value in the Lippmann process. A similar process was tried with 4μ and 15μ emulsions with no observable changes in the readout spectum. It is evident that we have not as yet attained the thickness at which this effect becomes important. It is expected that 50μ and 100μ emulsions will require this process.

A preliminary investigation has been made into the effect of different developers. Kodak D-8, D-19, and Amidol were investigated, and D-19 appears to give the best results.

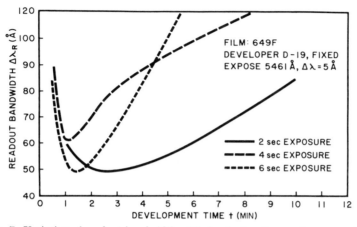

F<small>IG</small>. 7. Variation of readout bandwidth with developing time and exposure time.

The effect of developing time was investigated, and it was found that the time for optimum reflection bandwidth was dependent on the exposure time. See Fig. 7. Very short exposures require more development, and longer exposures require less development. In general, the optimum time was in the 1 to 5 min range with the variation in resulting bandwidth being only 10 per cent. If, however, the samples were unfixed, it was found that over the same range of exposures, the dependency on time relaxed. See Fig. 8. Consequently, a 2-min process in D-19 developer has been adopted unless further work indicates otherwise.

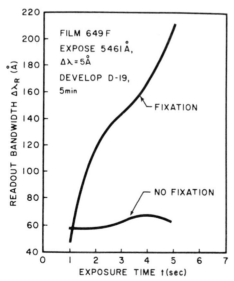

F<small>IG</small>. 8. Variation of readout bandwidth with exposure time for fixation and no fixation conditions.

When the latent image consists of discrete exposure spots, cells in this case, there will exist a discontinuous change in optical density as the emulsion surface is scanned. Such a discontinuity of latent image structure will give rise to adjacency effects.[3] One of these effects will appear as a line or border of high density surrounding the actual exposed spot. This is created by the developer that has penetrated the unexposed regions and hence is acting around the sides of the exposed region. Therefore, the image has greater access to fresh developer around its border than in the center resulting in a high-density border. This effect has been observed in Lippmann exposures and appears as a colored border around the exposed regions. It is expected that this effect will vanish as the spot size becomes very small due to the penetration depth of the developer from the sides becoming larger

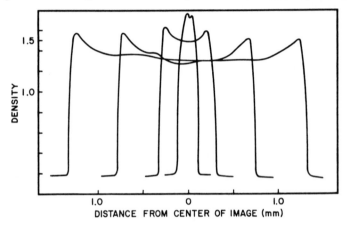

Fig. 9. Adjacency effect.

than the spot diameter. This will result in a very uniform reduction of the latent image. The effect may create problems only if the desired spot size is of the order of 0.5 mm or larger. See Fig. 9.

Rinsing

Following the development of the latent image, it is necessary to neutralize the action of the developer by placing it in a rinse bath. This may be either water or an acid stop bath. It is desirable to stop the development rapidly to prevent overdevelopment. For this, the acid stop bath is commonly used. This, however, presents a problem as the change in pH from developer to stop bath is very large (pH D-19 is 10.3, pH STOP is 3.3). This sudden change in pH can cause rapid and/or uneven swelling and contraction of the emulsion creating an effect called reticulation. It is expected that the separation of the silver planes will also be affected by relative swelling and/or contraction of the gelatin. If a permanent deformation or surface irregularity is produced, then the plane separation will vary correspondingly. This will cause the readout spectrum to vary according to the degree of deformation at the location being interrogated.

Fixation

The fixing bath must fulfill the primary function of dissolving the unexposed light-sensitive silver halide, prevent organic stain, and harden the gelatin to check its further swelling.

It is the removal of the unexposed silver halide that causes the emulsion to contract, decreasing the separation of the silver planes. As a result, the readout spectrum shifts to shorter wavelengths (toward the blue). This shift may be as large as 1000 Å depending on the total exposure. As the exposure or number of exposures is increased, more silver halide is reduced, leaving less unexposed silver halide to be dissolved, resulting in less contraction. It has been observed experimentally that the degree of wavelength shift does decrease as the number of exposed colors increases.

This effect can be greatly reduced by elimination of the fixation step completely; the unexposed silver halide is left in the emulsion causing the thickness to be relatively independent of exposure. Figure 10 shows the

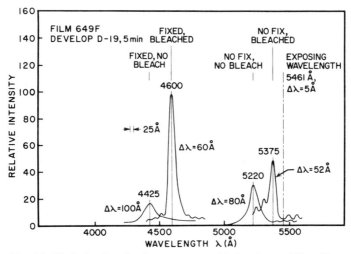

Fig. 10. Variation in reflection spectrum with fixation and bleaching.

degree of wavelength shift for a one-color exposure for fixed and unfixed conditions.

Included in the fixation bath is a hardener to provide emulsion stability against further swelling. Without hardening, the emulsion is more susceptible to variations in thickness due to the moisture absorption from the surrounding atmosphere.

Washing

Washing operations are used to remove reagents which might adversely affect later reactions and to eliminate all soluble compounds which might impair the stability of the exposed emulsion. The common purpose of the final washing is to remove the fixing salts that are contaminated with dissolved silver compounds. Failure to remove these compounds would eventually cause stain and fog. The efficiency of the washing process can be increased by using a hypo-eliminator bath partway through the washing step. This is an alkali solution that oxidizes the fixing reagents to a harmless chemical having increased solubility in water.

Bleaching

If the exposed emulsion is dried after the previous washing step, it will be black in appearance and show only a faint reflection. Analysis of the reflection spectrum indicates that bandwidths of the individual lines are considerably larger than theory predicts. This is attributed to the density of the individual silver planes being too large to allow the interrogating light to penetrate to the lower lying silver planes. The reflection spectrum is thus derived from a fraction of the total number of planes available.

The transmission of the individual planes can be increased by a bleaching process. This is done by bathing the plates (before drying) in a solution of mercuric chloride to convert the silver grains to silver-chloride grains. This produces a semitransparent image and allows the light to penetrate to all silver planes giving a more intense and narrower bandwidth reflection. There is a corresponding improvement in signal-to-noise ratio. The best bandwidth observed in an unbleached sample was approximately 80 Å, whereas a comparable bleached sample exhibits a 50 Å bandwidth. Figure 10 shows the effect of bleaching on the relative intensity and bandwidth of a one-color exposure.

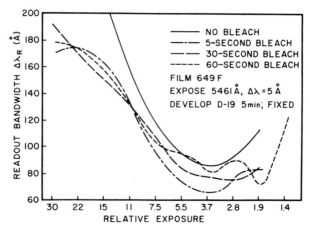

Fig. 11. Variation in readout bandwidth with exposure time and bleach time.

Other types of bleaching and reducing solutions have been tried but none of those investigated gave results comparable to mercuric chloride.

The bleaching process has been observed to cause a swelling of the emulsion resulting in a shift of the reflection spectrum to the longer wavelengths (toward the red end of the spectrum). If the degree of swelling can be controlled, it may provide us with a means of counteracting the shrinkage created by the fixing bath. See Fig. 10.

Figure 11 shows the effect of bleaching time and exposure on the readout bandwidth. It is seen that regulation of the bleaching time is not sufficient to compensate for overexposure. Such a compensation would require an additional change in the developing time. This again indicates an optimum range of exposure times for a given, fixed, developing time.

Emulsion Coating

A preliminary investigation has been made into the coating of photographic emulsions. Using a formula given by Ives,[4] samples were coated and exposed in the standard manner. A reflection bandwidth of approximately 100 Å was obtained indicating an emulsion thickness of about 9μ.

Circuits and Opto-Electric Devices

In this section we discuss light sources, detectors, and driving and control circuits. Their compatibility with information storage by the Lippmann process was investigated and various criteria for evaluation were established.

Light Emitters

Light emitters are primarily gallium arsenide (GaAs) p-n junction diodes, which when forward biased emit a relatively narrow, primarily noncoherent, 8970 Å wavelength light band.

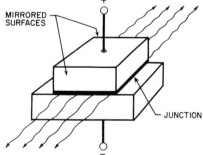

FIG. 12. Forward-biased light-emitting diode.

Electrons that flow into the junction give up energy upon recombination with holes. This energy exhibits itself in the form of photons, Fig. 12. The photons produced radiate from the surface in a cosine distribution (Lambertian source).

The energy of the photons radiated corresponds closely to the energy band gap of the semiconductor material used in the junction. Pure GaAs has a 1.513-eV band gap.[5] The frequency corresponding to this energy band gap is given by the equation:

$$\nu = \frac{E}{h} \tag{1}$$

where ν is the frequency, E is the energy of the photons, and h is Planck's constant.

Using Eq. 1 and $\lambda = c/\nu$ one can obtain the relation

$$\lambda = \frac{1.24 \times 10^4}{E} \tag{2}$$

where λ is the wavelength of the light in Angstrom units (Å) and E is the energy in eV. Therefore, assuming a constant speed of light throughout, one can approximate the wavelength of emission of a diode. The 1.513-eV band gives a wavelength of 8190 Å. Emissions have also been reported in the 1.47-eV (8450-Å) band. The shift in wavelength can be attributed to the doping of the GaAs.

The energy output rate of a light-emitting diode ranges from 0.5×10^{14} to 2×10^{14} photons per sec for 100 mA in the diode. Light output increases linearly with current after a few milliamperes in the diode.

The injection laser differs from the light-emitting diode in that a cavity is needed to obtain light amplification. This cavity is usually obtained by cleavage of the semiconductor material, although there have been reports of grinding and polishing to obtain this cavity.

The threshold current to produce stimulated emission varies from 0.400 to 10 A. This variation is a function of the material, manufacturer, and operating temperature. The band gaps and possible lasing frequency of various materials are shown in Fig. 13. This figure also shows the relative

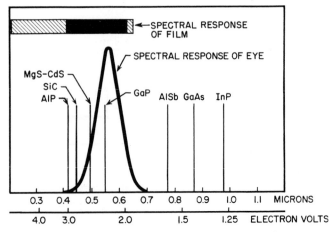

FIG. 13. Band gaps of various possible injection lasers.

position of the response of the film to be used in the Standing Wave Read Only Memory (SWROM). The response of the eye is also shown for reference. The voltage across the GaAs diode at 10 A is between 2 and 5 V. Therefore, worst case drive conditions would be a 15-A peak into a 0.132 Ω load.

Light Detectors

A light detector can be an electro-optic tube or a solid-state device. Examples are the photomultiplier tube (PMT) and the silicon photodiode.

PMT's are capable of operating in a spectral range between 0.1 and 1.0μ; however, this cannot be done with one photosensitive surface.

The quantum efficiency of a PMT photocathode varies between 0.1 to 20 per cent over the spectral range. The ultimate frequency-response limit of a commercial PMT is about 500 Mc. These characteristics are compared to solid-state devices in Table 2.

TABLE 2 COMPARISON OF LIGHT DETECTORS

Device	Upper Frequency Limit	Quantum Efficiency	Operating Voltages	Volume in.[3]
PMT	500 Mc	0.1–20%	1500 V	4.72
Photodiodes	5 kMc	25–85%	3–90 V	0.001

While PMT's have a very high gain, they also occupy a larger volume than solid-state devices.

Solid-state light detectors are silicon photodiodes and silicon phototransistors. The diodes offer less gain, although they are faster than their transistor counterparts. Since all solid-state devices are made from similar materials with closely matched band gaps, the spectral range of the detectors closely matches that of the injection laser, Fig. 14.

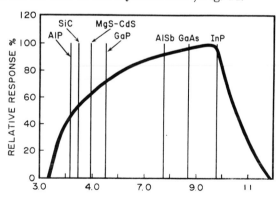

FIG. 14. Spectral response of silicon.

A photodiode is operated with reverse bias into a suitable sense amplifier. A photon entering the junction creates hole-electron pairs, which cause a current to flow in the diode. The number of photons needed to give a usable output to a sense amplifier is 1.81×10^7 to 4.32×10^7. The best quantum efficiencies of solid-state photo devices reported are from 25 to 85 per cent. These devices can be compared to the PMT in Table 2.

Sense Amplifier

The capacitance of a photodiode for various bias voltages is shown in Fig. 15. A preliminary design for a sense amplifier would employ an emitter

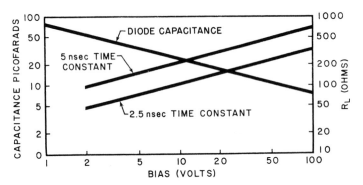

Fig. 15. Diode capacitance and load resistance versus bias voltage.

follower for impedance matching into a grounded-base amplifier. From this circuit, the signal could be fed into a conventional high-frequency amplifier.

Injection Laser Drives

A preliminary specification for a driver would be

Peak current	3 A
Rise time	25 nsec
Fall time	25 nsec
Duty cycle	25 per cent

A driver with these specifications could be built with existing components. An ultimate specification that one could expect would be

Peak current	3 A
Rise time	2 nsec
Fall time	2 nsec
Duty cycle	50 per cent

With a driver specification such as this, one could predict a 10 to 20 nsec cycle time.

Logic

The SWROM as presently conceived does not need decode logic. However, input and output registers and some pulse-shaping and delay circuits will be needed. These logic circuits could be implemented with ACP 2 nsec solid logic circuitry.[6] These circuits would also be adequate for higher speed models.

Deflection Circuits

Positioning of the accessing light beam will employ a KDP-calcite crystal deflector.[7] For 1000 spot positions, a 10-stage deflector would be needed. Each KDP crystal would need its own driver circuit; therefore, for 10^6 positions, 20 drivers would have to be constructed.

Deuterated KDP (KD_2PO_4) could be used for the electro-optic switches in the deflector. The electrical properties of this material are

$$V\lambda/2 \qquad \text{Capacitance}$$
$$3.5 \text{ kV} \qquad 80 \text{ pF}$$

In order to reduce the half-wave voltage $V\lambda/2$, two KDP crystals could be placed electrically in parallel, optically in series. The driving voltage would then be 1.7 kV, and the drivers would drive a 160 pF capacitance.

Systems

Systems Configurations

Six possible systems organizations have been studied for the SWROM:

1. Random word selection   parallel bit readout
2. Random word selection   serial bit readout
3. Sequential word selection   parallel bit readout
4. Sequential word selection   serial bit readout
5. Parallel word selection   parallel bit readout
6. Parallel word selection   serial bit readout

RANDOM WORD SELECTION. Random word selection requires a summation of various injection lasers, as shown in Fig. 16, or the use of a white light source in which all colors are present. This source is then deflected to the selected location by the electro-optic deflector. The output from the memory plane is then separated into the various colors by means of a prism or other dispersive medium for a parallel bit readout. This technique requires a detector and amplifier per bit (color).

The output could also be sent through a tunable filter. These filters would select the colors as a function of time and would, therefore, give a serial bit readout as in Fig. 17. This method requires only one detector-amplifier; however, it would be slower than parallel readout.

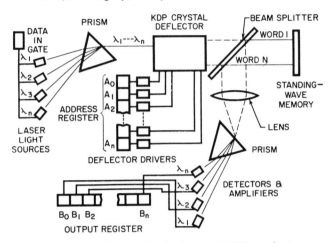

FIG. 16. Random word selection parallel bit readout.

SEQUENTIAL WORD SELECTION.   Another approach to systems organization is to scan a line or area sequentially in time. See Figs. 18 and 19. This method provides simplicity in deflector circuits at the expense of access time but may be useful in machines which would use drum or disk type organization and require strings of fixed data serially by bit or record.

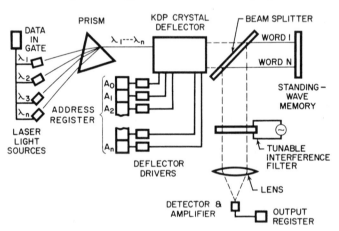

FIG. 17. Random word selection serial bit readout.

Sequential word selection is also a special case of random word selection as mentioned previously: a memory could also be implemented as a random store and be used sequentially. A sequential word-selected memory could also be implemented as in the photoscopic disk memory.*

* Contract AF 30(602)1832: Computer AN/GSQ-16 (XW-1), in which the information is stored on a disk. The disk is rotated and the information moves past a recording area.

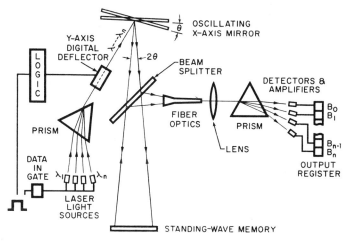

FIG. 18. Sequential word selection parallel bit readout.

PARALLEL WORD SELECTION. Parallel word selection is organized in a manner similar to the random word selection, the difference being that words (i.e., cell location) may be selected in parallel. This selection could be accomplished by fiber-optic light splitting. It could also be accomplished by flooding the area to be read out with monochromatic light whose fre-

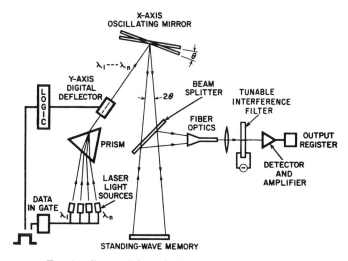

FIG. 19. Sequential word selection serial bit readout.

quency is that of the bit or series of bits to be selected. This type of word selection would be useful for associative word selection. See Figs. 20 and 21.

INDEXING AND REGISTRATION. In large-capacity memories, the problems of indexing and registration become important.

Registration of the film into its proper position after a change can be achieved by using a number of columns and rows reserved for this purpose. Several approaches are possible. One is to scan particular areas and use

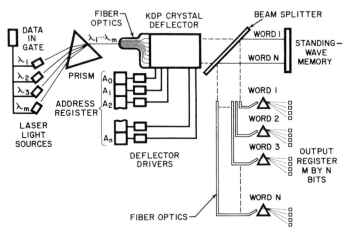

FIG. 20. Parallel word selection parallel bit readout.

the readout to set up a conversion matrix from virtual address to actual address and compensate for a misorientation of the film. Another is to break the film up in regular areas into an address hierarchy.

Indexing could be achieved by reserving lines and columns and numbering them so that the position corresponded to the number written in memory.

BAD BIT PROBLEMS.   In any large memory, there is inevitably the prob-

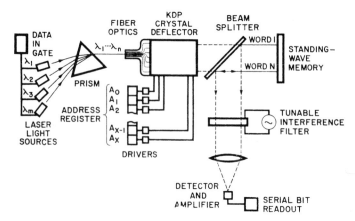

FIG. 21. Parallel word selection serial bit readout.

lem of what to do with "bad bits." In the case of the SWROM, there are two basic types of bad bits: (1) the whole cell is not usable, or (2) a particular color is in error. The first error could be due to imperfections, specks of dirt, etc.; while the latter could be caused by an error in writing.

In both cases it would be necessary to scan the entire memory and determine the bad addresses. If there is a reasonable upper limit, a buffer memory could be used to establish that the desired address was an error address and then select an unused portion of the memory to place and retrieve information for that address. This buffer memory would have a cycle time much less than the memory cycle time. This buffer memory could be implemented in tunnel diodes or thin films depending upon the desired size and speed.

System Components

LIGHT SOURCES. Two basic schemes can be considered: a white light source and monochromatic sources, one for each color.

For a white light source, the zirconium arc lamp provides a relatively small area of high intensity and relatively flat response over the visible band down to 4000 Å.

The problem associated with a white light source is the difficulty in obtaining very small collimated beams of light with enough intensity over the bandwidth associated with any one color.

Inherently monochromatic light sources, such as lasers, turn out to be very convenient for the SWROM requirements. The injection laser in particular with its small size and fast response could be very useful. Fortunately, the source dimensions are relatively small ($\approx 30\mu$) and reasonably well collimated, 2° by 10°.

Circuit problems in pulsing injection laser diodes are also relatively simple and within the capabilities of existing transistors (20 A at 2 V).

COLOR COMBINATION AND SEPARATION. Two basic approaches have been investigated. By using dichroic mirrors which reflect certain wavelengths and transmit others, the separate colors associated with each bit can be separated and combined. However, the losses in this type of system increase as the power of the number of colors. Present mirrors are neither very efficient nor of very narrow band, and both properties are required for this system.

The other approach is to use a dispersive prism or diffraction grating to combine and separate the light so that the separate colors can be combined uniaxially and then separated to the different photodetectors. Gratings offer the advantage of constant dispersion over the band without too much complication.

For a practical grating of 1000 lines/mm and a bandwidth of 50 Å, we have a dispersion of 5×10^{-3} rad for the first-order lines.

So, for example, with injection lasers or photodiodes of 2.5 mm center-to-center spacing, the distance from the grating will be 50 cm. This represents a reasonable working distance.

DEFLECTION.   Four aspects of the digital deflector* have been considered: these are spot size, signal-to-noise ratio (intensity of the spot with respect to background), light attenuation, and drive requirements.

1. Spot size is controlled or degraded by the following conditions:

   a. Effective light source collimated (effective area of source).
   b. The diffraction limit due to the aperture of the deflector and associated optics.
   c. Distortions.
   d. Optical purity of the crystals.

The smallest f number available with a deflector of active area of 20×20 mm and 1000×1000 positions of 20μ diameter is $f/22$. This seems practical with present convergent beam deflector design. For a 10:1 signal-to-noise ratio, this means a maximum source size of 0.2 mm diameter. This size is easy to obtain with an injection laser diode, but an aperture would have to be used with white light sources resulting in loss of light.

2. The signal-to-noise ratio at the output of the deflector is affected by the half-wave voltages $(V\lambda/2)$. The tolerance of $V\lambda/2$ is determined during the manufacturing of the crystal and can be controlled somewhat by the drive circuitry. A 10:1 ratio could probably be tolerated by using thresholds in the sense amplifiers. Since the half-wave voltage is a function of wavelength, it may be necessary to use two optical rotator crystals per stage to obtain the 10:1 signal-to-noise ratio.

3. Light attenuation. Because of the requirement that the RC time constant of the switching crystals be small enough to allow high-speed operation, low-resistance contacts to the crystal are necessary. Where a longitudinal effect rotator (i.e., KDP) is used, the transparency of the electrodes becomes very important. A transmission of (0.95) per crystal is presently available commercially with low enough resistance to satisfy speed requirements. This gives a total transmission for a 20-stage deflector of $(0.95)^{20} = (0.36)$. Surface reflections are reduced by broadband antireflective coatings and matching indices of refraction.

4. Drive requirements. Two things control drive requirements: half-wave voltage, $V\lambda/2$, which is dependent on the material used, and capacitance of the switching crystal C, which is a function of the dielectric constant and of crystal dimension. The design aims are to minimize capacitance, since the peak current I required to drive the deflectors is

$$ I \approx \frac{C \cdot V\lambda/2}{T} $$

where T = time. For high-speed operation, direct drive is impractical because of the power requirements:

* U.S. Army Contract No. DA-36-039-ACM-00118(E), and paper on "Convergent Beam Digital Light Deflector," by W. Kulcke, K. Kosanke, E. Max, H. Fleisher, and T. J. Harris, this volume, p. 371.

$$P \approx V \cdot I \approx \frac{CV^2\lambda/2}{T}$$

The dissipation factor of the crystal is important as this determines power dissipated in the crystal and, hence, the cooling requirements and optical distortions due to temperature gradients.

DETECTION. Photodiodes or photomultiplier tubes may be used to detect the Lippmann reflections from the film. Photomultiplier tubes are used where low signals are present. Therefore, very high amplification is needed. Photodiodes offer wideband responses, simple sense amplifier circuitry, and compact size.

Systems Applications

Major systems applications of high-capacity, high-speed, random-access, read-only memories appear to stem from table lookup operations. In various forms, these applications include microprograming, journal keeping, and arithmetic and logic manipulations.

A feature of the SWROM which appears to be unique is its capability of storing both digital and video (analog) information. This feature, combined with the capability of the memory for simultaneous, multibit readout with minimal cross talk, will give the SWROM an even wider range of application than mentioned earlier.

Conclusions

We have succeeded in reproducibly verifying the physical principles on which the standing-wave memory is based, and have established basic design principles in the areas of writing and reading the information, control of the process, opto-electronic circuitry, and systems organizations.

APPENDIX I
Coherence Length and Exposure

We know from Fourier analysis that a reciprocal relationship exists between frequency ν and time t, namely,

$$\Delta\nu \, \Delta t \approx 1$$

Since for light, $\nu\lambda = c$, we can manipulate this to

$$\Delta\nu = c\frac{\Delta\lambda}{\lambda^2}$$

and substituting into the first expression we have

$$c \, \Delta t = \frac{\lambda^2}{\Delta\lambda}$$

or

$$\Delta l = \frac{\lambda^2}{\Delta\lambda} = \lambda\,\frac{\lambda}{\Delta\lambda}$$

where Δl is called the "coherence length" of the wave train. This is not a rigorous definition, nor does it have a definite value, but is a very useful expression. In any material, the coherence length would be modified as $\Delta l' = \Delta l/n$, thus

$$\Delta l' = \frac{\lambda^2}{n\,\Delta\lambda}$$

For the standing wave to be fully effective throughout the entire emulsion, we must have

$$\Delta l' \geq 2t_0$$

where t_0 is the emulsion thickness. Hence

$$t_0 \leq \frac{\lambda_w{}^2}{2n\,\Delta\lambda_w}$$

where λ_w is the writing wavelength. The optimal condition of

$$t = \frac{\lambda_w{}^2}{2n\,\Delta\lambda_w}$$

would be desirable if the coherence length had a definite value (no "tails"). However, because it does not, the inequality above must hold, where the emulsion thickness is smaller than one-half the coherence length. Rewriting the expression as

$$t_0 \leq \left(\frac{\lambda_w}{2n}\right)\left(\frac{\lambda_w}{\Delta\lambda_w}\right)$$

we can see the following terms:

$$\frac{\lambda_w}{2n} = \text{separation between layers within the emulsion}$$

$$\frac{\lambda_w}{\Delta\lambda_w} = \text{characteristic of the source}$$

The number of layers set up is

$$\frac{t_0}{(\lambda_w/2n)} = \frac{2nt_0}{\lambda_w} = N$$

For a fully utilized emulsion, the number of layers set up is

$$N = \frac{\lambda_w}{\Delta\lambda_w}$$

We may summarize the foregoing conditions:

$$t_0 > \left(\frac{\lambda_w}{2n}\right)\left(\frac{\lambda_w}{\Delta\lambda_w}\right), \qquad N = \frac{\lambda_w}{\Delta\lambda_w}, \text{ source limited}$$

$$t_0 \leq \left(\frac{\lambda_w}{2n}\right)\left(\frac{\lambda_w}{\Delta\lambda_w}\right), \qquad N = \frac{2nt_0}{\lambda_w}, \text{ emulsion thickness limited}$$

In any case, once N has been determined, it becomes an invariant, e.g., unaffected by shrinkage.

In addition to the standing wave within the emulsion, there is, because of absorption, a traveling wave that causes an over-all exposure. This decreases the transmission and hence limits the minimum bandwidth of the reflected light signal.

APPENDIX II
Analysis of Reflected Light

The reflection of light from a multilayered structure, such as a Lippmann filter, may be analyzed, at least approximately. One of the best treatments is Delcroix's in *Revue d' Optique*.[8] He assumes no absorption or multiple reflections within a multilayer structure. By adding up all reflected rays, accounting for the relative phases, an expression for the reflected intensity is derived:

$$I = I_0 \left(\frac{\sin Nz}{\sin z} \right)^2$$

where

$$z = \text{phase difference of successive rays.}$$

Also

$$z = \frac{\pi \lambda_w}{\lambda_R}$$

where

$$\lambda_w = \text{exposing wavelength}$$
$$\lambda_R = \text{reflected wavelength}$$

This expression assumes no shrinkage. It is a typical interference term of the diffraction grating. The curve of this function peaks to a value $N^2 I_0$ whenever

$$z = \frac{\pi \lambda_w}{\lambda_R} = l\pi$$

where l is an integer. At points between the peaks, the function is oscillatory, but if N is large, the magnitude of the signal in these regions is very small.

The bandwidth of reflected light is usefully defined as the difference in wavelength (or frequency) at the half-intensity points of the reflected light. This can be found by solving the following equation for Δz:

$$\frac{N^2 I_0}{2} = I_0 \left(\frac{\sin N(\Delta z/2)}{\sin (\Delta z/2)} \right)^2$$

The results are, approximately,

$$\Delta z = \frac{2}{\sqrt{2} N}$$

or in terms of bandwidth,

$$\Delta \lambda \approx \frac{0.9 \lambda_R}{N}$$

If we consider the case in which the emulsion is fully utilized, then

$$N = \frac{2n t_0}{\lambda_w}$$

And,

$$\Delta\lambda_R = \frac{0.9\lambda_R\lambda_w}{2nt_0}$$

Unless the spacing of the layers has changed during processing or aging, $\lambda_R = \lambda_w$. We can connect these factors by introducing a shrinkage term k and writing the expression in terms of the reflected wavelength alone. If the shrinkage factor k is defined as

$$k = \frac{\lambda_w}{\lambda_R}$$

then

$$\Delta\lambda_R = \frac{0.9\lambda_R^2}{2nt_0}k$$

Since we can also write

$$\Delta\lambda_R = \frac{0.9\lambda_R^2}{2nt}$$

by lumping all shrinkage in terms of the thickness change, we have

$$k = \frac{t_0}{t}$$

Here t is emulsion thickness at the time of observing the reflected light. Thus, the shrinkage can be observed by comparing the reflected and exposing light wavelength as well as by the physical thickness change.

APPENDIX III
Bragg Effect

As the angle of incident light on a multilayer changes, the phase condition for interference in the reflected light changes. The phase condition is

$$\frac{2\pi}{\lambda_R} d \cos \theta = m\pi$$

where

d = layer spacing
m = integer 1, 2, 3, $\cdots$
λ_R = reflected light wavelength
θ = angle of incidence and reflection measured from the normal

Rewriting, we have

$$2d \cos \theta = m\lambda_R$$

or

$$\lambda_R = \frac{2d}{m} \cos \theta$$

when

$$\theta = 0, \lambda_R = \lambda_0$$

therefore

$$\frac{2d}{m} = \lambda_0$$

when $m = 1$, we can see that the spacing is just the exposing wavelength; i.e., $2d = \lambda_w$.

So

$$\lambda_R = \lambda_0 \cos \theta$$

Hence the wavelength of the light reflected from a multilayered structure decreases toward the blue as the angle of incidence increases. Figure 22 illustrates a possible

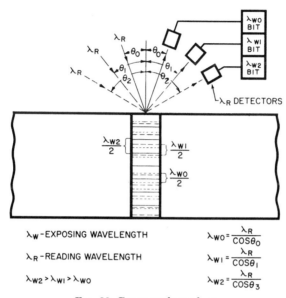

λ_w - EXPOSING WAVELENGTH $\lambda_{wo} = \dfrac{\lambda_R}{\cos \theta_0}$

λ_R - READING WAVELENGTH $\lambda_{w1} = \dfrac{\lambda_R}{\cos \theta_1}$

$\lambda_{w2} > \lambda_{w1} > \lambda_{wo}$ $\lambda_{w2} = \dfrac{\lambda_R}{\cos \theta_3}$

Fig. 22. Bragg angle readout.

use of this effect. Here monochromatic sources are arranged at suitable angles above the memory cell containing a like number or recorded colors, or bits. Because of the foregoing relation, the source nearest the normal (at θ_0) will cause the color $\lambda_{w0} = \lambda_R / \cos \theta_0$ to be reflected at the wavelength λ_R. At θ_2, the reflected light will still have wavelength λ_R but will correspond to the exposed color $\lambda_{w2} = \lambda_R / \cos \theta_2$. Hence a single wavelength source can be used to read out all recorded colors or bits. This ideally suits the character of a laser, but it requires the readout wavelength to be below all recorded colors.

REFERENCES

1. MEES, C. E. K., *The Theory of the Photographic Process*, Macmillan Company, New York, 1954, p. 23.
2. GARFIELD, JOHN F., "Apparatus and a Laboratory for Processing Thick Nuclear Track Emulsions," *Phot. Sci. Eng.*, *2*, No. 2, 85 (August 1958).
3. NEBLETTE, C. B., *Photography: Its Materials and Processes*, D. van Nostrand, Princeton, New Jersey, 1962, p. 338.
4. IVES, H. E., "An Experimental Study of the Lippmann Color Photograph," *Astrophys. J.*, *27*, 325–352 (1908).

5. NATHAN, M. E., AND G. BURNS, "GaAs Injection Laser," *IBM Research Report NC 202*, 1 February 1963.
6. BUELOW, F. K., et al., "A Circuit Packaging Model for High Speed Computer Technology," *IBM J. Res. Develop.*, No. 3, 182 (July 1963).
7. U.S. Army Contract No. DA-36-039-ACM-00118 (E), and paper on "Convergent Beam Digital Light Deflector," by W. Kulcke, K. Kosanke, E. Max, H. Fleisher, and T. J. Harris, this symposium, p. 371.
8. DELCROIX, J. L., "Utilisation des Plaques Lippmann Comme Filtres," *Rev. Opt. 27*, 493–509 (1948).

CHAPTER 2

A QUANTUM OPTICAL PHENOMENON: IMPLICATIONS FOR LOGIC *

E. M. Ring and H. L. Fox†

Boston University, Boston, Massachusetts

L. C. Clapp‡

Bolt Beranek and Newman Inc., Cambridge, Massachusetts

Introduction

There are two approaches that can be taken in the search for new devices and techniques for digital information processing. One approach consists of having an *a priori* conception of a logic structure for the implementation of general logical statements. The other approach is to examine appropriate devices and physical processes and to determine which logical statements they might represent. The first approach is the most common. It is usual to reduce all logical statements to Boolean algebra and then to seek devices and physical processes which will perform the function of a binary "store" or "nor" or "and," etc. This more common approach has the obvious advantage that one can concern himself only with devices and need not construct a new algebra of logical statements. However, as new physical processes and resultant devices are explored, such an approach may result in an inefficient utilization of these new techniques. The alternate approach is explored in the present paper. We examine a physical process which we believe has the potential for high-speed and accurate optical information

* This work was supported in part by the Office of Naval Research under contract NONR-4445 (000).

† NSF Fellow 1963–1964; present address, Bolt Beranek and Newman Inc., Cambridge, Massachusetts.

‡ Present address, Computer Research Corporation, Belmont, Massachusetts.

processing.[1] We then examine some of the logical functions such a device could perform. In investigating these we attempt to avoid any *a priori* bias for the realization of binary logic.

Logic Structures

There appear to be two stages in the development of a new computer device. There is the description of the elemental device, its physical properties and signal characteristics. Then there is a second stage where one explores the rules for interconnecting the elemental devices in a manner that will provide useful computer functions. In discussing these two stages of development with respect to the prototype described in the following section, we want to place the emphasis on the approach and methodology rather than on a particular device. To clarify that approach, we briefly discuss various types of logic.

The most widely known and used type of computing logic is conventional binary logic. We assume the reader has a general knowledge of such logic and of the basic devices used for its implementation. For our purposes it is important only to emphasize that the signals in such systems are characterized by one of two states. The basic devices for implementing binary logic are the three gates illustrated in Fig. 1. Their great virtue lies in the remarkable fact that in principle any logical statement can be reduced to a sequence of Boolean logical statements, each element of which can be realized by interconnecting the three logic elements as shown in Fig. 1.

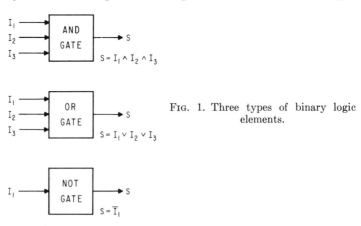

FIG. 1. Three types of binary logic elements.

This is not the only type of logic in current usage. Another type which is becoming increasingly important is majority decision logic. One example of such an element is shown in Fig. 2. The output signal S is 1 if and only if a majority of the input signals are also 1. In this particular example at least three of the input signals must be in the 1 state for S to be 1.

There exist other generalizations of the above types of logic, such as multivalued logic of which the simplest order above binary is ternary logic. As the name implies the information is contained in signals having three possible states. It is of interest in considering other multivalued logics to question what the limiting case is when the information signals have vir-

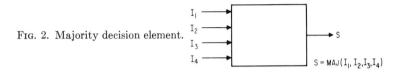

FIG. 2. Majority decision element.

tually an infinite number of states. Such a logic is essentially the basis of the analog computer. In this rather unconventional description one can therefore characterize an analog computer as the limit of a multivalued logical system. Other logic structures exist which cannot conveniently be placed in the above categories. One example is the "neural logic" which can be implemented by the types of devices being constructed by Kosonocky[2] and others.

We have tried to emphasize that there are a wide diversity of possible logic structures which might be used to translate optical and quantum principles into useful information processing devices. With such a diversity of logic structures available, one ought to examine the logic structures suggested by devices themselves. For it well may be that optical devices which do not appear at all suitable as binary computer elements may be very effective computing elements in the context of some other logic structure.

Thus far, we have used the expression "information signal" or "information carrying signal" as if one could precisely ascribe to a signal a very limited number of states. But it is generally true that actual signals carry more information than is used by any one computing device. For example, it is characteristic to use the amplitude of a signal in binary logic by describing it as having two states. Very often, such a signal also has phase and this information is not used. Alternatively, in certain devices, such as the Parametron,[3] logical decisions are dependent upon the phase (or frequency) of a signal, but then the amplitude is ignored. Thus one must consider not only whether the logical possibilities of a new device are ignored when one is restricted to a binary logic, but also whether one is efficiently using the signals when only one of the parameters characterizing that signal is used.

The Dither Effect in Optical Pumping of Rubidium

Having emphasized in the last section the wide diversity of logic structures which are available or which can be conceived we wish now to describe a quantum optical phenomenon. With it we show that an unbiased attitude toward the logical possibilities may permit one to discover a greater potential for the device as a computing element than might be obtained by using only a binary approach. The phenomenon is the "dither effect," and the experiment we describe involves optical pumping in rubidium vapor.

A complete discussion of the "dither effect" requires a fairly complicated analysis which is developed in a forthcoming paper.[1] It suffices here to display its essential features by means of a simplified model. Consider the three-level system illustrated in Fig. 3. Of course there are implicitly many other levels present which may even take part in the process but this model is adequate to describe the phenomenon of the "dither effect."

Circularly polarized radiation is applied corresponding to the energy difference between level E_1 and E_3. By virtue of the angular momentum conservation laws this radiation can only be absorbed in transitions from E_1 to E_3. This results in the absorption of a photon γ_1 as indicated in Fig. 3.

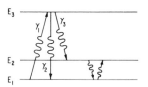

FIG. 3. Simplified level diagram for illustrating "dither effect."

If the radiation is sufficiently intense or if the relaxation time for the level E_3 is sufficiently long, an overwhelming majority of the atomic systems in a given sample having the level structure indicated in Fig. 3 will ultimately be in the excited state E_3.

One must consider decay by interaction with a thermal reservoir and spontaneous emission. These are indicated by the photons γ_2 and γ_3. Those systems which decay by the emission of photons γ_2 go into the state E_1 and by subsequent absorption of a photon γ_1 will again go to the excited state E_3. However, those systems which decay by emission of a photon γ_3 go into the state E_2. From E_2 they cannot be excited by the incident radiation. Thus, after a period of time associated with the intensity of the radiation and the relaxation time, the overwhelming number of atomic systems in a sample find themselves in a state E_2. In this manner the system is pumped into a population inversion ("population inversion" because a distribution of energy in thermal equilibrium would have the majority of systems in the state E_1, whereas the population just described has the majority of the systems in the state E_2). When the majority of systems in a given sample are in the state E_2 there are very few atomic systems which can absorb the incident radiation and therefore the sample becomes transparent to such radiation.

We examine now the manner by which one can apply other fields which change the sample's transmissibility, that is, cause the system again to absorb the radiation corresponding to the photons γ_1. One way is to cause transitions by a "probe" radiation field between the levels E_2 and E_1, such that some of the systems in E_2 are placed in the state E_1 and are thereby again accessible to the radiation γ_1. The sample therefore absorbs the radiation γ_1 and its transmissibility for γ_1 is reduced.

Consider the level separation between E_1 and E_2 to be a function of an applied field. This applied field might be a static field such as a magnetic field in the Zeeman effect or an electric field in the Stark effect. Then that applied field "tunes" the system by establishing the separation between E_1 and E_2. That is, the "probe" radiation field causes the system to oscillate between E_1 and E_2 when its frequency is ω such that $\hbar\omega = (E_2 - E_1)$. As described in the foregoing such a situation can be a condition for absorption of photons γ_1.

The "dither effect" can occur when the field that causes the level separation between E_1 and E_2 has an oscillating component. One can then show that if the relaxation time associated with the process of absorbing the photon γ_1 has the appropriate relationship to the frequencies involved in the transitions between E_2 and E_1 and to the rate at which the separation between E_2 and E_1 is varied, then the absorption occurs not at one frequency $\omega = (E_2 - E_1)/\hbar$, but in general at several frequencies. These are separated from $\omega = (E_2 - E_1)/\hbar$ by integral multiples of the frequency at which the level separation of E_2 and E_1 is varied. This is illustrated in Fig. 4. Here the first absorption spectrum is that for the usual Zeeman or

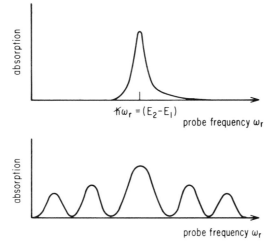

FIG. 4. Absorption spectra without and with "dither effect."

Stark effect in optical pumping, and the second absorption spectrum is characteristic of the "dither effect."

When analysis of the "dither effect" is carried out in detail, one can show that every peak in the spectrum may not be present. The presence of the peaks in the spectrum has to do with the relationships of the intensities and frequencies of the various radiation fields present. Expressions for the line width can be obtained which also relate to the intensities of these radiation fields. An approximate expression for the absorption of radiation γ_1 as a function of the various parameters is

$$\text{absorption} \simeq \sum_n \frac{\omega_0^2 \beta^2 / 2 \left[J_n \left(\frac{\epsilon \omega_0}{\omega_d} \right) \right]^2}{\omega_0^2 \beta^2 + (\omega_r - \omega_0 - n\omega_d)^2} \tag{1}$$

In this expression ω_0 is the resonant frequency corresponding to the mean separation of levels E_1 and E_2 ($\hbar\omega_0 = E_2 - E_1$); β is a measure of the intensity of the field used to cause transitions between E_2 and E_1; ϵ is a measure of the relative intensity of the "dither" field, that field which causes the separation $E_2 - E_1$ to be time-dependent; ω_d is the frequency of the "dither" field and ω_r is the frequency of the probe field used to cause transitions between E_2 and E_1; n is an integer and J_n is the Bessel function. Note that by varying these parameters independently a considerable variety of responses can be obtained in the absorption.

In spite of the apparent simplicity of the above model it serves quite adequately to describe the experimental results in a real system having more than two levels, particularly that of rubidium 87. A readable account of the process of optical pumping in such a system is given in a paper by deZafra.[4] Under the influence of a constant magnetic field, the energy-level diagram of Fig. 5 is applicable. The ground state has an $F = 1$ triplet and

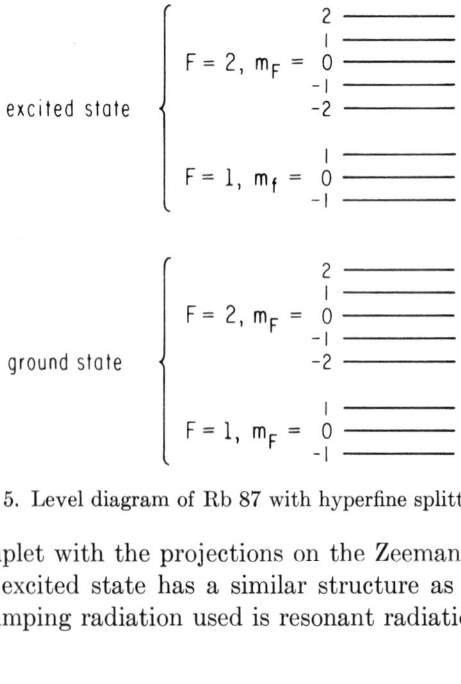

FIG. 5. Level diagram of Rb 87 with hyperfine splitting.

an $F = 2$ quintuplet with the projections on the Zeeman axis m_F as indicated. The first excited state has a similar structure as indicated in the diagram. The pumping radiation used is resonant radiation from a rubidium vapor lamp which is passed through a circular polarizer such that the angular momentum selection rule ($\Delta m_F = +1$) is applicable. By careful examination of Fig. 5 one can determine that because of the selection rule, transitions out of every one of the members of the multiplet in the ground state are possible except $m_F = 2$. Thus atoms which decay by spontaneous emission into the $m_F = 2$ ground state cannot be raised by the incident radiation to any level of the first excited state. Since the radiation spectrum is not energetic enough to involve the other excited states, one can see that eventually the sample becomes saturated in the $m_F = 2$ level of the ground state.

For low-intensity Zeeman fields, the separations between the terms in the multiplet are almost identical and cannot be resolved with usual detection equipment. Furthermore, since in a pumped condition the overwhelming majority of the systems are in the $m_F = 2$ level of the ground state, the application of a radiation field which causes transitions among the levels of the ground state can be considered to cause transitions only between the $F = 2, m_F = 2$ level and the $F = 2, m_F = 1$ level, providing the frequency of the field is not too high.

This discussion has not included the dither field. One way to visualize the dither field is that it makes the separation between the $F = 2, m_F = 2$ and the $F = 2, m_F = 1$ levels vary sinusoidally in time. Of course such a picture does not obtain an understanding of the complex details which cause the ultimately simple resonance phenomena.

The experimental apparatus* is based on the work of Franzen and Emslie.[5] A schematic description is given in Fig. 6. The important element

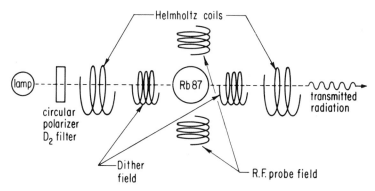

FIG. 6. Schematic of apparatus for "dither effect" in Rb 87.

of this apparatus which distinguishes it from other optical pumping experiments is the additional set of coils which produces the time-dependent

* The apparatus used in this experiment was originally set up at Boston University for student demonstrations under the supervision of Professor Franzen with funds from NSF.

variation in the Zeeman field, that is, along the axis of the Helmholtz coils. Figure 7 is a photograph of the apparatus showing the various components. The resonant response was observed on an oscilloscope and plotted with a graphic level recorder. Typical response curves are given in Fig. 8. The

FIG. 7. Photograph of apparatus for Rb 87 "dither effect" (courtesy of Professor W. Franzen, Boston University).

second curve in Fig. 8 is an example of how the parameter $\epsilon\omega_0/\omega_d$ can be adjusted to yield full transmission at $\omega_r = \omega_o$ and yet have several absorption side bands.

Logical Implications of the Dither Effect

Now consider some of the logical implications of the optical device described in the previous section. A block diagram of this experimental device in logical terms is shown in Fig. 9. The signal i represents the light source. In the following development i is not manipulated. It is to be regarded in the nature of a power source or steering signal which must be present for the device to function. Each of the two input signals I_1 and I_2 are shown as having two components. The symbol δ represents the frequency of I_1 and β represents its intensity. Similarly, d and ϵ represent the frequency and intensity respectively of signal I_2; σ represents the output signal of the device.

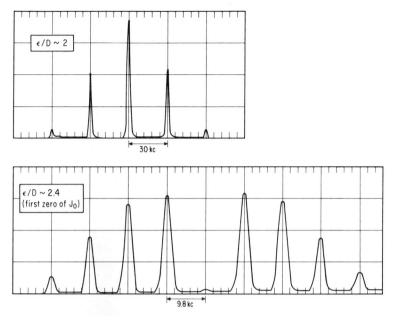

FIG. 8. Experimental data on "dither effect."

From a physical point of view, the characteristics of the device are described by Eq. 1, which shows the relationship between the light absorption of the device and the input signal conditions. How does one proceed from these physical relations to logical relations? The logical conditions or signals which must be applied at the input terminals in order to obtain a specified signal at the output terminal constitute a logical algebra for the device. The specification of a logical algebra implies certain restrictions on, and relations between, the input signals. Although in conventional binary devices there are usually only a small number of input relationships available, in the dither effect device and in other quantum optical systems there may

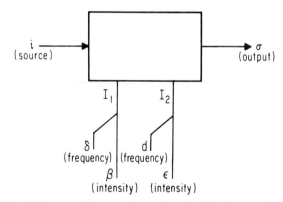

FIG. 9. Block diagram of the experimental optical device as a logic element.

be a very large number of relationships and sets of restrictions from which one can choose. Each of these sets may lead to a particular type of logic, generally nonbinary.

Often the simplest signal configuration yields binary logic. Consider the particularly simple case when there is no input signal $I_2, (\epsilon = 0)$. The device is dependent only upon signal I_1. If one keeps the intensity β constant and varies the frequency δ, an absorption curve such as that sketched in Fig. 4a is obtained. Light is transmitted through the system for all values of δ except in the vicinity of a specific value δ_0. At $\delta = \delta_0$ absorption occurs, then the device is sensitive only to signals I_1 that have a frequency near δ_0. Such a device is strongly suggestive of the NOT gate described in Fig. 1. By cascading elements one can construct in an analogous manner "and," "or," and "nor" gates. But the implementation of these simple logic functions does not utilize the full range of input-state configurations possible. The configuration when both signals I_1 and I_2 are present and one varies δ, yields more interesting and useful results. The characteristic result is as illustrated in Fig. 4b (ω_r corresponds to δ). Note here that the absorption curve has a number of peaks of differing amplitudes. The amplitude of a peak is dependent on both the frequency and intensity of I_2. Thus the device is sensitive to a restricted number of the possible input signal combinations. Were this device followed by an optical intensity sensitive element, then it could be considered a rudimentary example of a multivalued logic element.

To recapitulate, the device could be used as a Boolean element to implement binary-logic statements. When so used it is compatible with existing computer configurations. However, by recognizing the device's broader logic capabilities and not restricting oneself to compatibility with usual computer configurations, one might be able to utilize the quantum optical phenomenon for the development of highly efficient devices. To demonstrate this concept, we pursue in some detail an example whereby a ternary logic is implemented by using an appropriate set of input signals.

In order to develop this example, we must implicitly assume that certain auxiliary technological problems are (or can be) solved. In particular we deal with optical level-logic (intensity levels) under the assumption that appropriate threshold devices can be constructed to follow the "dither" apparatus such that well-defined states correspond to each level. The intensity levels that are available can be evaluated using the expression for the absorption, Eq. 1. The calculations can be greatly simplified by utilizing certain properties of the infinite sum in this expression. If $\beta\omega_0 \ll \omega_d$, then the sum has an overwhelming dominant term whenever $\omega_r - \omega_0 \simeq n\omega_d$ (n is an integer). Consequently, we restrict $\omega_r - \omega_0$ to the set of values $\{n\omega_d\}$ and thereby obtain the approximate absorption $\frac{1}{2}J_n{}^2(\epsilon\omega_0/\omega_d)$ for each value of n. Note, however, that one is still free to choose the argument of J_n, and this is most simply accomplished by varying ϵ. For convenience let $\epsilon\omega_0/\omega_d = x$.

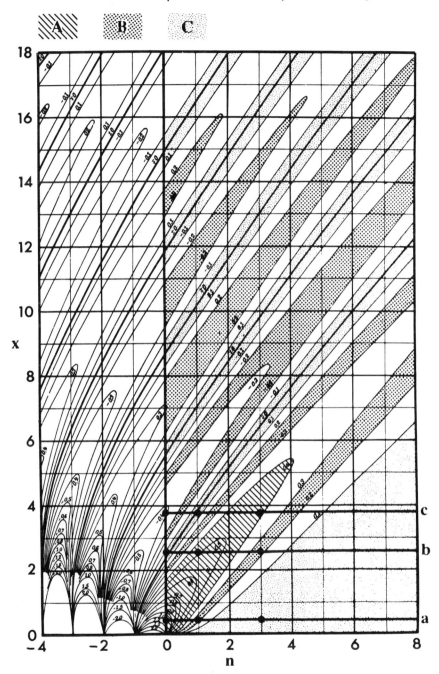

FIG. 10. Contour curves of $J_n(x)$ with truth table construct.

To implement an l-valued logic one must choose l distinct output states. We illustrate ternary logic by selecting three distinct ranges of $J_n^2(x)$. It is also necessary that the input be three-valued. This is accomplished by selecting three appropriate values of x and three of the integers defining the order of the Bessel function. Then a truth table may be generated in which the inputs are the parameters n and x, each restricted to three values and the output the three distinct ranges of $J_n^2(x)$. We employ contour curves of $J_n(x)$, Fig. 10, to construct the truth table.[6] We arbitrarily choose output levels by specifying regions on the contour map as follows:

$$A \quad \text{corresponds to} \quad 0.4 < J$$
$$B \quad \text{corresponds to} \quad 0.2 < J < 0.3$$
$$C \quad \text{corresponds to} \quad J < 0.1$$

The basis of this choice is to preserve output discrimination while providing some flexibility in choosing values of x and n. A truth table is obtained by selecting three values each of x and n such that each of the points determined by these coordinates lies in one of the regions A, B, or C in the contour plane. As an example consider the three lines $x = a, b, c$ and the integers $n = 0, 1, 3$ (see Fig. 10). The resulting truth table is shown in Fig. 11.

Fig. 11. Ternary truth table.

Other truth tables may be constructed in an analogous fashion. Given a complete basis set of such ternary truth tables, it is possible to implement any logical statement. We have not yet determined those conditions under which a complete basis set can be obtained with the present system. This is one of the areas presently being studied. We are also studying the increases in logic flexibility that might be obtained by cascading systems.

Before a practical all-optical logic device based on these principles can be realized further research is necessary. Among the areas to be investigated are: (1) polarization states of the off-axis scattering, (2) materials with $E_1 - E_2$ optical transitions, (3) refinement of the mathematical theory, and (4) the application of generalized logic to optical information processing.

REFERENCES

1. RING, E. M., AND H. L. FOX, "The Dither Effect," in preparation.
2. KOSONOCKY, W. F., "Feasibility of Neuristor Laser Computers," *Optical Processing of Information*, Donald K. Pollock, Charles J. Koester, and James T. Tippett, Eds., Spartan Books, Inc., Baltimore, Md., 1963, p. 255.

3. Goto, E., "The Parametron, A Digital Computing Element which Utilizes Parametric Oscillation," *Proc. IRE*, 1304 (August 1959).

4. DeZafra, R. L., *Am. J. Phys.*, *28*, No. 7, 646 (1960).

5. Franzen, W., and A. G. Emslie, *Phys. Rev.*, *108*, 1453 (1957).

6. Jahnke, E., and F. Emde, *Tables of Functions*, Dover Publications, New York, 1945, p. 152.

CHAPTER 3

RESEARCH IN PICTURE PROCESSING *

T. S. Huang and O. J. Tretiak

Department of Electrical Engineering and Research Laboratory of Electronics
Massachusetts Institute of Technology
Cambridge, Massachusetts

I. Introduction

In 1960, Professor W. F. Schreiber founded the Picture Processing Research group (now a part of the Cognitive Information Processing Group) at the Research Laboratory of Electronics at Massachusetts Institute of Technology. The research program of this group has been to investigate schemes for reducing bandwidth required for picture transmission. It was realized that in order to solve this problem, it is necessary to better understand how the human observer perceives the image, what features of the picture are important, so that a collateral interest of the group has been to investigate ways of mathematically representing pictorial data, of finding out details of what features of the picture are important.

Professor Schreiber's philosophy is to treat the picture as a function of several dimensions: to represent the image as a function of the spatial directions as well as time, since it seems impossible to realize much bandwidth saving from only video signal obtained in picture scanning. The investigation was not directed only to systems that are feasible at the current state of the electronics art. It is imperative to carry on the investigation experimentally, since the merit of a picture-transmitting system can only be judged from the actual appearance of the received pictures. The experiments were carried out by computer simulation. The flexibility of a digital computer enables one to try out complicated picture processing

* This work was supported in part by the Joint Services Electronics Program under Contract DA36-039-AMC-03200(E); and in part by the National Science Foundation (Grant GP-2495), the National Institutes of Health (Grant MH-04737-04), and the National Aeronautics and Space Administration (Grant NsG-496). Part of this work was done at the Computation Center, Massachusetts Institute of Technology.

schemes with a relatively small amount of effort. To facilitate this simulation, a digital picture scanner and cathode-ray tube display was constructed. Pictures were scanned with this system, the signal was recorded on a computer magnetic tape, and this tape was used as input to a program that simulated a picture-transmitting system. The program wrote the simulated picture onto a second magnetic tape, and this tape was photographed with the digital display system.

This paper summarizes the research carried on by our group over the past four years. The topics fall into roughly two categories: bandwidth reduction schemes, and studies of picture quality. Several projects have aimed to extend Schreiber's synthetic highs system to two dimensions, and work in this direction is still going on. Other experiments aimed at reducing the redundancy in motion pictures, and at the optimum coding of digital color pictures. The relation between the two-dimensional power spectrum of noise and its objectionability was investigated, and experimental investigation of optimum picture sampling systems was related to an analytical optimization of the problem.

II. The Digital Scanner-Display System

A digital scanner-display system was constructed to provide input-output for computer simulation of picture-transmitting systems. A block diagram of the scanner is shown in Fig. 1. A cathode-ray tube flying spot scanner

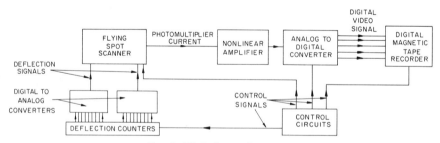

Fig. 1. Digital scanning system.

was used to scan a transparency. The scanner was operated in a point-by-point display mode, after the fashion of computer displays. The deflection was positioned while the cathode-ray tube was blanked, and a single point on the tube face was intensified while the beam was stationary. The light passing through the transparency was picked up by a photomultiplier tube, and the photomultiplier current was integrated during the intensification period. The integrated signal was passed through a nonlinear amplifier that was adjusted to give an output proportional to the density of the transparency. This signal was converted to a digital code, and the bit pattern was recorded on a computer magnetic tape.

The system used to obtain photographs from computer tapes is shown in the block diagram of Fig. 2. A digital video signal was read from tape,

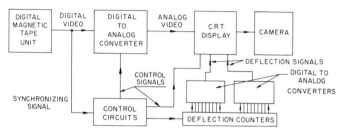

FIG. 2. Digital display system.

converted to analog form, and used to modulate the brightness of a cathode-ray tube. The cathode-ray tube deflection was operated in the same way as that in the scanner. As a matter of operational economy, the same cathode-ray tube and deflection system was used both for scanning and for display.

The compelling reason for using a point-by-point scanning and display system was that the tape unit had a large amount of velocity variation, and, if a conventional continuous deflection were used, this variation would cause either deflection distortion or shading.

The deflection signal was obtained from digital-to-analog converters connected to binary counters. Each of the converters and counters had ten bits, so that one could step to one of 1024 horizontal and vertical positions. The counters were interconnected with plug wires, so that with appropriate interconnections one could scan over rasters whose number of horizontal or vertical increments equal to any power of two. The system intensified the cathode-ray tube at a 7.5-kc rate. This rate was chosen to make the data on the magnetic tape conform with an IBM tape format. Since the number of data points per line or per frame could be varied by changing the deflection counter interconnections, the frame rate of the system depended on the resolution.

The video signal was quantized to eight bits before being recorded on the magnetic tape. The quantization is finer than that normally thought necessary for perfect reproduction of video signals. A light feedback system was used on the cathode-ray tube. This reduced the effects of phosphor variations and of tube transfer characteristic changes.

III. Bandwidth Compression

We are concerned mainly with the transmission of digital pictures. To transmit a picture digitally, one has to take discrete samples from a continuous picture and to quantize the brightness of each sample to a finite number of levels. To get a digital picture with quality comparable to that of commercial television pictures, one needs about 500×500 samples and 6 bits (64 levels) for each sample: hence 1.5×10^6 bits per picture. Since the bandwidth required of a channel increases with an increase in the number of bits one has to send through it, one would like to reduce the number of bits needed to transmit a picture.

A bandwidth compression is possible because of the following two facts.

1. There are statistical constraints among the picture samples. Therefore, the information content[1] R of a class of pictures is less than 6 bits/sample. Up to third order probability distributions of pictures have been measured.[2] From these measurements, one would guess that, by using only intraframe statistical constraints, a bandwidth reduction of 5:1 to 10:1 can be achieved. However, elaborate block codes and hence huge code books are necessary.

2. If the received picture is to be viewed by humans, then one can take advantage of the properties of human vision. Here, the purpose is to distort the picture in such a way that the distorted picture can be described by a smaller number of bits, yet the change is not noticeable to human viewers.

We have been working mainly with monochrome still pictures, trying to extend Schreiber's synthetic highs system[3,4] to two dimensions. However, some preliminary work was done on motion and color pictures.

A. Schreiber's Synthetic Highs System

Schreiber's synthetic highs system took advantage of the fact that the human eye tends to emphasize edges (abrupt changes in brightness) in a picture but is relatively insensitive to the amount of changes in the brightness over edges; on the other hand, in areas where the brightness changes slowly, quantization noise is easily discernible. Therefore, edges and the slowly varying part of a picture were treated differently. Figure 3 shows a

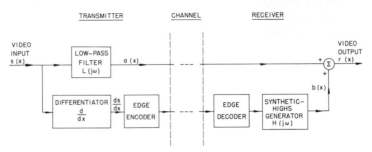

FIG. 3. Block diagram of Schreiber's synthetic highs system.

block diagram of the system. The video signal, derived from a picture by scanning, is passed through a low-pass filter with frequency response $L(j\omega)$.

If the bandwidth of the low-pass filter is $\frac{1}{10}$ of that of the original video signal $s(x)$, then the output $a(x)$ needs to be sampled only $\frac{1}{10}$ as often as $s(x)$; each sample of $a(x)$ still has to have 6 bits to avoid quantization noise. The video signal $s(x)$ is also passed through a differentiator; since ds/dx is large at the edges, this signal contains mainly edge information. If both $a(x)$ and ds/dx are transmitted exactly (and if the channel is noiseless), then we can synthesize the high-frequency part of $s(x)$ by passing ds/dx through a "synthetic highs generator" with a frequency response

$$H(j\omega) = \frac{1 - L(j\omega)}{j\omega}$$

The output of $H(j\omega)$ will be

$$b(x) = s(x) - a(x)$$

and the sum of $a(x)$ and $b(x)$ is exactly $s(x)$, the original picture. In Schreiber's system, the edge signal ds/dx was quantized to eight levels (3 bits); the first level was chosen high enough so that only a few noise points were mistaken to be edges, yet it was low enough so that no significant edge points were missed. The edge information was sent by run-length coding (essentially, the magnitude and the position of each edge point were transmitted). A reduction of 4 : 1 was achieved with rather good received pictures.

To obtain more reduction, an obvious step would be to extend Schreiber's system to two dimensions.

B. Huang's Two-Dimensional Edge-Detection Scheme

A picture coding scheme investigated by Huang[5] could be considered as an extension of Schreiber's system to two dimensions. Figure 4 shows an

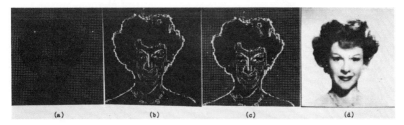

FIG. 4. Pictures pertaining to Huang's two-dimensional edge-detection scheme. (*a*) Basic points. (*b*) Edge points. (*c*) Points sent from the transmitter = (*a*) + (*b*). (*d*) Reconstructed picture. Bandwidth reduction = 7:1.

anatomy of this scheme. A set of basic points (e.g., one out of every sixteen samples as in Fig. 4*a*) were transmitted for all picture frames. These points essentially constituted the low-frequency part of the picture. In addition, extra edge points (see Fig. 4*b*) were sent for each frame. Whether any given point was an edge point or not was determined by a threshold function which depended only on the basic points. Therefore, if the transmitter and receiver agreed on the threshold beforehand, the positions of the edge points need not be sent. At the receiver the blanks were filled in by linear interpolation. For the particular picture shown in Fig. 4d, the reduction was about 7:1.

C. Pan's Two-Dimensional Edge-Detection-and-Approximation Scheme

Pan[6] attempted to extend Schreiber's system to two dimensions. The low-frequency part of the picture was obtained by passing the picture through a two-dimensional low-pass filter. The edges in the picture were obtained by a two-dimensional edge detector. Whether any given point was an edge point or not was determined by a threshold function which depended on the neighboring points. The edges were then approximated by straight line segments, and only the end points of the segments (plus the information on how to connect them) were transmitted. With this scheme, it was possible to achieve reductions of from 10:1 to 20:1 (see Fig. 5).

FIG. 5. Picture from Pan's two-dimensional edge-detection-and-approximation scheme. Bandwidth reduction = 15:1.

However, the received pictures had rather poor (though still respectable) quality, even in cases where the reductions were small. It is thought that this defect is caused by the ad hoc procedure used to obtain and to encode the edges.

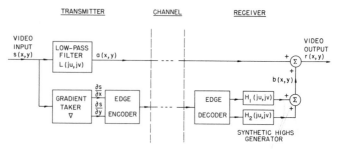

FIG. 6. Block diagram of two-dimensional synthetic highs system.

D. A Mathematical Formulation of Two-Dimensional Synthetic Highs System

Recently, Schreiber[7] suggested a direct mathematical extension of his synthetic highs system to two dimensions. The block diagram of this extended scheme is shown in Fig. 6. Here, the differentiator is replaced by a gradient operator, and a pair of two-dimensional filters, H_1 and H_2, are required to synthesize the high-frequency part. It can be shown readily that if the low-frequency part $a(x, y)$ and the gradient components $\partial s/\partial x$ and $\partial s/\partial y$ are sent exactly (and if the channel is noiseless), then one can synthesize the high-frequency part, *viz.*, $s(x, y) - a(x, y)$, exactly, by using appropriate $H_1(ju, jv)$ and $H_2(ju, jv)$, and the original picture will be reproduced exactly. This was simulated and verified on a digital computer (see Fig. 7). Graham[8] is now working on the problem of how to approximate

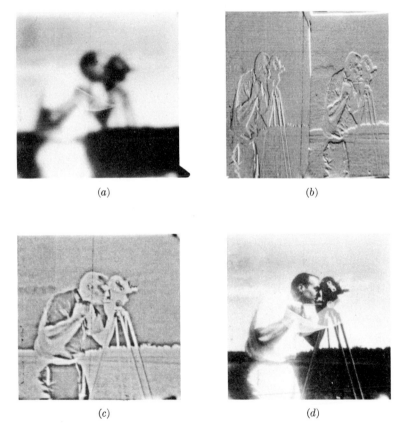

(a) (b)

(c) (d)

FIG. 7. Pictures pertaining to two-dimensional synthetic highs system. (*a*) Low-passed picture, $a(x)$. (*b*) Gradient pictures. Left is $\partial s/\partial x$. Right is $\partial s/\partial y$. (*c*) High-frequency part of picture synthesized from gradient. (*d*) Reconstructed picture.

the gradient so that we can achieve a large amount of reduction and also at the same time obtain good received pictures.

E. Motion and Color Pictures

Cunningham[9] investigated several systems of transmitting monochrome motion pictures. Some of the systems used lower frame rates than in standard practice. Besides introducing temporal filtering as a band-limiting process, the systems transmitted picture sequences by correcting a fixed fraction of the picture sample points during each frame transmission time. The results indicate that a saving of 6:1 in bandwidth is possible using such methods.

The coding of color still pictures was studied by Gronemann.[10] Pictures were obtained for various combinations of the numbers of samples and the numbers of quantum levels for the luminance and for the chrominance. It was found that a normal monochrome picture can be converted to a full color picture of the same apparent sharpness by transmitting additionally only a fraction of a bit per sample. For some purposes (e.g., recognizing objects), inclusion of color may result in a smaller over-all bandwidth requirement than that required to get the same quality in a monochrome system.

IV. Research in Picture Quality Evaluation

The relative merits of different television systems have been, and still are, a major point of contention. It is currently not possible to analytically evaluate the subjective quality of a picture received through a system: one must use tests with human observers. There also is no single test procedure used to evaluate picture quality, so that it is not surprising when different laboratories come up with different conclusions when evaluating similar systems.

We are concerned with investigating test procedures for evaluating the subjective quality of pictures, and would like to develop a mathematical criterion for calculating this quality. Two projects dealing with this problem have been carried out to date.

A. Subjective Effect of Noise

Huang[11] studied the subjective effect of pictorial noise. The main goal was in finding out how the objectionability of a two-dimensional low-pass noise depends on its bandwidth. Three original pictures, varying in the amount of details, were used. The noise was additive Gaussian, stationary, and independent of the picture; hence, it was completely specified by its two-dimensional power density spectrum. Noisy pictures were presented to observers to be rank-ordered according to noise objectionability. The noise used had a power density spectrum.

$$\Phi(u, v) = \begin{cases} \text{constant}, & \text{for } -k_1 \leq u \leq k_1, \ -k_2 \leq v \leq k_2 \\ 0, & \text{elsewhere} \end{cases} \qquad (1)$$

where u and v are angular spatial frequencies. Examples of noisy pictures are shown in Fig. 8. Each picture consists of 256×256 sample points. The distance between two successive points is taken as the unit length; therefore, the bandwidth is expressed in terms of cycles per point. We tried

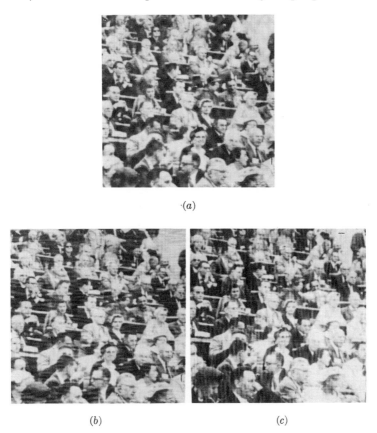

·(a)

(b)   (c)

FIG. 8. Some noisy pictures. Noise is low-pass Gaussian and independent of signal. Peak-signal-to-rms-noise ratio is 26 dB. Bandwidth (in cycles per point $\times$ 40) of the noise is: (a) 4×4. (b) 10×2. (c) 2×10.

to find the isopreference surfaces in the 3-space $\sigma - k_1 - k_2$, where σ is the rms value and k_1 and k_2 are the bandwidths of the noise in the horizontal and the vertical directions, respectively. Any noise whose spectrum is of the form of Eq. 1 can be represented as a point in the $\sigma - k_1 - k_2$ space. An isopreference surface is defined as a surface whose points represent noises of equal objectionability. It was found that the general shapes of the isopreference surfaces are quite similar for the three pictures. In particular, we note the following general trends which are true of all three pictures:

1. If we keep the noise power constant and go radially outward from the

origin in the $k_1 - k_2$ plane (i.e., keeping k_1/k_2 constant), the objectionability will first increase, then reach a maximum and finally fall off again.

2. Noises with vertical streaks (vertical bandwidth is smaller than horizontal bandwidth) are more objectionable than noises with horizontal streaks.

The details of the isopreference surfaces, however, are quite different for different pictures. Generally, it seems that noises which contain frequencies similar to those of the pictures are less annoying. For example, in Fig. 8a, the picture bandwidth and the noise bandwidth are almost the same, and one may observe that the noise is practically masked by the signal.

B. Optimum Picture Sampling

Tretiak[12] carried out a study to find an optimum sampled-data picture transmitting system. When a picture must be sent over a sampled-data channel, the source picture, a function of several dimensions, has to be represented by a sampled-data signal, which is just a collection of numbers. The question asked in this investigation was: What is the best way of abstracting a certain number of samples from the source picture, and of reconstructing a second picture from these samples? The study was restricted to still monochrome pictures.

The problem of finding an optimum system was approached analytically by postulating that the subjective picture quality can be calculated from a certain mathematical criterion. The fidelity criterion was based on two properties of human vision:

1. The human eye seems to respond linearly to the logarithm of the observed brightness.

2. The human eye sensitivity depends on the spatial frequency of the stimulus.[13]

It was supposed that the highest quality picture that one can see is an identical reproduction of the original scene's brightness variation, and that any departure from this degrades the picture. The criterion used is represented in the following mathematical terms. Let the brightness as a function of position in the original image be given by $b_s(x, y)$ and the brightness distribution in the picture received through some system be $b_r(x, y)$. We will suppose that the "subjective" appearance of the picture is found by convolving the logarithm of the stimulus brightness distribution with a two-dimensional weighting function $w(x, y)$. In this terminology, it is postulated that the degradation of a picture is a function of

$$\int dx \int dy \left[\int dx_1 \int dx_2\, w(x - x_1, y - y_1)(\log b_s(x_1, y_1) - \log b_r(x_2, y_2)\right]^2$$

One can find many faults with the above criterion, for example, the dimensions (x, y) are not clearly defined—it is implied that they are chosen so that the source and received pictures overlap. The criterion is probably useless when the picture suffers from geometrical distortions, such as deflection nonlinearity. The criterion is, however, analytically tractable, and it embodies the intuitive notion that quality of reproduction is linked with fidelity.

The sampled data picture-transmitting system was modeled by the block diagram shown in Fig. 9. The logarithm of the source picture brightness

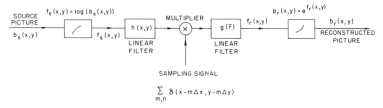

SAMPLING SIGNAL

$$\sum_{m,n} \delta(x - m\Delta x, y - m\Delta y)$$

Fɪɢ. 9. Block diagram of picture sampling system.

was put through a two-dimensional filter, and the sample values were modeled by multiplying the prefiltered picture with a two-dimensional periodic impulse train. Thus the sampling was carried out over a regular grid. The received picture was reconstructed by passing the two-dimensional pattern of sample-modulated impulses through a second two-dimensional filter. The first filter causes the sample values to be the weighted averages of the source picture brightness in the vicinity of the sampling point. The second filter smooths out the brightness distribution, interpolating between the sample values.

The above combination of system and error criterion can be optimized analytically.[14] It is found that the presampling filter should be a two-dimensional low-pass filter that band-limits the source signal in such a way that the sampling process does not alias any of the spatial frequencies. The filter used to interpolate between the sample values should have an identical spatial frequency response. It is interesting that as long as the Fourier transform of $w(x, y)$, the subjective weighting function mentioned in the foregoing, does not become too large for high spatial frequencies, the above result is independent of the shape of the weighting function.

The proposed system was simulated with a digital computer. A picture scanned over a 256 × 256 dot raster was fed into a program that simulated filtering and sampling over a rectangular 64 × 64 point raster. The simulated output pictures were obtained by interpolating 256 × 256 point pictures from the sample values. Many filtering functions were simulated. A few of these pictures are shown in Fig. 10. The original 256 × 256 sample version of one of the pictures is shown in Fig. 10a. This is a photograph of the signal used as input to the computer. The same picture, when band-limited to 64 × 64 samples, sampled and the sample values interpolated with a band-limiting filter is shown in Fig. 10b. The picture in Fig. 10d was

produced from the same sample values as that in Fig. 10*b*, but the interpolation between sample values was done with a filter that band-limited to
32 cycles per picture height and picture width, but these spatial frequencies
were accentuated by a factor of two over the filter gain at zero frequency.
A simpler system was used to produce the picture in Fig. 10*c*. The sample
values were taken directly from the source picture, and linear interpolation

(a)   (b)

(c)   (d)

FIG. 10. Pictures received through simulated sampling system.

between the sample values was used for reconstruction. It is evident that
the boundaries in this picture are both more jagged and less sharp than
those in the band-limiting system. Sixteen different filter combinations
were simulated, and subjective rank-ordering tests were run to find the
best pictures. The tests were run at two viewing distances. In the tests at
a two-foot viewing distance, the picture that was band-limited to the
Nyquist rate before and after sampling was chosen as best. In tests at a

ten-foot viewing distance, about half of the observers ranked the picture in Fig. 10*d* in first place; the other observers did not have a strong consensus of opinion.

The over-all study indicates that for best quality sampled data picture transmission, one should band-limit before and after sampling. The test and data analysis were not extensive enough to conclude to what extent the criterion used in the analysis is to be trusted. The results of the tests carried out at the extended viewing distance were not in agreement with the criterion, yet it was found that the appearance of the original pictures used in the experiments can be improved by an appropriate "crispening"—a process that accentuates the high spatial frequencies, so that the picture used as input to the programs was not the best signal representing the scene, and the criterion may be modified to take account of this fact. It is encouraging that the results of the tests at a close distance are in agreement with the theory.

REFERENCES

1. SHANNON, C. E., AND W. WEAVER, *The Mathematical Theory of Communication,* University of Illinois Press, Urbana, Ill., 1949.
2. SCHREIBER, W. F., "Third Order Probability Distribution of Television Signals," *IRE Trans. Inform. Theory,* IT-2, 94 (1956).
3. SCHREIBER, W. F., AND C. F. KNAPP, "TV Bandwidth Reduction by Digital Coding," *IRE Nat. Conv. Record,* Part 4, 88 (1958).
4. SCHREIBER, W. F., C. F. KNAPP, AND N. D. KAY, "Synthetic Highs—an Experimental TV Bandwidth Reduction System," *J. Soc. Motion Picture Television Engrs.,* *68*, 525 (1959).
5. HUANG, T. S., "A Method of Picture Coding," *Quarterly Progress Report of the Research Laboratory of Electronics, Mass. Inst. of Technology,* No. 57, 109 (April 1960).
6. PAN, J. W., "Picture Processing," *Quarterly Progress Report of the Research Laboratory of Electronics, Mass. Inst. of Technology,* No. 66, 229 (July 1962).
7. SCHREIBER, W. F., "The Mathematical Foundation of the Synthetic Highs System," *Quarterly Progress Report of the Research Laboratory of Electronics, Mass. Inst. of Technology,* No. 68, 140 (January 1963).
8. GRAHAM, D. N., "Two-Dimensional Synthetic Highs System," *Quarterly Progress Report of the Research Laboratory of Electronics, Mass. Inst. of Technology,* No. 75, 131 (October 1964).
9. CUNNINGHAM, J. E., "Image Correction—Transmission Experiments," *Quarterly Progress Report of the Research Laboratory of Electronics, Mass. Inst. of Technology,* No. 70, 244 (July 1963).
10. GRONEMANN, U. F., *Coding Color Pictures,* Technical Report No. 422, Research Laboratory of Electronics, Mass. Inst. of Technology (June 1964).
11. HUANG, T. S., "The Subjective Effect of Pictorial Noise," *Quarterly Progress Report of the Research Laboratory of Electronics, Mass. Inst. of Technology,* No. 72, 194 (January 1964).
12. TRETIAK, O. J., *The Picture Sampling Process,* Sc.D. Thesis, Department of Electrical Engineering, Massachusetts Institute of Technology, 1963.
13. SCHADE, O. H., *J. Soc. Motion Picture Television Engrs.,* *67*, 801 (1958).
14. PETERSON, D. P., AND D. MIDDLETON, *Information and Control,* *5*, 279 (1962).

CHAPTER 4

USE OF THE FOURIER TRANSFORMABLE PROPERTIES OF LENSES FOR SIGNAL SPECTRUM ANALYSIS

K. Preston, Jr.

Perkin-Elmer Corporation, Norwalk, Connecticut

In a coherently illuminated ideal optical system there exists a Fourier transform relationship between the light amplitude distributions in the front and back focal planes of each lens. The purpose of this paper is to describe analytically the conditions which must be fulfilled so that this relationship occurs in a manner which preserves phase and achieves diffraction limited resolution.

Due to the Fourier transformable property of optical systems, it is possible to produce the two-dimensional spectrum of an arbitrary function assuming that this function can properly be introduced in the input focal plane of an optical spectrum analyzer. This paper discusses methods suitable for the introduction of two-dimensional functions or "signals" and gives illustrative examples.

Consider, now, the optical system shown in Fig. 1. The x, y plane to the left of an ideal lens of aperture D is illuminated by a planar, unpolarized, unmodulated monochromatic electromagnetic wave of uniform spatial amplitude propagating in the z direction. Letting the maximum amplitude of the electromagnetic vector be E_0, we can express the incident wave in the x, y plane by the equation:

$$E_i(t) = E_0 \exp [j\omega t] \tag{1}$$

where ω is the radian frequency of the electromagnetic radiation. Let us assume that the x, y plane contains a light modulator $\bar{f}(x, y)$ which operates upon $E_i(t)$ to produce $E_d(t)$ given by

$$E_d(x, y, t) = E_0 \bar{f}(x, y) \exp [j\omega t] \tag{2}$$

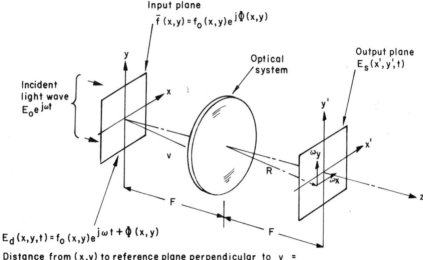

Input plane
$$\bar{f}(x,y) = f_0(x,y)e^{j\phi(x,y)}$$

Output plane
$E_s(x',y',t)$

Optical
system

Incident
light wave
$E_0 e^{j\omega t}$

$E_d(x,y,t) = f_0(x,y)e^{j\omega t + \phi(x,y)}$

Distance from (x,y) to reference plane perpendicular to v =

$a_1 x + a_2 y$ where $a_1 = x'/R$; $a_2 = y'/R$

FIG. 1. The optical spectrum analyzer.

In general, $\bar{f}(x, y)$ is complex; i.e., it acts upon both the amplitude and phase of $E_i(t)$ so that Eq. 2 can be expressed as

$$E_d(x, y, t) = E_0 f_0(x, y) \exp j[\omega t + \phi(x, y)] \tag{3}$$

This operation represents diffraction of the incident wave $E_i(t)$ by $\bar{f}(x, y)$.

Geometrical optics tell us that an ideal lens of aperture D will sum the diffracted electromagnetic energy arriving within its aperture in the direction $\mathbf{v}$ to a point in its back focal plane (Fig. 1). In order to evaluate this summation at all points in the focal plane, the phase of the diffracted electromagnetic energy at all points in a reference plane perpendicular to $\mathbf{v}$ through the origin of the x, y plane must be determined. The equation of this reference plane is

$$a_1 x + a_2 y + a_3 z = 0 \tag{4}$$

where (a_1, a_2, a_3) are the direction cosines of the perpendicular to the plane, i.e., of $\mathbf{v}$. The perpendicular distance from a point (x, y) in the x, y plane to the reference plane is given by

$$d = a_1 x + a_2 y \tag{5}$$

Therefore at the reference plane the phase of the diffracted electromagnetic energy is given by

$$\phi = \phi(x, y) + \frac{2\pi d}{\lambda} = \phi(x, y) + \frac{2\pi}{\lambda}(a_1 x + a_2 y) \tag{6}$$

where λ is the electromagnetic wavelength and $\phi(x, y)$ is the phase function defined by Eq. 3.

The location of the summation point in the focal plane which corresponds to a particular set (a_1, a_2, a_3) can be obtained from the geometrical optical theorem which states that light in the **v** direction passing through the center of an ideal lens is not diverted. Let R be the distance from the center of the lens to the summing point (Fig. 1). Then

$$a_1 = x'/R$$
$$a_2 = y'/R$$
$$a_3 = F/R \qquad (7)$$

where x' and y' are coordinates in the focal plane and F is the effective focal length of the lens.

Combining Eqs. 6 and 7 and letting L be the optical path length from the origin of the x, y plane to the summing point (x', y') yields

$$\phi = \phi(x, y) + \frac{2\pi a_3}{\lambda F} (x'x + y'y) + \frac{2\pi L}{\lambda} \qquad (8)$$

We can now write for the composite electric field $E_s(t)$ at the summation point:

$$E_s(x', y', t) = E_0 \exp\left[j\omega t\right] \iint_P f_0(x, y)$$

$$\exp j \left[\phi(x, y) + \frac{2\pi a_3}{\lambda F} (x'x + y'y) + \frac{2\pi L(x', y')}{\lambda} \right] dx\, dy \qquad (9)$$

where the integration is taken over some pupil P in the x, y plane.

The quantities $2\pi x'/\lambda F$ and $2\pi y'/\lambda F$ are usually defined as the radian spatial frequencies ω_x and ω_y. Equation 9 is not completely general in that it neglects:

1. The effect of the direction of the Poynting vector in the x', y' plane upon the integration which yields E_s, i.e., the "obliquity factor" of references 1 and 2.
2. The effect on E_s of vignetting by the finite aperture D.*
3. The effect of lens aberrations.

These effects are small in most cases of interest where a_3 is close to unity, i.e., for small diffraction angles.

If the x, y plane is placed one focal length from the lens, $L(x', y')$ is a constant for all x' and y'. Thus the term in Eq. 9 involving $L(x', y')$ can be discarded as representing a constant phase shift over the x', y' plane. Furthermore, as the user of an optical spectrum analyzer is primarily interested in the long-term integration of the light intensity—long term in the sense of integration over many cycles at the electromagnetic frequency—we can replace $E_0 \exp\left[j\omega t\right]$ with its rms value, which we shall call E_a.

---

* For an interesting one-dimensional analysis of vignetting, the reader is referred to Appendix B, reference 3.

With these simplifying assumptions, Eq. 9 becomes

$$E_s(x, y) = E_a \iint_P f_0(x, y) \exp j[\phi(x, y) + a_3(\omega_x, \omega_y)(\omega_x x + \omega_y y)] \, dx \, dy \quad (10)$$

If we normalize by dividing by E_a and let $a_3(\omega_x, \omega_y)$ equal unity by assuming small diffraction angles, Eq. 10 becomes

$$E_s'(x, y) = \iint_P \bar{f}(x, y) \exp j[\omega_x x + \omega_y y] \, dx \, dy \quad (11)$$

which is in fact the two-dimensional bounded Fourier transform of the complex function $\bar{f}(x, y)$. This expression further simplifies to

$$E_s'(x, y) = \iint_P f_0(x, y) \exp j[\omega_x x + \omega_y y] \, dx \, dy \quad (12)$$

if we assume $\phi(x, y) = 0$, i.e., only spatial amplitude modulation (no phase modulation) in the x, y plane.

Since P is finite, the above operations are of interest to the user of an optical spectrum analyzer only when the value of $\bar{f}(x, y)$ is insignificant outside of P.

Let us now consider methods for introducing the signal $\bar{f}(x, y)$ into the input focal plane. The transducer required is often called a spatial light modulator. Photographic film is traditionally used as a spatial light modulator when $\bar{f}(x, y)$ is real. Thermoplastic film may be used when $\bar{f}(x, y)$ is purely imaginary, i.e., when only phase modulation is required in the input plane. Satisfactory media for introducing a complex function are not readily available although Leith and others have experimented with methods for using photographic film for this purpose by mixing $\bar{f}(x, y)$ with a spatial carrier frequency.[4] Inhomogeneities in both photographic and thermoplastic film limit their dynamic range. Other media such as photochromic, polymer, and diazo materials are more homogeneous but suffer in comparison with standard silver-halide emulsions in that the input energy required for recording is high.

This brings us to the question of the speed of introduction of the input signal. Both photographic and thermoplastic film require mechanical motion from the point of recording to the input plane as well as either chemical or thermal processing in transit. When the time delay which results from the above processes is intolerable, other methods of signal introduction must be sought. One attractive alternative, when $\bar{f}(x, y)$ is imaginary and one-dimensional, is to use a beam of ultrasound in the input plane as a spatial light modulator. An electrical signal may be directly transduced into ultrasound by means of a piezoelectric driver so as to create a traveling pressure wave in an optically transparent medium. Both transparent liquids and solids may be used for this purpose. As the sound wave traverses the input plane, optical index changes due to the fluctuation in sonic pressure cause the input light to be phase-modulated spatially. The delay time between the introduction of the signal and the production of the spectrum of the signal in the output plane is merely the length of time required for the sound wave to enter the aperture. This may be as short as a few microseconds. For a single transducer the $\bar{f}(x, y)$ introduced in this manner can vary only in one dimension, i.e., the dimension in the direction of ultrasonic propagation. Parallel ultrasonic transducers may be used to produce two-dimensional signal distributions in the input plane. Other methods for instantaneous two-dimensional signal introduction are still under exploratory investigation. They include spatial light modulation by thin films using such effects as the Pockels electro-optic effect, Kerr magneto-optic effect, etc.

Figure 2 gives an illustration of a one-dimensional signal recorded on photographic film and its Wiener spectrum or $|E_s'(x,y)|^2$. In this case the

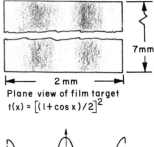

Plane view of film target
$t(x) = \left[(1 + \cos x)/2\right]^2$

FIG. 2. Illustration of input and output distributions.

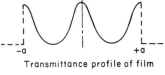

Transmittance profile of film

signal is $f(x) = \left[(1 + \cos x)/2\right]$ which results when the transmittance of the photographic film is recorded as $t(x) = \left[(1 + \cos x)/2\right]^2$. This is due to the fact that $f(x)$ refers to electric field which is the square root of the light intensity to which transmittance is related. The strong signal at $\omega_x = \omega_y = 0$ is the "zero-order frequency" or bias term characteristic of photographic film recordings. Such a term would not appear in an appropriately made recording upon thermoplastic film. Figure 3 shows another example where $t(x) = \left[(1 + \cos 2x)/2\right]$ and thus $f(x) = \left[(1 + \cos 2x)/2\right]^{1/2} =$

$|\cos x/2|$. Note the spurious harmonics created by the square root relationship between $t(x)$ and $f(x)$. These illustrations are given in order to emphasize that the equations derived above relate to light amplitude distributions rather than light intensity distributions. To illustrate quantita-

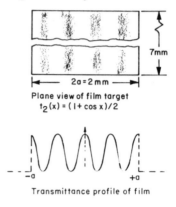

Plane view of film target
$t_2(x) = (1 + \cos x)/2$

Transmittance profile of film

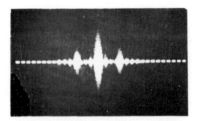

FIG. 3. Illustration of spurious harmonics due to square root effect.

tively the error which can be introduced by neglecting this phenomenon, consider the light intensity distribution given by

$$I_1(x) = \begin{cases} \frac{1}{2}\left(1 + \cos \frac{2\pi}{\lambda_s} x\right) & -\frac{\lambda_s}{2} \leq x \leq +\frac{\lambda_s}{2} \\ 0 & \text{elsewhere} \end{cases} \tag{13}$$

where λ_s is the spatial period.

To obtain the light amplitude distribution we must take the square root of Eq. 13 which yields

$$f(x) = \sqrt{\frac{1}{2}\left(1 + \cos \frac{2\pi}{\lambda_s} x\right)}$$

$$= \cos \frac{\pi}{\lambda_s} x \tag{14}$$

over the interval $-\lambda_s/2 \leq x \leq +\lambda_s/2$.

Combining Eqs. 13 and 14 yields the light amplitude distribution in the x', y' plane as

$$E_s(\omega_x) = \int_{-\lambda_s/2}^{+\lambda_s/2} \cos \frac{\pi}{\lambda_s} x \exp [j\omega_x x] \, dx \qquad (15)$$

Applying the classic relationship $e^{ja} = \cos a + j \sin a$ as well as the well-known trigonometric sum and difference formulas to Eq. 15 permits us to write

$$E_s(\omega_x) = \frac{1}{2} \int_{-\lambda_s 2}^{+\lambda_s/2} \left[\left(\omega_x + \frac{\pi}{\lambda_s}\right) x + \exp j / \exp j \left(\omega_x - \frac{\pi}{\lambda_s}\right) x \right] dx \quad (16)$$

which can readily be integrated and simplified to yield

$$E_s(\omega_x) = \frac{[(\omega_x + \pi/\lambda_s)\lambda_s/2]}{(\omega_x + \pi/\lambda_s)} + \frac{[(\omega_x - \pi/\lambda_s)\lambda_s/2]}{(\omega_x - \pi/\lambda_s)} \qquad (17)$$

The resultant light intensity distribution, i.e., $|E_s(\omega_x)|^2$, is plotted in Fig. 4.

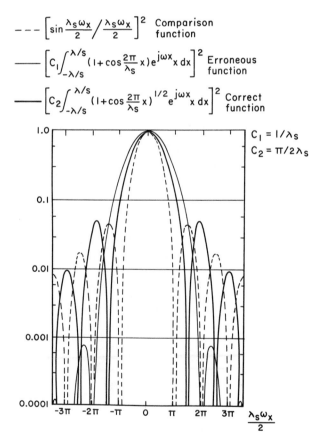

FIG. 4. Plots of several spectra.

Now if the square root effect had been neglected in our derivation and Eq. 15 written in error as

$$E_s'(\omega_x) = \int_{-\lambda_s/2}^{+\lambda_s/2} \frac{1}{2}\left(1 + \cos\frac{2\pi}{\lambda_s}x\right)\exp\left[j\omega_x x\right]dx\ x \tag{18}$$

it can be shown that the resultant (and erroneous) expression, $E_s'(\omega_x)$, would become

$$E_s'(\omega_x) = \frac{\sin \omega_x\lambda_s/2}{\omega_x} + \frac{1}{2}\frac{\sin (\omega_x + 2\pi/\lambda_s)[\lambda_s/2]}{\omega_x + 2\pi/\lambda_s} + \frac{1}{2}\frac{\sin (\omega_x - 2\pi/\lambda_s)[\lambda_s/2]}{\omega_x - 2\pi/\lambda_s} \tag{19}$$

which is also plotted in Fig. 4.

The magnitude of the error is immediately apparent. The first-order fringes of the correct distribution are 13 dB down from the zero-order peak and occur at $\lambda_s\omega_x/2 \approx 2\pi$, whereas the first-order fringes of the erroneous distribution are 31 dB down from the zero order and occur at $\lambda_s\omega_x/2 \approx 5\pi/2$. The limit of the correct function as $\omega_x \to 0$ is $2\lambda_s/\pi$ while the same limit of the incorrect function is $\lambda_s/2$. This yields an absolute error of 2 dB between the peak magnitudes of the corresponding light intensity levels of the main lobes. (This has been taken into account by the normalizing factors C_1 and C_2 in Fig. 4.) Figure 4 shows a sinc x function for com-

FIG. 5. Aerial photograph and its Fourier transform.

parison with $E_s(\omega_x)$ and $E_s'(\omega_x)$. Note that the main lobe broadening at the 6-dB points of the correct distribution, $E_s(\omega_x)$, is 25 per cent while for $E_s'(\omega_x)$ it is 50 per cent.

As a more general illustration of two-dimensional Fourier transforms, consider Fig. 5. This figure shows an aerial photograph with its two-dimensional spectrum (inset). The bright central region of the spectrum is again the zero-order or dc term characteristic of photographic film recordings. The pattern superimposed upon the zero order is clearly due to the periodic structure of the images of the parked automobiles. In the direction of high spatial frequency, i.e., perpendicular to the narrow dimension of the automobiles, the higher order harmonics are clearly visible. In the direction of lower spatial frequency, i.e., perpendicular to the long direction of the automobiles, the harmonics are present but are not resolved, indicating either a certain degree of spatial incoherence in the illuminating light or optical aberrations.

From the above discussion it is clear that a lens is a useful device for performing certain mathematical operations upon a light amplitude input function in its input focal plane. The reader has been exposed to some of the subtleties of this operation in the above discussion. The reader should also be aware that, in terms of lens design, the optics must not contribute spurious phase variations. The optical system must provide for collimation of point sources in the input plane as well as for the focusing of collimated light to points in the output plane over all possible angles associated with **v** (Fig. 1) and over the field determined $(\pm x_{max}, \pm y_{max})$ and $(\pm x'_{max}, \pm y'_{max})$. This is an important requirement in that it restricts the optical system to symmetrical designs, such as are shown in Figs. 6a and 6b. The doublet

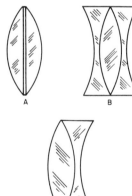

FIG. 6. Symmetrical and asymmetrical
lenses.

shown in Fig. 6c is an example of a lens which, in general, could not be used to take Fourier transforms within the restrictions of the above analysis.

Lens raw material should be strain- and bubble-free and have maximum surface quality. For example, it can be shown that the amplitude of light scattered from the surface of a lens is given by

$$I_s \approx \psi_{\text{rms}}^2 \approx \left[\frac{2\pi(n-1)}{\lambda}\right]^2 \delta_{\text{rms}}^2 \qquad (20)$$

where ψ_{rms} is the rms value of the phase variations produced by δ_{rms} surface ripple. For scattered light intensity to be 40 dB below the average intensity of the signal in the output focal plane, Eq. 20 implies an rms value of surface ripple of about 20 Å per cycle.

Thus, in summary, it is clear that to design and use optical systems for optical spectrum analysis requires a thorough understanding of the theory involved as well as an appreciation of the peculiar lens design and manufacturing tolerances which must be placed upon such systems.

REFERENCES

1. BORN, M., AND E. WOLF, *Principles of Optics*, Pergamon Press, New York, 1959, Chap. 8.
2. CUTRONA, L. J. *et al.*, "Optical Data Processing and Filtering Systems," *IRE Trans. Inform. Theory*, IT-6, 386 (1960).
3. VANDER LUGT, A. B., *Signal Detection by Complex Spatial Filtering*, Report 4594-22-T, Institute of Science and Technology, University of Michigan, Ann Arbor, Mich.
4. LEITH, E. N., AND J. UPATNIEKS, *J. Opt. Soc. Am.*, 53, 1377–1381 (1963).

CHAPTER 5

CONTRIBUTION OF DIFFRACTION OPTICS TO OPTICAL INFORMATION TECHNOLOGY

Guy Lansraux

National Research Council, Ottawa, Canada

Introduction

Technical processes in science, engineering, etc., dependent on optical instruments are often bounded in the field of their performances by the resolution limit of the involved optical systems. Therefore to improve image quality by enhancing the resolving power of instruments is not only a fundamental problem in optics but should also contribute to the progress of many techniques.

It is well known that the image of a point formed in the observation plane of any optical system is never a point but a distribution of light, a so-called diffraction pattern. The consequences of this are: limitation of resolution, degradation of contrasts, etc.

The larger the diffraction pattern, the more degrading are the effects. Conversely, image quality increases if the radiant energy is more concentrated in the central region of the diffraction pattern. Moreover, one supposes that the most favorable energy distribution is that where the greatest concentration of energy is in the close vicinity of the observation focus, i.e., the center of the diffraction pattern.

The general aim of this paper is to show how *amplitude filtering* improves image quality and enhances resolving power.[1] This now well-known technique consists in varying locally the transmission factor of any optical system in order to provide a nonuniform illumination of the wavefronts emerging from the exit pupil. These wavefronts are then propagated toward the image plane where they form the utmost concentrated diffraction pattern.

Secondarily this paper includes a contribution in the field of information storage.

Remarks on Optical Information Storage

In the field of optical information storage one of the basic techniques consists in recording photographically: letters, numbers, sigils, ideograms, and generally speaking any symbolic drawings which will be simply called *symbols* in this paper. These symbols are distributed in a so-called *input information plane*. Then by means of an optical system, named *image-forming system*, a considerably reduced image of this plane is projected on a film where information is definitively stored after processing. At any time the initial information can be reconstructed in an *output information* by a *reading system*.

The optimized storage is that where the total amount of information per unit area of film is maximum. Such a result depends on four factors at least: nature of the input information, quality of the image projected on the film, recording performances of the photographic material, and resolution of the reading system. The determination of the optimum over-all device, including the image-forming system, the film with its processing, and the reading system, is somewhat intricate because each of the four factors mentioned is more or less dependent upon the others.

Now let us analyze in detail an example in order to illustrate the previous remarks. The information to be stored is a geometrical arrangement of luminous points whose brightnesses are almost uniform. The image of each point is a diffraction pattern, which is supposed to be widely spread in the plane of the film, with a large amount of diffracted light surrounding the luminous central disk. Such diffraction patterns are produced by an optical system which should be estimated, in this case, to have low performances. Consequently, the over-all image is a geometrical arrangement of widely overlapping diffraction patterns.

On the other hand let us imagine that the photographic material offers simultaneously two facilities: an ultrafine grain and a very high contrast. The grain is supposed small enough to avoid breaking up the images of diffraction patterns. Then, according to a technique used for line image sharpening, the high-contrast film is underexposed in order to cut off the background of diffracted light. By locating adequately the emulsion threshold in the image density range one can reasonably expect the film to show a geometrical arrangement of circular spots definitely separated. Moreover the spots might be resolved even if the distances from one to another are slightly shorter than the Rayleigh's limit of resolution. Nevertheless such an image recording would fail if the symbol brightness in the input information plane is not almost uniform.

However idealized this example may be, it illustrates the importance of associating the nature of information, the optical systems, and the recording process.

In fact most of the emulsions, available at the present time, have either ultrafine grain with a low gamma or a very high gamma with a coarse grain. Consequently, the effective density of information storage is far below that expected. It is only when the size of stored symbols is large with respect to diffraction patterns that one can correct a poor image quality by an adequate use of the emulsion facilities.

In conclusion the only way remaining to increase the storage density is by improving the optical performances of the image-forming system.

Moreover in the given example the symbols, which must be uniformly illuminated, are identified by means of their own shape. This is a restrictive condition and in order to increase the storage density one can change symbols for points which differ from one another only by their brightnesses. Information is then contained in a set of spots distributed inside an area of film smaller than the minimum area required by any conventional one-tone symbols.

Nevertheless such a code implies two independent conditions: a photographic process recording brightnesses with fidelity, and images where each spot is definitely isolated from its neighbors in order to avoid luminous interactions of close spots, and, consequently, misreading. The first condition is easily met with a low gamma emulsion by distributing the image brightness range inside the limits of the straight line in the characteristic curve. The second condition is met by suppressing the far diffracted light surrounding any details. This requirement brings us back to the general problem of diffraction optics mentioned in the Introduction.

The Image Quality Criterion

In this paper any diffraction pattern has a radial symmetry and is therefore represented by the radial intensity $I(W)$. According to the requirements previously mentioned, the diffraction pattern has to be a luminous disk without outer diffracted light. In other words the whole luminous energy of the diffraction pattern must be concentrated inside a circle C as small as possible. Rigorously speaking it is impossible to suppress the diffraction effect, but, in practice, one can gather the highest possible amount of energy inside the circle C.

The energy concentration is represented by the *factor of encircled energy*:

$$E(W) = \frac{\int_0^W I(W)\, d(W^2)}{\int_0^\infty I(W)\, d(W^2)} \tag{1}$$

which is the ratio of the energy distributed inside the circle of radius W to the total amount of energy in the diffraction pattern[2-5] (Figs. 1 and 4).

Maximizing $E(W)$ for $W = W_m$ means that the diffraction pattern is a disk of radius W_m as far as: $1 - E(W_m)$, i.e., the light diffracted outside the circle W_m is negligible.

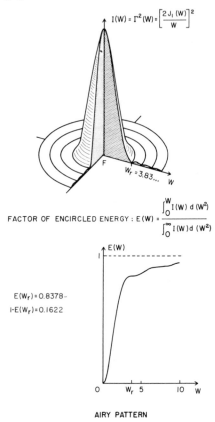

FIG. 1. View in perspective of the Airy pattern. The factor of encircled energy $E(W)$ is the ratio of the energy distributed within a circle of radius W centered at F to the total energy in the diffraction pattern.

A detailed determination of the optimum instrument providing a maximized factor of encircled energy will be established in other papers. Nevertheless the successive steps of this study are briefly described here.

Expressions for Diffraction Optics

For a given focusing the diffraction pattern corresponding to the object point H is distributed on the observation plane, normal to the optical axis at the focus F (Fig. 2).

The spherical wavefront S propagated from H is transformed into an emergent wavefront centered on O and limited by a circular diaphragm whose normalized radius is equal to unity.

The sphere centered on F and intersected by the optical axis at O is a reference surface used to determine the spherical aberration, i.e., the departure $\overline{PM}$ from S to Ω along any oriented straight line PMF. However

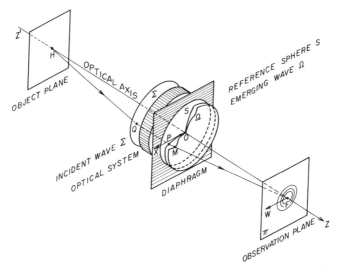

Fig. 2. Schematic diagram of the formation of a diffraction pattern in an optical instrument.

the aberration is generally represented by its phase $\psi(P) = (n2\pi)/\lambda,\ \overline{PM}$.

On the other hand, the transmittance of the optical system is supposed to vary by means of an *amplitude filter*, and along any optical path $HQPMF$ the *transmission factor* is $T(P) = $ amplitude emergent at P/amplitude incident at Q.

The normalized radial abscissas in the pupil and the diffraction pattern are respectively X, and $W = n2\pi Rr/\lambda D$, where n, λ, R, D, and r (measured simultaneously with any unit of length) are respectively the refractive index of the medium, the wavelength, the radius of the diaphragm, the distance OF, and the radial abscissa in the observation plane. Incidentally, $W = 3.83$ is the normalized radius of the central disk in the Airy pattern, and is consequently the resolution limit according to Rayleigh's criterion.

The complex amplitude in the diffraction pattern $\gamma(W)$ is then related to the pupil by the well-known expression:

$$\gamma(W) = \int_0^1 T(X)e^{i\psi(X)}J_0(WX)\ d(X^2) \qquad (2)$$

This expression has to be transformed for easier use. In any case one can expand the complex amplitude of the pupil in a development:[6,7]

$$T(X)e^{i\psi(X)} = \sum_{n=1}^{n=\infty} a_n(1 - X^2)^{n-1} \tag{3}$$

The corresponding complex amplitude in the diffraction pattern is then

$$\gamma(W) = \sum_{n=1}^{n=\infty} \frac{a_n}{n} L_n(W) \tag{4}$$

where $L_n(W)$ are functions defined in terms of Bessel functions of first kind by the relations:

$$L_n(W) = 2^n \cdot n! \frac{J_n(W)}{W^n} = \sum_{k=0}^{k=\infty} (-1)^k \frac{n!}{k!n+k!} \left(\frac{W}{2}\right)^{2k} \tag{5}$$

The expression 1 of the factor of encircled energy may be written

$$E(W) = \frac{\int_0^W I(W)\,d(W^2)}{\int_0^\infty I(W)\,d(W^2)} = \frac{\int_0^W |\gamma(W)|^2\,d(W^2)}{\int_0^\infty |\gamma(W)|^2\,d(W^2)} = \frac{\int_0^W \left|\sum_{n=1}^{n=\infty} \frac{a_n}{n} L_n(W)\right|^2 d(W^2)}{\int_0^\infty \left|\sum_{n=1}^{n=\infty} \frac{a_n}{n} L_n(W)\right|^2 d(W^2)} \tag{6}$$

Determination of the Pupil Providing a Maximized E(W)

The pupil is completely determined when the coefficients a_n are known. They may be calculated by associating with Eq. 6 the conditions which make $E(W)$ an absolute maximum for $W = W_m$, i.e., the infinite set

$$\left[\frac{\partial E}{\partial a_1} = 0\right]_{W=W_m} \cdots \left[\frac{\partial E}{\partial a_n} = 0\right]_{W=W_m} \tag{7}$$

Here one can prove that for a given W_m, the absolute maximum $E(W_m)$ is obtained when, and only when, the optical system is aberration-free and correctly focused. Consequently $\psi(X)$ vanishes, the coefficients a_n are real, and the expression 3 is reduced to the distribution $T(X)$ of the amplitude in the pupil. Moreover, one can determine only one function $T(X)$ corresponding to a given W_m.

Figure 3 shows $T(X)$ calculated for $W_m = 5$ and the corresponding curve $E(W)$ passing by the point whose ordinate $E(5) = 0.9953$ is the absolute maximum at the abscissa $W_m = 5$.

A Property of T(X) and Its Application to Lasers

Between $T(X)$ and $E(W)$, Fig. 3 shows $\Gamma(W)$ which is derived from $\gamma(W)$, i.e., the radial amplitude in the diffraction pattern, by means of a double normalization. First, normalization of amplitude by changing $\gamma(W)$ for $\Gamma(W) = \nu \cdot \gamma(W)$, where ν is a normalization factor such that $\Gamma(0) = T(0)$.

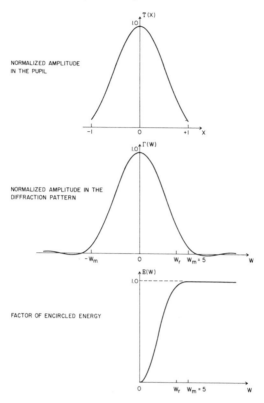

FIG. 3. Normalized curves $T(X)$, (W), and $E(W)$. With a suitable normalization of abscissas and amplitudes, the curve $T(W)$ can be superimposed directly upon the curve (W).

Secondly, normalization of abscissas such that the range $0 \leq W \leq W_m$ covers exactly the range $0 \leq X \leq 1$.

The curve $T(X)$ can be superimposed upon the curve $\Gamma(W)$ according to the analytical identity

$$T(X) \equiv \Gamma(W) \qquad \text{when} \qquad W = W_m X \qquad (8)$$

In other words by means of a suitable normalization the light distribution in the pupil is identical to that of the diffraction pattern inside the circle of radius W_m.

In a previous paper[8] the author showed that an emergent spherical wavefront, as S on Fig. 1, produces an Airy diffraction pattern, whose wavefront is not plane, but almost spherical and confocal with S. This property remains whatever amplitude filtering there may be. Consequently $T(X)$ and the amplitude $\Gamma(W)$ distributed inside the circular area of radius W_m are identical light distributions on confocal spheres. Moreover they correspond evidently to the light distributions on the confocal mirrors of a laser for the TEM_{00} mode.

Computations carried out by the author of the cases studied by A. G. Fox and Tingye Li are in perfect agreement.[9]

Recently M. J. Taylor, G. R. Hanes, and K. M. Baird studied experimentally the diffraction loss and the beam size of the TEM_{00} mode in two different gas lasers. Their results are in agreement with the theoretically predicted values to within the experimental error.[10]

T(X) Is the Equilibrium Distribution in an Iterated Diffraction Process

The *iterated diffraction process* consists in cutting off the marginal region of a diffraction pattern with a diaphragm and in inverting the spherical curvature of its wavefront in order to provide a new pupil, producing the next diffraction pattern, and so on.

The author proved that any first pupil, whatever its amplitude distribution may be, tends toward $T(X)$ in the infinite iterated diffraction process using circular diaphragms of radius W_m. In other words $T(X)$ is a steady-state distribution, and for that reason is called *equilibrium distribution*.

Miscellaneous Properties

1. The normalization coefficient is related to the absolute maximum of the factor of encircled energy $E(W_m)$ by

$$\nu = \frac{W_m}{2\sqrt{E(W_m)}} \tag{9}$$

2. $E(W_m)$ is related to the marginal amplitude in the pupil $T(1)$ by

$$E(W_m) = 1 - T^2(1) \tag{10}$$

In other words the amount of diffracted light distributed outside the circle of radius W_m is equal to the normalized intensity transmitted at the edge of the amplitude filter: $1 - E(W_m) = T^2(1)$.

3. The amplitude is maximum at $X = 0$ and $W = 0$ in the pupil and diffraction pattern respectively.

4. The amplitude in the pupil decreases as X varies from 0 to 1.

5. When $W_m \to 0$, $\Gamma(W)$ becomes an Airy pattern.

6. For small W_m, one can use the approximate expression:

$$T(X) \sim 1 - \frac{W_m^2}{8} X^2 \qquad E(W_m) \sim \frac{W_m^2}{4} \qquad \nu \sim 1 \tag{11}$$

7. When W_m increases, $T(X)$ becomes, in the limit, a delta function, because when $W_m \to \infty$, then $T(X) \to 0$ whenever $x = 0$; however, $T(0) = 1$ still holds.

8. For large W_m, $T(X)$ is approximately Gaussian:

$$T(X) \sim \exp\left(-\frac{W_m}{2} X^2\right) \qquad \Gamma(W) \sim \frac{2}{W_m} \exp\left(-\frac{W^2}{2W_m}\right) \qquad \nu \sim \frac{W_m}{2}$$

The Relationship: $W_m, 1 - E(W_m)$

In Fig. 4 are shown various curves $E(W)$ for different W_m, including the classical Airy pattern curve $W_m = 0$. Each curve passes by a point whose ordinate $E(W_m)$ is the absolute maximum at the abscissa W_m. At this point the curve $E(W)$ is tangent to the envelope $M(W)$ of all the curves $E(W)$.

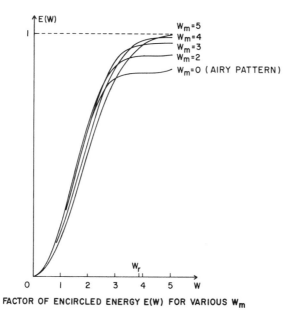

FACTOR OF ENCIRCLED ENERGY E(W) FOR VARIOUS W_m

FIG. 4. Family of curves $E(W)$.

In other words $M(W)$ is also the locus of the points whose coordinates are W_m and $E(W_m)$. Therefore $M(W)$ represents the greatest possible concentrations of radiant energy in diffraction patterns, and may be considered as the limit of optical system performances.

Several numerical values of $E(W_m)$ and $1 - E(W_m)$ are given in Table 1 with respect to W_m.

As previously mentioned, maximizing $E(W)$ for $W = W_m$ means that the diffraction pattern is a disk of radius W_m, as far as $1 - E(W_m)$; i.e., the light diffracted outside the circle W_m is negligible. The quantities W_m and $1 - E(W_m)$ being related together by means of the function $M(W)$, when W_m is chosen too small, $1 - E(W_m)$ cannot be neglected. As it is obvious that the smaller W_m the more favorable the diffraction pattern, one has to consider first the highest amount of diffracted light which is tolerable in the studied problem; then W_m is determined. In each case a compromise must be found between small W_m but large $1 - E(W_m)$ and small $1 - E(W_m)$ but large W_m.

TABLE 1   NUMERICAL VALUES OF THE ABSOLUTE MAXIMUM $E(W_m)$ AS A FUNCTION OF W_m. COMPLEMENTARY VALUES OF $1 - E(W_m)$

W_m	$E(W_m)$	$1 - E(W_m)$
0	0.0000	1.0000
0.5	0.0606	0.9394
1	0.2211	0.7789
1.5	0.4295	0.5705
2	0.6296	0.3704
2.5	0.7851	0.2149
3	0.8871	0.1129
3.5	0.9452	0.0548
4	0.9750	0.0250
4.5	0.9890	0.0110
5	0.9953	0.0047
5.5	0.9981	0.0019
6	0.9992	0.0008
6.5	0.9997	0.0003
7	0.99987	0.00013
7.5	0.99995	0.00005
8	0.99998	0.00002
8.5	0.99999	0.00001
9	0.999997	0.000003
9.5	0.999999	0.000001
10	0.9999995	0.0000005

The experiments carried out by the author are based on $W_m = 5$. The chosen W_m is slightly greater than the Rayleigh's limit of resolution: $W_R = 3.83 \cdots$. On the other hand, the diffracted light: $1 - E(W_m)$ is considerably reduced with respect to that in the Airy pattern where $1 - E(5) = 0.1388$ (Fig. 5). In conclusion such an amplitude filtering is supposed to improve image quality when a great reduction of the far diffracted light is required.

General Applications in Diffraction Optics

The photographs of Fig. 6 show the Airy pattern and the maximized diffraction pattern corresponding to $W_m = 5$. By comparing one to the other, one can estimate how low is the background of diffracted light. As predicted, the diffraction pattern is restricted, in practice, to a central disk, whose radius is roughly 5, without outer rings.

A first consequence in diffraction optics is an enhanced resolving power in most cases. Generally speaking the sharpness of images improves the image quality of most optical systems, mainly metrological instruments.

On the other hand the low background of diffracted light is particularly suitable in spectroscopy for isolating very faint lines in the vicinity of

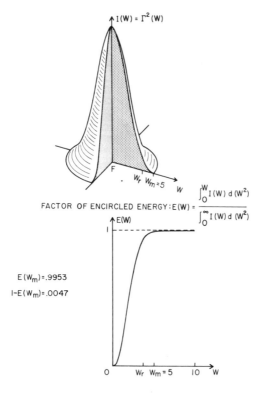

$$I(W) = \Gamma^2(W)$$

W_r $W_m = 5$

FACTOR OF ENCIRCLED ENERGY : $E(W) = \dfrac{\int_0^W I(W)\,d(W^2)}{\int_0^\infty I(W)\,d(W^2)}$

$E(W_m) = .9953$

$1 - E(W_m) = .0047$

$E(W)$

W_r $W_m = 5$ 10 W

EQUILIBRIUM DIFFRACTION PATTERN FOR $W_m = 5$

FIG. 5. View in perspective of the diffraction pattern corresponding to the absolute maximum of the factor of encircled energy for $W_m = 5$.

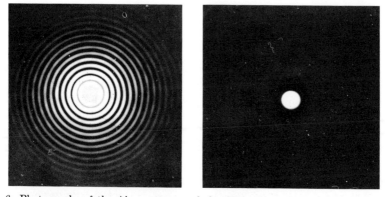

FIG. 6. Photographs of the Airy pattern and the diffraction pattern corresponding to the absolute maximum of the factor of encircled energy for $W_m = 5$.

bright lines and in astronomy for resolving groups of stars whose brightnesses differ by several magnitudes.

Moreover geometrical aberrations are more or less reduced. It is then possible to envision a new field of optical instruments with wider apertures, whose aberrations are corrected by amplitude filtering. The loss in clarity due to the amplitude filter is balanced or exceeded by the gain due to aperture. The resolving power is then considerably enhanced.

Applications in Optical Information Storage Technology

As mentioned previously, amplitude filtering improves that basic technique which consists in recording photographically information symbols. The photographs of Fig. 7 show the "lucky! number" with or without

FIG. 7. Photographs of the "lucky! number" with and without amplitude filtering in a case where symbol size is almost comparable to that of diffraction pattern.

amplitude filtering in a case where symbol size is almost comparable to that of diffraction pattern.

One can note the line broadening on the one hand and the reduction of diffracted light on the other hand. With this example it appears that Rayleigh's theory is definitely inadequate for estimating resolution. Failure of such a classical criterion is more striking in Fig. 8 which illustrates a successful application of amplitude filtering to a spot coding process.

In the image produced by the conventional optical system the interaction of the bright spots against a very faint one makes the code useless. On the contrary amplitude filtering permits accurate measurements of the absolute density at the center of each spot, and assigns therefore a given symbol to each spot according to a precalibrated characteristic curve.

Moreover the spot diameter is related to the density and may be used as an auxiliary coding process.

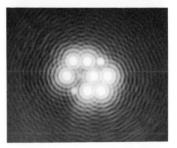

Fig. 8. Photographs, with or without amplitude filtering, of luminous spots whose brightnesses have varied magnitudes. They can be used for a code by assigning a given symbol to the photometric density of each spot. Such spots would be liable to be misread were there no amplitude filtering, due to the interaction of the diffracted light.

The photographs of Figs. 7 and 8 have been obtained with the same image-forming system in identical conditions. One can therefore estimate the gain in storage density, which can reach, in the actual state of the art, one million symbol spots per millimeter square.

REFERENCES

1. LANSRAUX, G., *Compt. Rend.*, *222*, 1434–1435 (1946).
2. LANSRAUX, G., *Rev. Opt.*, *31*, 321–333 (1952); *31*, 444–456 (1952); *31*, 545–560 (1952); *32*, 72–90 (1953); *32*, 313–225 (1953).
3. LANSRAUX, G., *Rev. Opt.*, *34*, 65–91 (1955).
4. LANSRAUX, G., AND G. BOIVIN, *Can. J. Phys.*, *36*, 1696–1709 (1958).
5. LANSRAUX, G., AND G. BOIVIN, *Can. J. Phys.*, *39*, 158–188 (1961).
6. LANSRAUX, G., *Rev. Opt.*, *26*, 24–25 (1947).
7. LANSRAUX, G., *J. Phys. Radium*, *7*, 29–39 (1953).
8. LANSRAUX, G., *Can. J. Phys.*, *40*, 1101–1112 (1962).
9. FOX, A. G., AND TINGYE LI, *Bell System Tech. J.*, *14*, 453–488 (1961).
10. TAYLOR, M. J., G. R. HANES, AND K. M. BAIRD, *J. Opt. Soc. Am.*, *43*, 1310–1414 (1964).

CHAPTER 6

RECENT DEVELOPMENTS
IN COHERENT OPTICAL TECHNOLOGY

Louis J. Cutrona

Conductron Corporation, Ann Arbor, Michigan

I. Introduction

Recently optical techniques have received increased attention from a growing number of physicists and engineers. This has stemmed in part from the invention of the laser and in part from a realization that optical configurations can be used to perform a large variety of operations on signals. Moreover, techniques have been devised whereby the two-dimensional nature of optical operations can be used as such or can be converted to a multiplicity of one-dimensional operations. Thus, optics has emerged as a powerful and versatile analog computing technique.

Both coherent and noncoherent computation techniques have been used for analog computations. Of these the use of coherent optical techniques is by far the more versatile and useful for such purposes.

In coherent configurations the phenomenon of diffraction is used. When a lens is placed a focal distance from a transparency, it will be found that the light a focal distance from the lens on its output side is distributed according to the two-dimensional Fourier transform of the object.

By the addition of a cylindrical lens to this configuration, the equipment is converted to one with multichannel capabilities. In this case, instead of a single two-dimensional analysis of the transparency, one obtains a multiplicity of one-dimensional spectral analyses.

In some cases the operation desired is that of spectral analysis. In such cases, one can use a spherical lens, or a spherical lens in conjunction with a cylinder lens to display either a two-dimensional spectral analysis or a multiplicity of one-dimensional spectral analyses.

Often it is desirable to do simple filtering operations on signals. For such cases one can arrange an optical system in which two configurations of either type described above are in tandem. One can operate upon the spectrum at an intermediate plane so that the output image reflects the effect of these changes. In one simple case, a passband in an optical filter is simply a transparent region in the spectral plane; a stopband is an opaque spot placed at the appropriate point in the spectrum plane.

Another operation of interest is that of multiplication. This operation arises in performing such operations as autocorrelation, cross-correlation, convolution, and other linear operations. Multiplication is achieved optically by imaging one transparency upon another.

As discussed in Sec. IVC, optical configurations are capable of performing linear operations on a function of a single variable. Among these linear operations are those of spectrum analysis, autocorrelation, cross-correlation, convolution, filtering, and matched filtering.

In most cases one has the choice of using the optics as a single two-dimensional channel or as a multiplicity of one-dimensional channels. In the latter case 50 channels per millimeter can be achieved easily and one has the capability of about 1350 channels using 35-mm optics with 27 mm of these active.

Thus one has in optics an extremely powerful and versatile tool.

II. Basic Diffraction Phenomena

The capability of optical equipment as a computing tool arises from diffraction phenomena. For this reason two basic configurations which appear repeatedly in computing configurations will be described. The two configurations referred to are:

1. A configuration using a spherical lens which produces two-dimensional diffraction.

2. A configuration consisting of a spherical lens in conjunction with a cylindrical lens which produces a multiplicity of one-dimensional diffraction patterns.

The basic configuration for obtaining two-dimensional diffraction patterns is shown in Fig. 1.

Fig. 1. Configuration for two-dimensional spectrum analysis.

In this figure S represents a source of light, L_1 represents a collimating lens, P_1 represents the input plane in which a transparency is placed, and lens L_2 is the spherical lens which is the essential element for producing a two-dimensional diffraction pattern. Plane P_2 is the plane in which the two-dimensional spectrum (of the transparency in plane P_1) is exhibited.

In order that the distribution of light in plane P_2 be the two-dimensional spectrum analysis of the density distribution of the transparency in plane P_1, it is necessary that planes P_1 and P_2 be spaced a focal length on either side of lens L_2. If $f(x, y)$ represents the amplitude of light emerging from plane P_1, then the distribution of light amplitude in plane P_2 is given by Eq. 1:

$$F(\alpha, \beta) = \iint f(x, y)e^{jk(\alpha x + \beta y)} \, dx \, dy \qquad (1)$$

In Eq. 1, the amplitude of the light in plane P_2 is given by $F(\alpha, \beta)$. Here k represents the wave number of the light while α and β represent the direction cosines of the diffracted beam with respect to the x and y axes.

Equation 1 is the fundamental relationship for two-dimensional diffraction. The configuration shown in Fig. 1 is used in a number of applications which are described in Secs. III and IV.

The configuration in Fig. 1 produces a single two-dimensional diffraction pattern. This equipment can be converted to a multichannel one-dimensional diffraction equipment by the addition of a cylindrical lens to the configuration of Fig. 1. This cylindrical lens is placed between planes P_1 and P_2 to give the configuration shown in Fig. 2.

FIG. 2. Configuration for one-dimensional spectrum analysis.

In this case the distribution of light in plane P_2 is given by Eq. 2. It will be noted that this expression indicates distribution of light corresponding to a multichannel spectrum analysis:

$$F(\alpha, y) = \int f(x, y)e^{jk\alpha x} \, dx \qquad (2)$$

The parameter y is an index referring to a given channel. The other parameters have been previously defined.

III. Filtering Operations and Spectrum Analysis

Optical equipment can be usefully employed in a number of filtering operations and in a number of spectrum analysis operations.

In many cases, a display of the spectrum is the desired output. In such a case configurations shown in Figs. 1 and 2 are used.

If a two-dimensional spectrum analysis is desired, the two-dimensional signal to be analyzed is recorded on a transparency by whatever means are appropriate to obtain this image (e.g., a photograph is taken of the object or line by line buildup of the image is used).

In the multichannel case a number of separate channels must be recorded. If a transparency is placed in plane P_1 of the optical configuration shown in Fig. 2, the output will consist of a multiplicity of spectral analyses; each input channel having its corresponding output channel in plane P_2.

In many cases it is desirable to perform filtering operations upon the recorded signals. In such cases, it is usually required to view the signals corresponding to these altered spectra. To achieve this alteration of the spectrum, and viewing of the result, it is necessary to modify the optical configurations shown in Figs. 1 and 2 to those shown in Figs. 3a and 3b respectively.

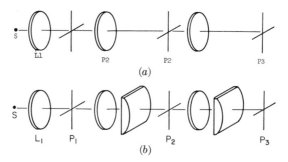

FIG. 3. Modified optical configurations.

The configurations in Figs. 3a and 3b permit operations on the spectra by filtering operations in plane P_2. A number of filtering operations are possible.

In the simplest case one can consider band-pass and band-stop filtering in plane P_2. A passband is achieved by having a transparent region at the appropriate location in plane P_2. A band stop is achieved by locating an opaque spot at the appropriate position in plane P_2. A number of important cases, in which such operations are useful, are described in the following.

One may have a photograph with a lower contrast than is desired. Low contrast is a consequence of an average illumination level which is large compared to the fluctuations in illumination level. A reduction of the average illumination level will increase the contrast of the image. This can be done using the configuration shown in Fig. 3a by placing an opaque spot or partially transparent spot on the optical axis in plane P_2. This will remove all or part of the dc component (average illumination). Examples of the improvement in contrast, which can be achieved by this means, are shown in Fig. 4.*

* The author wishes to express his gratitude to Dr. E. O'Neill and to the Professional Technical Group on Information Theory of the IEEE for permission to reproduce Figs. 4 and 5. These figures were taken from Dr. O'Neill's paper entitled "Spatial Filtering in Optics."

FIG. 4. Contrast improvement.

In the contrast improvement application described above, a spot on the optical axis was used to remove or reduce the dc (average component of the signal). In the multichannel one-dimensional case for which the configuration of Fig. 3b is appropriate, a wire can be used to remove the dc simultaneously from all of the channels.

A more complicated filtering operation can be achieved by placing in plane P_2 a transparency having a density varying as a function of position. Since position in plane P_2 corresponds to specific values of the spectral variables, this corresponds to a filter which changes the relative magnitudes of the spectral components.

In some cases the desired filter can be made in the equipment configurations shown as Figs. 3a and 3b. In this case, an object, whose spectrum is desired, is placed in plane P_1. An unexposed photographic plate is placed in plane P_2 and exposed by the light incident upon this plane. This film, processed as a positive (by reversal or by contact printing of a negative) is then the spectrum corresponding to the object.

This spectrum has passbands at appropriate locations for passing the spectrum corresponding to the object used in making the filter. Such a filter is extremely useful for enhancing a given object while suppressing other objects in the field.

Examples in which the signal-to-noise ratio corresponding to a number of objects is improved, are shown in Fig. 5.*

A more difficult filter to make is one in which phase variations are desired. The difficulties in making filters of this kind arise largely from the short wavelengths of light.

In the most general case, a filter is desired in which both the magnitude and the phase shift of the spectra can be varied. In this case one can place two transparencies in contact in plane P_2; one of the transparencies has a varying density while the other has a varying phase shift. This permits the most general filtering operation to be performed optically.

There are many instances in which this type of filtering is useful. Infor-

* See footnote on previous page.

mation theory indicates that in a number of cases a desirable signal operation is that of passing a signal through a matched filter. In general the matched filter will require a variation of both magnitude and phase, hence the general filter consisting of variable magnitude and phase is required.

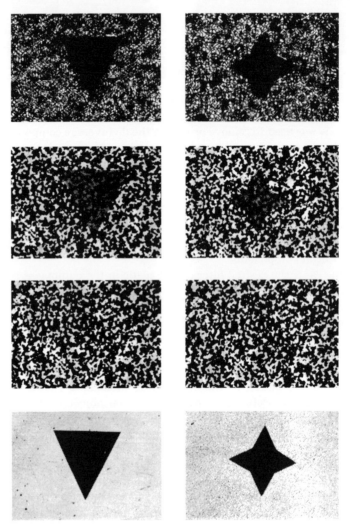

Fig. 5. Isolated signal in the presence of "noise."

The difficulty of achieving sufficient accuracy in the phase filter, however, has motivated a search for techniques which are equivalent but in which the recording of density alone is sufficient.

At least two such techniques have been successfully demonstrated. In one case, use is made of the fact that the Fourier transforms of a symmetric function is real. The object whose spectrum is desired is printed with appropriate symmetry so that its transform is real.

A second scheme for achieving the equivalent of a complex filter (magnitude and phase shift both variable) makes use of a technique recently demonstrated by Leith and Upatnieks[1] and Vander Lugt.[2]

In this case a recording is made in which both phase and magnitude are preserved but in which this information can be recovered from a transparency having density variations only.

The configuration required in this case is shown in Fig. 6.* In this equip-

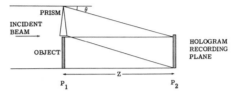

Fig. 6. (*a*) Wedge technique for producing a two-beam hologram.

ment the object whose spectrum is desired is illuminated with coherent light.

A hologram is produced by recording on photographic film the interference pattern resulting from the illumination of some object with a wavefront from the same source. In using the technique, the reference wavefront is made to be incident upon the recording film at an angle so that the phase of the incident light progresses linearly across the film. This becomes a carrier for the information bearing part of the signal.

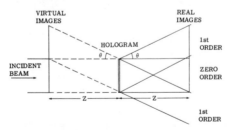

Fig. 6. (*b*) The reconstruction process. Low-quality conventional reconstructions occur on hologram axis. High-quality reconstructions occur in the first-order diffracted waves.

Let $A_1 e^{j\phi_1}$ represent the signals incident upon the photographic plate which have come from the transparency. Both A_1 and ϕ_1 are to be considered as functions of x and y. Let the reference signal have the form

* The author gratefully acknowledges permission given him by E. N. Leith and J. Upatnieks and the Optical Society of America for permission to use Figs. 6a–6g. These figures are taken in part from "Wavefront Reconstruction with Continuous-Tone Objects," and from unpublished material supplied by these authors.

$A_0 e^{j\phi_0}$. Here, too, A_0 and ϕ_0 are functions of x and y. The amplitude of the light incident on the photographic plate will be given by Eq. 3:

$$A(x, y) = A_1 e^{j\phi_1} + A_0 e^{j\phi_0} \tag{3}$$

The intensity I recorded on the film will be given by Eq. 4:

$$I = |A|^2 = |A_1 e^{j\phi_1} + A_0 e^{j\phi_0}|^2$$
$$|A_1|^2 + |A_0|^2 + 2 |A_0| \cdot |A_1| \cos (\phi_1 - \phi_0) \tag{4}$$

It will be noted that the recorded intensity contains terms dependent

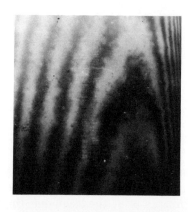

FIG. 6. (*c*) Hologram and reconstruction of transparent lettering on dark background. Top: Hologram. Middle: Reconstruction. Bottom: Original object. The original object was about 1.5 cm in length; the distance between objects and hologram planes was about 2 ft. The hologram was made with Kodak Spectroscopic Plates, Type 649-F.

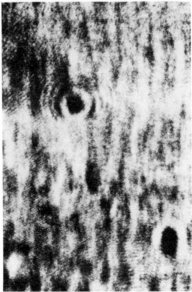

FIG. 6. (*d*) Hologram and reconstruction of a scene. The object was about 1.5 cm in height, and the distance between object and hologram was made with Kodak High Contrast Copy.

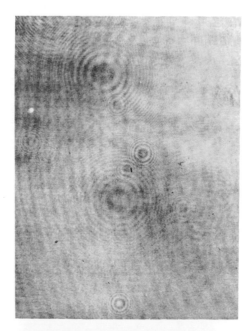

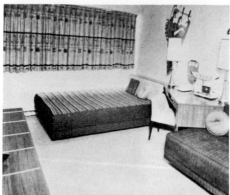

Fig. 6. (*e*) Hologram of a scene (made from a photographic transparency of the scene). Reconstruction of the scene.

both upon the amplitudes and upon the phases of the signals. The recorded hologram has the form given by Eq. 4.

Let us consider next the effect of illuminating a transparency upon which this signal has been recorded in a configuration appropriate to the reconstruction of the image. Let attention be given to the result of performing a two-dimensional spectrum analysis upon each of the terms in Eq. 4. To do this, however, it is useful to be more specific regarding the nature of A_0 and ϕ_0.

The reference signal used in recording the hologram is a plane wave incident at some angle upon the photographic plate. This implies that A_0 and ϕ_0 are of the form given by Eqs. 5:

$$A_0 = \text{constant} \qquad \phi_0 = kx \sin \theta = \omega_0 x \tag{5}$$

The phase ϕ_0 becomes a carrier for the phase information contained in ϕ_1.

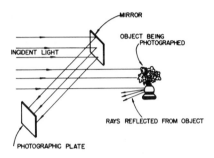

Fig. 6. (*f*) Making of hologram.

It is important to choose the effective carrier frequency ω_0 so that it is higher than the frequency content in A_1.

Under these circumstances the signals in plane P_2 of Fig. 1 will have the following characteristics.

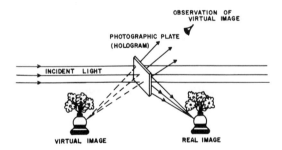

Fig. 6. (*g*) Reconstruction of image.

The term corresponding to $|A_0|^2$ will correspond to a distribution of light near the optical axis; the light corresponding to the $|A_1|^2$ will, to a greater or less extent, resemble the image on the transparency in Fig. 6a. The signals resulting from the third term of the final expression in Eq. 4 can be considered as the result of two terms as given by Eq. 6:

$$2A_0A_1 \cos (\phi_1 + \phi_0) = A_0A_1[e^{j(\omega_0 x - \phi_1)} + e^{-j(\omega_0 x - \phi_1)}] \tag{6}$$

Each of the terms in Eq. 6 represents the signal $A_1 e^{j\phi_1}$ with all its phase and amplitude information. The carriers indicate signals traveling in different directions. Two images are produced, one to the left of the optical axis and one to the right. To arrive at this conclusion, use is made of the translation theory of Fourier analysis which states that a multiplying factor of the form $e^{j\omega_0 x}$ results in a translation of its transform.

Of importance is the fact that the light incident upon the plane P_2 at the location of each of these images contains information having both the phase and the amplitude of the original image. If one arranges stops in the optical system to remove terms arising from the spectrum of the terms $|A_0|^2$ and $|A_1|^2$ and one of the terms corresponding to the third term of the last equation of Eq. 4, a reconstruction is achieved which reproduces both the amplitude and phase of the object. This technique can be used for generating a complex signal.

Since a signal of this type is the most general form of signal, this technique is very powerful and should find application in general filtering problems.

It is to be noted that although the reconstruction produced an image with both the phase and the amplitude characteristics of the original object, nonetheless, the recorded signals were positive real quantities, namely, the intensities given by Eq. 4.

IV. Linear Operations

Optical techniques can be used for performing a large number of linear operations. Some of these operations have been described in Secs. II and III.

It is possible to assemble optical equipment which perform other linear operations including such operations as autocorrelation, cross-correlation, convolution, matched filtering, ambiguity function display, and integration. In this section the configurations for performing these operations will be given together with a brief discussion of their operation.

A. Spectrum Analysis and Filtering

The operation of displaying the spectrum of the function has been discussed in Secs. II and III. Also discussed in Sec. III were some details of types of filtering that can be performed.

B. Autocorrelation and Cross-Correlation

Important linear operations are those of autocorrelation and cross-correlation. These functions will be considered together since the equipment needed to mechanize the operations is identical. In performing a cross-correlation the operations performed are those indicated by Eq. 7 while an autocorrelation is given by Eq. 8:

$$\phi_{fg}(x_0) = \int f(x)g(x - x_0)\, dx \qquad (7)$$

$$\phi_{ff}(x_0) = \int f(x)f(x - x_0)\, dx \qquad (8)$$

It will be noted from Eqs. 7 and 8 that to mechanize these operations, techniques are needed for performing multiplication, translation, and integration. A configuration capable of performing a multiplicity of autocorrelations or cross-correlations is given in Fig. 7. In this figure the source and

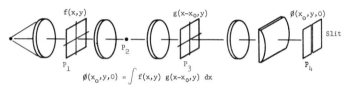

$$\phi(x_0, y, 0) = \int f(x,y)\, g(x - x_0, y)\, dx$$

FIG. 7. Cross-correlator configuration.

collimating lens to the left of the plane P_1 causes a plane coherent wave to be incident on the transparency $f(x, y)$.

The optics between planes P_1 and P_2 causes the spectrum analysis of $f(x, y)$ to appear in the plane P_2. The optics between planes P_2 and P_3 performs a second spectrum analysis of the signals in plane P_2. Thus, incident upon P_3 is the function $f(x, y)$. If one looks through plane P_3 toward the source, the distribution of light will be the product $f(x, y)g(x, y)$.

Let the holder which contains the function $f(x, y)$ have provision for transporting this transparency along the x axes. If this displacement is through a distance x_0, then the distribution of light in plane P_3 looking toward the source will be the product $f(x, y)g(x - x_0, y)$.

The combination of spherical and cylindrical optics between planes P_3 and P_4 cause a multichannel spectrum analysis of the light distribution emerging from plane P_3. Hence, the distribution of light in plane P_4 is described by Eq. 9:

where

$$\left.\begin{aligned} \phi(x_0, y; \alpha) &= \int f(x, y)g(x - x_0, y)e^{i\alpha z}\, dx \\[2ex] \alpha &= \frac{2\pi}{\lambda} \sin \theta \end{aligned}\right\} \qquad (9)$$

It will be noted that this equation resembles Eq. 7 except that a multiplicity of operations is performed (one for each value of y) and that the factor $e^{i\alpha z}$ appears as a factor in the integrand. In Eq. 9, $\alpha = 0$ corresponds to the light in a slit parallel to the y axis. If only the light in this slit is recorded, the exponential factor in Eq. 9 assumes the value unity.

In this case, Eq. 9 becomes identical with Eq. 7 except for its multichannel feature. This result is written as Eq. 10:

$$\phi(x_0, y, 0) = \phi_{fg}(x_0, y) \tag{10}$$

As the plane P_3 is transported, at a given position in plane P_4, there will appear an amplitude of light corresponding to the value of the cross-correlation function for that value of the displacement x_0. This autocorrelation function can be recorded by transporting a film past the slit. The configuration in Fig. 7 is, thus, capable of performing a multiplicity of simultaneous correlations.

To perform an autocorrelation using the configuration of Fig. 7, one uses a second copy of $f(x, y)$ in plane P_3.

In the mechanization shown as Fig. 7 a relatively complicated optical arrangement was shown to image plane P_1 onto plane P_3. It is necessary to use this configuration in order to remove errors arising from bias levels used in recording the signals in planes P_1 and P_3.

Autocorrelations and cross-correlations are important operations, and there are many instances for which information theory indicates these as optimum signal detection and/or parameter estimation operations. It will be noted that the configuration of Fig. 7 performs a multiplicity of such autocorrelations or cross-correlations simultaneously. There is no difficulty in recording onto film a density of 50 cycles per mm. Hence 35-mm film can be used in configuration of Fig. 7 to perform simultaneously more than 1000 simultaneous autocorrelations or cross-correlations. Equipments having the configuration of Fig. 7 are commercially available.

C. Optical Technique for Implementing a General Linear Operation

The most general linear operation [0] on a function $f(t)$ to produce an output $g(t)$ can be written in the form given by Eq. 11:

$$g(t) = 0[f(t)] = \int h(\tau, t)f(\tau) \, d\tau \tag{11}$$

In this equation, the nature of the operation to be performed determines the kernel function $h(\tau, t)$. The fact that Eq. 11 represents a general linear operation is discussed in texts dealing with functional analysis.[3] Pertinent discussions have also been given in publications by L. A. Zadeh.[4]

In order to mechanize the operation given by Eq. 11, the configuration shown in Fig. 8 may be used

$$g(t) = \int h(\tau, t)f(\tau) \, d\tau \tag{11'}$$

If one looks toward the left, the light amplitudes in the plane containing $f(\tau)$ contains the product of $h(\tau, t)$ with $f(\tau)$.

Between the transparency $f(\tau)$ and the output slit in which $g(t)$ is found, is a pair of lenses, one of which is spherical, the other of which is cylindrical. This configuration performs the function of causing the line-by-line spectral analysis of the light in the $f(\tau)$ plane to be displayed in the output plane. The distribution of light in the output plane is described by Eq. 12.[5] It will

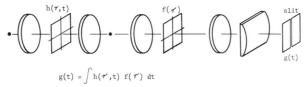

$$g(t) = \int h(\tau, t) f(\tau)\, dt$$

Fig. 8. General linear operation configuration.

be noted that Eq. 12 is a somewhat more general operation than that described by Eq. 11, and that it describes a two-dimensional distribution of light in the output plane:

$$I(t, \omega) = \int h(\tau, t)f(\tau)e^{-i\omega\tau}\, d\tau \tag{12}$$

It will be further noted that Eq. 12 becomes identical with Eq. 11 if ω is set equal to 0 in Eq. 12. Thus, the performing of a linear operation expressed as Eq. 11 is accomplished simply by observing the light in the output plane which is present in the central slit. The location of this slit corresponds to ω equals 0 in Eq. 13. The relationship that $g(t)$ is obtained from Eq. 12 by setting $\omega = 0$ is written as Eq. 13:

$$g(t) = I(t, 0) \tag{13}$$

Thus, the performing of a general linear operation optically requires the configuration shown in Fig. 8 together with the ability to record on two transparencies the functions $h(\tau, t)$, which represents the operations to be performed, and the function $f(\tau)$, which represents the function upon which the operation is to be performed. The result of the operation is present in a centrally located slit in the output plane of the equipment.

It can be shown that, if a number of linear operations are to be performed in tandem, one can represent the tandem sequence of operations by a single equivalent operation. Hence, Eq. 11 represents not only a single operation but a sequence of linear operations, if such is the desired operation.

The optical technique has been successfully used in a number of signal processing situations. Such operations as spectrum analysis, autocorrelation, cross-correlation, and matched filtering are all special cases of linear operations as are also such operations as differentiation and integration. It is believed that the optical computing technique is a very powerful and versatile means of performing operations on large volumes of data.

D. Matrix Multiplication

Equation 11 and Fig. 8 are pertinent when a general linear operation or a function of one variable is to be performed. It is useful, however, to consider the case in which a linear operation is to be performed in a space of a finite number of dimensions. In this case each input and output quantity of interest will be a vector (n-tuple) and will be that of matrix multiplication. If V_1 and V_2 represent two vectors and if M represents a matrix, one may write

$$V_2 = MV_1 \tag{14}$$

to indicate that V_2 is derived by a linear operation on V_1.

In Eq. 14 V_1 and V_2 are vectors (column matrices) whereas M is a k by n matrix. These matrices may be of the form given by Eqs. 15 and 16:

$$V_1 = \left| \begin{pmatrix} v_{11} \\ \cdot \\ \cdot \\ \cdot \\ v_{1n} \end{pmatrix} \right|$$

$$V_2 = \left| \begin{pmatrix} v_{21} \\ \cdot \\ \cdot \\ \cdot \\ v_{2n} \end{pmatrix} \right| \tag{15}$$

$$M = \left| \begin{pmatrix} m_{11} & \cdots & m_{1n} \\ \cdot & & \cdot \\ \cdot & & \cdot \\ m_{n1} & & m_{nn} \end{pmatrix} \right| \tag{16}$$

The operation indicated by Eq. 14 can be performed by the optical configuration shown in Fig. 8. In this case the transparency $h(\tau + t)$ is replaced by a rectangular array representing the matrix M and $f(\tau)$ is replaced by V_1. The output slit now contains the values of V_2 instead of $g(t)$.

Thus Eq. 11 and Fig. 8 make possible the general linear operation on t, which can be either a continuous or discrete variable.

V. Applications

Important applications for these optical techniques include spectrum analysis, filtering, autocorrelation, and antenna pattern simulation.

In the use of optical techniques for spectrum analysis the techniques have been applied to vibration analysis problems. Here recordings of vibration data onto photographic film have been made using density modulation of the film. The result is a recorded format of density (representing vibration amplitude) versus time (represented by distance along the film). The insertion of such a record with a multiplicity of traces into plane P_1 of Fig. 2 gives the corresponding frequency analysis in plane P_2. This can be recorded onto a film in plane P_2, or photoelectric readout can be performed. These components mounted on an optical bench designed for ease of rearrangement of components are commercially available. A photograph of such equipment is shown in Fig. 9.

Other applications of coherent optics in filtering have been illustrated in Figs. 4 and 5 of Sec. III. Here contrast improvement and signal-to-noise improvement were illustrated.

The use of optics as a cross-correlation device is another important appli-

Fig. 9. Spectrum analysis equipment.

cation. Here again vibration analysis has provided an example. Vibration data from a number of points have been recorded. The cross-correlation of vibration data from different points has been desired and performed.

A configuration utilizing a component configuration similar to that of Fig. 7 is commercially available and is shown in Fig. 10. In this case the

Fig. 10. Equipment for cross-correlation of vibration data.

components are mounted on an optical bench for easy rearrangement and the output may be sensed either photographically or by photoelectric means.

In other cases pseudorandom codes have been recorded and cross-correlated. The result observed experimentally duplicates closely the results predicted by the theory.

Finally with respect to many problems, the optical configuration remains relatively invariant; to change a problem one simply changes the signals recorded on the transparencies.

A number of examples of optical computations using the appropriate optical configuration follows.

A. Antenna Simulation

The far field pattern of an antenna can be computed from its illumination function $f(x, y)$ by the use of

$$F(\alpha, \beta) = \iint_{\substack{\text{over} \\ \text{aperture}}} f(x, y)e^{-jk(\alpha x + \beta y)} \, dx \, dy \tag{17}$$

In this equation α and β are direction cosines of the beam, $F(\alpha, \beta)$ is the far field pattern, and k is defined by

$$k = \frac{2\pi}{\lambda} \tag{18}$$

This quantity is the wave number and λ represents the wavelength used. If Eq. 17 is compared with Eq. 1 it will be seen to have the same form. Thus the optical configuration shown in Fig. 1 can be used to display the far

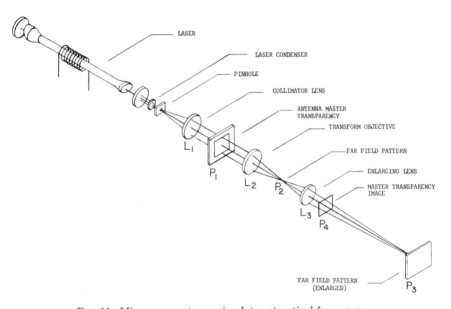

FIG. 11. Microwave antenna simulator at optical frequency.

field pattern of an antenna. In this case a transparency containing the aperture function $f(x, y)$ is placed in plane P_1 and the far field pattern is observed in plane P_2.

While the configuration of Fig. 1 is usually satisfactory, in some cases, the far field pattern found in plane P_2 may be too small. In this case it is desirable to use another lens to magnify the image found in plane P_2. Such a configuration is shown in Fig. 11 where an enlarged image of the field in plane P_2 is displayed in plane P_3.

In Fig. 11 one finds that an image of plane P_1 occurs between lenses L_3 and plane P_3 at plane P_4. Thus between planes P_4 and P_3 one has an opportunity to observe the pattern as it emerges from the illumination function through the near field until at plane P_3 the far field pattern is obtained. With this configuration, studies of the relationship between near field and far field can be made. In addition, by inserting perturbations into the regions between plane P_4 and P_3, for example by simulating a nonhomogeneous medium it is possible to observe the effects of perturbations on the far field pattern.

A series of photographs showing the far field developing from the illumination function for an array antenna[6] is shown in Figs. 12 through 17.

FIG. 12. Antenna illumination function.

This set of photographs is the optical simulation of an antenna array being built by J. P. Wild in Australia. The array consists of 96 parabolas arranged on a circle whose diameter is about $1\frac{1}{2}$ miles. Each parabola has a diameter of 45 ft. The frequency of operation is 80 Mc.

Assuming that the far field pattern begins at a distance $2D^2/\lambda$, the far field pattern begins approximately 2400 miles from earth. This poses real problems for measurement of the far field pattern. The configuration of Fig. 11, however, enables one to obtain not only the far field pattern shown in Figs. 16 and 17 but also views of the near field pattern are obtained. Additional examples of illumination functions and the corresponding far field patterns are shown in Figs. 18 through 21. In Fig. 18 a one-dimensional array is shown and the corresponding pattern is shown in Fig. 20. Similarly Figs. 19 and 21 show a two-dimensional array and pattern, respectively. For the one-dimensional pattern the digital computer computation of the far field pattern is shown in Fig. 22.

FIG. 13. Near field pattern.

Thus antenna simulation is another demonstration of the versatility of optical equipments.

B. Display of Ambiguity Functions

A useful function associated with a function of time is its ambiguity function. The ambiguity function $\psi(\tau, \omega)$ associated with $f(t)$ has been defined by Woodward[7] in accordance with Eq. 19

$$\psi(\tau, \omega) = \int_{-\infty}^{\infty} f(t)f(t + \tau)e^{-i\omega t}\, dt \tag{19}$$

The optical configuration shown in Fig. 7 can be used to observe the ambiguity function. In this case a function $f(t)$ is located in plane P_1 with $f(t + \tau)$ in plane P_3. Looking to the left through plane P_3 one has the prod-

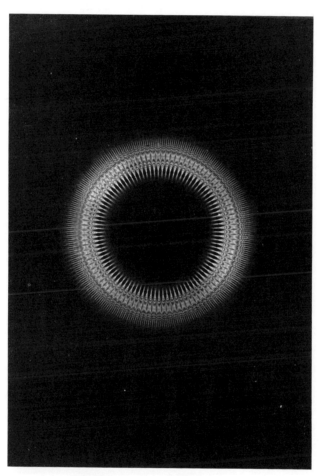

Fig. 14. Near field pattern.

uct $f(t)f(t + \tau)$. The combination of spherical and cylindrical optics to the right of plane P_3 generates a line-by-line spectrum analysis of this product. Thus the distribution of light in plane P_4 is that given by Eq. 19 and the output light distribution represents the ambiguity function both in amplitude and phase. To display the ambiguity function the entire function is recorded in plane P_4 instead of only the light in the slit.

This gives further evidence of the flexibility of optical computation.

C. Filtering

It has been shown in Sec. III how the spectrum of a signal can be displayed. As an example of a problem solved by spectral analysis, consider the testing of a film transport device.

In this case one is desirous of measuring the uniformity of transport of film through the device. One can use the film transport to generate ampli-

Fig. 15. Near field pattern.

tude grating by exposing a uniformly flashing light on the moving film. If the film transport is uniform one will obtain a perfect grating of equally spaced lines on the film. The spectral analysis of this signal will be a positive and negative frequency line and their harmonics. Nonuniform translation will destroy the periodicity. This will cause frequencies in the output not present in the input. Figure 23 shows two test patterns obtained in testing two film transports and their spectra. In the first case (top channel) uniformity of motion was excellent as reflected in the single harmonic present in the spectrum. In the second case (bottom channel), erratic motion of the film transport caused extraneous lines in the spectrum; the fundamental

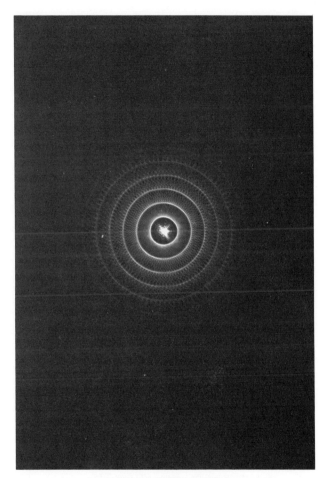

Fig. 16. Far field pattern.

frequencies and their second harmonics are clearly visible. The two lines between the fundamental frequency and the "dc" line indicate erratic motion. By measuring the frequency of these extra lines, it was also possible to trace the source of the error and correct that error.

D. Cross-Correlation Example

While many examples of cross-correlation can be given, two rather interesting ones have been selected for illustration. In one case the cross-correlation of a pseudorandom code of length 31 is correlated with itself and with two dissimilar codes of the same length. The optical configuration used is shown in Fig. 7. The signals are shown in Figs. 24 through 27. As a second example of cross-correlation, half a zone plate is correlated with

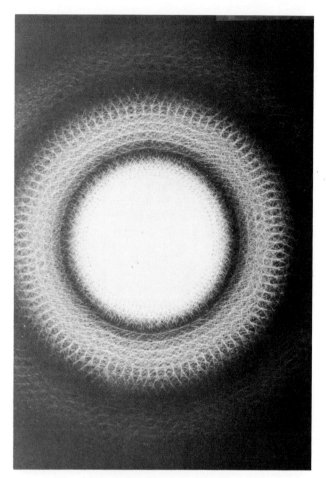

FIG. 17. Far field pattern (increased exposure).

itself in the presence of noise and without noise. The result of the auto-correlation is shown in Figs. 28 through 31.

VI. Optical Transfer Function

There is at present a lack of uniformity in what is meant by the term optical transfer function. It is the purpose of this discussion to indicate what these differences are and to suggest a philosophy whereby a single definition can be made of optical transfer functions from which the behavior of an optical system can be derived. At least two optical transfer functions

FIG. 18. Master drawing for one-dimen-   .   . . .
sional array.

have been defined. One of these transfer functions is defined for the case in which the light is noncoherent; the other is defined for the case that the light is fully coherent. The transfer function for partially coherent light, to the author's knowledge, has not been defined.

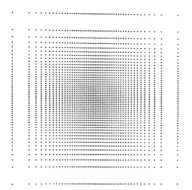

FIG. 19. Master drawing for two-dimensional array.

For the case of noncoherent light there exists an international agreement in which the transfer function is obtained by taking the two-dimensional

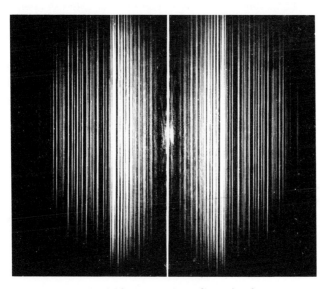

FIG. 20. Far field pattern of one-dimensional array.

Fourier transform of the *intensity* of the output plane and dividing it by the two-dimensional Fourier transform of the intensity of the input plane.

For the case of totally coherent light a second definition of transfer function has been stated or implied in which the transfer function is the ratio

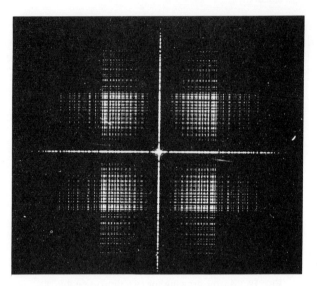

FIG. 21. Far field pattern of two-dimensional array.

of the Fourier transform of the output *amplitude* divided by the two-dimensional Fourier transform of the *amplitude* in the input plane. For the case of partially coherent light, the author has heard comments which stated in effect that an optical equipment had no transfer function for partially coherent light.

Because of this confusion and lack of uniformity in the meaning of terms it is the author's conviction that a transfer function should be defined so

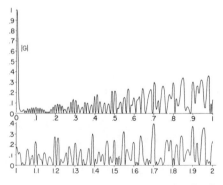

FIG. 22. Array factor for quadratic distribution.

that it has a single definition and so that the transfer function is *independent* of the signal passed through the device. For this reason a transfer function definition should be sought which does not depend upon whether the light is coherent, noncoherent, or partially coherent.

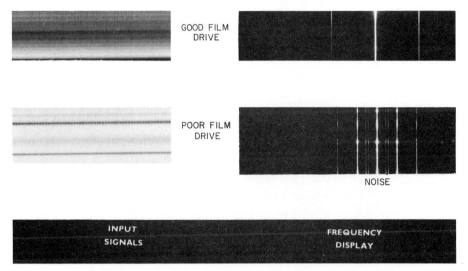

FIG. 23. Test patterns obtained in testing two film transports and their spectra.

It is believed that such a satisfactory definition of transfer function can be obtained by accepting as the transfer function for an optical equipment a definition in terms of operations on *amplitudes* rather than on intensities. This statement is based upon the fact that the output of any optical device

FIG. 24. Cross-correlation signals.

results from the interference at the output due to propagation of the signals from the input plane to the output plane. Thus the geometry and structure of the instrument should completely determine its transfer function.

Unfortunately, there is a further difficulty in defining optical transfer functions. This arises from the fact that optical systems do not have in general the property of stationarity. This statement refers to the fact that the translation of a point in the input does not produce an equal translation in the output. In other words, the image produced by one point in an input scene differs from the image of any other point in the input scene. Mathematically this means that the transfer function of an optical equipment

Fig. 25. Cross-correlation signals.

cannot be written as a function of differences of coordinates of points in the input and output planes.

If an analogy to electrical filters is made, optical transfer functions are analogous to time-varying filters rather than to time-invariant filters. For

Fig. 26. Cross-correlation signals.

time-invariant filters the impulse response of the filter is a function of the difference of parameters. For the nontime-invariant case the impulse response of a filter is a more general function of two parameters (not of their differences). The analogous situation for optics is one in which the impulse

     Fig. 27. Cross-correlation signals.

response (output due to a point source) cannot be described as a function of differences of coordinates.

This fact both for time-varying filters and for optics makes the role of the Fourier transform much less important than the role played by this transform for the time-invariant filter. The extreme usefulness and importance of the Fourier transform arises when the impulse response is a func-

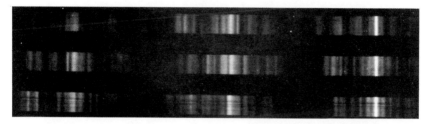

FIG. 28. Cross-correlation of signal with itself and two other signals.

tion of the difference of parameters. For this case a linear operation can be written as a convolution and the Fourier transform of the convolution gives a multiplication of the Fourier transforms. Thus for stationary systems (defined as systems whose impulse response is a function of the differ-

FIG. 29. Signal and the result of the autocorrelation.

ences of parameters) the Fourier transform gives a multiplicative relationship. This is not true for the nonstationary case.

In order to obtain a multiplicative relationship, one must expand the input and output function in terms of eigenfunctions for the operation performed. If this is done one obtains a result in which the transform of the output becomes the product of the transform of the input by the transform

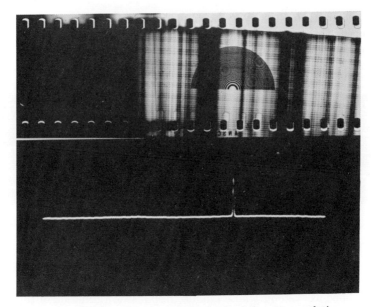

FIG. 30. Signal with noise and the result of the autocorrelation.

of the system. Only for stationary systems is this transform the Fourier transform.

Thus if one makes use of the fact that an optical system is linear and that a transfer function should be independent of the signals passed through it

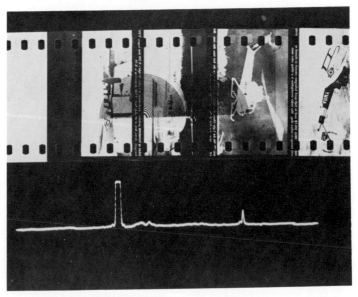

FIG. 31. Two signals with noise and the result of the autocorrelation.

one finds that the theory of linear functionals is the appropriate mathematics and that expansion in terms of the eigenfunctions is the indicated transform.

Thus far the discussion has concerned itself with operations upon the amplitude of the signals rather than operations upon the intensity. For the case of noncoherent light or for the case of partially coherent light an additional factor must be taken into account, namely, the effect of a random component of light. This situation can be treated in exactly the same manner as is done in information theory where a random component is present. In this case one is generally not interested in the instantaneous value of a random function but rather with certain statistical averages of the function. Among these statistical quantities are such quantities as average, standard deviation, variance, and the various moments.

In dealing with these quantities when passed through linear systems, one is concerned with an appropriate statistical parameter value for the input signal and the appropriate statistical parameter value for the output. Thus in putting a partial or completely random signal through a linear operation the nature of the output can be obtained in part from a knowledge of the transfer function of the device and in part from the statistical behavior of the signal. The present international definition for transfer function in terms of intensity combines into the same definition of the *effect of the instrument* and the *averaging* over the signal. It is proposed by the author that the transfer function of the instrument should not include the averaging process inasmuch as the averaging process depends upon the statistics of the signal and the transfer function definition should not depend upon the signal passed through it. However, if a random or partially random signal is passed through a linear device and this is followed by appropriate averaging one can obtain the behavior of the system to that signal. Thus in effect it is proposed that a transfer function in terms of amplitude should be adopted and that the necessary statistical operations be performed as a subsequent step, *not* as part of the transfer function. It is the author's belief that a transfer function based upon this philosophy will be applicable to all light coherence cases whether coherent, noncoherent, or partially coherent. A brief derivation of the appropriate mathematical relationships is discussed in Appendix I.

The optical transfer function based upon the philosophy above and that of Appendix I can be derived from the computations usually performed for optical systems. In these computations one traces ray paths through the equipment from an object point to its image. Hamilton's characteristic functions play a dominant role in this analysis. These quantities also play dominant roles in computing the optical transfer functions in which the amplitude and phase of the signal in this output plane are obtained given the phase and amplitude in the input plane and the structure of the optical system.

In many cases, however, one is interested in the distribution of light amplitude in planes other than the image plane. In this case it is desirable to have transfer functions which take one from one plane to another. Such transfer functions can readily be computed for homogeneous media. Thus if the lens computation permits one to go from an object plane to an image plane one can use the transfer function between any two other planes separated by a homogeneous medium to get the transfer function from any plane to any other plane.

The transfer function for a homogeneous region in space does have the stationary property; therefore, Fourier transforms are appropriate for this part of an optical system. By a combination of the optical systems for most stationary systems with that for homogeneous regions one can easily adapt lens computation from any desired input plane to any desired output plane.

One can summarize the considerations above to indicate that it is possible to define transfer functions so that any planes can be input or output planes. Ordinary lens computation can be used as a tool. The transfer function is independent of the input and statistical properties of both inputs and outputs can be derived. These will provide the required information whether the light is coherent, noncoherent, or partially coherent.

Summarizing Remarks

In this paper an attempt has been made to describe the properties and techniques of coherent light which are useful for performing a number of operations on signals. It has been shown that optics is a very versatile and powerful tool for performing these operations. The basic phenomenon of diffraction is described. Both the single channel two-dimensional situations and the multichannel one-dimensional situations have been described.

Because of their importance, the problems of spectral analysis and filtering have been highlighted. However, optics is capable of performing many linear operations. Among the linear operations are those of autocorrelation, cross-correlation, ambiguity function display, convolution, matched filtering, and spectrum analysis. Since the optical equipments display the information successively in spatial domain and frequency domain planes, operations in either of these planes can be performed. Techniques have been described both for producing complex signals and for achieving complex filtering. Thus the most general signals and the most general filtering operations can be treated.

The configurations and operations described in this paper are by no means exhaustive. It is hoped, however, that sufficient information regarding fundamentals has been presented so that the reader can proceed to use optical computing as a means to solve those problems appropriate to the technique.

ACKNOWLEDGMENTS

The author wishes to gratefully acknowledge the contributions of E. O'Neill, of E. N. Leith and J. Upatnieks, and of B. A. Vander Lugt. Specifically, much of the author's initial exposure to coherent light was the result of conversations with E. O'Neill. Moreover, Figs. 4 and 5 are taken from Dr. O'Neill's paper, Reference 8.

I am also indebted to E. N. Leith and J. Upatnieks, and to B. A. Vander Lugt for many discussions involving coherent optics as computing devices. Specifically, I am indebted to E. N. Leith and J. Upatnieks for Figs. 6a through 6g. Most of these figures are from Reference 1. A significant contribution to wavefront reconstruction by B. A. Vander Lugt is contained in Reference 2.

The author wishes also to acknowledge the assistance by his colleagues at Conductron Corporation, Mr. A. L. Ingalls, Dr. I. Kay, Mr. C. Thomas, and Mr. J. King. Some of the work reported herein is their work and not that of the author.

APPENDIX I

A. *Introductory Remarks*

The purpose of this Appendix is to discuss an approach which will be useful for the definition and computation of optical transfer functions. There is currently a great deal of activity in optics which makes the definition of such terms important.

Both coherent and noncoherent techniques are used. A body of literature dealing with these special areas exists. However, in many instances, the coherent optical configurations are analyzed by workers in that field using an implied set of definitions for transfer functions whereas workers with noncoherent optical systems have adopted a different set of definitions for optical transfer functions. It is the belief of the author that there should be only one transfer function defined for optical systems, and that this optical transfer function should be independent of whether the light is coherent, noncoherent, or partially coherent.

In this Appendix, an approach is suggested to meet this requirement. In essence, it is proposed to define the optical transfer function in terms of amplitudes, not in terms of intensity. A definition of this type clearly permits interference phenomena which a definition in terms of intensities does not permit.

Such a definition is useful for optical equipments using a noncoherent or partially coherent light, as well as for those using coherent light. In either of these cases, the presence of a noncoherent component of light means that one is not interested in the instantaneous value of an input function, or of an output function, but rather that one is concerned with some averages of these functions. In the text, it is shown that the use of a transfer function based upon amplitudes followed by the appropriate averaging of the quantities of interest give the quantities desired in computing the behavior of systems with a noncoherent component of light.

In defining optical transfer functions, it is shown that a multidimensional Fourier transform is the appropriate transform for cases in which a translation property, defined later, is valid. It is further shown, when this translation property is not valid, that a more general transform is required. In either case, provided the proper transform is used, it is shown that transforms which are multiplicative and independent of the input function are obtained.

If the multiplicative property of the transfer functions is combined with the remarks concerning the averaging process when a noncoherent component of light is present, one obtains the highly desirable situation in which:

1. The transfer functions of components in tandem are multiplicative;

2. The transfer functions are independent of the input functions and of the coherence of the source; and

3. The transfer function, followed by appropriate averaging, can be used to compute the desired output quantities for coherent, partially coherent, and noncoherent light.

In considering optical transfer functions, two situations arise. In one case, the light distribution over the output surface depends only upon differences of coordinates; that is, the amplitude of the light at a point on the output surface coming from a given point on the input surface depends upon the differences of the coordinates of the points. In this case, Fourier transforms are the appropriate transforms.

In the second case, the amplitude of the light at a point on the output surface is a function of the coordinates of that point and of a point on the input surface by some function other than that of differences of coordinates. In this case, an expansion in terms of eigenfunctions is necessary.

The situation in which a homogeneous medium is present between the input surface and the output surface is an example of the first case. A situation in which there is a change in medium or a nonhomogeneous medium (such as going through a lens) is an example of the second case.

In the sections which follow, these cases are discussed separately. In Sec. B, an analysis is made for the case in which the translation property holds and in which the Fourier transform is the appropriate transform. This section also discusses the averaging which is appropriate as an additional operation for those cases in which a noncoherent component of light is present.

Section C discusses the modification which must be made in computing the transfer function for those cases in which the translation property is not valid. In this case, the transforms must be expressed in terms of expressions involving eigenfunctions of the optical system. If this is done, the multiplicative property and the independence of the transfer function on the input function are retained.

B. *Optical Transfer Functions: Case I (Translation Property Is Valid)*

It is the purpose of this Appendix to propose a philosophy from which a definition for the optical transfer function can be made to derive some properties of the transfer function for the case in which the transfer function depends only on differences of coordinates.

1. It will be shown that the definitions are applicable to all cases; namely, for light sources which are noncoherent, partially coherent, or fully coherent.

2. It will also be shown that the transfer function of a number of components

in tandem is the product of their transfer functions if and only if an expansion is made in terms of eigenfunctions.

3. It will also be shown that the transfer function so defined is independent of the signal passed through the system.

Initially, it will be assumed that the transfer operation has a translation property stated explicitly in the text which follows. This will be followed by an analysis of the more general case in Sec. C.

The definition for an optical transfer function for the present case is arrived at from the following considerations.

Let some finite surface be considered as the input, and let a second finite surface be defined as the output. At some instant of time t there is a distribution of amplitudes over the input surface and over the output surface.

Let $f_1(x_1, y_1, z_1, t)$ be the amplitude of light over the input surface, and let $f_2(x_2, y_2, z_2, t)$ be the distribution of amplitudes over the output surface. Let $F_1(\alpha, \beta, \gamma, \omega)$ be the four-dimensional Fourier transform of $f_1(x_1, y_1, z_1, t)$ and let $F_2(\alpha, \beta, \gamma, \omega)$ be the four-dimensional Fourier transform of $f_2(x_2, y_2, z_2, t)$. These transforms are defined by Eqs. A-1 and A-2:

$$F_1(\alpha, \beta, \gamma, \omega) = \int f_1(x_1, y_1, z_1, t) \exp\left[-j(\alpha x_1 + \beta y_1 + \gamma z_1 + \omega t)\right] dx_1\, dy_1\, dz_1\, dt$$
(A-1)

$$F_2(\alpha, \beta, \gamma, \omega) = \int f_2(x_2, y_2, z_2, t) \exp\left[-j(\alpha x_2 + \beta y_2 + \gamma z_2 + \omega t)\right] dx_2\, dy_2\, dz_2\, dt$$
(A-2)

The optical transfer function T for the system between the input surface and the output surface is defined by Eq. A-3:

$$T = \frac{F_2(\alpha, \beta, \gamma, \omega)}{F_1(\alpha, \beta, \gamma, \omega)}$$
(A-3)

This transfer function (Eq. A-3) is independent of $F_1(\alpha, \beta, \gamma, \omega)$. This can be shown as follows.

The distribution of amplitudes over the output surface can be derived from the distribution over the input surface by the use of Eq. A-4:

$$f_2 = \int f_1\left(x_1, y_1, z_1, t - \frac{K}{c}\right) dx_1\, dy_1\, dz_1$$
(A-4)

This expression states that the distribution of light over the output surface is the result of individual amplitudes over surface 1 delayed by the transit time from a specific point in the input surface to a point in the output surface. In Eq. A-4, $K(x_1, y_1, z_1; x_2, y_2, z_2)$ is the path length for a ray from the point x_1, y_1, z_1 in the input surface to the point x_2, y_2, z_2 in the output surface. Substitution of Eq. A-4 into Eq. A-2 gives Eq. A-5:

$$F_2(\alpha, \beta, \gamma, \omega) = \iint f_1\left(x_1, y_1, z_1, t - \frac{K}{c}\right)$$
(A-5)

$$\exp\left[-j(\alpha x_2 + \beta y_2 + \gamma z_2 + \omega t)\right] dx_1\, dy_1\, dz_1\, dx_2\, dy_2\, dz_2\, dt$$

For generality, the input and output surfaces have not been defined as planes. Ideally, however, these surfaces will be defined as planes normal to the optical axis of the device.

Equation A-5 can be rewritten in the form given by Eq. A-6:

$$F_2(\alpha, \beta, \gamma, \omega) = \iint f_1\left(x_1, y_1, z_1, t_1 - \frac{K}{c}\right) \exp\left[j(\alpha x_1 + \beta y_1 + \gamma z_1)\right] dx_1 \, dy_1 \, dz_1$$

$$\text{(A-6)}$$

$$\exp\left\{j[\alpha(x_2 - x_1) + \beta(y_2 - y_1) + \gamma(z_2 - z_1) + \omega t]\right\} dx_2 \, dy_2 \, dz_2 \, dt$$

Let us consider the nature of the function K. In many cases, K will be a function only of differences in the coordinates of points in the input and output surfaces. In particular, K will be a function of $x_2 - x_1$, $y_2 - y_1$, and $z_2 - z_1$. Where K is of this form, it will be said to have the translational property. If this is the case, a new set of variables, q_1, q_2, and q_3 can be defined by Eqs. A-7:

$$\begin{cases} q_1 = x_2 - x_1 \\ q_2 = y_2 - y_1 \\ q_3 = z_2 - z_1 \end{cases} \tag{A-7}$$

In terms of these variables, Eq. A-6 can be rewritten as Eq. A-8.

$$F_2(\alpha, \beta, \gamma, \omega) = \iint f_1\left(x_1, y_1, z_1, t - \frac{K}{c}\right) \exp\left[j(\alpha x_1 + \beta y_1 + \gamma z_1)\right] dx_1 \, dy_1 \, dz_1$$

$$\text{(A-8)}$$

$$\exp\left[j(\alpha q_1 + \beta q_2 + \gamma q_3 + \omega t)\right] dq_1 \, dq_2 \, dq_3 \, dt$$

If the integrations with respect to x_1, y_1, z_1, and t are performed, one obtains the result given by Eq. A-9:

$$F_2(\alpha,\beta,\gamma,\omega) = \int F_1(\alpha,\beta,\gamma,\omega) \exp\left[-j\left(\frac{\omega K}{c}\right)\right] \exp\left[j(\alpha q_1 + \beta q_2 + \gamma q_3)\right] dq_1 \, dq_2 \, dq$$

$$\text{(A-9)}$$

In writing Eq. A-9, use was made of the well-known result in Fourier transform theorem expressed by Eq. A-10:

$$\int f(t - \tau)e^{-j\omega t} \, dt = F(\omega)e^{-j\omega \tau}$$

where

$$\left. \begin{array}{c} \\ \\ \end{array} \right\} \tag{A-10}_3$$

$$F(\omega) = \int f(t)e^{-j\omega t} \, dt$$

Since $F_1(\alpha, \beta, \gamma, \omega)$ is independent of the variables of integration, q_1, q_2, and q_3, $F_1(\alpha, \beta, \gamma, \omega)$ can be brought outside the integration sign. Therefore, the transfer function T is given by Eq. A-11:

$$T = \frac{F_2(\alpha, \beta, \gamma, \omega)}{F_1(\alpha, \beta, \gamma, \omega)} = \int \exp\left[-j\left(\frac{\omega K}{c}\right)\right] \exp\left[j(\alpha q_1 + \beta q_2 + \gamma q_3)\right] dq_1 \, dq_2 \, dq_3 \quad \text{(A-11)}$$

It will be noted that the transfer function depends only on geometrical quantities and does not depend on the input function. This establishes the third of the characteristics desired in transfer functions; namely, the independence of the transfer function on the signals being passed through the system. It will be noted that this result depends upon the function K being a function only of differences of coordinates and upon the use of Fourier transforms.

If an optical equipment consists of a number of components in tandem, the output of one component can be considered as the input to the next component. Application of this idea can be shown to result in the transfer function of a tandem configuration to be the product of the transfer functions of each of the components. This establishes the second characteristic desired in transfer functions.

It remains now to consider the nature of the light source. The transfer function defined is related to the instantaneous value of amplitudes as a function of time. No reference has been made nor is it necessary to describe whether the light source was coherent, partially coherent, or noncoherent for the analysis to this point. If the light is coherent, the expressions as given are those of interest. If the light is noncoherent or partially noncoherent, then various statistical measures of these signals become of interest. Of particular value is the average of the squared amplitude of the signal at each point of the input surface and of the output surface.

In discussing the statistical behavior of the signals, an extremely useful quantity is the correlation function, ϕ_{ff}, which is defined as the average or expected value of the product of a function when its variables have one value with the function when its variables have a second set of values. This expectation is given as Eq. A-12:

$$\phi_{ff} = \langle f_1(x_1, y_1, z_1, t) f_1(x_1', y_1', z_1', t') \rangle \tag{A-12}$$

where the brackets $\langle \ \rangle$ indicate expected values.

In the theory of random processes, one encounters the notion of stationarity. This notion states that the expected value in Eq. A-12 depends only on the difference in parameter values; i.e., if the variables q_1, q_2, q_3, and τ are defined in accordance with Eq. A-13, then ϕ_{ff} is a function of these new variables only (Equation A-14):

$$
\begin{aligned}
q_1 &= x_1 - x_1' \\
q_2 &= y_1 - y_1' \\
q_3 &= z_1 - z_1' \\
\tau &= t - t'
\end{aligned}
\tag{A-13}
$$

$$\phi_{ff}(x_1, y_1, z_1, t; x_1', y_1', z_1', t') = \phi(q_1, q_2, q_3, \tau) \tag{A-14}$$

It can be shown that the four-dimensional Fourier transform of the correlation function for a stationary random process gives the magnitude squared of the four-dimensional Fourier transform of $f_1(x_1, y_1, z_1, t)$. The result is given by Eq. A-15:

$$|F_1(\alpha,\beta,\gamma,\omega)|^2 = \int \phi_{ff} \exp\left[-j(\alpha q_1 + \beta q_2 + \gamma q_3 + \omega \tau)\right] dq_1 \, dq_2 \, dq_3 \, d\tau \tag{A-15}$$

Conversely, Eq. A-15 can be inverted so that a correlation function ϕ_{ff} can be computed from the squared magnitude of the spectrum, $|F_1(\alpha, \beta, \gamma, \omega)|^2$. The result is given as Eq. A-16:

$$\phi_{ff} = \int |F_1(\alpha, \beta, \gamma, \omega)|^2 \exp\left[j(\alpha q_1 + \beta q_2 + \gamma q_3 + \omega \tau)\right] d\alpha \, d\beta \, d\gamma \, d\omega \tag{A-16}$$

Thus far, the coherency characteristics of the light have not been used other than as considerations in which average values rather than instantaneous values become the quantities of interest. To illustrate the additional considerations when the light is partially coherent, one can write an expression for a function as the sum of a coherent f_{1c} and an incoherent part f_{1n}. This is done in Eq. A-17:

$$f_1(x_1, y_1, z_1, t) = f_{1c}(x_1, y_1, z_1, t) + f_{1n}(x_1, y_1, z_1, t) \tag{A-17}$$

If Eq. A-17 is substituted in Eq. A-12, the result is Eq. A-18:

$$
\begin{aligned}
\phi_{ff} &= \langle (f_{1c} + f_{1n})(f_{1c}' + f_{1n}') \rangle \\
&= \langle f_{1c}f_{1c}' \rangle + \langle f_{1n}f_{1n}' \rangle + \langle f_{1c}f_{1n}' \rangle + \langle f_{1n}f_{1c}' \rangle
\end{aligned} \tag{A-18}
$$

In this equation, the primes on the function have been used to indicate complex conjugates of the variables and also different values of variables: x_1', y_1', z_1', t'. Usually, the cross-correlation function of the coherent part with the incoherent part will be zero, so that the last two terms of the second line of Eq. A-18 will vanish. In this case, the correlation function reduces to the sum of the correlation function of the coherent part of the illumination plus the correlation function of the noncoherent part of the illumination.

It is useful to compare the quantities of interest for the cases of totally coherent and totally noncoherent light. Let this be done with reference to Fig. 32. In this

$$f_1(x_1, y_1, z_1, t) \qquad\qquad f_2(x_2, y_2, z_2, t)$$

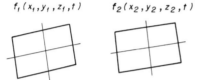

Fig. 32. Calculation of transfer functions.

figure, an input surface is described by $f_1(x_1, y_1, z_1, t)$, whereas the output surface is defined by $f_2(x_2, y_2, z_2, t)$. The transfer function is defined in Eq. A-19:

$$F_2 = TF_1 \tag{A-19}$$

If the light is totally noncoherent, the quantities of interest are the mean squares of the functions.

The transfer function for the totally noncoherent case may be defined in terms of the four-dimensional transfer function of the instantaneous (mean-squared) values of the amplitude. Rewriting Eq. A-15 for the input function $f_1(x_1, y_1, z_1, t)$ and the output function $f_2(x_2, y_2, z_2, t)$, Eqs. A-20 and A-21, respectively, are obtained:

$$|F_1|^2 = \int \langle f_1{}^2 \rangle \exp\left[-j(\alpha q_1 + \beta q_2 + \gamma q_3 + \omega \tau)\right] dq_1\, dq_2\, dq_3\, d\tau \tag{A-20}$$

$$|F_2|^2 = \int \langle f_2{}^2 \rangle \exp\left[-j(\alpha q_1 + \beta q_2 + \gamma q_3 + \omega \tau)\right] dq_1\, dq_2\, dq_3\, d\tau \tag{A-21}$$

The ratio of these quantities may be defined as the transfer function for noncoherent light. This ratio is written as Eq. A-22:

$$T_{\text{noncoherent}} = \frac{|F_2|^2}{|F_1|} = T^2 \tag{A-22}$$

It will be noticed that for this case the noncoherent transfer function is equal to the squared magnitude of the transfer function defined by Eq. A-3.

C. *Optical Transfer Functions: Case II (Translation Property Does Not Hold)*

In arriving at Eq. A-11 for the transfer function of an optical system, it was necessary to assume that the function K depended only upon differences of coordinates. However, one can get multiplicative transfer functions by the use of a generalization of transfer functions from those used in ordinary filter theory. In doing this, it is necessary to make use of the theory of linear operators and to express the results in terms of eigenfunctions and eigenvalues.

To illustrate the approach, an analysis is carried out for a function of a single variable so that the ideas involved can be pointed out.

The most general linear operation on a function $f(t)$ to produce an output $e_0(t)$ can be written as Eq. A-23:

$$e_0(t) = \int g(t, \tau) f(\tau) \, d\tau \qquad \text{(A-23)}$$

In this equation, the function $g(t, \tau)$ is a two-dimensional kernel function whose form depends on the linear operation to be performed.

It is useful to consider solutions of Eq. A-23 in terms of the eigenfunctions and eigenvalues of this kernel function. Let $Q(\omega, \tau)$ be the eigenfunction for this kernel function, and let $A(\omega)$ be the eigenvalue. Then, these eigenfunctions would be solutions of Eq. A-24 with eigenvalues $A(\omega)$:

$$\int g(t, \tau) Q(\omega, \tau) \, d\tau = A(\omega) Q(\omega, t) \qquad \text{(A-24)}$$

A generalized transform for $f(t)$ and for $e_0(t)$ to give $F(\omega)$ and $E_0(\omega)$ is given by Eqs. A-25 and A-26:

$$f(t) = \int F(\omega) Q(\omega, t) \, d\omega \qquad \text{(A-25)}$$

$$e_0(t) = \int E_0(\omega) Q(\omega, t) \, d\omega \qquad \text{(A-26)}$$

These are expressions of the time functions in terms of the eigenfunctions. If Eqs. A-25 and A-26 are substituted into Eq. A-23, the result is given by Eq. A-27. It will be noted that the integration with respect to τ in the right-hand term of Eq. A-27 contains the left-hand side of Eq. A-24:

$$\int E_0(\omega) Q(\omega, t) \, d\omega = \iint g(t, \tau) F(\omega) Q(\omega, \tau) \, d\omega \, d\tau \qquad \text{(A-27)}$$

If Eq. A-24 is used to rewrite the right-hand side of Eq. A-27, one obtains Eq. A-28:

$$\int E_0(\omega) Q(\omega, t) \, d\omega = \int A(\omega) Q(\omega, t) F(\omega) \, d\omega \qquad \text{(A-28)}$$

It will be noted that each term of Eq. A-28 contains as a factor the quantity $Q(\omega, t)$. Since $Q(\omega, t)$ is not identically equal to 0, and since the expression must remain valid for arbitrary $E_0(\omega)$ and $F(\omega)$, it follows that the coefficient of $Q(\omega, t)$ must vanish. This result is written as Eq. A-29:

$$\int [E_0(\omega) - A(\omega) F(\omega)] Q(\omega, t) \, d\omega = 0$$

$$E_0(\omega) - A(\omega) F(\omega) = 0 \qquad \text{(A-29)}$$

This is the desired result. Thus, a definition of the transforms in terms of the eigenfunctions leads to a result in which the transform of the output is equal to the product of the transform of the input by the transfer function of the system. In this case, the transfer function of the system, $A(\omega)$, is seen to be the set of eigenvalues associated with the kernel function $g(t, \tau)$.

In applying this to optics, instead of the use of functions of a single variable, functions of three space variables and a time variable must be used. However, expressions analogous to Eqs. A-23 to A-29 can be written. By this means, multiplicative transfer functions can be obtained which do not require the translation property used in deriving Eq. A-11.

In those cases in which the translation property is valid, an expression such as Eq. A-11 is still valid.

An interesting and possibly useful set of surfaces between which transfer functions might be defined are surfaces at which the index of refraction changes. For example, one could derive the transfer function from a point just outside of a lens to a point just outside the next lens. One could use the boundary conditions to get from just outside the lens to just inside the lens. One could define a second transfer function from just inside one surface of the lens to just inside the other surface of the lens. Boundary conditions could again be used to get to the medium outside the lens, etc.

Only experience will indicate whether the choice of surfaces of this kind is useful or leads to simplification of the analysis. However, the flexibility of input and output surfaces, it is believed, is useful even if the specific surfaces referred to here do not add any simplification.

It is believed that definitions of optical transfer functions as defined in this paper are useful. It is believed that the transfer functions which now form the basis for the international agreement are contained in these definitions. It is believed that interferometric processes which are becoming an important part of optical technology are included herein. For this reason, it is urged that serious considerations be given to definitions of optical transfer functions based on considerations such as those which are given in this paper.

References

1. LEITH, EMMETT N., AND JURIS UPATNIEKS, "Wavefront Reconstruction with Continuous Tone Objects," *J. Opt. Soc. Am.*, *53*, No. 12, 1377–1381 (December 1963).
2. VANDER LUGT, B. A., "Signal Detection for Complex Spatial Filtering," *IEEE Trans. Inform. Theory*, IT-10, No. 2, 139–145 (April 1964).
3. FRIEDMAN, BERNARD, *Principles and Techniques of Applied Mathematics*, John Wiley & Sons, Inc., New York and London, 1956.
4. ZADEH, L. A., "A General Theory of Linear Signal Transmission Systems," *J. Franklin Inst.*, *253*, 293–312 (January June 1952).
5. CUTRONA, L. J., E. N. LEITH, C. J. PALERMO, AND L. J. PORCELLO, "Optical Data Processing and Filtering Systems," *IRE Trans. Inform. Theory*, 386–400 (June 1960).
6. INGALLS, A. L., "Optical Simulation of Microwave Antennas," presented at the 1964 PTGAP International Symposium, 21–24 September 1964, JFK International Airport, Long Island, N.Y., and published in the *Program and Digest*, pp. 203–208.
7. WOODWARD, P. M., *Probability and Information Theory, with Applications to Radar*, Pergamon Press, New York, 1960.
8. O'NEILL, E., "Spatial Filtering in Optics," *IRE Trans. Inform. Theory*, IT-2, 56–65 (June 1956).

General References

BORN, M., AND E. WOLF, *Principles of Optics*, Pergamon Press, New York, 1959.
CHEATHAM, T. P., JR., AND A. KOHLENBERG, *Analysis and Synthesis of Optical Processes*,

Technical Note 84, Part I, Boston University Physics Research Laboratories, Boston, Mass., March 1952.

CHEATHAM, T. P., JR., AND A. KOHLENBERG, "Optical Filters—Their Equivalence to and Differences from Electrical Networks," *IRE Nat. Conv. Record*, 6–12 (1954).

CUTRONA, L. J., E. N. LEITH, AND L. J. PORCELLO, "Coherent Optical Data Processing," *IRE WESCON Conv. Record*, Part 4, 141–153 (1959); and *IRE Trans. Auto. Control*, *AC-4*, No. 2, 137–149 (November 1959).

CUTRONA, L. J., E. N. LEITH, AND L. J. PORCELLO, "Data Processing by Optical Techniques," paper presented at the 3rd National Convention on Military Electronics, Washington, D.C., *1959 Conference Proceedings* (June 1959).

CUTRONA, L. J., E. N. LEITH, AND L. J. PORCELLO, "Filtering Operations Using Coherent Optics," *Proc. Nat. Electron. Conf.*, 15 (October 1959).

ELIAS, P., "Optics and Communication Theory," *J. Opt. Soc. Am.*, *43*, 229–232 (April 1953).

ELIAS, P., D. GREY, AND D. ROBINSON, "Fourier Treatment of Optical Processes," *J. Opt. Soc. Am.*, *42*, 127–134 (February 1952).

O'NEILL, E., *The Analysis and Synthesis of Linear Coherent and Incoherent Optical Systems*, Technical Note 122, Boston University Physics Research Laboratories, Boston, Mass., September 1955.

O'NEILL, E., *Selected Topics in Optics and Communication Theory*, Technical Note 133, Boston University Physics Research Laboratories, Boston, Mass., October 1957.

RHODES, J., "Analysis and Synthesis of Optical Images," *Am. J. Phys.*, *21*, 337–343 (January 1953).

CHAPTER 7

CHARACTER-READING BY OPTICAL SPATIAL FILTERING *

A. Vander Lugt, F. B. Rotz, and A. Klooster, Jr.

Radar Laboratory, Institute of Science and Technology
The University of Michigan, Ann Arbor, Michigan

1. Introduction

The problem of automatic character-reading is a broad one. The central problem is the recognition of individual characters when various kinds of noise are introduced into the system. If that problem is solved, techniques must be found to incorporate the character-recognition subsystem into a system that will achieve integrated processing of data from its generation to the final use of the processed output.

Several methods for recognizing characters have been used, including template matching, curve-following techniques, vector crossings, and moment calculation.[1] In this paper we focus attention on the potential of matched filtering in coherent optical systems. Although the use of these systems has been proposed for certain operations in the character-recognition problem (Reference 1, p. 88), matched filtering has not been employed to any great extent. The reason for this neglect is that the required filter for the recognition of most characters must be a complex-valued function. However, a recently developed technique for the practical construction of such filters opens the way for a re-evaluation of coherent optical systems as an element in the character-reading problem.[2]

Some problems normally encountered in various character-recognition schemes do not arise, or are easily eliminated, in coherent systems. Scanning of the input by a filter or a template is not required, a small error in the location of the character is not disastrous, a fair amount of variation in size and orientation can be tolerated, the degree of selectivity between characters can be controlled by varying the frequency content of the filter,

* The work reported here was made possible in part by research contracts with the Department of the Army and the Department of the Air Force.

and the system's output is a two-dimensional distribution of light mapped from the input.

The use of coherent systems does involve some difficulties, however. Preparing the data for presentation to the optical system is a complicated matter. Other problems are met in connecting the output of the optical system to a computer for logical operations or for transfer to tape. These problems are probably no more difficult to solve for this system than for most systems that are now in operation or that have been proposed.

In this paper we will briefly review the theory of coherent systems and the technique for constructing complex-valued filters. Experimental results are given that illustrate the concepts and show the system's performance when the characters are noisy. The concepts are then extended so that a single filter can recognize all the characters in a printed page. An example of word detection is also presented.

In the Appendix we discuss two problems that must be solved if we are to realize the potential of this subsystem. The first is concerned with transforming the input data from its original form to one suitable for processing in the optical system. The second is concerned with connecting the light distribution in the system's output to a computer for logical operations and preparation for ultimate use of the processed output.

II. Matched Filter Theory as Applied to Character-Reading

The problem of reading characters begins with the identification of a particular character when it is known to be an element in a set of characters. Identification is made difficult because of the noise present in the system. Noise can take the form of corrupted symbols produced by faulty printing techniques and/or can be considered to be everything in the input which is not of interest for the moment. If we assume that the signal (the character to be identified) and the noise are linearly additive* and that the noise is homogeneous, the optimum linear processing for maximizing the ratio of peak signal to mean square noise energy is the so-called matched filtering operation.[3] We denote the signal by $s(x, y)$ and the noise by $n(x, y)$. Since the signal is a known function, it has Fourier transforms $S(p, q)$, where

$$S(p, q) = \iint_{-\infty}^{\infty} s(x, y)e^{j(px+qy)} \, dx \, dy \tag{1}$$

The noise is a random function characterized by its autocorrelation function $R_n(x, y)$ where

$$R_n(x, y) = \iint_{-\infty}^{\infty} n(u, v)n^*(u + x, v + y) \, du \, dv \tag{2}$$

---

* The fact that signal and noise are not always additive but may be mutually exclusive does not seem to affect the experimental results materially in this application.

and its spectral density function $N(p, q)$ where

$$N(p, q) = \iint_{-\infty}^{\infty} R_n(x, y)e^{j(px+qy)}\, dx\, dy \qquad (3)$$

Under the conditions mentioned in the foregoing, the optimum filtering process is represented by

$$H(p, q) = \frac{S^*(p, q)}{N(p, q)} \qquad (4)$$

Let $f(x, y)$ represent the input function, and let $F(p, q)$ denote the Fourier transform of $f(x, y)$. To perform the optimum process we multiply $F(p, q)$ by $H(p, q)$ and then take the Fourier transform of the product. The input is mapped into the output point by point, but is modified by the filtering operation.

Coherent optical systems, such as that shown in Fig. 1, are well suited

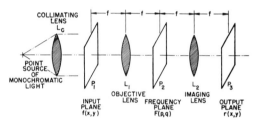

FIG. 1. A coherent optical system.

for carrying out this operation. Systems of this general type have been described elsewhere,[4,5] so we will only treat them in sufficient detail to serve our purposes. A point source of monochromatic light is collimated by lens L_c. The input function $f(x, y)$ is placed in plane P_1 and lens L_1 displays its Fourier transform in plane P_2; i.e., the light distribution in plane P_2 is

$$F(p, q) = \iint_{-\infty}^{\infty} f(x, y)e^{j(px+qy)}\, dx\, dy$$

A filter having (possibly) complex-valued transmission is placed in plane P_2 to modify $F(p, q)$. Lens L_2 takes the Fourier transform of the product. If the filter function is denoted by $H(p, q)$ and the output of the system by $r(x, y)$ then

$$r(x, y) = \frac{1}{4\pi^2} \iint_{-\infty}^{\infty} F(p, q)H(p, q)e^{j(px+qy)}dp\, dq \qquad (5)$$

which represents the output from an optimum filtering system. Thus, the system shown in Fig. 1 can be implemented to carry out the desired operation for two-dimensional matched filtering, provided we can realize the required filter.

The problem has two aspects: (1) to determine mathematically the filter function from knowledge about the signal, and (2) to construct the filter by some practical method. In each case it is the phase response required of the filter that causes difficulty. We will briefly describe a technique that avoids both problems and has the advantage that the filtering is recorded on photographic film.[2] Photographic film is, of course, a medium sensitive to energy and as such cannot record phase information. The key to recording a complex-valued function on photographic film is to transform the phase information into intensity information so that it can be recorded. This is accomplished by recording the complex-valued function as a real-valued function modulating a carrier frequency.[3]

Before describing such a technique we simplify the notation by rewriting Eq. 4 as the product of two functions:

$$H(p, q) = \frac{k_1}{N(p, q)} \cdot k_2 S^*(p, q) \qquad (6)$$

where k_1 and k_2 are constants chosen to make the filter passive. Since $N(p, q)$ is the Fourier transform of an autocorrelation function, it is a nonnegative function, and can be recorded on a separate piece of photographic film. The film can be placed in contact with the one that records $k_2 S^*(p, q)$ to complete the realization of the desired filter function.* Hence, we turn our attention to the method for recording $k_2 S^*(p, q)$.

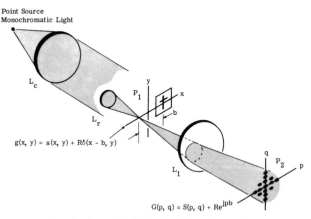

FIG. 2. A modified Rayleigh interferometer.

A method for recording the complex-valued function $k_2 S^*(p, q)$ on photographic film is given in Reference 2. It uses a modified Mach-Zehnder interferometer. An alternate but equivalent method is to use the modified Rayleigh interferometer shown in Fig. 2. The signal $s(x, y)$ is placed in one half

---

* When photographic films are placed in contact their transmissions are multiplicative. Also, throughout this paper the word "transmission" refers to the specular amplitude transmission of the film.

of the beam in plane P_1. In the other half of the system a lens L_r is positioned so that the collimated light comes to focus in plane P_1 at distance b from the center of the signal. Aside from the effects of the limited aperture, the distribution in P_1 due to the reference lens L_r can be denoted by $R\delta(x - b, y)$. The total distribution in plane P_1 is then

$$g(x, y) = s(x, y) + R\delta(x - b, y) \tag{7}$$

Lens L_1 takes the Fourier transform of $g(x, y)$ and displays it in plane P_2. That is, the distribution in P_2 is

$$G(p, q) = \iint_{-\infty}^{\infty} [s(x, y) + R\delta(x - b, y)]e^{j(px+qy)}\, dx\, dy \tag{8}$$

$$= S(p, q) + Re^{jpb} \tag{9}$$

A sheet of photographic film placed in plane P_2 acts as a square-law detector and will record $|G(p, q)|^2$ which is

$$|G(p, q)|^2 = |S(p, q) + Re^{jpb}|^2$$
$$= |S(p, q)|^2 + R^2 + Re^{-jpb}S(p, q) + Re^{jpb}S^*(p, q) \tag{10}$$

The last term of Eq. 10 is the desired function (if we set $R = k_2$) except that it is multiplied by the linear phase term e^{jpb}. However, this linear phase term is exactly what is needed to separate the effect of the last term from all the others when the photographic film is inserted into plane P_2 of the system shown in Fig. 1.

Suppose we now introduce the film which has $k_1/N(p, q)$ recorded on it and form a new function

$$T(p, q) = \frac{k_1}{N(p, q)} \cdot |G(p, q)|^2 \tag{11}$$

Substitute $T(p, q)$ for $H(p, q)$ in Eq. 5 to get

$$r_1(x, y) = \frac{1}{4\pi^2} \iint F(p, q) \frac{k_1}{N(p, q)} \cdot |G(p, q)|^2 e^{j(px+qy)}\, dp\, dq \tag{12}$$

By expanding $|G|^2$ into its component terms we have

$$r_1(x, y) = \frac{1}{4\pi^2} \iint \frac{k_1 F(p, q)[|S(p, q)|^2 + k_2^2]}{N(p, q)} e^{j(px+qy)}\, dp\, dq$$

$$+ \frac{1}{4\pi^2} \iint F(p, q)H^*(p, q)e^{j[p(x-b)+qy]}\, dp\, dq \tag{13}$$

$$+ \frac{1}{4\pi^2} \iint F(p, q)H(p, q)e^{j[p(x+b)+qy]}\, dp\, dq$$

The first term of Eq. 13 is centered on the optical axis and is of no particular interest in this discussion. The second term is centered at $x = -b$, $y = 0$ and represents the cross-correlation of the input data with the conjugate of the impulse response of the filter. The final term is centered at $x = b$,

$y = 0$, and is the convolution of the input data with the impulse response of the filter. Except for its location, this term is identical to that represented by Eq. 5, i.e., the output of a matched filtering system. If the value of b is chosen to be sufficiently large, no overlap of the three outputs occurs.

This completes a brief introduction to coherent optical processing systems and to a method for realizing complex-valued filter functions. We now present a method for reading characters based on the matched-filtering capability of these systems. Basically the method involves optically cross-correlating an unknown character and an array of known characters, and determining which known character gives maximum correlation.

III. Implementation of a Character-Reading Device

A. Introduction

The simplest implementation of a character-reading device is to record each character on a separate filter and to process the input sequentially.* The locations of the correlation peaks are stored in a computer, are read out in the proper order at the end of a cycle, and are recorded on magnetic tape. The disadvantage of this method is that mechanical filter changing is required. Such a technique could be very useful, however, if one is searching for words or a sequence of words, in which case the filter would not have to be changed rapidly. Some of our experimental results were obtained by this technique, as will be indicated later.

Another approach is to record all possible characters on a single filter and submit only one unknown character to the input at one time. This method is obviously the same as the previous method except that the roles of the input and the frequency planes are interchanged. The advantage of this method is that the positional tolerance of the input character is generally less severe than that on the filter. However, this advantage would accrue only if the method of presenting the unknown characters sequentially is less complex than the method for changing filters.

Some reflection on the problem will clearly show that sequential operations are needed in both of these methods because of limited space-bandwidth products. In the first method, a sufficient product was gained by using multiple filters, i.e., time-sharing the system bandwidth. In the second method, the product was increased by sequential input display, i.e., time-sharing the system space. If we can employ the available space-bandwidth product efficiently, we should be able to do the reading without time-sharing in the domains of frequency and space. Later we will give examples that show how this is done.

---

* What is meant, of course, is that the character is recorded on the filter via its complex-valued Fourier transform.

B. Illustration of Ideas and Some Experimental Results

In this section we present experimental results that illustrate the ideas already suggested. These results are also useful in estimating the system's performance. The experiments are exploratory in nature, and the estimate of the system's performance is limited to visual observations. No claim is made that these results are optimum, although we do feel that the results are realistic.

In the design of any practical system, one must know how the system performs when the input characters are noisy. Three kinds of noise are considered; changes in the signal size, changes in the signal orientation, and changes in the signal quality. This knowledge must be coupled with knowledge about the mean-square noise energy to determine a threshold. The detection and false alarm rates can then be determined.

We begin with experiments that show how the single-character filter operates, and at the same time illustrate the effects that changes in the size, the orientation, and the quality of an input character have on system performance.

For these experiments we chose the character 5 because it consists of both straight line segments and curved segments. Two matched filters for this character were constructed, one that responds well throughout the frequency range, and one in which the low-to-intermediate frequencies were

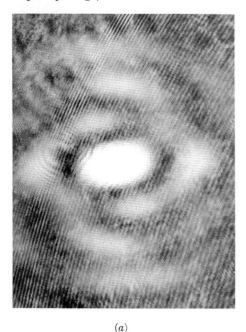

(a)

(b)

FIG. 3. Broadband spatial filter and impulse response. (a) Broadband filter of "5"
(b) Impulse response of filter.

attenuated. The first, hereafter called the broadband filter, is shown in Fig. 3a, with the corresponding impulse response shown in Fig. 3b. The second, called the high-pass filter, is shown in Fig. 4a, with its impulse response shown in Fig. 4b. Note that the second filter produces an impulse response having more emphasis on the edge information.

The first experiment illustrates the effect of variations in signal size on the output of the system. Figure 5a shows a set of 5's containing signals at ±7.5 per cent and ±15 per cent of the nominal (center character) scale. The system output, when the broadband filter is used, is shown in Fig. 5b,

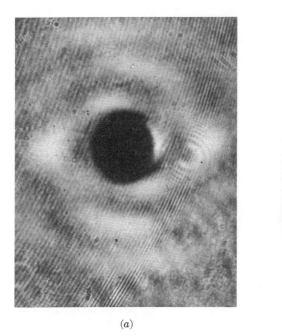

(a)

(b)

FIG. 4. High-pass spatial filter and impulse response. (a) High-pass filter of "5." (b) Impulse response of filter.

and that for the high-pass filter is shown in Fig. 5c. From these results it can be seen that the response decreases as the signal size departs from the nominal scale, and that the decrease is accentuated when the high-pass filter is used. Under a change in scale of the input character, the system's performance tends to be independent of the shape of the character.

The results of the second experiment, however, are highly dependent on the character's shape. The character O has no preferred orientation while the character 1 has a large amount of what one might call "orientativeness." The character 5 was chosen to fall somewhere in between. Figure 6a shows a set of 5's oriented at angles of 2°, 4°, 8°, and 16° relative to the character at the extreme left. The results for the broadband filter are shown in Fig. 6c. Again we see that the response decreases as the departure from normal inclination increases and that the decrease in response is faster for the high-pass filter.

The final experiment in this set shows the effect of signal deterioration on the system output. Figure 7a shows a sequence of 5's in order of decreasing quality. The respective outputs are shown in Figs. 7b and 7c. The

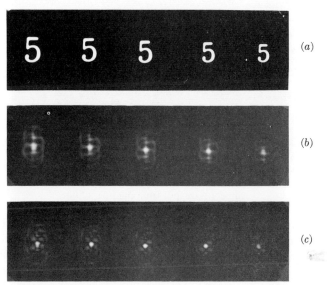

FIG. 5. Effect of variations in signal size. (a) Input. (b) Output from broadband filter. (c) Output from high-pass filter.

change in the system's response as a function of the quality of the input is far greater than are the effects of the changes in input size or orientation. Unfortunately it is also more probable that degraded images such as these will be encountered in some practical systems and steps should be taken to obtain inputs of reasonably consistent quality.

The results of this set of experiments can only be interpreted in terms of the ability of the system to discriminate between signal and noise. The question of how much size, orientation, and quality variation can be tolerated cannot be answered until we know what the maximum response is to nonsignals. The maximum response to nonsignals will determine the threshold for any character. This level, in turn, will determine the allowable variation in the parameters cited above.

Having presented a simple example that illustrates the operation of the system, we now proceed to one of the more interesting problems cited before. How can we implement the system so that a single filter can contain information about many characters, and yet process an appreciable amount of data? Our next example will show how this can be done in principle. The

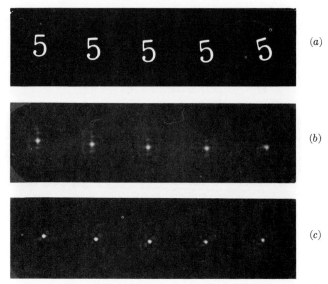

FIG. 6. Effect of variations in signal orientation. (*a*) Input. (*b*) Output from broadband filter. (*c*) Output from high-pass filter.

extension to even higher space-bandwidth products is obvious. Recall from the discussion of Eq. 13 that we must choose a sufficiently high carrier frequency to prevent overlap of the three outputs represented by the three terms in the equation. In our previous examples this implied that the value

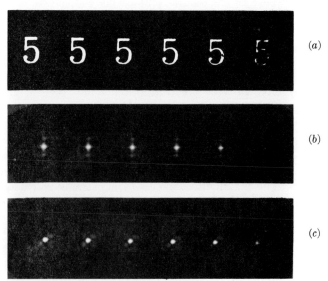

FIG. 7. Effect of variations in signal quality. (*a*) Input. (*b*) Output from broadband filter. (*c*) Output from high-pass filter.

of b was slightly larger than the length of the various sequences of the 5's. More precisely, the central image (the first term of Eq. 13) occupies a region equal to the length of the sequence plus four times the length of a single character. This can be seen readily by rewriting the first term of Eq. 13, using the convolution theorem and, for purposes of this discussion, letting $N(p, q) = N_0$. We then have

$$r'(x, y) = \frac{k_1}{N_0} \iint_{-\infty}^{\infty} [R_s(u, v) + k_2^2 \delta(u, v)] f(u - x, v - y) \, du \, dv \qquad (14)$$

or

$$r'(x, y) = k_1 \frac{k_2^2}{N_0} f(x, y) + \frac{k_1}{N_0} \iint_{-\infty}^{\infty} R_s(u, v) f(u - x, v - y) \, du \, dv \qquad (15)$$

where

$$R_s(u, v) = \iint_{-\infty}^{\infty} s(x, y) s^*(x + u, y + v) \, dx \, dy \qquad (16)$$

The first term of Eq. 15 clearly occupies a length equal to the length of the input sequence (with unity system magnification). The second term occupies that same length plus twice the length of R_s. Since R_s is the autocorrelation function of a single character, its length can be no greater than twice the length of the character itself. Thus we arrive at a maximum total length for the central image equal to the length of input data plus four times the signal length.

The length of the side image of interest (the last term of Eq. 13) is, by similar analysis, equal to the input data length plus two times the signal length. If we choose the value of b so that the central and side images are just separated, its value must be equal to the length of the input data plus three times the length of the signal. This line of reasoning sets the minimum value of b, the distance from the center of the signal to the reference beam, as shown in Fig. 2.

If we wish to record multiple symbols on the filter, we must not only ensure that the distance from the center of the set of symbols to the reference beam is large, but that the distances between the symbols is large enough to contain whatever size signal we wish to process.

What has taken many words to describe perhaps can be more quickly demonstrated with a few pictures. Suppose we wish to implement our optical system to identify a set of symbols where each symbol might take on one of nine different shapes. The set of nine shapes (arranged conveniently) is shown in Fig. 8a. A filter, shown in Fig. 8b, was constructed to record this set of symbols and its impulse response is shown in Fig. 8c. Although not shown in this figure, a sufficiently high value of b has been chosen to satisfy the first requirement that the three output images be separated. Further, the separation between the nine symbols is large enough so that a nine-digit sequence, such as that shown in Fig. 9, can be processed. We

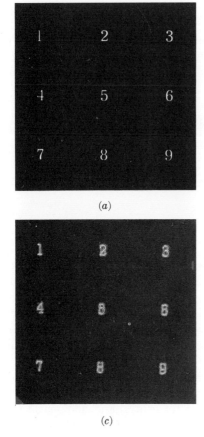

(a)

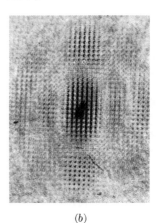

(b)

(c)

FIG. 8. Multiple character filter. (a) Set of symbols. (b) Broadband filter for symbols. (c) Impulse response of filter.

chose this sequence so that the output will show how well each symbol correlates with itself, and also show how well the filter rejects the other symbol.

Actually, two filters were constructed, one with wideband frequency

FIG. 9. Nine-digit sequence.

content and one with more emphasis on the high-frequency content. What we expect to gain from the latter filter is increased shape selectivity (or, alternately, more noise rejection). However, we gain this selectivity at the expense of tolerance to variations in signal size, orientation, and quality. Such tolerance is reduced, as demonstrated in the previous examples.

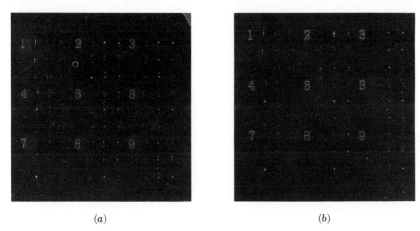

(a)   (b)

Fig. 10. System output. (*a*) Output from broadband filter. (*b*) Output from high-pass filter.

The results are shown in Fig. 10*a* for the broadband filter and in Fig. 10*b* for the high-pass filter. To make the results somewhat more illuminating, we have included the impulse responses of the respective filters in the output by using a double exposure. Let us discuss Fig. 10*a* in some detail so that the results are clearly understood. First, we see the filter's impulse response, which is similar to that shown in Fig. 8*c*. To the right and below each symbol we see the output corresponding to the cross-correlation of that symbol with the input sequence that was shown in Fig. 9. For example, to the right and below the symbol 4 in Fig. 10*a*, we see that the brightest spot of light occurs in the first column, second row. Referring to Fig. 9 we see that this is indeed the location of the symbol 4. A similar check with the other symbols shows that maximum correlation occurs at the point where that symbol occurs in the input. Also, within each subportion of the output, one can see how well the filter rejects the other (nonsignal) symbols.

It should be observed that the *relative* amount of light in the autocorrelation peak for each signal varies. This is because the original signals do not contain equal energies, and is most clearly illustrated in the output for the symbol 1. If photodetectors were used to sense the correlation peaks, they could be biased properly to compensate for the inequalities of signal energy. The compensation could also be made when the filter is constructed.

OPTICS.   The study of optics is usually divided
into three parts: physical optics, physiological optics
and geometrical optics.   Physical optics is primarily
concerned with the nature and properties of light itself
and is treated under LIGHT.   Physiological optics deals
with the mechanism of vision, and is treated under
VISION.

Geometrical optics, which is the subject of this
article, is the name applied to that part of optics which
deals with the properties of optical instruments such as
telescopes, microscopes, photographic lenses, spectroscopes
and the elementary lenses, mirrors and prisms from
which they are constructed.

(a)

(b)

FIG. 11. Detection of key word. (a) Input text. (b) Detection of the word "optics."

The significance of Fig. 10*b* is that the *selectivity* of the filtering process has been improved; i.e., the difference between the maximum correlation peaks (denoting detection) and all other peaks has been increased. As pointed out before, this increase in selectivity must be weighed against the increased sensitivity to symbol variations in any practical system.

It is clear how this method could be extended so that a much larger set of test symbols could be used, say, the entire English alphabet plus the Arabic numeral system and miscellaneous characters. At the same time we may wish to read an entire printed page. The key is to separate the symbols so that an entire printed page can "fit" between them. The letters will become very small, of course, and some problems with the light levels might arise.

A final example of the use of spatial filtering in coherent optical systems is to construct filters for the detection of key words in printed material. Such a system might be used in the Post Office Department for routing mail to given areas by using the Zip Code. It might also be useful in abstracting and cataloging operations where one looks for certain descriptor words. Figure 11*a* gives a portion of text taken from the *Encyclopaedia Britannica*. The key word is *optics*. Figure 11*b* shows the system output with the relative positions of the word *optics* clearly indicated. One also gets partial response to the word *optical* which is to be expected. The reader is left to discover why the word *applied* also gives a fair response. However, neither response is as great as that to the word *optics*, and some thresholding device could easily separate them on the basis of the amount of energy in the relative correlation peaks.

Summary

In this paper we have illustrated how some new developments in the construction of complex-valued spatial filters can be applied to the character-reading problem. Using a simple implementation of the system we have given experimental results that show the system's performance when there is variation in the size, the orientation, or the quality of the character. The effect of varying filter frequency response is also evident in these experiments.

The system was also implemented so that a single filter can be used to identify all the characters within a given set. In concept the system could be used to identify all the characters on a printed page simultaneously (in parallel). Finally, an example of the detection of groups of characters was given.

These experiments were performed under laboratory conditions using photographic film as the input medium and as a sensing medium in the output. To attain reasonable data rates the photographic film must be replaced in both the input and the output by other devices. Some considerations of these problems are given in the Appendix.

APPENDIX

A Note on the Input and the Output

In this section we will look at some of the requirements of the readin and readout systems. The discussion will be suggestive in nature, with no definite solutions to the problem given. We first look at the requirements of a real-time readin device suitable for a coherent optical system.

The first, and most important, requirement is that the medium used to spatially modulate the light in the processor have a coherent substrate, i.e., the thickness variation (or phase variation) must be below certain tolerances to obtain satisfactory system performance. Second, the medium must possess sufficient resolving power to record the data with minimum degradation in quality. Third, the time interval between readin and erasure must be consistent with the expected data rates. Fourth, the medium must be reusable over many cycles, and should remain free from dust, dirt, or other foreign material. Finally, the average transmission of the medium should be as high as possible to utilize available light efficiently and also possess good diffracting characteristics. A schematic of how such a readin system would be incorporated into the processing system is shown in Fig. 12.

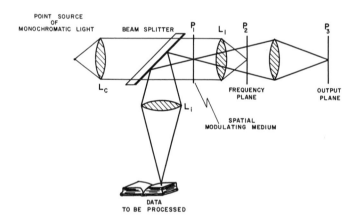

FIG. 12. A suggested readin system.

Several commercial processes possess some of these requirements, but to the best of our knowledge no one has all of them. This is an important area for development, not only for application to this problem, but to a multitude of others as well.

Passing to the readout problem, we have the following requirements. First, the capacity of the readout must be adequate. Suppose our alphabet consisted of a 26-letter alphabet plus the 10 numerals and 14 miscellaneous characters to give a 50-character test alphabet. Suppose that one line of type might contain 100 possible characters and that a page can contain 35 lines of type. We then have $50 \times 100 \times 35 = 175,000$ points to evaluate in the output of the system. The output sensor must be able to detect this number of points easily. Second, the readout system must provide some kind of thresholding (or decision-making) level. Also, it may be necessary to be able to bias the individual detectors to compensate for different amounts of energy in the test symbols unless this compensation is made in filter construction. Third, the readout must have adequate sensitivity to detect the light distribution in the output. Finally, the readout system must be connected to a computer so that it can carry out the required processes of logic and record the results on magnetic tape or use the information to activate other devices.

REFERENCES

1. STEVENS, M. E., *et al.*, *Automatic Character Recognition*, NBS Technical Note No. 112, U.S. Department of Commerce, OTS, Washington, D.C., 1961.
2. VANDER LUGT, A., "Signal Detection by Complex Spatial Filtering," *IEEE Trans. Inform. Theory, IT-10*, Vol. 2, 139–145 (April 1964).
3. BROWN, W. M., *Analysis of Linear Time-Invariant Systems*, McGraw-Hill Book Co., Inc., New York, 1963.
4. O'NEILL, E. L., "Spatial Filtering in Optics," *IRE Trans. Inform. Theory, IT-2*, 56–65 (June 1956).
5. CUTRONA, L. J., *et al.*, "Optical Data Processing and Filtering Systems," *IRE Trans. Inform. Theory, IT-6*, 386–400 (June 1960).

CHAPTER 8

COHERENT OPTICAL SYSTEMS FOR DATA PROCESSING, SPATIAL FILTERING, AND WAVEFRONT RECONSTRUCTION

Emmett N. Leith, Adam Kozma, and Juris Upatnieks

Radar Laboratory, Institute of Science and Technology
The University of Michigan, Ann Arbor, Michigan

I. Introduction

For the past decade, the Radar Laboratory of the Institute of Science and Technology at The University of Michigan has been engaged in the study of coherent optical systems. These studies have centered on the idea, advanced by Duffieux,[1] Maréchal[2] and others in Europe, and among others, O'Neill[3] in the United States, that there is an analogy between optical systems and linear electric filters. The application of this basic idea has enabled engineers at the Radar Laboratory to develop sophisticated coherent optical systems of great practical utility, for multichannel data processing and for processing of inherently two-dimensional data.

The work cannot be covered here in its entirety; therefore, this partial survey is focused on a single theme: the recording of Fraunhofer and Fresnel diffraction patterns in such a way that both the phase and amplitude of the diffraction pattern are completely contained in the recording.

Around this simple theme have evolved several significant efforts, producing results which, to the authors' knowledge, have not been previously achieved. These efforts fall into two main categories.

One category is the extension of the wavefront reconstruction method of Gabor. By combining conventional wavefront reconstruction techniques with interferometry, it has been possible to produce holograms from which high-quality reconstructions can be obtained. These reconstructions bear a close likeness to the original object, complete with three-dimensional characteristics.

The second category is that of complex spatial filtering. This work is based on optical spatial filtering techniques used by Maréchal, O'Neill, and others. These researchers demonstrated, by means of spatial filtering, such phenomena as edge sharpening and noise reduction in photographic transparencies. However, these filters were, in most cases, *amplitude only* filters; they modified only the amplitude of the spatial-frequency components of the picture. The spatial filters described here incorporate phase as well as amplitude, and give to optical spatial filters the same broad capabilities possessed by their electrical counterparts.

The work in complex spatial filtering falls into two categories. Kozma and Kelly[4] have constructed such filters by conventional photographic techniques from data calculated by digital computers. The area of application is general multichannel data processing. Vander Lugt developed techniques for producing complex filters by optical interferometric methods.[5] His main areas of application are image interpretation and character recognition. The present paper is concerned only with the former category; the latter is described in a separate paper by Vander Lugt *et al.*

II. The Recording of Complex Functions

The complex function, $ae^{j\phi}$, whether it be a diffraction pattern in an optical system, the transfer function of a complex filter, or some other quantity, is to be recorded in a way as to preserve its phase and amplitude. The most straightforward way, conceptually, of recording this function is to produce a photographic variable-density mask having a transmittance proportional to the amplitude a, to produce a transparency with thickness varying in proportion to ϕ, and then to superimpose the two masks. Such a combination represents a complete recording of the complex function, which can readily be converted into a complex distribution of coherent light by placing the mask in a beam of monochromatic, spatially coherent light. The light, upon transmission through this complex mask, is amplitude-modulated in accordance with a and phase-modulated in accordance with ϕ. The general impracticality of producing the phase part of the mask limits this method to relatively simple and special cases.

In order to carry out the desired program without the obvious practical limitations, an alternative method is utilized. It is known to communication engineers[6] that a complex function of frequency bandwidth B can be represented as a real function with bandwidth $2B$. The real function is derived from the complex one by placing the complex function on a carrier and taking the real part; thus we have

$$f = ae^{j\phi} \rightarrow \tfrac{1}{2}(fe^{j\alpha x} + f^*e^{-j\alpha x}) = a \cos (\alpha x + \phi) \qquad (1)$$

as the complex function and its real-function equivalent. The carrier α must be at least as great as some minimum value which is determined by the bandwidth of f, in order that the complex function can be unambiguously recovered from the real-function counterpart.

Let the complex signal $f(x)$ have the Fourier spectrum $F(\xi)$. Here we adopt the notation, to be used throughout the paper, of using lower case letters for spatial domain functions and the corresponding upper case letters for the Fourier transforms; the letters ξ, η represent the spatial frequency coordinates corresponding to x, y, the spatial coordinates of the signal.

The spectrum of the complex function and its real function representation are shown in Fig. 1. The spectrum $F(\xi)$ becomes $F(\xi - \alpha)$ when the signal

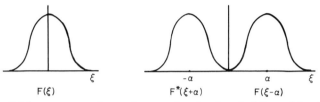

$$F(\xi) \qquad\qquad F^*(\xi+\alpha) \qquad\qquad F(\xi-\alpha)$$

FIG. 1. Spatial-frequency spectrum of a complex signal and of its real-function representation.

is placed on a carrier. Taking the real part of the signal corresponds to adding to the signal its complex conjugate. If a function $f(x)$ has a Fourier transform $F(\xi)$, then its complex conjugate $f^*(x)$ has the Fourier transform $F^*(-\xi)$. Thus, Eq. 1 has the equivalent frequency-domain statement

$$F(\xi) \rightarrow F(\xi - \alpha) + F^*(\xi + \alpha) \tag{2}$$

which is shown in Fig. 1. The purpose of the carrier is to shift the spectrum F so that addition of the complex conjugate does not contaminate the original spectrum. Obviously, $\alpha = B/2$ is the minimum value of α that accomplishes this objective. Also, the real signal has the minimum bandwidth $2B$, which is twice the bandwidth of the complex signal.

The real function thus generated is to be recorded as transmittance on a photographic transparency for insertion into an optical system. Since photographic transmittance is restricted to positive values, a bias term s_b is added to the signal $a \cos (\alpha x + \phi)$. This adds a delta function to the spectrum shown in Fig. 1b, which, being located at $\omega = 0$, does not fall into the signal spectrum.

In the optical system, the complex signal is to be recovered from its real function representation. This is accomplished in various ways, all of which are a variant of the method illustrated in Fig. 2. The coherent light passing

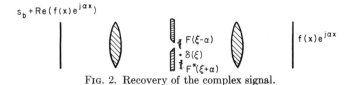

FIG. 2. Recovery of the complex signal.

through the transparency is spatially modulated in accordance with the transmittance function recorded on the transparency. A lens produces, at its focal plane, the Fraunhofer diffraction pattern of the transparency, thus displaying at this plane the signal spectrum shown in Fig. 1b. A slit at this position removes the delta function and one of the sideband terms, for example, $F^*(\xi - \alpha)$. What remains is the spectrum of the required complex function. If the function $ae^{j\phi}$ rather than its spectrum is required, a second lens may take a Fourier transformation, thus producing $f(x)e^{-j\alpha x}$. The residual term $e^{-j\alpha x}$ represents only a progressive linear phase shift across the aperture and is of no practical consequence.

III. Complex Spatial Filtering

The principles described in the previous section can be applied to the construction of spatial filters having both amplitude and phase components in their transfer function.* Such control enables spatial filters of any desired transfer function to be realized in practice, thus giving to the optical researcher a capability long enjoyed by electronic engineers.

The concept of spatial filtering is shown in Fig. 3. A beam of monochro-

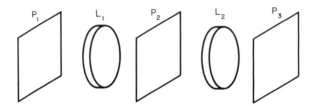

FIG. 3. Basic system for spatial filtering.

matic light derived from a point source illuminates a transparency. This transparency may be a photograph or electrically recorded multichannel or two-dimensional data. We designate the amplitude transmittance of this transparency as the input signal $s(x, y)$. At plane P_2, the Fraunhofer diffraction pattern of the signal is displayed. The complex amplitude of this light distribution represents the Fourier transform, $S(\xi, \eta)$ of the signal $s(x, y)$ where, as before, we adopt the notation of using lower case letters for spatial-domain functions, while the corresponding upper case letters designate the Fourier transforms.

The lens L_2 takes a second Fourier transform, thus restoring the original signal $s(x, y)$. This is an instance of the well-known fact that an imaging process can be formulated as two successive Fourier transformations.† This

---

* The use of these principles for the construction of complex filters was suggested to the authors by C. J. Palermo, of our laboratory.

† Here it is assumed that the lenses are well corrected and that the structure of the object is sufficiently coarse so that the low-pass characteristic of the imaging process may be neglected.

formulation is correct regardless of the lens arrangement used; however, the above arrangement is particularly convenient for discussion purposes.

The spatial filtering process involves placing, at plane P_2, a transparency mask whose amplitude transmittance we designate as $F(\xi, \eta)$. Placing this mask at P_2 causes the light distribution present there to be multiplied by $F(\xi, \eta)$, producing the product $S(\xi, \eta)F(\xi, \eta)$. The "image" of $s(x, y)$, as displayed at plane P_3, has the amplitude distribution $s(x, y)*f(x, y)$, where $f(x, y)$ is the Fourier transform of $F(\xi, \eta)$, and the * denotes the convolution operation. Designating the new image as $s_0(x, y)$, we have

$$s_0(x, y) = s(x, y)*f(x, y) = \iint s(\alpha, \beta)f(x - \alpha, y - \beta)\, d\alpha\, d\beta \qquad (3)$$

The transparency, $F(\xi, \eta)$ thus modifies the spatial-frequency content of the signal $s(x, y)$ and is thus directly analogous to an electrical filter, which modifies the temporal-frequency content of an electrical signal. The function $f(x, y)$ is called the impulse response of the filter, since, if the signal $s(x, y)$ is an impulse, or delta function, the output signal $s_0(x, y)$ is just $f(x, y)$.

Generally $F(\xi, \eta)$ is a complex transmittance function

$$F(\xi, \eta) = |F(\xi, \eta)|e^{j\phi(\xi, \eta)} \qquad (4)$$

The amplitude modulus portion $|F|$ produces attenuation of the spectrum $S(\xi, \eta)$, while the phase portion produces phase shifts in the spectrum.

The practical difficulties involved in producing masks with complex transmittance has previously limited their construction to such simple forms as two-level phase plates and to a few other special cases. Application of the spatial carrier method removes the difficulty. To produce a filter which is equivalent to the complex filter, a mask bearing the function

$$F_B + \text{Re}[F(\xi, \eta)e^{jx_0\xi}] = F_B + |F(\xi, \eta)| \cos [x_0\xi + \phi(\xi, \eta)] \qquad (5)$$

is inserted in the Fraunhofer diffraction plane P_2. F_B is a bias term, providing the gray level about which the transmittance variations are written. The signal spectrum $S(\xi, \eta)$ is multiplied with this transmittance function, producing three terms:

$$F_B S(\xi, \eta) + \tfrac{1}{2}F(\xi, \eta)S(\xi, \eta)e^{jx_0\xi} + \tfrac{1}{2}F^*(\xi, \eta)S(\xi, \eta)e^{-jx_0\xi} \qquad (6)$$

where the middle term is the desired result, i.e., the result that would be obtained if the filter transparency had been synthesized in its complex transmittance form.

At the image plane P_3 three terms are produced:

$$F_B s(x, y) + f(x - x_0, y)*s(x - x_0, y) + f^*(-x_0 + x, -y)*s(-x + x_0, -y) \qquad (7)$$

These terms arise, respectively, from the three terms of the filter given by Eq. 6. The first term is merely the original signal, attenuated by the factor F_B. The second term is the desired result; *viz.*, the original signal modified by the required complex filter. This term is displaced from the first one by an amount x_0; this displacement is the result of the term $e^{jx_0\xi}$ used in constructing the filter. The requirement on x_0 is that it be sufficiently large as to prevent overlapping of the two output terms; this means approximately that

$$x_0 \geq L \qquad (8)$$

where L is the length of the signal $s(x, y)$ along the x dimension.

The third term is displaced from the original signal by $-x_0$ and represents the original signal modified by a filter which is conjugate to the desired filter. Its presence may be useful or not, depending on the application. Since it is physically separated from the desired output term, its presence is not harmful.

Using this technique, one can produce any desired filter; for instance, optimum smoothing filters if an obscured object is to be detected in its original form or a matched filter if only recognition of the object is desired. The filter which has the most interest in our work is the matched filter which is used for detection of a signal immersed in an additive noise background. It operates by suppressing, to a degree, the noisy background, while enhancing the signal by causing the energy contained in the signal to be concentrated into a small area, roughly, a point. This description is quite oversimplified, but basically correct.

The matched filter is defined to be one whose modulation transfer function is proportional to the complex conjugate of the signal spectrum. Thus, using the previous notation, the matched filter for a signal $s(x, y)$ is one whose modulation transfer function is defined by

$$F(\xi, \eta) = KS^*(\xi, \eta) \qquad (9)$$

Consider the signal $s(x, y)$ to be an element or elements of the transparency at plane P_1. Let all other elements of the transparency be considered noise $n(x, y)$. This may be random noise, or it may be other signals which tend to obscure the desired signal. In either case it is desired to enhance $s(x, y)$ and suppress $n(x, y)$.

To see how the matched filter does this, consider the signal $s(x, y)$, with spectrum $S(\xi, \eta) = |S(\xi, \eta)|e^{j\phi(\xi,\eta)}$, a complex quantity. The spectrum $S(\xi, \eta)$ exists in the vicinity of the frequency plane P_2 as a distorted wavefront, whose contour is defined by the function $\phi(\xi, \eta)$. The matched filter introduces the compensating phase factor $e^{-j\phi(\xi,\eta)}$, thereby converting the distorted wavefront into a plane wavefront. The lens L_2 then tends to bring this wavefront to a point focus. This is exactly what happens, from a geometrical optics viewpoint. From the viewpoint of physical optics, the collapsing to a point is only approximate, because of diffraction effects. The broader the spectrum $S(\xi, \eta)$, the larger the extent of the wavefront corresponding to $S(\xi, \eta)$, and the smaller will be the collapsed point.

The collapsed point appears in the output image at the same relative position where the original signal is located on the input transparency. Thus, the matched filter not only detects a signal in noise by collapsing it to a point, thus causing a large buildup of intensity at that point, but it also detects the location of the signal. If several such displaced signals are present, each is detected simultaneously and brought to a point focus at the appropriate position.

This describes the action of the phase portion of the matched filter. The amplitude portion has a transmittance proportional to the amplitude of the signal spectrum $S(\xi, \eta)$. This portion gives the noise-suppression characteristic. Wherever the signal spectrum is weak, the filter attenuates. It is evident that the filter discriminates in favor of the signal as opposed to the noise.

IV. Experimental Results

An example of a matched filter application, described by Kozma and Kelly,[4] arises when pulse compression techniques are used to increase the probability of detection of a known signal in a background of noise. The process amounts to deliberately lengthening a signal, originally narrow in the time extent, in such a way that upon reception it can be compressed to the original length. The lengthening amounts to coding the original pulse and the matched filtering is a decoding or compression operation.

To demonstrate the method, a matched filter was constructed to compress a signal which was derived from a linear shift register. To simplify the filter construction, the spatial-frequency-shifted transfer function was quantized to two levels. This corresponds to "hard clipping" of the filter, resulting in a filter with transmittance

$$t = F_b + \frac{k \cos \left[x_0 \xi + \phi(\xi) \right]}{\left| \cos \left[x_0 \xi + \phi(\xi) \right] \right|} \tag{10}$$

We see that this quantizing discards the amplitude information and also produces intermodulation terms.

Discarding the amplitude portion of the filter function generally results in little loss, since in designing the signals for this purpose care is taken to make the amplitude of the signal spectrum nearly uniform over the frequency band of interest. For this particular signal, discarding the amplitude portion of the matched filter resulted in a signal-to-noise ratio loss of only 1 dB.

The intermodulation terms produced by the hard clipping have no effect on the resulting filtering operation if x_0 is made sufficiently large, since the generated terms will appear in the "image" separated from the desired result. The signal and its matched filter are shown in Fig. 4. The filter was constructed as a series of opaque and transparent strips of large scale and reduced photographically to the correct size.

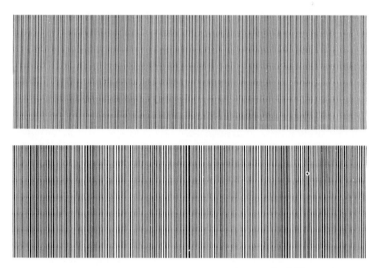

Fɪɢ. 4. Shift-register sequence and its matched filter.

Figure 5 shows the result of this filtering operation. The broad area on the left is the term $F_Bs(x)$, the image of the signal. The bright line on the right is the desired matched filter output. Figure 6 shows the same signal immersed in noise, with a signal-to-noise ratio of -7.5 dB. The signal is

Fɪɢ. 5. Result of matched filtering of shift-register sequence. (Left) Signal in noise. (Right) Filtered signal.

completely submerged in the noise, but the matched filtering operation has successfully pulled the signal out of the noise.

A method of producing complex spatial filters directly from the impulse function of the signal, by the use of optical interferometric techniques, has been developed by A. Vander Lugt of our laboratory. This very elegant method enables filters that are enormously complicated in their structure to be built with no more effort than the exposure and development of a photographic plate. The application of these techniques in the area described here should prove to be fruitful.

Fig. 6. Detection of signal in noise, signal-to-noise ratio $= -7.5$ dB.

V. Wavefront Reconstruction

Wavefront reconstruction is another area in which the spatial-frequency carrier methods have been applied, with favorable results.

In wavefront reconstruction, the diffraction pattern of an object is recorded and this record is then used to produce an image of the original object. The object can be a transparency, or it can be a solid, three-dimensional object.

The wavefront reconstruction method of image formation was first announced by Gabor in 1948.[7] Haine,[8,9] Dyson,[8] Bragg,[10] Rogers,[10,11] and Lohmann[12] in Europe, and Kirkpatrick[13] and El-Sum[13-15] in the United States are among the various researchers who further developed the wavefront reconstruction method.

A two-beam interferometric technique developed by Leith and Upatnieks[16] has resulted in reconstructions of much higher quality than have, to the authors' knowledge, previously been achieved.* Continuous-tone transparencies have been converted into holograms from which reconstructions of quality comparable to the originals have been obtained. Holograms made from solid, three-dimensional objects have produced reconstructions which are a faithful reproduction of the original object, complete with

---

* The development of this method stems originally from conversations of the authors with C. J. Palermo and L. J. Porcello, of our laboratory.

three-dimensional appearance, parallax between near and distant parts of the object, etc.

The Leith-Upatnieks method for producing a hologram of a transparency is shown in Fig. 7. An object, located at plane P_1, is illuminated with spa-

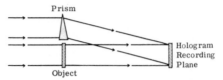

FIG. 7. Two-beam method for hologram construction.

tially coherent, monochromatic light, and a Fresnel diffraction pattern of the object is formed at plane P_2. Adjacent to the object is a prism, which deviates a portion of the incident light through an angle θ, thus combining this light with the lower portion of the beam. This combining of the two beams results in a fringe pattern which is superimposed on the Fresnel diffraction pattern of the object. Let the diffraction pattern of the object be

$$u(x, y) = a(x, y)e^{j\phi(x,y)} \tag{11}$$

and the auxiliary or reference beam from the prism be

$$u_0 = a_0 e^{j\alpha x} \tag{12}$$

where the term $e^{j\alpha x}$ arises because the reference beam impinges obliquely on the plate, thus producing a linear phase shift across the hologram recording aperture. The photographic plate records the intensity of the sum of the two beams,

$$\begin{aligned} I &= |u_0 + u|^2 \\ &= a_0^2 + a^2 + a_0 a \cos (\alpha x + \phi) \end{aligned} \tag{13}$$

The photograph has, by virtue of its square-law recording characteristic, performed a square-law detection or heterodyning operation, in which the diffraction pattern has been translated from a temporal carrier to a spatial carrier $\cos \alpha x$. This operation has produced the real-function representation of the complex function which describes the diffraction pattern. In addition, the process has produced a_0^2, the bias or gray level about which the diffraction is recorded. Finally, the process has produced the intermodulation-product term a^2, which is extraneous. It can be made small by a sufficiently strong reference beam, or its presence can be made tolerable by a sufficiently large value of carrier frequency α.

In the reconstruction process (Fig. 8) the photographic plate is illuminated with a beam of collimated monochromatic coherent light. The manner in which this light interacts with the density variations on the plate can conveniently be described by thinking of the plate as a diffraction grating, which indeed it is. The bias term a_0^2 and the intermodulation term a^2 combine to form a zero-order diffracted wave, while the signal-bearing term produces a pair of first-order diffracted waves. One of these waves is $a_0 a e^{-j\alpha x + \phi}$, which is just the original waveform recorded by the plate, except for the phase factor $e^{-j\alpha x}$ which shows that the wave is radiated

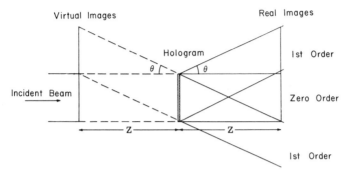

FIG. 8. Reconstruction from the hologram.

obliquely. An observer (human eye or camera) intercepting these waves will see them as emanating from a virtual object located behind the plate, in the same location with respect to the plate as was occupied by the object when the plate was exposed. The other first-order diffracted wave carries the term $a_0 a e^{j(\alpha x + \phi)}$, which represents a real image.

In the conventional Gabor type of hologram the real and virtual images are inseparable; one must be viewed against the defocused background of the other. The two-beam interferometric method, however, achieves complete separation of these images.

For a three-dimensional object viewed in reflected light, the theory is the same, but the procedure is appropriately modified.* The object is illuminated with coherent, monochromatic light and the light scattered by the object is captured by the recording plate as in Fig. 9.

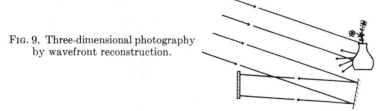

FIG. 9. Three-dimensional photography by wavefront reconstruction.

The reconstructed image is striking, in that it is entirely three-dimensional, complete with parallax effects, change of perspective with viewing

---

* For holograms made in reflected light, scalar theory is incomplete, since polarized light is depolarized upon diffuse reflection. A linearly polarized reference beam records only that component of reflected light whose polarization matches that of the reference beam. Polarization effects are currently under study by K. Stetson, of our laboratory.

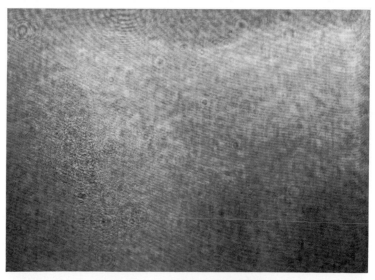

Fig. 10. Hologram and reconstruction of a transparency.

position, etc. That such should be the case is apparent from the nature of the wavefront reconstruction method, and was recognized by Gabor.[5] Nonetheless, the viewing of a high-quality reconstructed image with these properties manifested is an interesting experience.

Examples of wavefront reconstruction are shown in Figs. 10 and 11.

Figure 10 shows the hologram and reconstruction of a transparency. The quality of the reconstruction is high, and there are no defects evident. The high quality is largely a result of placing a diffuser between the source and transparency. Figure 11 shows the reconstruction from solid objects: an

Fig. 11. Reconstruction of a solid, three-dimensional object. (Courtesy *Journal of the Optical Society of America.*)

HO gauge model train. The three-dimensional properties are, of course, lost in photographing the reconstruction.

VI. Microscopy by Reconstructed Wavefronts

Gabor and others[5] have proposed the use of the wavefront reconstruction method to produce a highly magnified image, using either a change in wavelength between recording of the hologram and its reconstruction, or by using diverging light for one or both steps of the process. The two-beam process is readily amenable to such magnification, as suggested by Gabor[7] and El-Sum.[15] The process is shown in Fig. 12. The magnification of the process is readily found to be

$$ M = \frac{Z_0 + Z_1}{Z_0} \left[1 \pm \frac{Z_a(Z_0 + Z_1)}{Z_1{}^2 + Z_1 Z_0 + Z_a Z_0} \right] \tag{14} $$

where the $(-)$ applies to the real image and the $(+)$ to the virtual.

Examples of magnified objects are shown in Figs. 13 and 14. Analysis shows that aberrations arise in the wavefront reconstruction method when-

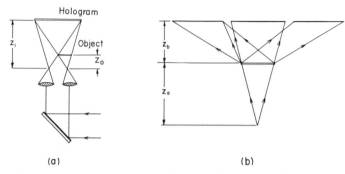

(a)   (b)

Fɪɢ. 12. Wavefront reconstruction in divergent light. (*a*) Hologram construction. (*b*) Reconstruction.

ever magnification is attempted, but it is apparent that the aberrations have not precluded good imagery.

The use of self-developing photochromic devices in place of the photographic plate would enhance the value of wavefront reconstruction micro-

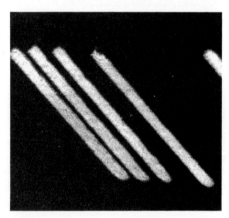

Fɪɢ. 13. Lensless magnification of a test chart. Magnification is 120 times. The spacing of the bars in the object was 10 microns.

scope by permitting nearly real-time operation and eliminating the chemical development process.*

---

* Karl Stetson, of our laboratory, has produced holograms using samples of Corning's photochromic glass.

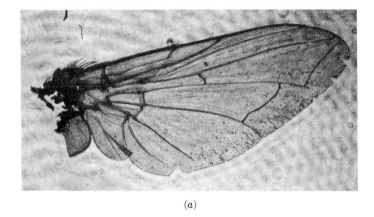

(a)

(b)

Fig. 14. Magnification of a fly's wing. (a) 16 × magnification. (b) 48 × magnification.

VII. Wavefront Reconstruction Throughout the Electromagnetic Spectrum

The wavefront reconstruction method offers the possibility of extending the highly developed imagery methods of visible-light optics to regions of the electromagnetic spectrum where high-quality imagery has not yet been achieved, or where the diffraction limits on resolution have not been realized. Indeed, this has been one of the broad aims of researchers in the wavefront reconstruction area, beginning with Gabor.

The present authors have demonstrated high-quality three-dimensional imagery in the visible region of the spectrum. The successes produced here should provide incentive to extend these results to other spectral regions, including x-ray, the far ultraviolet, and the infrared. In some of these regions, the lack of lenses or their equivalent have prohibited the realization of imagery of the quality that is theoretically possible.

In carrying out such a program, the holograms would be produced at these nonvisible wavelengths, while the reconstructions would be made at visible wavelengths, thereby providing an image which can be observed visually. Further, in the visible region, high-quality lenses exist and aberrations can be corrected. This is the program proposed by Gabor for electron microscopy and by Baez and El-Sum for x rays and other wavelengths.

We have embarked on a program of doing these things. The task is by no means a simple one, and we certainly encourage exchange of ideas in the efforts to achieve these goals.

REFERENCES

1. DUFFIEUX, P. M., "l'Intégrale de Fourier et ses Applications à l'Optique," chez l'Auteur, Université de Besançon, 1946.
2. MARÉCHAL, A., "Optical Filtering by Double Diffraction," *Optical Processing of Information*, Donald K. Pollack, Charles J. Koester, and James T. Tippett, Eds., Spartan Books, Inc., Baltimore, Md., 1963.
3. O'NEILL, E., "Spatial Filtering in Optics," *IRE Trans. Inform. Theory, IT-2*, 55–56 (June, 1956).
4. KOZMA, A., AND D. L. KELLY, *J. Opt. Soc. Am., 54*, 1395 (1964).
5. VANDER LUGT, A., *IEEE Trans. Inform. Theory, IT-10*, 139 (1964).
6. CUTRONA, L. J., E. N. LEITH, C. J. PALERMO, AND L. J. PORCELLO, *IRE Trans. Inform. Theory, IT-6*, 386 (1960).
7. GABOR, D., *Nature, 161*, 777 (1948); *Proc. Roy. Soc. (London), A197*, 454 (1949); *Proc. Phys. Soc. (London), B64*, 449 (1951).
8. HAINE, M. E., AND J. DYSON, *Nature, 166*, 315 (1950).
9. HAINE, M. E., AND T. MULVEY, *J. Opt. Soc. Am., 42*, 763 (1952).
10. BRAGG, W. L., AND G. L. ROGERS, *Nature, 167*, 190 (1951).
11. ROGERS, G. L., *Proc. Roy. Soc. Edinburgh, A63*, 193 and 313 (1952).
12. LOHMANN, A., *Opt. Acta, 3*, 97 (1956).
13. KIRKPATRICK, P., AND H. M. A. EL-SUM, *J. Opt. Soc. Am., 46*, 825 (1956).
14. BAEZ, A. V., AND H. M. A. EL-SUM, "Effect of Finite Source Size, Radiation Bandwidth and Object Transmission in Microscopy by Reconstructed Wavefronts," *X-Ray Microscopy and Microradiography*, Academic Press, Inc., New York, 1957, pp. 347–366.
15. EL-SUM, H. M. A., "Information Retrieval from Phase Modulating Media," *Optical Processing of Information*, Donald K. Pollock, Charles J. Koester, and James T. Tippett, Eds., Spartan Books, Inc., Baltimore, Maryland, 1958, p. 85.
16. LEITH, E. N., AND J. UPATNIEKS, *J. Opt. Soc. Am., 52*, 1123 (1963); *53*, 1377 (1963); *54*, 579 (1964); *54*, 1295 (1964).

CHAPTER 9

MACHINE PERCEPTION OF THREE-DIMENSIONAL SOLIDS *

L. G. Roberts

Massachusetts Institute of Technology, Lincoln Laboratory, Lexington, Massachusetts

I. Introduction

The problem of machine recognition of pictorial data has long been a challenging goal, but has seldom been attempted with anything more complex than alphabetic characters. Many people have felt that research on character recognition would be a first step, leading the way to a more general pattern recognition system. However, the multitudinous attempts at character recognition, including my own, have not led very far. The reason, I feel, is that the study of abstract, two-dimensional forms leads us away from, not toward, the techniques necessary for the recognition of three-dimensional objects. The perception of solid objects is a process which can be based on the properties of three-dimensional transformations and the laws of nature. By carefully utilizing these properties, a procedure has been developed which not only identifies objects, but also determines their orientation and position in space.

Three main processes have been developed and programed in this report. The input process produces a line drawing from a photograph. Then the three-dimensional construction program produces a three-dimensional object list from the line drawing. When this is completed, the three-dimensional display program can produce a two-dimensional projection of the objects from any point of view. Of these processes, the input program is the most restrictive, whereas the two-dimensional to three-dimensional and three-dimensional to two-dimensional programs are capable of handling almost any array of planar-surfaced objects.

* This report is based on a thesis of the same title submitted to the Department of Electrical Engineering at the Massachusetts Institute of Technology on 10 May 1963, in partial fulfillment of the requirements for the degree of Doctor of Philosophy.

In order to implement the three-dimensional processing of pictures, perspective effects must be considered. For this reason, a four-dimensional, homogeneous system of coordinates will be used. In this system a single 4×4 matrix can modify a position vector by a linear transform, a translation, and a perspective transformation. Although many books discuss this homogeneous system of coordinates, their presentations are either incomplete or too involved for our purposes.[1] Therefore, the system is explained in Appendix A. Without the notational simplicity provided by using homogeneous transformations, most of the following analysis would not have been accomplished.

II. Background

A. Pattern Recognition by Computer

There have been numerous attempts to recognize simple patterns by machine. There is the work with neuronlike nets of threshold elements which divide the set of all input patterns into a number of classes by correlating a set of adaptive weights with some functions of multiple input cells. For this type of system there may not be many output classes and the transformations of the patterns must be minimal or nonexistent. Because of these restrictions, the patterns worked on so far have been those which, although complex, are not subject to much transformation such as characters and spoken digits. My paper on character recognition is typical and gives the other references.[2] This type of system would be of no value for multiple object recognition, except perhaps for finding the lines originally.

In the work by Selfridge and Neisser *et al.*,[3] a more useful set of tests is made on the input, whereas the output processing is similar to that of the system described earlier. That is, computation routines are developed to extract the useful information from the input, and their outputs are weighted to determine the most likely output class. Here again a small set of outputs is expected and characters were the patterns tested. One problem with both these methods is that they were intended for specific groups of abstract patterns, such as characters, and not for the well-defined geometry of photographs. They are better suited for looking at my resultant list structure of objects and deciding whether a group of objects is a chair or a table.

The closest that any researcher has come to the problem I propose is Leo Hodes in his work on processing line drawings.[4] His main result was to produce a list of lines and vertices by following out lines. Then he suggested a few simple tests which might be made on this list to find triangles, etc. Although his main purpose was to study abstract line patterns, he did describe a working line follower which was of value to me in this part of my effort.

The only work I know of on machine depth perception is that on binocular images. Julesz has reported a procedure which shifts the binocular pictures to find the areas at different depths.[5] This procedure uses only texture, not edges, to develop the depth information and shows that the binocular information alone is sufficient for depth perception. This work is similar in goal but completely different in procedure from mine. Other work in machine photograph processing has mainly been in the field of information reduction for bandwidth compression and my paper in this area summarizes this work.[6]

B. Psychophysical Theory

There has been a large volume of psychophysical research on human depth perception and shape recognition. From all this I have tried to isolate the ideas and theories which are used to explain our monocular perception of a three-dimensional world. It will be apparent, however, that the work of Gibson is dominant in my mind, since his book is both clear and complete.[7]

Of all the monocular depth cues perhaps the most written about is that of known object size. Ittelson reports experiments in which only one object could be seen, thus eliminating other depth cues.[8] Although the assumed size of objects such as playing cards tended to vary, the subjects would judge the depth reasonably well for normal-sized cards and proportionately shorter for jumbo cards. Thus he, for one, showed that the size of familiar objects is a good relative depth cue and fair for absolute depth. Gibson points out, however, that this type of distance perception is rarely used in the everyday world, since we look at arrays of objects rather than at single objects and can use more general depth cues.

Gibson's favorite cue is that of texture gradient. This is the effect of perspective on the grain or fine structure of large surfaces. As these surfaces recede, the apparent grain becomes finer. Another gradient cue is the illumination variation which puts curved surfaces in relief. This shows us the surface depth variations. The final depth cues are those of aerial perspective or blur with depth, and the angular upward position of objects toward the horizon which is a depth measure in most outdoor scenes.

Recognition of forms, shapes, and objects is often discussed from the Gestalt point of view, where shadowy forms and plane geometry figures are the forms to be recognized. Attneave and Arnoult spend many pages explaining random shape generation and the useful procedures for analyzing them.[9] They discuss contour following, differentiating pictures, and some of the simple measures of shape complexity. If they were discussing character recognition, it might be reasonable to use these tools; however, they say they are investigating "natural forms." This preoccupation with the abstract projected form is strongly attacked by Gibson. He feels that the visual world of objects and surfaces should be studied rather than the visual field on the retina. A perspective transformation does not reduce a solid object to a shadowy form. Rather, it defines the set of shapes which go with a single perception.

Perspective variations in a cube were tested by Langdon in an experiment on three-dimensional solids.[10] He found that perspective plays only a minor part in the perception of the size and depth and that the subjects always saw a cube, even when it was badly distorted by the perspective transform. The continual perception of a cube, even when transformed, is consistent with Gibson's idea that shape perception is and must be invariant under perspective transformation. My idea of models also follows from this, since each model represents an invariant percept, and can be identified with any projection of itself.

III. Depth Perception

The perception of depth in a monocular picture is based completely upon the assumptions of the observer. Some of the assumptions are about the nature of the real world and some are based on the observer's familiarity with the objects. Without these assumptions the picture is just another two-dimensional image, whereas with them the human is rarely confused about the depth relationships represented in the picture. Since humans agree so closely on their depth impressions, it is fair to assume that their major assumptions are the same, and are therefore subject to identification and analysis. The following is an attempt to set down some of the likely assumptions and derive what depth information can be obtained if they were used.

A. Transformation of Real World

The first assumption is that the picture is a view of the real world recorded by a camera or comparable device and therefore that the image is a perspective transformation of a three-dimensional field. This transformation is a projection of each point in the viewing space, toward a focal point, onto a plane. The transformation will be represented with a homogeneous, 4×4 transformation matrix P such that the points in the real world are transformed into points on the photograph (see Appendix A for an explanation of homogeneous coordinates). The transformation depends on the camera used, the enlargement printing process, and, of course, the coordinate system the real world is referred to. Let us fix the real world coordinates by assuming that the focal plane is the $x = 0$ plane and that the focal point is at $x = f$, $y = 0$, $z = 0$. In order that the picture not be a reflection, we choose the focal plane in front of the camera. Then the objects seen will be in the x half-space. Thus the focal plane is really the plane of the print, not of the negative. Figure 1 shows this arrangement.

A particular camera will have some focal distance f. We shall consider the square on the focal plane which was enlarged to create the print. The center of this square will be at some coordinates y_0, z_0, and the size of the square from the center to an edge will be some distance S. The actual size to which the square is enlarged is unimportant, since we shall measure the print with a normalized system which has the origin at the center and the

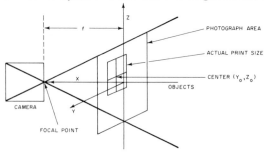

FIG. 1. Camera transformation.

edges at $y, z = \pm 1$. Normally, the whole film area is printed, and in this case $y_0 = z_0 = 0$ and S is equal to half the film size. For standard cameras without special lenses, the ratio of focal distance to film size is usually the same since this corresponds to a fixed viewing angle. Thus the ratio S/f is fairly constant at about $\frac{1}{4}$. In my case, the ratio is known if the camera is known and could be supplied with the photo.

It is not necessary to know the variables y_0, z_0, f, and S since they can be computed from the picture, given other assumptions later on. However, for the sake of simplicity we shall assume that S/f is known and that $y_0 = z_0 = 0$. The numerical values of S and f alone are not necessary, since this just affects the scale of the real world. Thus we can assume that $S = 1$ and with $r = S/f$ obtain a simple transformation P,

$$P = \begin{bmatrix} 1 & & & -r \\ & 1 & & \\ & & 1 & \\ & & & 1 \end{bmatrix}$$

If $\bar{v}$ is a point in real space, then $\bar{v}P$ is a point in a perspective space such that its Y and Z coordinates are the original point's projection in the picture plane. The X coordinate of $\bar{v}P$ is also obtained and will be useful for hidden line computation during display of three-dimensional objects.

Thus a transformation from the real world to a picture has been described, and to go the other way simply requires the inverse transformation P^{-1}. Of course, the x component of the real-world points will not be known in this case.

B. *Objects Observed*

We shall further assume that the three-dimensional field observed consists of a set of solid objects which occupy a definite region of space. Since we realize that it is usually possible to pick out the lines which define the boundaries of the objects and their surfaces, we shall assume that this has been accomplished and that the picture has been reduced to a line drawing. Because the objects are solid, we do not expect to see the boundaries which are hidden from the focal point by another solid.

Second, we shall assume that the objects seen could be constructed out of parts with which we are familiar. That is, either the whole object is a transformation of a preconceived model, or else it can be broken into parts that are. The models could be anything from a cube to a human body; the only requirement is that we have a complete description of the three-dimensional structure of each model.

The transformation from the model to the real world object will be a suitably restricted homogeneous transformation matrix R. We must allow an arbitrary rotation and translation of the model in order to position it properly in space. We should also like to allow three degrees of freedom for size change of the model so that a cube model can represent any parallelepiped. So far we have allowed nine degrees of freedom. The 4×4 matrix R can allow fifteen degrees of freedom since it has 16 elements and the total scale of the matrix is arbitrary in the homogeneous coordinate system. The last six degrees of freedom represent skew and perspective deformations. Skew deformations are size changes in the x, y, and z directions after the model has been rotated and will change the sides of a cube to parallelograms. A perspective deformation is most easily visualized as a compression of one end of the model. Objects that have been deformed in either way are not usually considered to be simple instances of the model. Furthermore, objects deformed in these ways could be constructed from smaller parts, so it is not necessary to allow skew and perspective deformations.

We cannot allow perspective deformation and still obtain a unique transform R from the picture; therefore, we require the top three elements in the last column of R to be zero. Skew variations can be allowed if we maintain very high accuracy in our computations, so our derivation will allow them, but later on they will be eliminated.

Now R transforms a model into an object and P transforms the object onto the picture so that if

$$H = RP$$

H transforms the model points into picture points. Therefore, in order to identify a group of points and lines in the picture with a particular model, we must find out if there is any transformation H which will take the model's points and lines into those of the picture. If such a model and transform are found, it can be said that the object represented in the picture could be that model under the transformation $R = HP^{-1}$.

C. Model Identification

Let us say that we are given a picture of a parallelepiped, and it has been reduced to a line drawing. We can then find the interior polygons which correspond to the surfaces of the object. There will normally be three quadrilaterals visible. These polygons all come together at one point which can be used for a reference point. If we look through our list of models, we find that a cube and perhaps other models have three quadrilaterals about one point. Therefore, we can pick a point in the cube model which has the proper polygons around it, pick a polygon from both the cube and the picture as starting points, and proceed to list topologically equivalent point pairs. When we have finished, we have a list of seven three-dimensional points from the model and a corresponding list of seven two-dimensional points from the picture. By adding a homogeneous coordinate $w = 1$ to each point vector, we obtain a 4×7 matrix of model points A and a 3×7 matrix of picture points B.

Now by means of the similarity test derived in Appendix B, we obtain the best transform H which will take A into B. We also obtain a mean-square error which indicates whether or not the model chosen really can fit the picture. We can then choose the model that causes the least error. For the parallelepiped, the cube model should fit with very little error. The transform obtained is a 3×4, since no depth data accompanied the picture points. Since we know P and thus P^{-1}, we can start to obtain R, the real space transform of the model. Since we have required that the three perspective components of R should be zero, we can specify the top three components of R in the first column as $(-1/r)$ times the corresponding elements of the last column of H.

$$R = HP^{-1}$$

$$H = \begin{bmatrix} y_1 & z_1 & w_1 \\ y_2 & z_2 & w_2 \\ y_3 & z_3 & w_3 \\ y_4 & z_4 & w_4 \end{bmatrix} \qquad P^{-1} = \begin{bmatrix} 1 & & & r \\ & 1 & & \\ & & 1 & \\ & & & 1 \end{bmatrix}$$

$$R_0 = \begin{bmatrix} -w_1/r & y_1 & z_1 & 0 \\ -w_2/r & y_2 & z_2 & 0 \\ -w_3/r & y_3 & z_3 & 0 \\ 0 & y_4 & z_4 & w_4 \end{bmatrix}$$

The lower left element of R still is not known since it is the x position of the whole object, and if an object grows in size as it moves away from us, it can maintain the same projection on the focal plane. Thus this depth value must be found some other way. For the present, we can call it zero and label the matrix R_0.

At this point, by assuming that an object in a picture is a transformation of a known model and by utilizing our knowledge of perspective geometry, we have been able to find the model and transformation which best represent the object. We know the precise orientation and position of the object except for one depth variable. We also know all the dimensions of the object relative to its total size. We also should know the skew deformation of the object, since we have obtained eleven variables. However, compression or expansion in the x direction produces only a slight change in the picture due to the perspective, since we are looking along the x axis. Thus the determination of the x skew can easily be in error. This problem of skew error in derived transformations was not realized until the computer program implementing these ideas began to produce distorted transformations of models. Even though the program could match every point in the picture with model points within one part in 4000, the x skew of the transformation might be off by a factor of 2. Thus it is clear that the x skew is not really obtainable from a picture, even though it can be derived mathematically.

If x skew deformations of the model must be restricted, it is logical to eliminate all skew variations for consistency. To restrict skew it is necessary to ask that the top three rows of R be orthogonal. Since the introduction of this requirement into the similarity test requires solving second-order equations, it is simplest to modify R after it has been computed. Thus the top three rows of R are forced to be orthogonal by modifying the first column, which is the one with the worst error. This means that the focal ratio r and w_1, w_2, and w_3 are not needed for the computation of the model transformation. Now in fact, r may be computed from the ratio of the new first column to the w_j.

Thus, by assuming that the objects seen in a picture are nondeformed transformations of known models, we can find the model and transformation without knowing the camera characteristics. Even if the picture is an orthogonal projection, as is almost the case with long telephoto lenses, we can compute the proper transformation. This would be impossible if we did not eliminate skew since r, w_1, w_2, and w_3 would all be zero. Thus the process accounts for, but does not depend on, perspective information.

The information required to obtain a transformation is obtained from the points in the line drawing. These points have two dimensions each and we need to determine eight degrees of freedom in the transformation. Therefore, at least four points from the picture must be used. These points cannot all lie in the same plane of the object or the equations will be degenerate. If more than four points are available, the mean-square error will indicate whether they are consistent with the model, and therefore help in the selection of the proper model.

D. Depth Information

After the matrix R_0 is obtained for an object or object part, it is still necessary to obtain the x translation or depth. Here we must resort to another assumption. There are several possibilities which I have chosen to ignore. If we were to assume that we know the models so well that we knew their size, this would fix their depth also; or, if we wished to interpret shadows, this might determine the depth if shadows existed. The fact that one object is partly in front of another supplies depth information, but only in the form of inequalities. Lastly, the various gradients—intensity, blur, and texture—might be useful for determining the depth gradients of each surface, but this information has already been found through the use of models. All these cues may be useful to humans, but each one is restricted in its generality and only useful in special cases.

The one depth perception concept which is suitably general, and sufficiently accurate to position all objects properly, is the use of a support theorem. We assume that each object must be supported somehow, either by another object or by a ground plane. This assumption allows us to project each object back in the x direction until it hits the ground plane or another object. While it is being projected back, it must be expanded so as to maintain the same image on the focal plane. The slope of the ground plane can be determined by examining each object for parallel planes, choosing a plane which goes under the focal point and is as parallel to the $z = 0$ plane as possible. When such a plane is found, we know only its slope, not its distance, from the origin. However, this single variable can be set arbitrarily, since it affects only the total scale of the picture. Actually it can be guessed rather accurately for the majority of pictures just by assuming or knowing the distance the camera was held from the ground and the focal ratio r. Since r may be computed, we could assume that the camera was held five feet above the floor, and now we can state the dimensions of each object in feet.

For compound objects, we know the pieces should fit together, so their relative depths are determined and the compound object can then be treated as one object and projected onto the ground plane. The whole procedure is relatively simple so long as the ground plane is really planar. If the ground curves, this could be taken care of by computing the curvature from the slopes of several objects. If there are breaks in the floor's slope such as walls, the breaks will be seen as lines and walls treated as objects. Thus the support assumption enables us to properly place all the objects in space.

To review the depth perception assumptions and results, we assumed that the picture was, in fact, a perspective view of the real world, that the objects shown in the picture could be described by means of one or more transformations of known models, and that all objects were supported by others or by a ground plane. The transformations allowed were restricted to rotation, translation, and size changes. Then, from a single picture, each object which has four or more points showing can be described in terms of the models and positioned in a three-dimensional space. The scale of this space in feet can even be determined if the distance of the camera from the floor can be supplied. The whole representation in three dimensions should be accurate, except for a simplification of hidden details and occasional problems due to the breakdown of the assumptions. However, humans have the same problems.

IV. Picture Input and Reduction to Lines

Pictures are presently being entered into the computer by means of a facsimile scanner, although many types of optical scanners would be suitable. The facsimile scanner, however, was already connected to the computer for some of my previous experiments.[6] A 4 × 5 photographic print is placed on the drum of the scanner and the computer made ready. Then, during each rotation of the drum, a photomultiplier output scans a line of the picture. An analog-to-digital converter samples the photomultiplier output at about 600 cps and sends the computer ten-bit digital intensity values. Thus, in about three minutes, a 256 × 256 raster of intensity samples can be read into the computer. Each sample is compressed to eight bits in the computer, so the storage of one picture requires about half a million bits of memory. Thus four pictures can be stored in the TX-2 memory. Figure 2*a* and *b* shows a picture before and after computer sampling.

When the scanning is completed, the picture is processed with a local differential operator to produce a new raster which has the appearance of a line drawing. The choice of a differential operator is very critical and many variations were tried. Three main criteria can be used to judge such an operation. The edges produced should be as sharp as possible, the background should produce as little noise as possible, and the intensity of the lines produced should correspond closely to a human's ability to perceive the edge in the original picture. Edge sharpness depends upon the number of samples used by the differential operator. Background noise seems to be reduced by using operators symmetric in x and y. In order to make equally apparent edges have equal derivatives, the intensity values of the picture can be subjected to a gamma change so as to make intensity differences proportional to a human's ability to perceive them. According to psychophysical theory, the square root of the intensities should be used in order to achieve the desired effect.[11]

Therefore, after a picture is read in, a differential picture is created according to the functions

$$y_{i,j} = \sqrt{x_{i,j}}$$
$$z_{i,j} = \sqrt{(y_{i,j} - y_{i+1,j+1})^2 + (y_{i+1,j} - y_{i,j+1})^2}$$

where $x_{i,j}$ is the initial intensity value, $z_{i,j}$ is the computed derivative value, and i and j are the coordinates in the two dimensions. The resulting z values indicate the probability of a line through that cell. Even though the square-

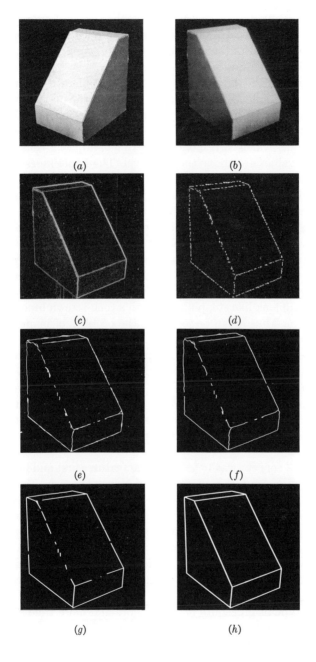

FIG. 2. Picture to line drawing. (*a*) Original picture. (*b*) Computer display of picture (reflected by mistake). (*c*) Differentiated picture. (*d*) Feature points selected. (*e*) Connected feature points. (*f*) After complexity reduction. (*g*) After initial line fitting. (*h*) Final line drawing.

root operation involved takes more time than several simpler operations which were tried, the extra line sharpness and background noise reduction obtained are well worth the additional time. Figure 2c is an example of the result of this differentiation.

After obtaining the differential picture, the problem is to determine a set of lines and end points which correlate well with the raster. It is no simple chore to obtain a list of lines and their end points from a half-million-bit array of data. A simple procedure might be to choose a clip level and start tracing out lines which correspond to a string of adjacent cells in the raster, all of whose values are above the clip level. The hopelessness of this procedure is easily seen when one looks at typical pictures and considers them as a three-dimensional surface where the z values are used as the height. Even a very clean input picture when viewed in this way looks like a bumpy, hilly landscape, with a broken-down stone wall representing the lines, and where some hills are higher than the top of other stone walls. If we imagine the clip level as a flood over this landscape, there is no water level which covers all the hills and yet does not submerge some stone walls. In fact, even by adjusting the water level to be optimal for a particular area, a line will look like stepping stones in a rock-strewn brook rather than a smooth dam. Thus it can be seen that the problem of mapping the walls is not a simple one.

The procedure I have developed for finding the lines from the differential picture makes mistakes in complex pictures and is a complex special-purpose program demonstrating very few general concepts. However, it does manage to produce accurate line drawings from a sufficient group of pictures so that the transformation techniques can be tested on data from real photographs. The description of this procedure will be rather general in nature.

The over-all concept was to look at local features first and build up to the determination of long lines in a series of steps. There are two reasons for this procedure. First, at each step the complexity of the processing goes up since more data are being considered, but at the same time the number of features to process is being reduced at each step. Thus the total time to process the picture is much less than if a one-step process were used. Such a one-step process was tried by Leo Hodes in an attempt to find the lines in black and white line drawings.[4] For each possible line a correlation with the raster was made, and then the line position was corrected and recorrelated. This type of procedure becomes more and more time consuming as the raster size, line length, and accuracy required increase, whereas a multistep process need not consume additional time.

The second reason for a multistep process is that the initial local feature extraction can take into consideration the local noise level and thus detect lines which an over-all clip level would miss.

The first step of the process looks for points in the differential picture which seem to be on a line. The maximum sample in each 4 × 4 square of raster points is considered as a possibility if its value exceeds a small threshold. This threshold is low enough to include all the lines and much of the noise but it does eliminate further processing of smooth areas of the picture. Its value has been determined by experiment to be about one-tenth of the maximum intensity in the original picture. After a point has been chosen in this way, four correlations are performed to find the direction of a line through the point which best fits the data. Four lines, having a length of five samples with slopes of 0, 1, ∞, −1, are correlated with the data around the point, and the ratio of the best to the worst fit is taken. If the ratio is greater than a second threshold (about 3), the point and the best direction are recorded. In this way a set of feature points is obtained, along with approximate line directions through them. The procedure can be considered to be a ridge detector which locates points along each ridge with limits on the height and width of the ridge. The number of feature points obtained is usually between 100 and 1000. Figure 2*d* shows a short line at each feature point, pointing in the recorded direction.

After the feature points are found, the next step is to connect lines between neighboring points. The line directions of the points are used to limit cross connections between adjacent lines. Specifically, a pair of points are connected if they are in touching 4 × 4 squares and if the line's direction will be within ±23° of the direction recorded for either point. Any points left unconnected are eliminated, thus filtering out most of those created by noise. The result is a preliminary line drawing composed of many short lines. There are two major problems with this line structure: sections of a long line may be missing, and sections may be complicated by multiple interconnections. The interconnections are most obvious at corners but also appear along a line as extra width. Figure 2*e* gives a more graphic illustration. To reduce these small networks of lines to a single line or neat corner, two reduction techniques are used. Their important property is that they do not change the over-all connectivity and topology of the line structure. First, the longest side of each triangle is deleted. A triangle is defined here as any three lines in a loop. This cleans out most of the unwanted lines; however, there are a few quadrilaterals left. Therefore, each group of four lines connected in a loop is compressed along its shortest diagonal; that is, the two closest, nonadjacent points are merged. There may still be a few pentagons left but most of the networks have been reduced. The last step in smoothing out the line structure is to remove all small tails or spurs which are unconnected at one end and connect to more than one line at the other end. These smoothing operations are all on short lines so no major features are changed. They do, however, limit the resolution of the input system to about four to eight samples out of 256. This restriction is on resolving short, close lines, not on the accuracy of longer lines. The result of smoothing Fig. 2e appears in Fig. 2f.

Now that a structural outline of the lines in the picture has been obtained, longer lines can be fitted to sections, missing segments filled in, and extra segments removed. The segments along the path of a true straight line may weave in and out but each point was obtained by the ridge detection technique and is accurate to about one sample width if it was caused by the edge. A sequence of singly connected points with no intersections will probably be caused by the same edge or sequence of edges. By a least-mean-square error-line-fitting routine, a straight line can be put through the points and result in a very high accuracy line. Curve segments could also be fitted to the points if this were desired; the main additional problem would be the choice of the type of curve to try—circle, parabolic, cubic, etc. It becomes more and more obvious, as one considers fitting curves to the picture edges, that it is advantageous to have a set of points already determined, through which to put a curve, instead of having to correlate various curves with the picture data.

To fit a straight line to a sequence of points, a sequential least-mean-square error-fitting routine is used. The problem is to find the best coefficients (a, b, c) for the line equation

$$ax + by = c$$

The data are supplied sequentially in the form of points (x, y) and it is desirable to recompute as little as possible each time a point is added. However, upon each addition of a point, the coefficients (a, b, c) and the new mean-square error E should be available. It is sufficient to keep a history of five numbers, the cumulative sums

$$\sum x, \quad \sum y, \quad \sum xy, \quad \sum x^2, \quad \sum y^2$$

and the number of entries made n. Then, after each addition of a new point (x, y), the coefficients are computed as

$$
\begin{aligned}
a &= \sum x \sum y^2 - \sum y \sum xy \\
b &= \sum y \sum x^2 - \sum x \sum xy \\
c &= \sum x^2 \sum y^2 - \sum xy \sum xy \\
E &= c(nc - a \sum x - b \sum y)/n(a^2 + b^2)
\end{aligned}
$$

Since these equations represent the mean-square best reduction of the unnormalized error $E(a^2 + b^2)$, they do not always produce the least-mean-square distance error as represented by E. However, the solution is much easier than the complete form and just as good in almost all cases.

The procedure for fitting a line to a series of connected points starts by choosing any small line segment as a starting place and moving in one direction until a point is reached with other than two line segments attached, or until the mean-square error exceeds a threshold. When the error threshold is reached, a bend in the true lines has probably been passed, so the procedure is to back up until the angle between the little line segments and the computed line has decreased by a factor of 2. Usually this condition will occur at the bend sought for, since on the other side of the bend the angles must be negative. This procedure works very well and needs no threshold adjustment because of the backup procedure.

When the line has been finished in one direction from the starting point, the other direction is investigated in the same manner, still modifying the same computed line. The method of using cumulative sums as the only history for the line computation allows points to be subtracted out during backup, eliminating the need for large tables of past history. Also, the procedure is fairly independent of the starting point since, during the second direction's backup, the starting point can be passed, thus creating a line totally to one side of the starting point. This will occur when a break point appears just after the starting point, and as the break point is passed in the forward direction, the error does not build up to threshold.

Thus the line-fitting procedure replaces groups of small line segments with longer, more accurate lines. The ends of these new lines are at the intersections of several lines, at break points as detected by the error criteria, or are free and unconnected. Each time a long line is computed, the points at its ends are moved onto the line since the line is more accurate than the points. If several long lines meet at a point, the point's coordinates are computed to be the intersection point of the two longest nonparallel lines. Thus the points become as accurate as the lines connected to them. A special case may come up due to the incomplete removal of a network of small lines: Two lines may be constructed between the same end points. These must be merged and the lines connected to the false intersections reprocessed into one line, if possible.

When all the lines have been fitted to the small segments, the representation of the picture consists of a set of lines and end points mapping the edges in the picture. There still may be sections of lines missing and extra segments near intersections. Figure 1*g* shows the result at this point. Now line filling and merging are done to complete the line drawing. Each line is considered for modification. If the line is of significant length, the nearest points to both ends of the line, which are within about three raster units of the extended line, are considered as possibilities for new end points. A new line is correlated with the differential picture between an end point and the new point and if the average value along the line is greater than a threshold, the line is put in. When a line is very short, it is not extended but is considered for merging or elimination. If the line's end points both connect to one other line, then the end points are merged, otherwise the line is deleted. After extending, merging, or deleting the proper lines, the whole line structure is again processed with the mean-square line-fitting program in order to eliminate extra joints which may have been created. The resulting line drawing is the finished version as shown in Fig. 1*h*.

The entire picture-to-line-drawing process is not optimal but works for simple pictures. It has several useful parts; the differentiation, the feature point extraction, and the mean-square line fitting are the best parts. In the future, I hope to recombine these sections to produce a more general system.

V. Construction of Three-Dimensional Objects from Line Drawing

The program described in this section starts with a planar line drawing and produces a three-dimensional description of the objects shown in the drawing in terms of models and their transformations. The line drawing may be one generated by the picture input process or some other computer program such as the three-dimensional display program (Sec. VI). The main restriction on the lines is that they should be a perspective projection of the surface boundaries of a set of three-dimensional objects with planar surfaces. Any line drawing produced by the three-dimensional display program is acceptable as an input to this program, and since this program's output is an input to the display program, the two programs can be used to check each other. The models used for construction can be any set of three-dimensional building blocks which seem useful so long as all their surfaces are planar. Since the models can be put together so that their joint lines disappear, almost any complex object can be constructed with a very few models. There are only three models presently used in the program: a cube, a wedge, and a hexagonal prism (Fig. 6, in Sec. VI illustrates these models). Section III describes the general procedure used for this two-dimensional to three-dimensional transformation, whereas we now wish to develop the specific mathematics and techniques used in the program.

A. Polygon Recognition

The line drawing which is produced by the three-dimensional display program is just a list of end-point pairs, one pair for each line. This type of input is specially processed to put it in the form wanted. Each line is assigned to a line block in a line list and each point to a point block. Each point indicates which lines are connected to it and each line block points to its end points. Thus, for each end-point pair in the input list, a line block is created and the point list searched for point values close to the end points. If the points already exist, the line is just tied into them; otherwise, a new point block is created. Upon completion of this phase, each point is checked against all lines to see if it lies on a line but is not connected to the line. If this occurs, the line is broken in two and both new ends are tied to the point. The list format produced is a good form for topology processing and is the same format as that produced by the picture input program.

The first problem is to find the polygons described by the lines. In order to trace the polygons easily, the lines tied to each point are ordered by their angle of exit. This allows us to start with any line, choose an adjacent line at one end point and continue around the polygon to the first line, without ever getting off the polygon. This procedure can be made to go clockwise or counterclockwise around polygons, and thus record two polygons for each line. A list of polygon blocks is prepared, each tied to the lines that compose it. The lines also point to their two polygons. As each polygon is produced, the exterior angle at each vertex is computed and the sum of these angles is kept for the polygon. These angles are computed in semicircles, so they are between +1 and −1. The sum will therefore be +2, if the polygon was hollow on its inside, but if the polygon was really an exterior boundary of an object, the "hollow" part is outside and the sum will be −2. Figure 3 shows the polygons of a cube projection and their exterior angles.

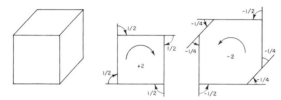

Fɪɢ. 3. Exterior angles. The exterior boundary of an object is separated from the normal polygons by the sum of the exterior angles, taking the unconnected direction as the inside. The direction of travel and the sum of the exterior angles appear in the center of (b) and (c). Angles are in semicircles. (a) Complete cube. (b) Interior polygon. (c) Exterior boundary.

It may not be apparent that exterior boundaries are difficult to separate from the real polygons, but as the computer traces a polygon, it has no concept of the inside; it just traces a closed path with all connecting lines on one side of the boundary. It must expect some negative angles because the polygon may be concave. Thus the sum of the exterior angles is necessary, if the computer is going to separate exterior boundaries from real polygons.

Some further information is obtained as the polygon is traced out: the number of sides of the polygon, the number of negative angles encountered, and the number of near-zero exterior angles. One or more negative angles indicate that the polygon is concave, whereas the zero angles indicate collinear joints which most likely were produced by another object partially hidden behind this one. Thus a first guess at the number of sides the surface really has is the number of lines minus the number of zero angles. The polygon is then marked as complete and convex if there are no negative angles, it is not an exterior boundary, and it does not include a point where a zero angle was observed on another polygon. The last condition eliminates from initial consideration polygons that are most likely partially hidden by another object. Figure 4 shows an example where each complete and convex polygon is labeled with its first-guess number of sides.

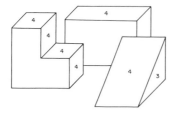

FIG. 4. Complete convex polygons. The polygon selection procedure would select the numbered polygons as complete and convex. The number indicates the probable number of sides. A polygon is incomplete if one of its points is a collinear joint of another polygon.

The reason concave polygons are not considered at first is that the models presently being used in the program are all convex. However, if a model with concave polygons is included, the appropriate concave polygons from the line drawing should be considered. In this connection, the rule is that both the number of positive angles and the number of negative angles of a polygon are invariant under any perspective transformation. Thus the only polygons which need be considered at this point are those which have the same number of plus and minus angles as some model surface. With the models included in the present program, the acceptable polygons are further restricted to have 3, 4, or 6 sides.

A comment on incomplete polygons may be useful at this point. A perfect projection of solid objects with visible width and no two-dimensional markings is being assumed for the input. Since such projections are completely composed of surface boundary projections, they will never contain any points connected to only one line, unless the points are on the boundaries of the picture. If a special external boundary square is included, there will be no incomplete polygons as is assumed. The three-dimensional display program will always generate acceptable input, but the picture input process could miss lines, generate false lines, or include two-dimensional markings. These cases could be taken care of by further checking the picture and other techniques, but at present this task was ignored. The program eliminates such problems by deleting all lines not connected in a closed polygon. Also any isolated polygon is considered to be a two-dimensional marking and is deleted. Thus all letters except *B* are deleted as well as most other simple two-dimensional markings. When the process is completed, these markings could be transferred to the appropriate surface, if desired, but this was not done.

One further computation is performed on each polygon even though it is used only to order the investigation of the polygons. The area of each polygon is found as the program moves clockwise around the points (x_j, y_j),

$$A = \tfrac{1}{2} \sum (x_{j+1}y_j - x_j y_{j+1})$$

This procedure, which is really summing the signed areas of the triangles formed by each line and the origin, is very simple and works for any shape polygon. If the motion is counterclockwise instead of clockwise, as is the case for external boundaries, the area will come out negative. This formula for the area of a polygon was derived by the author since no suitable formulation could be found easily.

B. Model Matching

The first tool used to match the polygon structure to the models is topology. Basically, we wish to find points in the line drawing which fit a transformation of some model. The polygon structure is used to find a suitable model with a set of topologically equivalent points. Then the mean-square error technique is used to find out whether the point positions are related by a simple transformation or not. Topology matching proceeds in four steps. First, each point is examined to see if it is completely surrounded by approved polygons. When such a point is found, the number of polygons of each type is counted. At present, since the only approved polygons are those with 3, 4, or 6 sides, three counts are obtained. A list of triads corresponding to distinct points on the models is maintained so that a quick search will indicate which model points are surrounded by the same polygon structure as the picture point. For example, if a point has three quadrilaterals around it, the list will specify a particular point on the cube model. The other points on the cube need not be listed because they are all similar to each other. Once a model point has been chosen, the program cycles around the picture and model points to line up the order of the polygons. If the orders cannot be matched, other listed model points are tested; however, if they are matched, a list of equivalent point pairs is constructed.

The computation of the optimal transformation matrix from the point pairs is presented in Appendix B. Besides producing the transformation, the procedure generates the mean-square error. A threshold is placed on this error to eliminate models which fit the picture topologically, but do not fit exactly without being deformed. Models having acceptably small error can now be transformed to produce the lines and points which were not part of the fitted area. The points are checked against the picture to make sure they do not fall outside the object's external boundary. If a point does exceed this boundary, the model must be discarded since it would produce new lines not in the picture. Models that pass this test, however, could represent at least part of the object, and are accepted. If a transformed model completely accounts for a group of connected lines, the transform and model are used to represent that object; however, if some lines are left, the procedure described under object construction must be used. Figure 5a through d shows the processing of a photograph in which a single cube model was used to describe the three-dimensional object, whereas Fig. 6a through d illustrates a situation in which two models were needed.

The examination of all points surrounded by polygons is only the first step of the topology matching. When all the points are tested, lines are examined for approved polygons on both sides. A second list of model information is searched for any models with such a pair of adjoining polygons. When a line and model are found, the polygons are aligned and a list of point pairs produced. From here on the transformation procedure is the same as before.

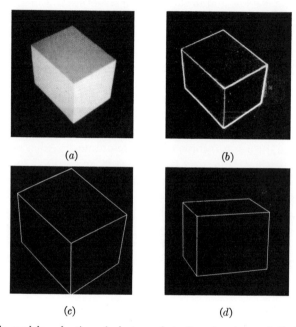

(a)   (b)

(c)   (d)

FIG. 5. Single model: reduction of photograph to line drawing and display of three-dimensional construction from another viewpoint. (a) Original picture. (b) Differentiated picture. (c) Line drawing. (d) Rotated view.

The third step, after all lines have been examined, is to test each remaining approved polygon. The polygon must have a line attached to one vertex. The model information lists each distinct model, polygon, and vertex for each type of polygon, and the point pair list is easily prepared. The fourth step, if necessary, is to take each point with three lines out of it and test these four points against each distinct vertex and line orientation in each model. This test is a last resort because there are so many model possibilities and in every case a transformation can be found which makes the mean-square error zero. Only finding a point outside the boundary can eliminate these cases.

The four steps are ideal for the cube model since the number of points found decrease by one with each step. Almost any visible piece of a cube will be processed with the maximum number of points possible. Even though this is not true for all models, the four steps are a good approximation to a comprehensive topology search. Topology tests and matching are very difficult to implement on a computer, even with the aid of a good list structure. Computer languages seem to be far superior at numerical and symbolic manipulation than the decision-loaded searching associated with topology. The inherent limitations of the serial processing of a line struc-

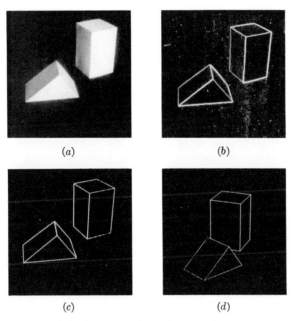

(a)   (b)

(c)   (d)

FIG. 6. Multiple objects: reduction of photograph to line drawing and three-dimensional construction, involving ground plane determination of depth. (a) Original picture. (b) Differentiated picture. (c) Line drawing. (d) Rotated view.

ture, without some global picture of what one is looking at, make specific tests such as the four steps far easier to achieve than any general procedure. Even to accomplish these steps without continual searching and backtracking, the list structure must be organized in a very special manner. At each vertex the connecting lines are ordered by angle of exit in a counterclockwise ring. Thus any time the program arrives on one line, it can easily exit on an adjacent line. Further, the lines in each polygon are ordered in a clockwise ring, with the end points of each line and the two polygons of the line specifically related. This is important because, upon arrival at an end point of a line, the program can immediately identify the right and left polygons and proceed around either one. Both the model structure and the line drawing are organized in this way. The definition of clockwise and counterclockwise in a three-dimensional model structure is not obvious but, for compatibility with the projections of a solid model, all such orderings are made while looking in from the outside.

C. Compound Object Construction

A compound object is a single solid object which is not a transformation of a single model, but must be formed by piecing together several models. Whenever two models are fitted together such that they have a frontal plane in common, the three-dimensional display program will eliminate any piece of line which touches both models and is in that plane. Since these joint lines do not reflect any surface discontinuity, it is expected that they will also be missing in the line drawing input. If joint lines happen to appear in the input, the resultant structure will probably be the same as if they were missing; therefore, the display will not include them. As models are found which fit a part of an object, their lines are projected back onto the drawing and the joint lines found. Thus the complex unapproved polygons are cut up by these joint lines into smaller polygons until each piece is approved. The following rules are for deleting an accepted model from an object and reforming the picture to make ready for the next model identification. The expression "*T* joint" refers to a vertex at which two collinear lines and one other line, the "stem," meet. During the process, parts of the drawing are deleted, but these changes are never allowed to modify the external boundary polygon since it must be used to test new models. The concept of a "visible" model line or point refers to the points and lines on the frontal surfaces of the model.

1. Each visible point of the transformed model is projected on the drawing.

    a. Any new point pairs disclosed by the proximity of model and picture points are used to recompute the transformation for better accuracy.

    b. If a model point falls on a picture line, the line is cut in two and the point inserted.

2. All the model lines and points are added to the picture if they are not already there. Any picture point which lies on a model line, but not on either end, is separated from the model line structure. Thus a picture line that ends in a T-joint stem may be extended to its proper end point, and the collinear T-joint lines unified into one line. Joint lines are those visible model lines which were not in the picture and which divide a picture polygon.

3. Each visible model point in the picture which does not connect to any nonmodel lines is now marked "used." Also, all points on polygons with more than two "used" points are marked "used." The joining polygon between parts is the polygon which includes the joint line but is not divided

by it, and all the points on such a polygon must be unmarked. Now all "used" points are deleted along with their attached lines and polygons. Also, any line in a joining polygon which is the stem of a T joint at both ends should be deleted.

4. All remaining model lines should be marked as unnecessary. If all lines left connected to them are unnecessary or if no lines are left connected, the object has been finished.

Each time a model is stripped from an object in this way, its transform and model name are saved as part of an object block. For each model, a point which was connected to the remainder of the object is remembered, so that the depth relations between the parts may be computed. When an object is finished, there will be a string of points connecting its parts. An object transformation is set up to position the depth of the whole object; hence, the first model can be assumed to have the correct depth. Then each model whose point connects to the first has its transformation modified so that the points have the same depth. Then the models connected to those are updated and so on.

To correct a transformation R_0 when a known point $\bar{v}$ should be equal to a point $\bar{p} = \bar{q}R_0$, the new lower-left element x of R_0 is computed as

$$x = \frac{q_4 v_1 w - p_1 v_4}{q_4(v_4 - r v_1)}$$

Here w is the present lower-right element of R_0 and the new $w' = w + rx$. Note that the focal ratio r for the picture must be known at this point. However, the accuracy of r will not affect the accuracy of positioning the parts with respect to each other.

Eclipsed objects, or objects partially hidden from view by other objects, are automatically taken care of by the construction rules. One case, however, needs further attention. When an object is so well hidden that a dimension cannot be determined, this dimension must be estimated. An example of this case would be when only the top of a building is visible over another. The first assumption we make is that the object is supported by the ground plane. But a second assumption is needed to place the object, and the program assumes that the hidden object just touches the object in front. This is not a very good assumption, but there are no good assumptions.

Figure 7 illustrates the construction of a compound object. The original line drawing appears in A1 and includes a compound object and a partially hidden object. Since there are no points surrounded by acceptable polygons, we must look for a line with good polygons on both sides. There is only one such line to which a model can be fitted and this is in the upper object. Both the cube and wedge models fit this object; however, the cube is always tested first to avoid splitting cubes into wedges. The lines of the cube model are then projected onto the line drawing as in A2, and the transformed model is entered into the three-dimensional structure as displayed in A3. After a model has been identified, the "used" points and lines are deleted, thus producing the line drawing in B1. Now a new search for fitting models is made. The lower-right quadrilateral and the bottom line adjoining it are found to fit a cube model, resulting in B2 and B3. Next, a cube is fitted at

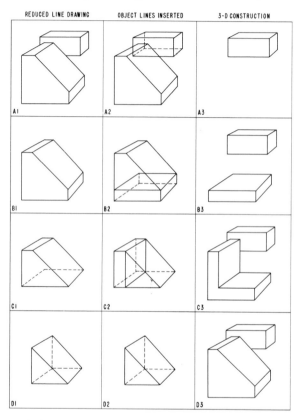

REDUCED LINE DRAWING   OBJECT LINES INSERTED   3-D CONSTRUCTION

Fig. 7. Compound object construction: original line drawing in A1 is processed to obtain three dimensions in D3 by sequential recognition and deletion of four models in steps A, B, C, and D.

the left, in C1, producing C2 and C3. Finally, just a wedge is left in D1 and since all the back lines have already been determined, D2 appears the same. When this model is added to the three-dimensional structure, the result is a complete description of the objects and can be displayed as in D3 or from any other point of view. Figure 8a through d shows the computer processing of a similar compound object from a photograph. The collection of models describing the three-dimensional object can then be rotated as in Fig. 8e through h.

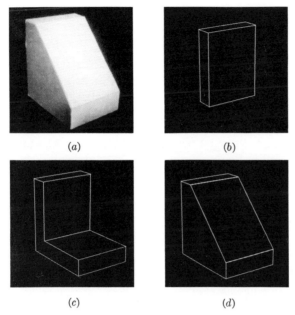

FIG. 8. (*a–d*) Compound object construction: processing of Fig. 2 to obtain three-dimensional description of compound object. (*a*) Original picture. (*b*) First construction model. (*c*) Two construction models. (*d*) Complete three-dimensional object.

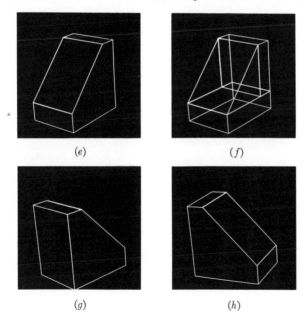

FIG. 8. (*e–h*) Compound object construction: rotated views of object obtained in Fig. 8(*d*). (*e*) Rotated view. (*f*) All lines of Fig. 8(*a*). (*g*) Second rotated view. (*h*) Third rotated view.

D. *Ground Plane Assumption*

When all the objects in the picture have been constructed, they still need their object transformations adjusted for depth. If an object consisted of a single model, the transformation listed is R_0. If the object was compound, an identity matrix was set down as the object transform and the model transforms all relate to it. In both cases each object has one free variable related to depth and size. The support theory would place each object on top of another or on a ground plane. In order to simplify the present program, the ground plane is the only support assumed. However, the addition of object support will not be very difficult.

Finding the ground plane is the most difficult part of the depth computation. Each object could be examined for possible support planes and all objects compared for a common plane. An object could be supported by anything from three points to a full plane in contact with the ground. To simplify this chore, it was assumed that the picture was upright and each object had a full plane in contact with the ground. A simple test of the slope of each plane of an object is used to determine if that plane is the bottom. This test merely asks that the bottom is not visible, that it faces the downward z direction, and that the tilts in the y and x directions are moderate. The best such plane is chosen from each object, and all are expected to agree. The slope of this plane is the only information available from the incomplete transformations, so the distance of the plane below the origin or focal point must be assumed. This distance just sets the numerical scale of all distances, so it might as well be unity. Thus a ground plane is determined and all the object bottoms are now made to lie in this plane.

With each model surface is stored its plane equation vector for the use of a three-dimensional display program. The dot product of this vector with any position vector is zero if the position is on the surface, and positive if the position is inside the solid. These plane vectors should be transformed by R^{-1} to become plane vectors of the transformed model. If the plane vector of an object plane is transformed by R_0^{-1}, it has the correct slope but not necessarily the correct length. In other words, its first three components are correct. These are used to find the ground plane. Now with the ground plane distance equal to one, we must find the depth x for each R. The lower-right component of R_0 we shall call w, and the same component in the final R, w'. We first set $x_1 = -w/2r$ and $w_1 = w/2$ to obtain R_1. If we transform the plane vector by R_0^{-1} and R_1^{-1}, we obtain $\bar{v}_0$ and $\bar{v}_1$. Normalizing these vectors so that the sum of the squares of the first three components is 1, we obtain normalized fourth components p_0 and p_1. The plane vector for R has a fourth component which is a linear combination of p_0 and p_1. Setting this combination equal to one and solving for the depth x, we obtain

$$x = \frac{w(p_0 - 1)}{r(1 + p_1 - 2p_0)}$$

$$w' = w + rx$$

Here again the focal ratio r is needed, and this time if r is zero, the computation of x blows up. This just reflects the fact that an infinite projection has infinite depths; however, it restricts r to nonzero for this procedure.

VI. Three-Dimensional Display

After a list of three-dimensional objects has been obtained in some manner, it should be possible to display them from any point of view. The sections of objects behind other objects should not be seen, nor should the back lines and construction lines of individual objects. The three-dimensional display program will do all this and more. It allows macrolike instances of objects so that a single object construction can be used many times with different transformations. It allows structures of models to be built up by the use of the knobs, push buttons, and light pen. Any object can be duplicated, deleted, or transformed. These extras make possible the construction of test cases for the two-dimensional to three-dimensional program to process. However, the most significant feature of this program is the mathematical technique which makes possible the hidden line removal.

A. Storage Structure

A good method of storing three-dimensional data is extremely important. The structure used is the basis for both the display program and the three-dimensional construction process. Therefore, the data necessary for hidden line removal must be quickly available and at the same time the topological structure must be suitable for model matching.

The list structure used is a list of tied blocks connected in rings. Ring list structures were developed for the TX-2 computer by Sutherland for his Sketchpad system.[12] Sketchpad allows a user to draw two-dimensional line drawings on the computer display with the aid of the light pen, knobs, and push buttons. An extension of this work to three dimensions is currently being completed by Johnson.[13] These two systems use ring list structure and, in order to be compatible with them, the same format is used in the three-dimensional display program. However, the exact block form used is different because of the different data requirements. In the ring structure, a block of registers is used for each item and contains pairs of ties to other blocks. Each pair of ties is part of a ring which allows the program to move from block to block around the ring in either direction.

The basis of all three-dimensional forms is the set of models. Each model block is tied to lists of its points, lines, and surfaces. The point blocks are tied to the lines connected to them and include a four-component position vector. Since a homogeneous vector can be normalized without changing the point, each component of the vector can be represented by a fixed-point, 36-bit number. The line blocks are tied to two point blocks and two surface blocks, since two planes determine a line. The surface blocks are tied to a ring of lines which represent the surface polygon and also include a plane vector. This detailed structure is needed for models only, since the objects are to be composed out of transformations of models. The models are always in the list structure and must be referred to by instances in order to be displayed. An instance is an intermediate block between a picture and either a model or another picture. Each instance includes a 4 × 4 transformation matrix and also the inverse of this matrix. The picture blocks may be referred to by any number of instances and have as their parts any number of instances. Thus each picture represents an object or a collection of objects and is composed of transformations of other pictures or models by means of instances. One picture is the current picture being displayed, and it has only one instance containing the picture transformation. Figure 9 shows a possible structure leading from the models to the current picture. The instances have been compressed to ties with matrices on them for simplicity.

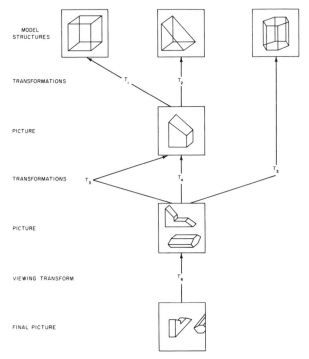

FIG. 9. List structure formation: representation of list structure formation of compound pictures. Each "picture" is composed of transformed versions of models and other pictures. There may be as many levels of pictures as necessary.

B. *Display Generation*

In order to display the picture represented by the current storage pattern, a recursive procedure is used, starting with the current picture. Each picture block has a temporary storage area to store the effective transformation and its inverse at that picture level. One recursion involves taking the transformation at one picture level, premultiplying by the matrix of one of the instances the picture refers to, and placing that transformation in the picture block referred to by the instance. The inverse matrices are carried along also, but postmultiplication must be used for them. If the instance refers to a model, the matrices obtained are put in a transform block along with the model name. Each time a model is reached, the process backs up to the last picture block and proceeds to the next instance, or if all instances have been processed, it backs up to the preceding picture block. In this way a list of transform blocks is obtained. Each transform block is now processed by tying to it a list of point-pair blocks obtained by transforming the end points of each line in the selected model. Each position vector is postmultiplied by the transformation in the transform block to obtain the new position vector. Also, the plane vectors of the model are transformed by the inverse matrix and collected as the columns of a volume matrix.

Thus a list of transform blocks is obtained, each block of which has a volume matrix and a list of point pairs. The point pairs represent all the lines in the display and can now be processed to eliminate the hidden lines. The display coordinates of a point are obtained from the four-component position vector $\bar{v}$ as

$$x = v_2/v_4$$
$$y = v_3/v_4$$

C. *Hidden Line Elimination*

Three steps are required to prepare a line for display. First, it is trimmed off at the edges of the display. Next, the back lines of each model are deleted. Third, the sections of each line which are hidden by other models are removed. It is the third part which is difficult and time-consuming. As far as I know, no one has ever devised a procedure for determining hidden line segments. One can imagine brute force methods such as calculating all the line intersections on the focal plane and then computing which lines were in which polygons and tracing out the frontal lines. But procedures such as this are hard to make complete for all cases, and the processing time could be fantastic. Therefore, a new mathematical method was conceived which utilizes volume inequality matrices to find out whether a point is inside or outside a volume. This test can then be extended by linear inequality solutions to tell which segment of a line is behind a volume. This is why the inverse transformations, plane vectors, and volume matrices are needed.

Since they are available, they can be used to advantage in the first two steps.

The volume matrix V of a model is a $4 \times n$ matrix with the n-plane vectors as columns. In the homogeneous coordinate system, a dot product of a position vector and a plane vector produces a measure of the distance of the point from the plane. The plane vectors of the models have had their signs adjusted so that the dot products will be negative if the point is outside the solid and positive if the point is inside. Thus, when a position vector $\bar{v}$ is postmultiplied by a volume matrix, the resulting vector $\bar{v}V$, since it is a collection of dot products, will have at least one negative term if the point is outside the volume. If any terms are zero, the point is on the model's surface, and if all are positive, the point is inside. In order that this test may work, the models must be convex. This is a small restriction, since the objects constructed with the models need not be convex,

$$(\bar{v}V \geq 0) \Rightarrow \bar{v} \text{ inside volume } V$$

In the expression above, the inequality sign means that all components of the vector should be nonnegative. Expressions and formulations of inequality matrices have been used in the field of linear programing to express the interior region of convex polyhedral cones where the general problem was the optimization of a function in such a region. However, literature in this field does not seem to cover the geometrical type of problem we are concerned with.

A volume matrix can be used for the first step of the line reduction: the elimination of lines from the display. As well as cutting off lines at the display edge, we wish to cut off lines in front of the focal plane. Thus a volume matrix can be designed which has planes at $y = \pm 1$, $z = \pm 1$, and $x = 0$. These planes form a semi-infinite box, and we wish to find the section of each line inside the box. First, we shall define the volume matrix V_0,

$$V_0 = \begin{bmatrix} 0 & 0 & 0 & 0 & -1 \\ 1 & -1 & 0 & 0 & 0 \\ 0 & 0 & 1 & -1 & 0 \\ 1 & 1 & 1 & 1 & 0 \end{bmatrix}$$

The set of all lines is the list of point-pair blocks. We shall want to use a line equation of the form

$$\bar{v} = \bar{s} + t\bar{d}, \qquad 0 \leq t \leq 1$$

where t is a running variable, moving the position $\bar{v}$ from $\bar{s}$ to $\bar{s} + \bar{d}$. A point-pair block has two points, $\bar{s}$ and $\bar{r}$. If the fourth component of these vectors is made to agree by normalizing one vector, the difference vector $\bar{d} = \bar{r} - \bar{s}$ can be formed. With this line representation we can proceed to find the values of the variable t for which the following inequalities are true:

$$\bar{s}V_0 + t\bar{d}V_0 \geq 0$$

This set of inequalities requires that the line be inside V_0 and we can solve for the minimum and maximum t. If we define

$$\bar{p} = \bar{s}V_0, \qquad \bar{q} = \bar{d}V_0$$

then for all j,

$$p_j + tq_j \geq 0$$

For $q_j > 0$, $t \geq -p_j/q_j$. For $q_j < 0$, $t \leq -p_j/q_j$. From these relations it is fairly obvious that we can obtain a minimum and maximum value for t and thus define the segment of line inside the volume. This segment then replaces the old point pair.

The second step of the line elimination is the removal of all the lines hidden by their own volume. Although this would be done automatically if we went right on to the third step and included the line's own volume among all the others, it is faster to eliminate these back lines ahead of time. The volume matrix associated with a line contains the plane vectors of the model, and two of these planes intersect to form the line. In each point-pair block we keep track of which columns of V are the line's plane vectors. The first component of a plane vector is the x component and will be negative if the plane faces toward the observer. Thus the second step is very simple: a line should be deleted if both the x components of its plane vectors are positive.

The third method of eliminating a line is to see if it is hidden by some other volume. For this test, each remaining line is tested against every volume matrix except its own. The procedure is similar to that of step one except that a two-variable inequality solution must be found this time. The segment of line found is the part to be deleted, and this may be an end, the center, or the complete line.

A volume matrix produces inequalities which tell if a point is in the volume. In step one we used a point with one degree of freedom t along a line. Now the line may be behind the volume so a second degree of freedom must be used to move the point forward through the volume. If a point on the line is moved forward in x in this transformed space, it will have to move through the volume, if it is hidden. The variable point will thus be represented as before with a variable t along the line, but also with a variable α, in the $\bar{x} = [1, 0, 0, 0]$ direction.

Variable point: $\bar{v} = \bar{s} + t\bar{d} + \alpha\bar{x}$
Inequalities: $\bar{v}V \geq 0$
Thus: $\bar{s}V + t\bar{d}V + \alpha\bar{x}V \geq 0$

Now $\bar{x}V$ is just the top row of V, which we can call $\bar{w}$, and $\bar{s}V$ and $\bar{d}V$ can be computed as before.

Define: $\bar{p} = \bar{s}V, \qquad \bar{q} = \bar{d}V, \qquad \bar{w} = \bar{x}V$
Thus for all j: $\cdot\, p_j + tq_j + \alpha w_j \geq 0$
Where: $0 \geq \alpha \geq 1, \qquad 0 \geq t \geq 1$

These inequalities must be solved for the minimum and maximum t for any nonnegative α. A few simple tests allow the removal of equations which are always satisfied or the termination of the test if an equation will never be satisfied. Ignore equation:

$$(q_j > 0) \wedge (p_j \geq 0) \wedge (p_j + w_j \geq 0) \tag{1}$$

$$(q_j < 0) \wedge (p_j > 0) \wedge (p_j + q_j \geq 0) \wedge (p_j + q_j + w_j \geq 0) \tag{2}$$

Quit, leave line:

$$(q_j > 0) \wedge (p_j < 0) \wedge (p_j + q_j \leq 0) \wedge (p_j + q_j + w_j \leq 0) \tag{3}$$

$$(q_j < 0) \wedge (p_j \leq 0) \wedge (p_j + w_j \leq 0) \tag{4}$$

These tests speed up the process considerably since only a few planes of each volume are really involved in the determination of t. To solve the remaining equations, many methods are possible and a very simple one was chosen. Each inequality is considered as an equality and all intersections between these equalities are found. Also, the intersections of these equalities with the boundaries, $\alpha = 0, 1$ and $t = 0, 1$, are found. Each intersection results in a pair (α, t), and these pairs are tested in the inequalities. Any pair satisfying all inequalities and the boundary conditions is used to compute a minimum and maximum t. Because the actual minimum and maximum t must occur at intersections, this is a complete solution. It is also fairly fast since there are usually very few equations. If no pair will satisfy all the inequalities, then the line is not hidden by the volume and is left intact. Otherwise, the section of line corresponding to the solution area, between minimum and maximum t, is deleted.

One case of interest can be modified during this process. We want to eliminate joint lines between touching, tangent objects. A joint line, when processed with the touching solid, is detectable since the inequality caused by the plane through the line will have $q_j = p_j = 0$. If this occurs, the solution space is limited to $\alpha = 0$. Thus the joint line can have a proper solution and will be eliminated. However, this also occurs for joints between objects where the planes are not tangent. We want these lines and must act to preserve them. Therefore, whenever $q_j = p_j = 0$, we make a special test to find out if either of the planes through the line from its own volume is parallel to the plane being tested. We also ask that the tangent planes face the same direction. If parallel planes facing the same way are not found, the line under consideration is kept intact and the rest of the test skipped.

This completes the testing of one line with one volume. The line is then tested against the other volumes. The final result of the complete hidden line removal is a modified list of point pairs. These lines are then displayed. The complete process tends to be time consuming for complicated displays, but the time does not seem to go up as the square of the number of objects, as might be expected. This is because objects far away from the line being processed are quickly disposed of by conditions (3) and (4). Thus the time consumed is on the order of one second per object for displays of up to thirty objects. It is not necessary to do the complete hidden line removal, though, if a faster moving display is required. The complete process can be reserved until the desired view is obtained.

D. Display Construction

Besides being able to display the list structure, the display program has provisions for modifying the list. The picture transformation in the first instance can always be changed by a rotation about each of three axes, a translation in three directions, or a size change. All transformation changes are obtained through the use of four shaft encoder knobs on the computer console. The function of these knobs is selected by means of push buttons. In addition to modifying the picture transformation, the light pen can be used to point out any instance transformation for modification. The pen is pointed at the object to be modified, and a level register indicates which instance level of the object to modify. This method is somewhat crude but does allow any instance to be modified. The transformation changes allowable for objects include rotation, translation, three size components, three skew components, and an over-all size factor. Beyond these transformation controls, any object can be deleted or duplicated. New instances of models can be generated and instances made of present pictures. These controls allow the construction of any list structure possible or the modification of any existing structure. Thus test pictures may be generated to facilitate the testing of this program and the three-dimensional construction program. Some sample pictures generated on the computer appear in Figs. 10*a* through *h*. These photographs illustrate the complexity of three-dimensional arrays which can be constructed on the computer in a few minutes.

VII. Conclusion

In the past, research in the pattern recognition field has been limited to the identification of two-dimensional shapes, mainly because it was thought that any three-dimensional analysis would be more difficult. The idea seems to have been that the two-dimensional work would pave the road for future three-dimensional work. However, progress has been slow and it may well be that the study of three-dimensional projections is an easier step. The human visual field is the result of a projective transformation, and the shapes perceived are independent of this transform. Thus it makes sense to utilize this transformation, since our goal is to recognize the same similarity classes which humans do.

The mathematics necessary to go from a photograph to an object list have been described. A set of transforms is found which takes a set of models

192   L. G. Roberts

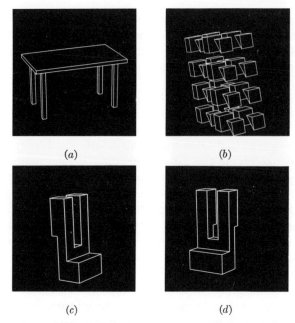

FIG. 10. (a–d) Three-dimensional displays: pictures constructed with three-dimensional display program. (a) Table. (b) Array made with instances. (c) Compound object. (d) Rotated view of object.

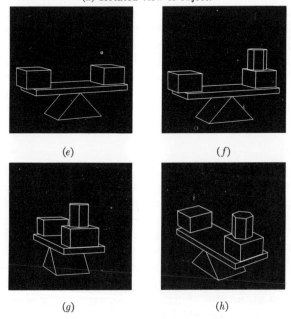

FIG. 10. (e–h) Three-dimensional displays: pictures constructed with three-dimensional display program showing hidden line elimination. (e) Seesaw. (f) With hexagonal prism. (g) Second view. (h) Balanced.

into the shapes observed. The models are then the invariant shapes which we perceive as the same object from any point of view. Individually or in specific groups, they could be given names.

The process of creating an object list from a picture is mainly mathematical, based on the natural laws of the space around us. It is based on the assumptions of model construction and object support and shows the theoretical implications of these concepts. Four or more points on an object must be seen in order to find the correct model and its transformation. Further, the depth relationships between objects depend on the focal ratio which can either be assumed as a camera constant, or calculated from the picture if the data are accurate enough. If the focal ratio used is wrong, the effect will be a contraction or expansion of the depth dimension. When both the focal ratio and the distance from the camera to the ground are known, the exact size of each object can be calculated.

The two-dimensional to three-dimensional and three-dimensional to two-dimensional programs are completely general, as long as the assumptions of model construction and support are not violated. The display program can handle any structure made up of transformations of models. The construction program will always produce a three-dimensional structure which projects to the given line drawing except that it will eliminate any two-dimensional markings, isolated polygons, and superfluous joint lines. Any drawing produced by the three-dimensional display program will be correctly reconstructed into the three-dimensional structure if the objects are properly supported and sufficiently visible.

The programs are all written for the TX-2 computer at Lincoln Laboratory. The TX-2 is ideal for this type of work because of its large memory for picture storage and its special input-output equipment. During the course of developing these programs, I designed a vector-drawing display for the computer which can draw line and circle segments. This display enables the computer to display a line drawing continuously and still spend most of its time computing new data. Thus it is possible to display rotating objects and have them move fairly smoothly.

The input program has about 5000 instructions and uses over 40,000 registers of data storage for its pictures and lists. It takes about one minute to process a picture into a line drawing of which half is for differentiation. The three-dimensional construction and display programs are each about 3000 instructions and use from 5000 to 40,000 registers of data storage depending upon the number of objects. Both construction and display take about one second per object. All told, a rotated view of the objects in a photograph might be obtained in two minutes.

I foresee at least two uses for this type of picture handling system. First, it could be used for an information reduction system to aid in the transmission of pictorial information. However, the necessity of an ultrahigh-speed computer will probably limit this use. Second, the computer programs will be useful input-output tools for future investigations of three-dimensional processes. The biggest benefit of this investigation, however, is an increased understanding of the possible processes of visual perception.

APPENDIX A
Homogeneous Coordinates

In a homogeneous coordinate system, a fourth coordinate, or scale factor, is used in such a way that the total scale of a vector is unimportant. That is,

$$k\bar{v} \equiv \bar{v}$$

I am using $\equiv$ to indicate that the same point is represented even though the individual components may not be equal. The above form is achieved by defining the point's coordinates, X, Y, Z, in terms of the homogeneous components x, y, z, w as below,

$$X = x/w, \qquad Y = y/w, \qquad Z = z/w$$

When new points are introduced into the system, w may be assigned to any nonzero value and these equations used to find x, y, and z. When points are to be displayed, the same equations are used to find X, Y, and Z. An added advantage for a fixed point computer is gained by using a homogeneous system: w may always be chosen so as to keep the numbers normalized.

A plane is represented by l, m, n, p such that on the plane

$$lx + my + nz + pw = 0$$

I have chosen to represent points by row vectors; therefore, to transform a set of points $\bar{v}_i$, each is postmultiplied by a 4×4 matrix H,

$$\bar{v}_i' = \bar{v}_i H$$

The advantage of homogeneous coordinates is that a single transform H can accomplish a full projective transformation. Normally, it is convenient to separate the various functions provided by a transform until they are needed and then multiply them. Below is a breakdown of a transform H, consisting of a rotation by a standard 3×3 R matrix, a translation by a vector $\bar{v} = (x, y, z, w)$, a perspective transform from a focal point at f on the x axis, a translation after perspective to a center (y_0, z_0), and a total picture scale factor S. This sequence might represent the transform made by taking a picture with an arbitrary camera orientation and making an enlargement of a section. The transform would take the real space points X, Y, Z into a Y', Z' on the print. An X' will be formed which can be used for eliminating object overlap.

$$
H = \begin{bmatrix} & & & 0 \\ & [R] & & 0 \\ & & & 0 \\ 0 & 0 & 0 & 1 \end{bmatrix} \begin{bmatrix} w & & & \\ & w & & \\ & & w & \\ x & y & z & w \end{bmatrix} \begin{bmatrix} f & & & -1 \\ & f & & \\ & & f & \\ & & & f \end{bmatrix} \begin{bmatrix} 1 & & & \\ & 1 & & \\ & & 1 & \\ & y_0 & z_0 & 1 \end{bmatrix} \begin{bmatrix} 1 & & & \\ & 1 & & \\ & & 1 & \\ & & & S \end{bmatrix}
$$
$$\quad\;\text{Rotation}\qquad\quad\text{Translation}\qquad\text{Perspective}\qquad\text{Translation}\qquad\quad\text{Scale}$$

It should be noted that a set of points $\bar{v}_i$ can be written as the successive rows of a matrix V and transformed by one matrix equation, $V' = VH$.

Also, a plane equation can be expressed as a scalar product in terms of $\bar{n} = (l, m, n, p)$,

$$\bar{v} \cdot \bar{n} = 0$$

A plane normal n can be transformed along with the points of a space,

$$\bar{v}' = \bar{v}H, \qquad \bar{n}' = \bar{n}(H^{-1})^T, \qquad \bar{v}' \cdot \bar{n}' = 0$$

Of course, if the transform is orthogonal, $(H^{-1})^T = H$.

APPENDIX B
Similarity Test

We are given a matrix A of n points (x, y, z, w) from a model and want to find a transform H that will most nearly fit n points (y, z, w) in a matrix B. Thus we hope for

$$AH \cong B$$

However, we cannot write an equality sign above without introducing a diagonal scale matrix D which will allow the w_i values of AH to differ from the w_i of B,

$$AH = DB$$

We now have 12 unknowns in H (3×4) and n unknowns in D ($n \times n$). Matrix A is $4 \times n$ and matrix B is $3 \times n$, creating $3n$ equations. Therefore, $n \geq 6$ should produce a complete solution. We shall use a minimum square-error technique to solve the equations. Thus we wish to minimize the squared error in each equation. We shall use A' to indicate the transpose of A,

$$\frac{\partial}{\partial h_{lm}} \left[\sum_i^n \sum_k^3 \left(\sum_j^4 a_{ij} h_{jk} - d_i b_{ik} \right)^2 \right] = 0$$

$$\sum_j^4 h_{jm} \sum_i^n a_{il} a_{ij} = \sum_i^n d_i a_{il} b_{im}$$

or $A'AH = A'DB$. Thus

$$H = (A'A)^{-1} A'DB$$

Now we must find D,

$$\frac{\partial}{\partial d_l} \left[\sum_i^n \sum_k^3 \left(\sum_j^4 a_{ij} h_{jk} - d_i b_{ik} \right)^2 \right] = 0$$

$$\sum_j^4 a_{lj} \sum_k^3 h_{jk} b_{lk} = d_l \sum_k^3 b_{lk}^2$$

Thus the diagonal terms of AHB' equal those of DBB'. Substituting for H and making the definition

$$G = A(A'A)^{-1}A' - I$$

we obtain a matrix $GDBB'$, which has zero diagonal terms.

Define: $Q = BB'$

If we now multiply the terms of G by those of Q', term by term, we get a new $n \times n$ matrix S,

$$S_{ij} = g_{ij}q_{ji}$$

Define: $\bar{d} = d_1 \cdots d_n$

Now the vector $\bar{d}$ or diagonal terms of D can be found by solving

$$Sd = 0$$

This equation requires S to be singular, with degeneracy at least one. If the degeneracy is one, the problem is solved since the common scale factor of D and H is unimportant. A degeneracy more than one means that too few equations were used ($n < 6$) or that the picture had no perspective. However, by assuming a value of unity for each undefined d_j, an accurate, but not complete solution, can be found.

When D is found, H can be found,

$$H = (A'A)^{-1}A'DB$$

It should be noted that for $n = 4$, A^{-1} will probably exist and in this case the best solution obtainable is one with no perspective,

$$H = A^{-1}B$$

If solutions without perspective are expected, the matrix D is unnecessary and the ordinary minimum square-error solution holds,

$$H = (A'A)^{-1}A'B$$

An error criteria can be found to indicate the mismatch of model and picture. An error matrix E is found,

$$E = AH - DB \quad \text{or} \quad E = GDB$$

Now if the sum of the squares of the components of E is taken, this number can be used to indicate the error magnitude. If one row of E contributes the main error, this point of B probably should not be mapped to the model A.

ACKNOWLEDGMENTS

I am indebted to Professor P. Elias for his valuable suggestions and criticisms in his capacity of Thesis Supervisor. His advice, as well as that of Professors Claude Shannon, Murray Eden, and Thomas Stockham, has been very helpful in encouraging and guiding this work. I also wish to thank Ivan Sutherland for his help and list structure subroutines; Leonard Hantman, who programed the major part of the three-dimensional display process; and the M.I.T. Lincoln Laboratory staff for their cooperation in the use of the TX-2 computer.

REFERENCES

1. SOMERVILLE, D. M. Y., *Analytical Geometry of Three Dimensions*, Cambridge University Press, 1959.
2. ROBERTS, L. G., "Pattern Recognition with an Adaptive Network," *IRE Intern. Conv. Record*, Pt. 2, 66–70 (1960).
3. SELFRIDGE, O. G., AND U. NEISSER, "Pattern Recognition by Machine," *Sci. Am.*, *203*, 60–68 (August 1960).
4. HODES, L., *Machine Processing of Line Drawings*, Report 54G-0028[U,] Lincoln Laboratory, Massachusetts Institute of Technology (March 1961).
5. JULESZ, B., "Toward the Automation of Binocular Depth Perception," *Proceedings of the I.F.I.P. Congress*, Munich (1962).
6. ROBERTS, L. G., "Picture Coding Using Pseudo-Random Noise," *IRE Trans.*, *IT-8*, 145–154 (1962).
7. GIBSON, J. J., *The Perception of the Visual World*, Houghton Mifflin Co., Boston, 1950.
8. ITTELSON, W. H., "Size As a Cue to Distance," *Am. J. Psychol.*, *64*, 54–67 (1951).
9. ATTNEAVE, F., AND M. D. ARNOULT, "The Quantitative Study of Shape and Pattern Perception," *Psychol. Bull.*, *53*, 452 (1956).
10. LANGDON, J., "The Perception of 3-D Solids," *Quart. J. Exptl. Psychol.*, *7*, 19–36 (1955).
11. STEVENS, S. S., "The Psychophysiology of Vision," *Sensory Communication*, W. Rosenblith, Ed., M.I.T. Press, Cambridge, and John Wiley & Sons, Inc., New York, 1961, p. 13.
12. SUTHERLAND, I. E., *Sketchpad: A Man-Machine Graphical Communication System*, Technical Report No. 296[U], Lincoln Laboratory, Massachusetts Institute of Technology, 30 January 1963.
13. JOHNSON, T., *Sketchpad III, 3-D, Graphical, Communication with a Digital Computer*, S.M. Thesis, Department of Mechanical Engineering, Massachusetts Institute of Technology, Cambridge, Massachusetts, June 1963.

CHAPTER 10

OPTICAL-ELECTRONIC SPATIAL FILTERING
FOR PATTERN RECOGNITION

W. S. Holmes, T. R. Babcock, G. E. Richmond, L. A. Pownall, and G. C. Vorie

Computer Research Department, Cornell Aeronautical Laboratory, Inc., Buffalo, New York

Introduction

This paper describes the application of optical-electronic spatial filtering as a method of isolating pictorial subarea properties. The objective was to automate the photointerpretation functions of object detection and whole-photo classification. The approach taken was (1) to find spatial property characteristics of subareas (of the order of 500 ft square), particularly relating to line structure, and (2) then to use these derived properties as inputs to a logical process which might behave like a recognition process.

The work was sponsored by the Geography Branch of the Office of Naval Research. This program has included research in imagery preprocessing using two-dimensional filters,[1] and the study of perceptron recognition processes for target classification. However, this paper will report only on the experimental aspects of the optical-electronic spatial filtering work. The results obtained are sufficient to indicate feasibility for detecting straight-line segments, but additional work is required to perfect the experiment.

The philosophy of experimental design was predicated on the assumption established by the CAL electro-optical spatial filtering research[2] that straight-line segments and other pictorial detail from man-made objects cause a particular peaking of the spectral energy in the frequency plane. The orientation of a wedge-shaped filter was used to test for the energy distribution of photographic subareas.

Several approaches can be suggested which use peaked spectral energy information from subareas, but this paper is based upon only two fundamental concepts, the first of which was not developed extensively. In the first case the two-dimensional spectral pattern is reproduced in all essential detail electronically using a vidicon or similar image converter. This process was demonstrated and will be described. The electronic image is then processed at video rates using computer-controlled gates to produce the desired filtering and processing functions.

In the second case a mechanical aperture filter is imposed at the image point. The spatially filtered spectral pattern represented by the emerging light is integrated in a light detector, and subsequently processed and displayed. The second system used a Nipkow disk which mechanically scanned the image, derived power spectrum properties with optical-wedge spatial filters, and collected the light with photomultipliers. Several specific filters were used for detecting the spectral frequency distribution of man-made objects in photographs. An oscilloscope was used as an intensified television-type monitor.

The relationship of this spatial filtering processing to the photointerpretation (PI) function is shown by the flow chart of Fig. 1. In the figure a

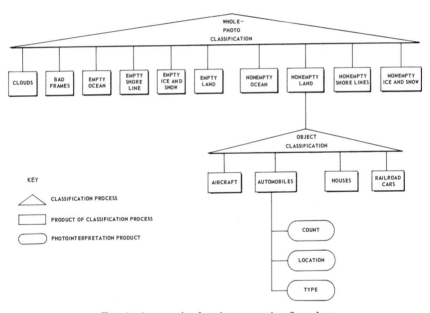

Fig. 1. Automatic photointerpretation flow chart.

triangle represents a classification process, a rectangle represents a product of a classification process, and ovals represent photointerpretation products. Two major functions represented are whole-photo classification and target classification. Now whole-photo classification is not necessarily a one-stage process. For example, all photos might be classified into CLOUDS and BAD FRAMES/VS/ICE AND SNOW, LAND, OCEAN, and SHORE LINES; after which the second group might be classified into EMPTY (of culture)/VS/NONEMPTY frames. The imagery is ultimately categorized into reject and useful areas, which one can appreciate by reviewing the individual titles of the classification products. This is the level of culture detection which hopefully can be achieved by electro-optical spatial filtering.

The next PI function of target classification is a more specific description of the man-made objects or area of interest. For example, the number of automobiles, their type, and location might be desired from all frames containing nonempty land culture. For this problem, other types of processing than spatial filtering would be more efficient and practical. Advanced hyperplane discriminators and other pattern recognition techniques hold more promise for this type of problem. However, these techniques will not be covered in this paper, but have been reported elsewhere.[3-5] Additional details of the electro-optical spatial filtering work is available in a recent CAL report.[6]

Electro-Optical Experimentation

First Experiment

The first experiment was initiated because earlier numerical filtering techniques by a general purpose computer indicated that useful properties could be derived. A schematic diagram of the spatial filter experimental setup "A" is shown in Fig. 2. The objective was to display the spatial-

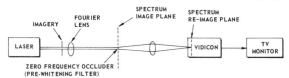

Fig. 2. Spatial filter experimental setup "A."

frequency plane of a portion of the stationary object film on a television monitor, and to examine their properties.

The setup consisted of the following optical train:

1. Source of parallel monochromatic light.
2. An adjustable aperture that selects the size of picture segment.
3. A movable film frame holder.
4. A converging lens to take the Fourier transform of selected segments.
5. A zero-frequency occluder to avoid dynamic range problems.
6. A re-imaging lens.
7. A vidicon placed at the spectrum re-image plane.
8. Scan-generation electronics, and television monitor.

Functions 1 and 2 are satisfied by using a narrow-beam laser source. These experiments were used to investigate the light source power levels required,

vidicon sensitivity, and other factors necessary for success. Photographs
were made of the TV monitor of images with and without culture. The
distinctive line structure of the photographs from man-made objects leads
to the speculation that this feature could be exploited for culture detection.
Copies of the input photos and the corresponding monitor image spectrum
are shown in Fig. 3. Note that the monitor image plane spectrum energies

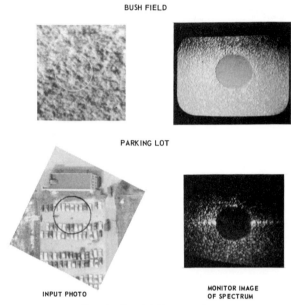

FIG. 3. Spatial filter results.

are concentrated and distributed at right angles to the natural image lines
for the parking lot. The bush field has a random textural pattern of energy
which is quite different from that with culture.

Second Experiment

Although the initial filtering approach showed promise, the subsequent
electronic processing would have been more expensive than could be justified on this project and an alternative approach was selected. The same sort
of results could be achieved using an optical filter in place of electronic
scanning and filtering of the vidicon. The filter could be easily changed or
rotated to detect line structure. A laser was used as a light source, as before.

A diagram of the second setup is shown in Fig. 4. The He-Ne laser output
is collimated into a 2-in. diameter beam, at 6328Å. The old standard
Nipkow disk causes a raster-type scanning of the test transparency. Timing
holes on the disk are used to generate the necessary horizontal and vertical
sweep syncs. A dual photomultiplier system P_1 and P_2 is used to collect
the reference and signal light from the Fourier lens. The beam splitter and
prism were used to achieve the proper input of reference light level without

conflicting with the signal. A comparison is made of the reference and signal photomultiplier outputs, and AGC action which is dependent on the reference PM minimizes the dynamic range images with different photograph densities. The Z axis of the oscilloscope was intensity modulated to pro-

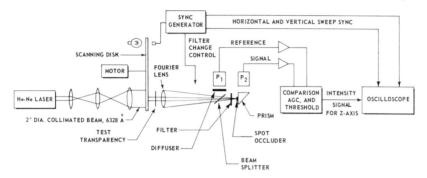

FIG. 4. Block diagram of electro-optical experimental apparatus.

duce a television-type raster synchronized to the scan of the objective, which was geometrically congruent to the original image.

The spatial relationship of the scanning disk, a typical test image, and the wedge filter are illustrated by Fig. 5. The experiments concentrated on

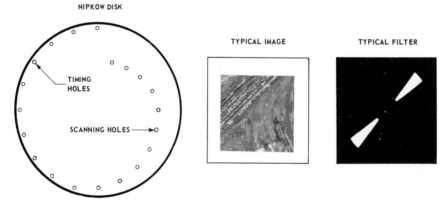

FIG. 5. Spatial relationships of the scanning disk, a typical image, and typical filter.

obtaining a good scanning signal from clear-cut images, and then actual photographs were used.

The video signals (top to bottom) and the intensified rasters (left to right) correspond to these object transparencies.

Condition	Object Transparency
A	Nothing
B	Applicable test pattern
C	Ronchi ruling (100 line/in.)

No adjustments of amplifier gains, threshold, etc., were made for the measurements recorded within a set of photographs. However, a larger diameter Fourier lens was used for Fig. 7 than for previous experiments on Fig. 6. Note that for each object transparency, the intensified raster scan

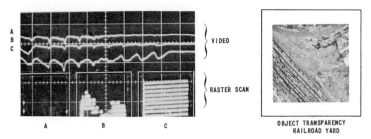

FIG. 6. Object slide, CRO video, and raster for railroad yard.

B corresponds to an area of culture or pseudoculture. The diagonal cut-out transparency of Fig. 7 produces the closest relationship between intensified raster and object. The actual image photograph of the railroad yard of Fig. 6 had poor contrast which made the sensitivity control difficult to adjust.

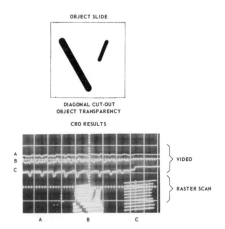

FIG. 7. Object slide, CRO video, and raster for diagonal cut-out.

Therefore, the lower left-hand corner of the intensified raster only generally corresponds to the area of culture. An actual photograph of the electro-optical experimental apparatus is given in Fig. 8. All units were mounted on a standard laboratory optical bench to maintain alignment and rigidity, and standard laboratory air-conditioned atmosphere prevailed. This was a diminishing of standards from the first experiment which was performed with higher grade optics, extremely rigid mounting fixtures, and a white room quality atmosphere.

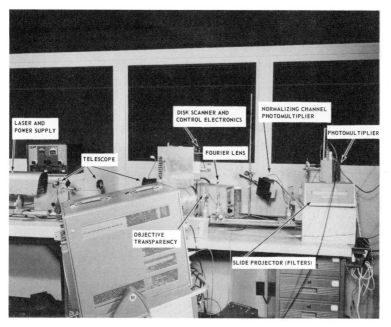

FIG. 8. Electro-optical experimental setup "B."

Discussion of Results and Problems

Problems encountered in this experiment which contributed to poor response separation for aerial photographs as contrasted to Ronchi rulings and drafted transparencies were as follows:

1. Difficulty with mechanical repeatability and stability because of object and optical components movement and lateral runout of the scanning disk.

2. Light scattering from lens imperfections and edges of mountings.

3. Drifts in laser mode and power output with time and temperature.

The experimental results, particularly those of Fig. 7, confirm that the electro-optical spatial filtering approach is potentially capable of detecting straight-line structure in photographs.

Conclusions

Electro-optical spatial filtering for detection of culture by spectral property analysis appears promising from this preliminary experimental investigation. The future use of the derived spatial filtering properties in an adaptive recognition system would be of great advantage in automating a routine but a time-consuming job of the human photointerpreter, for whole-photo classification and object detection.

The first experiment with electronic processing of the two-dimensional power spectrum indicated feasibility of the approach without completion of the closed-loop television electronic gating system. The second experiment used optical band-pass filters, a collimated laser beam, a mechanical Nipkow disk for image scanning, photomultipliers for light collection, and oscilloscope television-type monitoring. Results were obtained of the intensified raster scan which compared favorably with clean-cut images. For low contrast images, general correspondence with expectations was obtained, but additional experiment perfection is required.

As with many experiments, some images of improved contrast were obtained but unfortunately not documented before adjustment drifts and equipment failures occurred. The wedge-shaped spectrum filters were not used in the second experiment, so that analysis of the results was done visually.

It is recommended that additional research be initiated for an improved prototype model of an electro-optical spatial filtering system which could provide rapid serial or parallel property filter output signals to a recognition system. The spatial filter properties of photograph subareas would serve as a matrix of input signals to a recognition system for recognition of culture in a subset of these subareas.

APPENDIX A

Light Level Calculations for Optical Spatial Frequency Analyzer

No satisfactory theory exists which permits the direct computation of illumination in the frequency phase of optical spatial frequency analyzers. The best one can do is scale from experiments with similar devices.

All other things equal, the spectral power density p (watts/sq mm), at a given frequency (ν_x, ν_y) will be proportional to the input power P (watts). Also for pictures of the same contrast and average density, the upper envelope of the spectral power density is approximately proportional to $(\nu_x{}^2 + \nu_y{}^2)^{-5/4}$. Thus we have

$$\bar{p}(\nu_x, \nu_y) \approx KP(\nu_x{}^2 + \nu_y{}^2)^{5/4}$$

where

$$s = \text{scale factor}$$
$$\rho(\lambda) = \text{relative response over wavelength}$$

The constant K, in terms of the noise level of the vidicon is to be found experimentally, by the rearrangement of the above to:

$$K = \frac{N(\bar{\nu})^{5/2}}{ps^2\rho(\lambda)}$$

where

$$N = \text{noise level of tube}$$
$$(\bar{\nu}) = \text{greatest spatial frequency at which a signal was visible}$$

For the laser experiment

$$\bar{\nu} = 11 \text{ cy/mm}$$
$$P = 1 \times 10^{-3} \text{ W}$$
$$s = 3.5 \text{ cy/mm/mm}$$
$$\rho(\lambda) = 0.0225 \mu A/\mu W$$

where $\rho(\lambda)$ was taken from RCA data, $\bar{\nu}$ and s are measured fairly readily, and P was obtained by measurement.

For an operating system, the fundamental design variables are the maximum spatial frequency to be observed ($\bar{\nu}$), and the signal-to-noise ratio at this frequency and the quantity to be calculated is the required source power. Table 1 has been calculated from

$$K = \frac{N(\bar{\nu})^{5/2}}{Ps^2\rho(\lambda)}$$

TABLE 1   LASER POWER REQUIREMENTS

Maximum Spatial Frequency (cy/mm)	Signal-to-Noise Ratio (dB)	Required Laser Power (mW)
20	10	13.3
30	10	36.8
20	20	133
30	20	368

REFERENCES

1. FRYER, W., AND G. E. RICHMOND, "Two-Dimensional Spatial Filtering and Computers," *Proc. Nat. Electron. Conf.*, 18, 529–535 (1962).
2. ROETLING, P. G., AND H. HAMMILL, *Study of Spatial Filtering by Optical Diffraction for Pattern Recognition*, Project CODART, RADC-TR-62-93, Cornell Aeronautical Laboratory Report No. VE-1522-G-1, 13 February 1962.
3. MURRAY, A. E., *Phase I Report, Perceptron Applicability to Photointerpretation (Project PICS)*, Cornell Aeronautical Laboratory Report No. VE-1446-G-1, Contract Nonr-3161(00), 1 November 1960.
4. HOLMES, W. S., H. R. LELAND, G. E. RICHMOND, AND M. G. SPOONER, *Status and Planning Report on Perceptron Applicability to Automatic Photointerpretation*, Cornell Aeronautical Laboratory Report No. VE-1446-G-2, Contract Nonr-3161(00), 30 August 1961.
5. LELAND, H. R., G. E. RICHMOND, and M. G. SPOONER, *Application of Perceptrons to Photointerpretation*, Cornell Aeronautical Laboratory Summary Report No. VE-1446-G-3, Contract Nonr-3161(00), August 1963.
6. BABCOCK, T. R., AND G. E. RICHMOND, *Application of Perceptrons to Photointerpretation*, Cornell Aeronautical Laboratory Report No. VE-1446-G-4, Contract Nonr-3161(00), July 1964.

CHAPTER 11

A HIGH DATA RATE OPTICAL CORRELATOR
WITH TIME VARIABLE CODING

A. V. Bunker

The Boeing Company, Aero-Space Division, Seattle, Washington

Optical ultrasonic delay lines used as correlators and matched filters show considerable promise of achieving large time-bandwidth products and high data rates. The matched filters described herein are used to correlate binary coded signals in the presence of noise with corresponding stored reference signals. The devices described have applications in advanced communication systems and pulse compression radar.

Two types of matched filters are discussed: a fixed-code version having a time-bandwidth product of 127 (21 dB process gain) with a 10 Mc/sec signal frequency, and a variable-code matched filter which has a time-bandwidth product of 1000 (30 dB process gain) and a signal frequency of 20 Mc/sec. The latter, which is undergoing preliminary testing, incorporates two countercurrent channels, each doubled on itself. Polarized light, transmitted through the delay line normal to the acoustic wave trains, produces a correlation pulse when the two code sequences are aligned.

The paper discusses both the results from the fixed-code correlator development program and the optical, mechanical, and electronic design and construction of the variable-code matched filter-correlator along with preliminary results.

Introduction

For the past several years The Boeing Company has been engaged in the study and development of correlation signal processing techniques for use in experimental antijam (A/J) communication systems and phase-coded pulse compression radars. Of considerable interest is the development of matched filters to provide enhancement of coded signals in the presence of noise. For applications requiring large time-bandwidth products and wideband signals, photoelastic delay line matched filters and correlators are very suitable. Generally speaking, time-bandwidth products greater than about 200 (23 dB process gain) at signal frequencies greater than about 10 Mc/sec are perhaps most efficiently achieved by this means.

In applications where the coded signal is invariant in time, the reference function may be stored in the form of a coded slit mask on the photoelastic delay line. A typical example of such an application is a phase-coded radar. The first matched filter described is of this type.

The second matched filter was developed for applications requiring the reference code stream to be continuously driven from a long (in comparison with the time delay of the delay line) pseudorandom code sequence.

It is noted that the difference between a "correlator" and "matched filter" as described in this paper merely refers to the nature of the reference signal. For a cross-correlator the reference is similar to the signal and is sequentially multiplied and integrated by the optical processing. Maximum correlation appears when the two signals are in synchronism. The reference stored in the matched filter consists of the time-inverse of the transmitted signal, thereby producing a maximum output when the signals pass through correlation. Thus the devices described may be used either as matched filters or correlators, depending upon the time polarity of the reference signal.

Fixed-Code Optical Matched Filter Correlator

As the first step in the projected optical correlator program, in 1963 a joint effort was initiated between The Boeing Company and the Corning Glass Works in the development and testing of a 10 Mc/sec fixed-code optical matched filter.

An optical diagram of this first system is shown in Fig. 1. It consisted

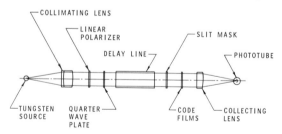

FIG. 1. Optical diagram fixed-code correlator.

of tungsten light source, an achromatic collimating lens, linear sheet polarizer, quarter-wave plate, fused silica delay line, coded analyzer mask, and phototube detector. Collimated light is first linearly polarized and then circularly polarized by the quarter-wave plate. The 90° phase shift or phase retardation caused by the quarter-wave plate is somewhat arbitrary, the purpose being to bias the operating point to the most linear portion of the intensity-phase retardation curve. The uncorrelated signal-plus-noise is used to suitably modulate and drive a piezoelectric ceramic transducer. The resulting compression and rarefaction perturbations either increase or decrease the phase retardation such that the circular polarization is changed to elliptical polarization.[1] This effect is shown in Fig. 2. It will be noted that

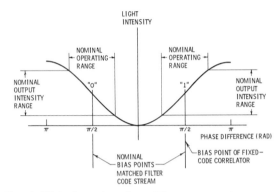

FIG. 2. Light intensity–phase difference operating curve.

a total retardation of 180° effectively rotates the polarization vector by 90°. Functioning of the coded analyzer mask depends upon this effect. If a 1 or a 0 is represented by the orientation of the polarization vector in each slit in the code mask, an instantaneous pulse of light will result when the acoustic wave train is aligned correctly with the coded analyzers.

The coded mask was constructed by Corning. A photographic mask was made containing 127 slits spaced one acoustical wavelength at 10 Mc/sec or about 0.015 in. apart. Each slit or opening was approximately 0.005 in. in width and 0.6 in. in height. The analyzer masks were made by placing polaroid Vectograph sheet film over the slit mask, and selectively dyeing each slit area in accordance with the matched filter code. Two thicknesses of Vectograph film were required, one layer representing the 1's and the other the 0's. The slit mask and two thicknesses of film were cemented together and then to the plano-convex collector lens.

The completed line with delay line, transducers, polarizer, and code mask is shown in Fig. 3. The fused silica line was 0.87 in. by 1.87 in. wide with the larger dimension parallel to the light path. The line was excited with a six-element series connected array of PZT lead zirconate-titanate transducers. Input impedance at 10 Mc/sec was approximately 16 ohms in parallel with 1300 pF.

The transducer array was driven by a seven-stage feedback shift register

FIG. 3. Assembled delay line fixed-code correlator.

producing a $2^n - 1$ or a 127 bit pseudorandom code. Various types of modulation of the transducer were tried, with the result that diphase modulation produced the best correlation peak-to-sidelobe ratio.

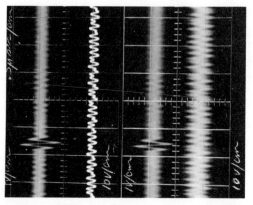

FIG. 4. Diphase code and correlator output fixed-code correlator.

Figure 4 shows the resulting diphase code and correlator output with correlation pulse. A process gain of about 18 dB was realized as against a theoretical process gain of 21 dB. The lower trace shows the same input with added noise.

The Optical Matched Filter with Time-Variable Coding

After testing the fixed-code matched filter it was decided to develop a correlator/matched filter which would have a considerably larger time-bandwidth product and wider signal bandwidth. At the same time it would feature electronic code switching. The latter was deemed necessary in some communication applications where the code reference must be continuously switched to prevent repeater jamming of the signal. In addition, other design features selected were

1. 15–20 Mc/sec signal frequencies.
2. 27–30 dB time-bandwidth product.
3. All solid-state electronics—micrologic modules where possible.
4. Higher quality optics and mounting structure with greater versatility.

As several different optical matched filter concepts were to be tried, mechanics, optics, and electronics had to be somewhat versatile. The configuration is shown in Figs. 5 and 6. The high cost of a first-class refracting

Fig. 5. Variable-code correlator.

collimator dictated the procurement and integration of a paraboloidal telescope mirror with a diameter of 6 in. and a focal length of 48 in. This required an extensive folding of the light path. This requirement plus the need for versatility resulted in a rather short, quite rigid optical bench arrangement. The optics and mechanics should be capable of handling a signal frequency of up to 50 Mc/sec.

Structure

The quality of the collimator mirror was the pacing item for both structure and additional optics. The ways were constructed of stainless steel tubing and all critical brackets fabricated of welded mild steel and then normalized.

Fig. 6. Optical-mechanical assembly: variable-code correlator.

Optics

SOURCE OPTICS. At signal frequencies of 20 Mc/sec and above, it becomes increasingly important that the "collimated" light beam impinging on the delay line approach spatial coherence. An Osram 100 W/2 100 watt high-pressure mercury arc lamp was selected for the source. Although lamps with higher wattages were available, the 100 W/2 has the smallest arc dimensions, 0.25 × 0.25 mm, and the highest mean luminance, 170,000 candles/cm². This could then yield the closest approximation to a point source without being forced to go to the added cost of a gas laser. The 4348/4358 Å blue line was chosen because of the combined integration of source, choice of available sheet polarizers, and spectral sensitivity of commercially available phototubes. The arc radiation is roughly collimated by a small fast achromatic lens, narrow-band filtered by an interference filter, and then focused on a 0.75-mm aperture by an $F/7$ plano-convex lens. The "pinhole" is also located at the focal point of the main collimating mirror. The source optics and interference filter were obtained from the Bausch & Lomb Optical Company.

COLLIMATING OPTICS. As mentioned previously, the choice of collimator optics was dictated largely by cost. The stringent spatial coherence requirements were complicated by the length of delay line to be illuminated, a minimum of 5 in. A parabolic Pyrex mirror accurate to $\frac{1}{4}$ wavelength with a diameter of 6 in. and a focal length of 48 in. was used. The schematic of the folded optical path is shown in Fig. 7. As noted, this requires the intervening brackets to straddle the light beam. The folding mirror consists of an aluminized optical flat accurate to $\frac{1}{4}$ wavelength. The collimating mirror is baffled in such a way as to emit a collimated beam approximately 1 in. high and 5.5 in. wide. To reduce coma, the mirror is used as an off-axis paraboloid.

POLARIZING ELEMENTS.   The choice of polarizing elements was limited to sheet polaroid by the long length of delay line to be illuminated. Both polarizer and analyzer were mounted in rotatable frames so that the polarizing vectors may be adjusted precisely with respect to each other and to the delay line. Three types of polaroid were considered, HN22, HN32, and HN38. Although possessing rather low transmittance in the uncrossed position, HN22 was selected as it has the highest crossed-uncrossed ratio, on the order of 10^5, in this spectral region.

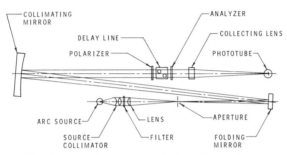

FIG. 7. Optical diagram variable-code correlator.

OPTICAL DELAY LINE.   Considerable care was taken in the design of the delay line. Fused silica or fused quartz is outstanding because of its high modulus of rigidity, high dimensional stability, extremely low acoustical attenuation, nonbirefringence, and high optical transmittance. Conversely, it is difficult to obtain large pieces and difficult to work. The finished line is 7 in. long and 1 in. in both height and width. It was made of Corning fused silica by the Davidson Manufacturing Company. The critical surfaces are flat to within one wavelength and are oriented to each other to an accuracy of one arc minute. The assembled line is shown in Fig. 8.

In order to minimize acoustical and electrostatic cross coupling, it would be considered desirable to incorporate two separate one-way delay lines each terminated in an absorbent wedge. However, the resulting critical alignment problem between the two delay lines resulted in the choice of a single line. It will be noted that one end of the line is terminated in a symmetrical wedge with an included angle of 90°. This was incorporated in order to determine the feasibility of doubling each acoustical wave train back on itself in the same vertical plane, but higher or lower in the line. This path is shown in Fig. 9. Obviously, this doubles the time-bandwidth product.

As was to be expected, selection, mounting, and driving the transducers at these frequencies turned out to require the most attention. Commercially available ferroelectric ceramics have a maximum fundamental resonant frequency of 10 Mc/sec. Therefore, the choice lay between driving compressional or longitudinal mode transducers at the third harmonic of

Fig. 8. Assembled delay line: variable-code correlator.

20 Mc/sec or a shear or transverse mode at either the second or third harmonic. Shear mode transducers are known to be much more effective in producing optical phase retardation than the compressional mode. In addition, one can expect less deleterious effects from mode changing caused

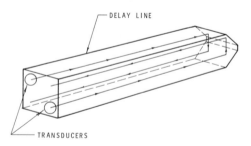

Fig. 9. Acoustical path variable-code correlator.

by acoustical beam spreading reflections. However, as stated by Arenburg, shear mode transducers are extremely difficult to couple to the delay line.[2]

Best results have been achieved with a lead zirconate titanate ferroelectric material, PZT-4, made by the Clevite Corporation. Several transducer-to-delay line bonding techniques have been used. Of the various techniques considered, furnace brazing with an indium alloy is the most promising at this time.

PHOTODETECTOR. In the far blue spectral region, the electron multiplier phototube is considered the most efficient detector. For the 4358 Å line, an RCA 1P21 nine-stage photomultiplier was selected for its high sensitivity and relatively low dark current.

Electronics

Items of electronic equipment required for both input and output of the delay line are the code generators, diphase modulators, transducer drivers, and a phototube amplifier. All ancillary electronics are of solid-state construction.

CODE GENERATOR. In communication applications information is transmitted using the coded sequence T intervals long, where T is the length of the delay line, from a pseudorandom code generator to represent a "mark" symbol. A "space" is usually denoted by the complement of the code sequence. In radar systems, the code stream length would denote the unambiguous range interval. A correlation pulse will occur for every n bits of the stream, n being the number of bits filling the delay line.

In the experimental system the correlation at the matched filter is performed by providing a reference signal in the form of a code sequence which is the time-inverse of the transmitted signal. The inverse is required because of the countercurrent nature of the acoustical wave trains in the line.

This type of encoder requires that the value of the bit being fed back is determined by the modulo-2 addition of two elements of the shift register, one of which is the last element in the register. The code sequence will be of maximal length if it can be described by an irreducible polynomial. This "m" sequence will then have a length of $2^n - 1$ bits or cycles. In this instance, as approximately 1000 A/J cycles are desired, a 10-stage shift register having a code sequence of 1023 bits is suitable. The polynomial describing this sequence is:

$$f(x) = x^{10} + x^3 + 1$$

The code generator for the matched filter code channel must generate the exact code but inverted in time. This may be accomplished by a feedback shift register whose output is characterized by a polynomial which is the conjugate of the polynomial describing the first code sequence:

$$f^*(x) = x^{10} + x^7 + 1$$

The logic diagrams for both code generators are shown in Fig. 10. The code generator logic design was simplified by utilizing micrologic modules for both flip-flops and gates. Motorola emitter coupled logic modules were selected. These are monolithic silicon epitaxial passivated integrated circuits. The modules are mounted on 37-pin printed circuit cards. This is shown in Fig. 11.

MODULATORS.   Diphase modulation was chosen over RZ or bipolar modulation because of the easing of the low-frequency requirements of the

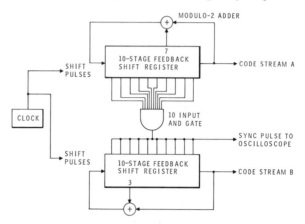

FIG. 10. Code generators: logic diagram variable-code correlator.

delay line. In diphase modulation a 1 is represented by one phase on the carrier and a 0 by a second phase displaced by 180°. In this application the modulating code bit rate equals the carrier frequency. The buffer amplifiers convert the complementary low-level logic inputs M and $\overline{M}$ to the

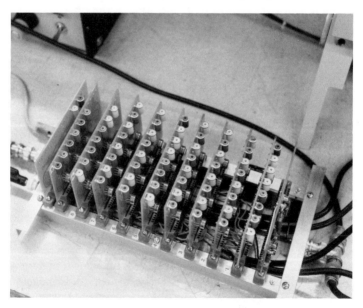

FIG. 11. Code generators: variable-code correlators.

proper level and polarity to drive the series switches. The switches then gate the direct or phase-inverted carrier to the summing circuit. To circumvent phasing problems, both clock pulses and carrier frequency are derived from the same source. An oscillograph of the output of both modulators is shown in Fig. 12.

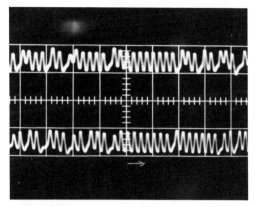

FIG. 12. Modulator output–variable code correlator.

TRANSDUCER DRIVER ELECTRONICS. The driver electronics for each channel consist primarily of untuned amplifiers, 2N2887 power transistor stage, and impedance matching networks. A special trifilar matching transformer is used to match the output of the power amplifier stage to the coaxial cable.

Obtaining a satisfactory impedance match between the power amplifier and the transducer proved to be difficult. The approach chosen was first to measure the input impedance as a function of frequency (5–30 Mc/sec) of the transducer delay line assembly on an automatic impedance plotter. Next, the fixed transducer capacitance was shunted with a suitable inductance resulting in a better match.

PHOTOTUBE AMPLIFIER. A single stage preamplifier was mounted adjacent to the photomultiplier. The main amplifier is a conventional broadband transistorized amplifier similar to that used with the fixed code optical correlator.

Experimental Results

At the present time, experiments have been performed using both compressional and shear mode propagation. Correlation over restricted bandwidths has been achieved in both modes. Present development is directed toward improving the transfer characteristics of the transducer by developing better bonding techniques for the shear mode.

Conclusions

Success with the fixed-code optical matched filter and preliminary results from the variable-code matched filter indicate that the use of photoelastic delay lines shows considerable promise in achieving large time-bandwidth products. Such devices are useful in high data rate communications and pulse compression radars to improve the operating signal-to-noise ratio while retaining time resolution.

A delay line used for these purposes must operate in a shear mode. The principal difficulty in the development of a shear mode optical matched filter is providing efficient coupling between a transducer and the ultrasonic delay line. Substantial progress has been made on this problem.

ACKNOWLEDGMENTS

The author would first like to acknowledge the help of D. H. Cofield in designing the modulator-driver electronics and also in the system checkout. Acknowledgment should also be made to W. R. Sanders for the design of the code generators, to Dr. D. Carter for theoretical support, and to Dr. J. L. Fitch for some of the novel concepts which went into the correlator, as well as to F. M. Lightfoot for constructive guidance.

REFERENCES

1. COKER, E. G., AND L. N. G. FILON, *Photo-Elasticity*, Cambridge University Press, New York, 1957.
2. ARENBURG, D. L., *J. Acoust. Soc. Am.*, *20*, 1 (1948).

CHAPTER 12

APPLICATION OF SEMICONDUCTOR TECHNOLOGY TO COHERENT OPTICAL TRANSDUCERS AND SPATIAL FILTERS

Dean B. Anderson

Autonetics, A Division of North American Aviation, Anaheim, California

Introduction

By far the strongest stimulus to develop an optical information process-ing technique is the potential enormous data-handling capacity. The optical data are distributed in two transverse dimensions and are processed simul-taneously by the integral transform operation of an optical system. Usually, the photographic plate is employed as the input, output, and spatial filter to demonstrate the processing concept. The chemical amplification of pho-tographic development provides high sensitivity, and the small grain size provides for the large spatial bandwidth.

With photography, it is possible to record, store, and observe data in a fast emulsion having a density of approximately 10^6 bits per square centi-meter. By sacrificing four orders of sensitivity, the information density may approach 10^9 bits per square centimeter. Such storage capacity is attractive for computer application. However, because the time required to develop the latent image is 10 sec or greater, access to current data is both dismally slow and cumbersome in comparison to electronic means. In order that optical information processing systems will be competitive with the existing electronic art, it is essential that the optical access time to current data be of the order 10^{-6} sec without compromise of data density. When real time optical processing is achieved, a further requirement arises for an adaptive capability.

Optical computers, sensors, and communication systems require the func-tions of amplification, modulation, and detection to be performed within the signal spatial field. In some cases, the amplification and modulation functions must preserve phase information. In parametric transducers the phase relations of amplification and frequency translation are preserved, whereas most optical transducers inherently include a square law detection process. These operations must be implemented not only for a single-mode channel but for any order and kind of mode compatible with the aperture. Thus, to synthesize a spatial filter rapidly and to change its characteristics with time require an array of independent transducers extending across the aperture field. The spacing between individual transducers must be comparable to their size and be of the order of the radiation wavelength to effectively synthesize the spatial filter and eliminate ambiguities due to grating lobes.

Some recent advances of photolithography for semiconductor technology are delineated herein for single-mode optical waveguide and optical arrays. An approach to implement optical parametric interactions in a back-biased semiconductor junction diode called a varactor is described. A heuristic description of design philosophy is included to show that reasonable expectations now exist to develop and apply coherent optical parametric transducers.

Planar Annular Varactor

A back-biased semiconductor varactor diode functions as the nonlinear capacity in microwave parametric amplifiers. In the optical spectral region where the semiconductor is transparent, the space-charge depletion layer can function as an optical dielectric waveguide. For use as an optical dielectric waveguide structure, junction dimensions must be comparable to the optical wavelength. In a varactor the depletion layer is bounded by p and n regions having free carriers that effectively act as metallic walls so that the depletion layer functions as an optical waveguide. The physical dimensions of the depletion layer are a function of the applied voltage. Voltage dependence of one junction dimension in a simple low-order mode transmission line or resonant cavity provides a simple control to change the velocity of propagation or resonant frequency. To support the contention that low-order mode optical cavities can be fabricated comparable to the wavelength, a brief description of a related technology follows.

To extend the parametric amplifier and parametric harmonic generator arts into the millimeter wave region, Autonetics has evolved a new configuration for the varactor identified by the planar annulus.[1] The planar annular structure is formed in a gallium arsenide semiconductor chip of 0.015 in. diameter and 0.002 in. thickness. The central region of a single planar annular varactor is shown in Fig. 1. The diode itself is embedded underneath a planar annular passivation of silicon monoxide which protects the exposed junction edge. A conductive gold surface is formed on the gallium arsenide chip, both internal and external to the passivation annulus. The outside diameter of the annulus is 11μ, and the inside diameter is 5μ, thus the total path length of conduction through the semiconductor to charge the depletion layer is 3μ. This extremely short path length should be contrasted with a conventional varactor diode which has a path length of the order of 300μ. It is this refinement of junction diode dimensions where the

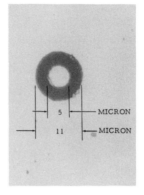

FIG. 1. The planar annulus.

fields are confined to the surface that leads to an increase of the figure of merit by 10 to 50 times and extends the parametric amplifier art through the millimeter wave region.

Figure 2 shows an array of unseparated planar annular varactor diodes.

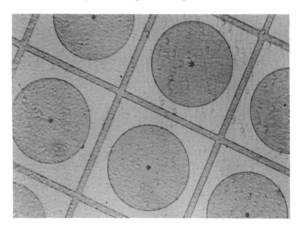

FIG. 2. An array of planar annular varactors prior to separation processing.

The photolithographic patterns contain 625 annuli arranged in a rectangular grid system spread over an area of 2 cm². The grid system is used for alignment purposes so that each step in the process to define the planar annulus matches within a fraction of a micron throughout the entire pattern area. Careful attention to the material properties and processing procedures is required to obtain semiconductor slices with a high degree of uniformity in all 625 varactors.

Optical Waveguide

Investigations of optical transmission lines have concentrated upon modes of propagation having extremely low loss. The glass fiber and the sequence of lenses are two such examples in cylindrical geometry. Recent attention has turned to the plane geometry of the electron injection laser.[2-4]

The dielectric annulus in Fig. 1 has a 0.5×3 micron rectangular cross section. The dielectric annulus is an optical waveguide in which radiation with wavelengths less than 9μ will propagate in the TE_{01} mode and only when the dielectric is transparent. For radiation confinement, the rectangular dielectric must be surrounded by a metal, highly doped semiconductor, or dielectric with a lower index of refraction.

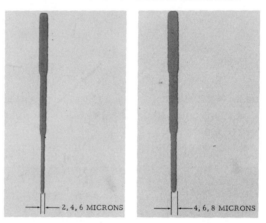

FIG. 3. Optical waveguide: step transformers.

Using advanced photolithography techniques that were developed for the planar annular varactor, a variety of optical waveguide components have been prepared using a 1μ thick, thermally grown silicon dioxide film on a highly doped silicon substrate. Figure 3 illustrates two examples of optical waveguides with successive steps in width which are utilized for impedance transformation. The largest width is 8μ, and the narrowest width is 2μ. Figure 4 illustrates an optical H-plane bend and an offset

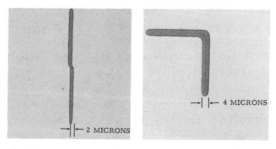

FIG. 4. Optical waveguide: offset susceptance step and H-plane bend.

junction to create an inductive susceptance. An *H*-plane branch directional coupler is illustrated in Fig. 5, together with a wedge pattern used to test the photolithography pattern definition. The original artwork apex is indicated. Inspection of the fine structure of the feathered edges indicates an

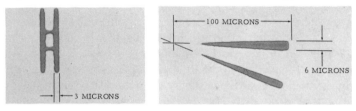

FIG. 5. Optical waveguide: branch coupler and pattern definition wedge.

rms variation of 0.2μ. The etched edges of the optical waveguide visually appear to be ideally normal to the substrate. An example of a hybrid junction known to the microwave art as a "rat-race" is shown in Fig. 6.

These examples of rectangular optical waveguides are of sufficient quality

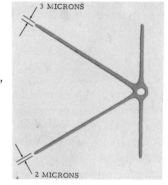

FIG. 6. Optical waveguide: "rat-race" hybrid junction.

to be useful in the near and intermediate regions of the infrared spectrum. They will be useful for coupling together various active optical transducers where it is absolutely essential that a single mode of propagation be realized. The losses of these rectangular dielectric waveguides far exceed those of an optical glass fiber, and therefore they will probably be restricted to interconnections. Inspection of the waveguide examples shows that a smoothing phenomenon occurs removing the sharp corners in the original artwork. This smoothing arises in part from the diffraction phenomena and in part from the chemical etching process. Techniques do exist to eliminate this smoothing phenomena.

Depletion Layer Optical Waveguide

Optical waves may also be bounded by the depletion layer in a semiconductor junction diode.[5-7] Such is the case in the electron injection laser because the recombination process induces a negative impedance layer near the junction interface. In the back-biased varactor diode, the depletion layer, sandwiched between the p and n region, can have a thickness comparable to optical wavelengths. The depletion layer boundary is defined by existent free carrier concentration and the field gradient. The free carriers in both p and n regions give rise to solid-state plasma having a reduced index of refraction which traps light in the depletion layer. The discontinuity in the real part of the index of refraction at the boundary is approximately 1 part in 10^2 to 10^3, depending upon the wavelength.

A linear strip junction diode similar in cross section to the planar annular varactor is illustrated in Fig. 7. The optical waveguide defined by the

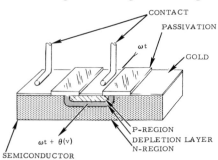

FIG. 7. Transmission optical phase shifter.

depletion layer is folded into a U channel (ridge waveguide). The dimensions of the optical waveguide are defined by the depletion layer thickness, diffusion depth, and the photolithography pattern width. Because the depletion layer thickness and width depend upon the bias voltage, the optical waveguide velocity is related to the applied field. Thus, as a transmission phase shifter, optical frequency modulation can be produced. The modulation bandwidth in such a varactor is limited only by the RC time constant, typically 10^{-9} to 10^{-10} sec.

In another manner the diode junction may be utilized as an optical phase shifter in the reflection mode as illustrated in Fig. 8. For this case, one

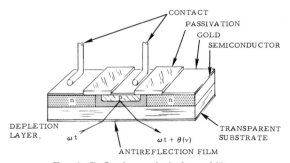

FIG. 8. Reflective optical phase shifter.

surface of the depletion layer discontinuity must be exposed to the light beam, which can be accomplished by confining one depletion layer interface by a transparent insulating substrate. The structure illustrated in Fig. 8 can be fabricated in a new material such as single-crystal silicon grown on an insulating substrate such as sapphire.[8,9] Obviously, an applied back-biased field will cause the depletion layer boundary, as a mirror, to move and shift the reflected phase. Because the discontinuity in the index of refraction is very small, the angle of incidence must be large.

These depletion layer type transmission and reflection phase shifters must be assembled into an array to function as a spatial filter/modulator. The spacing between phase shifters in the array must be comparable to the wavelength to suppress grating lobes in the diffraction pattern. To test the art of photolithography for semiconductors, an array of linear varactor diodes has been developed, as shown in Fig. 9. The array of linear diodes

FIG. 9. A linear array of junctions diodes (SiO₂ and Au over Si).

shows the individual gold contacts between the passivation grating. The diffused junctions under the gold have a geometry identical to that in Fig. 7. Each junction is 4μ wide, and is separated from adjacent junctions by 8μ. This linear varactor diode array configuration as transmission phase shifter is confined to a single dimension, whereas the reflection configuration may be expanded into an array in two dimensions. Another pattern has been investigated which can be repeated in an array of two dimensions and operated in the transmission mode. An island of silicon-on-sapphire is shown in Fig. 10 which has two parallel junctions spaced 6μ apart under the silicon dioxide passivation film.

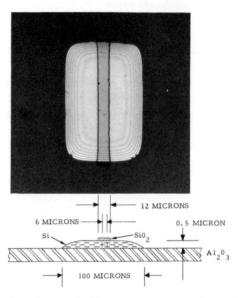

FIG. 10. An island of single-crystal silicon grown on a sapphire substrate with cross section of two junctions.

In the preceding paragraphs, it has been tacitly assumed that the wavelength of the radiation bounded to the depletion layer is between the intrinsic absorption and the lattice absorption or free carrier absorption regions so that the semiconductor appears essentially as a lossless dielectric. Naturally, careful attention must be given to the selection of doping elements and their concentrations which give rise to extrinsic absorption.

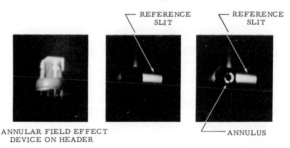

FIG. 11. Demonstration optical absorption modulation (Franz-Keldysh effect).

The semiconductor junction diode geometry may be used as an optical absorption modulator by utilizing the Franz-Keldysh effect.[10] The band-edge absorption may be shifted to a longer wavelength by the application of an electric field. This effect is demonstrated in an annular structure photographed through an image converter. (See Fig. 11.) A portion of the source slit (out of focus) serves as a reference to indicate the modulation depth. Note the interference pattern surrounding the annulus. A part of this pattern is obscured by the contact structure.

Parametric Wave Interaction

The frequency of radiation produced by the stimulated emission process is assigned to the natural frequencies within the atomic structure and may be altered only slightly by changes in the atomic environment (Stark and Zeeman effect). The privilege of selecting a specific frequency from a stimulated emission source is severely limited. Parametric techniques which depend upon optical nonlinear phenomena remove restrictions upon frequency assignment and permit translation of signals across various portions of the spectrum.

Parametric wave interaction involves the mixing of one or more signal frequencies with an intense source called a "pump," producing sum and difference combinations. For an optical parametric transducer, the intense field of a focused laser is used as the pump. Typical resonant circuits for parametric transducers are usually resonant at three or four specific combinations. The signal and idler frequencies need not be confined to atomic resonances, but are rather related to the mode structure within the optical waveguide. Since the resonant frequency of the modes depends upon the dimensions of the depletion layer waveguide, it is easily controlled; and, when the depletion layer is utilized in a parametric amplifier/oscillator as a cavity, it permits their tuning over a wide range.

Parametric interaction depends upon a nonlinear phenomenon usually in the polarization susceptibility tensor.[11] Because the first nonlinear coefficient is of the order of 10^{-9} esu, brute force excitation with fields approaching dielectric strength breakdown has been required to generate the optical second harmonic. The paraelectrics KDP, ADP, and KTN exhibit the largest nonlinear coefficients.[12] Worthwhile second harmonic efficiencies have been achieved only under traveling wave conditions by index matching.[13] Because optical dielectric materials are frequency dispersive, the birefringence in some crystals is used to maximize the wave interaction length by index matching. With two frequencies (pump, degenerate signal or harmonic), index matching is possible; but, with a third frequency necessary for tunability, index matching is impossible. The search for materials with higher nonlinear coefficients continues.

Observations of the first-order nonlinear susceptibility in the band-edge absorption shows the coefficient to be at least two orders larger for gallium arsenide than for KDP.[14] However, the parametric interaction region will be confined to the surface boundary because of the large absorption.[15,16] It is this type of nonlinear interaction which will be utilized in the following discussion.

Conspicuous by its absence in the investigation of optical nonlinearities has been the use of the four-frequency parametric amplifier technology developed in the microwave region. To achieve successful optical nonlinear interaction requires that each frequency generated be properly terminated, as well as selecting the proper impedance level for the desired frequency component. When means exist to control the impedance level of each frequency component, the requirements for a material having a high nonlinear interaction coefficient are reduced. In the conventional optical sense, an impedance level is not recognized except insofar as the index of refraction influences the velocity of propagation of all modes.

To achieve impedance control requires the technology to fabricate single-mode optical transmission lines, with sufficiently precise dimensions to permit control of waveguide cutoff frequency. The use of photolithographic technology and the planar annular varactor configuration represented by the photographs will implement the required control of impedance.

The parametric interaction concept is described by the Manley and Rowe general energy relations.[17] These energy relations show that there are two basic mechanisms which may yield useful gain. These amplification mechanisms are distinguished by the manner in which the signal and pump frequencies are permitted to combine. The operational mode spectrum for either mechanism contains only three frequencies. The mode spectrum containing the difference between signal and pump frequency designates one parametric amplification mechanism which creates an effective negative conductance and results in a signal spectrum inversion. Such a parametric amplifier is typically characterized by a constant gain–bandwidth product and is potentially unstable. The mode spectrum containing the sum of the signal and pump frequency designates a second parametric amplification mechanism which is due to a frequency conversion process by pumping a nonlinear reactance. This frequency conversion does not invert the signal spectrum. Such an amplifier is typically characterized by an unconditionally stable gain which is limited to the ratio of output-to-input frequency.

The distinctive attributes of each mechanism in three-frequency parametric transducers are realized only when each frequency port is properly terminated in a real impedance and the nonlinear element is terminated reactively elsewhere throughout the frequency spectrum. The interaction of the signal frequency with the pump frequency in the nonlinear element produces frequency components as sidebands located symmetrically about the pump frequency and each of its harmonics. A specific operational mode spectrum defines the ports where real terminations must exist. The other spectral components generated in the nonlinear element due to the mixing process must be terminated by either zero or infinite impedance, depending upon the equivalent circuit configuration. Failure to terminate these frequency ports properly outside the operational mode spectrum drastically influences the performance of the transducer. The requirement for proper termination of all frequency ports is difficult or impossible to achieve when the nonlinear reactive element losses become significant.

In the microwave portion of the spectrum, each frequency port usually contains a well-defined single propagation mode defined by boundary conditions. The usual optical propagation path supports a variety of modes, which may exist simultaneously. Three modes may be distinguished by their polarization character, their axial variation, and their transverse spatial variation. In optical parametric transducers, it is mandatory that the signal frequency port and the pump frequency port of the operational mode spectrum be identical in order and kind to fulfill the termination requirements of all other frequency ports in both kind and order. The implications of this latter fact are not generally recognized. The number of frequency ports may be two, three, or more, provided that coupling to the additional ports induces a useful effect, rather than just dispersing the signal and pump energy. The significant features[18] of both amplification processes may simultaneously exist in a parametric transducer, and are designated by the adjective "four-frequency." Such a device has separate ports for each signal sideband surrounding the pump frequency.

Probably the single most important factor supporting the belief that optical parametric amplification is feasible comes from an inspection of the transducer gain K_T expression which contains a factor of the form

$$K_T \propto \frac{\omega_2/\omega_1}{(1 - a_{12} + a_{13})^2}$$

where

$$a_{1m} = \frac{\omega_1 \omega_m C_1{}^2}{4 G_m (G_1 + G_g)}$$

The pumping parameters a_{12} and a_{13} arise from the pumping of the nonlinear reactance. In order that large parametric gains be realized, the denominator must approach zero by the difference in the pumping parameters a_{12} and a_{13}. Inspection of these parameters shows that after the nonlinear coefficient C_1 has been maximized by material selection and pump power, the only way available to alter the pumping parameters to approach the zero condition in the denominator is through changing the conductance loading G_m and G_1 and G_g in each of the frequency ω_m and ω_1 ports. Impedance changes are easily accomplished in the microwave spectrum.

In the optical region the coupling may be changed, but changes of the impedance level are not normally considered because the optical guide is much larger than a wavelength. If the optical guide is operated somewhat near the cutoff frequency, the characteristic impedance of that mode of propagation is changed. Thus, the designer is given another freedom to control the pumping parameter. It is this control by choice of optical guide configuration coupled with the maximization of the interaction parameter which supports the belief that optical parametric amplification will be realized.

A possible configuration of an optical parametric amplifier-oscillator is illustrated in Fig. 12. The microwave planar annular structure deformed

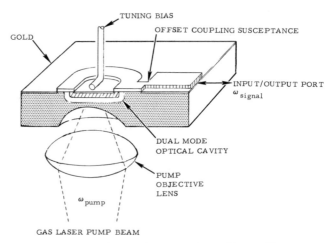

FIG. 12. Proposed optical parametric amplifier-oscillator.

into a rectangular shape is illustrated as the optical cavity resonant at both the signal and idle frequencies. Coupling to the amplifier is provided by the passivation layer in forms of rectangular waveguide. Control of the signal coupling coefficient is provided by the offset designed into the photolithographic pattern. The semiconductor material is gallium arsenide, which has the largest known first-order nonlinear susceptibility. A gas laser is used for pumping because of its spatial mode purity, coherency, and continuous operation. An objective lens is provided for focusing to achieve the high electric field intensity. The base of the semiconductor chip is etched away to form a complementary lens, and to create a plane wavefront in the depletion layer interaction with the signal and idle fields.

Conclusion

Within the constraints of presently known optical nonlinear coefficients, photolithographic, and semiconductor material technologies, it appears that a coherent infrared parametric amplifier is possible. It further appears that functions of oscillation, frequency translation, modulation, and detection can be generated from the amplifier, both singly and in arrays. The potential exists for formation of spatial filters and holograms having arbitrary transfer functions, controlled by an optical information field in real time.

ACKNOWLEDGMENTS

Although the conclusions are those of the author, he is indebted to many colleagues in the Autonetics Research Center for the privilege of presenting, collectively, their achievements. In particular, sincere appreciation is expressed to Mr. R. R. August for the many stimulating discussions of optical semiconductor technology. The photolithography definition and the processing of the planar annular varactor are largely due to Mr. August.

Thanks are also due to Mr. S. G. Plonski for the processing of the optical waveguides; to Mr. R. L. Palmquist for the demonstration of the Franz-Keldysh effect; to J. C. Aukland for discussions on parametric transducers; to D. Medellin for the photomicrography; and to Dr. Arnold Miller, Director of the Physical Research Department, and his associates, Dr. H. M. Manasevit and Mr. P. H. Hagon, for their silicon-on-sapphire materials and devices contributions.

REFERENCES

1. ANDERSON, D. B., R. R. AUGUST, J. C. AUKLAND, R. L. PALMQUIST, AND S. G. PLONSKI, "The Planar Annular Varactor and Its Application to Millimeter Wave Parametric Transducers," presented at 1964 Electron Devices Conference, Washington, D.C., 31 October 1964 (to be published).
2. KAPLAN, R. E., "Optical Waveguide of Macroscopic Dimensions in Single-Mode Operation," *Proc. IEEE*, *51*, 1144 (1963).
3. YARIV, A., AND R. C. C. LEITE, "Dielectric-Waveguide Mode of Light Propagation in *p-n* Junctions," *Appl. Phys. Letters*, *2*, 55 (1963).
4. BOND, W. L., B. G. COHEN, R. C. C. LEITE, AND A. YARIV, "Observation of the Dielectric Waveguide Mode of Light Propagation in *p-n* Junctions," *Appl. Phys. Letters*, *2*, 57 (1963).
5. ASHKIN, A., AND M. GERSHENZON, "Reflection and Guiding of Light on *p-n* Junctions," *J. Appl. Phys.*, *34*, 2116 (1963).
6. LEITE, R. C. C., AND A. YARIV, "On-Mode Confinement in *p-n* Junctions," *Proc. IEEE*, *51*, 1035 (1963).
7. WEISER, K., AND F. STERN, "High-Order Transverse Modes in GaAs Lasers," *Appl. Phys. Letters*, *5*, 115 (1964).
8. MANASEVIT, H. M., AND W. I. SIMPSON, "Single-Crystal Silicon on a Sapphire Substrate," *J. Appl. Phys.*, *35*, 1349 (1964).
9. MANASEVIT, H. M., A. MILLER, F. L. MORRITZ, AND R. L. NOLDER, "Heleroepitaxial Silicon-Aluminum Oxide Interface, I. Experimental Evidence for Epitaxial Relationships of Single Crystal Silicon on Sapphire—An Overview of the Growth Mechanism," *Trans. Met. Soc. AIME*, *233*, 540 (1965).
10. RACETTE, G., "Absorption Edge Modulator Utilizing a *p-n* Junction," *Proc. IEEE*, *52*, 716 (1964).

11. ARMSTRONG, J. A., N. BLOEMBERGEN, J. DUCING, AND P. S. PERSHAN, "Interactions Between Light Waves in a Nonlinear Dielectric," *Phys. Rev., 127*, 1918 (1962).
12. MILLER, R. C., "Optical Second Harmonic Generation in Piezoelectric Crystals," *Appl. Phys. Letters, 5*, 17 (1964).
13. TERHUNE, R. W., "Non-Linear Optics," *solid/state/design*, 38–46 (November 1963).
14. ARMSTRONG, J. A., M. J. NATHAN, AND A. W. SMITH, "Harmonic Generation in GaAs Injection Lasers," *Appl. Phys. Letters, 3*, 68 (1963).
15. DUCING, J., AND N. BLOEMBERGEN, "Observation of Reflected Light Harmonics at the Boundary of Piezoelectric Crystals," *Phys. Rev. Letters, 10*, 474 (1963).
16. BLOEMBERGEN, N., AND P. S. PERSHAN, "Light Waves at the Boundary of Nonlinear Media," *Phys. Rev., 128*, 606 (1962).
17. MANLEY, J. M., AND H. E. ROWE, "Some General Properties of Nonlinear Elements—Part I General Energy Relations," *Proc. IRE, 44*, 9041 (1956).
18. ANDERSON, D. B., AND J. C. AUKLAND, "A General Catalogue of Gain, Bandwidth and Noise Temperature Expressions for Four-Frequency Parametric Devices," *IEEE Trans. Electron Devices, ED-10*, 13 (1963).

CHAPTER 13

PRINCIPLES OF INJECTION LASERS

Robert H. Rediker

Lincoln Laboratory,* Massachusetts Institute of Technology, Lexington, Massachusetts

Introduction

The semiconductor diode laser has the advantages over the gas and paramagnetic-ion lasers that its size is small, that it converts electric power directly into coherent light, and that its output can be modulated by simply modulating the diode current. The diode laser also has advantages when compared to diodes which emit incoherent radiation. The radiation emitted by the laser is directional while incoherent radiation is emitted isotropically. While the directionality is of itself important, much of the isotropic incoherent radiation is trapped inside the high-dielectric-constant (~ 11) semiconductor unless the surfaces are very carefully shaped, while the directional laser beam is normal to the surface and therefore does not suffer the difficulties of total internal reflection. Therefore the external power efficiency (ratio of light power emitted to power input) of a laser is usually significantly larger than that of a diode emitting incoherent radiation. The spectral width of the laser radiation is very much narrower than that of the incoherent diode. In addition, if the application requires that the light be modulated at the highest possible frequency or that the light pulse have the shortest rise time, laser radiation, which is associated with the stimulated lifetime of the carriers, is preferable to the incoherent radiation which is limited by the larger spontaneous lifetime of the carriers.

Figure 1 shows an artist's sketch of a GaAs diode laser in a pill-type package. Such a laser when operated at 4 to 20°K has emitted up to 6 W of continuous coherent radiation at close to 50 per cent power efficiency[1] and the radiation has been modulated[2] at frequencies up to 4 Gc. At room temperature such a laser can be used on a pulse basis and 20 W of coherent

*Operated with support from the U.S. Air Force.

radiation can be emitted in 50 nsec pulses.[3] When operated continuously at currents not too high above threshold, GaAs lasers can operate stably in one mode of the Fabry-Perot cavity formed by the cleaved face, shown in Fig. 1, and the parallel face on the opposite end of laser. The width of such

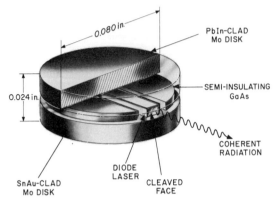

FIG. 1. An artist's sketch of a GaAs diode laser in a pill-type package. The diode laser is a rectangular parallelepiped whose dimensions are typically 0.010 in. × 0.030 in. × 0.003 in. thick.

a cavity mode has been measured[4] to be less than 50 Mc/sec, or less than 1.5 parts in 10^7 of the output frequency.

The use of semiconductor lasers in room temperature computers may not be feasible today because of the very large threshold current densities required at this temperature to obtain laser action. The lowest threshold current density reported[5] at the time of this writing was 40,000 A/cm². Thus, continuous operation of a diode laser has not been achieved at room temperature. Computer operation at 77°K for which threshold current densities are about 2000 A/cm² is a question computer engineers will have to answer when they compare the advantages of electro-optical processing of information using diode lasers with all the inherent disadvantages (some of which are psychological) of a low temperature computer. In any case, the injection laser is but two years old, and advances may occur which will make the laser a practical computer component.

In this paper the principles of laser action will be described. The following questions will be answered: What is the mechanism by which the output radiation is produced by the input current? Where in the semiconductor is the radiation produced? How does the coherent output radiation propagate? In conclusion some of the properties of injection lasers will be described.

The Radiative Transition

The mechanism by which radiation is produced is the same whether or not the output radiation is coherent. The *sine qua non* of the injection laser is that the radiative process be an efficient one. To this time with the exception of the controversial SiC,[6,7] laser action has only been reported for *p-n* junctions in direct gap semiconductors, semiconductors in which the crystal momentum **k** is the same at the bottom of the conduction band and at the top of the valence band. The transition probability for radiative recombination is at least three orders of magnitude larger for the direct transition than it is for the indirect transitions which occur in indirect gap semiconductors such as Ge, Si, GaP, and SiC.

Possible radiative transitions associated with laser action in semiconductors are shown in Fig. 2. In the upper left-hand corner of the figure is

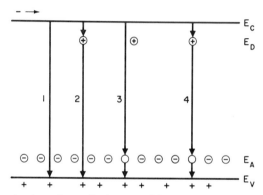

Fig. 2. Four mechanisms for radiative transitions: 1, conduction to valence band; 2, donor to valence band; 3, conduction band to acceptor; 4, donor to acceptor.

shown an electron which has been injected into *p*-type material. (The injection of an electron into *p*-type material is for illustrative purposes only.) The *p*-type material is compensated, as are almost all real semiconductors, there being some donors present as well as the predominant acceptors. The four mechanisms by which the injected electron can recombine with a hole in the valence band and emit the observed infrared radiation are: 1, direct radiative recombination from the conduction band to the valence band; 2, recombination via a donor level, the electron is first captured by one of the compensating donor levels and then makes a radiative transition to the valence band; 3, recombination via an acceptor level, the electron makes a radiative transition to an acceptor level and then recombines with a hole in the valence band; 4, recombination via both a donor and an acceptor level in which the radiative transition is from donor level to acceptor level. In addition, in each of these four mechanisms there may be the intermediate step of exciton formation. Laser action has been observed over a large range of impurity concentrations. At higher concentrations where the impurity levels form impurity bands which merge into the conduction or valence band and produce band tailing, it may be academic to differentiate between the four mechanisms.

Diode lasers in which the radiation is believed due to band-to-band transitions (mechanism 1) have been reported in lightly doped ($N_d \sim 10^{16}$ cm^{-3}) GaAs,[8] in InAs,[9] and in InSb.[10] In all these cases the intermediate step of exciton formation could not be excluded. In most lasers of GaAs and InAs, however, the radiation is believed to stem from transitions between the conduction band and an acceptor (zinc) level (mechanism 3). Again, exciton formation cannot be excluded. In the "band-to-band" GaAs lasers, the energy of the stimulated emission is 1.505 eV (77°K), and this emission is believed to be associated with spontaneous emission whose spectrum can be correlated with the absorption edge by the principle of detailed balance.[11] In the "conduction band-to-acceptor" GaAs lasers the energy of the stimulated emission is about 0.020 eV smaller. Similarly the photon energy associated with the "band-to-band" laser radiation in InAs lasers is 0.020 eV larger than the energy associated with the "band-to-acceptor" laser radiation.[9] Thus the mechanism of the radiative transition is not unique; and even in the same laser diode, it may be possible by changing the junction current to change the recombination mechanism. The mechanisms should be studied for themselves and also with the hope that further understanding may allow us to produce more useful lasers, i.e., lasers with lower threshold currents at the higher temperatures.

Population Inversion

In Fig. 3a is shown an equilibrium band diagram of a p-n junction in which both p and n regions have been assumed to be degenerate, as

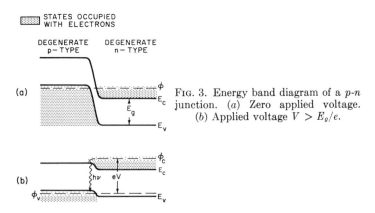

FIG. 3. Energy band diagram of a p-n junction. (a) Zero applied voltage. (b) Applied voltage $V > E_g/e$.

illustrated by the Fermi level ϕ, being below the top of valence band in the p region and above bottom of the conduction band in the n region. By applying a forward bias V across the junction, a region of population inversion is produced at the junction as illustrated in Fig. 3b. In the inversion region more quanta are emitted than are absorbed in radiative transitions between conduction and valence bands, and this region presents a negative conductivity to the electromagnetic wave.

In the above discussion the recombination mechanism has been assumed to be a band-to-band transition, but a similar argument would hold for the other transitions.

Guided Mode Laser Action

The laser action occurs in even TE or TM modes guided along the plane of population inversion as shown in the idealized model of Fig. 4. Energy

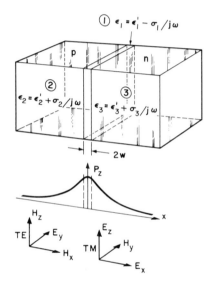

FIG. 4. Laser diode showing region of inverted population at junction labeled (1) and lossy dielectric regions on either side labeled (2) and (3). Sketch of x dependence of symmetrical electromagnetic field is also shown. Field components of TE and TM modes are indicated for propagation in z direction between reflecting faces of Fabry-Perot type cavity.

is fed into the modes in the inverted population region labeled 1 which is taken to be of width $2w$ and is assumed to be characterized by a constant negative conductivity of magnitude σ_1. Energy is lost by the modes in the p and n regions (labeled 2 and 3) on either side of the junction. These regions are characterized by constant positive conductivities σ_2 and σ_3. The electromagnetic problem involves determining by matching boundary conditions the exact x dependence of the mode and in this way ascertaining how far into lossy regions 2 and 3 the modes extend and hence how much energy is taken from the mode in these regions. The results of McWhorter[12]

FIG. 5. Photograph of GaAs laser emitting in three filaments. (Courtesy A. E. Michel.)

show that the extent to which the mode penetrates the lossy regions depends on the difference in the value of the real part of the dielectric constant, ϵ', in region 1 and its value in regions 2 and 3.

As the diode current is increased, the population inversion in region 1 is increased and more energy is fed into the mode. When this energy be-

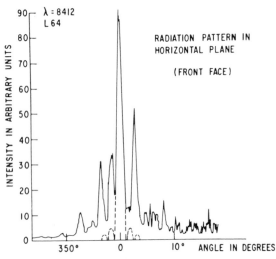

FIG. 6. Radiation pattern in plane of junction of GaAs diode laser at 77°K. (After G. E. Fenner and J. D. Kingsley, Reference 13.)

comes larger than the energy absorbed from the mode in regions 2 and 3, the wave grows in amplitude as it propagates in the z direction between the reflecting surfaces shown shaded in Fig. 4. When the product of the bulk amplification per pass and the reflection coefficient becomes larger than unity, laser oscillations are observed.

Generally the guided TE or TM modes propagate in filaments along the junction plane rather than uniformly along the plane as suggested by Fig. 4. Figure 5 is a photograph of a GaAs laser that is radiating from three filaments. This photograph was obtained using an image converter tube focused on one of the faces defining the Fabry-Perot cavity. The cross-sectional dimensions of the filaments (the area of the spots in Fig. 5) have been determined from radiation patterns. Typical radiation patterns for GaAs lasers are complex and show that the radiation is usually emitted in many beams.[13] A radiation pattern in the plane parallel to the junction is shown in Fig. 6 and the corresponding radiation pattern in the plane perpendicular to the junction in Fig. 7. Simpler patterns have been obtained

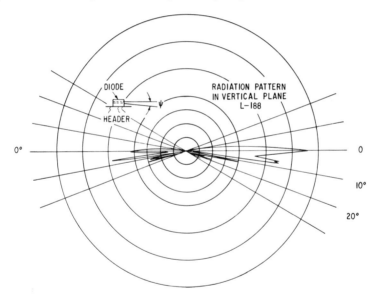

FIG. 7. Radiation pattern in a plane perpendicular to junction of GaAs diode laser at 77°K. (After G. E. Fenner and J. D. Kingsley, Reference 13.)

and beam angles as narrow as 1 deg in the plane of the junction and 10 deg in the perpendicular direction have been reported. Such beam angles correspond (using $d \approx \lambda/\theta$) to a coherently emitting filament of 50μ in the plane of the junction and of 5μ in the plane perpendicular to the junction. The explanation of this filamentary behavior is not completely clear. Similar effects are observed in optically pumped solid-state lasers.

Optical inhomogeneities or variations in current density are possible explanations.

Opto-Electronic Properties of Injection Lasers

To illustrate the opto-electronic properties of injection lasers, results obtained by Melngailis and collaborators[14,15] for InAs lasers will be presented. These results are similar to results for all diode lasers of III-V compounds which have a Fabry-Perot cavity, as illustrated in Fig. 1, formed by one set of faces perpendicular to the junction plane. The infrared emission from one of these faces is plotted as a function of diode current in Fig. 8. As shown in the figure, at 77°K the emitted radiation

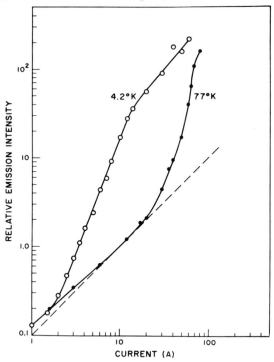

FIG. 8. Infrared emission from cleaved surface of InAs diode at 77°K and at 4.2°K as a function of the amplitude of 0.4-μsec-duration current pulses. (After I. Melngailis, Reference 14.)

varied close to linearly with current until the current reached a threshold value above which the intensity increased radically. At 4.2°K the threshold for stimulated emission is lowered considerably. Well above threshold the light output again becomes linear with current indicating that a limiting quantum efficiency has set in. The spectra of the emission below and above the threshold for laser action are illustrated in Fig. 9. The laser spectrum shows mode structure which becomes more pronounced at higher currents. The inset in the figure shows the laser spectra in more detail for two currents. The 35 Å line width measured for the individual modes corresponds to the resolution of the spectrometer used. The actual line width

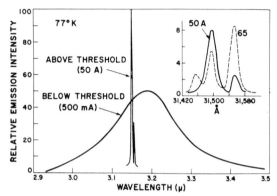

FIG. 9. Spectra of infrared emission from cleaved surface of InAs diode at 77°K for currents below and above threshold. The spontaneous emission spectra are not drawn to the same intensity scale as the stimulated emission spectra. In the inset the stimulated emission spectra at 50 and 65 A are shown on an expanded wavelength scale. (After I. Melngailis, Reference 14.)

is much narrower—as mentioned in the introduction, line widths about 1.5 parts in 10^7 of the output wavelength have been measured and these measurements have just yielded an upper bound!

Figure 10 illustrates magnetic tuning of an InAs diode laser and also illustrates well the mode structure of the laser output spectrum. For laser action to occur there must be an integral number of half-wavelengths m between the reflecting faces of the Fabry-Perot cavity, and the adjacent modes have values of m differing by one. Magnetic tuning is more effective for lasers which operate farther into the infrared. Thus the magnetic tuning of an InAs laser, which is illustrated, is larger than that of a GaAs laser, which radiates at 0.84μ, but smaller than that of an InSb laser which radiates at 5.2μ. (The InAs laser radiates at 3.15μ as illustrated in Fig. 9.) In addition to magnetic tuning, one can tune the output wavelength of a semiconductor laser with temperature or with pressure.

The magnetic field, temperature, or pressure affects the refractive index n of the semiconductor and thus changes the effective length nL of the cavity. The cavity mode itself can be excited only if its wavelength is close to that of the peak of the spontaneous emission. For all the transitions shown in Fig. 2 (if the pertinent impurity levels are relatively shallow as they have been in all lasers so far) the spontaneous line will change as the band gap changes. The temperature, magnetic field, or pressure changes have a larger effect on the band gap than on the cavity modes. Thus as shown in

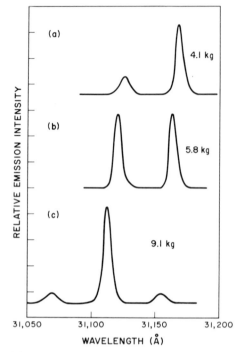

FIG. 10. Spectra of laser emission from cleaved surface of InAs diode at 4.2°K for three different values of magnetic field. (After I. Melngailis and R. H. Rediker, Reference 15.)

Fig. 10, there are small changes in the wavelength of the excited cavity modes as well as switching of these modes as the spontaneous line "moves through" and excites new cavity modes.

New Developments

I have described in this paper the semiconductor junction laser. Very recently, diode lasers of InSb have been reported[16] in which the coherent radiation emanates from the bulk of the semiconductor in which an electron-hole plasma has been established. The possibility of obtaining relatively large coherently emitting areas implies smaller beam angles $(\theta \approx \lambda/d)$. The large radiating volume is better suited for light amplification, higher output power may be attainable and because the population is inverted over a large volume, threshold current densities may be lower. Also very recently, laser action has been reported[17-19] when electron-hole pairs were generated by means of a beam of high-energy electrons.

These developments plus improvements in the junction laser may eliminate some of the many reservations computer engineers now have when considering the injection laser as a computer component. The injection laser field is but two years old, and further new developments and improvements may show the way to practical computer components which can compete favorably in performance and price with the more conventional components now in use.

REFERENCES

1. QUIST, T. M., private communication.
2. GOLDSTEIN, B. S., AND J. D. WELCH, private communication.
3. GALLAGHER, C. C., P. C. TANDY, B. S. GOLDSTEIN, AND J. D. WELCH, *Proc. IEEE*, *52*, 717 (1964).
4. ARMSTRONG, J. A., AND A. W. SMITH, *Appl. Phys. Letters*, *4*, 196 (1964).
5. DOUSMANIS, G. C., H. NELSON, AND D. L. STAEBLER, *Appl. Phys. Letters*, *5*, 174 (1964).
6. GRIFFITHS, L. B., A. I. MLAVSKY, G. RUPPRECHT, A. J. ROSENBERG, P. H. SMAKULA, AND M. A. WRIGHT, *Proc. IEEE*, *51*, 1374 (1963).
7. HALL, R. N., *Proc. IEEE*, *52*, 91 (1964).
8. WILSON, D. K., *Appl. Phys. Letters*, *3*, 127 (1963).
9. MELNGAILIS, I., *Symp. Radiative Recombination in Semiconductors*, Paris, 27–28 July 1964.
10. PHELAN, R. J., JR., A. R. CALAWA, R. H. REDIKER, R. J. KEYES, AND B. LAX, *Appl. Phys. Letters*, *3*, 143 (1963).
11. SARACE, J. C., R. H. KAISER, J. M. WHELAN, AND R. C. C. LEITE, *Phys. Rev.*, *137*, A623 (1965).
12. McWHORTER, A. L., *Solid-State Electron.*, *6*, 417 (1963).
13. FENNER, G. E., AND J. D. KINGSLEY, *J. Appl. Phys.*, *34*, 3204 (1963).
14. MELNGAILIS, I., *Appl. Phys. Letters*, *2*, 176 (1963).
15. MELNGAILIS, I., AND R. H. REDIKER, *Appl. Phys. Letters*, *2*, 202 (1963).
16. MELNGAILIS, I., R. J. PHELAN, JR., AND R. H. REDIKER, *Appl. Phys. Letters*, *5*, 89 (1964).
17. BENOÎT À LA GUILLAUME, C., AND J. M. DEBEVER, *Symp. Radiative Recombination in Semiconductors*, Paris, 27–28 July 1964.
18. HURWITZ, C. E., AND R. J. KEYES, *Appl. Phys. Letters*, *5*, 139 (1964).
19. BENOÎT À LA GUILLAUME, C., AND J. M. DEBEVER, *Compt. Rend.*, *259*, 2200 (1964).

CHAPTER 14

ON ALL-OPTICAL COMPUTER TECHNIQUES

Oskar A. Reimann

Information Processing Branch, RADC, Rome, New York

High-speed electronic computer circuitry is becoming interconnection limited. The reactance associated with the mounting and interconnections of the devices, rather than the response of the active components, is becoming the main factor limiting the speed of operation of the circuits.[1] A possible approach to computer development that might circumvent interconnection limitations is the use of optical digital devices rather than electronic devices as active components. This paper reviews some of the research that is being carried out to develop techniques that may lead to an all-optical computer.

Although it is premature to give conclusive results on the basis of research conducted so far, excluding the area of optical image processing (which is a separate subject), several points can be mentioned:

1. In optical transmission lines, the wavelength of the signals will be much shorter than any of the circuit dimensions; therefore, one could eliminate, for example, all the reactive effects in the interconnections. One might still have to be content with mismatched transmission lines, but this is not a major problem since the decay times are very short.

2. The possibility of signal connection between parts of the system without electrical or actual physical contacts are very attractive for integrated circuit techniques. With optical signals, a totally new approach to the interconnection of digital devices is possible.

3. Laser devices show promise of very fast switching speeds. These fast-switching laser devices together with optical interconnections could provide digital circuits that are faster than electronic circuits.

4. Finally, new circuit techniques may give additional degrees of freedom to the computer engineer and may increase the computing power of future information processing systems.

"All-Optical" and Opto-Electronic Approaches

At this point, distinction should be made between the "all-optical" laser digital devices and opto-electronic circuits. Laser digital devices are devices whose operation is based on the interaction of optical signals with laser materials. Only optical signals are used as the inputs and the outputs of these devices. Therefore, laser digital circuits should be capable of taking full advantage of the very fast switching speed of laser materials in response to intense optical signals.

Opto-electronic circuits, on the other hand, require conversions between optical and electrical energies. Such circuits are already established in the digital technology for specific applications. A typical example is the case where the transfer of signals without mechanical connection or with perfect electrical isolation is of great importance. Opto-electronic digital circuits using electroluminescent materials and photoconductors have a long history in their application to digital logic. Present components provide a minimum switching time of approximately 50 msec, with a power consumption (per element) of approximately 10^{-5} W. This type of device is very slow and therefore has only a limited application in digital logic. It is useful in image processing and character recognition. With the advent of the laser, efficient light-emitting diodes, and high-speed photodetectors, interest in the application of higher speed opto-electronic circuits to digital logic has increased. The work of Biard[2] in applying opto-electronic circuits to integrated electronics is representative of this type of an effort. In general, however, opto-electronic circuits cannot compete in performance with their electronic counterparts. The high losses associated with converting the signal between optical and electrical energies require a high-gain electronic amplification which slows down the operation of these circuits. The above situation could be changed if the amplification were provided by a laser amplifier. Therefore, we may in the future expect to see opto-electronic circuits which will combine laser amplifiers with other high-speed semiconductor devices.

Several years ago RADC undertook an investigation of various optical effects that would lead to development of an optical digital device for use in an all-optical computer. The concept of an all-optical computer is a novel and "far out" idea. The motivation for research in the area of all-optical devices, as mentioned previously, was to circumvent some of the problems that are presently being encountered in computer engineering and to start a long-range program for the development of an optical computer. Although the idea of an optical computer is very ambitious, the payoff for success would be very great.

As part of this investigation, American Optical Company undertook to explore for RADC* the use of optical fibers for performing digital functions.

* This work was done under Contract AF30(602)-2440.

Initial investigations were concerned with more or less classical optical effects, among them the Faraday and Kerr effects. With the development of the glass-fiber laser by Elias Snitzer of American Optical Company, research work turned to the exploration of the use of laser fibers for performing digital functions. At approximately the same time, the neuristor laser computer was conceived at RCA, which was awarded a contract to study the feasibility of a laser computer employing neuristor laser components.*

Glass-Fiber Laser

The attempt to use the Faraday or Kerr effect to make glass-fiber light switches gave marginal results.[3] Both effects are unattractive for computer application because they involve a high magnetic or electric field. Also, both effects require optical to electrical transducing. The experimental results also showed that the Faraday effect in glass is small at room temperature. The material with the greatest known Kerr constant is a liquid, which in its own right is not very appealing for computer application. Subsequently, the laser quenching effect was first demonstrated by C. J. Koester with neodymium-doped glass lasers.[3] This experimental result was significant, because it demonstrated that one laser signal can affect the output of another laser. In the quenching effect, the quenching beam robs energy from the quenched laser and thus is amplified, while the population inversion in the quenched laser drops below that necessary for laser oscillation. An analysis of the laser quenching effect was made and it was concluded that, in principle, the effect can be fast and exhibit gain.[4] The quenching effect was also demonstrated by Fowler of IBM[5] using GaAs lasers, and, more recently, efficient GaAs laser quenching has been achieved at RCA Laboratories with a dual laser oscillator. In this last device, the laser oscillator and the quenching oscillator are combined in the same GaAs wafer.[6]

The work at American Optical Company also included a study of pulse propagation in fiber lasers and of resonant coupling between two fiber lasers in the same cladding.† Amplification of low-level signal pulses on the order of 10^4 were exhibited in a one-meter fiber laser. High input signals exhibited saturated amplification in which the first pulse is amplified more than the second and the first pulse approaches a steady-state pulse with varying input signals. The results of the fiber-laser-coupling experiments showed that two fiber lasers with a diameter of 5μ and length of 10 cm in the same cladding and separated by approximately 5μ exhibited very strong coupling (time coincidence). On the other hand, similar fibers but with 11μ separation exhibited no coupling. These results are described in more

---

* This work was done under Contract AF30(602)-2761.
† This work was done under Contract AF30(602)-2829.

detail in RADC-TDR-64-79 and in the paper "Some Laser Effects Potentially Useful in Optical Logic" by C. J. Koester and C. H. Swope.[7]

The Neuristor Laser Computer

The neuristor laser computer, conceived at RCA, is an "all-optical" computer in which all information and control signals are in the form of optical energy. Fiber-optic elements with appropriate concentrations of active emissive ions and passive absorptive ions are the basic components of this system. The computer is powered by being in a continuous light environment that provides a constant pump power for maintaining an inverted population of the emissive ions. Among the potentially attractive features of such a system are the freedom from power-supply connections for individual circuits, the possibility of transmission of signals without actual connections between certain locations, and a promise of high-speed operation.

A theoretical study of the neuristor concept in form of Fiberglas lasers concluded that the fundamental requirements of a neuristor line could, at least in principle, be met with lasers. A laser traveling-wave transmission line that has a linear scattering-loss mechanism possesses inherent stability, as evidenced by the existence of steady-state pulses that propagate down the line with a constant velocity. If the line includes saturable absorber ions (in addition to the emissive ions) and linear losses, a line that propagates steady-state pulses can be obtained by a proper choice of system parameters. Such a line may possess a stimulation threshold such that weak incident pulses are attenuated while strong incident pulses develop into steady-state pulses characteristic only of the line itself.[12] Following the steady-state pulse, the laser neuristor line has a refractory period. The duration of this period (length of the refractory region) depends directly on the recovery times of the ions of the emitter and the saturable absorber. In view of present emphasis on saturable absorber material for Q-switched lasers,[8-10] it is reasonable to assume that a saturable absorber will be developed for the neodymium glass laser.

The major limitation of the laser neuristor is the pump power requirement. It appears that the shortest refractory (or recovery) time that may be expected within the foreseeable future is on the order of 1 to 100 μsec. Thus, optically pumped lasers could be used for digital operations only at kilocycle repetition rates and only in form of resonators and not as continuous transmissions lines. Open-loop or closed-loop Fiberglas lasers could form such laser-resonator digital devices. It also appears that it should be more efficient to use these laser resonators in a bistable or monostable circuit mode of operation rather than in the form of neuristor transmission lines.

The main result of the laser neuristor feasibility study was the conclusion that lasers are capable of satisfying all the requirements for digital devices. It was shown that, in addition to the neuristor-type logic, lasers in form of resonators and amplifiers can have input-output characteristics that resemble those of conventional logic circuits, such as gates or flip-flops. The concept of saturable optical absorber material that can provide a threshold function for laser digital devices was suggested early in the program.[11] Saturable absorption at optical frequency was first demonstrated with an unpumped ruby crystal.[12] Spectroscopic tests of saturable absorber materials were then expanded to the studies of solutions of phthalocyanine. Operation of a laser resonator with a saturable absorber as a Q switch had been predicted by W. F. Kosonocky.[11] This idea has been verified experimentally and is presented by him in more detail in "Laser Digital Devices."[6]

A significant contribution of the neuristor laser feasibility study to the laser field is Wittke's analysis of pulse propagation in a laser transmission line without[13] and with[12] a saturable absorber material. This was the first correct formulation of signal-pulse shaping by an infinitely long laser amplifier. The surprising result of this study is that the steady-state pulse developed by such an amplifier tends to leave behind a transparent rather than an absorptive line. Therefore this pulse is a "90° pulse" rather than the "180° pulse" initially expected.

The duration of the steady-state pulse is a function only of the loss to gain ratio and, for a large range of this ratio, the pulse duration T is on the order of $(\pi \Delta \nu)^{-1}$ where $\Delta \nu$ is the homogeneously broadened line width in cps. Thus, if a high-gain laser amplifier is used for pulse forming in laser digital circuits, most laser materials at room temperature would have to be operated with pulses on the order of 10^{-11} sec in duration to exhibit a steady-state pulse.

Once the basic limitation of low repetition rates with optically pumped lasers was realized, interest shifted toward semiconductor lasers as components for laser digital devices. The basic performance characteristics of laser digital devices have been considered and examples presented to show how semiconductor laser oscillators and amplifiers could be used as laser digital devices.[6] The operation of a ruby laser as a monostable (i.e., triggerable) oscillator was demonstrated to illustrate the possibility of laser digital devices using optical saturable absorbers.[6]

Conclusions

In view of the progress at RCA, and the work at IBM, as can be inferred from recent publications,[14–16] we may in the near future expect to see experimental semiconductor laser digital devices. The basic techniques employing fiber optics, Fiberglas lasers, and fiber laser amplifiers can also be expected to be used in laser digital devices or opto-electronic devices.

REFERENCES

1. AMODEI, J. J., "High Speed Address and Computers Using Transistors and Tunnel Diodes," *IEEE Trans. Electron. Computers*, 197 (2 October 1964).
2. *Opto-Electronic Functional Electronic Blocks*, Interim Engineering Report No. 03-64-53, Contract No. AF33(657)-11552, BPS No: 4-6799-415910, Texas Instruments Corp., 4 August 1964.
   Opto-Electronic Functional Electronic Blocks, Interim Engineering Report No. 03-64-56, Contract No. AF33(657)-11552, BPS No: 4-6733-415310, Texas Instruments Corp., 27 August 1964.
3. *Study of Optical Fiber Techniques for Data Processing*, RADC-TDR-62-478, AD 299 007, Final Report on Contract AF30(602)-2440, prepared by C. J. Koester, American Optical Co., August 1962.
4. *Development of Glass Fiber Lasers*, RADC-TDR-64-79, Final Report on Contract AF30(602)-2829, prepared by C. J. Koester, American Optical Co., May 1964.
5. FOWLER, A. B., "Quenching of Gallium-Arsenide Injection Lasers," *Appl. Phys. Letters*, *3*, No. 1, 1 (1 July 1963).
6. KOSONOCKY, W. F., "Laser Digital Devices," Chapter 16, this volume.
7. C. J. KOESTER, AND C. H. SWOPE, "Some Laser Effects Potentially Useful in Optical Logic," Chapter 15, this volume.
8. SOROKIN, P. P., J. J. LAZZI, J. R. LANKARD, AND G. D. PETTIT, "Ruby Laser Q-Switching Elements Using Phthalocyanine Molecules in Solution," *IBM J. Res. Develop.*, *8*, No. 2, 182 (April 1964).
9. STARK, P. E., L. A. CROSS, AND J. F. HOBART, *Saturable Filter Investigation*, Semi-Annual Tech Report (July 63–Dec. 63), NOnr-4125(00), NRO 15-702, ARPA Order No. 306-62, Program Code No. 3730, Lear Seigler, Inc., Laser System Center, 19 February 1964.
10. BRET, G., AND F. GIRES, "Giant—Pulse Laser and Light Amplifier, Using Variable Transmission Co-efficient Glasses as Light Switches," *Appl. Phys. Letters*, *4*, No. 10, 175 (15 May 1964).
11. KOSONOCKY, W. F., "Feasibility of Neuristor Laser Computers," *Optical Processing of Information*, Donald K. Pollock, Charles J. Koester, and James T. Tippett, Eds., Spartan Books, Inc., Baltimore, Md., 1963, p. 255.
12. *Neuristor Logic Technology*, RADC-TDR-64-123, Final Report Prepared under Contract AF30-(602)-2761 by Applied Research Dept., Defense Electronic Products, RCA, Camden, N.J., June 1964.
13. WITTKE, J. P., AND P. J. WARTER, "Pulse Propagation in Laser Amplifier," *J. Appl. Phys.*, *35*, No. 6, 1668–1672 (June 1964).
14. NATHAN, M. I., J. C. MARINACE, R. F. RUTZ, A. E. MICHEL, AND G. J. LASHER, "A GaAs Injection Laser with Novel Mode Control and Switching Properties," *Solid State Device Conference*, Boulder, Colo., July 1964.
15. LASHER, G. J., AND A. B. FOWLER, "Mutually Quenched Injection Lasers as Bi-Stable Devices," *IBM J. Res. Develop.*, *8*, No. 4 (September 1964).
16. KELLY, C. E., "Interactions Between Closely Coupled GaAs Injection Lasers," *Electron Devices Meeting*, Washington, D.C., 29–31 October 1964.

CHAPTER 15

SOME LASER EFFECTS POTENTIALLY USEFUL IN OPTICAL LOGIC FUNCTIONS *

Charles J. Koester and C. Hermas Swope

Research Division, American Optical Company, Southbridge, Massachusetts

Introduction

It is useful to distinguish the three broad categories which have emerged in the field of optical processing of information. First, there is the coherent optical processing technique, having its origins in the spatial filtering studies of Maréchal[1] and of O'Neill.[2] This technology has reached a certain maturity in the sense of being an already useful method of processing data. The second category includes all the electro-optical effects and devices which are useful in logic, memory, or input-output. This is also a field in which practical use has already been made of certain principles and techniques.[3]

The third category is all-optical processing, in which the signals are carried by light and logic is performed by interaction between light beams. The status of this category must be described as exploratory. The current activity is directed primarily toward uncovering effects which show promise in optical logic or storage.

In this paper several optical interaction effects employing lasers are discussed. The emphasis is on fiber lasers, because of the possibilities of compactness and relatively low pumping power.

Saturated Amplification in a Fiber Laser

In a traveling-wave laser amplifier a saturation effect is expected when the input signal is sufficiently intense to reduce the inversion measurably.

* This work was supported by the U.S. Air Force Systems Command, Rome Air Development Center.

254   C. J. Koester and C. Hermas Swope

There are several ways in which this effect can be manifested. Under steady-state conditions the high-signal gain has been shown to be less than the low-signal gain.[4] With a pulse input signal, pulse sharpening is predicted[4,5] and observed[6] under certain conditions. On the other hand, using a density matrix approach, Wittke and Warter[7] have shown that all input pulses, as they propagate in a traveling-wave laser, approach a steady-state pulse which has a unique peak intensity and shape. Finally, with a series of input pulses, the first of which contains sufficient energy to reduce the inversion, the succeeding pulses should receive less amplification than the first. The latter effect has been used in this study.

Fiber lasers of a nominal 1-meter length, 10μ core diameter were wound into a helical form and pumped by means of a straight flash tube (G.E. FT 91/L). As in an earlier study of linear amplification,[8] the ends were beveled to prevent feedback and the resulting oscillation. The signal source was a Nd^{3+} doped glass laser rod with the reproducible damped oscillation output shown in Fig. 1, lower trace. For high input signal levels, a lens was

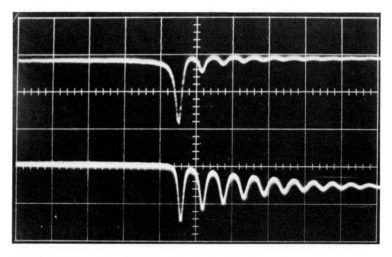

FIG. 1. Saturated amplification in a fiber laser. Length 123 cm; core diameter 9.4μ; barium crown with 2.55 wt per cent Nd_2O_3; cladding glass, soda lime. Input end of fiber beveled at 5°, output end at 20°. Sweep speed: 5 μsec per cm. Upper trace: output of fiber laser. Lower trace: monitor of input signal. Time runs left to right.

used to concentrate the output of the signal rod onto the entrance end of the fiber laser. For lower signal inputs, the lens was removed and attenuating filters were inserted as required.

The measurement consisted of recording the signal output of the fiber laser when pumped and when unpumped. The ratio of signal levels is the gross gain,

$$G_0 = \exp\left[\int_0^l \beta(x, t)\, dx\right] \qquad (1)$$

where β is the gain per unit length due to the active ions at point x at time t, and l is the pumped length of the fiber. The net gain is somewhat less due to scattering and absorption losses within the fiber laser.[8] Figure 1, upper trace, shows the largest saturation effect observed in these experiments in a 1-meter long fiber laser.

Figure 2 summarizes the data obtained. At low input signal the measured

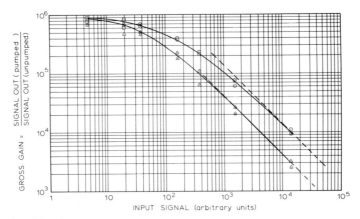

FIG. 2. Amplification as a function of input signal. Same fiber as described in Fig. 1. Approximate conversion values for input signal: 1 arbitrary unit on graph = 10^{-10} joule total input signal energy; = 1.5×10^{-6} joule/mm^2 total input signal energy density; = 1.9×10^{-8} joule/mm^2 energy density in first spike; = 3.5×10^{-2} watt/mm^2 max power density in first spike.

gross gain is the same within experimental error for the first and second spikes; i.e., $G_0 = 8 \times 10^5$. As the signal level is increased, the gain of the second spike drops more rapidly than that of the first spike. After the gain G_2 of the second spike has dropped to about 10^5, the gain G_1 of the first spike decreases at about the same rate as G_2. Both curves appear to approach a slope of -1, which would imply a constant output, independent of input signal level.

The curves of Fig. 2 are very similar in appearance to those shown by Schulz-DuBois.[4] However, since the latter were based on steady-state, constant signal conditions, the explanation must be somewhat different for the transient situation of the present experiment.

In addition to the reduction of gain of the second spike relative to the first, two additional effects can be seen in Fig. 1, upper trace. The spontaneous emission level is substantially lower after the passage of the first spike than before. This provides confirmation that passage of the first spike reduces the inversion in the fiber laser. The other effect is that the peak of the first output spike is shifted slightly to the left (earlier time) relative to the peak of the first input spike. The shift is seen in all time traces exhibiting saturated gain, but is absent in traces obtained when the fiber laser was not pumped. The shift increased with increasing signal input power, and measured 0.28 ± 0.06 μsec at the highest signal used.

Saturated amplification is a logic function in the broad sense, in that the second pulse is strongly influenced by the presence or absence of the first pulse. Saturated amplification is also an important ingredient for the neuristor concept[9] as applied to the fiber laser.[10]

Dual Fiber Optical Coupling Experiments

By fabricating laser fibers with two small, closely spaced cores in a common cladding, it has been possible to demonstrate optical coupling between two fiber lasers.

Several 1-m long dual-core fiber lasers were fabricated, differing in core diameters and core spacing. Each was wound into a helix and mounted in a silver-plated brass cavity. The cavity containing the coiled fiber was placed in the optical system shown in Fig. 3. White light was focused onto

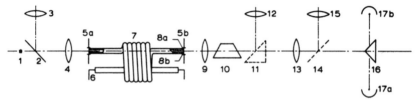

FIG. 3. Schematic diagram of optical system for dual fiber coupling experiments. 1, Light source; 2, beamsplitter; 3, microscope eyepiece; 4, microscope objective; 5, (a) and (b) end caps with pinholes; 6, flash lamp—GE FT-91 3-in. arc length; 7, fiber coil; 8, (a) and (b) ends of cores; 9, microscope objective; 10, dove prism; 11, removable reflector; 12, microscope eyepiece; 13, microscope objective; 14, removable reflector; 15, microscope eyepiece; 16, reflecting prism; 17, (a) and (b) photomultipliers.

one end of the cores, and the visible transmitted light was viewed at the other ends by means of a microscope. The ends were aligned to the optical axis of the system and their images, rotated into the horizontal plane by a dove prism, were viewed again by a second microscope in series with the first. The light transmitted by the fiber was then separated by a reflecting prism and directed into photomultipliers. This completed the lineup procedure. When the fiber lased, the outputs from the photomultipliers were displayed simultaneously on a dual-beam oscilloscope. The oscilloscope traces appeared as a series of spikes 1 or 2 μsec apart and varying from one to another in amplitude. When the system was properly aligned and the spikes from the two oscilloscope traces appeared simultaneously, it was concluded that the fibers were coupled. Table 1 summarizes the characteristics of three 1-m long dual core fibers. Figures 4, 5, and 7 show the different degrees of coupling between the cores.

In the case of Fiber No. 3 where strong coupling was observed, a photographic plate was placed at a position intermediate between the near field

TABLE 1 RESULTS

	Fiber No. 1 (See Fig. 4)	Fiber No. 2 (See Figs. 5 and 6)	Fiber No. 3 (See Fig. 7)
Core Diameter = d	3.7μ and 3.9μ	4.9μ and 5.2μ	4.4μ and 4.5μ
Core Separation (edge to edge) = D	11.0μ	5.2μ	5.3μ
D/d	2.9	1.0	1.1
Core Glass	Barium crown 2.55 wt % Nd_2O_3	Barium crown 2.55 wt % Nd_2O_3	Barium crown 2.55 wt % Nd_2O_3
Cladding Glass	Soda lime	Soda lime	Soda lime
Total Fiber Length	120 cm	123 cm	120 cm
Total Pumped Length	108 cm	111 cm	108 cm
Ends	Polished normal	Polished normal	Polished normal
Threshold	Approximately 125 joules	143 joules for one core and 150 joules for the other See Fig. 5	160 joules
Coupling	No coupling	Intermediate: general time coincidence of spikes, but core in which spike originates can generally be identified	Strong: traces are nearly identical; core in which a spike originated cannot be identified

and the far field of the lasers. Exposures of this quasi far field showed fringes with spacings on the order of magnitude as predicted by Young's theory of the double slit. This was taken as further evidence of coupling. (See Fig. 7.)

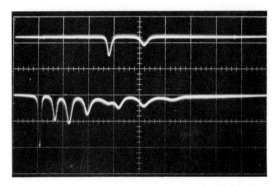

FIG. 4.(a) Oscillogram for Fiber No. 1 pumped near threshold. Pumping energy: 125 joules. Sweep speed: 10 μsec/div. Note lack of coincidence of spikes indicating that there is no coupling and that the cores have different thresholds.

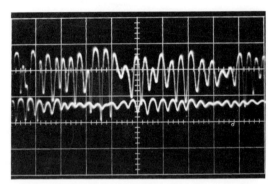

FIG. 4.(b) Oscillogram for Fiber No. 1 pumped 2.8 times threshold. Pumping energy: 335 joules. Sweep speed: 5 μsec/div. Note general lack of correlation of spikes although occasional correspondence does occur.

In order to verify that the cores were actually coupled in the case of Fiber No. 2, a series of oscilloscope traces were taken for various positions of the reflecting prism as it was moved across the field. The prism was initially centered and the position verified photographically. The photographic exposure also clearly showed that the core images were well separated at the reflecting prism. At one extreme of its motion, the prism was located so that one photomultiplier received light from both cores and the other photomultiplier received part of the light from just one core (see Fig. 6a); at the other extreme, the situation for the photomultipliers was reversed (Fig. 6c). Inspection of the corresponding oscillograms (Figs. 6a, b, c) show that the cores must indeed be coupled.

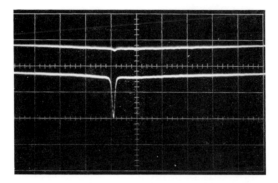

FIG. 5.(a) Oscillogram for Fiber No. 2 pumped at threshold for one core. Pumping energy: 142 joules. Sweep speed: 20 μsec/div. Note that only one spike appears and that it appears in both traces at the same time. From other data (Fig. 5b) one can say that only one laser core is at threshold.

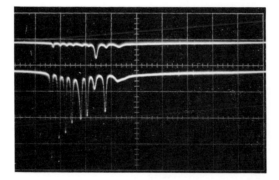

FIG. 5.(b) Oscillogram for Fiber No. 2 pumped at threshold for second core. Pumping energy: 150 joules. Sweep speed: 20 μsec/div. Note that in the upper trace one large spike appears and that a corresponding spike appears in the lower trace. Because of the spikes' relative amplitudes it is concluded that the single large spike in the upper trace originates in one core and is coupled into the second core, whereas the smaller spikes in the upper trace originate in the second core and are coupled into the first core. The second core (lower trace) has a slightly lower threshold than the first one (see Fig. 5a).

Analysis of the Laser Quenching Effect

In order to be useful in optical logic functions, an interaction effect should fulfill several requirements. One is that the signal input power is no greater

FIG. 6.(a) Oscillogram for Fiber No. 2 with prism edge at one extreme. Pumping energy: 350 j; Sweep speed: 2 μsec/div. The diagram at the right shows the relative position of the reflecting prism with respect to the core images. Note that the lower trace records light from *only* one core, and note time correlation of spikes.

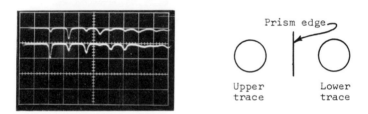

FIG. 6.(b) Oscillogram for Fiber No. 2 with prism edge in central position. Pumping energy: 350 j; Sweep speed: 2 μsec/div. Just as in Fig. 5b we can identify from which core a spike originates.

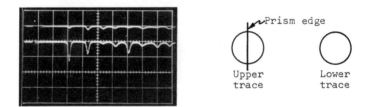

FIG. 6.(c) Oscillogram for Fiber No. 2 with prism edge at other extreme. Pumping energy: 350 j; Sweep speed: 2 μsec/div. Note that the upper trace records light from only one core, and note time correlation of spikes. These facts along with the data in Fig. 6a show that the fibers are indeed coupled.

than and preferably less than the controlled output power. Another requirement is that the effect be fast. The following analysis shows that the laser quenching effect[11] in principle can be made fast, since the rate of depletion of inversion is proportional to the input signal power. The analysis also shows that if the time constants of the oscillating mode and the

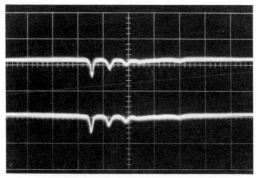

FIG. 7.(*a*) Oscillogram for Fiber No. 3 pumped near threshold. Pumping energy: approximately 160 joules. Sweep speed: 5 μsec/div. Note time correlation and relative amplitude correlation of spikes.

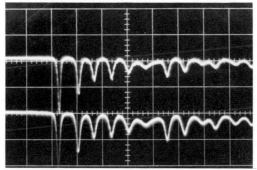

FIG. 7.(*b*) Oscillogram for Fiber No. 3 pumped at 1.1 times threshold. Pumping energy: 175 joules. Sweep speed: 5 μsec/div. Note the close correlation between spikes in upper and lower traces. This is taken as evidence of very close coupling between the cores.

so-called quenching mode are not too different, the required quenching power is less than the power which is turned off.

Mathematical Formulation

In order to analyze the laser quenching effect, we assume the following conditions:

1. There is a mode (or modes) in which oscillation occurs, and this mode has a *time constant* T_1 for decay of radiation in the cavity. Let the *energy density of radiation* in this mode be denoted by ρ_1.

2. There is another mode(s) in which the quenching light is injected, and this mode has a *time constant* T_2. Assume $T_2 < T_1$. The *energy density of radiation* in this mode is denoted by ρ_2.

3. The volumes occupied by these modes overlap completely, so that each mode interacts with the same atoms.

4. During oscillation the laser reaches a steady-state condition.

The rate equation governing the *number N_2 of ions per unit volume in the upper laser level is*

$$\frac{dN_2}{dt} = -A_{21}N_2 - (\rho_1 + \rho_2)B_{21}(N_2 - N_1) + \phi \tag{2}$$

where A_{21} *and B_{21} are the Einstein A and B coefficients for the transition,* and ϕ *is the number of atoms per second per unit volume raised to the upper laser level,* i.e., the pumping rate.

The equation governing the number of photons in the oscillation mode is

$$\frac{1}{h\nu}\frac{d\rho_1}{dt} = \rho_1 B_{21}(N_2 - N_1) - \frac{\rho_1}{h\nu T_1} \tag{3}$$

Equations 2 and 3 are basically the same as those used by Makhov[12] and Sinnett,[13] and by Statz and deMars.[14] The exception is the term ρ_2 in Eq. 2, which expresses the interaction of the externally incident radiation field. The equation which governs the number of photons per unit volume, $\rho_2/h\nu$, in this mode is

$$\frac{1}{h\nu}\frac{d\rho_2}{dt} = \eta + \rho_2 B_{21}(N_2 - N_1) - \frac{\rho_2}{h\nu T_2} \tag{4}$$

Here η *is the number of photons per unit volume added to the cavity per second* by the external source, i.e., $\eta = (P_q/h\nu V)$ where P_q *is the incident quenching power,* V *is the volume of the laser.* The second term gives the number of photons per second per unit volume added to this mode due to stimulated emission. The third term expresses the loss of energy out of the cavity.

Before the quenching light is turned on, η is 0, and the laser oscillates in mode 1 only. When steady state is reached, Eqs. 2 and 3 give

$$\frac{dN_2}{dt} = 0 = -A_{21}N_2 - \rho_1 B_{21}(N_2 - N_1) + \phi \tag{5}$$

$$\frac{1}{h\nu}\frac{d\rho_1}{dt} = 0 = \rho_1 B_{21}(N_2 - N_1) - \frac{\rho_1}{h\nu T_1} \tag{6}$$

The steady-state inversion is found from Eq. 6:

$$(N_2 - N_1)_a = \frac{1}{B_{21}h\nu T_1} \tag{7}$$

The subscript "a" *denotes steady state with mode 1 oscillating.*

Now when the quenching light is turned on at time $t = 0$, Eq. 4 governs the rate at which the energy density ρ_2 in mode 2 increases in the cavity. The initial rate of increase is seen to be

$$\frac{1}{h\nu}\left(\frac{d\rho_2}{dt}\right)_0 = \eta$$

Therefore to a first approximation $(1/h\nu)\rho_2 = \eta t$.

If this expression for ρ_2 is substituted in Eq. 2, we have

$$\frac{dN_2}{dt} = -A_{21}N_2 - \rho_1 B_{21}(N_2 - N_1)_a + \phi - h\nu\eta t B_{21}(N_2 - N_1)_a$$

$$= -\frac{\eta t}{T_1}$$

from Eqs. 5 and 6. Therefore we see that the initial rate dN_2/dt at which the inversion is reduced is directly proportional to the intensity of the quenching light.

Required Quenching Power

If the quenching radiation is continued at a constant level, and if it is of sufficient power, a steady state will be reached when the spontaneous emission together with the stimulated emission due to ρ_2 just balance the pumping rate, i.e., from Eq. 2:

$$\left(\frac{dN_2}{dt}\right)_b = 0 = -A_{21}(N_2)_b - \rho_2 B_{21}(N_2 - N_1)_b + \phi \tag{8}$$

and from Eq. 4

$$\frac{1}{h\nu}\frac{d\rho_2}{dt} = 0 = \eta + \rho_2 B_{21}(N_2 - N_1)_b - \frac{\rho_2}{h\nu T_2} \tag{9}$$

The subscript "*b*" *denotes steady state in the quenched condition.*

From Eqs. 8 and 9 we can calculate the *minimum quenching power,* P_{qm}. This is the power which reduces the inversion to a value just infinitesimally below the threshold inversion

$$(N_2 - N_1)_a = \frac{1}{B_{21}h\nu T_1}$$

Putting $(N_2 - N_1)_b = (N_2 - N_1)_a$, and solving Eqs. 8 and 9 for $\eta_{\min}$ yields

$$\eta_{\min} = \left(T_1\phi - \frac{A_{21}}{h\nu B_{21}}\right)\left(\frac{1}{T_2} - \frac{1}{T_1}\right)$$

$$P_{qm} = Vh\nu\eta_{\min} = V\left(h\nu T_1\phi - \frac{A_{21}}{B_{21}}\right)\left(\frac{1}{T_2} - \frac{1}{T_1}\right)$$

If the quenching power is less than this value, quenching will not be complete. If it is greater than this value, the inversion will be reduced below threshold, and quenching should be complete.

However, since we have not yet established how far below threshold the inversion must be reduced, in the development which follows we define a *ratio, k,* which we retain as a parameter.

$$k \equiv \frac{(N_2 - N_1)_b}{(N_2 - N_1)_a}$$

Here the numerator is the inversion in the quenched state (from Eq. 8) and the denominator is the inversion at threshold for oscillation.

It is obvious that the quenching effect will be most valuable if a relatively small signal can quench a laser oscillation of larger power. Therefore, we wish to compare the *required quenching power* P_q with the *power* P_a, *which is turned off*. Then Eq. 8 becomes, if we assume again that $N_1 \ll N_2$,

$$-A_{21} \frac{k}{B_{21} h\nu T_1} - \rho_2 B_{21} \frac{k}{B_{21} h\nu T_1} + \phi = 0$$

$$\rho_2 = \frac{h\nu T_1 \phi}{k} - \frac{A_{21}}{B_{21}}$$

Substitution of this value of ρ_2 into Eq. 9 yields the required value of η

$$\eta + \left(\frac{h\nu T_1 \phi}{k} - \frac{A_{21}}{B_{21}}\right) B_{21} \frac{k}{B_{21} h\nu T_1} - \left(\frac{h\nu T_1 \phi}{k} - \frac{A_{21}}{B_{21}}\right) \frac{1}{h\nu T_2} = 0$$

$$\eta = \left(\frac{T_1 \phi}{k} - \frac{A_{21}}{h\nu B_{21}}\right) \left(\frac{1}{T_2} - \frac{k}{T_1}\right)$$

Therefore the required quenching power is

$$P_q = h\nu V \eta = V \left(\frac{h\nu T_1 \phi}{k} - \frac{A_{21}}{B_{21}}\right) \left(\frac{1}{T_2} - \frac{k}{T_1}\right) \tag{10}$$

(Note that if k is set equal to unity, Eq. 10 reduces to the previously derived expression for minimum quenching power P_{qm}.)

From Eqs. 5 and 7 we find the power generated in the laser cavity (steady state, before quenching),

$$P_a = V \frac{\rho_1}{T_1} = \frac{V}{T_1} \frac{\phi - A_{21} N_2}{B_{21}(N_2 - N_1)_a} = V \left(h\nu\phi - \frac{A_{21}}{B_{21} T_1}\right) \tag{11}$$

Finally, the ratio of power quenched to required quenching power is

$$\frac{P_a}{P_q} = \frac{\dfrac{V}{T_1} \left(h\nu T_1 \phi - \dfrac{A_{21}}{B_{21}}\right)}{V \left(\dfrac{h\nu T_1 \phi}{k} - \dfrac{A_{21}}{B_{21}}\right) \left(\dfrac{1}{T_2} - \dfrac{k}{T_1}\right)}$$

$$= \frac{\left(h\nu T_1 \phi - \dfrac{A_{21}}{B_{21}}\right)}{\left(\dfrac{h\nu T_1 \phi}{k} - \dfrac{A_{21}}{B_{21}}\right) \left(\dfrac{T_1}{T_2} - k\right)} \tag{12}$$

This expression could be evaluated exactly for specific cases, but we can gain some insight as follows. Note that just at threshold (for mode 1), when $\rho_1 = 0$, Eq. 5 yields

$$\phi_{th} = A_{21} N_2$$

Assuming that $N_1 \ll N_2$ and substituting the threshold value for N_2 from Eq. 7 into this expression we have

$$\phi_{th} = \frac{A_{21}}{B_{21} h\nu T_1}$$

Now suppose that we pump at a rate equal to m *times threshold;* i.e.,

$$\phi = m \frac{A_{21}}{B_{21}h\nu T_1}$$

Then Eq. 12 becomes

$$\frac{P_a}{P_q} = \frac{m-1}{\left(\frac{m}{k}-1\right)\left(\frac{T_1}{T_2}-k\right)} \quad (13)$$

This ratio can be interpreted as the gain in going through one logic element. It is plotted as a function of pumping power in Fig. 8. The major

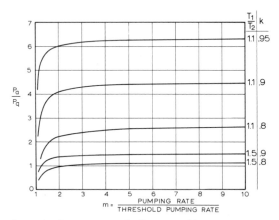

FIG. 8. Power gain: ratio of power turned off to quenching power.

$k = \dfrac{\text{inversion (quenched)}}{\text{inversion (threshold)}}$

T_1 = time constant for decay of radiation in the oscillation mode (s).
T_2 = time constant for decay of radiation in the quenching mode (s).
P_a = power output of oscillating laser.
P_q = quenching power required to reduce inversion to the specified value of k.

conclusion from this plot is that P_a/P_q can be greater than one for a range of values of T_1/T_2, k, and m.

It is apparent from Fig. 8 that the ratio approaches an asymptotic value as m increases. From Eq. 13 this value is seen to be

$$\left(\frac{P_a}{P_q}\right)_{m\to\infty} = \frac{k}{(T_1/T_2)-k} \quad (14a)$$

Therefore for high pumping rates (m large) the gain, P_a/P_q, will be greater than unity so long as

$$2k > \frac{T_1}{T_2}$$

Since k is by definition less than unity, T_1/T_2 must be less than 2.

Furthermore, the curves and Eq. 14a show that in the limit $k \to 1$, the power gain, P_a/P_q is simply given by

$$\left(\frac{P_a}{P_q}\right)_{m\to\infty} = \frac{T_2}{T_1 - T_2} \tag{14b}$$

For a cavity in which $T_2 = \frac{2}{3}T_1$, P_a/P_q is equal to 2; i.e., an output power of unity could be quenched by half of that power.

The above analysis is admittedly only a first approximation, in that it ignores the spiking behavior of many solid-state laser materials and assumes steady-state conditions. The next step should include a time-dependent solution of Eqs. 2, 3, and 4.

The laser quenching effect has also been demonstrated with diode lasers.[12] Recently, combinations of quenchable diode lasers have been proposed[13] as bistable devices.

Another possibility for a bistable optical device is the combination of a laser with a saturable absorber having a sufficiently long lifetime. The laser cavity includes the saturable absorber, as shown in the upper diagram of Fig. 9, so that the laser can oscillate only when the absorber is saturated.

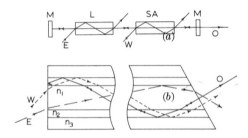

FIG. 9. Bistable optical devices. (a) Conventional laser (L) with saturable absorber (SA) between reflectors (M). W is a write signal, E is an erase signal, and O is the laser output. (b) Fiber laser greatly enlarged. The core is of laser glass with index of refraction n_1. The first cladding is of saturable absorbing material with index n_2. The outer cladding is of clear glass with index n_3. The indices obey the relation $n_1 > n_2 > n_3$.

The bistable device is switched on by an external signal which saturates the absorber, allowing the laser to start to oscillate and thereby keep the absorber saturated. The device is switched off by sending into the laser a signal which quenches the laser, thus allowing the absorber to return to its original absorbing state. In the case of the bistable fiber laser, one end is beveled at such an angle that oscillation can occur only for high-angle rays, as illustrated in the lower diagram of Fig. 9. These rays are not totally reflected at the first interface. Therefore they must penetrate into the first cladding which is the saturable absorber, where they are totally reflected at the second interface. To switch the device on, a signal is sent into one end at a high angle; it passes into the first cladding and saturates the absorber. To switch the device off, a signal is sent at low angle into the core. It quenches oscillation and allows the absorber to return to its original absorbing state.

Such devices require a saturable absorber having the necessary long lifetime in the saturated state. It will also be important to adjust the other parameters of the system, such as NA of the fiber, so that the presence of the saturable absorption does not produce an instability or a series of relaxation oscillations[14] in the system.

ACKNOWLEDGMENTS

The authors wish to thank C. W. Ask, who obtained experimental data, and W. P. Bazinet, who fabricated the fiber lasers.

Stimulating discussions with E. Snitzer, C. G. Young, H. M. Teager, O. A. Reimann, and D. R. Maynard are also appreciated.

REFERENCES

1. MARÉCHAL, A., AND P. CROCE, *Compt. Rend., 237*, 607 (1953).
2. O'NEILL, E., *IRE Trans. Inform. Theory, IT-2*, 56 (1956); for recent review papers on coherent optical processing, see L. J. Cutrona *et al., IRE Trans. Inform. Theory, IT-6*, 386 (1960), and L. J. Cutrona, *IEEE Spectrum, 1*, 101 (1964).
3. See, for example, *Optical Processing of Information*, Donald K. Pollock, Charles J. Koester, and James T. Tippett, Eds., Spartan Books, Inc., Baltimore, Md., 1963, papers by R. J. Potter, p. 168; T. R. Babcock, p. 145, and T. E. Bray, p. 216.
4. SCHULZ-DUBOIS, E. O., *Bell System Tech. J., 43*, 625 (1964).
5. FRANTZ, L. M., AND J. S. NODVIK, *J. Appl. Phys., 34*, 2346 (1963).
6. GEUSIC, J. E., AND H. E. D. SCOVIL, *Quantum Electronics*, Columbia University Press, New York, 1964, p. 1211.
7. WITTKE, J. P., AND P. J. WARTER, *J. Appl. Phys., 35*, 1668 (1964).
8. KOESTER, C. J., AND E. SNITZER, *Appl. Opt. 3*, 1182 (1964).
9. CRANE, H. D., *Proc. IRE, 50*, 2048 (1962).
10. KOSONOCKY, W. F., "Feasibility of Neuristor Laser Computers," *Optical Processing of Information*, Donald K. Pollock, Charles J. Koester, and James T. Tippett, Eds., Spartan Books, Inc., Baltimore, Md., 1963, p. 255.
11. KOESTER, C. J., R. F. WOODCOCK, E. SNITZER, AND H. M. TEAGER, *J. Opt. Soc. Am., 52*, 1323 (1962); also *Optical Processing of Information*, p. 74.
12. FOWLER, A. B., *Appl. Phys. Letters, 3*, 1 (1963).
13. LASHER, G. J., AND A. B. FOWLER, *IBM J. Res. Develop., 8*, 471 (1964).
14. SNITZER, E., "Glass Lasers," ICO Tokyo, September 1964 (proceedings to be published).

CHAPTER 16

LASER DIGITAL DEVICES *†

Walter F. Kosonocky

RCA Laboratories, Princeton, New Jersey

Introduction

An investigation of the use of lasers as digital devices for processing of information was begun in 1962 as a feasibility study of a neuristor laser computer.[1] Early in this study we realized that laser materials similar to those required for the laser neuristor lines could, when used in laser oscillators and laser amplifiers, result in digital devices whose input-output characteristics would resemble the conventional switching circuits. Such laser digital devices could be used as general purpose logic circuits in very much the same way as transistors are presently used for this purpose, except that all of the processing would be done with optical rather than electrical signals. The operation of these laser digital devices is based on nonlinear (saturable) interaction of intense optical signals with laser materials. The two basic nonlinear processes are the quenching of gain in a laser, and saturation of optical absorption.

This report describes the status of our work on the laser digital devices. A simplified model is developed in Sec. I for large signal response of laser materials. This model was verified by spectroscopic measurements of saturable absorbers illuminated by outputs of ruby lasers described in Sec. II. Results are given of studies of two saturable absorbers: (a) R transitions of an unpumped ruby crystal, and (b) singlet transitions of phthalocyanine solutions.

* The research reported in this paper was sponsored by the Air Force Systems Command, Rome Air Development Center, Griffiss Air Force Base, New York, under Contract Number AF30(602)-3169.

† This work done as a partial requirement for Eng.Sc.D. at Columbia University.

The applications of semiconductor lasers for digital devices are considered in Sec. III. The semiconductor, current-injection lasers are ideal for this purpose because of their small size, high quantum efficiency, and fast switching speed. In Secs. IV, V, and VI, a laser inverter circuit, a laser bistable circuit, and a laser monostable circuit are examined as typical switching circuits that could be implemented with semiconductor lasers. Efficient quenching of a GaAs oscillator using a dual oscillator structure is described. Ruby lasers with phthalocyanine solutions as saturable absorbers were operated as relaxation oscillators and as monostable circuits.

I. Large-Signal Response of Laser Materials*

A discussion of the operation of digital laser devices must be preceded by a review of the large-signal transient response of laser materials.

The interaction of an electromagnetic wave with a "saturable" absorber material (the absorber) or a continuously pumped laser material (the emitter) can be described by a two-energy-state model. In Fig. 1 the stim-

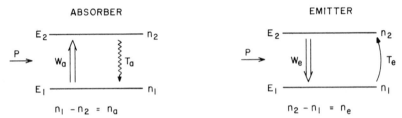

Fig. 1. Model for the interaction of an electromagnetic wave with a two-energy-state material.

ulated transitions are represented by a transition rate $w = \frac{1}{2}BP$, where B is an interaction constant and P is the signal flux-power density in watts/cm². For a two-level absorber this interaction constant is equivalent to the absorption cross section σ; i.e., $B = (2\sigma/h\nu) = (2\alpha/h\nu N)$, where α is absorption coefficient in cm⁻¹, N is the concentration of the ground state, E_1 in ions/cm³ when $P = 0$, and $h\nu$ is in joules. The interaction constant can also be expressed in terms of homogeneously broadened line width $\Delta\nu$ and spontaneous emission time constant T_r by

$$B = 0.085 \frac{\lambda^3}{\eta^2 \, \Delta\nu \, T_r} \tag{1}$$

where λ, wavelength, is in microns; η is the index of refraction; $\Delta\nu$ is in wave numbers, cm⁻¹; and T_r is in seconds.

The spontaneous transitions of the absorber toward the ground state are represented by an effective recovery time T_a. The effective recovery

* See References 2 and 7 for more details.

time of the emitter T_e represents the effective pumping rate of the laser material. Equivalent two-energy-state representations of three-level and four-level lasers are shown in Fig. 2. When, as in Fig. 1, absorption population difference for the absorber, $n_a = n_1 - n_2$, is defined to correspond

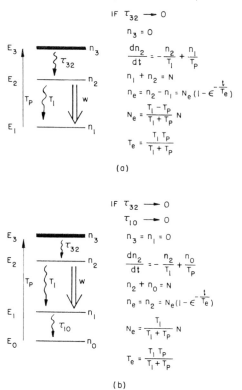

(a)

(b)

Fig. 2. Equivalent two-energy-state representations for three-level and four-level lasers. (a) 3-level laser. (b) 4-level laser.

to the inverted population for the emitter, $n_e = n_2 - n_1$. The responses of both materials to an applied optical signal P can be expressed by similar differential equations,

$$\frac{dn}{dt} = \frac{N - n}{T_1} = -nBP \tag{2}$$

Let us consider two laser signals incident on a two-energy-state absorber material. The absorption spectrum of this material matches the emission spectrum of the emitter material that produces the input laser signals (see Fig. 3). The absorber material can be characterized by a concentration of absorptive ions per cm^3, N_a, a lifetime of the excited state T_a, and an interaction constant B_a. The constant B_a relates the stimulated transitions probability per unit time w_a to the flux power density P of the optical signal at the resonant frequency, $\nu_0 = (E_2 - E_1)/h$. (The absorber will be referred to as a saturable absorber if it can be saturated by the signal intensity that is produced by the laser source under consideration.) The effect on the applied signal due to interaction with the saturable absorber

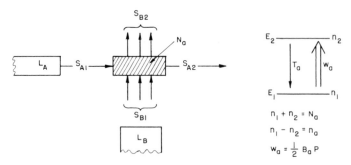

FIG. 3. Schematic for test of a saturable absorber.

can best be shown if signal S_{A1} in Fig. 3 is assumed to have a much smaller intensity than signal S_{B1}. Also, due to geometry, signal S_{B1} is not as strongly affected by the absorber. Under these conditions, the following equations apply:

$$\frac{dn_a}{dt} = \frac{N_a - n_a}{T_a} - n_a B_a P \tag{3}$$

and

$$\frac{dP_A}{dx} = -\frac{1}{2} h\nu n_a B_a P_A \tag{4}$$

where

$$P = P_A + P_B$$

The absorption coefficient α_A can be defined as

$$\alpha_A = -\frac{dP_A}{P_A \, dx} = \frac{1}{2} h\nu n_a B_a \tag{5}$$

The steady-state solution of Eq. 3 is

$$n_a = \frac{N_a}{1 + B_a T_a P_B} \tag{6}$$

Therefore, the steady-state absorption coefficient is

$$\alpha_A = \frac{\alpha_A(0)}{1 + B_a T_a P_B} \tag{7}$$

where $\alpha_A(0) = \frac{1}{2} h\nu N_a B_a$ is the low signal absorption coefficient. The curve of α_A versus P_B is sketched in Fig. 4a.

Equations 6 and 7 apply for steady-state modulation of the absorption coefficients by signals with durations that are much longer than the recovery time, $t \gg T_a$. The transient effect on α_A when the signal S_B is in the form of a pulse with a duration $T \ll T_a$ can be expressed simply, from Eq. 2, by

$$n_a = N_a \exp\left(-B_a \int_0^T P_B \, dt\right) \tag{8}$$

and

$$\alpha_A = \alpha_A(0) \exp\left(-B_a W_B\right) \tag{9}$$

where $W_B = \int_0^T P_B \, dt$ is the energy density in joules/cm² of the saturating pulse. The curve of α_A as a function of time for the transient response is

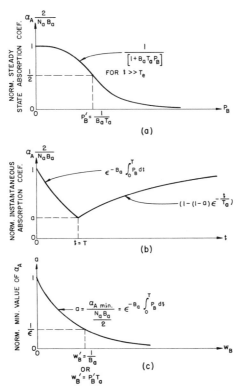

(a)

(b)

(c)

Fig. 4. Response of the saturable absorber in Fig. 3. (a) Normalized steady-state absorption coefficient α_A as a function of flux power intensity P_B of signal S_B. (b) Normalized instantaneous absorption coefficient α_A as a function of time for pulse signal S_B with duration T and energy W_B. (c) Normalized minimum value of α_A, a, as a function of W_B.

given in Fig. 4b. The curve in Fig. 4c shows the normalized minimum value of α_A as a function of the energy W_B of the signal S_B. When the signal S_B is removed, the material has an exponential recovery with the time constant T_a.

Three types of saturable absorbers can be considered (see Fig. 5). Figure 5a shows a two-energy-level absorber with a radiative recovery time

$T_a = T_r$. In Fig. 5b a two-energy-level absorber is shown that has a re-covery time T_a, which is composed of both a radiative time constant T_r and a nonradiative time constant τ. The absorber in Fig. 5b requires higher signal intensities to reach steady-state saturation than does the

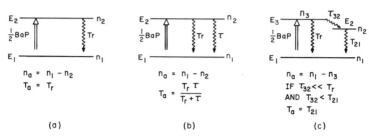

FIG. 5. Representation of saturable absorber. (a) Two-energy-level absorber with radiative lifetime. (b) Two-energy-level absorber with nonradiative recovery time. (c) Three-energy-level absorber.

absorber in Fig. 5a if both have the same interaction constant B_a and the same radiative lifetime T_r. The three-energy-level absorber in Fig. 5c, on the other hand, can reach steady-state saturation at much lower signal intensity.

In the three types of absorbers described above, steady-state saturation is reached; i.e., $\alpha_A = \frac{1}{2}\alpha_A(0)$, when $P_B' = 1/BT_a$, or, using Eq. 1, when

$$P_B' \approx \frac{12\eta^2 \, \Delta\nu}{\lambda^3} \left(\frac{T_r}{T_a}\right) \tag{10}$$

In general, steady-state saturation begins when the rate due to stimulated transitions becomes comparable to the recovery rate associated with spontaneous transitions. In the two-level absorber, T_a/T_r is the fluorescent quantum efficiency. In other words, in the case of the two-level absorber with a purely radiative recovery, $T_a = T_r$, the signal-flux-power spectral density (in watts/cm²/cycle) must exceed the flux-power density associated with the so-called zero-point fluctuations of all possible radiation modes. According to Eq. 10, the signal-flux-power spectral density must be

$$\frac{P'}{\Delta\nu} = \frac{12\eta^2}{\lambda^3} \text{ watts/cm}^2/\text{cm}^{-1} \tag{11}$$

or

$$\frac{F'}{\Delta\nu} = \frac{6 \times 10^{19}\eta^2}{\lambda^2} \text{ photons/sec/cm}^2/\text{cm}^{-1} \tag{12}$$

where

$$\eta = \text{index of refraction}$$
$$\lambda = \text{wavelength in microns}$$

and

$$\Delta\nu = \text{cm}^{-1}$$

The foregoing relationships point out that it would be relatively easy to reach saturation in resonant systems at microwave and lower frequencies. It is also very easy to reach saturation with gas lasers, due to their very narrow line widths. In solid-state lasers, however, the line widths are usually broadened due to coupling with the phonon spectrum. For a line width $\Delta\nu$ of the order of 10 cm^{-1}, for instance, a signal-flux-power density of the order of a kilowatt/cm^2 would be required to produce a pronounced saturation effect.

The energy density, $W_B' = 1/B_a$, required for transient saturation, i.e., for $\alpha_A = \alpha_A(0)/\epsilon$ when $T \ll T_a$, depends only on the interaction constant B_a. According to Eq. 1, W_B' should depend only on the homogeneously broadened line width $\Delta\nu$ and radiative lifetime T_r; i.e.,

$$W_B' = \frac{4\eta^2}{\lambda^3} \, \Delta\nu \, T_r \text{ joules/cm} \tag{13}$$

II. Saturable Absorber Experiments

A. Saturation of Absorption in R_1 and R_2 Lines of Ruby

The concepts of saturable absorption developed in the previous section were verified by a study of the absorption and fluorescence spectra of an unpumped ruby crystal during illumination by a ruby laser. The results of the tests of saturation of absorption and of spontaneous emission made on a $\frac{1}{4}$-inch ruby cube placed inside the resonant cavity of a ruby laser showed that the R_1 and R_2 lines of ruby behave at room temperature as a single homogeneously broadened band. Both lines can be saturated by a laser pulse (at 6941.5 Å) having a duration of 0.2 msec according to a simple exponential function. A ruby laser beam with energy density of 3 joules/cm^2 reduces the absorption in a ruby crystal to 37 per cent of the original, small signal value. The saturation can be described by the solution of a simple rate equation using an interaction constant determined from the value of the absorption coefficient. It was shown that, at room temperature, the model is valid down to nanosecond time durations. The lifetime of the excited state of ruby is about 3.6 msec and independent of the degree of saturation. The ratio of the excited populations corresponding to the R_1 and R_2 lines obeys the Boltzmann distribution and is independent of the degree of the saturation.

1. THE EXPERIMENT. The schematic layout of this experiment is shown in Fig. 6. In all of the measurements the $\frac{1}{2}$ meter, Jarrell Ash spectrometer was used with a slit width of 50μ giving a resolution of about 0.5 Å. It was found that reliable absorption measurements could be done only by focusing the entrance slits of the monochrometer across the width of a large flashtube such as an FT524-GE.

Typical waveforms used for the measurements of the increase of the monochromatic signal through the ruby cube are shown in Fig. 7. The energy density of the laser beam in this test was estimated to be about 10 joules/cm² in a beam with a 0.5-cm diameter. The results of this experiment are shown in Fig. 8. The increase in the detected monochromatic signal is expressed in terms of the amount of absorption per unit length which was saturated, or removed, as a result of the ruby cube being illuminated by the laser beam. These points computed from the experimental data are compared with an absorption curve for the same crystal measured by a Jarrell Ash 3.4-m, plane grating photospectrometer with resolution of less than 0.1 Å.

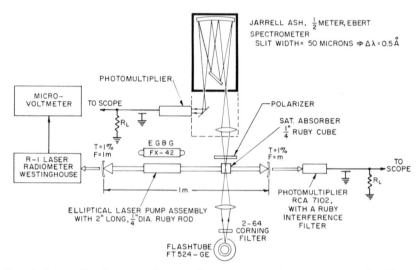

Fig. 6. Schematic of an experiment using a spectrometer to measure saturation of absorption in ruby.

The wave shapes in Fig. 9 represent typical measurements of the spontaneous emission caused by illumination of the ruby cube by a laser beam. The ratio of the peak values of the spontaneous emission of R_1 and R_2 lines was found, within the experimental accuracy, to be constant and independent of the degree of saturation. The spontaneous emission decay time of 3.6 msec was independent of the wavelength. The variation of the total spontaneous emission with the wavelength is shown as the experimental points in Fig. 10.

These points are compared with a fluorescence of the same ruby cube produced by a mercury lamp and also recorded by the same spectrometer, but using a chopper and a locked-in amplifier.

The variation of the spontaneous emission with the degree of saturation was investigated by changing the relative orientations between the c axes of the laser ruby and the absorbing ruby cube. The total spontaneous emission at the peaks of R_1 line (6941.5 Å) and R_2 line (6926.5 Å) is plotted

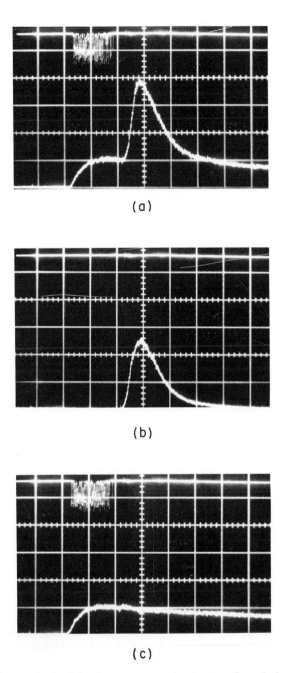

FIG. 7. Waveforms obtained in the measurements of saturation of absorption using monochrometer (at 6927 Å). (a) Laser fired: spontaneous emission and monitoring signal. (b) Laser not fired: monitoring signal only. (c) Laser fired: monitoring signal stopped, spontaneous emission only. Horizontal scale: 0.2 msec/div. Upper trace: Laser output; 0.5 V/div, $R_L = 1$ kohm. Lower trace: Output of the monochrometer; 20 mV/div, $R_L = 1$ kohm.

277

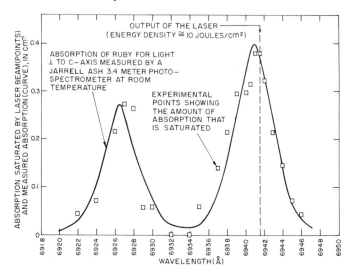

FIG. 8. Comparison of absorption measured on the ¼-in. ruby cube and the amount of absorption saturated (removed) due to a laser beam with energy density of 10 joules/cm illuminating the cube.

in Fig. 11, as a function of the transient saturation parameter S_{tr}. The choice of this saturation parameter as $S_{\text{tr}} = 0.33\ W$ is discussed in Sec. IIA3. The energy density W is 11.2 joules/cm² and the maximum value of the interaction constant B_{12} for ruby is 0.172 cm²/joule. The reduction in the interaction as a function of the angle between the c axis of the laser ruby and the c axis of the absorber ruby is taken from the measured curve for R_1 line in Fig. 12 which is described in the following section.

2. VARIATION OF ABSORPTION COEFFICIENT OF R_1 AND R_2 LINES OF RUBY WITH THE ANGLE BETWEEN THE INCIDENT LIGHT AND c AXIS. Since no conclusive data were found in the literature on the variation of absorp-

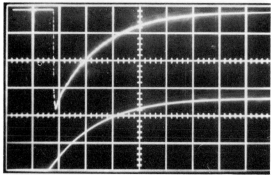

FIG. 9. Spontaneous emission of ruby at 6941.5 Å. (a) Upper trace: spontaneous emission, $R_L = 100$ kohm, vert. scale = 0.2 V/div, horizontal scale = 2 msec/div. (b) Lower trace: integrated spontaneous emission, vertical scale = 50 mV/div, horizontal scale = 2 msec/div.

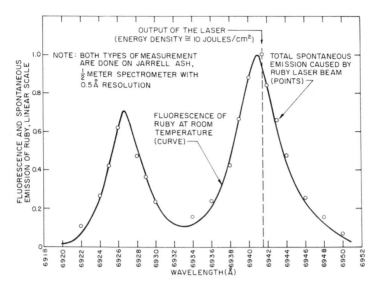

FIG. 10. Comparison of fluorescence of ruby and spontaneous emission of ruby caused
by ruby laser illumination.

tion of R_1 line of ruby as a function of the angle between the polarization
of the incident light and the c axis of ruby,[3,4] this variation was carefully
measured for both the R_1 and R_2 lines. To avoid errors due to possible
crystallographic imperfections in longer ruby crystals, the absorption
measurements were done on the $\frac{1}{4}$-in. ruby cube that was used as the
saturable absorber in the experiments. The best available method found

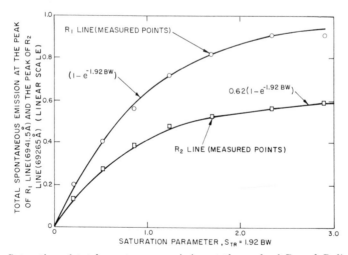

FIG. 11. Saturation of total spontaneous emission at the peak of R_1 and R_2 lines as a
function of the transient saturation parameter, $S_{tr} = 1.92\ BW$; W in joules/cm²,
$B_{max} = 0.172$ cm²/joules.

for such measurements was the following: A Jarrell Ash, 3.4-m, plane grating photospectrometer was used with a tungsten lamp as a light source. To avoid depolarizing effects of the grating during the measurement, the ruby crystal was turned in a calibrated holder while the polarizer was kept in a fixed position. The absorption spectrum for R_1 and R_2 lines was photographed on a Kodak I-L emulsion plate and then was recorded using a densitometer. It should be noted, however, that the smallest values of absorption by the $\frac{1}{4}$-in. ruby cube were less than 2 per cent and were comparable to the noise due to the graininess of the emulsion. The results of this test are shown in Fig. 12. No explanation is offered for the differ-

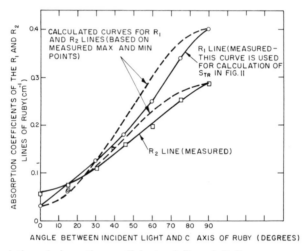

Fig. 12. Variation of absorption coefficients of R_1 and R_2 lines measured for a $\frac{1}{4}$-in. ruby cube as a function of the angle between incident light and c axis of ruby.

ence between the measured curves and the curves computed on the basis of the extreme points. However, it should be noted that the saturation of fluorescence of R_1 and R_2 lines shown in Fig. 11 follows a simple exponential curve for the variation of absorption chosen in Fig. 12 for the measured R_1 line. For the ruby cube the ratio of absorption coefficient for the R_1 line for a light perpendicular and parallel to the c axis was found to be about 13; i.e.,

$$\alpha^{\perp}(R_1):\alpha^{\parallel}(R_1) = 13$$

3. TEST OF THERMALIZATION TIME BETWEEN R_1 AND R_2 LINES OF RUBY. The thermalization time, or coupling time, between R_1 and R_2 lines of ruby was tested by measuring the fluorescence of ruby as a function of time resulting from the illumination of the ruby cube by a Q-switched ruby laser. The laser pulse had a half-width of 20 nsec and energy of 200 millijoules. The fluorescence was measured using a $\frac{1}{2}$-m Jarrell Ash spectrometer, 6275 RCA photomultiplier with 50-ohm termination, and

585 Tektronix oscilloscope. The tests showed that the thermalization time between the R_1 and R_2 lines is less than 20 nsec, the duration of the laser pulse.

According to the work of McCumber and Sturge,[5] above 77 °K the R lines of ruby are homogeneously broadened due to two-phonon Raman process. Since at room temperature these lines are partially overlapping, the thermalization time between the R_1 and R_2 lines is expected to be on the order of 10^{-11} sec, being comparable to the transverse relaxation time T_2.

4. ANALYSIS OF THE RESULT ON SATURABLE ABSORPTION OF RUBY. The results of the tests described in Sec. A demonstrate that, at room temperature, the R_1 and R_2 lines of ruby behave as a single homogeneously broadened band. Therefore, the expression for the saturation parameter must be reexamined.

The analysis of the absorption of a ruby laser signal by an unpumped ruby must consider three energy states. These are: the ground state with a population of n_1, the excited state corresponding to the R_1 transition with a population n_2, and the excited state corresponding to the transition R_2 with a population n_3. The experimental results point out that (as it might be expected) at room temperature the population n_2 and n_3 are in thermal equilibrium following the Boltzmann distribution. Therefore

$$n_3 = 0.866n_2 \qquad (14)$$

and

$$n_1 + n_2 + n_3 = N \qquad (15)$$

where N is the concentration of chromium ions.

Since the duration of the saturating laser pulse of 0.2 msec is much shorter than the lifetime of the excited states of 3.6 msec, the condition of transient saturation is applicable:

$$\frac{dn_2}{dt} = \left(n_1 - \frac{g_1}{g_2} n_2\right) \frac{B_{12}P}{2} \qquad (16)$$

but

$$n_1 = N - 1.866n_2 \qquad \text{and} \qquad \frac{g_1}{g_2} = \frac{4}{2} = 2*$$

Therefore

$$\frac{dn_2}{dt} = (N - 3.866n_2) \frac{B_{12}P}{2} \qquad (17)$$

$$n_2 = 0.35N[1 - \exp(-1.92\,B_{12}W)] \qquad (18)$$

and

$$S_{\text{tr}} = 1.92\,B_{12}W \qquad (19)$$

where W is the energy density in joules/cm² and B_{12} is the interaction con-

* See Reference 6.

stant in cm^2/joules. The interaction constant B_{12} can be found from the low-signal absorption coefficient α as

$$B_{12} = \frac{2\alpha}{h\nu N}$$

For ruby with 0.05 per cent of chromium $h\nu N = 4.65$ joules/cm^2, this gives $B_{12} = 0.172$ cm^2/joule for the case when the c axes of the laser ruby and the absorber ruby are parallel.

The experimental curve for saturation of the total spontaneous emission in Fig. 11, plotted as a function of the derived saturation parameter S_{tr}, points out that the saturation of fluorescence of R lines of ruby by a ruby laser signal follows a simple exponential curve. It should be noted that the experimental points in Fig. 11 are in very good agreement with the computed exponential curves for which the reduction in the saturation parameter S_{tr} was obtained from the measured curve for the variation of the peak absorption coefficient of R_1 line with the angle of the incident light and the c axis of ruby as shown in Fig. 12.

The factor of 0.62 defining the ratio between the spontaneous emissions at the peak of R_1 line and the peak of R_2 line can be explained as the Boltzmann factor (0.866) divided by the ratio $\alpha^\perp(R_1)/\alpha^\perp(R_2) = 1.4$. The ratio of the rates of the spontaneous emissions of R_1 and R_2 lines are expected to be related by this ratio.

The measured value for the energy density required to cause transient saturation corresponding to $S_{tr} = 1$ was found to be quite close to $W' = 3.0$ joules/cm^2, the value computed from the absorption coefficient $\alpha^\perp(R_1) = 0.4$ cm^{-1}. The same energy density estimated by Eq. 1 is $W' = 2.0$ joules/cm^2 by assuming that at room temperature the radiative lifetime T_r for ruby is 5.0 msec and the line width for the R_1 transition $\Delta\nu$ is 10 cm^{-1}. However, as the R_1 and R_2 transitions behave as a single homogeneously broadened band, they must jointly be considered in the determination of the effective line width. It is interesting to note that if the effective line width $\Delta\nu'$ is taken as $\Delta\nu' = \Delta\nu(R_1) + 0.62 \, \Delta\nu(R_2) = 15.3$ cm^{-1} the composite homogeneously broadened line width, then the simplified relationship of Eq. 1 can give a very good prediction for the value of W'.

B. Saturation of Absorption of Solutions of Phthalocyanine*

As a further test of the mechanism of saturable absorption, spectroscopic measurements were made of solutions of phthalocyanine[8] illuminated by giant ruby laser pulses. Q-switched ruby lasers with saturable absorbers, such as VOPc in toluene, in their cavities were used as the saturating sources. The equipment used for this experiment is shown in Fig. 13. Figure 14 illustrates typical waveforms obtained in the dual-beam

* A complete description of this experiment will be published in Reference 7.

absorption tests. A curve for saturation of absorption of VOPc in toluene is shown in Fig. 15. The tested solutions include: H_2Pc in toluene, benzene, and chloronaphthalene, H_2Pc in quinoline, VOPc in toluene, and CuPc in chloronaphthalene.

All of the metal-free phthalocyanines had strong spontaneous emission corresponding roughly to the absorption band of the first singlet state S_1. In all cases the emission of the S_1 line showed a Franck-Condon shift of

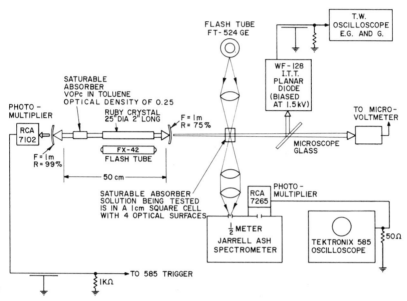

Fig. 13. Equipment used for study of saturation of emission and absorption spectrum of solutions of phthalocyanine.

about 50 Å. The emission lifetime was found to be less than 20 nsec, i.e., the duration of the shortest laser pulse used. The absorption bands of both singlet states of the metal-free solutions (S_1 at about 6390 Å and S_2 at about 6640 Å) in chloronaphthalene and in quinoline were completely saturated by the laser pulse. This saturation had a recovery time of about 1 μsec at room temperature and about 200 μsec at 77 °K. Very small emission from the S_2 band and complete saturation of absorption of S_1 and S_2 bands indicates that the ground state is emptied by the laser pulse. The 1-μsec recovery time of the absorption bands S_1 and S_2 suggests that following the laser pulse all excitation is transferred to a triplet state. The temperature variation of the recovery time from the triplet to ground state and the fact that no fluorescence was observed out to 10,000 Å supports the theory that the transition from the triplet to ground state is nonradiative. VOPc in toluene and CuPc in chloronaphthalene gave no spontaneous

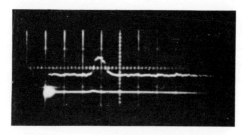

(I)

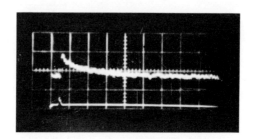

(II a)

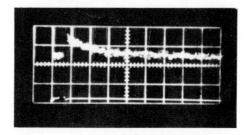

(II b)

FIG. 14. Signal waveforms obtained in the test of saturation of absorption.
I. VOPc in toluene at 6910 Å, low signal optical density of 0.3. Scale: horizontal, 0.1 μsec/div; vertical, 0.2 volt/div. Upper trace: laser and flashtube is fired. Lower trace: only laser is fired.
II. H₂Pc in chloronaphthalene at (a) 6640 Å, low signal optical density of 0.2. (b) 6990 Å, low signal optical density of 0.224. Scale: horizontal, 0.5 μsec/div; vertical, 0.2 volt/div. Upper trace: laser and flashtube is fired. Lower trace: only laser is fired.

emission and their absorption spectra were completely saturated by the laser pulse. The recovery times of this saturation could not be measured, being shorter than the durations of the laser pulses used.

These spectroscopic tests under illuminations of a giant laser pulse point out that the saturation of absorption of the phthalocyanine solutions could be explained in terms of a three-level absorber. The three-level-absorber response has been clearly shown for the metal-free solutions. In the metal solutions, the stronger spin-orbit coupling, as compared to the metal-free solutions, should give shorter nonradiative transitions, thus resulting in a more efficient three-level system. This experiment is con-

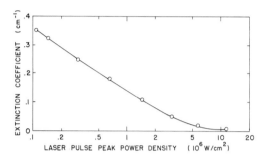

Fig. 15. Saturation of absorption of VOPc in toluene at 6910 Å (low signal absorption coefficient, $\alpha(0) = 0.92$ cm^{-1}).

sistent with the lower energy needed to saturate the absorption of the metal solutions compared to the metal-free solutions.

Although the results of the tests of saturation of absorptions of the phthalocyanine solutions are not as straightforward as tests of an unpumped ruby, they are consistent with the theoretical analysis of saturable absorbers.

III. Semiconductor Lasers for Digital Devices

The operation of laser digital devices such as the laser neuristors[1] or the laser resonator switching devices to be described is based on a large signal response of emissive and saturable absorber materials. A saturable absorber, to be useful as a laser switching device, must be easy to saturate by the optical signals developed by the laser. Therefore, the minimum energy density W (in joules/cm^2) that must be developed within the active region of the laser device to saturate the emitter material should be comparable to the energy density required to cause one switching operation of the device. It turns out that this energy density $W = PT_1$ is about the same whether the switching time is much shorter or comparable to the effective recovery time T_1. The value for this energy density is given by Eq. 13. It should be noted that it depends only on the homogeneously broadened line width $\Delta\nu$ and the radiative lifetime T_r, which is inversely proportional to the dipole moment or the oscillator strength of the transition. It is apparent then that, for very-high-speed switching devices, materials with very strong transitions or very short radiative lifetimes are desirable. Current injection semiconductor lasers employ such materials.

The energy density required to cause one switching operation in optically pumped lasers such as the ruby or the neodymium laser should be roughly six orders of magnitude higher than for GaAs lasers. The other favorable attribute of semiconductor lasers is that their pumping efficiency is several orders of magnitude higher than that of the optically pumped lasers.

There is at present no verified theory available to describe the details of the radiative recombination processes in GaAs lasers.[9] In general, however, laser action in GaAs diodes is explained by radiative transitions between overlapping degenerate n and p regions at the junction. Emission takes place from filled states in the conduction band to empty states in the valence band at a frequency corresponding to the emission energy E_e. The material in the active region is relatively transparent, since its absorption edge E_a corresponds to a higher frequency; that is, $E_a > E_e$. The following simple phenomenological model is convenient for the prediction of large-optical-signal response of continuously pumped GaAs lasers.

Assuming that the degenerate valence band is essentially empty, the operation of GaAs can be interpreted in terms of a four-level laser, as shown in Fig. 16a. The laser action takes place between energy states E_2 and E_1. The relaxation times τ_{32} and τ_{10} correspond to the diffusion time of the majority carriers, which can be considered equal to the carrier scattering time (of the order of 10^{-13} to 10^{-12} second). The fictitious energy states E_0 and E_3, in combination with the relaxation times τ_{32} and τ_{10}, represent the most conductive regions of the diode. Both E_1 and E_2 are impurity "tails," which are not really separate from E_3 and E_0, respectively. The external source supplies a constant current I for the population inversion for the active region. The ground energy state E_0 can be thought of as an infinite source of carriers from which the external current source transfers carriers to energy state E_3 at a rate I, in electrons per second, assuming that the process is 100 per cent efficient. These carriers will repopulate energy state E_2 with a carrier scattering time constant τ_{32}. The time constant T_1 represents the spontaneous emission time of n_2. It is further assumed that all of the recombination takes place in the idealized active region, which is situated at the junction and which contains a uniform distribution of the inverted population, $n_2 - n_1$. Assuming further that the laser state E_1 is normally empty, any population n_1 will be transferred to the ground state E_0 with a carrier scattering time constant τ_{10}. Thus, n_2 is the inverted population and n_1 is equal to zero.

If the radiative recombination is in the form of band-to-band recombination of free carriers, it should be proportional to a product of these two carriers.[10–12] There is strong evidence, however, that the emission in these diodes results from a recombination in the p regions involving injected electrons and acceptor (zinc) centers or an equivalent but large number of free holes whose density is not greatly affected by the bias voltage.[13–16] The rate of change of the inverted population n_2 can then be expressed by

$$\frac{dn_2}{dt} = -\frac{n_2}{T_1} - n_2 w_{21} + I \tag{20}$$

where w_{21} represents the stimulated transition probability per unit time resulting from a signal present in the active region. By letting $I = N_2/T_1$, Eq. 20 will assume the familiar form

$$\frac{dn_2}{dt} = \frac{N_2 - n_2}{T_1} - n_2 w_{21} \tag{21}$$

If we consider the relation between spontaneous and stimulated émission, w_{21} can be expressed using Eq. 1 by

$$w_{21} = \frac{\lambda^3 P}{24\eta^2 \Delta \nu T_1} \tag{22}$$

where T_1 is the radiative lifetime in seconds, P is the flux power intensity

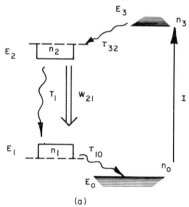

(a)

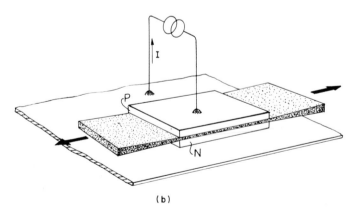

(b)

FIG. 16. (a) A four-energy-level representation of a GaAs laser. (b) Pictorial view of a GaAs laser.

in watts/cm^2, $\Delta\nu$ is the homogeneously broadened line width in cm^{-1}, λ is the wavelength in microns, and η is the refractive index. Then

$$w_{21} = \frac{P}{P'T_1} \tag{23}$$

For $\eta = 3.6$ and $\lambda = 0.84$ micron,

$$P' = 515\Delta\nu \text{ watts/cm}^2$$

From Eq. 21, we have

$$\frac{dn_2}{dt} = \frac{N_2 - n_2}{T_1} - \frac{n_2 P}{P'T_1} \tag{24}$$

where $N_2 = IT_1$, with I in electrons/sec/cm^3. P' is the flux power density at which the rate of stimulated emission equals the rate of spontaneous emission.

In terms of the band-filling model,[14,16] n_2 represents only the inverted population that corresponds to the homogeneously broadened part of the emission band. In other words, n_2 is the part of the inverted population that for particular doping levels, forward bias current, and temperature contributes directly to the stimulated emission. The homogeneously broadened line width $\Delta\nu$ then could be estimated to be equivalent to kT, where k is the Boltzmann constant and T is absolute temperature. At liquid nitrogen temperature, 78°K, $\Delta\nu$ would be equal to about 30 cm^{-1} and the flux-power density P' would then be of the order of 104 watts/cm^2. This estimate is consistent with experimental results showing that as the current of a GaAs diode is increased above the laser threshold the stimulated emission dominates the recombination process by maintaining the inverted population n_2 at a fixed level. The accompanying "lifetime-shortening effect" can be expressed conveniently by defining $T_s = 1/w_{21}$ as the lifetime of the injected carriers in the active region due to stimulated emission recombination. According to Eq. 20,

$$\frac{dn_2}{dt} = -\frac{n_2}{T_1} - \frac{n_2}{T_s} + I \tag{25}$$

or

$$\frac{dn_2}{dt} = \frac{N_2^* - n_2}{T_1^*} \tag{26}$$

where

$$T_1^* = \frac{T_1 T_s}{T_1 + T_s} \quad \text{and} \quad N_2^* = IT_1^*$$

This lifetime-shortening effect could be caused by superradiance, the amplified stimulated emission, or by externally applied signals. In the operation of continuously pumped laser digital devices, the time constant T_1^* of Eq. 26 determines the upper limit on the switching times. In GaAs lasers this time can be well under 1 nsec.[17] Although continuously pumped room-temperature operation would be desirable, at the present state of development of GaAs lasers only liquid nitrogen cw operation is easy to achieve.[18]

IV. Laser Inverter Circuit

The quenching of oscillations of one laser oscillator by an output of another laser oscillator[19-21] suggests a possibility of a laser inverter that as a NOR circuit could be used as a basic building block for optical computers. Let us consider a continuously pumped laser oscillator as shown in Fig. 17. The laser material is represented by an effective emissive pop-

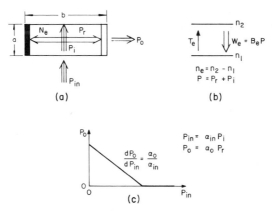

FIG. 17. NOR laser circuit. (a) Schematic of the circuit. (b) Model for the laser material. (c) P_o versus P_{in}.

ulation N_e, a recovery time T_e, representing the effective pumping rate, and an interaction constant B_e, representing the stimulated transition probability w_e, where $w_e = B_e P$. The total flux power P consists of two parts: (1) a flux power P_r, developed within the laser oscillator due to the resonant modes that produce an output signal P_o, where $P_o = \alpha_o P_r$; and (2) a flux power P_i that passes by the emissive population N_e as a result of an applied input signal P_{in}, which is not directly coupled into the resonant modes producing the output, P_o, $P_{in} = \alpha_{in} P_i$. The linear loss produced within the resonator due to P_r will be designated as $\alpha_r P_r$, and the total loss will be designated as αP_r, where $\alpha = \alpha_r + \alpha_o$ and $P_o = \alpha_o P_r$.

The simplest way to describe the input-output relation for circuit in Fig. 17 is to use Eq. 7 for the variation of the effective gain coefficient α_e with the total flux power density $P = P_r + P_i$. The steady-state solution for the resonator requires that

$$\alpha = \frac{\alpha_e(0)}{1 + BT_1 P} \tag{27}$$

or

$$P_r = \frac{\alpha_e(0) - \alpha}{T_1 B \alpha} - P_i \tag{28}$$

Equation 28 suggests a linear variation between the input P_{in} and the output P_o, with incremental gain of $-\alpha_o/\alpha_{in}$, see Fig. 17c. It might appear that by making $\alpha_o/\alpha_{in} > 1$ it should be possible to obtain a linear gain in the circuit of Fig. 17. However, according to this analysis, the inequality $\alpha_o/\alpha_{in} < b/a$ is required to assure that the signal P_i will be forced by P_{in} and will not be self-sustained. Since P_o and P_{in} are power densities, the maximum over-all gain of the output to input signals is still -1. Thus this circuit gives inverting operation and an isolation between input and output, it is capable of a fan-in, but it is not capable of fan-out or a digital gain. It might appear that the laser inverter circuit does not have a threshold for gain, as is required for stable digital circuits. However, if a gain is provided, even by a linear laser amplifier, the input-output transfer curve for two such inverters in series will give threshold for gain for small signals as well as saturation of output for large signals.

When implemented with semiconductor lasers, such as GaAs, the inverter circuit should have a very fast response. The turnoff time for a large input signal, the fall time, is the decay time of the resonator. The rise time would be determined by the effective recovery time of the emissive population T_e, and would be somewhat longer than the fall time. The rise time could be shorter than the lifetime of the minority carriers in the semiconductor lasers, which for GaAs lasers is on the order of 10^{-9} to 10^{-10} sec.[17]

NOR laser logic circuits, then, could be visualized in the form of continuously pumped laser oscillators whose outputs can be quenched by signals coupled from similar oscillators via laser amplifiers. The amplifier-oscillator-amplifier combination must be stable, free of self-oscillations, and must have sufficient gain to allow the output of one circuit to inhibit at least two other oscillators, i.e., fan-out of two. There is a good possibility that a single, bilateral laser amplifier might be sufficient for this purpose, since in the NOR circuit the output signal is isolated from the input signal. A true unidirectional amplifier using some nonreciprocal effect, such as Faraday rotation, though desirable, may not be necessary.

A GaAs laser inverter circuit is currently being developed at RCA Laboratories.* By performing logic operations such as OR-NOT or AND-NOT, this device can serve as a basic building block for optical logic circuits. The laser inverter circuit consists of an amplifier and an oscillator. The oscillator junction area is a part of the amplifier junction area. The operation of the inverter is the following. In the absence of an input, the oscillator section of the device produces an output signal; but when an input signal is applied to the amplifier section, this signal is amplified to an intensity high enough to lower the gain in the oscillator section to the point where the output of the laser oscillator is quenched.

The construction and the operation of the laser inverter is sketched in

* The results of this work will be described at the Solid-State Circuits Conference, Philadelphia, Pennsylvania, February, 1965.

Fig. 18. A pictorial view of the device is shown in Fig. 18a. The active laser region of the above structure is represented in Fig. 18b. A laser amplifier is formed between sides 1 and 2 by use of nonreflective coatings[22] or by destroying the laser cavity between these two sides[23,24] when side 2

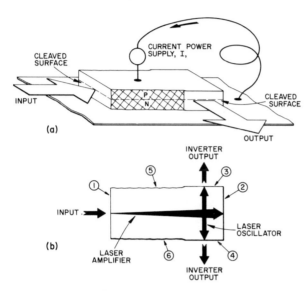

FIG. 18. Laser inverter.

is lapped at a horizontal or a vertical angle with respect to side 1. The laser oscillator is formed between two cleaved sides 3 and 4. The sides 5 and 6 are roughened or angled to prevent internal oscillations in the laser structure.

Efficient quenching of the output of a GaAs laser oscillator by means of a laser signal was demonstrated using a dual laser oscillator shown in Fig. 19. The dual laser oscillator contains two laser resonators within one laser structure. The dual laser was made by carefully roughening part of the longer sides of a diode cleaved on all four sides leaving two perpendicular resonators with the following dimensions: one typically 10 by 4 mils and the other 30 by 10 mils. The resonators can be pumped separately with two current sources. Isolation was achieved by sawing a groove through the top metal contact into part of the semiconductor material while monitoring the leakage conductance. Typical isolation resistance between the two diodes is about 1 ohm.

The tested dual laser oscillators were made from a GaAs wafer which yielded diodes that lased uniformly across the whole junction region. A typical operation of a dual laser oscillator is illustrated by Figs. 20, 21, and 22. In Fig. 20a are shown the waveforms of the applied currents to the large oscillator I_L and to the small oscillator I_S. In Fig. 20b are shown

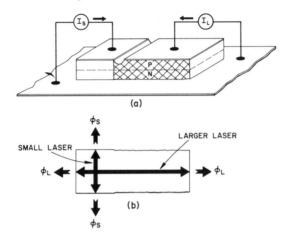

FIG. 19. Dual laser oscillator.

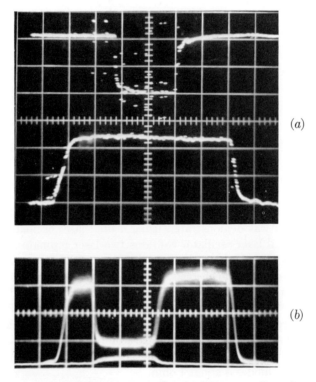

FIG. 20. Signal waveforms for dual laser oscillator. (a) Top trace: Large laser current I_L, 2 A/div. Bottom trace: Small laser current I_s, 1.6 A/div. (b) Output of the small laser ϕ_s for $I_L = I_s = 4$ A and $I_L = 4$ A, $I_s = 0$. Vertical scale: 0.1 V/div into 50-ohm load. Horizontal scale: 50 nsec/div for (a) and (b).

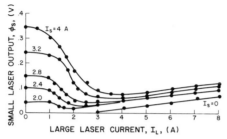

FIG. 21. Output of small laser ϕ_s versus large laser current I_L for fixed values of small laser current, I_s. *Note:* ϕ_s in Fig. 21 and ϕ_L in Fig. 22 were detected with the same photomultiplier, RCA 7102, terminated into 50-ohm load, at power supply voltage of 1.4 kV, neutral density filter of 2 and numerical aperture of 0.08.

the waveforms of the output of the small laser. The family of curves in Fig. 21 shows a typical variation of the output of the small laser as a function of the large laser current. The family of curves of the output of the large laser current for fixed values of small laser current is shown in Fig. 22.

The operation of the dual laser oscillator demonstrated that, as expected, the laser quenching effect can give an inversion operation. Isolation between the input and the output is provided but the device lacks the amplification required for digital circuits. By destroying the large laser cavity and thus converting it into a laser amplifier, the desired gain can be obtained.

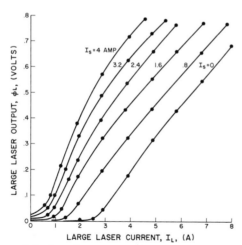

FIG. 22. Output of the large laser ϕ_L as a function of I_L for fixed values of I_s.

V. Bistable Circuit

A bistable laser circuit such as a flip-flop can be made from laser inverters or a single laser oscillator (see Fig. 23) that has a bistable operation if it has within its resonator a saturable absorber whose relation to the emitter is as shown in Fig. 24. In this figure the total loss coefficient α_T and the gain coefficient α_e are plotted as a function of the power density P_r in the resonator. The nonsaturable loss coefficient, $\alpha = \alpha_r + \alpha_0$ (where α_r represents the linear losses within the resonator and $\alpha_0 = (2 - R_1 - R_2)/2L$), represents an effective loss per cm length due to the reflectivities R_1 and R_2.

Note that point S is a stable equilibrium point. It gives the value of the

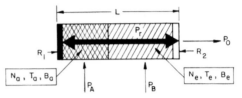

FIG. 23. Schematic of laser resonator containing a saturable absorber.

steady-state signal $P_r^{(S)}$. Point U is an unstable equilibrium point. Inspection of Fig. 24 shows that $P_r = 0$ is another stable operating point. Operation of such a bistable, start-stop laser oscillator is sketched in Fig. 25. The saturable absorber recovery time T_a in Fig. 25 is chosen to be longer than the emitter recovery time T_e to assure a bistable rather than an astable operation. Initially, if the circuit is in the "0" stable state, it can be switched into the "1" state by input A. The oscillations of the circuit

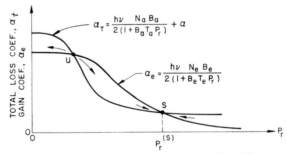

FIG. 24. Bistable operation of laser resonator in Fig. 23. (Total loss coefficient $\alpha_t = \alpha_a$ and gain coefficient α_e are plotted against resonator flux-power density P_r.)

can be quenched by input B, thus returning the circuit to state "0." The outputs of such bistable circuits can control the threshold of the monostable circuits described in the next section. The inputs A and B can be provided by these monostable circuits.

If a three-level saturable absorber is used for the bistable circuit, a digital gain may be possible between the input A and the output. A large digital gain cannot be expected from the bistable circuits, however, unless they are used in conjunction with laser amplifiers. The operation of a

GaAs laser as a bistable circuit has been reported by IBM[25] using a GaAs laser device very similar to the large oscillator of the dual oscillator device described previously. More efficient bistable semiconductor laser circuits should be possible if special measures are taken to introduce an appropriate

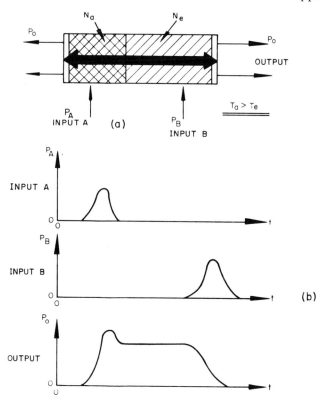

FIG. 25. Bistable circuit: (*a*) Schematic of the circuit. (*b*) Time variations of input *A*, input *B*, and output *P*. (Input *A* turns on laser oscillator; input *B* turns it off.)

saturable absorber in the laser cavity. The repetition rate of a bistable circuit will be determined by the recovery time of the saturable absorber T_a.

VI. Monostable Circuit

If a saturable absorber material placed inside the laser resonator has $N_a B_a > N_e B_e$, $N_a < N_e$, and $T_a < T_e$ a monostable laser circuit is obtained. Such a circuit can be triggered by an input pulse signal to produce an output pulse. The operation of a monostable circuit is illustrated in Fig. 26. Figure 26*a* shows a monostable laser resonator with an input *A*, an input flux power density P_A, and an output flux power density P_o. The input signal as a function of time is shown in Fig. 26*b*. It starts at time $t = t_{A1}$. The total loss coefficient $\alpha_t = \alpha_a + \alpha$ and the gain coefficient

α_e of the circuit are sketched as a function of time in Fig. 26c. Note that at time $t = t_{A2}$ the circuit reaches the condition for laser threshold; i.e., $\alpha_e = \alpha_t$. The input energy W_A' required to reach laser threshold is designated by the shaded area in Fig. 26b. Here W_A' represents the lower limit of the input energy needed for triggering the circuit. The input pulse triggers

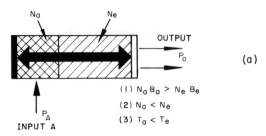

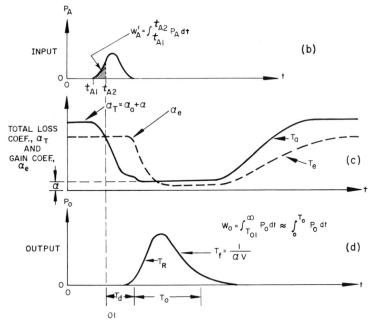

FIG. 26. Monostable circuit. (a) Schematic of the circuit. (b) Input signal as a function of time. (c) Time variation of total loss coefficient α_t and gain coefficient α_e. (d) Output signal as a function of time.

the laser oscillator into a regenerative state which in turn produces the output pulse shown in Fig. 26d. The output has a delay time T_d, a rise time T_r, a fall time T_f, and a duration T_0. The pulse output can be of very short duration. The duration will be largely a function of the fall time T_f, which is determined by the total loss of the resonator; i.e., $T_f = 1/v\alpha$. The repetition rate will depend on the recovery time of the emissive population T_e. For the semiconductor lasers, the recovery time corresponds to the minority carrier lifetime, which in the case of GaAs lasers is in the range of 10^{-9} to 10^{-10} sec.

A rough estimation of the energy gain G_w produced by this circuit is

$$G_w = \frac{W_0}{W_A} = \frac{N_e}{N_a} = \frac{B_a}{B_e}$$

A higher gain could be obtained if the strong regenerative action occurred before the saturable absorber is saturated by the input.

Since more than one input could be applied, the circuit of Fig. 26 can be used as a monostable OR gate. Any one of a number of inputs could trigger the circuit to produce a pulse output, the shape of the output pulse being essentially independent of the input. Since the input cannot be coupled directly into the output, this circuit also provides isolation between the input and output.

A monostable laser resonator is shown in Fig. 27. Input A can lower the threshold for regenerative action, and input B can increase this threshold. If both inputs are in the form of pulses, as in Fig. 27b, a large input pulse B will make the circuit inactive for the duration of the recovery time of the circuit. Since input A can be inhibited by input B, input B controls the transmission of input A. If input A is an unconditional clock pulse, the circuit acts as an inverter for signal B. As indicated in this figure, the circuit is not expected to provide "digital gain" as an inverter. Therefore, input B must be obtained from a monostable amplifier circuit.

If both inputs A and B are continuous bias signals, the operation of the circuit can be most conveniently described by the idealized transfer curves shown in Fig. 27c. The solid curve in 27c represents the response of the circuit in the absence of bias signals. Bias signal A will reduce the threshold T, while bias signal B will increase the threshold. The output can be completely inhibited by a large bias signal B. It has been shown that with continuous control signals bias A and bias B this circuit would perform the function of a threshold gate, with isolation between the inputs and the output. The control signals dictate whether or not a clock pulse is transmitted through the circuit. The control signals could be derived from the bistable circuits discussed in the previous section.

At the present time it is not clear whether or not a good saturable absorber can be found to give a semiconductor laser monostable circuits. The operation of a monostable laser circuit, however, was demonstrated using ruby lasers with solutions of phthalocyanine as saturable absorbers.[8,26,27] Equipment used for demonstration of a monostable laser circuit is shown in Fig. 28. In this figure Laser 1, operating as an astable self-triggered oscillator, is used as a trigger source for Laser 2 operating as a monostable laser circuit. Typical operation of Laser 1 as an astable circuit, or a relaxation oscillator is described by Figs. 29, 30, and 31. In

Fig. 29 a comparison is made of the output energy of the ruby laser against the flashtube power supply voltage for (a) without a saturable absorber, (b) with H_2Pc in toluene having low-signal optical density of 0.2, and (c) with H_2Pc in toluene having low-signal optical density of 0.3. The operation of this relaxation oscillator as a function of time is shown in

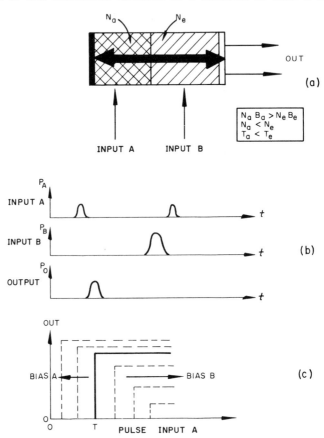

FIG. 27. Monostable circuit with two types of inputs (input A enables the circuit; input B inhibits the circuit). (a) Schematic of the circuit. (b) Time variation of input A, input B, and output. (c) Idealized transfer curve representing the operation of a variable threshold monostable gate for pulse input A and bias inputs A and B.

Fig. 30. In this figure the integrated laser output is recorded by an oscilloscope for the conditions a, b, and c of Fig. 29 and for the flashtube power supply voltage of 1.7 kV. In Fig. 31 is shown a TW oscilloscope picture of an output pulse wave shape detected by ITT W-128 diode which has a subnanosecond rise time.

From Fig. 28, the output waveforms of Laser 1 and Laser 2 are shown in Fig. 32. Both lasers were fired at flashtube power supply voltage of 1.8 kV. The delay of the output of Laser 2 is a function of the inverted

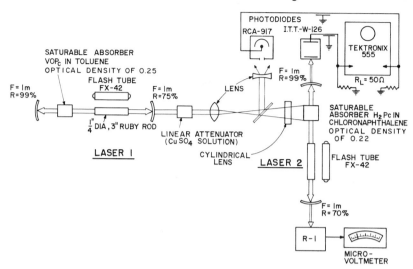

Fig. 28. Experiment for demonstration of ruby laser with phthalocyanine saturable absorbers operating as relaxation oscillator (Laser 1) and monostable circuit (Laser 2).

population and also it could be increased by increasing the distance between the spherical mirrors of Laser 2. Delays were obtained from 0.1 to 0.5 μsec. Operation of a monostable circuit with such a long delay is only possible with metal-free solutions of phthalocyanine which when saturated have recovery times of about 1 μsec.

The transfer curve for the monostable Laser 2 is shown in Fig. 33. A gain of two was demonstrated even though Laser 2 appeared to be less efficient than Laser 1. Operating as a relaxation oscillator with VOPc in

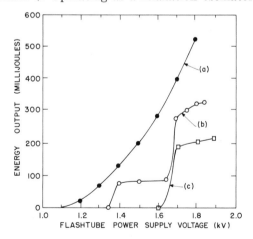

Fig. 29. Output energy of a ruby laser as a function of flashtube supply voltage. ($C =$ 400 μF.) (*a*) Without a saturated absorber. (*b*) With H_2Pc in toluene, optical density of 0.2. (*c*) With H_2Pc in toluene, optical density of 0.3.

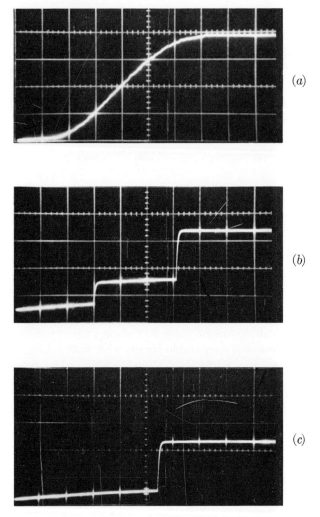

FIG. 30. Integrated output of a ruby laser, detected by a linear diode ITT W-128 Tektronix O-Unit. Horizontal scale: 50 μsec/div. Vertical scale: 0.5 V/div. Power supply voltage = 1.7 kV. (a) No saturable absorber. (b) H_2Pc in toluene, optical density of 0.2. (c) H_2Pc in toluene, optical density of 0.3.

toluene as a saturable absorber, Laser 2 produced also only 30 millijoule output pulses.

A triggerable operation was obtained without a delay time between the input and the output using a similar ruby laser system but aligned so that the output of Laser 1 couples into the resonant modes of Laser 2. In this case the c axes of both ruby crystals were made to be parallel and the two laser pump assemblies while positioned within two confocal spherical mirrors were separated by a flat mirror with 80 per cent reflectivity.

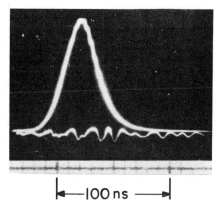

FIG. 31. Output pulse of a Q-switched laser. Detector: ITT W-128 planar dioded biased with 1.5 kV. Scope: EG and GTW oscilloscope.

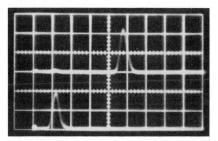

FIG. 32. Output waveforms of Laser 1 and Laser 2 in Fig. 28 displayed on Tektronix 555 oscilloscope. Horizontal scale: 0.1 μsec/div. Upper trace: Laser 2, 10 V/div. Lower trace: Laser 1, 5 V/div. Both traces have the same sweep internally triggered by the lower trace signal (Laser 1).

Initially, an attempt was also made to use an unpumped ruby as a saturable absorber for a ruby laser. The desired relation between the matrix elements of the unpumped ruby absorber and the pumped ruby emitter was to be obtained by having a resonant laser cavity only for one

FIG. 33. Input-output curve for the monostable Laser 2 triggered by output of Laser 1 (Fig. 28).

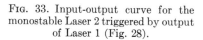
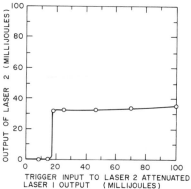

polarization and an appropriate orientation of the c axis of the crystals. At room temperature, the performance of this triggerable laser oscillator, using a ruby as the saturable absorber, was only marginal. In liquid nitrogen environment, however, this approach is expected to be more successful.

VII. Conclusions

The operation of the laser digital devices considered here is based on the nonlinear (saturable) response of materials to laser signals. The quenching of gain and the saturation of optical absorption in laser materials are the two basic nonlinear processes involved. It was shown, using a simple two-energy-state model, that (a) the flux power density (in W/cm^2) required to produce saturation of stimulated emission or saturation of optical absorption should be directly proportional to the homogeneously broadened line width and inversely proportional to the fluorescent efficiency of the transitions and (b) the energy density (in $joules/cm^2$) of the laser digital devices should be inversely proportional to the emission, or the absorption, cross section of the optical transitions. The validity of the above model was verified by studies of saturation of absorption of the R lines of ruby and the singlet absorption bands of phthalocyanine solutions.

Operation of a laser inverter, a laser bistable circuit, and a laser monostable circuit are examples of switching circuits that can be implemented with semiconductor lasers. It is assumed that the efficiency of the semiconductor laser will eventually be improved to make continuously pumped operation easier to obtain.

Efficient quenching of a GaAs laser oscillator was demonstrated using a dual oscillator laser structure. Ruby lasers with solutions of phthalocyanine as saturable absorbers were operated as astable and as monostable circuits. A digital signal gain of two was demonstrated by the operation of the laser monostable circuit.

The semiconductor, current injection lasers are ideal for digital devices because of their small size, high quantum efficiency, and high speed of operation. Two approaches recommended for the development of semiconductor laser digital devices are (a) the development of NOR laser circuits in the form of stable laser-amplifier-laser-oscillator combinations, and (b) the study of semiconductor laser devices that make use of the saturation of optical absorption in addition to the laser amplification and laser quenching effects. Semiconductor laser materials technology has arrived at a stage where more emphasis is being placed on research in the area of useful devices and their applications. Laser digital circuits will be one of these applications. In the next year or so, we should be in a better position to ascertain the role lasers will play in the digital computer field. We are optimistic that in the near future some forms of working laser digital circuits will be developed.

ACKNOWLEDGMENTS

The author wishes to thank Dr. J. A. Rajchman and G. B. Herzog for their support in this work.

The solutions of phthalocyanine were provided by Dr. S. E. Harrison. R. H. Cornely and R. C. Ballard helped in the development of the dual oscillator laser for which the GaAs wafers were provided by H. Nelson and F. Z. Hawrylo. The enthusiastic assistance of H. H. Whitaker in the ruby absorption measurements using the 3.4-m Jarrell Ash spectrometer is acknowledged. The proofreading of the manuscript by R. H. Ciafone is greatly appreciated.

REFERENCES

1. KOSONOCKY, W. F., "Feasibility of Neuristor Laser Computers," *Optical Processing of Information*, Donald K. Pollock, Charles J. Koester, and James T. Tippett, Eds., Spartan Books, Inc., Baltimore, Md., 1963, p. 255.
2. *Neuristor Logic Technology*, RADC-TDR-64-123, Final Report prepared under Contract AF30(602)-2761 by Applied Research Dept., Defense Electronic Products, RCA Camden, N.J., June 1964.
3. SUGANO, S., AND Y. TANABE, "Absorption Spectra of Cr^{3+} in Al_2O_3: Part A—Theoretical Studies of Absorption Bands and Lines," *J. Phys. Soc. Japan, 13*, No. 8, 880–899 (August 1958).
4. SUGANO, S., AND I. TSUJIKAWA, "Absorption Spectra of Cr^{3+} in Al_2O_3: Part B—Experimental Studies of the Zeeman Effect and Other Properties of the Line Spectra," *J. Phys. Soc. Japan, 13*, No. 8, 899–910 (August 1958).
5. McCUMBER, D. E., AND M. D. STURGE, "Linewidth and Temperature Shifts of the *R* Lines in Ruby," *J. Appl. Phys., 34*, 1682–1684 (1963).
6. DAVIS, J. I., AND SOOY, W. R., "The Effects of Saturation and Regeneration in Ruby Laser Amplifiers," *Appl. Optics, 3*, No. 6 (June 1964).
7. KOSONOCKY, W. F., "On Laser Digital Devices," *Doctoral Dissertation*, School of Engineering and Applied Science, Columbia University, 1965.
8. SOROKIN, P. P., J. J. LAZZI, J. R. LANKARD, AND G. D. PETTIT, "Ruby Laser *Q*-Switching Elements Using Phthalocyanine Molecules in Solution," *IBM J. Res. Develop., 8*, No. 2, 182 (April 1964).
9. BURNS, G., AND M. I. NATHAN, "*P-N* Junction Lasers," *Proc. IEEE, 52*, No. 7, 770–794 (July 1964).
10. HALL, R. N., "Recombination Processes in Semiconductors," *Proc. Inst. Elec. Eng. (London)*, Paper No. 3047E, 923 (March 1960).
11. MAYBURG, S., AND J. BLACK, "Dependence of Recombination Radiation on Current in GaAs Diodes," *J. Appl. Phys., 34*, No. 5, 1521 (May 1963).
12. MAYBURG, S., "Direct Recombination in GaAs and Some Consequences in Transistor Design," *Solid-State Electron., 2*, 195 (1961).
13. NATHAN, M. I., AND G. BURNS, "Recombination Radiation in GaAs by Optical and Electrical Injection," *Appl. Phys. Letters, 1*, No. 4 (December 1, 1962).
14. NELSON, D. F., M. GERSHENZAN, A. ASKIN, L. A. D'ASARO, AND J. C. SARACE, "Band-Filling Model for GaAs Injection Luminescence," *Appl. Phys. Letters, 2* (May 1, 1963).
15. DOUSMANIS, G. C., C. W. MUELLER, AND H. NELSON, "Effect of Doping on Frequency of Stimulated and Incoherent Emission in GaAs Diodes," *Appl. Phys. Letters, 3*, No. 8, 133–135 (October 15, 1963).

16. DOUSMANIS, G. C., NELSON, H., AND STAEBLER, D.L ., "Temperature Dependence of Threshold Current in GaAs Lasers," *Appl. Phys. Letters, 5*, No. 9, 174–176 (November 1, 1964).

17. KONNERTH, K., AND LANZA, C., "Delay Between Current Pulse and Light Emission of a Gallium Arsenide Injection Laser," *Appl. Phys. Letters, 4*, No. 7, 120–121 (April 1964).

18. MARINACE, J. C., "High Power CW Operation of GaAs Injection Lasers at 77 °K," *IBM J. Res. Develop., 8*, No. 5, 543–544 (November 1964).

19. KOESTER, C. J., "Some Properties of Fiber Optics and Lasers (Part B)," *Optical Processing of Information*, Donald K. Pollock, Charles J. Koester, and James T. Tippett, Eds., Spartan Books, Inc., Baltimore, Md., 1963, p. 74.

20. KOESTER, C. J., "Possible Use of Lasers in Optical Logic Functions," *Proceedings of the 1963 Pacific Computer Conference IEEE*, Pasadena, Calif., 15–16 March, 1963, p. 54.

21. FOWLER, A. B., "Quenching of Gallium-Arsenide Injection Lasers," *Appl. Phys. Letters, 3*, No. 1, 1 (1 July 1963).

22. CROWE, J. W., AND R. M. CRAIG, "Small-Signal Amplification in GaAs Lasers," *Appl. Phys. Letters, 4*, No. 3 (February 1964).

23. *Development of Glass Fiber Lasers*, RADC-TDR-64-79, Final Report on Contract No. AF30(602)-2829, prepared by C. J. Koester, American Optical Co., May 1964.

24. KOESTER, C. J., AND E. SNITZER, "Amplification in a Fiber Laser," *J. Appl. Phys., 3*, 1182 (October 1964).

25. NATHAN, M. I., J. C. MARINACE, R. F. RUTZ, A. E. MICHEL, AND G. J. LASHER, "A GaAs Injection Laser with Novel Mode Control and Switching Properties " *Solid State Device Conference*, Boulder, Colo., July 1964.

26. *Saturable Filter Investigation*, NONR-4125(00), NRO 15-702, ARPA Order No. 306-62, Program Code No. 3730, Semi-Annual Tech. Rept. (July 1963–December 1963), P. E. Stark, L. A. Cross, J. F. Hobart, Lear Siegler Inc., Laser System Center, 19 February 1964.

27. BRET, GEORGE, AND FRANÇOIS GIRES, "Pulse Laser and Light Amplifier, Using Variable Transmission Coefficient Glasses as Light Switches," *Appl. Phys. Letters, 4*, No. 10, 175 (May 1964).

CHAPTER 17

LIGHT AMPLIFICATION AND SWITCHING USING FIBER OPTICS AND LASER *

N. S. Kapany, G. M. Burgwald, and J. J. Burke, Jr.

Optics Technology, Inc., Palo Alto, California

I. Introduction

Present-day all-electronic computers employ logic gates that perform the switching operation in approximately 10^{-8} sec and are capable of storing 10^4 to 10^7 bits of information which are accessible in 10^{-6} to 10^{-7} sec. It now appears that in order to achieve higher speeds in micrologic gates, some basically new phenomena need to be explored. To this end extensive effort has recently been devoted to the exploration of the possibility of optical computer logic elements.

As a means for transferring radiation from one element to another, waveguide coupling[1] between adjacent parallel fibers has been investigated both theoretically and experimentally. Approximate expressions for the degree of coupling between two closely spaced slabs and fibers have been developed. Such coupling effects are also demonstrated and beat length variation studied as a function of the wavelength of incident radiation. Photometric studies have been undertaken in order to measure the relative intensities of two coupled fibers as a function of the wavelength, and a high degree of modulation has been achieved. Configurations that would provide waveguide coupling are under consideration, not only for closely spaced passive fibers that are excited by an external source, but also between active fibers such as a fiber laser.

With the advent of lasers[2] and fiber optics[3] it appears possible to perform high-speed optical switching function in conjunction with some well-known electro-optical effects. With the development of neodymium-doped glass

* This work supported by the Mathematical Sciences Division, Office of Naval Research, Washington, D.C., under Contract ONR-Nonr-4333(00).

lasers[4] it has now become possible to draw lasing fibers. The characteristics of these fibers have been studied in some detail with respect to the pumping configurations and output characteristics for both coated and uncoated fibers. For use in optical switching elements that are cascaded in series the development of laser amplifiers[5,6] is also necessary in order to compensate for light losses within the elements. Various experiments on the amplification of a signal from one fiber laser by another have been investigated and various parameters which govern the amplification factor and efficiency as well as fiber reflectivity are discussed.

Another mechanism which seems to hold considerable promise for optical switching applications is similar to the "hair-trigger mode"[7] operation performed in ruby lasers. Two configurations of hair-trigger mode operation between lasing fibers are being considered, one of which consists of the lasing fiber preceded by an intense light source, the energy from which is end-pumped into the lasing fiber. The second configuration consists of the waveguide coupling of the trigger pulse from a closely spaced fiber into the lasing fiber, which is pumped by a primary source to a level slightly below its threshold.

Yet another novel approach to high-speed triggering of optical pulse by an incident optical signal consists of the use of an absorbing cell (liquid dye or solid) in the laser cavity which is pumped by a primary source to a level slightly below its threshold. The pulse from another laser is side-pumped into the absorbing cell thereby causing instantaneous bleaching and consequent triggering of a Q-switched pulse from the first laser.

II. Waveguide Coupling Theory

A configuration that seems to hold promise for the switching of optical energy from one element to another makes use of waveguide coupling between two closely spaced optical waveguides. Energy is excited in one fiber by end feeding from an auxiliary source if a passive fiber is being used. On the other hand, if lasing fibers are used, then pumping radiation can be fed from the side walls with a high degree of efficiency. The degree of coupling between two closely spaced waveguides is a function of the fiber diameter d, fiber spacing t, length L, the refractive index of the fiber cores n_1, surround n_2, the wavelength of the exciting radiation λ and the particular mode excited in the guide. It can be shown that the "beat length" or the relative intensities of the two waveguides can be varied by varying any of the above-mentioned parameters. However, without regard to an efficient and fast mechanism for achieving this coupling, for the present, let us investigate the theory of resonant coupling between two identical waveguides.

Two fibers are illustrated schematically in Fig. 1. Each is of radius a

and index of refraction n_1. The center-to-center spacing between them is t, and they are imbedded in a medium of refractive index $n_2 < n_1$.

In experiments at optical frequencies a number of substantially different situations may occur when only one of the two fibers in such a geometry is illuminated. If the radius a is much greater than the wavelength of light and the illumination is incoherent, energy will slowly transfer from the illuminated fiber to the other by frustrated total reflection[8] until an equilibrium is established. If the radiation is completely coherent, the phenomenon of beating will occur, that is, almost all the energy will transfer to the unexcited fiber in a length $L/2$, and then back to the excited fiber in another length $L/2$, where L is the beat length. However, unless the radii a are of the order of the wavelength, the beat length will be too long to be observable experimentally, and, unless the radiation is highly coherent

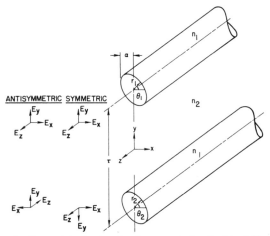

FIG. 1. Geometrical setup for two coupled cylindrical fibers.

over the end of the illuminated fiber, beating will not be observed even in small diameter fibers.

The phenomenon of beating between parallel waveguides or different modes in waveguides is familiar to microwave investigators.[9,10] Snitzer[11] has also reported observations of beating between optical waveguides and has described a general theoretical approach to the problem of coupling between two or more fibers. The purpose of the present study is to predict the beat length to be expected as a function of the radii of the fibers, the indices of refraction of the core and coating glass, and the separation between the fibers.

For the isolated fiber or slab, each component of the electric or magnetic field satisfies the equation

$$(\nabla_t^2 + k^2)\psi_0 = h_0^2\psi_0 \tag{1}$$

where $\nabla_t^2 = \partial^2/\partial x^2 + \partial^2/\partial y^2$, $k = (2\pi n/\lambda)$, and h_0 is the propagation constant of the mode. For example, the longitudinal component of the electric field in the $HE_{1,1}$ mode in an isolated fiber can be described by

$$\psi_0 \equiv E_Z = J_1\left(u_{1,1}\frac{r}{a}\right) \exp\left(i\theta + i\omega t - ih_{1,1}z\right)$$

where J_1 is the Bessel function of the first kind of order 1, $h_0 \equiv h_{1,1}$,

$$\frac{u_{1,1}}{a} = \left[\left(\frac{2\pi n_1}{\lambda}\right)^2 - h_{1,1}^2\right]^{1/2}$$

Two closely spaced fibers provide a system whose normal modes are symmetric or antisymmetric about the midplane that separates the fibers. For "tight"[9] coupling, one can approximate the modes of the two fiber system by symmetric and antisymmetric combinations of the modes of the isolated fiber, assuming that the interaction is weak enough so that only identical modes of the isolated fibers couple together. Then

$$\psi_S \simeq \psi_0(1) + \psi_0(2)$$

$$\psi_A \simeq \psi_0(1) - \psi_0(2)$$

where ψ_S and ψ_A indicate the symmetric and antisymmetric modes of the system respectively, and the numbers 1 and 2 represent the coordinates of the first and second fiber respectively. Now ψ_S satisfies the equation

$$(\nabla_t^2 + k^2)\psi_S = h_S^2\psi_S \qquad (2)$$

and ψ_A satisfies a similar equation. By multiplying Eq. 1 by ψ_S and Eq. 2 by $\psi_0(1)$, and subtracting and integrating over the half-plane that contains fiber 1, we have

$$\int_R (\psi_S\nabla_t^2\psi_0(1) - \psi_0(1)\nabla_t^2\psi_S)\,dR = (h_0^2 - h_S^2)\int_R \psi_0(1)\psi_S\,dR$$

Now, over the half-plane that contains fiber 1, $\psi_S\psi_0(1) \simeq \psi_0^2(1)$. The area integral on the left can be separated into two integrals, one over the fiber core cross section and one over the surround. Each of these can, in turn, be transformed to line integrals

$$\int_B (\psi_S\nabla\psi_0(1) - \psi_0(1)\nabla\psi_S)\cdot\mathbf{n}\,dB$$

around the corresponding boundaries B. One gets contributions from the integral along the midline, where $\psi_S = 2\psi_0(1)$ and $\nabla\psi_S\cdot\mathbf{n} = 0$, and contributions from the line integrals around the fiber that arise from the discontinuities in the derivatives of $\psi_0(1)$. The integrals can be evaluated by using asymptotic expansions of the Bessel functions along the midline and "addition theorem" representations around the fiber. Thus one has the general result:

$$h_0{}^2 - h_{S,A}^2 \simeq \mp 2h_0\Delta h \simeq \frac{\int_R (\psi_S \nabla_t{}^2 \psi_0 - \psi_0 \nabla_t{}^2 \psi_S)\, dR}{\int_R \psi_0{}^2\, dR} \tag{3}$$

where

$$\Delta h = h_S - h_0 = -(h_A - h_0)$$

As is clear from the preceding discussion, the theory gives a result similar to that which would be obtained when formal variational methods are used. The accuracy to be expected depends on the choice of the approximate eigenfunction ψ_0. The particular method of approximation described here was suggested by Landau and Lifshitz's technique[12] for determining the energy levels of adjacent, identical, one-dimensional potential wells.

The choice of $\psi_0(1)$ and $\psi_0(2)$ from the various degenerate eigenfunctions can be a problem. For a *TE* mode in a slab, it is sufficient to set $\psi_0(1) = \psi_0(2)$ equal to the transverse component of the electric field. For the rod, the terms "symmetric" and "antisymmetric" refer to reflection of the electric vector in the midplane. It is thus necessary, for the symmetric mode, that the electric vector on one fiber be the mirror image of the electric vector on the other, as illustrated in Fig. 1. To consider appropriately the discontinuous boundary conditions in this case, it is necessary to recast the foregoing theory in vector form.

By inserting the eigenfunctions into Eq. 3 one obtains expressions for the fractional change $\Delta h/h$ in propagation constant, from which the beat length, $L = (\pi/\Delta h)$, can be calculated.

For *TE* modes in the slab,

$$\frac{\Delta h}{h} \simeq \frac{\mp u^2 q^2 e^{-2qt/d}}{h^2 a^2 (u^2 + q^2)(1 + q)} \tag{4}$$

where

$$\cot(2u) = \frac{u^2 - q^2}{2uq}$$

$$u^2 + q^2 = \left(\frac{\pi\, d n_2}{\lambda}\right)^2 (K - 1)$$

$$K = \frac{n_1{}^2}{n_2{}^2}$$

$$h^2 a^2 = \left(\frac{\pi\, d n_2}{\lambda}\right)^2 + q^2$$

It is clear from Eq. 4 that the beat length is an exponential function of the separation between the slabs. In Fig. 2, the beat length is plotted as a function of separation, each expressed in number of diameters, for the lowest order *TE* in dielectric slabs with $(\pi\, d n_2/\lambda) = 4$, $n_2 = 1.52$, and

$n_1 = 1.53, 1.56, 1.62, 1.69$, and 1.75. Since d/λ is of the order of one optical wavelength, the ordinate covers a range of approximately 0.1 mm to 1 m.

Further computations are being undertaken to predict the relative intensities of coupled fibers of fixed length for variable wavelength. This is

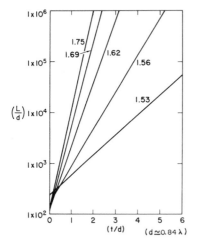

FIG. 2. Graphs of beat length as a function of slab separation for TE modes in closely spaced slabs.

the kind of data most readily obtained experimentally. As the wavelength is varied in a fixed system, all the mode parameters vary in a rather complicated manner. It is of course clear, however, that the coupling increases with increasing wavelength while the beat length decreases. In fibers longer than one beat length at some fixed wavelength, therefore, the relative output of the excited and unexcited fibers for adjacent wavelengths will vary. The experiments that confirm this will now be described.

III. Passive Waveguide Coupling

To demonstrate resonance coupling between two parallel fibers, the following experimental system was set up. Light from a Pek 100-watt xenon arc source, combined with an Engis S-05 monochromator, serves as a monochromatic light source. A combination of lenses is used to focus the light on a 50μ aperture, which is followed by a $10\times$ objective lens to obtain the required spot size. The output end of the fiber array is viewed with a $44\times$ microscope, with a $10\times$ Huygenian eyepiece, to see the beating effects.

The fiber pair being evaluated has a length of 2 inches; the fiber cores, drawn from Corning "signal yellow" filter glass ($n = 1.525$), are approximately 7μ in diameter and spaced by approximately 20μ on center. The imbedding glass is soda lime ($n_2 = 1.5188$). The fibers are slightly elliptical, the major axis being approximately 25 per cent longer than the minor axis. For this particular fiber combination, a two lobe pattern ($TM_{0,1}$ or

$TE_{0,1} + HE_{2,1}$) is seen at the output of the excited fiber at 5260 Å. At 5440 Å the two lobe pattern is equally intense in both fibers, and an increase to 5520 Å causes the two lobe pattern to appear only at the output of the unexcited fiber. A further increase in wavelength causes a single spot ($HE_{1,1}$ mode) to appear at the output of the excited fiber. Photographs of the output for these conditions are shown in Fig. 3.

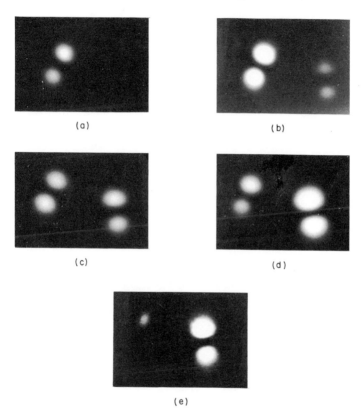

FIG. 3. Chromatic variation of beat length in two closely spaced glass fibers. (a) $\lambda =$ 526 mμ. (b) $\lambda = 536$ mμ. (c) $\lambda = 544$ mμ. (d) $\lambda = 548$ mμ. (e) $\lambda = 552$ mμ.

In Fig. 4 are shown plots of the normalized radiant flux from the excited (crosses) and unexcited (circles) fibers as a function of wavelength. This data was obtained photometrically by exposing an EMI-9558 photomultiplier behind the eyepiece to total flux from both fibers for varying wavelength, and then to the flux from each fiber separately. For this experiment, a 1-mm circular aperture was placed between the lenses of the eyepiece at the focal plane of the microscope-field lens combination. Since the aperture exposed the phototube to some of the background light in the coating around the fibers, and since the particular portion exposed varied

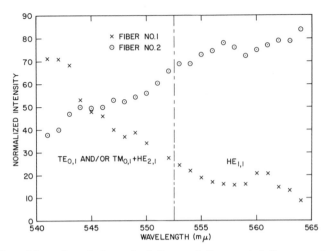

FIG. 4. Plot of intensity of the excited fiber and the coupled fiber as a function of wavelength of incident radiation.

for the three runs, certain experimental inaccuracies exist. Other fiber pairs are now under study.

IV. Fiber Lasers

Since the active and passive systems being considered for the switching operations also require the use of lasing fibers and fiber laser amplifiers, a search for lasing materials suited to fiber drawing was undertaken. Various domestic and foreign neodymium-doped glasses were evaluated both for devitrification and thermal compatibility with the coating glasses. Several acceptable combinations have been found, and both coated and uncoated fibers have been drawn and tested for laser action.

Long lengths of fibers were tightly wrapped against a xenon flash lamp with aluminum foil. The fiber ends were ground and polished, but not with the precision normally required in laser rods. Coated fibers, with multilayer dielectric end reflectors, pumped over 3-in. lengths, showed thresholds of less than 10 joules, while uncoated fibers had thresholds of about 20 joules. Coated fibers without end reflectors, pumped over a 12-in. length, gave thresholds of approximately 200 joules. Fibers of long length were hot-wound into a helical shape so that they would be easier to handle and shorter flash lamps could be used. Both the coated and uncoated fibers exhibited very regular pulse spacing, as shown in Figs. 5 and 6, respectively. The particular fiber used for Fig. 6 had a core diameter of 75 microns and index of refraction of 1.54 and 1.52 for the core and coating, respectively. The scope traces are for pumping levels of 1.25, 1.5, and 2 times threshold. Figure 6 shows the output of a 0.030-in. diameter, uncoated fiber pumped

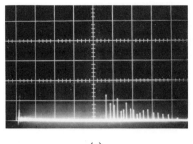

(a)

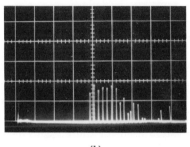

(b)

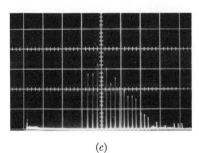

(c)

FIG. 5. Scope traces of output of a coated lasing glass fiber. Scale: 20 μsec/cm. (a) $E = 1.25E_T$. (b) $E = 1.5 E_T$. (c) $E = 2.0E_T$.

FIG. 6. Scope traces of output of un-coated lasing glass fiber. Scale: 20 μsec/cm. $E = 4E_T$.

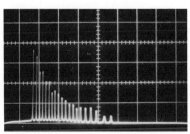

to 4 times threshold. In conjunction with the resonant coupling experiments already described and the hair-trigger mode experiments to be described, pairs of fibers have been drawn down to 3 to 10μ core sizes, with one or both cores being of neodymium-doped glass.

V. Fiber Laser Amplifiers

Fiber laser amplifiers appear to be ideally suited for use in overcoming the light losses in the resonant coupling systems proposed. The amplifier gain is dependent on degree of population inversion, the length and reflectivity of the fiber, and the loss coefficient of the glass at the laser wavelength. Gain, for our purpose, is defined as the ratio of the pumped to unpumped output of the amplifier, and is a constant only for small signal input. For fibers with plane parallel ends, the maximum gain is limited by the pumping level for laser action. In the region just below threshold, the gain is higher than would be expected for single pass gain because of multiple passes through the system. For higher gains, the reflectivity at one end of the fiber must be made as low as possible, in order that true traveling-wave amplification be achieved.

The experimental system used for the measurement of amplifier gain is shown in Fig. 7. The fiber laser shown on the left has dielectric end coatings,

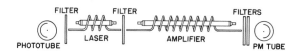

FIG. 7. Fiber amplifier setup.

permits the light signal to be amplified. A phototube views the output of the left end of the laser; a neutral density filter and monopass filter are included at the entrance to the phototube. The output of the amplifier is measured with a photomultiplier tube and associated filters.

Figure 8 shows the experimental results. Both the laser and amplifier had a 75μ core diameter and 0.030-in. outer diameter. The lasing fiber was 5 in. long and was pumped over a 3-in. length. The fiber amplifier was 15 in. long and the pumping length was 12 in. Figure 8a shows the input and output of the amplifier for the unpumped condition. The voltage on the photomultiplier tube was adjusted so that the signals presented to the oscilloscope were approximately the same size. In Fig. 8b the laser and amplifier are both pumped, and the scope sensitivity and transmission of neutral density filter were adjusted to give proper deflection. The gain for this particular figure is approximately 300; note the excellent correspondence of input and output.

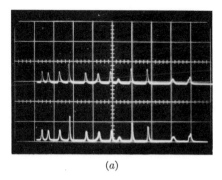

(a)

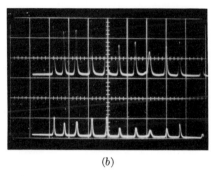

(b)

Fɪɢ. 8. Showing traces of the signal fiber output and the amplifier output. Scale: 10 μsec/cm. (a) Unpumped. (b) pumped.

VI. Hair-Trigger Operation in Fibers

As a first step in achieving hair-trigger mode through coupling of trigger light from a parallel fiber, the pulse was introduced directly into the end of the active fiber. This was done for two reasons: (1) it simplifies the setting up of the experiment; and (2) it permits the determination of the magnitude of the trigger pulse required to cause triggering action.

Assuming nominal indices of 1.54 and 1.52 for the core and coating glasses, the combination has a numerical aperture of 0.26, so that the total acceptance angle of light is approximately 30 degrees. This means that it is difficult to efficiently use the light from the trigger lamp. Also, for a fiber of 3-in. active length and 75μ core diameter, the ratio of side area to end area is approximately 4000.

For this arrangement, it is apparent that a low lasing threshold is desirable, since it minimizes the intensity of the trigger pulse required. Fibers of 3-in. active length with multilayer dielectric coatings have thresholds of approximately 10 joules whereas the threshold increases to several hundred joules when the coating is removed from one end. Advantage was taken of the fact that a multilayer dielectric coating, with 99 per cent reflectivity at 1.06μ, still has appreciable transmission in the visible region. The three main pumping regions of neodymium-doped glass occur at 2500, 5700, and 8000 Å, and by slightly shifting the wavelength of maximum reflectivity, it was possible to achieve almost 90 per cent transmission in the band centered at 8000 Å. Some difficulty was encountered, however, because the dielectric reflector was damaged by ultraviolet light from the xenon flash lamp. Triggering was finally achieved by using an evaporated reflective coating of silver on the core (but not on the cladding) at the triggering end. The experimental arrangement is shown in Fig. 9.

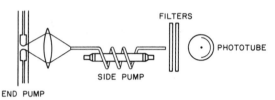

FIG. 9. Setup for demonstrating hair-trigger mode operation in lasing fiber.

Pumping light concentrated on the end of the fiber traveled down the coating and refracted into the core causing triggering.

The traces of the hair trigger mode are shown in Fig. 10. The upper trace in the figure shows the output of the laser when pumped in conventional fashion to a value of 1.05 times threshold. The lower trace shows the output when the laser is operated in the hair-trigger mode. A small portion of the white light from both flash lamps was allowed to enter the phototube housing in order to better illustrate the shapes of the pumping pulses.

In hair-trigger mode, both scope sweeps were started when the side pump was triggered. A time delay generator provided a pulse after 180 μsec, which was used to trigger the end-pump lamp, as shown in the center trace of Fig. 10. The shape of the end-pump pulse and the manner in which laser action was induced can be seen in the figure. Threshold for the laser action was approximately 37 joules, and triggering was achieved with the side-pumping level set slightly below this level.

In the figure showing hair-trigger operation, the laser output is not a single pulse, but rather a burst of pulses. This is, in part, due to the time duration of the end-pumping pulse. The RC time constant of this was 50 μsec, which is long compared to the width of the individual laser pulses. In other words, a shorter, higher intensity pulse would result in only a few output pulses. It is, of course, desirable to have single pulse output for switching applications.

Another approach which is being considered for the achievement of a single pulse is that of passive Q-spoiling. For example, liquids such as vanadium thalocyanine[13] are used with ruby lasers to provide nonelectronic Q-switching. Nonpermanent bleaching occurs in the liquid, resulting in

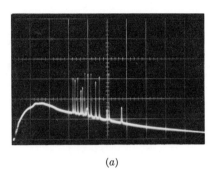

(a)

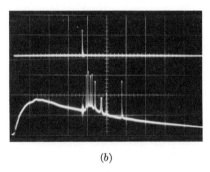

(b)

Fig. 10. Scope traces of hair-trigger mode operation in lasing fibers. Scale: 50 μsec/cm. (a) Output slightly above threshold $E = 1.05E_T$. (b) The trigger pulse (top) and fiber laser radiation output (bottom).

single pulse output as short as a few nanoseconds. This type of switching has also been accomplished using special glasses, and means for incorporating these techniques into fiber optics systems are being considered.

Experiments are also in progress to achieve hair-trigger mode through resonance coupling. As was mentioned previously, pairs of fibers, of which one is neodymium-doped, have been fabricated with core diameters as small as 2μ and 6μ center-to-center distance. The neodymium fiber is side-pumped to a value slightly below threshold, and resonance coupling used to transfer trigger light from the passive to active fiber.

VII. Other Methods of Optical Switching

A. *Variation of Beat Length*

At the time that we were setting up an experiment to demonstrate the change in coupling due to Kerr effect, a paper which describes such an experiment[14] appeared in the literature. The geometry of this experiment is shown in Fig. 11a, and it will be noted that the electric field is applied

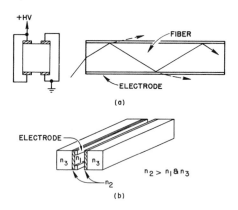

FIG. 11. Optical switching using electro-optical effects.

parallel to the glass-nitrobenzene interface. In the experiment, 22 per cent of the energy was coupled out of the slab in 28 internal reflections, using an electric field of 13×16^6 volts per meter.

Experimental efforts are now in progress to reduce the size of a slab coupling system to wavelength dimensions by using the Kerr effect in a nitrobenzene spacer as a means of controlling coupling. The experimental arrangement is shown in Fig. 11b. Note that the two elements are sandwiched together with a nitrobenzene interlayer. Two methods of fabrication are being attempted. In the first method, the conventional fiber optics drawing technique is used to achieve slab thicknesses of the order of a few wavelengths. Electrodes for application of the electric field are evaporated onto the slabs and define the physical separation of the two slabs. In the second method, the coupling slabs are evaporated thin film layers of optically transparent material, at least optically transparent at a particular wavelength. The materials that are being tested are silicon monoxide and cerium dioxide. After the thin films are deposited, the ends of the elements are ground and polished to provide a suitable entrance and exit surface for the light. Variable wavelength light, from the monochromator system described, will be used to establish beating in the absence of an electric field. An electric field will then be applied to the nitrobenzene to change the coupling.

B. *Passive Q-Switching Elements*

A means of optical switching that is being considered takes advantage of a change in transmission of a medium, as contrasted to the change in coupling which has been described previously. The technique takes advantage of the characteristics of a passive Q-switching material. Figure 12a shows the arrangement of a passive Q-switch ruby laser, and this figure will serve to illustrate the switching principle. The laser consists of a ruby

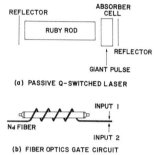

Fig. 12. Arrangement for triggering the primary laser by a secondary laser output. (a) A dye cell is placed in the laser cavity and the output of the secondary laser is used for triggering. (b) The same principle applied in lasing fiber system.

crystal with external mirrors. A cell that contains a material such as vanadium thalocyanine is placed within the cavity and serves as the Q-switching element. The liquid has an absorption band at approximately 7000 Å, and a typical cell has a transmission of 40 per cent, at the ruby wavelength. Under intense illumination, the transmission of the cell rapidly increases and serves as the Q switch. The ruby is pumped well above its normal threshold, but the start of oscillation is delayed because of losses in the cell. When a much higher population inversion than normal is reached, the gain is high enough to permit oscillation. The material in the cell is then quickly bleached and Q-switching takes place.

To achieve switching, the laser is pumped to a level slightly below threshold. The output of a second Q-switch laser is passed through the cell at right angles, causing bleaching of the liquid. The increased transmissivity permits Q-switching to take place. The switching is therefore activated optically, and at a speed determined by the bleaching time of the liquid. The minimum time between pulses is determined by the recovery rate of the liquid and the time required for the population inversion to build up on the laser.

Figure 12b illustrates the extension of this technique to an optical logic circuit. The laser material here is neodymium-doped glass in fiber form and it is used with a suitably bleached absorber. As an example, this configuration can be used as an OR gate by having the absorbing region common to the outputs of several other gates. Outputs from any of the other gates would result in bleaching of the absorber and Q-switch action in the OR gate. The output of the gate is suitable for direct activation of other gates. This configuration can also be extended to an AND gate by increasing the amount of absorber, such that one input pulse would not cause sufficient bleaching to allow triggering, but two inputs in time coincidence would induce switching.

REFERENCES

1. KAPANY, N. S., AND J. J. BURKE, *J. Opt. Soc. Am.*, *51*, 1067 (1961).
2. SCHAWLOW, A. L., AND C. H. TOWNES, *Phys. Rev.*, *112*, 1940 (1958).
3. KAPANY, N. S., *Sci. Am.*, *203*, 72 (1960).
4. SNITZER, E., *Phys. Rev. Letters*, *7*, 444 (1961).
5. KOESTER, C. J., AND E. SNITZER, *Appl. Opt.*, *3*, 1182 (1964).
6. KAPANY, N. S., "Fiber Optics and the Laser," Paper presented at the New York Academy of Sciences Conference on the Laser, New York, N.Y., 4–5 May 1964 (to be published in the Proceedings).
7. STITCH, M. L., E. J. WOODBURY, AND J. H. MORSE, *IRE WESCON Conv. Record*, 1961.
8. KAPANY, N. S., *J. Opt. Soc. Am.*, *49*, 770 (1959).
9. MILLER, S. E., *Bell System Tech. J.*, 661 (1954).
10. BRACEY, M. F., A. L. CULLEN, E. F. F. GILLESPIE, AND J. A. STANIFORTH, *IRE Trans. Antennas Propagation*, 219 (1959).
11. SNITZER, E., *Advances in Quantum Electronics*, Columbia University Press, New York, 1961.
12. LANDAU, L. D., AND E. M. LIFSHITZ, *Quantum Mechanics*, Pergamon Press, Ltd., London, 1958, p. 176.
13. SOROKIN, P. P., *et al.*, *IBM J. Res. Develop.*, *8*, 182 (1964).
14. UJHELYI, G. K., AND S. T. RIBERIRO, *Proc. IEEE*, *52*, 845 (1964).

CHAPTER 18

A PROPOSED OPTO-ELECTRONIC METHOD OF ACHIEVING VERY FAST DIGITAL LOGIC

E. H. Cooke-Yarborough, P. E. Gibbons, and P. Iredale

Electronics Division, AERE, Harwell, Didcot, Berkshire, England

As the speed of digital computers increases, electrical wiring becomes less attractive as a means of transmitting information between the many logic elements, and it has at various times been suggested that the use of light may be worth considering. Among the possible advantages of light we may note that a light beam is able to carry many information channels in parallel and that impedance matching problems are reduced, since the light reflection at an air/glass interface is only about 4 per cent. We shall, however, avoid discussion of the advantages or otherwise of using light as a medium, and concentrate instead on possible means of realizing logic and storage elements suitable for use with light. An objection hitherto has been the low speed of realizable elements. We believe that this is not necessarily valid.

Photomultipliers are capable of speeds in the nanosecond region, as are gallium arsenide electroluminescent diodes, while image intensifiers can act as high-gain light amplifiers with a very large number of independent channels.

An optical image, or information pattern, can be regenerated by imaging the phosphor of an image intensifier back onto the photocathode as shown in Fig. 1. We note that the gain needed to provide regeneration and an out-

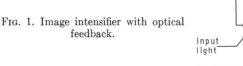

Fig. 1. Image intensifier with optical feedback.

put light signal is realized because each electron passing between the photo-cathode and the phosphor is accelerated to a high energy and generates many photons in the phosphor. The electron transit time may be quite small; in the case of one type of infrared image converter which has been made in quantity, the electron transit time is about 230 psec.

Such a system could, in principle, act as a parallel store. A serial store could be realized by slightly displacing the image at the photocathode so that the information would circulate through many paths before returning eventually to its point of arrival, as in Fig. 2.

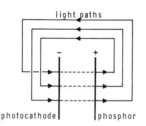

FIG. 2. Image intensifier with displaced optical feedback.

Such arrangements would not be practical for a number of reasons, the most important of which is that they do not have the logical apparatus necessary for setting 1 to 0, that is, for turning from light to dark.

These objections could be overcome if the phosphor could be replaced by what one might term an electro-optical inverter. This would have the property of emitting light except when an electron beam was falling on it, when the light would be extinguished. Thus, information at a point in a system like that of Fig. 3 would be characterized by rapid alternations

FIG. 3. Image inverter used for storage.

between light and dark with a period equal to twice the time delay round the regenerative loop. A pulse of light falling onto the photocathode during a dark period would reverse the phase of the alternations between light and dark and thus change 1 to 0 or vice versa, the difference between 1 and 0 now being determined by the timing of the light with respect to a reference phase.

We now consider the properties of the combination of photocathode, electron-accelerating region, and electro-optical inverter as a logic element. This functions as a NOR gate, since light falling at a given point on the photocathode from any one or more of several different sources will ex-tinguish the light at the corresponding point of the inverter. Light is only given out by a point of the inverter if the light input from all sources at the corresponding point of the photocathode is zero. To enable such logic elements to be interconnected, it is also necessary that the light output from any logic element be large enough to cause extinction of the light output of at least two and preferably more other similar logic elements receiving this light. We can then envisage logic arrangements such as shown in Fig. 4.

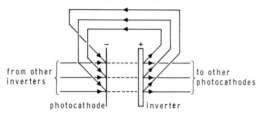

Fig. 4. Image inverter used for logic.

We sought in vain some physical phenomenon which would yield the properties required of the inverter, but regretfully had to fall back on inverters made up of discrete elements, as shown in Fig. 5 and formed into

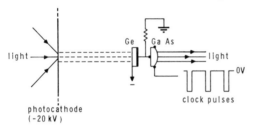

Fig. 5. Inverter made up of discrete elements.

an array as in Fig. 6. Here a germanium junction electron detector and a gallium arsenide electroluminescent diode at liquid nitrogen temperature share a common current source. When electrons strike the detector, a displacement current flows which causes the emitter potential of the gallium arsenide diode to fall, preventing the injection of carriers and the production of light by recombination radiation.

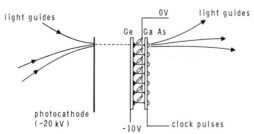

Fig. 6. Array of discrete-element inverters.

The likely performance of such a system is not easy to calculate because it depends upon many variables interrelated in a complicated manner and upon some data not accurately known, at least to us. We made an attempt at an approximate evaluation in a recent *Proc. Inst. Elec. Engrs.* (London) paper.[1] The data of Table 1 are derived from this paper.

TABLE 1   Gains and Delays of Opto-Electronic Logic System

	Quantum Gain	Delay
Photocathode:	0.003	Negligible
Statistical variations	0.43	
Acceleration of photoelectrons: (10 kV/cm)	1	460 psec
Detector: (20 keV electrons) power dissipation <13 mW	8000	200 psec
Total for conversion of light to current	10.4	660 psec
Electroluminescent diode		
Current transfer (detector to diode)	−1	Negligible
Quantum efficiency (external) at 77 °K:	0.15	1000 psec?
Optical losses		
Light guide packing factor:	0.5	Optical transmission
Interfaces and absorption	0.65	delays considered separately
Over-all:	−0.51	1.66 nsec
Continuous-channel electron multiplier: (near photocathode)	10	<400 psec
Gain available for fan-out:	−5.1	2.06 nsec

The low photocathode efficiency is the best currently available at GaAs wavelength and is perhaps the least satisfactory aspect of the whole proposal. A further factor has to be allowed for statistical uncertainties in photoelectron emission, because we are aiming to work at the lowest possible currents.

The time to accelerate electrons to a given energy (in this case 20 keV) depends on the electric field strength. The figure of 460 psec is based on 10 kV/cm, a field known to be practical in proximity-focused infrared image converters.

The germanium detector efficiently converts the kinetic energy of the accelerated electrons into electron-hole pairs at the rate of about one for every 2.5 eV of incident electron energy, yielding a current gain of 8000 at 20 kV.

A displacement current starts to flow in the electrical circuit as soon as electron-hole pairs are formed, but does not reach its maximum value until the first carriers are collected, so we include a delay equal to the collection time, which, allowing for both enhanced low-temperature electron mobility and high-field saturation,[2] is about 200 psec.

Despite the very low photocathode efficiency, we have a useful gain of 10 and a delay of under 0.7 nsec.

The low-current properties achievable in GaAs electroluminescent diodes are not well known to us. The combination of speed and efficiency predicted by early workers does not seem yet to have been realized. Our own measurements on diodes made at and kindly supplied by the Services Electronic Research Laboratory at Baldock, England, show light decay times of 2 to 3 nsec at liquid nitrogen temperature. The figure of 1 nsec given in Table 1 may therefore depend upon further development. The figure of 15 per cent external quantum efficiency is believed to be realistic at liquid nitrogen temperature.

The figure for optical losses may well be pessimistic, but it is clear that with present photocathode quantum efficiencies a fan-out ratio of even 1 will not be obtained, unless extra gain can be provided. A continuous-channel electron multiplier near the photocathode is one solution. The delay given in Table 1 should be treated with reserve; a delay figure for a published design[3] was calculated indirectly and this was then used to calculate the delay for a scaled-down geometry.[4]

An alternative way of obtaining extra gain would be to use avalanche multiplication[5] in the electron detector, but it might place too severe restrictions on detector design and operation. Undoubtedly the most attractive solution would be a development resulting in better compatibility between the wavelength characteristics of a fast electroluminescent diode and the photocathode.

Logic interconnection by fiber light guides is assumed; a standard length introducing a further 1 nsec delay would allow any logic element to be connected directly to any of about 400 others. This will present practical difficulties in manufacture; other means of achieving a complex combination of fixed low-loss light paths need study.

Fast opto-electronic logic is fraught with many problems, but their solution would allow high logic speeds to be realized. We hope that this paper and the I.E.E.E. paper to which we have referred may help to define the problems and to encourage their further study.

REFERENCES

1. COOKE-YARBOROUGH, E. H., P. E. GIBBONS, AND P. IREDALE, "Proposed Optoelectronic Method of Achieving Very Fast Digital Logic," *Proc. Inst. Elec. Engrs. (London), 111,* No. 10, 1641 (19 October 1964).
2. CONWELL, E. M., "The Properties of Silicon and Germanium" (Fig. 6), *Proc. IRE,* 46, 1327 (1952).

3. Goodritch, G. W., and W. C. Wiley, "Continuous-Channel Electron Multiplier," *Rev. Sci. Instr., 33*, 761 (1962).
4. Iredale, P., *Calculations of Electron Transit Times in Two Electron-Optical Structures*, Atomic Energy Research Establishment Memorandum 1410.
5. Lee, C. A., R. A. Logan, R. L. Batdorf, J. J. Kleimack, and W. Wiegmann, "Ionization Rates of Holes and Electrons in Silicon," *Phys. Rev., 134*, No. 3A, A761–A773 (4 May 1964).

CHAPTER 19

A THIN MAGNETIC FILM TECHNIQUE FOR WALL PANEL DISPLAY *

Harrison W. Fuller, Robert Jay Spain, Harvey I. Jauvtis, and Ronald J. Webber

LFE Electronics, Boston, Massachusetts

Introduction

There are growing requirements for large wall displays in command and control systems where most or all of the information entered on the display arrives in digital form. Among the most important characteristics of a technique used in such applications are: compatibility with digital data representation and control; low cost and power consumption; high reliability, writing speed, brightness, and contrast ratio; and great ruggedness. Display elements, furthermore, should possess permanent nonvolatile memory, and should not interact with neighboring elements.

This paper describes some progress made in a program aimed at the development of a particular electro-optical matrix display technique using thin magnetic films that promises to provide a comprehensive solution to many large wall panel display problems with operational performance that excels in all the characteristics listed.

Objectives

The end objective of the development program described in this paper is the construction of an electro-optical matrix display panel composed of 2048 by 2048 discrete display elements with a total activation time of 2 seconds. Each element must be capable of individually reflecting externally generated light on receipt of coincident X and Y signals applied through a matrix array of access wires. Access signals are in the form of 10-volt,

* This work was supported in part by contracts with the U.S. Navy Bureau of Ships and the Air Force Cambridge Research Laboratory.

10-microsecond pulses, and panel writing takes place one panel line at a time. The display panel density is 16 elements per linear inch, and the resolution must be sufficient so that no cross modulation or element-to-element interaction occurs. An element must retain the coincident signal applied to it until new data are supplied and must remain in the written state in the event of power failure. The display brightness must be sufficient for viewing in a normally lighted ambient environment, and the contrast ratio of on and off elements must be at least 50:1. The display access drive signals must be of sufficiently low voltage and current to allow use of economical semiconductor driver circuitry. Fabrication of the display panel must be modular, in suitable groups of elements, using modules which are capable of assembly without intervening spacing. Economical materials and low-cost fabrication techniques are required for panel construction to achieve an objective of full panels at a cost of less than 1 cent per element. The lifetime of a full panel must ultimately be 10,000 hr before any module needs to be replaced. Display panels must ultimately meet the following environmental specifications: MIL-E-16400E, Temperature Class I, Humidity 0 to 85 per cent, Shock 20G, Vibration per MIL-STD-107.

Description of Technique

The technique being developed at LFE for fulfilling the display panel objectives described above utilizes a magnetic microstructure, occurring in a class of thin magnetic films, to form an optical diffraction grating. Display elements are switched on or off by coincident-current selection as in a thin magnetic film matrix memory. The display panel is side lighted by a source of illumination, and the elements that are switched on brightly reflect light in the direction of normal viewing of the panel, while the elements that are switched off remain dark. Characters and contours are formed by switching on the proper pattern of display elements.

Figure 1 schematically shows the magnetic thin film where the magnetization has been switched with a magnetic field into a direction parallel to the x axis. The aforementioned microstructure gives rise to the magnetic

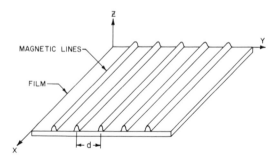

Fig. 1. Thin magnetic film with magnetic lines that give rise to diffraction effects.

lines of spacing d running parallel to the direction of magnetization. When the surface of the film is illuminated, the lines give rise to diffraction images, as shown in Fig. 2; a collimated light beam in the y, z plane arriving at an

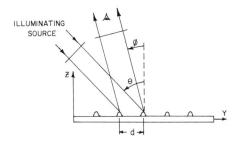

FIG. 2. Geometry for diffraction effects.

angle θ with respect to the film normal results in constructive interference and a diffraction image at an angle ϕ when

$$n\lambda = d(\sin \theta + \sin \phi) \tag{1}$$

where n is an integer and λ is the wavelength of the (monochromatic) light. If in Fig. 2 the lines were made to run in the y-axis direction (by switching the film magnetization ninety degrees) instead of in the x-axis direction, then no diffraction images could occur, except for the zero-order image ($n = 0$, normal reflection), and only a small amount of light would appear by diffuse scattering at angles other than $-\theta$.

Figure 3 shows the geometry for observation of a display panel (labeled

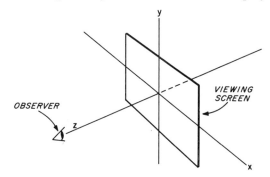

FIG. 3. Geometry for display panel viewing.

viewing screen) using the thin magnetic film technique. In Fig. 4 the display panel is shown side lighted with an illumination source, and the bright and dark conditions are illustrated at left and right, respectively, depending on the direction of the magnetization of the thin film making up the display panel.

In a practical application the illumination source(s) would be made a line

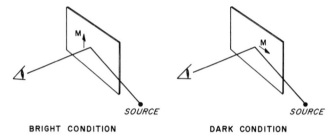

BRIGHT CONDITION   DARK CONDITION

FIG. 4. Dependence of display panel brightness on thin film magnetization direction.

source to make the angle of panel viewing uncritical. This is illustrated in Fig. 5, where the use of baffles is also shown for both eliminating direct

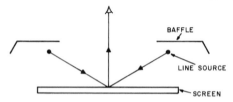

FIG. 5. Practical display panel arrangement.

light paths from the light sources to the observer and trapping light specularly reflected from the display panel. Figure 6 suggests a scheme for making

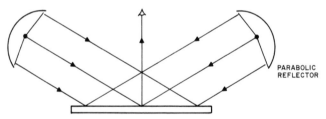

FIG. 6. Method of uniformly illuminating display panel.

the illumination of the display uniform over the entire panel, using parabolic reflections to produce collimated light beams. Figure 7 shows how

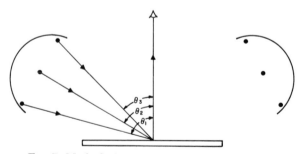

FIG. 7. Method of achieving white-on-dark display.

multiple line sources could be used to produce a superposition of diffraction images with different wavelengths at the point of observation; white images on a dark background could be achieved in this fashion.

Fabrication of Display Panel Modules

The thin magnetic film display technique is well suited to batch fabrication of rectangular arrays of display elements in sufficiently large modules to result in a small fabrication cost per element. Figure 8 shows a 2 × 2

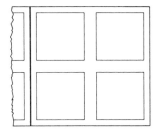

FIG. 8. Design of display panel modules permitting modular assembly of display panel.

element module placed against one edge of the adjacent module to illustrate how modules can be assembled to make a large display panel without introducing unusual spacing between adjacent elements in different modules; it is seen from the figure that the window-frame border of a module is made half as wide as the internal window-frame bars separating display

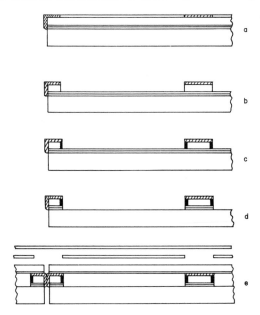

FIG. 9. Steps in fabrication of a display panel module.

elements to allow display panel assembly. An actual module would consist of up to 4096 elements in a square array, and modules would be assembled onto, and in registration with, a batch-fabricated matrix wiring pattern.

Display panel modules are fabricated by a sequence of operations including laminating of sheet materials, photoetching, and thin film deposition. The sequence of fabrication steps is indicated in Fig. 9, where in *a*, a thin sheet of etchable material, e.g. aluminum, has been bonded with photoresist material onto a glass substrate carrying a thin reflective film. The window-frame pattern has been used as a mask for exposure of a layer of photoresist on top of the sandwich. In *b* the windows have been etched out leaving the window-frame bars, and in *c* the edges of the aluminum bars have been anodized. In *d* the photoresist and reflective film have been removed in the windows. In *e* a glass substrate carrying the pretested thin magnetic film has been bonded to the window frame. Figure 9*e* also shows the row and column strip conductors; the vertical scale in Fig. 9 is exaggerated for clarity.

Experimental Results

Experiments have been performed to test line-at-a-time coincident-current writing into display panel models. Figure 10 shows the 5 × 7 strip

Fig. 10. Experimental 5 × 7 wiring pattern.

conductor pattern used in the experiments; the conductors are spaced one-tenth inch center to center. In Fig. 11 is shown the result of writing line-at-a-time into all 5 × 7 display element locations, where a line of writing is five elements long.

Fig. 11. Spot patterns on display panel model written line-at-a-time.

Figure 12 shows a 2 written into the display panel model. It can be seen that the contrast between light and dark display elements is great. The variations in spot size and shape that occur in Figs. 11 and 12 are due to

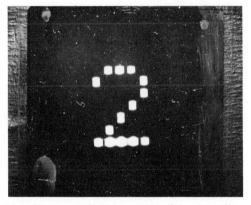

Fig. 12. Spot patterns on display panel model written line-at-a-time.

lack of flatness of both the matrix wiring pattern and the thin film substrate placed upon it. Figure 13a shows a 5 × 7 pattern of spots written into the display panel model wherein the picture was taken using a normal exposure time. Figure 13b is a long exposure of the display panel model following line-at-a-time erasure of a 5 × 7 spot pattern; Fig. 13b shows that an erased spot returns to essentially the same intensity as the undisturbed background.

Measurements performed on experimental panels indicate an element switching speed of less than 10 μsec, a brightness of over 100 ft-L, and a contrast ratio of 70:1. The conversion efficiency of illuminating light into display-image light is between 1 and 5 per cent. Pulse driver voltages for a

(a)

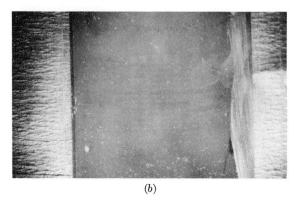

(b)

Fig. 13. Demonstration of line-at-a-time erasure of spot pattern.

full 2048 × 2048 display panel would be in the order of 1 V, while the pulse driver power required would be in the order of 100 W for maximum activity.

Technique Extensions

It is apparent from the experimental results shown in the figures that a display element resolution of 16/inch is easily achieved with the thin magnetic film technique. Display element resolutions of 100/inch or more appear to be quite feasible. Physically smaller high-resolution display panels appear to be well suited to projection display.

Advantage can be taken of the diffraction effect upon which the technique depends to construct multicolor display panels. A uniform gray scale is also possible. Figure 14 shows a photograph of an experimental display

Fig. 14. Patterns and characters manually written on a display panel model using magnetic probe.

panel (one inch square) on which characters have been handwritten using a magnetic probe. This technique of manual entry could be refined to usefully augment electrical entry on a memory-display panel; it is possible to electrically read out of the memory-display panel, and together with manual entry this capability could furnish a useful tool for improving man-machine communication.

ACKNOWLEDGMENTS

The authors would like to acknowledge the contributions of staff members of the Solid State Electronics Laboratory, LFE Electronics, in particular those of Floyd T. Gould and Curtis C. Deininger.

CHAPTER 20

UTILIZATION OF LIGHT EMISSION FROM GaAs TUNNEL DIODES TO PERFORM COMPUTER FUNCTIONS

B. T. French

Autonetics, A Division of North American Aviation, Inc., Anaheim, California

Introduction

As a result of developments in the field of solid-state light-emitting devices, it has become possible to construct a large number of opto-electronic digital logic circuits, such as "and" gates, "or" gates, latching circuits, opto-electronic amplifiers, and data links. All of these devices utilize the unilateral nature of opto-electronic power transfer processes to more efficiently perform logic functions. However, if these devices are to be used to yield computer function blocks that can replace conventional integrated circuit function blocks, they must incorporate much faster over-all transient response into the systems to which they are applied.

The primary reason for a consideration of opto-electronic techniques is the expectation of nanosecond computation and data processing techniques. There has not been, however, a high-speed dynamic storage element which interfaces suitably with opto-electronic devices. Thus it appears that this lack of storage function, combined with low emission and detection efficiencies of semiconductor opto-electronic devices, has limited the operating speed and thus has reduced the relative importance of semiconductor opto-electronic devices in the development of high-speed data processing systems.

An exemplary high-speed computer storage element with little present commercial usage is the tunnel diode. It possesses both bistability and high switching speed. However, when it is employed in a circuit as a bistable device, the state of the device must be determined, either by measuring the voltage across the device or the current through it directly; or by applying a stimulus and observing the presence or absence of a switching transient. These are difficult processes to perform at high data flow rates because of the negative resistance and small bias voltage of the device, and because of the complexity of the required readout circuitry.

The subject of this paper is the utilization of the recombination emission process in direct semiconductor devices to realize high-speed nondestructive readout from tunnel diodes without direct measurement or perturbation.

The method described makes use of the fact that two dominant current mechanisms shape the tunnel diode characteristic and that the dominance of one or the other of these mechanisms can be distinguished externally by opto-electronic techniques.

I. Basic Operating Concept

The current flow through a gallium arsenide or other direct semiconductor tunnel diode is composed of two primary components; tunnel current and injection current. Each of the current modes varies with voltage in a well-known manner such that tunnel current is dominant at voltages below the valley, and injection current is dominant at voltages above the valley. Coupled to the injection mode of current flow is the characteristic infrared recombination which can be observed to vary exponentially with applied voltage.

The construction of a bistable storage element requires only that a direct semiconductor tunnel diode be placed in the elementary circuit shown in Fig. 1. The values of R_L and V_0 are chosen to permit the circuit to have two

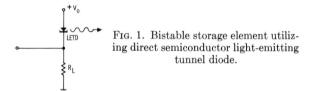

Fig. 1. Bistable storage element utilizing direct semiconductor light-emitting tunnel diode.

stable states and one unstable state as shown in Fig. 2. Note that one state occurs in the tunnel current region where no observable light is emitted

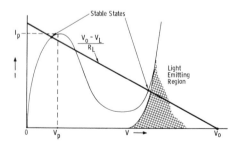

Fig. 2. Schematic V-I plot of GaAs tunnel diode (showing load line, stable states, and region of light emission).

while the other state occurs in a region of detectable light emission. Thus the state of this bistable storage circuit can be determined unambiguously by coupling a suitable photodetector to the circuit.

Because of the extremely rapid transient response of both the tunneling mechanism and the direct recombination mechanism, it is possible to design high-speed nondestructive readout (NDRO) storage cells and related circuitry utilizing this device concept. The first step in this procedure is a characterization of the various devices which are applicable to the problem.

II. Radiation from GaAs Tunnel Diodes

The most convenient devices for such experiments as these are GaAs tunnel diodes. The radiation from those devices matches the high-efficiency detection band of both S-1 photomultipliers and silicon photodetectors. Furthermore, they exhibit the extremely rapid switching response desired for such devices. The radiation from GaAs tunnel diodes has been considered previously in the literature. Anderson[1] has shown evidence that light emission from a tunnel diode is a function of injection current alone and that other currents do not contribute to the emission of light. The measurements made by Hoover and Zucker show radiation occurring in the tunnel region which has its peak at 0.4 volt forward bias and is quite intense.[2]

Because of the implications of this observation and because of the need for quantitative photon output data, several devices were obtained and their optical emission characteristics determined. The most fruitful measurements were made utilizing RCA 40058 GaAs tunnel diodes. These are diffused tunnel diodes in a low inductance ceramic package. The contact to the n region of the device is a gold-plated screen or flexible grating which is imbedded in the device ohmic contact.

The sealed package was opened by breaking four welds which hold the case top on the cathode side of the device. With entry thus gained, optical emission data were obtained in considerable detail. No emission was observed which was visible through an infrared snooperscope, but radiation output was sufficient to drive an IR photomultiplier, even when the light was passed through a prism spectrometer. Understandably, the resolution obtainable, using the spectrometer, was quite broad.

After measurement of the voltage-current characteristics shown in Fig. 3, the radiation output as a function of voltage was measured and the curve shown in Fig. 4 was obtained. Because the tunnel region radiation was observed only in the negative resistance portion of the voltage-current characteristic, the output voltmeter was replaced by an oscilloscope and the radiation output was examined for possible oscillations. As the tunnel diode bias was increased from zero to the peak value, no radiation was observed. A further increase of voltage to 0.3 V caused the current to decrease to

30 mA and radiation was detected which is shown as *A* in Fig. 5. Note the oscillations in optical output which occurred when the device was operated in this negative resistance region. Increasing the bias to 0.8 V caused the

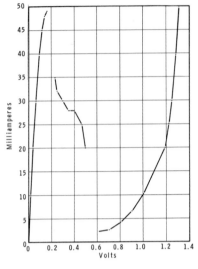

Fɪɢ. 3. V-I plot of RCA 40058 GaAs tunnel diode (300°K).

current to drop to 5 mA in the valley, and the radiation output dropped to *B* (Fig. 5), the zero level. Increasing the bias into the injection region caused the strong radiation shown as *C* (Fig. 5) at an injection current of 38 mA.

The frequency of oscillations observed in the negative resistance region is a function of applied bias varying from zero at the peak, increasing to

Fɪɢ. 4. Emitted intensity as a function of applied voltage for a GaAs 40058.

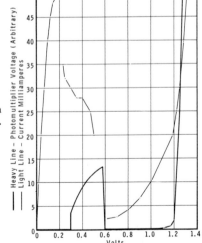

about 1.5 Mc at half the peak value, and then decreasing to zero and extinction at the valley. It is believed this oscillating radiation arises from the instability of the negative resistance region. The oscillations are limited in size by their encroachment into the injection region, which is a positive

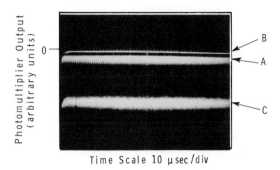

Time Scale 10 μ sec /div

FIG. 5. Photomultiplier response to GaAs tunnel diode radiation at various positions on the V-I plot. A. 1 = 30 mA (tunnel current) B. 1 = 5 mA (valley) C. 1 = 38 mA (injection).

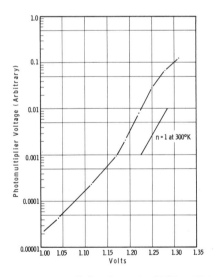

FIG. 6. Radiation output versus applied voltage for RCA 40058 GaAs tunnel diode.

resistance region. Part of the energy dissipated in the injection region appears as recombination radiation. If the assumption is made that the radiation observed in the tunnel region is caused by this instability, then the radiation from this tunnel diode (shown in Fig. 6) appears to be due entirely to recombination emission. It varies exponentially with voltage according to the standard form

$$\rho = \rho_0 e^{qV/nkt}$$

where $0.95 < n < 2$.

Room temperature emission intensity as a function of wavelength was plotted for a number of current levels. The curves, shown in Fig. 7, seem

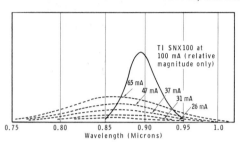

FIG. 7. Spectral plot of radiation emitted by RCA 40058 GaAs tunnel diode.

to peak at 0.865μ as opposed to the 0.89 to 0.9μ peaks usually seen at room temperature with gallium arsenide light-emitting diodes.

After evaluation of the optical output of a readily available commercial device, an attempt was made to fabricate some more efficient experimental devices.

Because of the transparency of n-type material to near band-gap emission in other devices, it was postulated that alloying p-regions into n-type base material would yield more efficient light emitters. Several attempts were made to fabricate efficient GaAs light-emitting tunnel diodes by this general method. The technique of alloying zinc spheres to 0.005Ω-cm Te doped n-type GaAs yields efficient light emitters with only slight tunneling or "backward" characteristics. Ostensibly this occurs because a sufficiently high n-type doping level cannot be grown into the GaAs.

The devices which most nearly met all the criteria for light-emitting tunnel diodes were some large zinc-diffused diodes which resulted from a laser-oriented project. It is believed that local zones of high Te concentration in the n-type base material may have been responsible for the appear-

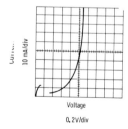

FIG. 8. Voltage current plot of GaAs "laser" tunnel diode.

ance of tunnel current in these devices. Although plagued by large excess current, these devices emitted sufficient light at a forward bias of 0.96 V (30 mA) to be easily visible with a snooperscope. Because the peak current of the best device was 12 mA (see Fig. 8), the high excess current observed

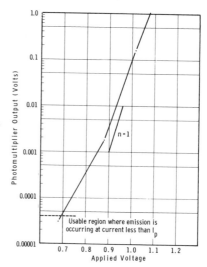

Fig. 9. Radiation from GaAs "laser" tunnel diode (300°K).

kept this device from being a useful LETD. At 11 mA in the injection region, photocurrent is just observable with an IR photomultiplier and a sensitive voltmeter. Nevertheless, observation of the photon output at such a low voltage (see Fig. 9) indicates that the concept of a GaAs LETD is feasible and that usable light-emitting tunnel diodes may indeed be realized.

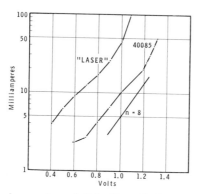

Fig. 10. Semi-log plot of excess current regions of two GaAs tunnel diodes showing exponential voltage dependence.

The large size of this "laser" diode (10^{-2} cm^2) may be responsible for its high excess and injection currents.

With respect to the excess tunnel current, it has been proposed that this current varies exponentially with voltage in GaAs tunnel diodes and that it is proportional to the density of occupied band-gap states in the junction region of the device.[3]

This indicates that a refinement of techniques, to reduce dislocations and other imperfection states, might increase the low quantum efficiency of GaAs light-emitting tunnel diodes. The apparent importance of this exponential excess current in the devices studied is shown in Fig. 10. Note that both of the devices are diffused and that their respective currents and light emissions are similar. In both devices, excess current predominates up to levels well above the peak value of tunnel current.

III. Recombination Emitter/Tunnel Diode Circuitry

Successful application of light-emitting tunnel diodes demands that a highly efficient radiation emitter with excellent tunnel diode characteristics be obtained. Since it has been shown that a GaAs light-emitting tunnel diode is basically a tunnel device superimposed upon an injecting device,

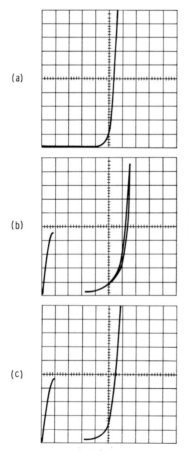

(a)

(b)

(c)

Fig. 11. Forward bias V-I characteristics of (a) TI SNX 100, (b) RCA 40058 TD, and (c) a and b in parallel (10 mA/div, vertical; 0.2 V/div, horizontal).

it was proposed that a simulated LETD be fabricated utilizing this technique. A TI SNX100 GaAs light-emitting diode was placed in parallel with an RCA 40058 GaAs tunnel diode (see Fig. 11) to obtain the resulting device. Note that the GaAs tunnel diode injection-current turns on at a higher voltage than the light-emitting diode. Thus in the injection mode almost all current flows through the light-emitting diode, while in the tunnel mode all current flows through the tunnel diode. This naturally occurring crossover due to the respective built-in potentials and relative junction areas of the two devices serves to make this approach to utilization of recombination emission in GaAs quite attractive. The photon output of this hybrid device at 40 mA is approximately 10^{14} photons/sec (15 μW) which is easily made visible by using an image converter (snooperscope). The peak tunnel-current of 50 mA renders this device feasible for demonstrations of circuit capability. Although the capacitance at zero bias of the light-emitting diode chosen was about 1000 pF, the hybrid device could be switched in about 10 nsec when used as the termination of a 50-ohm line. Figure 12 shows the device response to square pulses of

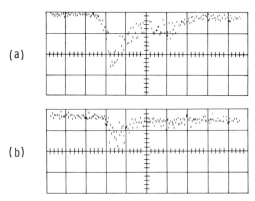

(a)

(b)

Fig. 12. Switching response of hybrid device to (*a*) 5 V and (*b*) 3.5 V pulses of 10 nsec duration when used as termination of a 50-ohm line (arbitrary units, vertical; 10 nsec/div, horizontal).

10-nsec duration in this setup. This response time is due to a combination of *R-C* effects, GaAs recombination time in the light emitter, and photomultiplier response time.

The over-all result of the device work which was performed indicates that a successful LETD might be a dual structure of some sort. This is consistent with the observed dependence of the degradation of GaAs tunnel diodes upon the ratio of maximum applied injection current to device capacitance. Theory states that tunneling is a high current density monoenergetic process while injection and recombination involve a considerable release of energy to the device structure. Thus the presence of high-density injection current in a tunnel junction may seriously degrade the tunnel diode structure. It appears that the proper design procedure for a light-emitting tunnel diode may begin with the assumption that the two functions must be generated separately, even if they are located on the same piece of material.

A. Memory Circuits

The basic LETD bistable storage circuit can be employed in various memory arrays which utilize its properties. The most basic array is a row of GaAs LETD's with series-connected load resistors, each connected in parallel with all the others across a bias supply. Optically coupled photodiodes read out each cell directly (see Fig. 13). Although this direct method

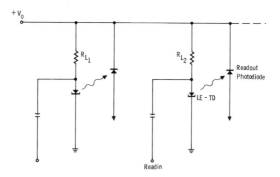

FIG. 13. Basic LRTD memory array.

yields a nondestructive readout memory capability, it is expensive to fabricate and requires a large continuous current for each bit.

The current drain of the memory can be greatly reduced by biasing each cell as shown in Fig. 14 so that current just greater than valley current

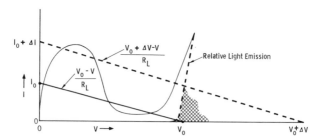

FIG. 14. Low-drain bias technique.

flows. When the output is to be read, a large voltage (ΔV) is introduced in series with the bias voltage which increases the current to the level shown by the dotted line. This does not change the state of the device; it does increase light emission if the device is in the light-emitting state.

A convenient memory array can be formed by connecting a number of bistable elements in series. Driving current may be provided by a current source such as a transistor amplifier. The current through the series array is maintained at a level that permits each device to be bistable. Each node between devices is ac grounded by a capacitor. Thus the array has the column-like appearance shown in Fig. 15. Switching of states is done by

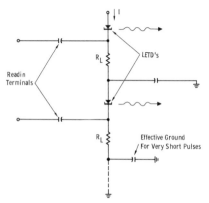

FIG. 15. Series-driven GaAs LETD memory column.

applying appropriate pulses to the load resistor of each bistable element. Two matrix arrangements have been postulated using this basic memory arrays. One matrix consumes only 3–6 mW/bit in quiescent operation, uses fewer components, but cannot be operated at very high speeds. It consists of a number of columns of bistable devices normally biased just above valley current and arranged side-by-side to form a basic matrix, as shown in Fig. 16. The state of each device is shown as "one" or "zero" corresponding to the light-emitting and tunneling states, respectively. Each row of devices is observed by a photodiode.

However, until a current (ΔI) is applied to a column, no detectable light is emitted regardless of the state of devices. In this manner, row-column indexing of the cell readout is achieved, but the speed of response is limited by the time required to charge the grounding capacitors. The alternate technique involves the operation of all the bistable devices at a current level such that each device in the 1 state can be detected at all times. Readout can be accomplished by interrogation of a matrix of phototransistors such as shown in Fig. 17, which is superimposed upon the matrix of tunnel emitters.

In both types of memories, readin would be accomplished by the coincidence of row current pulses with an alteration in current level in a column. These two signals would be chosen in such a manner that neither, alone, is sufficient to change the state of any cell, but in combination they must unambiguously place the device into the desired state. Although a relatively high current drain is necessary to conserve stored information, the arrays

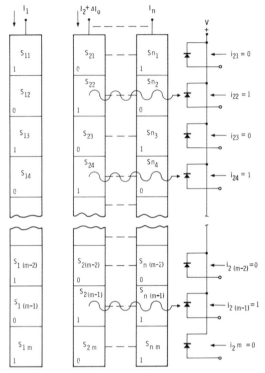

FIG. 16. Low-power matrix with column 2 activated for readout.

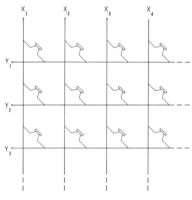

FIG. 17. Phototransistor matrix for high-speed NDRO LETD memory.

described here do represent methods of obtaining a high-speed opto-electronic NDRO memory.

B. *Flip-Flop Circuit*

A flip-flop is a logic component capable of observable bistable behavior which can be influenced to rest in one of its two stable states only during certain times. These readin times may be determined by the flip-flop itself (dynamic flip-flop) or they may be determined by the injection of an outside stimulus usually called a clock.

By the addition of a few components, a flip-flop with photon input and output was fabricated using the bistable circuit previously described. This flip-flop is most conveniently switched by the action of an external clock pulse upon some detecting circuit which determines what state the device will be in. The flip-flop circuit is shown in Fig. 18. In this circuit,

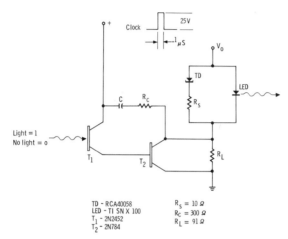

FIG. 18. Flip-flop circuit design.

the input and output functions are the presence or absence of a light signal. They are labeled 1 and 0, respectively. If no light is presented to the input, the clock pulse will pass through Rs and R_L to ground, increase the voltage drop across R_L to at least V_0, and unambiguously switch the LETD into the tunnel (0) state. If a sufficiently strong light signal is presented to the input phototransistor (T_1), T_2 saturates upon application of the clock and R_L is effectively short-circuited. This causes the current through the tunnel diode to increase to more than the tunnel current peak value. Thus the LETD is unambiguously switched into the 1 or light-emitting state. An experimental circuit was attempted using a 2N2452 phototransistor ($\beta = 130$) and a 2N784 driver. In the Darlington configuration, these transistors enabled the simulated LETD to switch on 0.1 μsec clock pulses at a 2-Mc rate. The input light was provided by a GaAs light-emitting diode.

In the circuit shown $R_C = 300 \; \Omega$. The capacitor C was required to keep the bias across R_C from activating T_1 between clock pulses, and $R_S = 10 \; \Omega$ was installed to tilt the tunnel characteristic and further concentrate the flow of current in the light-emitting diode when the circuit is in the 1 state.

The fabrication of a shift register by optically coupling a sequence of flip-flops has been contemplated. This application requires that each flip-flop possess optical switching gain greater than unity. Also a delay must be built into each module so that when turned on, all bits do not propagate out of the register. Naturally occurring transistor and capacitance delays seem to fulfill this requirement, but they greatly degrade transient response. It is felt that an avalanche photodiode coupled optically to an LETD might provide the unity gain optical power transfer necessary for very high speed shift register operation from a sequence of LETD flip-flops.

IV. Conclusion

Several devices and circuits have been described which show that recombination emission from tunnel diodes and hybrid devices can be used to perform certain computer functions requiring dynamic data storage. Although certain drawbacks exist, light-emitting tunnel diode circuitry may be used to synthesize certain high-speed digital computer function blocks.

REFERENCES

1. ANDERSON, R. L., *Proc. IEEE, 51,* 610 (1963).
2. HOOVER, G. J., AND R. S. ZUCKER, *Proc. IEEE, 51,* 1237 (1963).
3. NANAVATI, R. P., *Proc. IEEE, 52,* 869 (1964).

CHAPTER 21

LASER DEFLECTION AND SCANNING

R. V. Pole, R. A. Myers, H. Wieder, and E. S. Barrekette

Thomas J. Watson Research Center, International Business Machines Corporation
Yorktown Heights, New York

Introduction

The use of laser devices in many information-processing applications requires the development of economical methods for rapidly scanning or deflecting a high-resolution spot of coherent light. Past approaches to laser deflection have usually been based on techniques which do not capitalize on the special properties of this unique device. For example, the electro-optic prism[1] and its derivative devices[2] simply treat the laser as a bright light source; while attractive in principle, these devices cannot be made practical until improved materials are developed. On the other hand, though the phased array concept is a proven method for deflecting coherent radar beams,[3] it is unsuitable for lasers, since the problem of coupling multiple laser beams coherently has defied solution. In none of these schemes is the full potential of the laser realized. To do so would require that an optical scanner have access times of better than a microsecond, with a potential of 10 to 100 nsec, capacities of 10^6 spots or better, and resolution of 5μ. The energy consumed (within the laser pump and the addressing circuitry) must be small enough for the device to be competitive; it is therefore desirable that the system be one in which the entire active volume emits light into the desired spot, and in which deflection is electrically controlled and requires a minimal expenditure of power.

This paper describes a new approach to the deflection of laser light—an approach which is unique to the laser and its special properties and which is potentially capable of satisfying or exceeding all of the above requirements. In this technique the laser beam is not actually deflected; instead, the laser is caused to emit in the particular desired direction at a given time. In order for such a system to be realizable, the resonator must initially be capable of emitting light in a multiplicity of directions, i.e., it must be *directionally*, or angularly degenerate. A single mode, or direction, is then chosen by lifting the degeneracy, thus permitting one mode to be favored over all others. Since a laser oscillator is a nonlinear device, mode selection is reduced to a perturbation problem and the energies needed to accomplish it may be relatively small.

In light of this approach, the principal objective of this paper is to describe a number of optical resonators which have a suitably high angular degeneracy, and to discuss some mode selection schemes by means of which this degeneracy can be lifted. The first section includes a discussion of a primitive, angularly degenerate cavity,[4,5] the "bidirectional rooftop laser," and of a simple generalization of the concept it embodies. Studies on this system provide a bridge between our work and that of others using diode lasers,[6,7] and prepare the way for the more sophisticated experiments that are described in the remaining sections. These experiments were performed on a class of cavities which have been termed[8–12] "conjugate laser resonators." Such resonators are characterized both by their directional degeneracy and by the fact that they employ an active element which also acts as a lens, imaging the mirror surfaces on one another. By means of such an "active lens," as many as 10^6 differently directed modes may be obtained in a cone of 22° half-angle from a single active element.

Associated with the description of each laser resonator is a companion mode selection mechanism. This mechanism, a "dynamic spatial filter," electrically selects the direction of emission in either a digital or analog fashion. Thus, the bidirectional rooftop laser is discussed in conjunction with a digital Kerr cell filter.[4,5] The "conjugate plano-concentric" (CPC) resonator, in which the active lens is used at infinite magnification and in which a large number of discrete directional modes can be established, is described with a discrete analog filter.[11,12] Both of these sections include data concerning experimental verification of the principles presented. The final section describes the highly degenerate "conjugate concentric" (CC) resonator,[8–10] which is the equivalent of the CPC resonator working at unit (or finite) magnification. This resonator, in conjunction with a continuously variable analog spatial filter, makes possible the first true laser scanning system,[13] called the "Scanlaser."

The results and interpretations presented here have been selected from some unreported work, as well as from some that has already been published, in order to clarify the general principles we find significant; more details may be found in the references.

Bidirectional Rooftop Laser

Consider a laser which is in the form of a rod with two low-angle chisel ends,[4,5] such that the opposite facets of the ends are parallel, as shown in

Fig. 1. If one end of the rod is silvered and the other covered with an anti-reflection (AR) coating, then by positioning plane mirrors parallel to the AR faces, one may form two crossed Fabry-Perot (FP) cavities which share a significant portion of the active volume. Using this simple bidirectional

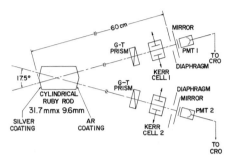

FIG. 1. Schematic diagram of bidirectional rooftop laser, showing switching mechanism.

laser, it is possible to demonstrate experimentally the principle of degeneracy-lifting, and also to obtain an estimate of the switching time between directions. In addition, the simultaneous output in the two directions yields information on the coupling between the two principal directional modes.

Experiments were performed on a 90° ruby rod 31.7 mm long and 9.6 mm in diameter, with a 17.45° chisel on each end and the c axis parallel to the chisel. In this geometry, about 40 per cent of the active volume in either cavity was shared by the other. The plane mirrors were about 60 cm from the end of the rod, as shown in the figure. Copious spiking was observed in both directions, with an observable temporal correlation between the output in the two directions; in a typical series of flashes about 50 per cent of the spikes occurred at approximately the same time in both directions. Their magnitudes, however, were random. Despite this correlation, the threshold in one direction was unchanged (within a 5 per cent experimental uncertainty) when the mirror in the other direction was either blocked or open. Because of this, and also because of the general properties of a spiking laser, it was possible to treat the system as a pair of independent oscillators. It will be seen in the succeeding sections of this paper that such a simplification cannot, in general, be made.

A bidirectional switching experiment was then performed with the full apparatus shown in Fig. 1. A Glan-Thomson polarizer, a nitrobenzene Kerr cell, and a variable aperture were positioned in each optical path, with all optical surfaces having AR coatings and aligned parallel to within 3 sec of arc. The polarizers were inserted to simplify the experiments, and ultimately were removed when the polarized emission of the laser was found to be sufficient to enable the Kerr cells to extinguish oscillation by inducing about $\frac{1}{6}$ wave ellipticity; the purpose of the apertures was to equalize the Q (and thus the threshold) in the two directions.

The Kerr cells were connected so that the high voltage (about 25 kV) could be switched rapidly from one to the other; the result of a typical switching experiment is shown in Fig. 2. Of particular interest was the time required to switch from one direction to the other; when the switch was

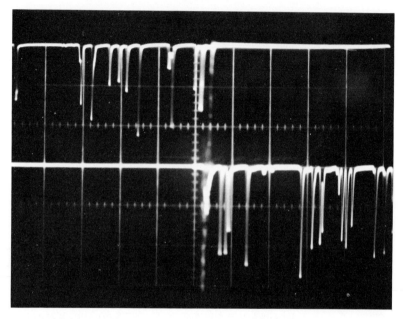

FIG. 2. Switching between channels of a bidirectional rooftop laser. (Scale: 20 μsec/div.)

triggered by a single spike, a switching time of the order of 1 μsec was observed. We were not able to measure shorter deflection times because the output of the laser was obscured by electrical pickup from the switch, but we are confident that the measured time was limited solely by the circuitry rather than by any coupling between the two directions. Thus, appropriate circuitry should make possible submicrosecond deflection times.

Note that a multifaceted active medium is not indispensable for obtaining multidirectional laser action; Fig. 3 shows how two (or more) crossed

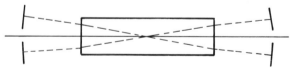

FIG. 3. Generalized bidirectional F-P cavity.

F-P cavities may share a portion of an active medium with plane-parallel ends. Although this geometry permits operation in more than two directions, as well as extensive variability of the directions, true degeneracy requires painstaking care in alignment. For this reason, no experiments were performed using this geometry. However, the experiments with the elementary rooftop realization of a bidirectional laser did show that: (1) the directional modes were probably independent, or at least sufficiently independent so as not to affect switching times, and (2) switching could be accomplished at megacycle rates. Extrapolations of this scheme, or of the plane-parallel one, to a multiplicity of directions, while possible in principle, are not especially attractive because the active volume associated with any particular direction of emission rapidly diminishes as the number of directions increases, and because the alignment of many F-P cavities would be a critical, time-consuming process. Neither limitation is so severe in the case of the conjugate plano-concentric (CPC) cavity which, like the rooftop, operates in a discrete set of directions.

Conjugate Plano-Concentric Laser

The CPC laser[11,12] is a generalization of the bidirectional laser depicted in Fig. 3. By capitalizing on the lenticular properties of the active medium, it allows a large portion of the active medium to contribute to the laser output in every direction and thus embodies a significant improvement over the bidirectional scheme. Furthermore, it has the advantage that the directions of emission are not predetermined by the orientation of the facets of the solid-state medium.

Let a solid-state laser be cut in the form of a sphere, or portion of a sphere, of radius r and index of refraction N. A basic property of such a spherical active lens is that it will focus parallel light incident from any direction onto a spherical focal surface whose radius R is given by

$$r/R = N'(1 - 2/N) + 1 \tag{1}$$

Here, N' is the index of refraction of the medium between the lens and the focal surface, and paraxial rays are assumed. Due to spherical aberrations, Eq. 1 must, in general, be modified for off-axis rays. Figure 4 shows typical ray paths for light incident along two different directions.

Two closed optical cavities will be formed if plane and spherical mirrors are inserted along the dashed surfaces shown in Fig. 4, resulting in a bidirectional CPC resonator. The spherical mirror of radius R must lie in the focal surface of the sphere, but the restrictions on the plane mirrors are minimal; they may be located anywhere in the right-hand space of the figure, provided only that they are orthogonally intersected by some line passing through the center of the lens. Under these conditions the mirror surfaces will be optical conjugates of one another, and any plane mirror will be imaged into a point on the spherical mirror. Note that a slight misalignment of the plane mirror changes the orientation of the resonator slightly, but does not prevent oscillation, as would be the case in a F-P cavity. Consequently, one may easily form a multidirectional laser of high degeneracy without any but the simplest alignment procedure. Furthermore, by using a back-surface meniscus mirror of proper outer radius, with the inner radius matched to the radius of the active medium, the focal sur-

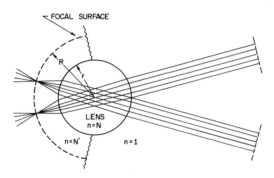

FIG. 4. Typical ray optics modes in a conjugate plano-concentric laser.

face mirror is automatically aligned when the meniscus is in contact with the active element, thus obviating the only difficult alignment inherent in the CPC geometry. Finally, by grinding a rod with concentric ends of radii r and R related by Eq. 1 with $N' = N$ so that $r = R(N - 1)$, the reflecting coating may be deposited directly on the laser medium.

In the actual experiment a 90° ruby rod 25.4 mm long and 9.6 mm in diameter was used. It had concentric ends and a back-surface glass meniscus mirror (of radius 15.8 mm) located at the focal surface. With a plane mirror positioned anywhere within the near 20° angular aperture of the ruby rod, "plano-concentric" laser emission was observed, i.e., light emerged normal to the plane mirror and was focused on the focal mirror.

Inasmuch as the system was designed to focus a zonal rather than a paraxial bundle of rays onto the spherical mirror, the near field pattern at the plane mirror should appear as a ring rather than a disk of light for certain modes. This ring was observed in early experiments when the plane mirror was placed normal to the axis of the rod and about 50 cm from the axis of the rod (Fig. 5). The angular variation in intensity seen in this figure is associated with a higher order mode, which was probably favored over the lower order modes because of the hole burned in the mirror by previous flashes of the laser. Once hole burning had been suppressed by means of a protective layer of SiO, near field patterns typical of conventional F-P lasers were observed. Threshold, too, was of the order of that observed for a F-P cavity of similar dimensions, and increased as the plane mirror was moved away from the rod.

Having demonstrated unidirectional emission, we turned our attention to multidirectional configurations. The simplest of these, the bidirectional laser, provided information on both the possible resolution of the system and on the effect of crosstalk within the resonator. Bidirectional emission was observed with separations varying from 20° to 10′; in no case was there an observable correlation between the outputs in the two directions when the system was operated well above threshold. However, the presence of

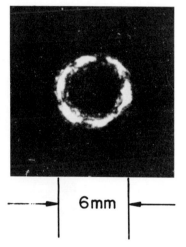

FIG. 5. Near field pattern at the plane mirror in the CPC laser.

6mm

an additional feedback path (the second mirror) was found to increase the unidirectional threshold by about 1 per cent for separations up to 18°.

The CPC laser was also operated in as many as six directions simultaneously. A photograph of the six-directional CPC laser and its multiplicity of components is shown in Fig. 6. The mirrors in this experiment were

FIG. 6. Apparatus used in a 6-channel CPC laser.

located about 90 cm from the ruby rod, with an angular spread of 8° in the horizontal plane and 2° in the vertical plane. The output of the six photomultipliers (as displayed on three dual-beam oscilloscopes) is shown in Fig. 7. Note the absence of any visible correlation between the traces, and

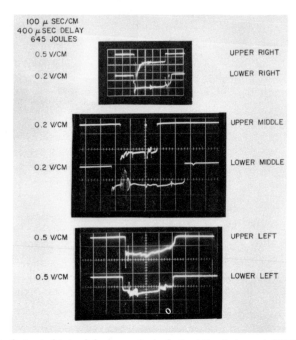

FIG. 7. Output obtained during a single flash of the 6-channel CPC laser.

the quasi-dc nature of the output. The latter, which is typical of single mode operation effected by very long resonators,[14] gradually changes to a spiking output as the mirror is brought closer to the ruby rod.

The CPC geometry is well suited for use with the analog version of the discrete switching technique. In this scheme there is a different fixed optical retardation plate in each optical path, and a single Kerr cell common to all paths. If the laser is operated close to threshold, the system will emit only along the direction for which the sum of the ellipticity induced by the Kerr cell and the fixed ellipticity induced by the retardation plate is zero; all other directions will be Q-spoiled. The direction of emission is then selected by means of a single parameter, the voltage on the Kerr cell. A tridirectional version of this technique is shown in Fig. 8.

This mode-selection mechanism was tested in a simple bidirectional CPC laser. The two paths, separated by about 5°, passed through a single plane-parallel Kerr cell and fixed retardation plates of either 0 or $\frac{1}{11}$ waves. By switching a voltage corresponding to a (negative) eleventh wave retardation across the common Kerr cell, the direction in which the laser emitted was switched. This switching technique was also demonstrated successfully with the rooftop laser, as was the discrete Kerr cell switch with the CPC laser.

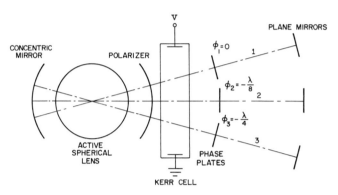

FIG. 8. A 3-channel, switchable, CPC laser with the discrete version of the Kerr-Babinet filter. The total phase retardation in the nth path is given by $\Gamma = 2[\Phi_n + (v/v_0)^2]$ where Φ_n is the fixed retardation of the nth phase plate and $(v/v_0)^2$ is the retardation introduced by the Kerr cell.

Although the experiments reviewed above were performed primarily as feasibility studies, it is interesting to speculate on the possibilities of a CPC-type laser in which the direction of emission may be electrically selected. Although 10' separations were attained, higher resolutions are certainly possible; our own experiments were limited by the physical size of the apparatus. Even with a 10' separation between directions, 10^5 discrete addresses are possible. A more severe limitation is imposed by the switching system, the reliability of which depends on the reproducibility of the laser threshold. Even in our pulsed lasers, air-cooled to ambient temperature, threshold is reproducible to better than one part in 400, and temperature-stabilized, cw lasers should certainly provide an order-of-magnitude improvement in this. Nevertheless, the inherent instabilities in the laser pump voltage and in the deflection voltage would probably limit the over-all system to about 10^4 locations.

The Conjugate-Concentric Resonator and the "Scanlaser"

The ultimate aim of the present work is the realization of a continuous scanning laser device, of which a possible embodiment, referred to as the "Scanlaser," [13] is shown schematically in Fig. 11. The Scanlaser consists of a resonator, called the "conjugate-concentric resonator," and a mode-selection mechanism, referred to as the "Kerr-Babinet filter." The geometry of the CC resonator is shown separately in Fig. 9. Once again the solid-state active medium is a sphere, or portion thereof, and its lenticular properties act to image one mirror surface on the other. However, in this case the magnification is finite, and the multiple plane mirrors are replaced by a

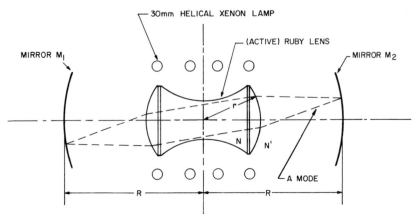

FIG. 9. Schematic diagram of the conjugate concentric laser, showing one of the "A"-type modes.

single (concentric) spherical mirror. While the CPC resonator lends itself to discrete directional switching or scanning, the CC geometry offers the possibility of truly continuous laser scanning. Restricting the discussion for the present to paraxial optics and unit magnification, one readily shows that the radii of the lens and mirrors are related by the equation

$$r/R = 1 - N'/N \qquad (2)$$

where the symbols are the same as in Eq. 1.

A detailed description of the CC resonator and its properties may be found in Reference 10. The following is a short summary of its basic properties. The most distinguishable characteristic of this resonator is its spherical symmetry which, together with the lenticular action of the active lens, leads to a set of modes which are highly angularly degenerate. Considerations of ray optics indicate that two extreme types of mutually degenerate modes can be supported in CC resonators: modes converging at the mirrors and modes converging in the vertical symmetry plane of the active lens. The former, referred to as "A" modes, are shown in Fig. 9. When the active lens is shaped in the form of a "biconical sphere" as in Fig. 11, all "A"-type modes will have nearly the same Q and gain, thus justifying the claim of directional degeneracy made for this cavity.

The integral equation satisfied by the one-dimensional eigenmodes ψ_i and eigenvalues σ_i is

$$\sigma_i \psi_i(x) = \int_{-1}^{1} \frac{\sin c(x - s)}{\pi(x - s)} \psi_i(s) \, ds \qquad (3)$$

where x and s are nondimensional coordinates which are unity at the edges of the mirrors. The parameter $c = 2\pi N a b / R \lambda$ is proportional to the product of the lens aperture $2b$ and the spatial bandwidth of the system $2aN/R\lambda$ (where $2a$ is the length of the mirror). Thus, c is a measure of the number of cells in the transverse phase space of the system and hence denotes the number of possible modes of the cavity. The mode with the lowest losses is the lowest order prolate spheroidal wave function,[15] a near-Gaussian function which is peaked on the axis of the system and falls to zero on the edges of the mirrors. In the case of complete degeneracy, of course, all axes of the system are equivalent, so that the eigenmodes of Eq. 3 form a natural set of basis functions with which to describe any mode of the cavity. Within the paraxial approximation, c can take on a value greater than 10^4. In practice, this number is somewhat lower due to the presence of spherical aberrations and some engineering restrictions.

Theoretically, the degeneracy of the system follows from the relationship among the eigenvalues σ_i of Eq. 3: $1 \approx \sigma_0 \approx \sigma_1 \approx \cdots \sigma_n$ for $n < c$. Experimentally this degeneracy was examined in a CC resonator consisting of a "dumbbell" shaped 90° ruby rod of radius of curvature 12.7 mm and two concentric mirrors of radius of curvature 28.3 mm. When properly aligned, the system showed a remarkable behavior—the output was quasi-continuous, i.e., nonspiking over its full duration.[9] Figure 10 shows the output

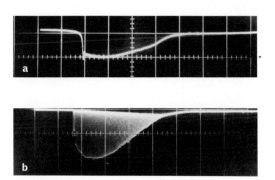

FIG. 10. Output of the CC resonator (*a*) with mirrors at conjugate positions; (*b*) with one mirror 1.5 mm from its conjugate position.

obtained in one case with the cavity in alignment and in the other with the system misaligned. From the theoretical calculations, this cavity is expected to support an enormous number of independent, but degenerate modes. The nonspiking behavior tends to confirm this. In a truly angularly degenerate system, no "A" mode is preferred over any other, and the modes which ultimately begin to oscillate will do so at random (influenced principally by the distribution of pumping energy). The initial combination of "A" modes will deplete some of the inverted population in the ruby but will leave a distribution of excited atoms which can support a different combination of "A" modes. Thus, it is possible for the resonator to radiate a sustained output by supporting first one such combination of modes, then another, and so on, while the initially depleted volume is being replenished by the pumping source. It was also observed that the quasi-continuous output does not burn any holes in the mirrors. This may be attributed to the fact that no individual mode is active for a long enough period to destroy the mirror surface. When the spiking was reintroduced by decreasing the degeneracy, holes were burned in one of the mirrors with the first spikes.

In terms of the applicability of the CC resonator to the fabrication of a Scanlaser, the quasi-continuous output, per se, plays no significant role. However, if the foregoing interpretation of the phenomenon is correct, then an important insight has been gained as to the ultimate prospects of the Scanlaser. In particular, the presence of a large number of modes proves the necessary degeneracy of the CC cavity, while the fast spontaneous switching indicates that very fast switching may also be obtainable under external control.

The mode selection mechanism of the Scanlaser is shown in Fig. 11.

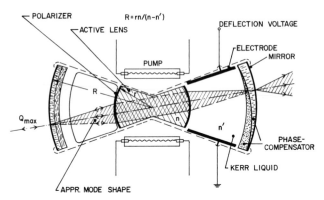

Fig. 11. Schematic diagram of the "Scanlaser," consisting of the CC resonator and the continuous version of the Kerr-Babinet filter.

On either side of the active spherical lens is a nitrobenzene Kerr cell. The electrodes of one cell are perpendicular to the electrodes of the other and, to minimize the losses of the system the active element is immersed in the liquid. Between each Kerr cell and concentric reflector there is a retardation wedge inducing an elliptical polarization which varies monotonically (and linearly, ideally) in a direction proceeding from one electrode to the other. The combination of Kerr cell and retardation wedge, the "Kerr-Babinet filter," is a dynamic spatial filter for polarized light; a polarizer is necessary if the laser emission is unpolarized. With a quarter-wave wedge and with a bias voltage of 20 kV on the Kerr cells, the full 45° aperture may be scanned with a 15-kV ac swing and negligible power dissipation in the cells, even at megacycle sweep rates.

The resolution of the system depends on the selectivity of the filtered CC resonator, and is discussed in detail in Reference 10 as well. As a measure of the mode discrimination ability of the resonator, the quantity D was defined in Reference 10, where

$$D = (Q_0 - Q_1)/Q_0 = (\delta_1 - \delta_0)/(\alpha + \delta_1) \tag{4}$$

Here, $Q_i(i = 0, 1)$ is the quality factor of the ith mode, δ_i is the diffraction loss $(1 - |\sigma_i{}^2(c)|)$ of the mode, and α represents all other nondiffraction losses. It was shown numerically in Reference 10 that for the value $\alpha = 0.05$ such a Kerr-Babinet filter will provide the discrimination plotted in Fig. 12

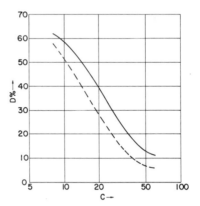

FIG. 12. The discrimination factor D of the filtered CC resonator as a function of c, the total number of possible modes. The broken curve corresponds to a single Kerr-Babinet filter, the full curve to two Kerr-Babinet filters in series.

as a function of c. Once the value of D required for selecting a single directional mode has been experimentally determined, these curves allow one to find the maximum number of resolvable spots in one dimension of the Scanlaser. If one employs two Kerr-Babinet filters in series, the discrimination will clearly be improved; this is also shown graphically in Fig. 12, for the simple case when the filters are identical.

Although we have not as yet operated a laser in this configuration, it is clear that, barring unforeseen difficulties, such a device should be operable in the near future.

Conclusions

In view of the results presented here, one can well be optimistic about the possibilities for laser deflection by means of multimode cavities with dynamic spatial filters. We believe that this offers the most promising approach to the problem of deflection, even though certain technological problems remain to be solved. For example, the high voltage required to operate a nitrobenzene Kerr cell is a difficulty that will be overcome only if strain-free cubic electro-optic crystals[1] can be grown to respectable dimensions (>1 cm^3). Another unfilled need is for a continuous solid-state laser with high numerical aperture. Finally, there is not yet available a truly linear, spherically shaped phase compensator. Nevertheless, it is our conviction that economical, high resolution, fast laser scanning devices should ultimately be practical using the techniques outlined in this paper.

REFERENCES

1. See, for example, F. S. Chen, *et al.*, *Proc. IEEE, 52*, 1258 (1964).
2. KULCKE, W., *et al.*, *IBM J. Res. Develop., 8*, 64 (1964); T. J. Nelson, *Bell System Tech. J., 43*, 821 (1964).
3. See, for example, *Microwaves, 3*, 6 (1964).
4. POLE, R. V., *et al.*, *J. Opt. Soc. Am., 54*, 559 (1964).
5. POLE, R. V., *et al.*, *Appl. Opt., 4*, 119 (1965).
6. FOWLER, A., *J. Appl. Phys., 35*, 2275 (1964).
7. KELLY, C. E., to be published.
8. POLE, R. V., *Bull. Am. Phys. Soc., 9*, 66 (1964).
9. POLE, R. V., AND H. WIEDER, *Appl. Opt., 3*, 1086 (1964).
10. POLE, R. V., *J. Opt. Soc. Am., 55*, 254 (1965).
11. MYERS, R. A., *et al.*, *J. Opt. Soc. Am., 54*, 1399 (1964).
12. MYERS, R. A., *et al.*, *Appl. Opt., 4*, 140 (1965).
13. POLE, R. V., *Z. Angew. Math. u. Physik, 16*, 173 (1965).
14. GÜRS, K., *Quantum Electronics, Proc. of Third International Congress* (Paris), Columbia University Press, New York, 1964, p. 1113.
15. SLEPIAN, D., AND H. O. POLLAK, *Bell System Tech. J., 40*, 43 (1961).

CHAPTER 22

LASER LIGHT REDISTRIBUTION IN ILLUMINATING OPTICAL SIGNAL PROCESSING SYSTEMS

Justin Kreuzer

Perkin-Elmer Corporation, Norwalk, Connecticut

It has been calculated and shown experimentally that the light intensity across a laser beam operating in the lowest order transverse mode is closely approximated by the Gaussian distribution as long as the reflectors subtend a large number of Fresnel zones.[1,2] Operation using a small number of Fresnel zones implies a large diffraction loss, and thus such configurations are seldom used. The Gaussian intensity distribution can be written

$$I(r) = e^{-r^2} \qquad (1)$$

where r is the normalized radius. In general, the relative phase is spherical; however, there is no loss in generality if we consider only the case of constant phase.

This natural nonuniform spatial intensity distribution of the laser is desirable for some applications, as when low side lobes around point images are important. However, some devices such as multichannel optical correlators require an intense coherent beam of light with a uniform spatial intensity. This paper compares four methods of forming a laser beam of greater uniformity.

First, one can utilize only the central portion of the beam where the intensity is comparatively uniform. If the ratio of the intensity at the edge to the central intensity is ρ, then the fraction of energy utilized is $(1 - \rho)$. For example, if the ratio of the intensities is $\rho = 0.8$, only 20 per cent of the energy is utilized while 80 per cent is lost.

As a second method, one can use a spatial filter of nonuniform transmission to attenuate the bright central region of the beam more than the edge and thus make the transmitted beam uniform. This is called apodization. By conventional optimization methods, one can show that a filter with transmission

$$T(r) = \begin{cases} e^{(r^2-1)} & r < 1 \\ 0 & r > 1 \end{cases} \qquad (2)$$

produces the uniform beam that utilizes a maximum of the incident energy, 37 per cent. The transmission of this filter is an inverse Gaussian function offset to have unity transmission at the edge. Again, most of the energy is lost.

Thirdly, the radial spatial modes of a confocal laser resonator that are independent of angle are degenerate in temporal frequency.[1] That is, all of these spatial modes can be resonant at the same temporal frequency. Thus a sum of spatial modes of the proper relative phases and amplitudes could provide greater uniformity than the Gaussian. It would be difficult to provide and maintain the proper sum and confocal resonator spacing. In any case, this cannot be done for a general resonator as the different spatial modes are resonant at different temporal frequencies.

This paper describes a fourth method that achieves beam uniformity at a minimum energy loss. Advantage may be taken of the spatial coherence of the laser beam to redistribute the energy to form a uniform beam. Figure 1 shows two optical surfaces redistributing the energy. The first

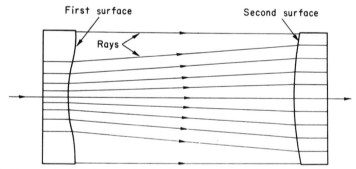

FIG. 1. Two optical surfaces redistributing laser energy (shown for $R = 2$, $n = 1.5$, $s = 8$).

element changes the initial direction of energy flow to form the desired uniform intensity some distance beyond. The direction of energy flow is in the direction shown by the optical rays. The redistribution is accomplished by spreading the high intensity out from the center to the peripheral region of weak intensity. The second element is located in the plane of the desired uniform intensity. It serves as a phase corrector to redirect the redistributed rays to form a new desired wavefront. If a collimated beam is desired, the phase corrector makes the rays parallel.

For example, let us find the surfaces required to redistribute the energy of a Gaussian intensity distribution inside a circle of radius R. The energy is redistributed to form a uniform intensity distribution inside a circle of the same radius located a distance s beyond. The geometry of the surfaces is shown in Fig. 2. Cylindrical coordinates (r, z) will be used with the z

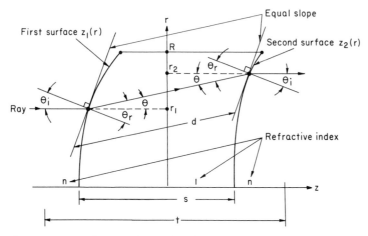

FIG. 2. Geometry of surfaces used to redistribute laser energy (angles are positive as shown).

axis coinciding with the optical axis. The equiphase surfaces will be taken to be planes. That is, the light enters and leaves collimated. The portion of the incident intensity distribution to be redistributed is

$$I_1(r) = \begin{cases} e^{-r^2} & r < R \\ 0 & r > R \end{cases} \tag{3}$$

The intensity of the redistributed beam, found from the law of conservation of energy, is

$$I_2(r) = \begin{cases} \left(\dfrac{1 - e^{-R^2}}{R^2}\right) & r < R \\ 0 & r > R \end{cases} \tag{4}$$

The intensity redistribution is shown in Fig. 1 by the change in ray spacings. The energy in the annulus of area $r_1\, dr_1$ at the input arrives in the annulus of area $r_2\, dr_2$ at the output. This may be expressed by the law of conservation of energy for each pair of annuli as

$$e^{-r_1^2} r_1\, dr_1 = \left(\frac{1 - e^{-R^2}}{R^2}\right) r_2\, dr_2 \tag{5}$$

Equation 5 may be integrated to yield r_1 and r_2, the pair of end points for one ray

$$r_2 = R \left(\frac{1 - e^{-r_1^2}}{1 - e^{-R^2}}\right)^{1/2} \tag{6}$$

Let the refractive index of the surrounding medium be n, and the index of the central region one. Let d be the distance from r_1 to r_2, and θ the angle between d and the optical axis; θ is the desired deflection angle. Then by geometric principles

$$r_2 - r_1 = d \sin \theta \qquad (7)$$

Consider two planes separated by a distance t. Let one of these planes be to the left of the surface $z_1(r)$, and let the other be to the right of $z_2(r)$. Let $p(r)$ be the optical path between these planes

$$p(r) = d + n(t - d \cos \theta) \qquad (8)$$

If all optical paths are equal, the light will leave with the desired equiphase plane. All rays are then recollimated. Thus the difference between the axial path for which $p(0)$ is simply $s + n(t - s)$ and any other path is zero and Eq. 8 becomes

$$s(n - 1) + d(1 - n \cos \theta) = 0 \qquad (9)$$

Snell's law for a ray incident at the first surface is

$$n \sin \theta_i = \sin \theta_r \qquad (10)$$

where θ_i and θ_r are respectively the conventional angles of incidence and refraction at the first surface. The angles of incidence and refraction are geometrically related to the desired deflection angle θ

$$\theta_i = \theta_r - \theta \qquad (11)$$

The angle θ_i defines the slope of the first lens surface $z_1(r)$ at $r = r_1$ and the second lens surface $z_2(r)$ at $r = r_2$. That is

$$\tan \theta_i = \frac{d}{dr_1} z_1(r_1) \qquad (12)$$

and

$$\tan \theta_i = \frac{d}{dr_2} z_2(r_2) \qquad (13)$$

Equations 7 and 9 to 13 may be combined algebraically to yield the equations for the two surfaces:

$$z_j(r) = \int_0^{r_j = r} \left((n^2 - 1) + \left[\frac{(n-1)s}{r_2 - r_1} \right]^2 \right)^{-1/2} dr_j \qquad j = 1, 2 \qquad (14)$$

The first and second surface correspond respectively to $j = 1$ and 2. The end points r_1 and r_2 are related by Eq. 6. If the separation s is sufficiently large, Eq. 14 may be approximated by

$$z_j(r) \approx \frac{1}{(n-1)s} \int_0^{r = r_j} (r_2 - r_1) \, dr_j \qquad j = 1, 2 \qquad (15)$$

The integrand in Eq. 15 is the radial displacement that the rays experience during the redistribution of energy.

The two surfaces given by Eq. 14 are unique except for the variation shown in Fig. 3 where the rays cross the optical axis. The surfaces for this variation may be found by replacing r_2 by $-r_2$ in Eq. 14, thereby inverting the second radius. In either case, the lens surfaces are often strongly as-

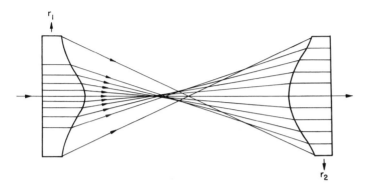

Fig. 3. A variation of the surfaces shown in Fig. 1 with the rays crossing the optical axis.

pheric. If additional surfaces are used, the solution is no longer unique. Thus the addition of more surfaces might permit a reduction in the severity of the aspherics.

In summary, this paper has considered four methods of forming a uniform beam from a typical laser resonator. The methods are (*i*) the use of only the central region of the beam, (*ii*) apodization, (*iii*) a sum of laser modes, and (*iv*) the use of a pair of aspheric elements. The last method is of even more general interest than indicated here because a derivation similar to the one shown will yield two surfaces to transform any given phase and amplitude distribution from a coherent light source into any other phase and amplitude distribution with minimum energy loss as long as the principles of geometric optics can be applied. This general redistribution of energy and phase may be achieved by redistributing the initial energy distribution into a new desired distribution while keeping constant the optical path between a given input equiphase surface and a desired output equiphase surface. Where the principles of geometric optics apply, this can be achieved with two active optical surfaces.

REFERENCES

1. Boyd, G. D., and H. Kogelnik, *Bell System Tech. J.*, *42*, 1347–1369 (1962).
2. Lotsch, H. K. V., *Physical Review Letters*, *12*, 99–101 (1964).

CHAPTER 23

CONVERGENT BEAM DIGITAL LIGHT DEFLECTOR *

W. Kulcke, K. Kosanke, E. Max, H. Fleisher, and T. J. Harris

Development Laboratory, Data Systems Division
International Business Machines Corporation, Poughkeepsie, New York

I. Introduction

A. Principle of Light Deflectors for Collimated and Convergent Beams

Light propagates through an isotropic medium in a straight line, independent of polarization. The direction of the light is changed only by changing the medium or by introducing anisotropy.

In the past, control of light deflection was performed mainly by mechanically changing the boundary conditions, e.g., changing the angle of incidence at the surface of a mirror. The mechanical inertia involved in this process of deflection limits the deflection speed to frequency responses in the range of 10^4 to 10^5 cps.

The electro-optic digital light deflector described in this report is based on the principle of generation of anisotropy in the medium. The generated anisotropy is without inertia up to microwave frequencies (at least 10^9 cps). Therefore, the electro-optic digital light deflector is operable up to very high deflection rates.

The digital electro-optic deflector utilizes a combination of two effects. One is the phenomenon of birefringence. An unpolarized collimated light beam, passing through a birefringent crystal such as calcite, splits into an ordinary and an extraordinary ray. These rays are linearly polarized, their directions of polarization being perpendicular to each other. While at normal incidence, the ordinary ray passes straight through the crystal, the extraordinary ray is diverted. Both rays leave the crystal in their

* The information contained in this paper was developed under contract with the U.S. Army Electronics Research and Development Laboratory, Fort Monmouth, New Jersey; Contract DA-36-039-AMC-00118(E).

original direction, but they are displaced by a distance proportional to the length of the crystal.

The other basic effect is the longitudinal electro-optic Pockels effect. Electro-optic switches employing this effect are capable of rotating the plane of polarization of linearly polarized light through 90°. The voltage required for this switching is the so-called half-wavelength voltage $V_{\lambda/2}$.

In the digital light deflector, linearly polarized light can be controlled by electro-optic switches to pass through calcite crystals as either the ordinary or the extraordinary ray. This principle is shown in Fig. 1, where

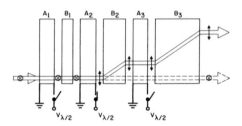

FIG. 1. Digital light deflector for collimated beams.

a linearily polarized collimated light beam of small diameter passes through an arrangement of electro-optic switches A and calcite crystals B. The original polarization direction is assumed to be horizontal. The electro-optic switches A change the direction of polarization from horizontal to vertical or vice versa after application of the half-wavelength voltage $V_{\lambda/2}$. For the switch positions shown in Fig. 1, no voltage is applied to A_1, and the polarization direction of the incident light beam remains horizontal traversing this switch. The light passes through the first calcite crystal B_1 as the ordinary ray. Since $V_{\lambda/2}$ is applied to the second switch A_2, the light leaves this switch vertically polarized and passes through calcite crystal B_2 as the extraordinary ray. No voltage is applied to A_3, and, therefore, the polarization direction of the beam remains vertical, the beam also traversing calcite crystal B_3 as the extraordinary ray.

In this way, with several switches and calcite crystals arranged as shown in Fig. 1, a multiplicity of different output loci can be switched digitally. In the digital deflector, the thickness of the calcite crystals increases in a binary sequence from stage to stage. In this case, a maximum of different output loci can be switched by a minimum of switches: 2^n positions can be controlled by n switches.

Two versions of the digital light deflector are possible—collimated beam and convergent beam. The deflector (Fig. 1) for a collimated beam is the simpler of the two, but it has some limitations with regard to intensity and resolution of the deflected beam. In order to achieve higher resolution and higher intensity, a second version of the digital light deflector (Fig. 2) can be used which involves sending a convergent beam through the device and focusing on the other side. In this way, we can make full use of the aperture a of the device and obtain smaller usable spots of light, thus increasing the number of deflection positions for a given crystal size. For demonstration, referring to Fig. 2, another selection of electro-optic switches is chosen by which the beam is deviated in the calcite crystals B_1 and B_3.

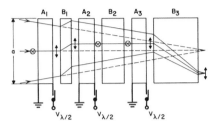

FIG. 2. Digital light deflector for convergent beams.

II. Orientation of the Birefringent Crystals

A. Calculation of the Maximum Angle of Splitting and the Corresponding Cutting Angle

In a properly oriented birefringent crystal, an unpolarized light beam normally incident onto the crystal is split into two rays—the ordinary and the extraordinary ray. Both rays travel through the crystal in different directions. The splitting angle between these two rays depends on the crystal material, the crystallographic orientation, and the wavelength of the light used. In an earlier report[1] the splitting angle ϵ was calculated as a function of the cutting angle γ, i.e., the angle between the surface normal and the optic axis of the crystal, for only one material and one wavelength ($CaCO_3$ at $\lambda = 546.1$ mμ).

Since then, two other crystal materials were considered to be important in the design of a light deflector: sodium nitrate ($NaNO_3$) and potassium dihydrogen phosphate (KH_2PO_4 or KDP). $NaNO_3$ is an artificially grown crystal which has a splitting angle being about 30 per cent larger than the one in calcite. KDP is of interest as a substitute for either calcite or sodium nitrate in the first few stages of a light deflector. In a high-resolution light deflector where a small beam separation is necessary, these crystals would have to be very thin if they would be designed of materials with a large splitting angle. Since the splitting angle of KDP is relatively small, the required thickness is much more practical to work with. Another possibility to increase the thickness and to use the same material throughout the deflector would be to change the cutting angle γ. For small splitting angles, ϵ depends much more on the angle of cutting than in the region of ϵ_{max}. Therefore, small variations in the orientation have a comparatively large influence on the separation of the beams.

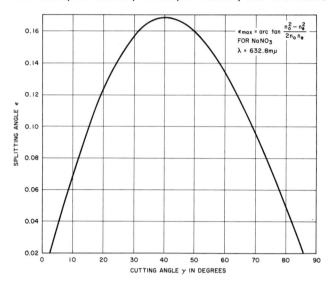

FIG. 3. Orientation of birefringent crystals for maximum angle of splitting of ordinary and extraordinary rays.

For three materials, $CaCO_3$, $NaNO_3$, and KDP, the splitting angle ϵ as a function of the cutting angle γ is shown in Figs. 3 through 5. Since the laser is of greater interest as a light source for the deflector than other sources, these calculations were made for $\lambda = 632.8$ mμ, the wavelength of the He–Ne gas laser.

The maximum splitting angle and the corresponding cutting angle are

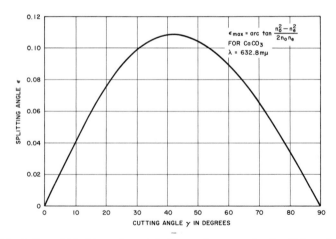

FIG. 4. Orientation of birefringent crystals for maximum angle of splitting of ordinary and extraordinary rays.

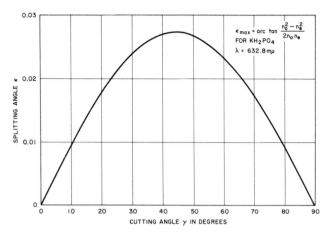

FIG. 5. Orientation of birefringent crystals for maximum angle of splitting of ordinary and extraordinary rays.

calculated for the three materials at $\lambda = 632.8$ mμ using the equation given in Reference 1.

$$\epsilon_{max} = -\frac{\pi}{2} + \text{arc sin } \frac{n_e}{\sqrt{n_e^2 + n_0^2}} + \text{arc tan}\left(\frac{n_e}{n_0}\right)$$

$$= -\text{arc tan } \frac{n_0^2 - n_e^2}{2n_0n_e}$$

and

$$\gamma_{max} = \text{arc sin } \frac{n_e}{\sqrt{n_e^2 + n_0^2}}$$

The results of these calculations are given in Table 1.

TABLE 1 MAXIMUM SPLITTING ANGLES AND COR-
RESPONDING CUTTING ANGLES

Crystal Material	ϵ_{max} (in degrees)	γ_{max} (in degrees)
NaNO$_3$	9.64	40.18
CaCO$_3$	6.22	41.89
KH$_2$PO$_4$	1.56	44.22

B. Calculation of the Isotropic Angle of Splitting and the Corresponding Cutting Angle

The light deflector, to be described in this paper, is designed for a convergent rather than a parallel light beam. Therefore, the influence of oblique incidence on the splitting angle ϵ was theoretically investigated.

In Fig. 6 a light beam LO is incident under an angle β onto a crystal surface which is cut at an angle γ relative to the optic axis of the crystal material. This beam is split into two components—the ordinary and the extraordinary. The ordinary component is refracted according to Snell's

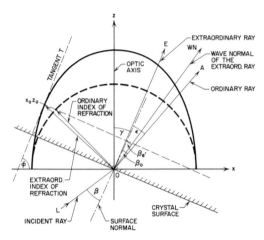

Fig. 6. Angle of incidence between ordinary and extraordinary ray for oblique incidence and arbitrary cutting angle.

law. In the extraordinary component, only the wave normal obeys this law whereas the ray vector of the extraordinary beam does not. In the ordinary component, the wave normal and the ray vector coincide. The path of the ordinary beam is OA and the direction of the extraordinary beam is OE, which is parallel to the tangent T on the index ellipsoid at the point $x_0 z_0$. The vector $O - x_0 z_0 = n_{e'}$ represents the index of refraction of the wave normal of the extraordinary component. From the equation of the index ellipsoid

$$\left(\frac{x}{n_0}\right)^2 + \left(\frac{z}{n_e}\right)^2 = 1$$

and the equations of Snell's law

$$n' \sin \beta = n_0 \sin \beta_0 = n_{e'} \sin \beta_{e'}$$

the equations of the coordinates x_0, z_0 can be derived

$$z_0 = \frac{1}{\cos \gamma} (n' \sin \beta - x_0 \sin \gamma)$$

$$x_0 = \frac{n_0^2 \cos \gamma}{n_0^2 \sin^2 \gamma + n_e^2 \cos^2 \gamma}$$

$$\left(n' \sin \beta \tan \gamma \pm \frac{n_e}{n_0} \sqrt{n_0^2 \sin^2 \gamma + n_e^2 \cos^2 \gamma - n'^2 \sin^2 \beta}\right)$$

n' is the index of refraction of the adjacent medium.

The direction of the tangent at this point is the derivative of the equation of the index ellipsoid

$$\tan \Phi = \frac{dz}{dx_{(x_0, z_0)}} = -\left(\frac{n_e}{n_0}\right)^2 \frac{x_0 \cos \gamma}{n' \sin \beta - x_0 \sin \gamma}$$

Using Fig. 6, the relation between the splitting angle ϵ, the angle of incidence β, and the cutting angle γ can be derived easily:

$$\epsilon = -\frac{\pi}{2} + \gamma + \beta_0 + \Phi$$

$$= -\frac{\pi}{2} + \gamma + \text{arc sin} \left(\frac{n'}{n_0} \sin \beta\right) + \text{arc tan} \left[-\left(\frac{n_e}{n_0}\right)^2 \frac{x_0 \cos \gamma}{n' \sin \beta - x_0 \sin \gamma}\right]$$

The equation used for the calculation of Figs. 3 through 6 is a special case of the last equation. There, the equation was derived for a beam of normal incidence ($\beta = 0$).

In Fig. 7, the graphical plot of $\epsilon = f(\beta, \gamma)$ is shown for $CaCO_3$ at $\lambda =$

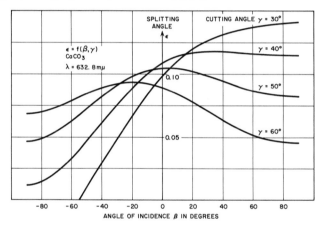

FIG. 7. Dependence of splitting angle of calcite on orientation and angle of incidence.

632.8 mμ. From this figure, it follows that an angle γ exists for which the function $\epsilon = f(\beta, \gamma)$ becomes symmetric (i.e., $f(\beta) \sim f(-\beta)$) (at least for small angles of incidence β). This cutting angle γ and the corresponding splitting angle ϵ for $\beta = 0$ will be called the isotropic angles ϵ_i and γ_i. These angles can be derived from the derivative of the above equation of the splitting angle:

$$\frac{d\epsilon}{d\beta_{(\beta=0)}} = 0$$

and results in

$$\sin^2 \gamma_i = -\frac{2n_e^4(n_0^2 + n_e^2) - n_0^4 n_e^2}{2(n_0^2 + n_e^2)(n_0^4 - n_e^4)}$$

$$\pm \sqrt{\frac{n_e^4}{n_0^4 - n_e^4} + \left(\frac{2n_e^4(n_0^2 + n_e^2) - n_0^4 n_e^2}{2(n_0^2 + n_e^2)(n_0^4 - n_e^4)}\right)^2}$$

and

$$\epsilon_i = \text{arc tan} \left(\frac{(n_0{}^2 - n_e{}^2) \sin \gamma_i \cos \gamma_i}{n_e{}^2 + (n_0{}^2 - n_e{}^2) \sin^2 \gamma_i} \right)$$

Table 2 shows the value of ϵ_i and γ_i for $\lambda = 632.8$ mμ calculated from

TABLE 2 ISOTROPIC SPLITTING ANGLE AND CRYSTAL
ORIENTATION OF DIFFERENT MATERIALS

Crystal Material	ϵ_i (in degrees)	γ_i (in degrees)
$NaNO_3$	9.17	49.34
$CaCO_3$	5.90	51.27
KH_2PO_4	1.48	53.87

the equations above. The graphical plot $\epsilon = f(\beta)$ for the isotropic angle of cutting γ_i is shown in Fig. 8 for the materials shown in Table 2.

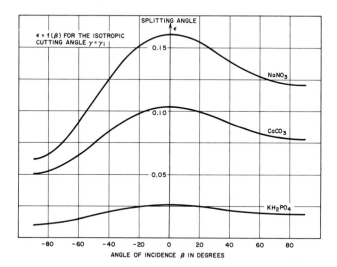

FIG. 8. Orientation of birefringent crystals for isotropic angle of splitting.

These calculations are concerned for rays with a plane of incidence coinciding with the principal plane of the crystal material. The resulting splitting angle might be called $\epsilon_{||} = f(\beta)$. For light in a plane of incidence perpendicular to the principal plane, the splitting angle $\epsilon_{\perp} = f(\beta)$ is equal to $\epsilon_{\perp} = f(-\beta)$ for reasons of symmetry. However, for angles of incidence other than $\beta = 0$, $\epsilon_{||}(\beta)$ is not equal to $\epsilon_{\perp}(\beta)$. This leads to a minor distortion of the shape of the spot in the output position.

III. Calculation of the Minimum Aperture and the Minimum Spot Diameter

In previous reports[1,2] the relation between the number of positions and the aperture was calculated. This relation is recalculated for the wavelength 632.8 mμ for several numbers of stages, and several lengths of space provided for the electro-optic rotators. Using the same variables, the

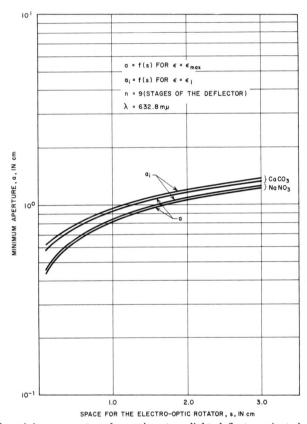

FIG. 9. The minimum aperture for a nine-stage light deflector oriented either for the maximum splitting angle or for the isotropic one.

minimum spot diameter obtainable from a light deflector with a certain aperture is recalculated. For path length compensation, the birefringent crystal of each deflection stage is assumed to be composed of two crystals. The principal planes of these crystals are rotated 90 degrees to each other as described in Reference 2.

The minimum aperture as well as the minimum spot diameter was calculated for the maximum splitting angle and for the isotropic angle of splitting, ϵ_{max} and ϵ_i. The equations used for these calculations are the same as reported in Reference 2 but are rewritten in a more general form.

(a) Minimum aperture

$$a = \frac{4\lambda K_1(2^n - 1)}{K_2}\left[1 + \sqrt{1 + \frac{K_2 ns}{4\lambda K_1^2(2^{n/2} - 2^{-n/2})^2}}\,\right]$$

(b) Minimum spot diameter

$$\delta = \frac{ns}{(a_0/4\lambda)K_2 - 2K_1(2^n - 1)}$$

The calculations for the minimum spot diameter are made assuming the aperture of the deflector $a_0 = 2$ cm. (For K_1 and K_2 see Table 3.)

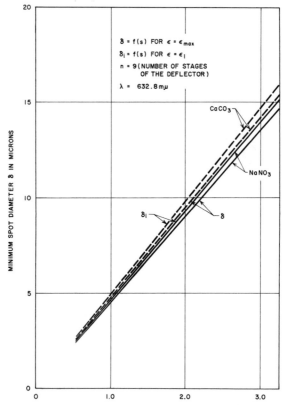

FIG. 10. The minimum spot diameter for a nine-stage light deflector oriented either for the maximum splitting angle or for the isotropic one.

Figures 9 and 10 show a comparison of the results of the calculations for the maximum angle of splitting ϵ_{max} and the isotropic angle of splitting ϵ_i for a 9-stage deflector whereas Figs. 11 through 14 show the results for the isotropic angle of splitting ϵ_i.

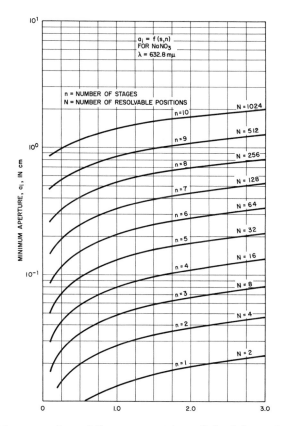

FIG. 11. Minimum aperture of the convergent beam light deflector for N resolvable spots calculated for the isotropic angle of splitting.

TABLE 3   EXPLANATION OF CONSTANTS K_1 AND K_2

	ϵ_{max}	ϵ_i
$K_1 = \left(\dfrac{1}{\sqrt{2}\tan\epsilon}\right)$	$\dfrac{n_e n_0}{n_0^2 - n_e^2}$	$\dfrac{n_e^2 + (n_0^2 - n_e^2)\sin^2\gamma_i}{\sqrt{2}(n_0^2 - n_e^2)\sin\gamma_i\cos\gamma_i}$
$K_2 =$	$n_0 + \sqrt{\dfrac{n_0^2 + n_e^2}{2}}$	$n_0\left(1 + \dfrac{n_e}{\sqrt{n_e^2 + (n_0^2 - n_e^2)\sin^2\gamma_i}}\right)$

IV. Determination of Output Position

A. *Calculation of Minimum Separation Between Two Adjacent Output Positions*

In order to compensate for the different optical path lengths of the ordinary and the extraordinary beams, a structure was proposed[2] in which the birefringent crystal of each stage is designed from two crystals of equal thickness. These crystals are cemented together in such a way that their principal planes make an angle of 90 degrees with respect to each other. A ray on passing through this crystal pair propagates first as an ordinary

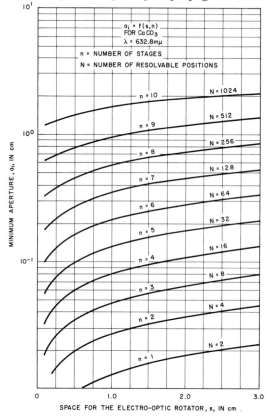

FIG. 12. Minimum aperture for the convergent beam light deflector for N resolvable spots calculated for the isotropic angle of splitting.

ray and then an extraordinary ray or vice versa. Thus the optical path through this crystal pair is invariant.

As a result of this method of compensation, the unit length l_0 of the birefringent crystals is:

1. For the maximum angle of splitting ϵ_{max}

$$l_{0max} = \frac{b}{\sqrt{2} \tan \epsilon_{max}} = \frac{\sqrt{2}\, n_e n_0}{n_0^2 - n_e^2}\, b$$

2. For the isotropic splitting angle ϵ_i

$$l_{0i} = \frac{b}{\sqrt{2} \tan \epsilon_i} = \frac{n_e^2 + (n_0^2 - n_e^2) \sin^2 \gamma_i}{\sqrt{2}\, (n_0^2 - n_e^2) \sin \gamma_i \cos \gamma_i}\, b$$

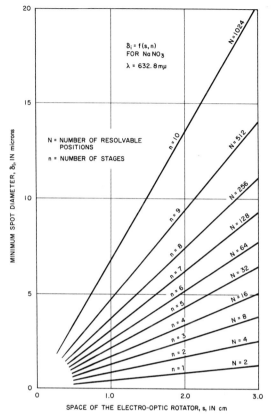

FIG. 13. Minimum spot size of a convergent beam light deflector for N resolvable spots for the isotropic angle of splitting.

where b is the smallest separation or distance between two adjacent spots.

The unit lengths l_{0max} and l_{0i} are calculated for some values of b and different crystal materials, and the results are shown in Table 4.

TABLE 4   UNIT LENGTH OF THE BIREFRINGENT CRYSTALS FOR DIFFERENT CRYSTAL MATERIALS AND DIFFERENT VALUES OF MINIMUM BEAM SEPARATION

	NaNO$_3$		CaCO$_3$		KH$_2$PO$_4$	
$b(\mu)$	l_{0max} (mm)	l_{0i} (mm)	l_{0max} (mm)	l_{0i} (mm)	l_{0max} (mm)	l_{0i} (mm)
10	0.042	0.044	0.065	0.068	0.260	0.275
50	0.208	0.219	0.324	0.342	1.295	1.375
100	0.417	0.438	0.649	0.685	2.595	2.750

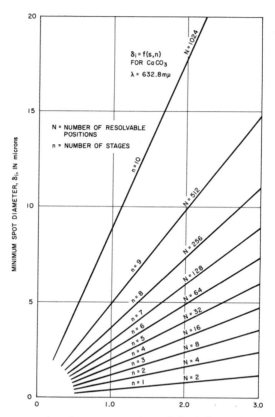

FIG. 14. Minimum spot size of a convergent beam light deflector for N resolvable spots for the isotropic angle of splitting.

B. Influence of the Fabrication Tolerances on the Minimum Separation of Two Output Positions

The accuracy of the separation between two adjacent positions of the light deflector depends mainly on the precision of fabrication of the birefringent crystals. The influence of variation of the specifications of the KDP crystals is negligible.

From the equation:

$$b = \sqrt{2}\, l_0 \tan \epsilon$$

the variation in b can be determined by the derivative of this equation:

$$\Delta b = \sqrt{2}\, [\tan \epsilon\, \Delta l + l_0(1 + \tan^2 \epsilon)\, \Delta\epsilon]$$

or for the relative variation

$$\frac{\Delta b}{b} = \frac{\Delta l}{l_0} + 2\, \frac{\Delta\epsilon}{\sin 2\epsilon}$$

The variation in ϵ can be derived as a function of a change in the direction of the optic axis $\Delta\gamma$ and a change in the angle of incidence $\Delta\beta$. The latter occurs by a misalignment of the crystal surfaces relative to the incident light beam. (A variation of the parallelness of the crystal leads to a similar change in the spot position, as the misalignment of the crystal.)

For the relation:

$$\Delta\epsilon = f(\Delta\gamma, \Delta\beta)$$

the general equation of the splitting angle is used

$$\epsilon = -\frac{\pi}{2} + \arcsin\left(\frac{n'}{n_0}\sin\beta\right) + \arctan\left[-\left(\frac{n_e}{n_0}\right)^2 \frac{x_0 \cos\gamma}{n'\sin\beta - x_0\sin\gamma}\right]$$

The relation is derived by means of a Taylor series

$$\Delta\epsilon = \frac{1}{1!}\left(\frac{\partial\epsilon}{\partial\gamma}\Delta\gamma + \frac{\partial\epsilon}{\partial\beta}\Delta\beta\right)$$

$$+ \frac{1}{2!}\left(\frac{\partial^2\epsilon}{\partial\gamma^2}\Delta\gamma^2 + 2\frac{\partial\epsilon}{\partial\gamma}\frac{\partial\epsilon}{\partial\beta}\Delta\gamma\,\Delta\beta + \frac{\partial^2\epsilon}{\partial\beta^2}\Delta\beta^2\right) + \cdots$$

As the values of the tolerances $\Delta\gamma$ and $\Delta\beta$ are small, only the first part of the Taylor series is of practical interest. From this, it follows that

$$\Delta\epsilon_{(\beta=0)} = \frac{\partial\epsilon}{\partial\gamma_{(\beta=0)}}\Delta\gamma + \frac{\partial\epsilon}{\partial\beta_{(\beta=0)}}\Delta\beta$$

$$\Delta\epsilon_{(\beta=0)} = \left(1 - \frac{n_e^2 n_0^2}{n_e^4 + (n_0^4 - n_e^4)\sin^2\gamma}\right)\Delta\gamma$$

$$+ \left(1 - \frac{n_e n_0^2 \sqrt{n_e^2 + (n_0^2 - n_e^2)\sin^2\gamma}}{n_e^4 + (n_0^4 - n_e^4)\sin^2\gamma}\right)\frac{n'}{n_0}\Delta\beta$$

For $\gamma = \gamma_m$ the derivative $\partial\epsilon/\partial\gamma_{(\beta=0)}$ equals zero. The same is true for $\partial\epsilon/\partial\beta_{(\beta=0)}$ when $\gamma = \gamma_i$.

Table 5 shows the values of the derivatives for both cutting angles γ_m and γ_i and for different crystal materials.

TABLE 5 $\partial\epsilon/\partial\gamma$ AND $\partial\epsilon/\partial\beta$ FOR DIFFERENT CRYSTAL MATERIALS

	$NaNO_3$		$CaCO_3$		KH_2PO_4	
	γ_m	γ_i	γ_m	γ_i	γ_m	γ_i'
$\dfrac{\partial\epsilon}{\partial\gamma_{(\beta=0)}}$	0	0.099	0	0.067	0	0.018'
$\dfrac{\partial\epsilon}{\partial\beta_{(\beta=0)}}$	$-0.08\dfrac{n'}{n_0}$	0	$-0.053\dfrac{n'}{n_0}$	0	$-0.014\dfrac{n'}{n_0}$	0

From Table 5 it follows that the linear influence of the tolerances of fabrication $\Delta\gamma$ and $\Delta\beta$ is very small and may be neglected compared with the variation in length Δl.

Therefore the relative variation of the output position depends mainly on the accuracy of the length of the crystals:

$$\frac{\Delta b}{b} = \frac{\Delta l}{l_0}$$

V. Background Light

In addition to the primary light beam in the controlled position of the light deflector, smaller amounts of light appear in some other positions of the output surface of the deflector. In the following calculations, the background light generated in the different parts of one stage of the deflector will be called q. As explained in the following, the main contribution to this background light is due to the convergence of the light beam. Both crystals, the electro-optic active one as well as the birefringent crystal, contribute to this background light. Some other sources of background light are the tolerances of fabrication of the crystals, the variation in amplitude of the applied voltage signal, and the bandwidth of the light to be used. As a laser is considered as a light source for the light deflector, the amount of background light from the bandwidth of the laser can be neglected.

A. *Background Light Originating from the Convergence of the Light Beam*

1. CONVERGENT LIGHT IN AN ELECTRO-OPTIC CRYSTAL.   In Fig. 15 a light beam is shown incident upon a crystal surface under an angle β.

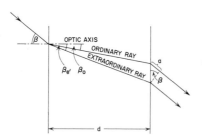

FIG. 15. Phase relation between the ordinary and extraordinary ray in an electro-optic crystal.

This beam normally is split into an ordinary and an extraordinary component traveling at different speeds through the crystal. Therefore, after leaving the crystal, a certain phase difference between the two components of the beam exists which leads to a change of the status of polarization. If the incident light beam is linearly polarized, after leaving the crystal, the light is elliptically polarized. The ellipticity depends on the angle of incidence and the thickness of the crystal material. Elliptically polarized light can be decomposed into two components polarized perpendicular to each other. Without any signal applied to the electro-optic crystal, the component of the light which is polarized parallel to the original polarization direction is directed into the selected position. The component which is polarized perpendicular is directed into some other positions and contributes to the background light of the deflector.

From Fig. 15, the phase difference ψ between the two components of the light beam is

$$\psi = \frac{1}{\lambda} \left(n_0 d_0 - n_{e'} d_{e'} + a \right)$$

where λ is the wavelength of the light, n_0 and $n_{e'}$ are the ordinary and extraordinary indices of refraction, $n_0 d_0$ and $n_{e'} d_{e'}$ are the corresponding optical path lengths, and "a" is the path difference occurring in the adjacent homogeneous medium. "a" can be derived from Fig. 15 as

$$a = n'(d_{e'} \sin \beta_{e'} - d_0 \sin \beta_0) \sin \beta$$

Using Snell's law of refraction

$$n' \sin \beta = n_0 \sin \beta_0 = n_{e'} \sin \beta_{e'}$$

and the equation of the extraordinary index of refraction for oblique incidence

$$n_{e'}{}^2 = n_0{}^2 + \left(\frac{n'}{n_e} \right)^2 (n_e{}^2 - n_0{}^2) \sin^2 \beta$$

the equation of the phase difference can be written as

$$\psi = n_0 \frac{d}{\lambda} \left(\sqrt{1 - \left(\frac{n'}{n_0} \right)^2 \sin^2 \beta} - \sqrt{1 - \left(\frac{n'}{n_e} \right)^2 \sin^2 \beta} \right)$$

The amplitudes of a linear polarized convergent light beam with the plane of polarization in the y direction can be expressed as

$$A_x = 0$$
$$A_y = \sin \omega t$$

In general, for a ray of this beam incident upon the crystal at an angle β, the corresponding principal plane does not coincide with the plane of polarization of this ray. The angle between the two planes is called η. As shown in Fig. 16, the ray is split into two components, one polarized par-

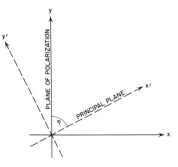

FIG. 16. Ordinary and extraordinary components of a linearly polarized light beam obliquely incident upon an electro-optic crystal.

allel to the principal plane, the other polarized perpendicular to this plane. The two components of the ray travel through the crystal as indicated in Fig. 15 and emerge from the crystal with a phase difference as derived above. The amplitudes of the two components after traveling through the crystal, in the $x'y'$ coordinate system, are

$$A_{x'} = A_y \cos \eta = \cos \eta \sin \omega t$$
$$A_{y'} = A_y \sin \eta = \sin \eta \sin (\omega t + \phi)$$

where $\phi = 2\pi\psi$ is the phase difference between the two components. Transformation onto the xy coordinate system leads to the following

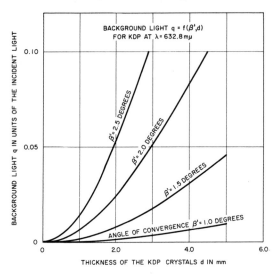

FIG. 17. Background light of a convergent beam in KDP.

equations for the intensities of the x and y components of the light, which are the squares of the corresponding amplitudes

$$I_x = A_x{}^2 = \sin^2 2\eta \sin^2 \frac{\phi}{2}$$

$$I_y = A_y{}^2 = 1 - \sin^2 2\eta \sin^2 \frac{\phi}{2} = 1 - I_x$$

The total light polarized in the x and in the y direction is given by the summation over the angle η, and the angle of convergence β. The range of summation is $0 \le \eta \le 2\pi$ and $0 \le \beta \le \beta'$

$$I_x(\beta') = \frac{1}{2\pi\beta'} \int_0^{2\pi} \int_0^{\beta'} A_x{}^2 \, d\eta \, d\beta$$

$$= \frac{1}{2\beta'} \int_0^{\beta'} \sin^2 \frac{\phi}{2} \, d\beta$$

In this calculation, the light polarized in the y direction is deflected into the selected position. The light which has its polarization direction in the x direction is the background light $q(\beta')$.

We calculate $q(\beta')$ by evaluating the integral by a numerical method (Simpson's rule). Figures 17 and 18 show the result of these calculations at $\lambda = 632.8$ mμ for different angles of convergence β' and varying thicknesses of the crystal.

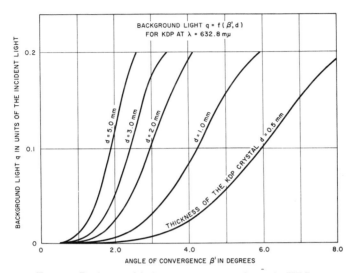

FIG. 18. Background light of a convergent beam in KDP.

2. CONVERGENT LIGHT IN A BIREFRINGENT CRYSTAL. In the birefringent crystal, a certain amount of background light is also generated when a convergent light beam is used. Figure 19 shows a convergent beam incident upon a birefringent crystal. The light is split into a part which travels the selected path and is polarized in the original direction and another part with a polarization direction perpendicular to the original direction. The latter part of the light is the background light.

In Fig. 19, the surface of a crystal is shown upon which a linearly polarized convergent light beam is incident. The crystallographic axes of the crystal are x, y, z.

The optic axis of the crystal is identical with the z axis. The coordinate system of the crystal surface and the incident light beam are denoted by x', y', z'. The x' axis is parallel to the x axis, and the z' axis coincides with the normal N to the surface, where N represents the axis of the convergent light beam as well. The angle of convergence is β', and γ is the cutting angle of the crystal.

The principal plane of a ray with the angular coordinates β, η intersects the circular cut of the index ellipsoid of the birefringent crystal under an angle ξ relative to the x axis. This angle ξ can be determined by constructing a plane through the origin of the coordinate system in such a way

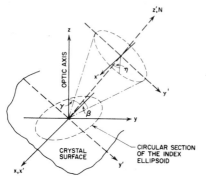

FIG. 19. Principal plane in a birefringent crystal for oblique incidence.

that this plane is perpendicular to the incident ray. This plane then determines the principal plane of this ray. The equation of this plane is

$$x' \sin \beta \cos \eta + y' \sin \beta \sin \eta + z' \cos \beta = 0$$

or written in the xyz coordinate system

$$x \sin \beta \cos \eta + y(\sin \beta \sin \eta \cos \gamma + \cos \beta \sin \gamma)$$
$$+ z(\cos \beta \cos \gamma - \sin \beta \sin \eta \sin \gamma) = 0$$

The equation of the circular cut of the index ellipsoid of the crystal is

$$z = 0$$

These two planes intersect with each other along a line

$$z = 0$$
$$x \sin \beta \cos \eta + y(\sin \beta \sin \eta \cos \gamma + \cos \beta \sin \gamma) = 0$$

The angle between this line and the x axis, respectively x' axis, is

$$\tan \xi = \frac{y}{x} = -\frac{\sin \beta \cos \eta}{\sin \beta \sin \eta \cos \gamma + \cos \beta \sin \gamma}$$

The plane of polarization of the light beam will be either in the x or in the y direction depending on whether it passes through the crystal as the ordinary or the extraordinary ray. The contrast ratio can be calculated for both cases similarly. In the case of a desired extraordinary path in the birefringent crystal, the amplitudes of the incident light beam are:

$$A_x = 0$$
$$A_y = \sin \omega t$$

for a unit amplitude beam.

Depending on the angular coordinates β and η of its rays, the light beam is decomposed into two paths x_1, and y_1, one parallel and the other perpendicular to the corresponding principal plane

$$A_{x_1} = A_y \sin \xi$$
$$A_{y_1} = A_y \cos \xi$$

While A_{y_1} passes through the crystal as the extraordinary ray, A_{x_1} passes as the ordinary ray and causes background light in an unselected position.

The intensities of the two paths of the incident light beam are the summation of the square of the amplitudes over the angles

$$0 \le \eta \le 2\pi \qquad \text{and} \qquad 0 \le \beta \le \beta'$$

$$I_x(\beta') = \frac{1}{2\pi\beta'} \int_0^{2\pi} \int_0^{\beta'} \sin^2 \xi \, d\eta \, d\beta$$

$$I_y(\beta') = \frac{1}{2\pi\beta'} \int_0^{2\pi} \int_0^{\beta'} \cos^2 \xi \, d\eta \, d\beta = 1 - I_x(\beta')$$

Using the equation of the angle ξ derived above the background intensity can be written as

$$I_x(\beta') = q(\beta') = \frac{1}{2\pi\beta'} \int_0^{2\pi} \int_0^{\beta'} \frac{d\eta \, d\beta}{1 + (1/\cos^2 \eta)(\sin \eta \cos \gamma + \cot \beta \sin \gamma)^2}$$

The background light for calcite at $\lambda = 632.8$ mμ is shown in Fig. 20.

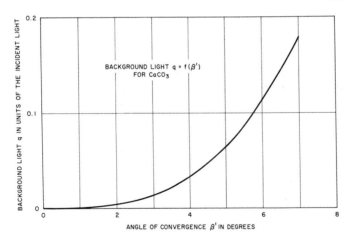

FIG. 20. Background light of a convergent beam in calcite.

B. Background Light Originating from the Fabrication
Tolerances of the Crystals

The amount of background light generated in the electro-optic active crystal, as well as in the birefringent one, depends on the precision of fabrication of these crystals. For the electro-optic crystal, this additional background light is a function of the deviations of at least four constants

$$q = f(\gamma, \beta, \theta_e, d)$$

and a function of the deviation of three constants for the birefringent crystal

$$q = f(\gamma, \beta, \theta_b)$$

For these functions, the constants are γ the angle between the optic axis and the normal to the surface, β the angle of incidence, θ_e the angle between the plane of polarization of the incident light and the crystallographic x and y axes, θ_b the direction of the principal plane relative to the edges of the birefringent crystal, and d the thickness of the electro-optic crystal.

All of these constants are influenced by the precision of fabrication. As follows from estimates, the contributions of the tolerances of the specific values γ, β, etc. to the background light can be neglected compared to the background light generated by the convergence of the light beam. Figure 17, for example, shows the influence of the variation in thickness of the electro-optic crystal. At $\beta = 2$ degrees and $d = 2$ mm, the additional background light q originating from a thickness variation Δd will be $q(\Delta d) \sim 0.002$ for $\Delta d = 0.05$ mm. The background light originating from the convergence of the light beam $q(\beta, d) \sim 0.02$ for $\beta = 2$ degrees and $d = 2$ mm. Therefore the influence of Δd can be neglected for small values of Δd.

C. Background Light Originating from an
   Amplitude Deviation of the Applied Signal

If a signal V is applied to an electro-optic crystal properly arranged between linear polarizers, the transmitted light can be written in terms of the intensities of two components polarized perpendicular to each other:

$$I_x = \sin^2 \frac{\pi}{2} \frac{V}{V_{\lambda/2}} \quad \text{and} \quad I_y = \cos^2 \frac{\pi}{2} \frac{V}{V_{\lambda/2}}$$

where $I_x + I_y = 1$ and is the intensity incident upon the electro-optic crystal, V is the amplitude of the applied signal, and $V_{\lambda/2}$ is the half-wave voltage of the crystal material. For $V = V_{\lambda/2}$ the induced phase retardation in the crystal is $\lambda/2$ and the polarization direction of the incident light is rotated 90 degrees. For this case the intensities of the two components become

$$I_x = 1; \quad I_y = 0$$

For a signal deviation of $\Delta V (V = V_{\lambda/2} \pm \Delta V)$ the retardation in the crystal differs from $\lambda/2$ and the light becomes elliptically polarized. The intensities of the two components change to

$$I_x = 1 - q(\Delta V)$$
$$I_y = q(\Delta V)$$

In the light deflector, only the x component of this light is deflected into the desired position whereas the y component contributes to the background light of the deflector. Written as a function of the signal deviation the y component is:

$$I_y = q(\Delta V) = \cos^2 \frac{\pi}{2} \left[\frac{(V_{\lambda/2} \pm \Delta V)}{V_{\lambda/2}} \right] = \sin^2 \frac{\pi}{2} \frac{\Delta V}{V_{\lambda/2}}$$

and is shown in Fig. 21 as a function of the signal deviation.

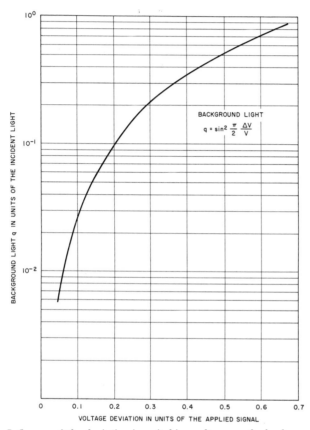

FIG. 21. Influence of the deviation in switching voltage on the background light.

D. Background Light Originating from the Dispersion of the Half-Wave Voltage of the Crystal Material

The half-wave voltage of the KH_2PO_4 and KD_2PO_4 crystal materials depends linearly on the wavelength of light.[1] Therefore for monochromatic light only a 90 degree rotation of plane of polarization can be achieved by applying a corresponding signal $V = V_{\lambda_0/2}$ to the crystal (λ_0 is the wavelength of the monochromatic light). If the light has a half-width $\Delta\lambda$, light of a wavelength λ will be elliptically polarized ($\lambda - \lambda_0 \leq |\Delta\lambda|$). The intensity of this elliptically polarized light can be written as the intensities of two components:

$$I_x = \sin^2 \frac{\pi}{2} \frac{V}{V_{\lambda/2}}$$

$$I_y = \cos^2 \frac{\pi}{2} \frac{V}{V_{\lambda/2}}$$

In the light deflector, again the y component contributes to the background light of the deflector, whereas the x component is deflected into the desired position. By applying a signal $V = V_{\lambda_0/2}$ to the crystal and using the equation $V_{\lambda/2} = c\lambda$ as an approximation for the wavelength dependence of the half-wave voltage, the intensity of the y component for a wavelength λ is

$$I_y(\lambda) = q(\lambda) = \cos^2 \frac{\pi}{2} \frac{\lambda_0}{\lambda}$$

Two different cases are considered in these calculations:

(a) The light is monochromatic but differs from λ_0, the wavelength which corresponds to the amplitude of the applied signal.

(b) The light has a certain half-width $\Delta\lambda$ centered at λ_0. The intensities are to be equal for all wavelengths in this region.

1. MONOCHROMATIC LIGHT. For $\lambda = \lambda_0 \pm \Delta\lambda$, the intensity of the y component is

$$q(\lambda_0 \pm \Delta\lambda) = \cos^2 \frac{\pi}{2} \frac{\lambda_0}{\lambda_0 \pm \Delta\lambda}$$

In Fig. 22 the relation between the $q(\lambda_0 \pm \Delta\lambda)$ and the deviation in wavelength is shown for two different wavelength λ_0

$$(\lambda_0 = 546.1 \text{ m}\mu \quad \text{and} \quad \lambda_0 = 632.8 \text{ m}\mu)$$

For small values of $\Delta\lambda$, a series expansion can be used which leads to

$$q(\lambda_0 \pm \Delta\lambda) = \sin^2 \frac{\pi}{2} \frac{\Delta\lambda}{\lambda}$$

This equation is the same as the one derived in Sec. VC for the voltage deviation.

2. POLYCHROMATIC LIGHT. To determine the background light originating from polychromatic light of a half-width $\Delta\lambda$, the intensity of the y component has to be integrated

$$q(\Delta\lambda) = \frac{1}{\Delta\lambda} \int_{\lambda_1}^{\lambda_2} I_y(\lambda) \, d\lambda$$

where the limits λ_1 and λ_2 are related to the half-width $\Delta\lambda$ by

$$\lambda_2 - \lambda_0 = \lambda_0 - \lambda_1 = \Delta\lambda/2$$

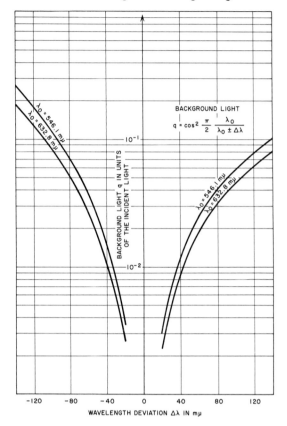

BACKGROUND LIGHT

$$q = \cos^2 \frac{\pi}{2} \frac{\lambda_0}{\lambda_0 \pm \Delta\lambda}$$

FIG. 22. Background light of a light beam with a definite bandwidth.

Using the relation

$$q(\lambda) = \cos^2 \frac{\pi}{2} \frac{\lambda_0}{\lambda}$$

the integral can be written as

$$q(\Delta\lambda) = \frac{1}{\Delta\lambda} \int_{\lambda_1}^{\lambda_2} \cos^2 \frac{\pi}{2} \frac{\lambda_0}{\lambda} \, d\lambda$$

$$= \frac{\lambda}{2\Delta\lambda} \left[2 \cos^2 \frac{x}{2} + x \left(x - \frac{x^3}{3.3!} + \frac{x^5}{5.5!} - \frac{x^7}{7.7!} + \cdots \right) \right]_{\lambda_1}^{\lambda_2}$$

$$x = \pi \frac{\lambda_0}{\lambda}$$

E. *Background Light in One Stage of the Light Deflector*

The background light generated in one stage of the light deflector is the algebraic sum of the different background lights described in this section. One stage of the light deflector is shown in Fig. 23. The electro-optic

switch is composed of two electro-optic crystals of equal thickness in
order to decrease the amplitude of the signal to be applied for 90 degree
rotation of the plane of polarization to half the value necessary for one
crystal. This has to be considered for the determination of the influence of
the thickness of the electro-optic crystals on the background light shown
in Figs. 17 and 18.

The total amount of background light is

$q_t = q(\beta, 2d) + q(\beta)$ background light by the convergence of the light

$+ q(\gamma, \beta, \theta_e, d) + q(\gamma, \beta, \theta_b)$ background light by the fabrication tolerances

$+ q(\Delta V)$ background light by voltage deviation

$+ q(\Delta\lambda)$ background light by wavelength deviation

The values of the different terms can be obtained from the corresponding
Figs. 17, 18, 20, 21, and 22 for any desired design.

VI. Specifications of the Crystals for a 256 × 256 Position Light Deflector

This light deflector will be designed for two-dimensional deflection with
256 × 256 addressable positions. This number of positions will be obtained
by an 8-stage linear light deflector for the x deflection direction and another 8-stage linear light deflector for the y deflection direction arranged
behind each other. Convergent light of a wavelength of $\lambda = 632.8$ mμ
(the wavelength of a He-Ne laser) will be used. The deflector will be compensated for the difference in optical path length between the ordinary and
the extraordinary beam using the compensation method described above.
The crystal material used for the design will be deuterated KDP(KD$_2$PO$_4$)
for the electro-optic crystals and calcite (CaCO$_3$) for the birefringent
crystals. As the total length of two 8-stage linear deflectors will be approx-

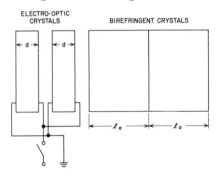

FIG. 23. One stage of the light deflector.

imately equal to the length of a 9-stage linear deflector, the minimum aperture and the minimum spot diameter can be obtained from Figs. 12 and 14 for $n = 9$. For a space $s = 20$ mm provided for the electro-optic crystals, the minimum aperture is $a_i = 12$ mm. The minimum aperture is derived by considering the diffraction at the entrance pupil only. Scattering from intermediate surfaces as electrodes etc. is neglected. This scattering leads to an increase of the minimum spot diameter of the deflector. There-fore, a larger aperture of 20 × 20 mm is chosen for this design. A mini-mum spot diameter of $\delta_i = 10\mu$ would be the theoretical limit for an aper-ture of 20 × 20 mm. The light deflector will be designed for a minimum spot separation between two adjacent spots of $b = 50\mu$. The correspond-ing display area at the exit surface of the deflector will be 12.8 × 12.8 mm².

The angle of convergence β in the light deflector can be calculated from the total length L and the aperture a,

$$\tan \beta = \frac{a}{2L}$$

The total length L can be expressed in terms of n, s, and l_0

$$L = 2[ns + (2^n - 1)2l_0]$$

where n is the number of stages of the linear deflector, s is the space pro-vided for the electro-optic crystals, and l_0 is the unit length of the bire-fringent crystals. For $n = 8$, $s = 10$ mm, $l_0 = 0.34$ mm, and $a = 20 \times 20$ mm² the angle of convergence will

$$\beta = 1.1 \text{ degrees}$$

The dimensions of the electro-optic crystals are shown in Fig. 24. The electro-optic switch of each stage will be designed from two electro-optic

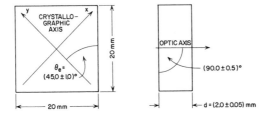

PARALLELITY OF THE TWO POLISHED SURFACES : ± 0.5°

FLATNESS OF THE POLISHED SURFACES : RADIUS OF CURVATURE R > 500 m

MATERIAL : KD✻P (KD₂PO₄)

Fɪɢ. 24. Dimensions of the electro-optic crystal.

crystals which will be arranged in series optically and electrically switched in parallel as shown in Fig. 23. Therefore, 32 electro-optic crystals will be necessary for the 16 switches of the light deflector. The thickness of the crystal d is derived from Fig. 17 for a background light of

$$q(\beta, 2d) \sim 0.01$$

Figure 25 shows the dimensions of the birefringent crystals. The different

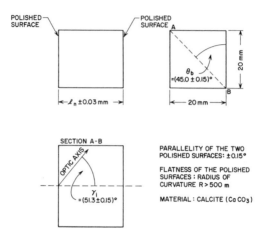

FIG. 25. Dimensions of the birefringent crystal.

lengths l_n of these crystals are calculated from the equation

$$l_n = 2^{n-1}l_{0i}$$

and listed in Table 6.

TABLE 6   LENGTH OF THE BIREFRINGENT CRYSTALS (MATERIAL CaCO₃)

n	l_n (mm)
1	0.34
2	0.69
3	1.37
4	2.74
5	5.47
6	10.94
7	21.89
8	43.78

In this equation l_{0i} is the unit length of calcite for a minimum separation of $b = 50\mu$ as listed in Table 4. To perform the compensation of focal depths each birefringent element is composed of two crystals of equal thickness (see Fig. 23). With the x and y deflector identical, four crystals of every length l_n are needed. This makes a total of 32 crystals.

The fabrication tolerances given in Figs. 24 and 25 are normal precision of optical fabrication. Only the tolerance $\Delta l = \pm0.03$ mm is calculated for an accuracy in spot position of $0.1b$ ($= 5\mu$).

The influence of the fabrication tolerances on the background light is assumed to be negligible. Also, because the light will be a He-Ne laser and therefore monochromatic, the term $(\Delta\lambda)$ in the total amount of background light in Sec. VE will be zero.

Therefore, from Figs. 17, 20, and 21 at $\beta = 1.1$ degrees, $d = 2$ mm, and $\Delta V/V = 0.06$ the background light generated in one stage of the light deflector will be

$$q_t = 0.022$$

VII. Addressing the Light Deflector

For many applications of the light deflector, one must know how to set the switches in order to have the light emerging from a certain position. For other applications, the inverse function is required, namely from what position does the light emerge if a certain signal is applied to the switches.

A. Graphical Method for Obtaining the Relation Between the Output Position and the Required Signal Combination

The relation between any output position and the required signal combination applied to the electro-optic switches can be obtained from the diagram shown in Fig. 29 for an 8×8 position light deflector, with compensation of optical path length. This diagram is explained by means of Figs. 26–28. In Fig. 26 a linearly polarized light beam enters the first

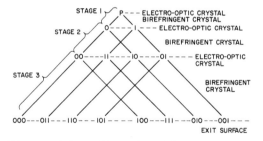

Fig. 26. Diagram of the positions of an eight-position light deflector.

stage of the light deflector at P and is emerging from the birefringent crystal of this stage either at 0 or at 1 as previously shown.[2] P-0 and P-1 are principal planes of the two parts of the crystal. The light beam emerges at 0 if no signal is applied to the electro-optic switch, or it emerges at 1 if a signal is applied and the polarization direction of the light beam is changed for 90 degrees. Therefore, symbols 1 or 0 indicate a change or no change in the status of polarization of the light beam and also indicate the status of the signal applied to the electro-optic crystal. Entering the second stage of the deflector from either one of the two positions 0 and 1, the light beam has four possible positions to leave this second stage:

00, 11, 10, and 01 depending on the status of the signal applied to the second electro-optic switch. The two digits of the binary number of the position represent the status of the signal applied to the corresponding switch. The light beam is deflected along the principal planes of the crystal which are indicated by the lines 0-00, 0-10, 1-11, and 1-01. The eight positions at the exit surface are obtained by entering the last stage of the deflector at any one of the four possible positions and applying a signal 1 or 0 to the electro-optic crystal at this stage.

The convergent-beam version of the light deflector is designed for the undeflected position to be in the middle of the output surface. In this case, the controlled deflections have to be in two directions, below and above the undeflected or zero position. In order to obtain this type of deflection, the largest stage of the deflector is rotated 180 degrees relative to the deflection directions of the other stages. This design was chosen to decrease internal reflections as much as possible, since minimum internal reflection is obtained when light is normally incident on a surface.

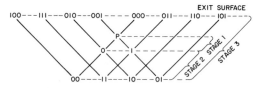

FIG. 27. Diagram of the positions of an eight-position light deflector with the largest stage turned 180 degrees.

Figure 27 shows a diagram of a three-stage light deflector, the last stage of which is rotated 180 degrees. The diagram is derived in the same way as the one shown in Fig. 26.

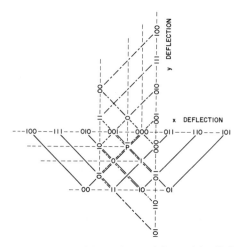

FIG. 28. Diagram of the positions of two eight-position light deflectors.

For a two-dimensional light deflector, two of these diagrams with deflections in x and y directions are superimposed as shown in Fig. 28. Figure 29 shows all possible positions of an 8×8 position light deflector. The positions are indicated by the related x and y signal combination which must be applied to the corresponding electro-optic crystals.

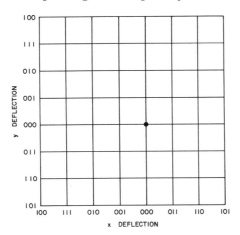

Fɪɢ. 29. Diagram of the positions of an eight-position light deflector.

This type of a diagram will be helpful in display applications of the light deflector. An example would be the determination of the signal combinations necessary for displaying any imagelike information (maps, graphics, etc.) by means of the light deflector.

B. *Analytical Method for Obtaining the Relation Between the Output Position and the Required Signal Combination*

The graphical method for obtaining the relation between input signal and output position makes use of the actual path of the light through the deflector. Therefore, the relationship can be clearly illustrated.

For some applications of the light deflector, however, it is more useful to have the input-output relation in an analytical form. The usefulness of this method will be shown in a later section where it is applied to the evaluation of the noise distribution of the deflector.

In the analytical method, the output position is denoted as "position address *PA*," and the combination of selected switches the "switch address, *SA*."

In the light deflector, an electro-optic switch either rotates the plane of polarization or leaves it unchanged. These are two possible states which will be called 1 and 0, respectively. Figure 30 shows a 3-stage light deflector. The switches are designated S_1, S_2, and S_3; S_1 belongs to the deflection stage with the smallest deflection, S_3 belongs to the stage with the greatest deflection. The position addresses *PA* are counted binary-wise from 000 at the bottom to 111 at the top. In the adjacent column are the switch addresses, written binary-wise in the order S_3, S_2, S_1, which correspond to the particular position addresses.

The task is to find the functional connection between the position address and the corresponding switch address, or the inverted connection. It is obvious from Fig. 30 that the lowest order bits of the two addresses

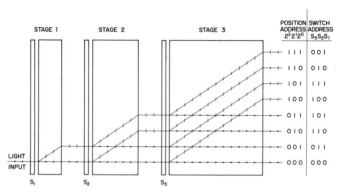

FIG. 30. Switch addresses and position addresses.

coincide. The second-order bit of the switch address is zero if the second-order bit of the position address equals the first-order bit. The second-order bit of the switch address is 1 if the second-order bit of the position address is not the same as the first-order bit. The same is true for the third-order bit

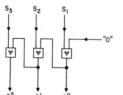

FIG. 31. Analog circuit for converting switch addresses to position addresses.

of the switch address. These features determine an exclusive OR function that is demonstrated in Fig. 31 in an equivalent circuit. The functional connection between the SA's and PA's is found similarly. The circuit for this case is shown in Fig. 32. It will be noted that in Figs. 31 and 32, the first element which connects the lowest order lines of the PA with that of

FIG. 32. Analog circuit for converting position addresses to switch addresses.

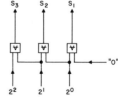

the *SA* is shown to be an exclusive OR. However, it would be sufficient to have a straight connector.

The addressing system developed above for a one-dimensional, 3-stage deflector can be expanded in a straightforward way for a two-dimensional light deflector. All position addresses *PA* now lie in one plane. We introduce *x* and *y* coordinates to distinguish the *PA*'s which now get two binary coordinate values: *PA-x* and *PA-y*. The horizontal coordinate is *PA-x* and is related to *SA-x*, which gives horizontal deflection. The vertical coordinates of *PA* and *SA*, respectively, are *PA-y* and *SA-y*. In Fig. 33

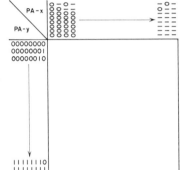

FIG. 33. Coordinates for deflector output positions.

the *PA* area is shown for an 8 × 8 stage light deflector, having 256 horizontal (*x*), and 256 vertical (*y*) coordinate values. In this light deflector, the eighth horizontal, and the eighth vertical deflection stages are inverted to give downward deflection as explained in Sec. VIIA. While deriving the

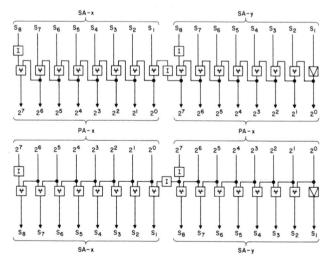

FIG. 34. Analog circuit for an 8 × 8 stage, two-dimensional light deflector with an inverted eighth stage.

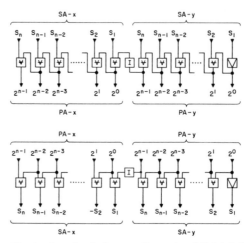

FIG. 35. Analog circuit for two-dimensional light deflector.

circuits of Figs. 31 and 32, deflection in only one direction was assumed.
However, in the equivalent circuits for this specific deflector, we put in-
verters in the signal lines that correspond to the eighth deflection stages.
This is shown in Fig. 34.

A generalization of the addressing system for an $n \times n$-stage deflector
by means of the equivalent circuits is given in Fig. 35. In the general
case, the kth stage of a deflector is inverted for downward deflection, as
shown in our addressing system in the equivalent circuits of Fig. 36.

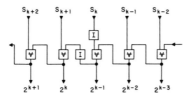

FIG. 36. Analog circuit for n-stage light
deflector with inverted kth stage.

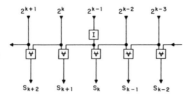

A feature of the addressing system developed is the parity of the switching address. The parity may be defined here as "even" or "odd" referring
to an even or odd number of 1's in the SA's. The special arrangement of
the deflector stages in increasing order of deflection enables us to use the
parity of the SA's to classify the PA's into groups which are spatially

separated. In Fig. 30, all switch addresses with even parity occur in the lower half of the addresses and odd parity switch addresses occur in the upper half. In the case of a two-dimensional light deflector, there is a classification of the PA's by means of the SA-parities into four quadrants as shown in Fig. 37. There is indicated that all position addresses PA given

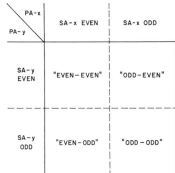

FIG. 37. Parity quadrants of the switch addresses in the position address area.

by PA-x and PA-y, with corresponding equal parity switch addresses $(SA$-x, SA-$y)$ are placed in the same quadrant. This feature is independent of the deflection direction of one or more stages, except that the quadrants become interchanged symmetrically.

VIII. The Noise Distribution

In Sec. V, it was explained that a light beam passing through a deflector stage loses some light to the nonswitched output positions. This undesired light is background light or noise.

For a light deflector with several deflector stages in series, each stage will contribute to the total noise. This yields an attenuation of the signal intensity and an increase of background light in the output positions, or position addresses, PA. The noise problem influences such light deflector applications as display, optical printing, optical access, or logical device.

The addressing system developed in Sec. VIIB and the parity criteria on the switch addresses, SA, are useful tools to analyze the noise problem.

To get a convenient model for the noise analysis, we made the assumption that each deflector stage gives an equal distribution to the total noise. This is justified by the analysis in Sec. V where the convergence of the light in the electro-optic crystals and the voltage fluctuations were found to be the main noise sources. As in Sec. V, we assume unit light intensity to enter the deflector. The fraction of light of an incident ray which goes the wrong way in a deflector stage is called q. The magnitude q is the total background light of one stage as derived in Sec. V. The light that goes the right way is called p. We state that $p + q = 1$, which means that we exclude (for these considerations) light losses by absorption, reflection, and scattering.

In Fig. 38, the noise distribution in a three-stage deflector is shown. The switch address chosen for this example is $SA^* - 101$ that corresponds

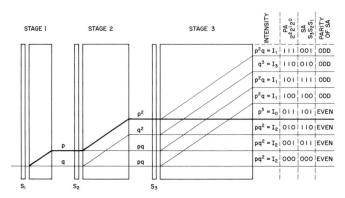

FIG. 38. Noise distribution in a three-stage light deflector.

to the addressed position $PA^* - 011$. The star on the SA and PA symbol refers to the actual switched address.

The sum of light behind each deflector stage is unity. The sums of the products of p and q behind each stage come out to be the terms of the binomial expansion $(p + q)^n$. That gives for the output of the third stage $(p + q)^3$. As indicated in Fig. 38, we will call

$$p^3 = I_0 \qquad \text{relative intensity in the addressed position } PA^*$$
$$p^2q = I_1 \qquad \text{first-order noise}$$
$$pq^2 = I_2 \qquad \text{second-order noise}$$
$$q^3 = I_3 \qquad \text{third-order noise}$$

In the other rows of Fig. 38, the PA's and SA's and the parity of the SA's are listed. It is obvious that the PA's with first-order noise I_1, and third-order noise I_3, have odd parity in their SA's and I_0 and I_2 have even parity. By taking a PA^* with odd SA^* parity, one finds that the second-order noise I_2 also occurs in PA's with odd SA-parity. Furthermore one sees that the SA's of those PA's in which first-order noise I_1 occurs differ in one digit from SA^*. The SA's of the PA's with second-order noise I_2 differ in two digits from the addressed switch address SA^*. The analog is true for the third-order noise I_3. The multitude of each noise level I_m is given by the number of combinations of the n bits in the SA^*, inverted m at a time, that is $\binom{n}{n-m} = \dfrac{n!}{(n-m)!\,m!}$.

For our example we have $n = 3$ and we find for

m	I_m	multitude
0	I_0	1
1	I_1	3
2	I_2	3
3	I_3	1

The numbers of multitude $\left(\begin{array}{c} n \\ n-m \end{array}\right)$ simply are the binomial coefficients of the expansion given above. The sum of these binomial numbers equals 2^n which is the total number of position addresses achieved by an n-stage digital light deflector.

In the case of a two-dimensional light deflector having n x-deflection stages and also n y-deflection stages there are $2n$ different noise levels. The noise is distributed upon the four parity quadrants of Fig. 37. If a position address PA^* is chosen with a switch address SA^*-x of odd parity, and SA^*-y of even parity, we can state the following facts. The PA^* lies in the quadrant "odd-even" of Fig. 37. Even indexed noise levels such as I_2, I_4, etc., occur only in this quadrant and in the diagonal quadrant. The odd indexed noise levels as I_1, I_3, I_5, etc., occur only in the off-diagonal quadrants "even-even" and "odd-odd." For reason of symmetry in the latter case there is a half-to-half distribution. This does not hold for the address quadrant and its diagonal quadrant. The distribution can be calculated by combinatorial means with the requirement that the parity does not change. These calculations have been made for the addressed quadrant for two-dimensional deflectors of 10, 12, 14, 16, 18, 20 stages. The results are coefficients C_{2k} which give the multitude of the even in-dexed noise levels in the address quadrant; these coefficients are listed in Table 7. The sum of all the noise in the address quadrant and the relative intensity I_0 in the PA^* is plotted in Fig. 39 as a function of the noise q in each deflector stage. The parameter of the curves is the total number of deflector stages $2n$.

The macroscopic noise distribution shows that there is no first-order noise in the quadrant in which the signal occurs. Second-order noise will be the brightest background noise. If we assume an 8×8 stage light deflector and a noise of $q = 0.1$ in each deflector stage, we find the relative signal intensity $I_0 = 0.185$, and the noise intensities $I_1 = 0.021$ and $I_2 = 0.002$. That means the brightest noise spots in the addressed quadrant have only about one-hundredth of the signal intensity. If we allow a 20 per cent noise contribution in each deflection stage, that is $q = 0.2$, we find $I_0 = 0.028$, $I_1 = 0.007$, $I_2 = 0.0018$, with a ratio $I_0/I_2 \sim 15$. In this case, the signal has 15 times the intensity of the brightest noise spot in the addressed quadrant. These are very favorable conditions for display ap-plications of the light deflector. Optical printing applications are also

TABLE 7 COEFFICIENTS FOR NOISE CALCULATION

C_{2k}	10 Stages	12 Stages	14 Stages	16 Stages	18 Stages	20 Stages
C_2	$2\binom{5}{2}$	$2\binom{6}{2}$	$2\binom{7}{2}$	$2\binom{8}{2}$	$2\binom{9}{2}$	$2\binom{10}{2}$
C_4	$2\binom{5}{4}+\binom{5}{2}^2$	$2\binom{6}{4}+\binom{6}{2}^2$	$2\binom{7}{4}+\binom{7}{2}^2$	$2\binom{8}{4}+\binom{8}{2}^2$	$2\binom{9}{4}+\binom{9}{2}^2$	$2\binom{10}{4}+\binom{10}{2}^2$
C_6	$2\binom{5}{4}\binom{5}{2}$	$2+2\binom{6}{4}\binom{6}{2}$	$2\binom{7}{6}+2\binom{7}{4}\binom{7}{2}$	$2\binom{8}{6}+2\binom{8}{4}\binom{8}{2}$	$2\binom{9}{6}+2\binom{9}{4}\binom{9}{2}$	$2\binom{10}{6}+2\binom{10}{4}\binom{10}{2}$
C_8	$\binom{5}{4}^2$	$2\binom{6}{2}+\binom{6}{4}^2$	$2\binom{7}{6}\binom{7}{2}+\binom{7}{4}^2$	$2+2\binom{8}{6}\binom{8}{2}+\binom{8}{4}^2$	$2\binom{9}{8}+2\binom{9}{6}\binom{9}{2}+\binom{9}{4}^2$	$2\binom{10}{8}+2\binom{10}{6}\binom{10}{2}+\binom{10}{4}^2$
C_{10}	0	$2\binom{6}{2}$	$2\binom{7}{6}\binom{7}{4}$	$2\binom{8}{2}+2\binom{8}{6}\binom{8}{4}$	$2\binom{9}{8}\binom{9}{2}+2\binom{9}{6}\binom{9}{4}$	$2+2\binom{10}{8}\binom{10}{2}+2\binom{10}{6}\binom{10}{4}$
C_{12}		1	$\binom{7}{6}^2$	$2\binom{8}{4}+\binom{8}{6}^2$	$2\binom{9}{2}+2\binom{9}{8}\binom{9}{4}+\binom{9}{6}^2$	$2\binom{10}{2}+2\binom{10}{8}\binom{10}{4}+\binom{10}{6}^2$
C_{14}			0	$2\binom{8}{6}$	$2\binom{9}{4}+2\binom{9}{8}\binom{9}{6}$	$2\binom{10}{4}+2\binom{10}{8}\binom{10}{6}$
C_{16}				1	$\binom{9}{8}^2$	$2\binom{10}{6}+\binom{10}{8}^2$
C_{18}					0	$2\binom{10}{8}$
C_{20}						1

$\binom{N}{M}$ are the binomial numbers. It is defined: $\binom{N}{M} = \dfrac{N(N-1)(N-2)\cdots(N-M+2)(N-M+1)}{M!}$

408

favored by this noise distribution. However, if a single integrating light detector is used for signal detection, the noise sums as shown in Fig. 39

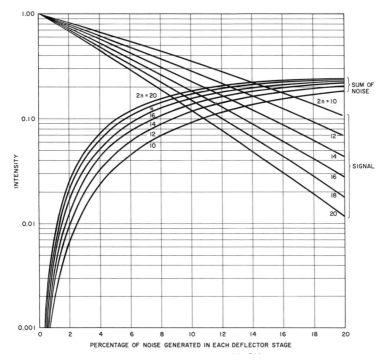

Fig. 39. Signal and noise in the address quadrant.

would distort the desired signal, and more sophisticated detection circuitry must be devised.

IX. Electrode Cementing

The switching of the electro-optic crystal requires transparent electrodes on both surfaces of the crystal. Since the light deflector uses many electro-optic crystals in series, very high transparency electrodes must be used. In addition, these electrodes must be good conductors to provide high-speed switching. There are no electrodes available with transmissivities higher than 90 per cent which can be deposited onto the crystal and which have reasonable electrical properties. Therefore, electrodes which are melted upon a glass or quartz substrate are attached to the crystal. Neither the crystal surface nor the electrode surface are so flat they will fit together without a tiny gap. Since such a gap will cause an electrical breakdown that will eventually destroy the crystal, the electrode must be cemented to the crystal with a conductive cement.

The cementing of the electrodes will make up a sandwich as shown in

Fig. 40. First, let us discuss the electrical properties of that electrode-crystal sandwich.

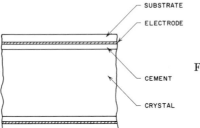

FIG. 40. Electrode mounting.

The crystal has a dielectric constant of $\epsilon_c = 50$ and its specific resistance is about $2 \times 10^{+10}$ ohm centimeters. The dielectric constant of the cement is about $\epsilon_L = 2.5$ and its specific resistance somewhere between 10^{+6} and 10^{+15} ohm centimeter.

The analog circuit for the electrode-crystal sandwich is shown in Fig. 41.

FIG. 41. Circuit used to determine the electrical properties of the cemented electrode shown in Fig. 40.

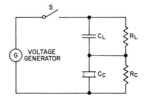

The crystal capacitance C_C is in series with the cement capacitance C_L. The respective resistors R_C and R_L, due to the material conductivities, are in parallel to the capacitances. The charging and discharging process of the capacitors depends on the time constants $\tau_c = \epsilon_0 \epsilon_c \rho_c = R_C C_C$ of the crystal, and $\tau_L = \epsilon_0 \epsilon_L \rho_L = R_L C_L$ for the cement. With the values above we have $\tau_C = 100$ msec. If we assume $\tau_L = \tau_C$, we have the case that at all times the ratio of the voltages V_C/V_L is constant and is only dependent upon the ratio of the respective capacitances:

$$\frac{V_c}{V_L} = \frac{C_L}{C_C}$$

where V_C is the voltage on the crystal, and V_L the voltage on the cement layer.

For $\tau_L \ll \tau_C$, the voltage on C_L will drop to zero very fast, causing all voltage to lie on the crystal. This case is highly desirable for very-low-frequency switching as well as for high-speed switching.

For $\tau_L \gg \tau_C$, the voltage across C_L will grow to about the supply voltage within the time τ_C, leaving the crystal uncharged. That happens if the switching cycle time is greater than τ_C. Therefore, this case is not applicable for very-low-speed switching. The maximum switching cycle time should be smaller than 1 per cent of τ_C, or about 1 msec.

Since the light deflector under construction is to be operable at very low switching speeds as well as at high switching speeds, τ_L must be less than τ_C, that is, τ_L must be as small as possible.

The second electrical feature to consider is the actual voltage on C_L:

$$V_L = \frac{C_C}{C_L} V_C$$

To switch the crystals economically $V_C/V_L = 100$ is a reasonable figure. We assume $\tau_C = \tau_L = 10^{-1}$ sec, for the worst allowable case. The capacitance C_C of KD*P crystals of 0.2 cm thickness and 4 cm² cross section is 100 $\mu\mu$F. From the voltage ratio $V_C/V_L = 100$ we get the capacitance of the cement layer as $C_L = 10^4\ \mu\mu$F.

The breakdown voltage of the cement should be large enough to stand the applied voltage $V_L = V_C/100$.

The dielectric constant of most transparent cements is in the range of $\epsilon_L \sim 2$ to 10. The time constant $\tau_L = \epsilon_0\epsilon_L\rho_L$ gives for the highest value of the dielectric constant of $\epsilon_L = 10$, the specific resistance to $\rho_L = 10^{11}$ ohm centimeters.

The required capacitance $C_L = 10^4\ \mu\mu$F gives us for a minimum dielectric constant of $\epsilon_L = 2$, a thickness d of the cement layer of $d = 0.72\mu$. The switching voltage V_C for the deflector will be about 2000 V. Due to $V_C/V_L = 100$, we get $V_L = 20$ V. For a cement layer thickness of 0.72μ, this gives a field strength of 28×10^4 V/cm which is 700 V per mil (VPM). That is about double the value of the breakdown voltage one can find for most cements. The parameters for the cement selection, therefore, are

1. High dielectric constant to get a high C_L.
2. Low resistivity, $\rho_L < 10^{11}$ ohm centimeters.
3. Dielectric strength as high as possible, at least 300 VPM.
4. Chemically neutral.
5. Not water-dissolved or hygroscopic.
6. Lowest light absorption for laser-light frequencies.
7. No shrinking of the cement, to avoid stress of the crystal.
8. Cementing below 150 °C (300 °F).

The last five points lead to polymers and it turned out that epoxy resins seemed to be the most promising cements if used in special formulation. The dielectric constant for epoxy resins is between $\epsilon_L = 2.5$ to 3.5, the dielectric strength for recommended formulations is between 250 and 450 VPM, and the resistivity for normal formulations is greater than 10^{11} ohm centimeter. However, ρ_L is very sensitive to the formulation of the compounds and the curing procedure.

The following epoxy resins have been investigated with respect to their resistivity. Various formulations of the resin components for different curing procedures have been investigated. Most of the cements were two-component epoxies.

It is well known that the insulating property of a cured polymer is better than that of the components. Unbalancing of the formulation, therefore, will give different dielectric properties.

From literature tables, the most promising epoxy resins were chosen as

	Supplier
ECCOGEL 1265	Emerson-Cuming, Inc.
STYCAST 1264	Emerson-Cuming, Inc.
ECCOBOND 45	Emerson-Cuming, Inc.
EPON 812 + Diethylene-triamine (DTA)	Miller Stephenson Chemical Co.
HE-79	Eastman Kodak Co.
HE-F-4	Eastman Kodak Co.

which have the properties given in Table 8.

TABLE 8   PROPERTIES OF CEMENT*

	Resistivity (ohm centimeter)	Dielectric Constant ϵ	Dielectric Strength (volts per mil)
ECCOGEL 1265	10^{12}	3	
STYCAST 1264	10^{14}	3.5	
ECCOBOND 45	3×10^{13}	3.2 − 2.9	410

* EPON 812 + Diethylenetriamine was chosen because of its high content of hydrochlorine that could possibly give low resistivities in unbalanced formulations. HE-79 and HE-F-4 were taken into consideration because it is used for electrode cementing by electro-optic crystal vendors.

The procedure for making samples was simply to cut square samples off the cured formulation. The square samples were electroded with silver paint. The resistance was measured by a high-voltage ohm meter.

Only formulations that become rigid, semirigid, or flexible after curing have been used for measurements. Sticky or syrupy cement is not considered useful for electrode cementing.

Table 9 shows the results on the test of the previously listed epoxy resins for various formulations and curing procedures. With respect to the resistivity, EPON 812 + Diethylenetriamine (DTA) in the formulation 12.5:1 by volume, cured at room temperature for 3 days and heated to 65 °C for 10 hours, showed the best results. Therefore this material has been chosen for more specific tests on the resistivity and on the dielectric strength.

TABLE 9 CEMENT TEST RESULTS

Sample No.	Material	Formulation	Curing Process	Status	Resistivity (ohm cm)	Remarks Regarding Color
1	ECCOGEL 1265 $A+B$	1:0.6	$A+C$	e		
2		1:0.8	$A+C$	c		Light yellow to colorless
3		1:1	$A+C$	b	$>10^{12}$	
4		1:1.2	$A+C$	c	$>10^{12}$	
5		1:1.5	$A+C$	d	$>10^{12}$	
6	STYCAST $A+B$	1:0.2	C	b	8×10^{11}	
7		1:0.4	C	a	$>10^{12}$	Greenish to colorless
8		1:0.6	C	b	$>10^{12}$	
9		1:0.8	C	d		
10		1:1	C	d		
11	ECCOBOND 45 $A+B$	1:0.25	A	e	$>10^{12}$	
12		1:0.5	A	a	$>10^{12}$	
13		1:0.75	A	a	$>10^{12}$	Yellow to orange
14		1:1	A	b	$>10^{12}$	
15		1:1.5	A	c		
16		1:2	A	d		
17	EPON 812 + Diethylene-triamine (DTA)	6:1	$A+D$	a	6×10^{11}	Orange
18		8:1	$A+D$	a	1×10^{10}	Orange
19		10:1	$A+C$	a	2.2×10^{9}	Yellow to orange
20	"	12.5:1	$A+C$	b	2.4×10^{8}	Light yellow
21	"	15:1	$A+C$	c	7×10^{7}	Yellow-greenish

TABLE 9 Cont'd

Sample No.	Material	Formulation	Curing Process	Status	Resistivity (ohm cm)	Remarks Regarding Color
22	EPON 812	20:1	$A + C$	d		
23	+ Diethlyene-triamine (DTA)	12.5:1	$A + D$	b	5×10^6	Yellow, curing at higher temperature darkens color
24	"	12.5:1	$A + C + D$	b	2×10^7	
25	"	12.5:1	$A + C + D$	b	4×10^9	
26	HE-79 $A + B$	100:2	$A + D$	a	4×10^{11}	
27	"		$A + C + D$	a	7×10^{11}	
28	{HE-F-4,		A	d		Colorless
29	one component		$A + C$	b	$> 10^{12}$	

Curing process:
A: 3 days room temperature
B: 5 hours at 65°C
C: 10 hours at 65°C
D: Evacuated before curing

Status:
a: Rigid
b: Semirigid
c: Flexible
d: Sticky (viscous)
e: Not homogeneous

The measurements were done on cement layers from 10 to 100μ thickness. The mounting for the samples is shown in Fig. 42. The cement layer

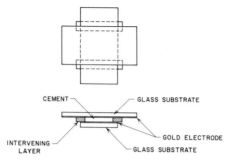

FIG. 42. Sample arrangement for dielectric strength measurement.

is in between two gold-plated glass substrates. The gap width is provided by an intervening layer of Mylar foil. Various curing procedures were followed. The voltage was applied in small steps up to the breakdown at some samples. Only dc voltage has been applied. The results are listed in Table 10.

EPON 812 + DTA in the formulation 12:1 by volume cured for 3 days at room temperature and after that heated for 10 hr at 65 °C gave the most promising result with respect to the resistivity and the dielectric strength.

These results will hold for dc voltage and very low switching speeds. However, they have to be confirmed for high-speed switching. Work is going on to find out the properties of the cement in the high-frequency range.

X. High-Speed Electronic Switches

In order to switch the light beam from one output position of the light deflector to another, the polarization direction of the beam has to be changed for 90° in at least one of the electro-optic switches. This change is accomplished by applying (or removing) the half-wavelength voltage $V_{\lambda/2}$ to (or from) at least one of the electro-optic crystals. As pointed out in Reference 3, the energy F to be stored or to be removed from one electro-optic switch for these operations is

$$F = \frac{1}{2} \epsilon\epsilon_0 \frac{a^2}{t} V_{\lambda/2}^2$$

where

ϵ_0 = absolute dielectric constant of vacuum
ϵ = relative dielectric constant of crystal material
t = thickness of the crystal
$V_{\lambda/2}$ = half-wavelength voltage of the crystal material
a = aperture of the deflector

TABLE 10 ELECTRICAL PROPERTIES OF EPON 812 + DTA IN FORMULATION 12:1 BY WEIGHT
All samples are cured for 3 days at room temperature followed by 10 hr at 65 °C. The breakdown voltage was applied only for 2 sec.

Sample No.	Curing Process	Thickness, μ	Resistivity (low voltage) (ohm × cm)	Resistivity at 100 V (ohm × cm)	Resistivity at 200 V (ohm × cm)	Breakdown Voltage (V)	Dielectric Strength (VPM)
1		80	2.5×10^9	9×10^9	10×10^9	>500	
2		46	3.2×10^9	1.7×10^9	2×10^9	550	270
3		23	6.5×10^8	7.6×10^9	10.5×10^9	450	490
4		56	3.7×10^8	1.7×10^9	2.4×10^9	>600	
5		25	6.3×10^8	4.8×10^9	6.9×10^9	450	450
6		38	2.6×10^8	1.1×10^9	3×10^9	500	330
7		34	2.2×10^8	1×10^9	1.7×10^9	400	290
8		40	3.2×10^8	2.7×10^9	2.7×10^9	500	310
9		11	1.1×10^9	4.7×10^9	9×10^9	300	680

Using the most recent data of Sliker and Burlage[4] for deuterated KD*P material, $\epsilon = 50$, $V_{\lambda/2} = 3.5$ kV at $\lambda = 632.8$ mμ, in a crystal of $a = 2$ cm aperture and $t = 0.2$ cm thickness, this energy amounts to

$$F = 0.55 \text{ millijoule}$$

In a typical way of operation, at ν deflections per second, each KD*P crystal will be charged in the average $\nu/2$ times per second. At the same rate, $\nu/2$, the energy F has to be removed. If F is removed by dissipation, then the power consumption W of each electro-optic switch at different deflection rates amounts to:

ν in defl/sec	W in watts
10^2	27.5×10^{-3}
10^3	0.275
10^4	2.75
10^5	27.5
10^6	275

At 4×10^4 defl/sec W exceeds 10 watts, and at some limit this method of operation becomes uneconomical.

It was pointed out in Reference 2 that the economical range can be extended to much higher deflection rates by using special circuitry in which removal of the switching voltage is accomplished by restoring the electric energy rather than by dissipating it. In this case, in the KD*P crystals only a small fraction of the energy is dissipated, and this is related to the loss tangent of the material. At ν deflections per second, corresponding to a sinusoidal operation at the frequency $\nu/2$, the power W_{sin} dissipated in each KD*P crystal is

$$W_{\text{sin}} = 2\pi \frac{\nu}{2} \epsilon\epsilon_0 \frac{a^2}{t} V_{\lambda/2}^2 \tan \delta$$

The $\tan \delta$ of deuterated KD*P was not yet reported in the literature. It is expected to be similar to that of normal KD*P. According to von Hippel[5] the latter is $\tan \delta \leq 5 \times 10^{-4}$ for frequencies between 10^4 and 10^7 cps. Sterzer et al.[6] reports $\tan \delta = 7.5 \times 10^{-3}$ at X band frequencies. Assuming $\tan \delta = 10^{-3}$, the power dissipated at ν is indicated below:

ν in cps	W_{sin} in watts
10^2	0.34×10^{-3}
10^3	3.4×10^{-3}
10^4	34×10^{-3}
10^5	0.34
10^6	3.4
10^7	34

The circuits with restoring capability will be discussed in another paper at a later date.

Conclusions

We have described the principles of digital light deflectors and discussed design criteria for a model with 256 × 256 output positions. For this purpose, general calculations of the optical and electro-optical properties of light deflectors have been performed. The calculations yield the specifications of the electro-optic and birefringent crystals for a 256 × 256 positions deflector.

Further investigations were concerned with the problem of addressing the deflector output. Graphical and analytical approaches relating the output position to the input signal are reported.

Consideration of light exiting from unswitched positions yields an important result about the distribution of background light (noise) over the output screen. No noise of first-order intensity is found in that quadrant of the screen from which the controlled beam exits. The different levels of noise have a special distribution over the quadrants of the output screen. This can be used to improve the signal-to-noise ratio in many applications.

Different optical cements were investigated for attaching the semi-transparent electrodes to the electro-optic crystals.

The problem of high-speed electronic switching of electro-optic crystals is discussed and the advantages of energy conserving switches are pointed out.

REFERENCES

1. KULCKE, W., AND H. FLEISHER, *Use of Optical Masers in Displays and Printers*, Quarterly Progress Report No. 1, contract DA-36-039-AMC-00118(E), IBM Poughkeepsie, N.Y., 7 January 1963 through 6 April 1963.*
2. KULCKE, W., AND H. FLEISHER, *Use of Optical Masers in Displays and Printers*, Final Report, contract DA-36-039-AMC-00118(E), IBM Poughkeepsie, N.Y., 7 July 1963 through 6 October 1963.*
3. KULCKE, W., AND H. FLEISHER, *Use of Optical Masers in Displays and Printers*, Quarterly Progress Report No. 2, contract DA-36-039-AMC-00118(E), IBM Poughkeepsie, N.Y., 7 April 1963 through 6 July 1963.*
4. SLIKER, T. R., AND S. R. BURLAGE, *J. Appl. Phys.*, *34*, 1837 (1963).
5. VON HIPPEL, A. R., *Dielectric Materials and Applications*, The Technology Press of M.I.T. and John Wiley & Sons, Inc., 1954, p. 301.
6. STERZER, F., D. BLATTNER, AND S. MINITER, *J. Opt. Soc. Am.*, *54*, 62 (1964).

GENERAL REFERENCE

FLEISHER, H., AND K. KOSANKE, *Use of Optical Masers in Displays and Printers*, Supplement to Final Report, contract DA-36-039-AMC-00118(E), IBM Poughkeepsie, N.Y., 7 October 1963 through 31 December 1963.*

* These reports can be obtained from the Defense Documentation Center, Arlington, Virginia.

CHAPTER 24

THIN FILM CONDUCTIVE MEMORY EFFECTS
APPLICABLE TO ELECTRON DEVICES *

Norman H. Lehrer and Richard D. Ketchpel

Hughes Research Laboratories, Malibu, California

I. Introduction

The conductivity of many insulating and semiconducting materials is increased by excitation with light or electron beams.[1,2] Generally these materials are substantially restored to their original low value of conductivity within fractions of a second when the excitation ceases. In some few cases,[3] a conductive hysteresis or persistence of the increased conductivity long after excitation ceases has been reported. In those cases heat treatment was required to restore the conductivity to its approximate original value. This paper describes a 2 to 4 orders of magnitude persistent increase in the conductivity of thin films of cadmium sulfide as a result of optical or electron beam excitation. This conductivity can be sustained for many minutes as long as the applied field is maintained and might well be described as field-sustained conductivity. The effect is completely reversible in that the momentary application of a reverse electric field or removal of the field restores the film to its pre-excited low value of conductivity. The field-sustained conductivity may result from a barrier which not only becomes reduced in height and width as a result of excitation but remains in that state after excitation ceases. The barrier is kept depressed by the injected currents that sustain themselves through continued neutralization of those charges which, if unneutralized, would restore the barrier to its pre-excited height and width. Reversal of the field stops the self-maintained current flow, re-establishing the barrier to its pre-excited condition. The

* The research reported here was partially supported by the Research and Technology Division, Air Force Systems Command, U. S. Air Force.

ability of these thin cadmium sulfide films to store these conductivity changes with almost photographic resolution suggests their application to electro-optical devices.

II. Experimental Procedure

These reversible conductive memory effects are observed in thin films of cadmium sulfide prepared by an evaporation process. Figure 1 is a

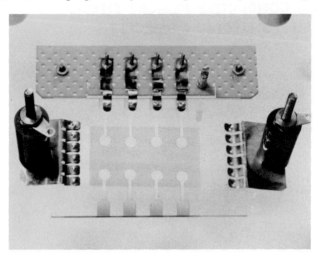

FIG. 1. Photograph of multielement field-sustained conductivity layer in testing fixture.

photograph of a multielement field-sustained conductivity layer held in a testing fixture. Figure 2 is a cross section of one of the elements.

The substrate is a glass microscope slide. The broad, rectangular-shaped bottom electrode is deposited directly onto the slide. The cadmium sulfide dielectric is deposited over the bottom electrode. The dielectric thickness is typically $\frac{1}{2}\mu$ but may vary between a fraction of a micron and several microns. The bottom conductor is completely covered by the cadmium sulfide except for a thin strip along one edge where contact is made. The top electrode is made to be transparent to the means of excitation. Several such $\frac{3}{16}$ in. diameter top electrodes are produced on each layer by appropriately masking the evaporation of the top electrode.

The barrier layer is produced by thermally processing the layer to diffuse some of the metal electrode into the dielectric. Although the cross section shown in Fig. 2 shows the barrier to be adjacent to the bottom electrode, it may also be formed adjacent to the top electrode.

A schematic of the simplified test circuit is shown in Fig. 3. A battery and a reversing switch are used to control the application of the field to the dielectric. A sensitive microammeter measures the current through the

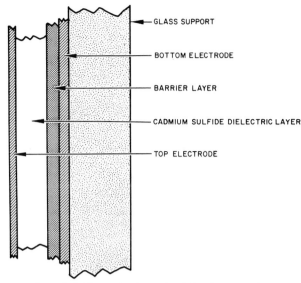

FIG. 2. Cross section of field-sustained conductivity layer with barrier adjacent to bottom electrode.

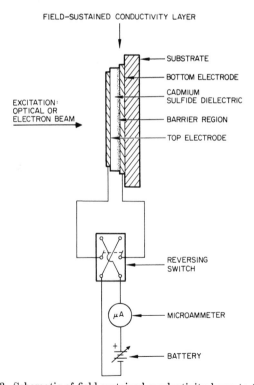

FIG. 3. Schematic of field-sustained conductivity layer test circuit.

field-sustained conductivity layer. In one position the reversing switch applies the desired field to the dielectric. In the other position the field can be momentarily reversed to restore the field-sustained conductivity layer to the low conductivity state. In the case of electron beam excitation the field-sustained conductivity layer was mounted with an electron gun in a demountable vacuum system.

The equivalent circuit of an elemental region of the layer is shown in Fig. 4. Its unexcited capacitance and unexcited conductance are repre-

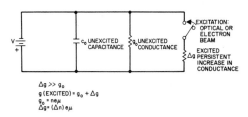

$\Delta g \gg g_0$
$g \text{ (EXCITED)} = g_0 + \Delta g$
$g_0 = n e \mu$
$\Delta g = (\Delta n) e \mu$

Fig. 4. Equivalent circuit of elemental region of field-sustained conductivity layer. Here n is the product of the free electron concentration and the area of the elemental region; e, the electron charge, and μ, the mobility.

sented by c_0 and g_0, respectively. The increased conductance which the region experiences as a result of excitation is represented by Δg, which is substantially larger than the unexcited conductance g_0. The unexcited conductance g_0 is in parallel with a series circuit which consists of this increased conductance Δg and a switch. When the field-sustained conductivity layer is in the low conductance or erased condition, the switch is open and the conductance of the region is the unexcited conductance g_0. The effect of excitation is to close the switch effectively by-passing g_0 with Δg. This is similar to the effect of light on conventional photoconductors. With conventional materials when the excitation ceases, the switch opens. However, because of the persistent nature of the field-sustained conductivity, the switch remains closed after excitation ceases and the conductance remains substantially unchanged. The switch is opened by momentarily removing or reversing the applied field which restores the conductance to its pre-excited value.

In actual practice the capacitance as well as the conductance of these field-sustained conductivity layers increases as a result of excitation. These changes are small compared to the changes in conductivity and have been ignored here.

III. Data and Results

The reversible conductive memory structures have, in the unexcited condition, an asymmetrical dc volt-ampere characteristic typically exhibited by diodes. Such a curve is shown in Fig. 5 for a $\frac{1}{2}\mu$ thick cadmium sulfide layer. Note that the applied voltage is defined as positive when the electrode on the glass substrate is positive. The current through the dielectric is orders of magnitude less when the electrode adjacent to the barrier is negative with respect to the top electrode. When the barrier layer

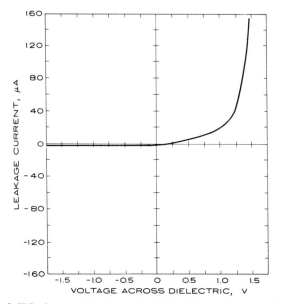

FIG. 5. Typical V-I characteristic for a $\frac{1}{2}\mu$ thick field-sustained conductivity layer.

is formed adjacent to the top electrode, the volt-ampere characteristic becomes reversed; i.e., the current in the negatively biased direction is greater than the current in the positively biased direction.

The sustained increase in conductance or conductive hysteresis is observed when the layers are in the low current condition, i.e., when the electrode adjacent to the barrier layer is at a negative potential and serves as the carrier injecting electrode. Then, pulsed excitation with light or electron beams increases the current through the excited region. The magnitude of the increased current during excitation is such as to make the excited reverse volt-ampere characteristic tend toward symmetry with the forward volt-ampere curve. This increased current is substantially maintained for many minutes after excitation ceases. Thus, the rectification ratio, or the ratio of the forward to the unexcited reverse current, is a factor in the magnitude of the relative sustained change in the conductance. The rectification ratio as a function of the absolute value of the applied voltage is shown in Fig. 6 for the curve in Fig. 5. The maximum rectification ratio obtained in this case was 7000, although values of 10^6 have been observed. Note that the rectification ratio increases with applied voltage and is limited by breakdown of the sample. In this case, when the dc voltage across the layer exceeds 1.5 V in the negative direction, irreversible break-down occurs. The result of this breakdown is to increase the leakage current in the reverse direction to such an extent that the volt-ampere characteristic becomes symmetrical and the memory is destroyed.

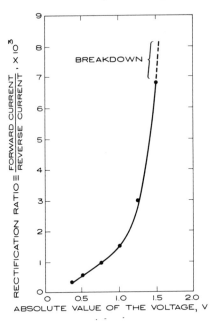

FIG. 6. Rectification ratio.

The ability of one element of these field-sustained conductivity layers to respond to optical excitation and store the conductivity changes is shown in Fig. 7. In this case the layer thickness is $\frac{1}{2}\mu$ and the applied voltage 1.5 V. The ratio of the forward-to-reverse current, or rectification ratio, is 300:1. Before the data for each one of these three curves shown in Fig. 7 were taken, the applied field was removed from the layer to erase it. This field was reapplied at $t = 0$. Note that the greatest increase in the unexcited current occurs during the first 60 to 90 sec after the field is reapplied. From that time on the unexcited current increases quite slowly for a period of minutes and even hours. The upper two curves indicate the rise and decay of the current as a result of exposure to optical excitation. In these two curves the excitation was turned on at $t = 0$ and then turned off after one minute. For both values of excitation the current increases quite rapidly at first but then tends to saturate, the saturation level depending upon the intensity of excitation. When the excitation is turned off, the current decays quite rapidly at first but then reaches a relatively constant value. Note that the level to which the current decays is related to the intensity and time of the initial excitation. Thus the stored conductance level is a function of the initial excitation. Although not shown in Fig. 7, it is possible at any time to re-excite the region and cause it to store at a higher level. In addition, by momentarily removing the applied voltage it is possible to partially or completely erase the increased conductance.

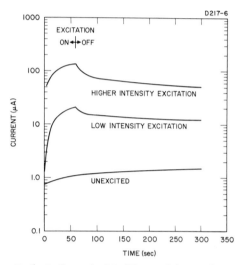

FIG. 7. Optically excited buildup and decay of current.

Comprehensive studies have been made on the effects of electron beam energy and applied voltage on field-sustained conductivity. These effects are most significantly measured in relation to the prebombarded conductance of the target. The sustained relative change in conductance

$$\frac{\Delta g}{g_0} = \frac{i_s - i_1}{i_l/4} \tag{1}$$

where i_s is the current flowing through the dielectric after bombardment has ceased and i_1 is the current flowing before excitation. Because only one-fourth of the area of the target was bombarded, $i_l/4$ appears in the denominator of Eq. 1.

In Fig. 8 $\Delta g/g_0$ is plotted as a function of the primary beam energy for a $\frac{1}{2}\mu$ thick cadmium sulfide layer with the barrier adjacent to the bottom electrode. The upper curve shows the change in conductivity immediately following a 10-sec bombardment with 600 pulses each of which was 150 μsec long and 1 μA in the beam current. Five seconds after bombardment has ceased, the conductive memory is still substantial, as indicated in the lower curve in Fig. 8. Note that the maximum conductivity obtained as a result of this excitation is almost four orders of magnitude greater than the prebombarded conductivity. The general shape of these curves for the sustained conductivity effect is similar to the curves obtained for the

instantaneous bombardment induced conductivity response. At low values
of beam energy, the effect is negligible. It increases sharply at 8 to 10 kV
and reaches a maximum at 14 to 16 kV, decreasing thereafter. These
measurements were made with an applied voltage of 1.5 V which gave the

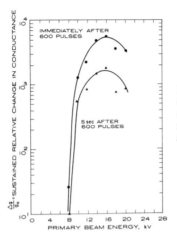

FIG. 8. Effect of electron beam energy
on conductance change. Primary beam
current 1 μA, pulse length 150 μsec,
number of pulses 600, electric field
across dielectric -3×10^4 V/cm, beam
diameter 0.25 cm.

greatest value of $\Delta g/g_0$. The effect of the applied voltage on the sustained
conductivity is shown in Fig. 9. As in the case of the bombardment-induced
conductivity instantaneous response, the sustained response is linear over
most of the applied voltage. However, there is some indication of saturation
at the highest applied fields; the unexcited leakage current increases more
rapidly at these high values of the field.

FIG. 9. Effect of applied field on conductance change with electron beam
excitation.

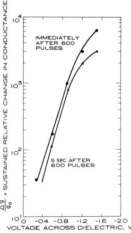

Substantial conductive memory effects can be obtained at much lower
values of the beam energy when the barrier is produced at the top electrode

rather than at the bottom electrode; this is because the electron beam does not have to penetrate the dielectric to excite the barrier. When the barrier is produced adjacent to the top electrodes, although not shown, the general shape of the curves in Fig. 8 is preserved but the maximum occurs at substantially lower values of the beam energy.

In Fig. 10, the change in conductivity is shown as a function of the number of excitation pulses for a bottom barrier structure. The effect of

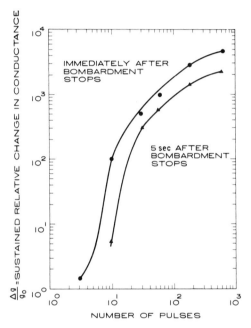

FIG. 10. Sensitivity to electron bombardment. Primary beam energy 14 kV, primary beam current 1 μA, pulse length 150 μsec, beam diameter 0.25 cm, applied field −3 × 10^4 V/cm.

the first few pulses is relatively negligible, although this is not evident in the curves. With succeeding pulses, the sensitivity increases. Saturation occurs for large numbers of pulses.

Computation of the energy delivered per unit area by each pulse can provide an indication of the sensitivity of the layers to electron beam excitation. The energy E contained in each 14 kV, 1 μA, 150 μsec pulse of electrons is given by

$$E = V_p I t = 21 \times 10^{-7} \text{ J} \tag{2}$$

where V_p is the primary beam energy, I is the primary beam current, and t is the pulse duration. The energy per unit area is given by

$$\frac{E}{A} = \frac{E}{\pi D^2/4} = 0.43 \times 10^{-4} \frac{\text{J}}{\text{cm}^2} \tag{3}$$

Thus, each pulse delivers 43 $\mu J/cm^2$. From the curves in Fig. 10, it can be seen that 50 such pulses or 2150 $\mu J/cm^2$ increases the conductance by a factor of 1000. If practical values are assumed for the spot size and current of the primary beam, an electron beam writing speed can be computed for the field-sustained conductivity layer.

The power per unit area P/A delivered by a 14 kV, 25 μA electron beam with a 0.01 in. spot size is

$$\frac{P}{A} = \frac{V_p I}{A} = 660 \ W/cm^2 \tag{4}$$

As noted previously, 2150 $\mu J/cm^2$ is required to change the conductance by a factor of 1000. The required pulse length T of the primary electron beam is therefore

$$T = \frac{2150 \times 10^{-6}}{660} \cong 3.2 \ \mu sec \tag{5}$$

Thus, with microsecond excitation from a high-energy electron beam it is possible to effect a three orders of magnitude stored change in the conductance level of these field-sustained conductivity layers. While the layer on which these data were taken may be considered typical of many, other layers have been made which exhibit greater as well as lesser sensitivity to electron beam excitation.

Brief investigations have been made of the effect of forward voltage pulses on the sustained currents when the dielectric is operated in the reverse bias condition. The conductance of the layer can be completely restored to its pre-excited value by the application of a forward voltage pulse several milliseconds long and equal in amplitude to the reverse voltage. The forward pulse must be applied for longer time periods as the amplitude of the pulse is reduced.

IV. Theoretical Aspects of Field-Sustained Conductivity

The principal phenomenological characteristics of the field-sustained conductivity effect can be summarized as follows:

1. Without external excitation, i.e., light or electron beam, very strong rectification effects are observed. Rectification ratios as high as 10^6 are obtained.

2. When the layer is in the low current condition, external excitation produces a substantial increase in the conductivity of the excited region. The amount of increase depends on the integrated excitation energy.

3. Upon removal of the external excitation but with continued application of the field, the high conductivity state is maintained in the previously excited region.

4. Momentary reversal or removal of the field restores the excited region of the layer to its low conductance state.

Of course, any valid theoretical model must be consistent with the above characteristics. The purpose of the following discussion is not to provide a complete model, which does not yet exist, but rather to indicate some of the relevant theoretical concepts to aid in understanding the phenomenon.

Item (1), the unexcited rectification effect, implies the existence of a barrier adjacent to the negative or injecting electrode, assuming n type conduction. The effect of the barrier layer is to produce a rectifying contact at the adjacent electrode, the other contact being ohmic. When the layer is back biased, excitation reduces the height of the barrier, permitting large currents to pass.

The present theory[4] of contacts and resultant barriers states that when two substances are brought together a redistribution of charge occurs. At equilibrium the Fermi levels of the two substances are at equal values at the interface. The dipole layer resulting from the charge redistribution must be distributed throughout part of the volume of one of the substances to form a barrier.

These concepts of the physics of metal-to-semiconductor contacts can be applied in the case of the field-sustained conductivity layers to produce a picture of the band structure as shown in Fig. 11.

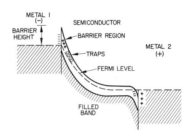

Fig. 11. Band structure of field-sustained conductivity layer.

If it is assumed that the work function of metal 2 is less than the work function of the semiconductor, then the electrons in metal 2 are in a higher energy state. Upon contact, these electrons can readily enter the semiconductor until the Fermi levels in both materials are at the same height. Because the barrier from the metal to the semiconductor is small, electrons can easily move in both directions and the contact is said to be ohmic.

It is further assumed that a result of the barrier layer produced by the thermal processing is to make the work function of metal 1 greater than the work function of the semiconductor. The electrons in the conduction band of the semiconductor are in a higher energy state than those in metal 1. For this reason, upon contact, electrons flow from the semiconductor into the metal until the Fermi levels in both materials are at the same height.

The flow of electrons from the semiconductor to the metal leaves a positive charge on the semiconductor. This positive charge is distributed throughout a part of the semiconductor volume while negative charge is contained near the surface of the metal. This charge distribution can be understood by considering that the density of donors in the semiconductor which contribute to the electrons is much less than the density of states in the conduction band of the metal which receive them. Because the donors are fixed in position, they remain spread out. This charge distribution produces a diffusion potential or barrier.

When a positive potential is applied to metal 2, the high density of donors in the barrier region becomes further depleted or ionized increasing the height of the barrier. This depleted region is one of high resistivity and most of the applied voltage drop is across it. In the presence of excitation these ionized donors will be partially neutralized by electrons excited into the conduction band. The barrier will be reduced in height and width, permitting large currents to pass.

If the electrons which are in the conduction band become trapped in the barrier region for periods longer than the excitation time, then the barrier will remain depressed by these trapped electrons after the excitation ceases. The concentration of trapped electrons will be more or less maintained by the continued flow of current in the conduction band. When the applied voltage is removed, the currents in the conduction band stop and the trapped electron concentration becomes reduced permitting the barrier to be re-established.

Thus, the principal characteristics of the field-sustained conductivity might be explained as follows:

1. Before excitation, the dielectric has one ohmic contact and one blocking contact, causing rectification.

2. During excitation, the blocking contact is converted to an injecting one through donor neutralization, and injection currents become possible.

3. Upon removal of the excitation, but with continuing application of the field, the injection currents maintain themselves by filling traps. These trapped electrons neutralize the ionized donor centers thereby keeping the barrier depressed.

4. Upon removal of the applied voltage, the injection currents cease, the traps empty, and the barrier is reestablished.

V. Readout Techniques

Readin of information to these field-sustained conductivity layers can be accomplished directly by means of excitation with electron beams, or light. For example, it is possible to scan the surface of the layer with a high energy electron beam and establish a two dimensional conductivity pattern with a resolution presumably determined by the electron beam and spot size. Because an electron beam or an optical image may attain resolution in the order of 3000 line/in., information may be stored with extremely high resolution. The essential problem in the application of these field-sustained conductivity layers to the electro-optical processing of information is the development of techniques capable of reading out the information stored in the field-sustained conductivity layer.

Electrical readout utilizes an electron beam. In Fig. 12, the field-

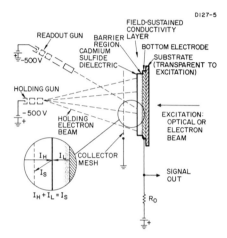

Fig. 12. Direct electrical readout schematic.

sustained conductivity layer is supported by a substrate which is transparent to the excitation. The input signals may be optical or electron beam or both. The barrier region is formed adjacent to the bottom electrode. An electron beam is used to establish the surface potential in place of the top electrode. A collector mesh serves to collimate the holding beam as well as collect the secondary electrons coming from the surface of the dielectric.

The holding beam strikes the surface of the layer with an energy such that more secondary electrons are emitted from the surface than are deposited by the holding beam. As long as the collector is more positive than the surface of the layer, the surface will be charged positively. When the surface arrives close to the potential of the collector, then the field is so reduced that most of the secondaries return to the surface of the layer, that is, the same number of electrons arrive at and leave the surface. This is the equilibrium potential. In the detail drawing of Fig. 12, the electron currents which flow to one elemental region under these conditions are indicated. Here I_H is the holding beam current, I_L the leakage current through layer, and I_s the collected secondary current. At equilibrium, potential I_H plus I_L equals I_s. The equilibrium value of the potential when the layer is unexcited is determined by the fact that I_L is essentially zero and I_s must equal I_H. When the field-sustained conductivity layer is excited, I_L substantially increases. The surface potential must now shift to a new equilibrium value which is closer to the negative potential of the bottom electrode. Thus, under the action of the holding beam, the effect of excitation is to establish a pattern of equilibrium potentials on the surface of the layer. These variations in turn produce modulations in the collecting field. The readout beam scans the surface of the field-sustained conductivity layer. The secondary electrons generated by this beam are redistributed in accordance with the modulations in the collecting field and develop a corresponding signal across the output resistor R_0. The field-sustained conductivity layer can be returned to the low conductivity condition at any time by momentarily interrupting the holding beam or bringing the bottom electrode to collector potential.

The feasibility of this technique has been demonstrated and investigations are under way to determine its ultimate limitations.

The information stored in the field-sustained conductivity layers may be read out by optical techniques. One such technique is shown in Fig. 13.

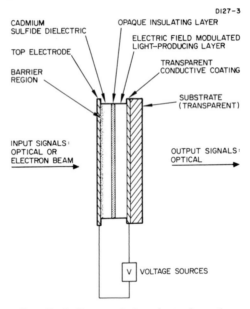

FIG. 13. Indirect optical readout schematic.

In this case, the conductivity variations in the field-sustained conductivity layer are used to modulate the voltage drop across a layer whose light output depends upon the applied field. The substrate is transparent to optical signals from the light-producing layer. One electrode is a transparent conductive coating applied to the substrate. Over this conductive coating the light-producing layer is deposited. A thin opaque insulating film is utilized between the field-sustained conductivity layer and the light-producing layer. This opaque layer prevents feedback of light from the light-producing layer to the field-sustained conductivity layer. The barrier region is produced adjacent to the top electrode. The input signals can take the form of either or both electron beam or optical excitation.

The operation of this indirect readout technique can be easily understood from a study of the equivalent circuit of an elemental region (Fig. 14).

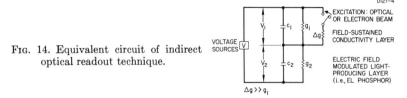

FIG. 14. Equivalent circuit of indirect optical readout technique.

The elemental capacitance and conductance of the field-sustained conductivity layer are represented by c_2 and g_2, respectively. The increased conductance which results from electron beam or optical excitation is Δg.

The elemental capacitance and conductance of the electric field modulated light-producing layer are represented by c_2 and g_2, respectively.

The impedance of the opaque insulating layer is small compared to the impedance of the other two layers and is therefore omitted.

The applied voltage is V with V_1 across the field-sustained conductivity layer and V_2 across the light-producing layer. Without going into detail, analysis indicates that if the capacitance and conductance of the two layers are properly chosen, then when the field-sustained conductivity layer is unexcited, most of the voltage drop will be across it, and the light-generating layer will be dark. When the sustained conductivity layer is excited by light or an electron beam, its conductivity increases substantially, thereby increasing the field across the light-generating layer causing it to generate the optical signals. Because the conductivity is sustained after the excitation has ceased (the switch remains closed), the light-generating layer remains excited. The optical display is erased by momentarily reversing the field across the combination layer; the pre-excited low value of conductance is then restored to the field-sustained conductivity layer and the voltage drop is restored across that layer.

V. Summary

An electron beam or optically induced conductive hysteresis effect in thin cadmium sulfide films was described. The effect is a form of field-sustained conductivity; i.e., the increased conductance exhibited by the excited regions of the film may persist for many minutes and even hours after the excitation ceases as long as the applied electric field is maintained. A momentary removal or reversal of the field restores the conductance of the film to its preexcited low value. While the effect is not completely understood, it appears that an unusual type of barrier makes possible the continued flow of increased current after excitation ceases.

The general characteristics of the field-sustained conductivity thin films make them promising as a high-resolution reusable storage medium. Their successful application to various electro-optical devices depends upon the ability to read out the conductivity modulations stored in the film.

An electrical readout method was described which utilizes an electron beam to scan the film. The feasibility of this technique has been demonstrated, but the ultimate performance remains to be determined.

A high-resolution optical (direct-view) readout method was also presented. The feasibility of this technique has not yet been established.

REFERENCES

1. BUBE, R. H., "Photoconductivity of the Sulfide, Selenide, and Telluride of Zinc and Cadmium," *Proc. IRE*, *43*, 1836–1850 (1955).
2. ROSE, A., "Performance of Photoconductors," *Proc. IRE*, *43*, 1850 (1955).
3. SCHULZE, R. G., AND B. A. KULP, "On the Conductivity of Cadmium Sulfide Following Electron Bombardment," *J. Appl. Phys.*, *33*, No. U, 2173–2175 (1962).
4. HENISCH, H., *Rectifying Semiconductor Contacts*, Clarendon Press, Oxford, 1957.

CHAPTER 25

THE GAIN ELEMENT IN OPTO-ELECTRONIC LOGIC BUILDING BLOCKS

Heinz Ruegg

Stanford University, Stanford, California

In order to obtain some design criteria for opto-electronic logic building blocks, different ways of indirectly amplifying light are compared with respect to signal propagation delay and power consumption. A system consisting of a junction detector, injection luminescent diodes, and an electronic amplifier is used as a model. Consistent with the gain-bandwidth limitations of the electronic amplifiers the propagation delay is shown to be proportional to the power gain required from the electronic amplifier. This power gain is equal to the product of the fan-out and the power efficiency of the opto-electronic block. For most arrangements, the propagation delay is found to increase with decreasing photon flux density in the system.

The photodiode is shown to be a fast detecting-amplifying device as long as the photon flux density is high. However, the corresponding propagation delay is inversely proportional to the square of the required gain. The photodiode therefore leads to a rather slow optoelectronic element if used in a system with a low efficiency.

By virtue of its current gain the phototransistor is capable of directly providing a quantum gain. Using it as the detecting amplifying device, propagation delays approaching the ones achievable with a photodiode can be obtained with less hardware and at a lower power.

The field-effect transistor is shown to be a detecting-amplifying device whose speed of response is to a first approximation independent of the photon flux density. This makes it very attractive for use in low-power opto-electronic systems.

The minimum propagation delay through present opto-electronic building blocks is estimated to be by about two orders of magnitude larger than the delay through electronic logic blocks operating at the same power level.

I. Introduction

A general opto-electronic logic building block is defined here as an element with several input ports and several output ports. If the discussion is restricted to binary logic elements, two standardized signal levels corresponding to the logic "1" and "0" respectively are defined. The signals of each output port are given in terms of the signals applied to the input ports by logic functions which are characteristic of the particular building block.

Self-compatibility of a logic building block requires that the output information be in the same form as the input information. Thus two basic types of opto-electronic building blocks can be distinguished according to the form of signals which they process:

1. A logic element with electrical input and output signals but optical internal information transfer.

2. A logic element with optical input and output signals but electrical internal information transfer.

While important for the hardware organization of an actual system, this distinction is insignificant for a discussion of the loss and gain mechanisms in a general opto-electronic building block. Therefore, without loss of generality, an opto-electronic element with optical inputs and outputs is considered. Two different photon-flux levels are assumed to represent the binary information.* For convenience they shall be denoted as ϕ_0 (photons/sec) for the logic "1" state and 0 for the logic "0" state. In order to guarantee some fan-out capability, N_{out}, the output photon flux for the "1" state must be equal to or greater than $N_{out}\ \phi_0$. Since self-compatibility requires equal photon energies at the input and at the output, the opto-electronic building block therefore has to provide a power gain equal to the fan-out.

With attention focused on this gain aspect, a simple "light amplifier" with a light power gain equal to N_{out} is considered rather than a specific opto-electronic element.† Such an amplifier in general consists of a light detector, an electronic amplifier and a light source (Fig. 1). In keeping with an opto-electronic amplifier as opposed to an optical one, this arrangement excludes a device capable of amplifying light directly. However,

* The conceptual possibility of representing binary data by two different light frequencies is not considered.
† This is an abstraction of an actual opto-electronic building block which is justifiable if only gain-delay relationships are discussed. A real opto-electronic element of course requires inversion and a means to limit the output signal.

systems where several of the three functions (detecting, amplifying, generating) are performed by the same device are not excluded.

The light generation, the light transport, and the light detection are associated with power losses. Denoting the corresponding power efficiencies[1]

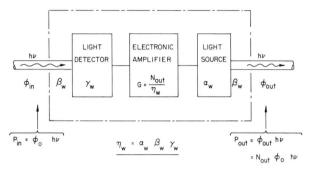

FIG. 1. Block diagram of a general opto-electronic light amplifier with a light power gain of N_{out}. The over-all power efficiency η_W is the product of the power efficiencies associated with detection γ_W, emission α_W, and transport β_W.

as α_W (emission), β_W (transport), and γ_W (detection), the over-all power efficiency is equal to $\eta_W = \alpha_W \beta_W \gamma_W$.* The power gain required from the electronic amplifier therefore is

$$G = \frac{N_{\text{out}}}{\eta_W} \tag{1}$$

II. Junction Detector—ILD System

The system shown in Fig. 1 is perfectly general and includes light bulbs, sparks, etc., as photon sources and photoconductors, photomultipliers, etc., as detectors. In order to have a more tractable model, however, the system to be considered is further specified as follows.

The light detector is assumed to be a reverse-biased p-n junction with a junction area A_d and a depletion capacitance $C_d = c_d A_d$. The light source is assumed to consist of one or several injection-luminescent diodes (ILD's) with junction areas A_s. The two logic states of an ILD are the off-state characterized by negligible current through the diode and the on-state characterized by a nominal diode current $I_s = j_s A_s$ and a forward voltage drop V_{Fs}.

* In what follows, η_W is assumed to be independent of the specific arrangement of the components in the light amplifier and of the current density of the system. This approximation is justifiable only in a very approximate treatment meant to reveal the key parameters which influence the gain-delay relationships of an opto-electronic element. In actuality the transport efficiency depends rather strongly upon the type and number of light interconnections. Also, the emission efficiency of injection luminescent diodes depends somewhat upon the current density in the system.

In Fig. 2 a simple arrangement is shown which should clarify the gain and loss mechanism in such a system. In keeping with the notation introduced for the general light amplifier, the optical power efficiency of this arrangement is also $\eta_W = \alpha_W \beta_W \gamma_W$.

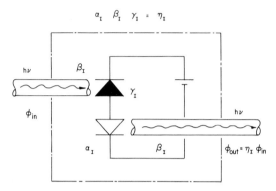

FIG. 2. A junction diode-ILD light amplifier with a power gain of $1/\eta_I$. The over-all quantum efficiency η_I is the product of the quantum efficiencies associated with detection γ_I, emission α_I, and transport β_I.

The quantum efficiency[1] can similarly be written as:*

$$\eta_I = \gamma_I \alpha_I \beta_I \qquad (2)$$

where

$$\gamma_I = \text{detection efficiency} = \frac{\text{electrons collected}}{\text{photons in}}$$

$$\alpha_I = \text{emission efficiency} = \frac{\text{photons emitted}}{\text{electrons recombined}}$$

$$\beta_I = \text{transport efficiency} = \frac{\text{photons out}}{\text{photons emitted}}$$

Since all the electrons collected in the detector recombine in the ILD, the input photon flux and the output photon flux are simply related by

$$\frac{\phi_{\text{out}}}{\phi_{\text{in}}} = \eta_I \qquad (3)$$

Likewise the light power ratio is

$$\frac{P_{\text{out}}}{P_{\text{in}}} = \frac{\phi_{\text{out}}}{\phi_{\text{in}}} = \eta_W G_1 = \eta_I \qquad (4)$$

where G_1 denotes the electronic gain. Thus it follows that the electronic gain of the arrangement of Fig. 2 is

* The photon transport losses have been lumped together at the output of the amplifier.

$$G_1 = \frac{\eta_I}{\eta_W} \tag{5}$$

The additional gain which must be provided in order to achieve the light power gain prescribed by Eq. 1 therefore is

$$G_a = \frac{G}{G_1} = \frac{N_{\text{out}}}{\eta_I} \tag{6}$$

This gain can be achieved in various ways. However, because of the finite gain over rise-time ratio of all electronic amplifiers, it must be obtained at the expense of an increased signal propagation delay through the logic block.

In the next paragraphs expressions for the propagation delays to be expected from different amplifier arrangements are derived. One purpose of this is to reveal the common dependence of the propagation delay upon some system parameters, regardless of the specific type of amplifier treated. A second purpose is achieved by selecting the examples in such a way as to also show some differences in the propagation delay arising from different configurations. Thus the question whether the electronic power gain prescribed by Eq. 6 should be obtained predominantly as a voltage gain or rather as a current gain is investigated in the next two sections.

III. Photodiode: ILD Light Amplifier

A reverse-biased photodiode has no current gain but can deliver an appreciable voltage gain. In an opto-electronic structure this voltage gain can be converted into a quantum gain by summing the output light of series-connected ILD's at the detector junction (Fig. 3). The maximum

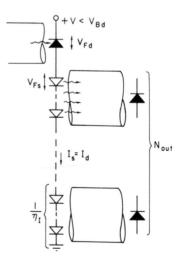

FIG. 3. Schematic diagram of a photodiode-ILD light amplifier.

achievable power gain of such an arrangement is limited by the forward voltage drop, V_{Fs}, of a fully turned-on ILD and the breakdown voltage, V_{Bd}, of the detector diode:

$$G < \frac{V_{Bd}}{V_{Fs}} \tag{7}$$

According to Eq. 6 the number of diodes required to achieve an over-all power gain of N_{out} is equal to N_{out}/η_I. They might conveniently be arranged into N_{out} groups of $1/\eta_I$ diodes, each group representing one output (Fig. 3).

The following effects contribute to the signal propagation delay through the light amplifier of Fig. 3:

1. The depletion capacitance C_d of the detector diode has to be charged and discharged to a voltage equal to $(N_{out}/\eta_I)V_{Fs}$ by the photocurrent I_d of the diode.

2. Carrier storage and carrier buildup effects in the ILD's delay the light output.

3. There is a voltage swing equal to V_{Fs} across each ILD. The depletion capacitances of the ILD's must be charged to this voltage by the photo-current.

It is found that effect 1 contributes the largest delay in systems with reasonably high amplification factors (many ILD's). Effects 2 and 3 are therefore neglected in an estimate of the propagation delay. It is also assumed that no recombination current flows through the ILD before a voltage equal to V_{Fs} is developed across it and that the whole photocurrent consists of ILD recombination current afterwards. Assuming furthermore that the light output follows the flow of the recombination current without delay, the propagation delay becomes

$$t_{pd} = \frac{N_{out}}{\eta_I} V_{Fs} \frac{C_d}{I_d} = \frac{N_{out}}{\eta_I} V_{Fs} \frac{c_d}{j_s} \frac{A_d}{A_s} \tag{8}$$

Since the parameters appearing in Eq. 8 are also common to other arrangements, it is worthwhile to examine their origin and the range of values which they can assume. The fan-out, N_{out}, is a systems requirement. The over-all quantum efficiency η_I is largely given by the state of the art of light generation, transport, and detection. The forward voltage across an ILD, V_{Fs}, is practically a materials constant. The current density in the ILD's, j_s, is a free variable with an upper limit given by considerations of power dissipation. The capacitance per unit detector area, c_d, can be minimized to a lower limit given by the width of the transition region where carrier transit times become appreciable.[2]

It is interesting to note that the propagation delay is directly proportional to the ratio of the detector and ILD junction areas. This is, of course, simply another way of stating that the propagation delay is inversely proportional to the photon flux density at the detector. The summation of the light generated by the $1/\eta_I$ ILD's belonging to one output group can be accomplished by mounting them opposite a large detector diode. The area ratio A_d/A_s is thus on the order of $1/\eta_I$, leading to a propagation delay of

$$t_{pd} = \frac{N_{out} V_{Fs}}{\eta_I^2} \frac{c_d}{j_s} \tag{9}$$

The power dissipation is

$$P = \frac{N_{out}}{\eta_I} V_{Fs} j_s A_s \tag{10}$$

The following features of the above expressions deserve some attention.

1. The propagation delay is inversely proportional to the square of the over-all quantum efficiency, indicating the necessity to minimize quantum losses in the system.

2. Within the framework of the assumptions made, the propagation delay is inversely proportional to the current density in the system. Thus a linear tradeoff between power consumption and speed exists. In order to increase the product of the power and the propagation delay, the dimensions of the devices must be reduced.

3. Expression 8 points out that the detector diode must be made as small as technologically possible if a fast logic element is desired.

In Fig. 7 the propagation delay given by expression 9 is plotted versus the over-all quantum efficiency for reasonably optimistic values of the other parameters involved.* Curve 1 indicates that due to the $1/\eta_I^2$ dependence a very high propagation delay results for present state-of-the-art quantum efficiencies. A more practical way to achieve a quantum gain is to use a device capable of current gain.

IV. Phototransistor—A ILD Light Amplifier

The phototransistor is a detecting-amplifying device capable of voltage gain as well as of current gain. Voltage gain leads to a signal delay because capacitors have to be charged and discharged to a certain output voltage swing. The speed of response of the current gain mechanism, on the other hand, is mainly limited by the carrier transit time. The phototransistor can therefore serve to illustrate the optimum balance between voltage gain and current gain which achieves a prescribed power gain with the minimum signal delay.

* The parameter values upon which the curves of Figs. 7 and 8 are based are thought to represent the present state of the art. Since they are not constants of nature, their choice might of course be subject to some discussion. While the absolute values of the propagation delays as well as the relative position of the curves with respect to each other depend upon the choice of these parameters, their dependence upon quantum efficiency and power dissipation does not. It is this latter feature which the curves are intended to show, while the absolute scale is only given to indicate the order of magnitude of the delays to be expected.

The arrangement to be considered realizes a voltage gain equal to nG_1 by connecting n ILD's in series with the collector of a phototransistor (Fig. 4). In order to attain the required power gain of N_{out}/η_W, the current gain of the transistor must be equal to*

$$\beta_0 = \frac{N_{\text{out}}}{\eta_W n G_1} = \frac{N_{\text{out}}}{n \eta_I} \tag{11}$$

In analyzing the propagation delay of the arrangement shown in Fig. 4, the same assumptions are made as for the photodiode. They are symbol-

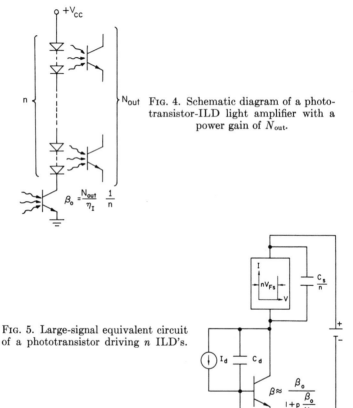

Fig. 4. Schematic diagram of a photo-transistor-ILD light amplifier with a power gain of N_{out}.

Fig. 5. Large-signal equivalent circuit of a phototransistor driving n ILD's.

ically included in the large-signal equivalent circuit shown in Fig. 5. In accordance with these assumptions, the light propagation delay is approximated by the time delay between the application of the input light step and the moment when I_s has reached 90 per cent of its nominal value.

As an alternative to a complete solution based upon an elaborate equiv-

* It is assumed that stable transistors with a current gain given by Eq. 12 can be made for all current levels considered.

alent circuit, a qualitative argumentation is used which divides the total propagation delay into three parts, each of them arising from a different effect. In treating these effects as if they would happen completely sequentially, the actual case is grossly idealized but a good understanding of the factors which cause the signal delay is obtained.

The base-emitter voltage of the phototransistor is essentially zero in the absence of light. After illumination, it must therefore rise by one diode forward drop (V_{Fd}) before any significant injection can take place. This leads to a delay time during which the base-collector capacitance, which is assumed to be identical to the detector capacitance, and the base-emitter transition capacitance are charged to V_{Fd} by the detector current I_d. Assuming that the base-emitter junction is made as small as technologically feasible, its capacitance is neglected and the delay time approximated by

$$t_1 = \frac{V_{Fd} C_d}{I_d} = \frac{V_{Fd} C_d \beta_0}{I_s} = V_{Fd} \beta_0 \frac{c_d}{j_s} \frac{A_d}{A_s} \tag{12}$$

With use of expression 12 for the current gain, the delay time for the case of $A_d/A_s = n/N_{\text{out}}$ calculates to be

$$t_1 = \frac{V_{Fd}}{\eta_I} \frac{c_d}{j_s} \tag{13}$$

After t_1 the transistor is at the edge of the active region. However, no collector current can flow until the collector voltage has changed by nV_{Fs}. Therefore no appreciable base current will flow for a time t_2 required to accomplish a voltage change of nV_{Fs} across the base-collector junction. If the equivalent load capacitance, $C_s/n\beta_0$ is much smaller than C_d, it can be neglected and one obtains in an analogous way to Eq. 13

$$t_2 = \frac{nV_{Fs}}{\eta_I} \frac{c_d}{j_s} \tag{14}$$

After t_2 the full detector current I_d is assumed to flow into the base, the transistor thus entering the active region, where its behavior can be approximately described by its small-signal parameters.[3] In terms of the angular gain-bandwidth product, $\omega_t = 2\pi f_t$, the rise time of the collector current to 90 per cent of its nominal value can be approximated by

$$t_3 = \ln 10 \frac{\beta_0}{\omega_t} = 2.3 \frac{N_{\text{out}}}{n\eta_I \omega_t} \tag{15}$$

If the light propagation delay is written as the sum of the three delay times calculated, the following expression is obtained:

$$t_{pd} = t_1 + t_2 + t_3 = \frac{V_{Fd} + nV_{Fs}}{\eta_I} \frac{c_d}{j_s} + \frac{2.3N_{\text{out}}}{\eta_I n\omega_t} \tag{16}$$

The optimum number n_0 of ILD's to be connected in series with the transistor in order to get the minimum propagation delay for fixed device and operating parameters is readily obtained as

$$n_0 = \left(\frac{2.3N_{\text{out}}j_s}{\omega_t V_{Fs} C_d}\right)^{1/2} \tag{17}$$

If a collector voltage equal to V_{Fs} is allowed in the on-state, the power dissipation of the arrangement shown in Fig. 4 is

$$P = (n+1)V_{Fs}j_s A_s \tag{18}$$

In Fig. 7 the propagation delay of the ILD-phototransistor light amplifier is plotted versus the over-all quantum efficiency for $n = 1$ and $n = n_0$. (The optimum number of ILD's for the parameter values on which Fig. 7 is based is approximately 10, i.e., 2 per output for a fan-out of 5.) In comparing these curves with the ones obtained for the photodiode amplifier it should be remembered that they represent the smallest achievable propagation delays for the device parameters being limited to the assumed values by the present state of the art. Nothing is of course implied about the practicality of actually achieving them. Thus the phototransistor with a single ILD (curve 2) is certainly a more practical light amplifier than the photodiode driving a large number of ILD's. Furthermore, the expense in power is also widely different for these two cases as illustrated in Fig. 8 where the propagation delays are plotted versus power dissipation.

V. FET—ILD Light Amplifier

The junction field-effect transistor (FET) is another example of a detecting amplifying device. One possible mode of operation is shown in Fig. 6.[4]

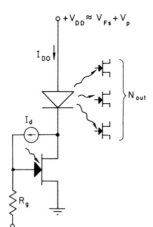

FIG. 6. Schematic diagram of an FET-ILD light amplifier with a power gain of N_{out}. The current generator between drain and gate represents the photocurrent generated in the gate-channel diode.

In the absence of light the gate voltage is equal to the pinch-off voltage V_p if the voltage drop across the gate resistor R_g caused by the junction leakage current is neglected. Since the drain to source resistance for this case is in the order of megohms, a negligibly small current flows through the ILD. Incoming light generates carriers near the gate-channel junction, and the resulting gate current causes a high enough voltage drop across the gate resistor to turn on the FET completely. A current equal to the drain to source saturation current then flows through the ILD.

The field-effect transistor connected in this way thus resembles a photo-transistor inasmuch as in both cases the light detection is accomplished by a junction which is also part of the amplifying device. Also, the capacitance of this junction in both cases leads to a signal delay which is proportional to the voltage swing across the junction and inversely proportional to the photon-flux density striking it. However, the gain of a phototransistor is independent of the size of the detector junction (base-collector junction) resulting in a gain over delay ratio which is proportional to the incoming photon-flux density. The transconductance of an FET on the other hand is proportional to the detector area (gate-channel area) for a constant channel length, leading to a gain over delay ratio which is to a first approximation independent of the photon-flux density. In our notation, this means that the propagation delay is independent of the current density in the ILD and hence independent of the power consumption. As shown in greater detail in the Appendix,

$$t_{pd} = \frac{N_{\text{out}}}{\eta_I} \frac{7L^2}{\mu_{\text{ch}} V_p} \tag{19}$$

L = channel length
μ_{ch} = majority carrier mobility in the channel

The corresponding curve 4 is included in Fig. 7 for comparison. The unique

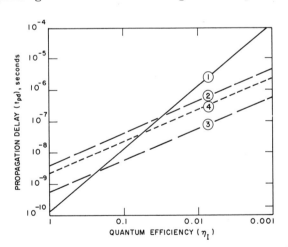

FIG. 7. Propagation delay versus over-all quantum efficiency for: 1, Photodiode; 2, Phototransistor driving one ILD ($n = 1$); 3, Phototransistor driving optimum number of ILD's ($n = n_0$); 4, Field-effect transistor driving one ILD. The curves are not drawn for equal power dissipation but are based upon the following values: $j_s = 200$ A/cm^2; $c_d = 5000$ pF/cm^2; $\omega_t = 3.10^9$ rad/sec (at all current levels considered); $L = 10\mu$; $V_p = -10$ V; $V_{Fs} = 1$ V (e.g., GaAs); $V_{Fd} = 0.5$ V (e.g., Si); $N_{\text{out}} = 5$.

feature of the field-effect transistor as a photodetector is illustrated in Fig. 8, where the propagation delays of the devices which were considered are plotted versus the power dissipation for a fixed quantum efficiency. The first-order theory put forward clearly indicates that in a low-power

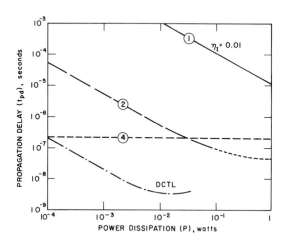

FIG. 8. Propagation delay versus power dissipation for $A_s = 10^{-4}$ cm². The DCTL curve included for comparison was obtained using 2N709 transistors.

system the field effect transistor might be capable of faster light amplification than any other detecting-amplifying device. Also included in Fig. 8 is the power delay curve for direct coupled transistor logic (DCTL) obtained with a commercial transistor type.[5] With the possible exception of the ILD-FET system at low powers, present-day opto-electronic systems are seen to be about two orders of magnitude slower than electronic systems at the same power level.

VI. Conclusions

In order to obtain some design criteria for opto-electronic building blocks, different ways of indirectly amplifying light were compared on the basis of signal delay and power consumption. An ILD-junction detector system with various electronic amplifiers was used as a model. Consistent with the gain-bandwidth limitations of the electronic amplifiers, the propagation delay for all arrangements was found to be proportional to the required gain and hence, for a given fan-out, inversely proportional to the over-all quantum efficiency of the system.* For most arrangements the propagation delay furthermore increases with decreasing photon-flux density.

---

* More accurately, the propagation delay is inversely proportional to the over-all power efficiency η_W. However, $G_1 = \eta_I/\eta_W$ has been treated as a constant given by the choice of the ILD- and detector material and was absorbed in the two diode forward drops V_{Fd} and V_{Fs}.

The photodiode was found to be a fast detecting-amplifying device as long as the photon flux density to be detected is high. However, the propagation delay varies as the reciprocal of the square of the over-all quantum efficiency, making the photodiode an undesirable device for systems with a low quantum efficiency.

By virtue of its current gain the phototransistor offers a means of achieving propagation delays shorter than the ones possible with the focused photodiode system. Moreover, a certain propagation delay can be obtained at the expense of less power than if a photodiode is used. Optimization of the current gain and the voltage gain leads to a minimum-delay amplifier for given device and operating characteristics.

In a field-effect transistor the gate-channel junction also serves as the detecting junction. This not only leads to an improved propagation delay (because the total capacitance to be charged is smaller than if separate junctions would be used) but also makes it independent of the incoming light intensity.

In conclusion it can be said that the propagation delay through an opto-electronic building block can be minimized by the choice of the optimum electronic amplifier and by proper design techniques. However, it will always be inversely proportional to the over-all quantum efficiency as long as linear electronic amplifiers are used. With present-day quantum efficiencies which are limited by the light generation efficiency of injection luminescent diodes and coupling losses, propagation delays result which are about two orders of magnitude higher than for electronic systems operating at the same power level. The only two possibilities to change this deplorable state of affairs is to either increase the over-all quantum efficiency considerably or else to find a much faster detecting-amplifying device. Both are quite formidable tasks.

APPENDIX

Propagation Delay Through an FET-ILD Light Amplifier

In estimating the propagation delay through an FET-ILD light amplifier, the following two effects must be considered:

1. The rate of change of the gate voltage is limited by an RC time constant τ_g.

2. The drain-gate capacitance adds a signal delay by transferring a voltage change at the drain back to the gate (Miller effect). However, this effect can be neglected regardless of the size of the drain-gate capacitance as long as the voltage swing of the drain is small compared to the pinch-off voltage. Therefore, assuming $V_{Fs} \ll |V_p|$, it is not considered here.

Returning therefore to effect 1, the time constant is approximated by

$$\tau_g = R_g \langle C_g \rangle \tag{20}$$

In this approximation the channel resistance has been neglected in comparison to

R_g. This is permissible as long as τ_g is much greater than the intrinsic FET time constant given by the channel resistance and $\langle C_g \rangle$.[6] $\langle C_g \rangle$ represents an average gate-channel capacitance defined as

$$\langle C_g \rangle = \int_0^{|V_p|} \frac{C_g(V_g)\, dV_g}{|V_p|} = \frac{Q_p}{|V_p|} \tag{21}$$

In Eq. 21 the pinch-off charge[7] Q_p has been introduced. According to the definition given in Eq. 21, the pinch-off charge is the charge with which the gate has to be provided in order to switch the FET from "off" ($V_g = V_p$) to "on" ($V_g = 0$) or vice versa. Over-all charge neutrality requires Q_p to be equal to the difference between the space charge in the channel of a turned-off device and a turned-on device. Therefore Q_p can be approximated by

$$Q_p \cong qLWTN_{ch} \tag{22}$$

L, W, T = length, width, and thickness, respectively of channel
N_{ch} = doping density in the channel (assumed uniform)
q = electronic charge

The approximation is valid as long as the pinch-off voltage is large compared with the diffusion voltage and as long as $L \gg T$. In order to equalize the turnon delay and the turnoff delay, the gate resistor is chosen such that

$$R_g I_d \approx |V_p| \tag{23}$$

If the propagation delay is defined as the time required by the gate voltage to reach 90 per cent of its final value, one obtains by using Eqs. 21, 22, and 24

$$t_{pd} = \tau_g \ln 10 = 2.3 R_g \langle C_g \rangle = 2.3 R_g \frac{Q_p}{|V_p|} = 2.3 \frac{Q_p}{I_d} \tag{24}$$

The current gain required from the FET is

$$\frac{I_{D0}}{I_d} = \frac{I_s}{I_d} = G_a = \frac{N_{out}}{\eta_I} \tag{25}$$

Thus from Eqs. 24 and 25 follows

$$t_{pd} = 2.3 \frac{Q_p}{I_{D0}} \frac{N_{out}}{\eta_I} \tag{26}$$

The drain-source saturation current for $V_g = 0$ can be expressed in terms of basic FET design parameters:[6]

$$I_{D0} = \frac{q^2 N_{ch}^2 \mu_{ch}}{24K} T^3 \frac{W}{L} \tag{27}$$

where

μ_{ch} = majority carrier mobility in channel
= 1400 cm²/V-sec for electrons in silicon
K = dielectric constant = $1.06 \cdot 10^{-12}$ f/cm for silicon.

Equation 27 can be expressed in terms of the pinch-off voltage and for an abrupt gate-channel junction with the gate being much heavier doped than the channel becomes

$$I_{D0} = \frac{|V_p|}{3} q N_{ch} \mu_{ch} T \frac{W}{L} \tag{28}$$

Inserting expressions 22 and 28 into 26 leads to expression 19 which is quoted in the text:

$$t_{pd} \approx \frac{N_{\text{out}}}{\eta_I} \frac{7L^2}{\mu_{\text{ch}}|V_p|} \tag{19}$$

REFERENCES

1. WUNDERMAN, I., *Characteristics of Photon-Coupled Systems*, Stanford Electronics Laboratories, Technical Report No. 4814-1.
2. RIESZ, R. P., "High Speed Semiconductor Photodiodes," *Rev. Sci. Instr., 33*, 994 (September 1962).
3. MOLL, J. L., "Large-Signal Transient Response of Junction Transistors," *Proc. IRE, 42*, 1773 (December 1954).
4. SHIPLEY, M., "Photofet Characteristics and Applications," *Solid State Design, 5*, 28 (April 1964).
5. BEESON, R., AND H. RUEGG, "New Forms of ALL Transistor Logic," *1962 International Solid State Circuits Conference*, Digest of Tech. Papers, p. 11.
6. SHOCKLEY, W., "A Unipolar Field-Effect Transistor," *Proc. IRE, 40*, 1365 (November 1952).
7. RUEGG, H., "An Integrated FET Analog Switch," *Proc. IEEE, 52*, 1572 (December 1964).

CHAPTER 26

DI-SCAN: VERSATILE IMAGE SENSOR

Reinald S. Nielsen and Michael A. Ford*

The MITRE Corporation, Bedford, Massachusetts

The potential of photographic film for digital data storage initiated the thinking that led to an improved image sensor. Other attempts to use photographic techniques for data storage have been successful; however, one can argue that these other attempts rely on geometrical relationships of the machinery handling the film rather than any peculiar advantage of the image itself. From these notions arose the idea of treating the photofilm data memory as a problem in image discrimination or pattern recognition. DI-SCAN, the sensing device that proved useful for the data memory problem, promises great utility in more general problems of image discrimination by machine.

1. The Image Discrimination Problem

Image discrimination is no problem to human beings in the majority of instances. Image discrimination is a problem for a machine. The discussion immediately following attempts to clarify the elements of mechanical image discrimination.

1.1. Defined Image Classes

The driver reacting to a dangerous oncoming automobile has singled out the dangerous automobile from the class of oncoming automobiles. If one considers the problem further, it is apparent that "oncoming automobiles" is a well-restricted class. That is, only those automobiles that are in the same highway, have speed and positions that permit a possible collision, etc., are considered by the threatened automobile driver. Machine discrimination of images must be based upon similarly restricted image classes.

In particular, since machines (computers) possess extremely limited

* Present address: Digital Equipment Corp., Maynard, Mass.

"intelligence," it is necessary to define carefully and extensively the class of images among which a machine discrimination is to be made. In practical terms, this necessity is illustrated by the fact that useful image discrimination machines have been limited, in most instances, to the class of alphanumeric symbols. The class of alphanumeric symbols is invariably further restricted to a few symbol styles (type fonts).

1.2. Image Measurements and Experience

Within the defined class of images, there must be some means for discriminating one image from another. Thus, in the class of oncoming automobiles, the driver recognizes the threatening automobile by its measurable position in the wrong traffic lane.

While measurable differences between images are necessary, they are insufficient, in themselves, for discriminating among images. That is, some means for defining the significant image measurements must be active. In the human, there is a faculty for predicting the result of an oncoming vehicle in the wrong lane. It is this faculty that enables the human to make a discrimination; the faculty implies data or information in addition to that implicit in the image measurements. For the human being, the additional data are the residue of past experience.

Machine discrimination of images requires the equivalent of human past experience. The logical structure of a computing machine can contain the reference data necessary for effective evaluation of image measurements. Recognize that a very close logical association must exist between the reference data and the image measurement data. If the two types of data do not exist in a common context, the machine discrimination can be no more conclusive than the thoughts of the driver seeing a flying saucer hovering over the highway.

1.3. Implementation of Image Discrimination

Many attempts have been made to implement mechanical discrimination among a class of images. A number of these attempts have been successful. However, the successful attempts have been those which possess least potential for extension to a larger or different class of images. Of the implementation attempts that might be classed as "failures," many seem to be easily extended to larger image classes. No one has yet found economic importance for "extensive failure," however.

The following summary gives only a slight indication of the multiplicity and ingenuity of the attempts to mechanize image discrimination. The bibliography lists several references that were particularly instructive for the authors.

1. Specialized characters. Several successful alphanumeric symbol readers have been based upon the use of a controlled, specialized set of symbols. Perhaps the most extreme specialization takes place in the reader systems

that employ magnetic inks. In this type of reader, the optical image of the character is irrelevant to the discrimination process. Instead of measuring the optical image, measurements are made of magnetic fields existing about each symbol to be read.

Symbol readers operating upon optical measurements of the symbol have been successful so long as the quality and style of the symbol are held to specified tolerances. There are many types of readers available differing primarily in capability to accept distorted or dirty symbols. These readers may be described as "template matchers." That is, the measurements from a particular symbol are compared with a file of symbol measurements; essentially, the file of measurements corresponds to templates of ideal symbols in the recognizable class. If a match of the unknown symbol measurements with a set of filed measurements can be made, the symbol is identified. If no match is made, that fact is indicated by an output signal from the machine.

This characteristic of these machines is a weakness. Since a match *must* be found to make a discrimination, symbols that are almost a match (differing in font or style, perhaps) are rejected. This means that many symbols are rejected that would be readily recognized by a human. To overcome this difficulty, a number of image discrimination schemes have been proposed.

2. "Unrestricted" symbols. "Unrestricted" is a poor word, since one can always point out some restriction upon the class of symbols that are acceptable to any symbol recognition scheme. Nonetheless, the word is used here to denote those schemes in which an attempt has been made to strip away dependence upon such restrictions as magnetic inks and narrowly defined type fonts. One author goes so far as to suggest that his machine recognizes "Gestalts"; apparently he concedes to the machine an intelligence superior to his own.

Many techniques have been proposed as a solution to discrimination of unrestricted alphanumeric symbols. All schemes, however, can be described in terms of a means for transforming the optical image of the symbol into a set of digital data representations followed by some manner of measuring a majority "vote" as to which of an agreed class of output signals shall be presented. Unfortunately, at least to my knowledge, none of these schemes has been successful, i.e., achieved practical utility.

One may divide the "unrestricted" symbol readers into two groups. The first group depends upon digital signals arising from a sensor composed of many elemental cells. Each elemental cell, in the well-defined array of cells, provides an individual signal defining the presence of a symbol "element" at the cell location. The second group of readers depends upon digital signals arising as a sensing device follows defined contours of the symbol. Most of the reported image discrimination work has been done with the first type of sensor.

The transformation of the sensor data to a form useful for symbol discrimination in a digital computer comprises the major distinction among the various "unrestricted" symbol readers. Transformations based on correlation and autocorrelation, random pairing of data, extraction of characteristic geometric data, moment of area calculations, and various transformations based upon ease of mechanization have all been used. Most of these transformations give rise to a range of output "values," with each value corresponding to a different symbol.

Thus, the manipulation of the transformed image measurements gives rise to a best symbol identification in every case. None of the unrestricted symbol readers approach the freedom from reading error that is possible with restricted symbols.

2. Idealized Solution to the Image Discrimination Problem

The difficulties that have plagued earlier workers yield some insight into an "ideal" image discrimination technique. One must still abide by the necessity to work in defined image classes with known image measurements; however, the relationship between particular image measurements and the measurement data transformation can be altered.

2.1. Image Measure Transform with Defined Characteristics

Many of the individuals proposing techniques for recognizing "unrestricted" alphanumeric symbols seem to be in the position of Oliver Heaviside. Heaviside's operational calculus constituted a set of calculation routines more powerful than classical mathematics long before there was any rigorous justification for the operational calculus. Most of Heaviside's techniques were proved valid by workers extending the theory of equations and the complex variable.

For many of the "unrestricted" symbol recognition schemes, however, there does not seem to be any possibility for proving a unique mapping of symbol measurements into symbol identifications via the particular transformation method. If such a unique mapping were proved, there would still remain a problem of economically implementing the transformation with digital computer machinery. Perhaps these problems will be solved for some of the existing image discrimination schemes; the necessity for solving these problems can be avoided by refusing to accept the utility of arbitrary data transforms.

Thus, the first requirement is an explicit data transform for the image discrimination problem. Though this requirement is easily stated, the task of describing a worthwhile transform is not simple. Therefore, a corollary requirement is a data transform that can be altered as greater understanding of the image discrimination problem is attained.

2.2. Image Measurements Dependent Upon Prior Measurements

A practical difficulty arising in many proposed "unrestricted" image discrimination schemes is the plethora of digital data that must be handled. One can recognize that much of the data is meaningless or redundant, but there is little opportunity to instruct the machine to discard useless data until the image discrimination is complete. Thus, a data processor capability is necessary that far exceeds the useful data implicit in the images.

The second requirement for an ideal image discrimination scheme becomes apparent. The image sensor shall carry out image measurements under control of the transformed measurement data. Essentially, the image measurement sequence should be controlled by feedback from the data discrimination routine. With such control over accession of image measurements, the data flow into the digital computer apparatus can be held nearer to the necessary minimum.

2.3. Ideal System

Figure 1 illustrates an ideal image discrimination scheme. An image sensor, prompted by the image measurement control, carries out measure-

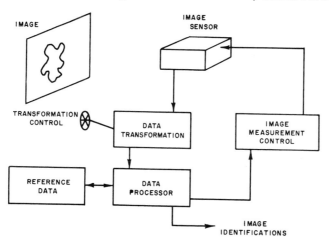

Fig. 1. Ideal image discrimination system.

ments and feeds the data to the data transformation device. Transformed data is fed to a data sorter where it is manipulated with reference data to derive control data for the image measurement control element and eventually, output data identifying the image. The handle labeled "Transformation Control" implies that the data transformation may be altered from time to time.

No restrictions are placed on the physical realization of the image discrimination system. It is apparent that the image sensor must be some manner of optical scanner or other physical realization of a shape sensitive device. However, the data transformation, transformation control, reference data, data processor, and image measurement control may all be realized with a digital computer just as well as physically distinct elements.

3. A Practical Image Sensor

Successful use of photographic data storage techniques has been achieved in at least two instances.[1,2] Each of these techniques depend strongly upon geometrical relationships established in the machine design as the basis for finding (addressing) particular data in the store. Geometrical relationships translate into dimensional tolerances on machinery; and, reasonable exploitation of photographic film capability meant difficult mechanical tolerance problems.

Rather than physically measurable relationships between an image and some sensing device external to the image, one requires physically measurable relationships among elements within the image. Measurement of image element relationships should be free of errors due to the measurement technique, insofar as possible.

3.1. The Data Image

Digital data, in binary number representation, can be implied by a succession of opaque and transparent areas on a film surface. One may define an opaque area to imply unity and a transparent area to imply zero. The relationships between opaque and transparent areas that will be accepted as proper implications of binary data can also be defined. For instance, a succession of binary digits can be represented by a series of spots strung over the film surface; the diameter of each significant opaque and transparent spot may be assumed approximately equal. These definitions and assumptions constitute the reference data that an image discriminator must employ.

3.1.1 DISCRIMINATION OF THE DATA IMAGE. Consider the data image as a succession of binary ONE's. A solid opaque line results. This data image can be discriminated by a sensing device operating to track a solid line. Consider Fig. 2 and the three-hole pattern labeled a, b, and c.

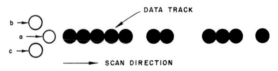

FIG. 2. Sensor tracking action.

Each hole provides an individual indication of image density; the geometrical relationship between the holes is fixed and independent of the image geometry. If the three-hole pattern moves over the data image, as shown, hole a will signal the presence of the opaque area, and holes b and c will signal transparent areas. Should the three-hole pattern fail to track the data image, hole b or hole c will intercept the solid line. Obviously, the signals arising from holes b and c can be used to correct the location of the three-hole pattern.

When the data image is not restricted to a solid opaque line, it becomes necessary to refine the description of the feedback tracking system. This refinement is straightforward and customarily necessary in design of feedback control systems.

3.1.2 PHYSICAL REALIZATION OF THE MULTIPLE APERTURE SENSING DEVICE. Early attempts to produce an all-electric television system prompted invention of the image dissector tube. Figure 3 is a schematic

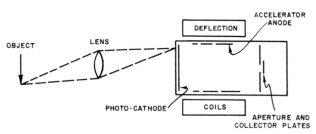

FIG. 3. Image dissector.

representation of the device. An image is focused upon a photocathode and the emitted electrons accelerated down the length of the tube to be magnetically focused upon an aperture plate. A small hole in the plate allows electrons to pass to an electron multiplier structure; suitable magnetic deflection fields cause the entire electron image to pass regularly before the aperture plate sampling hole. Hence the electron multiplier output signal is an acceptable television system video signal.

Rather than a single hole in the aperture plate, it is possible to use several holes; each hole must have an associated, independent electron multiplier. The DI-SCAN tube is derived from this simple idea; the idea and its ramifications seemed too simple. As a result, early considerations of the tube led to the name, DI-SCAN: Damned Instrument—Something's Clearly Amiss Now.

The Industrial Laboratories Division of ITT Corporation, Fort Wayne, Indiana, was chosen to build the first devices incorporating the DI-SCAN principle. Figure 4 illustrates one of the tubes furnished by ITT Industrial Labs.

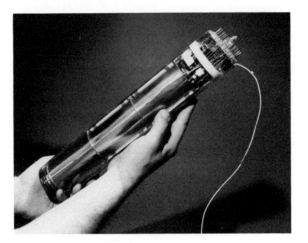

FIG. 4. DI-SCAN tube.

4. DI-SCAN Experimental Evaluation

This section describes the DI-SCAN tube and the apparatus that was built to test the tube performance and operating characteristics. Finally the experimental results and the conclusions that were drawn are presented. The Appendix presents an analysis of electron trajectories under simplified electric and magnetic field conditions assumed inside the tube.

Although there is still much to be learned, the results of this yearlong project were quite satisfactory in that they showed quite clearly in what direction we must go to develop the DI-SCAN into a useful laboratory tool.

4.1. Description of Apparatus

4.1.1 GENERAL DESCRIPTION.   The DI-SCAN tube is an electron multiplier phototube containing a photocathode, drift section, aperture plate, deflector plate and separator, and three electron multipliers as illustrated by Fig. 5 and described in detail in Secs. 4.1.1.1 to 4.1.1.3.

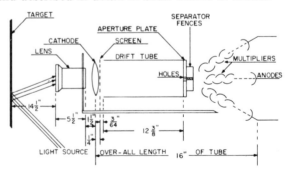

FIG. 5. DI-SCAN tube schematic.

An optical image is focused through a lens onto the front surface of the photocathode. The photosensitive material from which the cathode is formed emits electrons from each point on the inside surface of the cathode proportional to the intensity of the light falling on that point on the front surface of the cathode. Thus the light image is transformed into an electron image of the same size by the photocathode.

The electron image cloud formed at the cathode is accelerated down the length of the tube under the influence of the electric field between the cathode and the cylindrical drift tube, which is positive relative to the cathode. In traveling the length of the tube the beam, whose cross section is the electron image, is subjected to a magnetic focus field and a magnetic deflection field as it passes through the drift section. The focus field, supplied by solenoidal coils completely enclosing the tube, focuses the electron image on the aperture plate that caps the drift cylinder near the rear end of the tube. The deflection field permits the beam to be deflected in two orthogonal directions in the plane of the aperture plate and is applied via deflection coils external to the tube between the cathode and aperture plate.

The aperture plate at the far end of the drift tube contains three 0.005-in. diameter holes on 0.010-in. centers arrayed so that the centers are the apices of an equilateral triangle (Fig. 6b). Each aperture passes only the portion of the focused electron image beam that enters the aperture. The remainder of the beam is absorbed by the aperture plate itself.

Thus each aperture passes a 0.005-in. cross section of the focused electron image beam and these three small beams are kept separated on the rear side of the aperture plate by the fence (Fig. 6a) and deflector structures. Each of the three beams enters an electron multiplier that multiplies the extremely low aperture currents (10^{-10} A) to currents more readily used by electronic circuits (10^{-5} A). The three amplified aperture currents are then available via pins at the rear of the tube.

4.1.1.1 Photocathode. The photocathode has an S-11 response and an active area of approximately two inches. It has a nominal sensitivity of 25 μA/lm and can withstand no more than 25 ft-c direct illumination for extended periods of time without detriment.

4.1.1.2 Deflector Plate and Separator Fence. Physically and electrically attached to the aperture plate are three triangular wedges with knife-edges meeting at the center of the triangle formed by the three holes (see Fig. 6b). These form fences that prevent electrons from one hole getting into an improper multiplier. Further, to help diverge the three aperture streams, a deflector plate has been attached to an insulator on the aperture plate between the fences. This deflector plate may be electrically positive with respect to the aperture plate to pull electrons away from the fences and into the electron multiplier.

4.1.1.3 High-Voltage Divider String. The voltages applied to the cath-

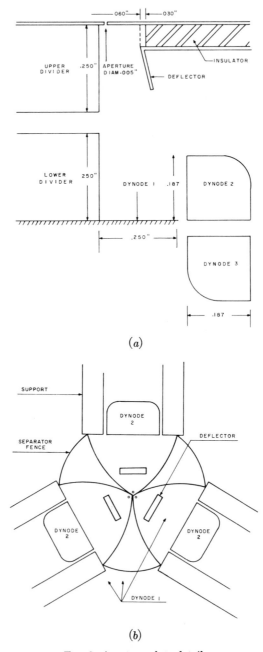

(a)

(b)

Fɪɢ. 6. Aperture plate detail.

ode, the drift tube deflector plates, and the electron multiplier dynodes are obtained from taps in a string of series resistors connected across a variable high-voltage supply. This voltage divider string is illustrated in Fig. 7. Several of the more critical voltages were taken from potentiometers to allow for experimental adjustment.

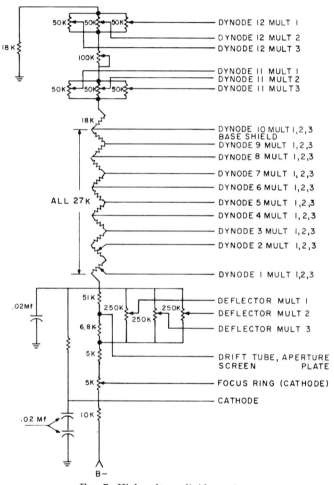

Fig. 7. High-voltage divider string.

4.1.2 DEFLECTION SYSTEM. The three apertures "see" only the portion of the electron image that is focused on the three apertures. For the three apertures to see the entire electron image (the whole photocathode active area) it is necessary to deflect the focused electron stream in two directions (*x* and *y*) so that the entire electron image is accessible to the three apertures.

4.1.2.1 Deflection Coils. The deflection coils are printed circuit coils bent into a cylindrical shape and placed inside the large focus coil between the inside of the focus coil and the outside surface of the tube. Each coil has an inductance of approximately 140 mH.

4.1.2.2 Deflection Amplifier. The deflection amplifier accepts a voltage from the digital-to-analog converters in the logic rack and converts this to current driven through the deflection coils. The unit used was the Celco ±3 A feedback driver (PDD-3).

4.1.3 FOCUS SYSTEM. To insure that all of the electrons emitted in various directions from each point on the photocathode converge to a corresponding point at the aperture plate a magnetic focus field is established parallel to the axis of the tube. Electron physics insures that any component of electron velocity normal to the focus field will cause the electron to spiral in a helix tangent to a line parallel to the focus field. The pitch of the helix is a function only of the strength of the focus field, and thus appropriate field adjustments cause the electron image to focus on the aperture plate.

The focus field is provided by a series of eight cylindrical coils wound on a common cylindrical form about 17.5 in. long. The tube is inserted inside this cylindrical form and since the form extends several inches beyond the front of the tube a nearly uniform field parallel to the tube axis exists in the drift space.

4.1.4 LOGIC RACK. The deflection of the electron image on the aperture plate and the corresponding action taken as a result of the output from the three electron multipliers is entirely controlled by the logical circuit modules contained in the Logic Rack pictured in Fig. 8. The control and data retrieval logic were designed so that a minimum of circuitry need be added to permit the tube to operate under control of a computer program.

At present, however, control of the tube operation is restricted to manipulation of the switches on the control and display panel at the top of the Logic Rack. One selects the operation desired by means of the six switches in the lower right-hand corner of the control panel and may start and stop the selected operation by means of the four switches in the lower left-hand corner of the Logic Rack. One may observe the measurements taken by the tube in the indicator lights above the switches. See Fig. 8. The function of all these switches is now described.

4.1.4.1 Program Selection Switches. Six switches in the lower right corner of the display panel select which of the available operations and their modifications are to be performed. These operations and modifications are described in the following.

4.1.4.1.1 HZ-VT Switch. This switch specifies the nature of the image scan, i.e., Horizontal Sweep or Vertical Sweep. For Horizontal Sweep, the sweep of the apertures relative to the image starts at the top of the image and as each horizontal scan is completed the apertures move one scan line down toward the bottom of the image. Likewise for Vertical Sweep the apertures move left to right relative to the image as each vertical scan is completed.

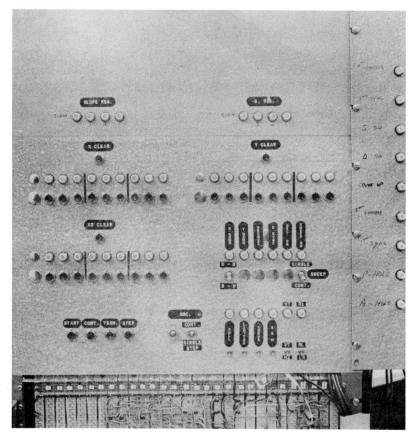

FIG. 8. DI-SCAN logic control panel.

4.1.4.1.2 LR-RL Switch. This switch specifies in which direction the fast sweep (horizontal for Horizontal Sweep Mode, vertical for Vertical Sweep Mode) shall occur. In the LR position, the LR-RL Switch will cause left-to-right horizontal sweep or top-to-bottom vertical sweep of the apertures relative to the electron image.

4.1.4.1.3 Full-Scale Slope Measurement. Whenever the edge of line image is encountered by two of the three holes, the slope of this edge is measured and recorded in the signed S_1 register. A slope measurement consists of a signed count in the three-bit register corresponding to one of eight increments of slope from 0° to 105° if the slope sign is positive and eight increments of slope from 105° to 180° if the sign is negative. The skewed Cartesian coordinates occur because the line between hole centers is at an angle of 105° with the direction of the sweep rather than 90° (Fig. 9).

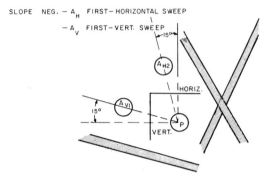

FIG. 9. Orientation of apertures for slope measurement.

In this and succeeding discussions, optical image dimensions are stated in terms of the electron image dimensions at the aperture plate. By this means, the unnecessary consideration of optical magnification can be ignored.

When full-scale slope has been selected and started, the full cross section of the electron image is swept over the aperture plate. Thus the apertures appear to move relative to a stationary image in the plane of the image. If we assume an image line width of at least 0.0025 in., the slope of the far edge of the line is also measured and the difference between this slope and the value in S_1 is recorded in the signed three bit S_2 register. The contents of the S_2 register are interpreted then as the difference between the leading-edge slope and the trailing-edge slope of a line image.

In the Full-Scale Slope mode, the focused image is continuously swept across the apertures and thus the full cathode image is viewed by the aperture.

4.1.4.1.4 Limited-Scale Slope Measurement. This mode differs from Full Slope mode only in that the apertures are restricted to a small portion of the cathode image. The apertures are swept from an initially specified point (x_0, y_0) to a point $(x_0 + \Delta x, y_0)$ and then returned to $(x_0, y_0 + 1)$, where a new scan is started. This results in a narrow raster which is continually swept as in Full-Scale Slope mode measuring the slopes of any images encountered in the narrow raster.

4.1.4.1.5 Curve Following Mode. This mode differs from Limited Slope mode in that the narrow raster is always positioned so that the measured line is centered in the narrow raster enabling the raster to "follow" a curved line (Fig. 10).

4.1.4.1.6 Stop On Measurement. SOM is a mode conditioning switch that causes the apparatus to stop after any complete slope measurement to allow the x and y position and the values in S_1 and S_2 registers to be observed. SOM is applicable in all modes of operation.

4.1.4.2 Operating Controls. The four switches described now are used to control the execution of the selected operations and are located in the lower left corner of the control panel.

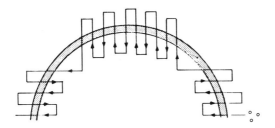

FIG. 10. Illustration of curve following mode.

4.1.4.2.1 Start Button. The Start button performs a master reset, clears all registers, and samples the six program switches to see if a new operation should be started.

4.1.4.2.2 Terminate Button. The Terminate button stops an opera- but does not perform a master reset.

4.1.4.2.3 Continue Button. The Continue button restarts the oscillator after a "Stop On Measurement" stop. The logic simply starts up from where it was interrupted by the SOM.

4.1.4.2.4 Step Button. The Step button provides one timing pulse each time it is operated in Single Cycle mode for logic maintenance purposes.

4.1.4.3 Registers. 4.1.4.3.1 Deflection Registers. The position of the focused image on the aperture plate relative to the apertures is determined at any time by the analog voltages decoded from the digital values standing in nine bit x and y registers. The scan is achieved by gating oscillator pulses into one of the registers to count the pulses and thus increase its digital value uniformly with time. When the fast counter overflows, the overflow pulse is fed into the other deflection register to increment its count by one step. When the slow counter overflows, a scan raster is complete and the process repeats.

Since the x and y registers are each nine bit registers and the oscillator frequency is about 1 Mc, the sweep rate is $1/512 \, \mu sec$ or about 2 kc.

4.1.4.3.2 Slope Registers. The slope registers consist of two signed three-bit counting registers containing sufficient logic to translate the se- quence of line edge detections into a binary count proportional to the slope of the line edges. The three DI-SCAN holes are grouped into two pairs, one of which is used for measuring slope during horizontal sweep

$(P - A_H$, Fig. 9), the other being used for measuring slope during vertical sweep $(P - A_v)$. During Horizontal Sweep if either P or A_H detects a line edge, both S_1 and S_2 are turned on. Each oscillator pulse that moves the hole pair farther onto the line is counted in both the S_1 and S_2 register.

In the normal situation, the measured linewidth will exceed 0.005 in. and the second hole will detect the leading edge before the first hole detects the far edge of the line (Case 1, Fig. 11).

In the illustration of Case 1 (Fig. 11) we see that both the S_1 register and S_2 register are turned off by the second hole detecting the leading edge, thus holding in S_1 and S_2 a count that is proportional to the angle the leading edge of the line makes with the line between the centers of P and A. Since this line is rotated 15° from the y axis, the Cartesian coordinates as seen by the holes will be distorted. The first quadrant will be from 0° to 105°, and the second quadrant will be from 105° to 180°.

When the first of the two holes passes off the line, S_2 is turned on again but this time it subtracts one from the value it holds for each oscillator pulse that steps the holes away from the line. If the far edge slope is equal to S_1, the value in S_2 will be counted to zero at the time the second hole passes off the line, and the value in S_2 corresponding to the difference between the leading and further edge slopes will be zero. In the illustration (Fig. 11), the far edge slope is larger than S_1 so the S_2 register will hold a difference value of two after the measurement is over.

Figure 12 illustrates the counter operations in the case where the line

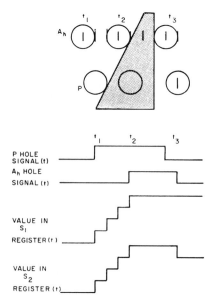

Fig. 11. Illustration of slope register control during slope measurement.

width is less than 0.005 in. and the line fits between the holes. It is seen that the S_2 register is controlled in such a way that it always contains the difference between the slope value in S_1 and a corresponding value for the far edge of the line.

Figure 13 shows oscilloscope traces illustrating the above discussion.

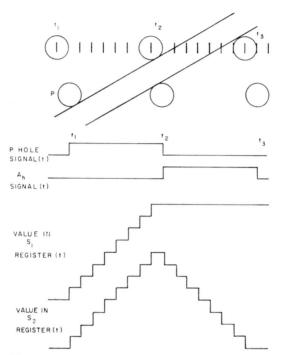

FIG. 12. Illustration of slope register control during slope measurement.

The top two traces are input signals from holes A_H and P. The third trace is the S_1 Counter On Flip-Flop and the length of time it is up is proportional to the binary count in S_1. The fourth trace is the S_1 sign flip-flop and illustrates that, for horizontal sweep, the sign is considered positive when the P hole detects the edge before the A_H hole.

4.1.4.4 Schmidt Trigger Circuits. The signals that are used to drive hole input logic in the DI-SCAN system are the anode currents from the tube. These signals vary from 1 μA dark current to 10 to 20 μA "light" current from an extremely high output impedance. Figure 14 shows the circuitry used to detect these currents and convert them to the logic levels used in the logic rack.

The anode current is converted to a small voltage across R_1, which is fed through an emitter follower to a common emitter amplifier with a gain of approximately ten. The amplified voltage level is then applied through

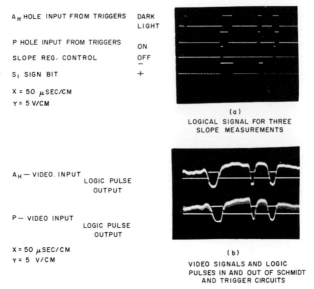

A_H HOLE INPUT FROM TRIGGERS   DARK / LIGHT

P HOLE INPUT FROM TRIGGERS   ON

SLOPE REG. CONTROL   OFF

S₁ SIGN BIT   +

X = 50 μSEC/CM

Y = 5 V/CM

(a)
LOGICAL SIGNAL FOR THREE SLOPE MEASUREMENTS

A_H — VIDEO INPUT   LOGIC PULSE OUTPUT

P — VIDEO INPUT   LOGIC PULSE OUTPUT

X = 50 μSEC/CM

Y = 5 V/CM

(b)
VIDEO SIGNALS AND LOGIC PULSES IN AND OUT OF SCHMIDT AND TRIGGER CIRCUITS

Fig. 13. Oscilloscope traces of input and control signals.

another emitter follower to the Schmidt trigger. The output of the Schmidt trigger drives an inverter that is similar to the inverters used in the logic rack and thus the correct logic levels are obtained.

Figure 13 shows the video output signals from the A_H and P holes as they sweep across several line images and the corresponding Schmidt

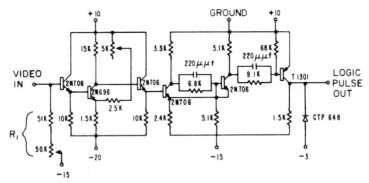

Fig. 14. Schmidt trigger circuit.

trigger output signals. The traces are positioned to show where the video pulses cross the threshold of the Schmidt triggers.

4.2. Experimental Results

The most significant experimental result obtained during the course of the project was the discovery, analysis, and reduction of spurious photocathode shading. Although the phenomenon was not completely understood, we made sufficient observations to construct a supposition as to the cause of the shadings. Another meaningful result of our experimentation was the observation that the inherent random noise in the tube corresponds to the theoretical estimates. Finally the observed resolution of the tube and slope measurement performance indicate where further engineering effort must be directed to develop the DI-SCAN system into a useful laboratory tool.

4.2.1 PHOTOCATHODE SHADING. One of the most important requirements on the DI-SCAN tube is that the output signals be of constant value as the three holes "look at" the image from a uniformly illuminated cathode. Nonuniform response during a sweep across the diameter of a uniformly illuminated cathode is called cathode shading.

4.2.1.1 Conditions Influencing Shading. Severe cathode shading was observed when the DI-SCAN tubes were first put into experimental operation. While we were trying to eliminate shading effects by adjustment of the operating conditions, shading appeared to be affected by

1. The magnetic focus field strength.
2. Cathode to drift tube voltage.
3. Deflector potential.
4. Aperture plate to dynode one voltage.

4.2.1.1.1 Effect on Shading of Focus Field Strength. Increasing the strength of the focus field tends to reduce the signal level and increase the degree of shading observed. The degree of shading is the ratio of the maximum signal to the minimum signal as the holes move along a cathode diameter. As the focus field is increased so also is the deflection stiffness and thus at moderately high focus fields one loses the ability to sweep the entire cathode diameter. As the focus field strength is made still stronger (40 gauss), the observed degree of shading is reduced.

4.2.1.1.2 Effect on Shading of Cathode to Drift Tube Potential. As the energy of the beam electrons is reduced by reducing the positive potential of the aperture plate and drift tube relative to the cathode, the degree of shading is reduced. The original drift voltage was set at 70 V, but reduction to 30 V or less reduced the degree of shading somewhat.

4.2.1.1.3 Effect of Deflector Potential on Shading. As the deflector plate potential relative to the aperture plate is varied from -12 to $+90$ V, the degree of shading does not change, but the shape of the shaded output signal does change; that is, the positions of the maxima and minima change along the cathode diameter. This leads us to believe that the shading is the result of electrons emerging from the aperture and striking either the separator fences or the deflector plate. The changing electric field in the region between the deflector plate and the fences as the deflector potential is varied will move the electron paths toward the fence or deflector plate. One can also assume from the foregoing that the paths of the electrons emerging from the aperture into this electric field have some angle to the axis of the tube that is proportional to the deflection of the electron image. This assumption is supported by observing that a given shape of shaded output signal is reversed end for end on the oscilloscope screen when the direction of image sweep is reversed along the cathode diameter.

4.2.1.1.4 Effect on Shading of Aperture to First Dynode Voltage. As the intensity of the electric field from the fence, aperture plate, and deflector plate to the first dynode is increased by varying the first dynode voltage, a slight reduction in the degree of shading is observed. The original first dynode voltage was set at 120 V, but as the voltage is increased to about 370 to 400 V a slight improvement in the shaded output signal can be observed.

4.2.1.2 Shading Elimination. The shading problem was corrected with the following operating conditions for the tube:

1. A very strong (50 gauss) magnetic focus field was added in the region of the photocathode in conjunction with a sleeve of magnetic shield material slipped over the entire focus coil assembly.

2. The Cathode to Drift Tube Potential was reduced from 70 to 30 V.

3. The Aperture Plate to First Dynode Potential was increased to 400 V.

4. The Deflector Potentials relative to the Aperture Plate were adjusted as required for a flat response ($+10$ to $+20$ V).

Under these conditions, the degree of shading was reduced to a point where most of the cathode area (70 per cent) gave a sufficiently flat response so that line images could be detected by the Schmidt trigger circuits. However, these adjustments are very critical and the flatness of the response leaves something to be desired.

4.2.1.3 Shading Explanation. Our understanding of the causes of the shading phenomenon is not complete. Our understanding of why the preceding steps eliminate the shading is even less complete. We have formed a supposition from the observed evidence which is partially supported by calculation and measurement, but which has not been satisfactorily proved.

Our supposition is that (*a*) the electrons pass through the aperture with a path angle proportional to the deflection of the image; (*b*) at certain of these angles the electron trajectories in the existing complex fields are directed toward the deflector plate and fences; (*c*) the emergence angular dependence on the deflection is the result of helical motion (not focus-type helical motion) that has been shown to exist in tubes with similar type of focus and deflection systems (Image Orthicon, for example. See RCA Technical Report PTR-20C summarized in Reference 3).

4.2.1.3.1 Evidence in Support of (*a*) and (*b*) of Shading Explanation. That there exists an emergence angle dependent on the deflection of the image is demonstrated by the discussion in 4.2.1.1.3. Unless such a varying emergence angle exists, one would not observe a variation in the output signal along the diameter of the cathode. A nonvarying angle or a non-varying distribution of angles would simply fix a particular invariant signal level as a uniformly illuminated diameter is swept assuming constant cathode sensitivity. To support the premise that the varying emergence angle of the aperture beam is responsible for the observed shading, we performed the electron optics analysis described in the Appendix. In this analysis the differential equations of motion were solved in the plane of the entrance to the electron multiplier to determine where on that plane the aperture beam strikes for various emergence angles, focus field strengths, and deflector voltages. For the analysis, a somewhat simplified field structure was assumed to facilitate the solution of the equations and the emergence angle was assumed to be the deflection angle of the beam from the axis. From the loci of beam position in the multiplier entrance plane as a function of deflector voltage for focus field strength $H = 10$, 50, 100 gauss (Figs. 24 and 25 in the Appendix) we plotted the estimated shading patterns shown in Figs. 15, 16, 17, and 18. Beside each of the

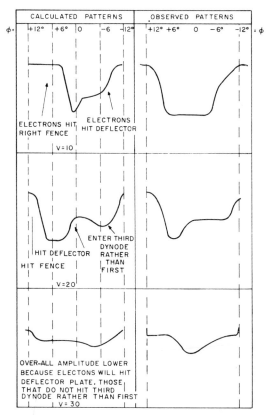

FIG. 15. Shading patterns, sweep parallel to deflector plate $H = 10$ gauss, $V_d = 10$, 20, 30 V.

theoretical patterns is pictured the pattern observed under corresponding operating conditions. One can see that there is good correspondence between the observed shading patterns and the patterns that were calculated based on the above premise.

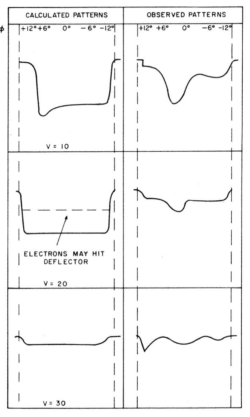

FIG. 16. Shading patterns, sweep parallel to deflector plate, $H = 50$ gauss, $V_d = 10$, 20, 30 V.

Further evidence to support the above premise is found from Figs. 24 and 25 in the Appendix. It is noticed that at higher values of focus field strength the position variation of the aperture beam in the multiplier entrance plane is reduced, thus reducing the degree of shading as shown by Figs. 16 and 18.

4.2.1.3.2   Evidence in Support of (c) of Shading Explanation.   We have shown in 4.2.1.3.1 that the shading appears to be caused by electrons emerging from the aperture along paths at some angle to the axis and that this angle is a function of image beam deflection. This section offers a qualitative explanation* for the existence of this emergence angle that is

* This explanation is taken from a summary of RCA PTR-20C given in Reference 3.

consistent with the observations listed in Sec. 4.2.1.1. This explanation arose during the development of the Image Orthicon tube, a tube with identical focus and deflection systems. RCA Laboratories' Technical Report PTR-20C contains a detailed and quantitative analysis of such tubes, and

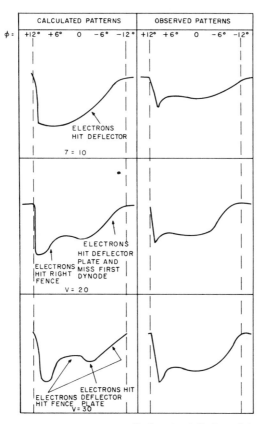

FIG. 17. Shading patterns, sweep perpendicular to deflector plate, $H = 10$ gauss, $V_d = 10, 20, 30$ V.

reference should be made to that report for specific details. The text below is a virtual quotation from a summary of PTR-20C written by Mr. E. H. Eberhardt as Research Memo No. 227, Capehart Farnsworth Company, Fort Wayne, Indiana. Since Mr. Eberhardt describes the phenomenon so well, we use his description almost verbatim.

When electrons are emitted from a Point P on the photocathode into a uniform axial magnetic focus field, the radial component of velocity of each electron causes helical motion tangent to a line parallel to the axis between the Point P and the aperture plate. Assuming no deflection fields, the cross section of the conical beam emitted from P is brought to a point again on the line between P and the aperture plate several times before reaching the aperture plate. When the focus field is appropriately adjusted, one of these points or nodes will occur at the aperture plate.

When a deflecting magnetic field is applied, considerable complication arises. The magnetic focus field lines are parallel to the tube axis until

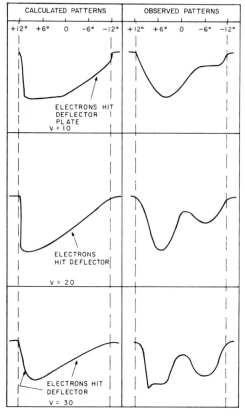

Fig. 18. Shading patterns, sweep perpendicular to deflector plate, $H = 50$ gauss, $V_d = 10, 20, 30$ V.

they reach the region of the deflection coils where they bend away from the direction parallel to the axis (Fig. 19). As the lines leave the deflection region they bend back to become parallel again with the tube axis. Consider the electron emitted from P with no radial velocity, i.e., the axial electron. This electron moves along the lines of force parallel to the axis until it reaches the first bend in the region of the deflection field. It attempts to follow the curved magnetic line but due to its inertia and the action of the magnetic field it "overshoots" the bend and begins to move in helical motion around the new direction of the original line it was following. Figure 19 illustrates the projection of this motion onto a plane through the tube axis. The motion is indicated in Fig. 20 on a cross-sectional plane

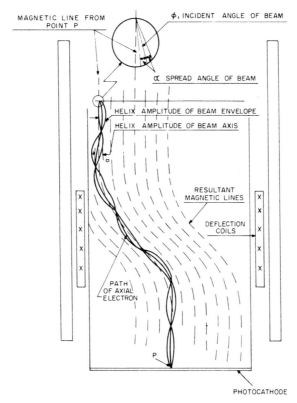

FIG. 19. Illustration of electron path in photomultiplier tube with magnetic focus and deflection.

showing that the axial electron rotates at a diameter a around the deflected magnetic line through point P. When this electron finally reaches the aperture plate, it will approach with an angle ϕ ($\phi \neq 90°$) which is a function of the deflection field strength.

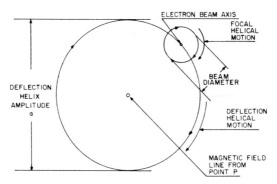

FIG. 20. Cross section of electron path after deflection in photomultiplier tube.

Having considered the axial electron (no radial velocity), let us now consider the conical beam of electrons normally emitted from P. The conical beam as a whole experiences approximately the same helical motion as the axial electron at the same time that each electron experiences its own helical motion due to its own radial velocity in the focus field. Thus, to a first approximation, the over-all beam will act as in Fig. 19 with the loops and nodes grouped along the central helical path of the axial electron. It should be emphasized that there are two separate helical motions described here. One is the helical motion of the beam "axis" proportional to deflection and the other is the helical motion of individual electrons making up the beam and proportional to their radial velocities. The former "deflection helical motion" is responsible for the electron angle of path emergence through an aperture varying with deflection.

According to the RCA report referenced earlier, deflection helical motion is unavoidable since it is produced whenever an electron is deflected in a magnetic field. It can be reduced in magnitude by reducing the energy of the electrons in the drift tube (reducing accelerating voltage), increasing the focus field strength, reducing the deflection angles, or by cancellation through the introduction of compensating electric or magnetic fields. As reported in Sec. 4.2.1.2, the observed shading effects were substantially reduced when the focus field was increased and the accelerating voltage was reduced and a large magnetic field was applied in the region of the cathode in conjunction with a magnetic shield completely enclosing the tube.

We feel that the magnetic field established by the large coil near the cathode and the magnetic shield surrounding the tube (Sec. 4.2.1.2) along with the reduction of the acceleration voltage, provides the required compensation and electron energy reduction to render insignificant this deflection helical motion and thus minimize observed shading.

4.2.2 RANDOM NOISE Inherent in any electron device is random "shot" noise. Also inherent in any laboratory electronic equipment is man-made noise (60 cycle, radar pickup, etc.). To insure ourselves that we had successfully eliminated all man-made noise and to determine the operational limitations imposed by noise, we measured the random noise output as a function of cathode current. The measured value of noise was converted to signal-to-noise ratio and compared with a computed estimate of signal-to-noise ratio. The computed estimate was obtained from Eq. 1, which is derived from the Shot Law and associated assumptions given in References 3 to 5, using measured values for I_k, Δf, ϵ, and σ. From Fig. 21 one can see that, indeed, the measured signal-to-noise ratios are sufficiently close to the estimated that we need not be concerned about the presence of extraneous noise.

$$\left(\frac{S}{N}\right)_{\text{anode}} = \frac{I_k}{2e\,\Delta f}\,\epsilon\,\frac{(\sigma - 1)}{\sigma} \tag{1}$$

where

I_k = cathode current for various values of dc illumination flooding the cathode

e = electronic charge

Δf = bandwidth at anode terminal under conditions of noise voltage measurement

ϵ = loss of cathode current in passing from cathode to first dynode

σ = gain per stage of electron multiplier

4.2.3 OBSERVATIONS CONCERNING DI-SCAN RESOLUTION. The theoretical upper limit on the resolution of the DI-SCAN tube is determined

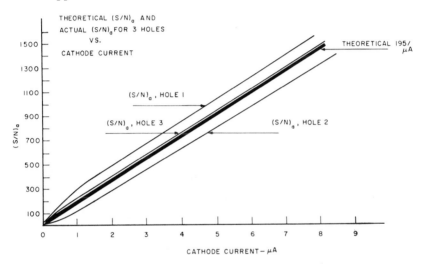

FIG. 21. Results of comparison of theoretical and actual signal-to-noise ratios.

by the aperture diameter 0.005 in., since the bandwidth of the photomultiplication process is very high (greater than 50 Mc) and the video amplifier input bandwidth is about 5 Mc (assuming anode resistance of 50 kΩ).

If we assume that a dark line image crossing an aperture must cause a video signal current change at the anode of at least 50 per cent of the "light" signal level, the 0.005-in. aperture requires a line width at the aperture plate of approximately 0.002 in. Since the image size at the aperture plate equals the image size on the cathode, the DI-SCAN is theoretically capable of discriminating no more than 250 alternate black-white line pairs per inch.

Experimental observation of the maximum resolution in our equipment shows that the DI-SCAN does not discriminate (50 per cent modulation of "light" level) more than 50 alternate black-white line pairs per inch.

However, experimental observation of the DI-SCAN resolution in manufacturer's test equipment showed that the DI-SCAN was, in fact, capable of discriminating almost 300 alternate black-white line pairs per inch.

The explanation for the failure of the tube to perform up to its theoretical limit in MITRE's apparatus lies in the fact that

1. The optical focus obtainable with the existing lens is not as good as it could be.

2. The magnetic focus obtained with the existing magnetic focus coils is not as good as it could be.

To improve the resolution performance of the DI-SCAN tube in the present test apparatus we must improve both the optical and magnetic focusing systems.

4.2.4   OBSERVATIONS CONCERNING DI-SCAN SLOPE MEASUREMENTS. After the reduction of the shading effects discussed in Sec. 4.2.1, the DI-SCAN tube was observed to measure slopes as described in Sec. 4.1.4.3.2 and as illustrated by Fig. 13.

Two related measures of the performance of the DI-SCAN in measuring slope are the sensitivity and the stability of the slope measurement. There are sixteen angular increments between 0 and 180° that the DI-SCAN can assign to a particular image being measured. The sensitivity of the DI-SCAN was observed to be much poorer than $180°/16 = 11.25°$. In general, the sensitivity was observed to be more like 30° in that the slope of a line could be varied about 30° before a change in the range of slope counts was observed. In addition, the stability of the slope count registered for repeated measurements of the same slope was observed to be plus or minus two counts.

Both the stability and sensitivity of the slope measurements are related to the shading problem. The sensitivity is dependent on the amplitude of the video pulse that corresponds to the Schmidt trigger threshold. Because shading still exists at the edges of the sweep, the thresholds are adjusted so that the Schmidt circuits are triggered close to the peak of the "dark" pulse. In this region of the pulse amplitude, the random noise is large enough relative to the "dark" pulse amplitude to cause a wide range of possible times that the Schmidt circuit is triggered. This causes the observed low measurement stability and contributes to the observed lack of sensitivity. Furthermore, shading effects prevent the adjustment of the triggering levels to exactly the same dark pulse amplitude in each of the three holes thus adding a constant error to the slope measurement.

It is believed that both sensitivity and stability of the slope measurements will be improved by

1. Increasing intensity of image illumination (further increasing the signal-to-noise ratio).

2. Improving optical and magnetic focusing systems.

3. Reducing further the shading effects at the edges of the sweep (so

that triggering levels can be adjusted for an optimum performance that is uniform in all three holes).

4.3. Conclusions

The experimental results discussed in Sec. 4.2 lead to the following conclusions:

1. Slope measurements are possible using a multiaperture photomultiplier tube such as the DI-SCAN.

2. The only problem inherent to the present DI-SCAN tube design is the shading problem discussed in Sec. 4.2.1. Further detailed analysis of this problem is not necessary to operate the DI-SCAN as a laboratory tool.

3. The present DI-SCAN tube and the apparatus built to operate it can be used as a tool for character recognition, etc., if the accessible improvements in shading, image focusing, and signal-to-noise ratio are exploited.

The existence of the shading problem suggests that the present design of the DI-SCAN, although suitable as a laboratory tool, is not the best possible design for a tube to satisfy the DI-SCAN applications. An alternative design that is worthy of future investigation is the channel-multiplier type of electron multiplier structure. The configuration of the channel multiplier tube is such that the aperture currents are coupled directly to the electron multipliers and thus the shading problem observed in the loosely coupled present design should be eliminated.

5. Elaboration of DI-SCAN Ideas

The DI-SCAN principle has been proven. Some rather straightforward elaboration of ideas associated with the principle should prove interesting.

5.1. Read-Only Digital Data Store

The three-hole prototype tubes can be employed to scan a surface carrying digital data patterns. Given an approximately 1.5-in. useful cathode diameter and the triangular array of three 0.005-in. diameter holes, straightforward calculation yields a data recording density of 9000 bits per square inch. Since only one hole is available for reading, one must depend upon transitions from opaque to transparent and vice versa to imply the binary one and zero. This implies approximately 0.010 in. in the data track for each binary digit.

In the preceding calculation, data density has been calculated in terms of the photocathode. If a lens is employed between the surface carrying the data and the cathode, it is possible to increase the data density on the surface. However, only one of the two surface dimensions can be exploited; the cathode diameter is fixed and hence the number of data tracks is fixed. Nonetheless, a 3.3 × magnification does provide 30,000 bits per inch of length in an approximate 0.45-in. wide band. On an approximate 10-in. diameter, the 0.45-in. band would accommodate 1,000,000 data bits.

Data storage numbers in the millions of bits begin to take on interest. The success of the early tubes delivered by ITT allowed us to ask for smaller holes in the aperture plate of two tubes. The 0.002-in. diameter holes in these tubes immediately imply better than 2,000,000 bits of data in our exemplary system. Consideration of the practical sizes of photo-cathodes (5-in. diameter or greater), smaller hole diameters (down to 0.001 in.), and the possibility for many more than three holes allows realistic anticipation of 500,000,000 bits of data on a two foot disk.

Practical realization of such large data stores is also dependent upon the technical feasibility of recording the data pattern and reading it fast enough to serve modern computing machinery. Reading speed should not be a problem. The bandwidth capabilities of the photocathode-electron multiplier process is ample to cope with current computers; access time delay to a given data record will be comparable to present magnetic drum and disk data stores (tens to hundreds of milliseconds).

The recording problem, with DI-SCAN, is eased relative to photographic data stores developed earlier. No dependence upon precise location of data on the recording surface exists for data patterns that are not adjacent. The track following action will cause the DI-SCAN to stay with the data track regardless of data surface distortions amounting to several per cent. A 2 per cent elongation of the data surface normal to the data track length will have negligible effect on a DI-SCAN tube reading nine tracks simultaneously.

Since the servo action employed with DI-SCAN does not depend on the fine structure of the recorded image, it is possible to accept rather wide tolerances on the opaque-transparent areas corresponding to binary digits. Further, the light flux illuminating the data surface can be provided by conventional lamps, thus minimizing signal-to-noise problems.

5.2. Alphanumeric Symbol Readers

Returning to the idea of image discrimination and measurement of parameters within a class of images, it is possible to recognize a unique feature of the DI-SCAN principle. Though we have not yet begun a systematic exploration of slope measurement utility in alphanumeric symbol recognition, there is good reason to think that slope measurement may unlock the symbol reading problem.

Consider the upper-case "K's" illustrated in Fig. 22. One may regard them as corresponding to different type fonts. If a corresponds to the prototype K, we may establish the following data as defining measures. (The numbers in Fig. 22a correspond to the following elements.)

Element 1. An element extending from the lower to upper extreme exists near the left extreme of the symbol.

Element 2. No continuous element exists near the upper extreme extending from the left to right extreme of the symbol.

Element 3. No continuous element exists near the right extreme extending from the lower extreme to the upper extreme of the symbol.

Element 4. No continuous element exists near the lower extreme extending from the left to right extreme of the symbol.

Element 5. An element with positive slope extends from Element 1.

Element 6. An element with negative slope exists to the right of Element 1 and below Element 3.

FIG. 22. Alphabet.

The measurement data descriptive of K can all be obtained by means of a slope measuring DI-SCAN apparatus. Upper, lower, left, and right extremes can be determined by an exploratory scan operation; existence of all six elements can then be determined. Consideration of Fig. 22b, 22c, 22d, and 22e reveals that all versions of the K satisfy the specification for the six elements.

Figures 22b and 22c constitute rotations of the prototype K; without an analysis of all letters, it is difficult to describe any general technique for obviating all effects of rotation. It is apparent that some rotation of the K does not destroy its legibility. One can consider a data processing routine that normalizes, to the vertical, the slope value at the leftmost element of a symbol. The same correction would be applied to all other slope values obtained from the symbol. A greater tolerance to symbol rotation may be secured.

If noise due to ink smears, ink voids, etc., corrupts the symbols, it is possible to create a data processing routine that requires multiple affirmations of each decision involved in recognizing a symbol. Using parallel affirmations, the data processor can react to lack of agreement in decisions by resorting to the image measurement control device. Taking one logical decision as correct, the processor can check the measurement giving rise to the conflict. In particular, the check measurement may be more refined than the original measurement (i.e., two measurements may have failed to affirm the existence of Element 6 for the K. A remeasurement may require that slope measurements be related to successive scan position measurements).

5.3. Miscellaneous

A number of opportunities for use of DI-SCAN ideas involve the use of the tube to discriminate colored symbols. Using techniques common in the television industry, DI-SCAN output signals can be related to color components of a scanned image. Hand lettering on preprinted documents could be quickly discriminated without recourse to a data processing routine.

In the event cathode shading effects are reduced sufficiently, it will be possible to translate image gray-level contours into digital representations of position coordinates. Such a capability would have immediate application to a variety of image evaluation tasks.

Finally, the demand for direct entry of graphic data into a digital data process may be more nearly practical with DI-SCAN. All the techniques described, digital data store, symbol recognition, contour plotting, etc., are specializations of graphic data input processes. If a general characterization of the graphic data entry problem comes into existence, DI-SCAN may be useful in the problem solution.

APPENDIX

Investigation of the Effect of Aperture Beam Current Angular Variations on Shading

The purpose of this Appendix is to investigate the theoretical contribution of angular variations of aperture beam current to the anode signal shading. To accomplish this we will derive expressions describing the trajectories of electrons emerging from the apertures into the complex electric and magnetic fields that exist between the aperture plate and first dynode of the electron multiplier. These expressions will be evaluated in the plane of the entrance to the first dynode to determine the position of the aperture current beam in that plane. The beam position is a function of deflector voltage, focus field, and orientation of the deflection coils with respect to the separator fences and deflector plate. By introducing the aperture current beam angular variation with deflection into the initial conditions of the trajectory equations, the effects of this angular variation on the input signal to the first dynode can be analyzed graphically to produce estimated shading patterns.

1. Equations of Motion

The actual fields that exist behind the aperture plate are a complex combination of the axial magnetic focus field, the fringes of the magnetic deflection field, the electric field between the deflector plate and the separator fences and aperture plate, and the electric field between the first dynode and the aperture plate, fences, and deflector plate. Since an accurate solution of the equations of motion including all of these fields would require a computer analysis, the fields in the region of interest will be assumed to be as shown in Fig. 23: an axial uniform magnetic focus field of field strength H_F along the z axis, a perpendicular uniform electric field intensity E_y along the y axis, and an axial uniform electric field intensity E_z along the z axis.

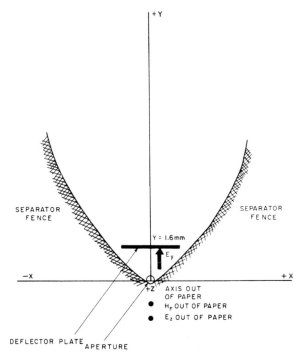

FIG. 23. Simplified fields assumed in trajectory analysis.

The differential equations of motion, for the fields and coordinate system illustrated in Fig. 23, are given as Eqs. 2, 3, and 4:

$$\left.\begin{aligned}
\ddot{z} &= \frac{e}{m} E_z \\[2mm]
\ddot{x} &= -\frac{e}{mc} \dot{y} H \\[2mm]
\ddot{y} &= -\frac{e}{mc} \dot{x} H + \frac{e}{m} E_y
\end{aligned}\right\} \tag{2}$$

with initial conditions:

$$x_0, y_0, z_0 = 0$$
$\dot{x}_0, \dot{y}_0$ specified by radial velocity V_r
$\dot{z}_0 = V_a$, the axial or drift velocity

Double integration of Eq. 2 with respect to time gives ($H = H_F$, E corresponds to E_y, $A = e/mc$):[6]

$$x(t) = \frac{cEt}{H} - \frac{\dot{y}_0}{AH}$$

$$+ \frac{1}{AH}\left[\left(\dot{x}_0 - \frac{cE}{H}\right)^2 + \dot{y}_0^2\right]^{1/2} \sin\left[AHt - \arctan\left(\frac{\dot{y}_0}{\frac{cE}{H} - \dot{x}_0}\right)\right]$$

$$y(t) = -\frac{1}{AH}\left(\frac{cE}{H} - \dot{x}_0\right)$$

$$- \frac{1}{AH}\left[\left(\dot{x}_0 - \frac{cE}{H}\right)^2 + \dot{y}_0^2\right]^{1/2} \cos\left[AHt - \arctan\left(\frac{\dot{y}_0}{\frac{cE}{H} - \dot{x}_0}\right)\right]$$

$$z(t) = \tfrac{1}{2}AcE_z t^2 + \dot{z}_0 t$$

$$\tag{3}$$

Let $cE/H = B$, then

$$x(t) = Bt - \frac{\dot{y}_0}{AH}$$

$$+ \frac{1}{AH}[(\dot{x}_0 - B)^2 + \dot{y}_0^2]^{1/2} \sin\left[AHt - \arctan\left(\frac{\dot{y}_0}{B - \dot{x}_0}\right)\right]$$

$$y(t) = -\frac{1}{AH}(B - \dot{x}_0)$$

$$- \frac{1}{AH}[(\dot{x}_0 - B)^2 + \dot{y}_0^2]^{1/2} \cos\left[AHt - \arctan\left(\frac{\dot{y}_0}{B - \dot{x}_0}\right)\right]$$

$$z(t) = \tfrac{1}{2}AcE_z t^2 + \dot{z}_0 t$$

$$\tag{4}$$

The projection on the x,y plane of the motion described by these equations may be visualized by imagining the cycloidal path of a point on the rim of a wheel in the x,y plane that starts at the origin and rolls away from the origin along the $+x$ axis with forward velocity $B = 10^8 E/H$ cm/sec and radius $R = B/AH = 5.68E/H^2$ cm (E in volts/cm, H in gauss).[5]

If the electron emerges from the hole with an initial radial velocity $V_r(\dot{x}_0, \dot{y}_0)$, the path is such as described by a point on the spoke of a wheel a distance $1/AH$ $[(\dot{x}_0 - B)^2 + \dot{y}_0^2]^{1/2}$ from the center. This may be greater or less than R giving rise to a prolate or curtate cycloid. Although the velocity of the wheel is unchanged, the track on which it rolls is shifted by an amount $\dot{x}_0/AH$.[6]

2. Evaluation of the Equations of Motion

To investigate the theoretical shading patterns we must evaluate Eq. 4 in the plane of the entrance to the first dynode. To accomplish this the initial conditions and field magnitudes must be specified and the constants A, B in Eq. 4 must be evaluated. We can then solve $z(t)$ for t_1 corresponding to $z_1 = 1.2$ cm, the distance between the aperture plate and the first dynode entrance plane. Using t_1 in Eq. 4, $x(t_1)$ and $y(t_1)$ can be found as a function of deflector voltage V_e for various values of H, deflection angle (reflected in initial conditions), and angular orientation of the deflection coils.

2.1. Initial Conditions

The initial conditions to be specified are $\dot{x}_0$, $\dot{y}_0$, and $\dot{z}_0$, where $\dot{z}_0$ corresponds to the axial velocity V_a that results from the acceleration of the beam from the cathode to the aperture plate through a voltage of 70 V.

Assuming conservation of energy, one can find the axial velocity of an electron accelerated to an energy of 70 eV according to Eqs. 5a, 5b, and 5c:

$$\tfrac{1}{2}mV_a{}^2 = eP, \qquad P = \text{accelerating voltage} \tag{5a}$$

$$V_a = \left(\frac{2eP}{m}\right)^{1/2} = 5.93 \times 10^7(P^{1/2}) \text{ cm/sec} \tag{5b}$$

$$V_a = \dot{z}_0 = 50.0 \times 10^7 \text{ cm/sec, for } P = 70 \text{ V} \tag{5c}$$

Any radial component of velocity, V_r, that exists as an electron enters the fields from the aperture will be the vector sum of $\dot{x}_0$ and $\dot{y}_0$. There are two contributions to this V_r:

(a) The V_r distribution that results from the initial random V_r that exists when an electron is emitted from the cathod,

(b) The V_r introduced during the deflection process that is proportional to the beam deflection.

2.1.1 CONTRIBUTIONS TO $\dot{x}_0$, $\dot{y}_0$ FROM CATHODE EMISSION. When electrons are emitted from the photocathode they are emitted with a distribution of energies, the average of which is about 0.75 eV.* They are also emitted with a distribution of angles to the axis of the tube. The average emission angle of the DI-SCAN photocathode is about 3°, resulting in an average radial velocity upon emission of about 2.5×10^6 cm/sec as determined in Eq. 6 using Eq. 5b:

$$\tan 3° = 0.05 = \frac{V_r}{V_a} = \frac{V_r}{5.93 \times 10^7 \text{ (eV)}^{1/2}} = \frac{V_r}{5.93 \times 10^7(0.75)^{1/2}} \tag{6}$$

$$V_r = (0.05)(5.05 \times 10^7) = 2.5 \times 10^6 \text{ cm/sec}$$

This same V_r exists when the electron emerges from an aperture. However, this radial velocity is now several orders of magnitude smaller than $\dot{z}_0$ since the electrons have been accelerated down the axis of the tube through 70 V. Thus the angle now formed by the $V_r = 2.5 \times 10^6$ cm/sec, and $\dot{z}_0 = 50 \times 10^7$ is about 0.28°. Since we will show that 2.5×10^6 cm/sec is very small relative to any radial velocity components introduced by beam deflection, the cathode emission contribution to $\dot{x}_0$, $\dot{y}_0$ will be considered nonexistent. Whenever there is no $\dot{x}_0$, $\dot{y}_0$ due to beam deflection, the $\dot{x}_0$, $\dot{y}_0$ terms due to cathode emission will be too small to consider in the expressions for $x(t)$, $y(t)$ given by Eq. 4.

2.1.2 CONTRIBUTION TO x_0, y_0 FROM BEAM DEFLECTION. The V_r that is proportional to the deflection of the beam off the tube axis is the vector sum of $\dot{x}_0$ and $\dot{y}_0$. The magnitudes of $\dot{x}_0$ and $\dot{y}_0$ will depend on the direction of V_r in the x, y plane (plane of the aperture plate). The direction of V_r will in turn depend on the orientation of the x and y deflection coils external to the tube. For the following analysis we will assume the deflection coils are arranged such that the image beam is sweeping: (a) along the x axis from positive x to negative x, and (b) along the y axis from $+y$ to $-y$. This corresponds to a sweep: (a) parallel to, and (b) perpendicular to the deflector plate. Thus for case (a) $\dot{x}_0 = V_r$, $\dot{y}_0 = 0$ and for case (b) $\dot{x}_0 = 0$, $\dot{y}_0 = V_r$.

The magnitude of V_r at any deflection is a function of the angle, ϕ, between the deflected image beam and the tube axis. Since the constant of proportionality is not known, we will arbitrarily choose a V_r such that $V_r(\phi)$ always satisfies

* Private communication, E. H. Eberhardt, ITT Laboratories, Fort Wayne, Indiana.

$(V_r/\dot{z}_0) = \tan\phi$, where ϕ ranges from $+12°$ to $-12°$ during a full sweep of the image beam.

Now for case (a) when the deflection is parallel to the deflector plate

$$\dot{x}_0 = V_r = \dot{z}_0 \tan\phi \tag{7}$$
$$\dot{y} = 0$$

For case (b) when deflection is perpendicular to the deflector plate

$$\dot{x} = 0$$
$$\dot{y} = V_r = \dot{z}_0 \tan\phi \tag{8}$$

We will evaluate Eq. 4 in the plane of the electron multipliers for $\phi = +12°$, $+6°$, $0°$, $-6°$, $-12°$, corresponding to five points along the sweep.

For these values of ϕ, Eqs. 7 and 8 become:

	$\phi = \pm 6°$	$\phi = \pm 12°$	$\phi = 0$	
Case (a)	$\dot{y}_0 = 0$	$\dot{y}_0 = 0$	$\dot{y}_0 = 0$	(9)
	$\dot{x}_0 = \pm 5 \times 10^7$ cm/sec	$\dot{x}_0 = \pm 10 \times 10^7$ cm/sec	$\dot{x}_0 = 0$	
Case (b)	$\dot{x}_0 = 0$	$\dot{x}_0 = 0$	$\dot{y}_0 = 0$	(10)
	$\dot{y}_0 = \pm 5 \times 10^7$ cm/sec	$\dot{y}_0 = \pm 10 \times 10^7$ cm/sec	$\dot{x}_0 = 0$	

2.2. Evaluation of Constants

The constants used to simplify the expressions in Eq. 4 are

$$A = \frac{e}{mc} = 1.73 \times 10^7$$

$$B = cE_y/H = \frac{6V_d}{H} \times 10^8 \tag{11}$$

The evaluation of A is a straightforward application of the physical constants available in any handbook of physics. The evaluation of B depends on the field magnitudes E_y and H. We can express E_y as

$$E_y = \frac{V_d = \text{deflector potential relative to aperture}}{\text{distance between separator fence and deflector plate}} = \frac{V_d}{0.16} = 6V_d \text{ V/cm}$$

2.3. Specification of Field Magnitudes

We will solve for $x(t_1)$, $y(t_1)$ under the following conditions:
Case (a) Sweep parallel to deflector plate:
$\dot{x}_0 = |V_r| \tan\phi$, $\dot{y}_0 = 0$

$H =$ 10 gauss, $\phi = +12°$, $+6°$, $0°$, $-6°$, $-12°$, $V_d = 0$ to $+40$ V
$H =$ 50 gauss, $\phi = +12°$, $+6°$, $0°$, $-6°$, $-12°$, $V_d = 0$ to $+40$ V
$H =$ 100 gauss, $\phi = +12°$, $+6°$, $0°$, $-6°$, $-12°$, $V_d = 0$ to $+40$ V

Case (b) Sweep perpendicular to deflector plate:
$\dot{x}_0 = 0$ $\dot{y}_0 = |V_r| \tan\phi$

$H =$ 10 gauss, $\phi = +12°$, $+6°$, $0°$, $-6°$, $-12°$, $V_d = 10, 20, 30$ V
$H =$ 50 gauss, $\phi = +12°$, $+6°$, $0°$, $-6°$, $-12°$, $V_d = 10, 20, 30$ V

2.4. Evaluation of Eq. 4

Application of Secs. 2.1, 2.2, and 2.3 to Eq. 4 gives Eq. 12:

$$z(t) = 0.87 \times 10^{17} t^2 + 5 \times 10^8 t \tag{12a}$$

$$x(t) = \frac{6V_d}{H} 10^8 t - \frac{\dot{y}_0 10^{-17}}{1.73H} \left[\left(\dot{x}_0 - \frac{6V_d}{H} 10^8 \right)^2 + \dot{y}_0^2 \right]^{1/2}$$

$$\sin \left\{ 1.73 H t 10^7 - \tan^{-1} \frac{\dot{y}_0}{[(6V_d/H)10^8 - \dot{x}_0]} \right\} \tag{12b}$$

$$y(t) = \frac{10^-}{1.73H} \left(\frac{6V_d}{H} 10^8 - \dot{x}_0 \right) - \frac{10^{-7}}{1.73H} \left[\left(\dot{x}_0 - \frac{6V_d}{H} 10^8 \right)^2 + \dot{y}_0^2 \right]^{1/2}$$

$$\cos \left\{ 1.73 H t 10^7 - \tan^{-1} \frac{\dot{y}_0}{[(6V_d/H)10^8 - \dot{x}_0]} \right\} \tag{12c}$$

We will first solve $z(t)$ for t_1 corresponding to $z_1 = 1.2$ cm [entrance to first dynode] giving from Eq. 12a:

$$E_z = \frac{150 \text{ V}}{1.5 \text{ cm}} = 100 \text{ V/cm} \tag{13}$$

$$z_1 = 1.2 \text{ cm at } t_1 = 1.76 \times 10^{-9} \text{ sec} \tag{14}$$

Using $t_1 = 1.76 \times 10^{-9}$ in Eqs. 12b and 12c gives $x(t_1)$, $y(t_1)$ as a function of H, V_d, and ϕ (through initial conditions). Solving $x(t_1)$, $y(t_1)$ according to Eqs. 12b

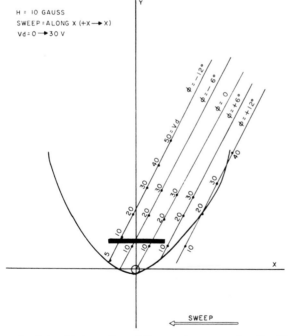

Fig. 24. Focus of points of intersection of the aperture current path with dynode one entrance plane as a function of deflector voltage V_d.

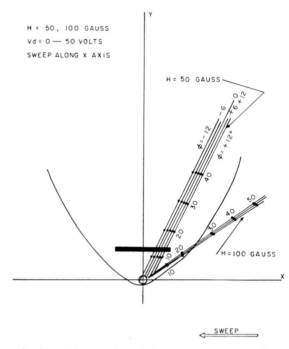

FIG. 25. Focus of points of intersection of the aperture current path with dynode one entrance plane as a function of deflector voltage V_d.

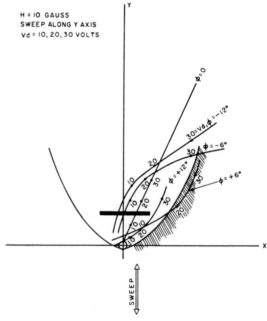

FIG. 26. Focus of points of intersection of the aperture current path with dynode one entrance plane as a function of deflector voltage V_d.

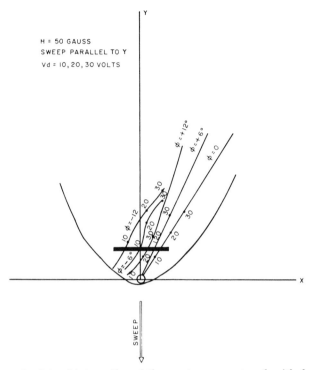

FIG. 27. Focus of points of intersection of the aperture current path with dynode one entrance plane as a function of deflector voltage V_d.

and 12c under the conditions listed in Sec. 2.3 gives the plots of the loci of aperture beam position in the first dynode plane as a function of V_d for given ϕ and H as shown in Figs. 24 through 27.

3.0. Estimation of Shading Patterns

Figures 24 through 27 represent the loci of the beam position on the electron multiplier entrance plane as V_d is varied from 0 to $+40$ V for various deflection angles and at various magnitudes of focus field H. These plots can be mapped into plots of input current to the electron multiplier as a function of ϕ by following the points of equal V_d from the $\phi = +12°$ line through the $\phi = 0°$ line to the $\phi = -12°$ line. Plots determined in this way for $V_d = 10, 20, 30$ V at $H = 10$ and 50 gauss appear in Figs. 15 through 18 of this article.

REFERENCES

1. HOOVER, C. W., G. HAUGK, AND D. R. HERRIOTT, "System Design of the Flying Spot Store," *Bell System Tech. J.*, *38*, 365–401 (1959).
2. KING, G. W., G. W. BROWN, AND L. J. RIDENOUR, "Photographic Techniques for Information Storage," *Proc. IRE*, *41*, No. 10, 1421–1428 (1953).
3. EBERHARDT, E. H., *Notes on Electron Beam Optics in Orthicon Type Tubes*, Research Memo #227, Capehart Farnsworth Co., Fort Wayne, Ind., 1952.

4. JENKINS, FRANCIS A., AND H. E. WHITE, *Fundamentals of Optics*, McGraw-Hill Book Co., New York, 1950, pp. 104–111.
5. ZWORYKIN, V. K., *et al.*, *Electron Optics and the Electron Microscope*, John Wiley & Sons, Inc., New York, 1961, pp. 521–523.
6. KLEMPERER, O., *Electron Physics*, Academic Press Inc., London, 1959, pp. 17–19.

GENERAL REFERENCES

BLOKH, E. L., "The Question of the Minimum Description," *Radiotechnica, 14,* No. 2, 10–14 (1960).
CHOW, C. K., "An Optimum Character Recognition System Using Decision Functions," *IRE Trans. Electron. Computers, EC-6,* 247–254 (1957).
CHOW, C. K., "A Recognition Method Using Neighbor Dependence," *IRE Trans. Electron. Computers, EC-11,* 683–690 (1962).
EBERHARDT, E. H., *Noise in Multiplier Phototubes,* ITT Laboratories Research Memo #309, 27 October 1959.
FARNSWORTH, P. T., "Television by Electron Image Scanning," *J. Franklin Inst., 218,* 411–444 (1934).
FISHER, R. A., "The Use of Multiple Measurements in Taxonomic Problems," *Ann. Eugenics, 7,* 179–188 (1936).
GREANIAS, E. C., P. F. MEAGHER, R. J. NORMAN, AND P. ESSINGER, "The Recognition of Handwritten Numerals by Contour Analysis," *IBM J. Res. Develop., 7,* 14–21 (1963).
GRIMSDALE, R. L., F. H. SUMNER, C. J. TUNIS, AND T. KILBURN, "A System for Automatic Recognition of Patterns," *Proc. Inst. Elec. Engrs. (London), Pt. B, 106,* 210–221 (1959).
KAMENTSKY, L. A., AND C. N. LIU, "Computer-Automated Design of Multifont Print Recognition Logic," *IBM J. Res. Develop., 7,* 2–13 (1963).
MacLACHLAN, DAN, JR., "Description Mechanics," *Inform. and Control, 1,* 240–266 (1958).
MARILL, T., AND D. M. GREEN, "On the Effectiveness of Receptors in Recognition Systems," *IRE Trans. Inform. Theory, IT-9,* 11–17 (1963).
MARILL, T., AND D. M. GREEN, "Statistical Recognition Functions and the Design of Pattern Recognizers," *IRE Trans. Electron. Computers, EC-9,* 472–477 (1960).
Reference Data for Radio Engineers, Fourth Edition, American Book Company–Stratford Press Inc., 1955, p. 372, p. 401, p. 420, p. 766.
SCHWARTZ, MISCHA, *Information Transmission Modulation and Noise,* McGraw-Hill Book Co., New York, 1959, pp. 21–80, pp. 200–259, pp. 373–384.
SHOCKLEY, W., AND J. R. PIERCE, "A Theory of Noise for Electron Multipliers." *Proc. IRE, 26,* No. 3, 321–332 (1938).

CHAPTER 27

RESEARCH ON OPTICAL MODULATION AND LEARNING AUTOMATA

Robert E. J. Moddes and Lewey O. Gilstrap, Jr.

Adaptronics, Inc., Alexandria, Virginia

Introduction

As an information processing system, a learning automaton presents unique problems to the system designer. In implementation, necessarily compact and efficient devices await development before truly sophisticated realization of concepts can be achieved.

The discussion of automata theory presented in this chapter is to be viewed as general background material in the problem area; readers desiring more thorough treatment are invited to pursue the appropriate citations to the literature.

Learning Automata

Definitions

A *learning automaton* (also referred to as a learning system, a learning computer, a self-organizing system, trainable system, or adaptive system) is one that changes its behavior on the basis of its past experience.[1-3] The changes in behavior are brought into or maintained in agreement with a criterion of performance which could be either built into the automaton or (more rarely) which could be autonomously evolved by the automaton.

Mathematically, every learning task can be viewed as the learning of a function or mapping. The domain of the function to be learned is some subset of the set of all possible sensory inputs to the automaton, and the range of the function is a subset of the set of all possible actions or outputs that the automaton can produce. For some purposes, this characterization of learning automata is somewhat narrow. It can be enlarged by changing the domain to the set of all possible input sequences and by changing the range to the set of possible output sequences.

For purposes of analysis, learning automata can be described as consisting of two primary subsystems: a *performance subsystem* and a *conditioning*

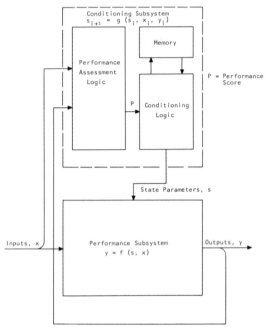

FIG. 1. A learning automaton partition by functional subsystems.

subsystem. (See Fig. 1.) The performance subsystem is a mechanization of the equation

$$y = f(x, s) \tag{1}$$

where

x is the automaton input
s is the automaton state
y is the automaton output

The conditioning subsystem is a mechanization of the equation

$$s_{i+1} = g(x_i, s_i) \tag{2}$$

where

x_i is the automaton input at instant i
s_i is the automaton state at instant i
s_{i+1} is the automaton state at instant $i + 1$

and assuming that state changes occur discretely. When the state of the system changes continuously, we can write

$$\dot{s} = \frac{ds}{dt} = g(x, s) \qquad (3)$$

Not all proposed or existing learning automata can be physically decomposed into these two distinct subsystems.

The purpose of an automaton is to provide us with some useful work or change in the environment; the performance subsystem provides this work.

Performance subsystems fall into one or more of five basic categories. These categories consist of subsystems that

1. Provide algebraic transformations on input signals.
2. Provide some type of compensation or phase-gain adjustment on input signals.
3. Provide some type of discrete or Boolean functions on the input signals.
4. Process digitally coded signals using arithmetic registers and either fixed or stored programs.
5. Generate signals coded in analog or digital form.

The conditioning subsystem must provide just the state such that the work provided by the automaton is in accordance with our specification of desired performance. Theoretically, it would be possible to construct an automaton that evolved its own criteria of performance (free automata). The need for constrained automata that provide performance in accordance with specified criteria is very much greater than the need for free automata at the present time; however, the free automata are of interest not only academically, but also in cases where only criteria for criteria are known, and the criteria themselves can be learned by the automaton.

Criteria of desired performance must be stated unambiguously so that the conditioning system can be implemented. Statements of criteria often take the form of a *score function* which is a continuously computed index of the closeness of actual performance with desired performance, and a *conditioning algorithm*, which provides a strategy for changing the automaton state in such a way that the performance tends to improve as measured by the score function.

In general, score functions must be functions of input and output variables, and it is often convenient to have a score function that is the difference between a *performance function* that measures the quality of the performance and a *penalty function* that measures the "cost" of obtaining improved performance. Any function or rule that indicates a next state or state change on the basis of a score function is called a *steering equation*.[4]

The training of automata requires the use of a *training sequence*, which is an input sequence selected to provide the desired system behavior, usually, but not necessarily, as efficiently or as rapidly as possible.

"Dimensionality" and "Size" of Automata

Since automata can be used to process sensor data derived from essentially one point in space, or from one-, two-, or three-dimensional regions of space, it is sometimes useful to characterize automata by their dimensionality. Inasmuch as inputs can vary with time, we define the dimensionality of an automaton as one plus the (spatial) dimensionality of its input data:

$$d_a = 1 + d_i \tag{4}$$

(When inputs do not vary with time, we can equate the dimensionality of the automaton with the dimensionality of its input data.)

The dimensionality of components for automata may be less than the dimensionality of the automaton. For example, image processing may be performed using a mosaic decomposition of images; each element of the mosaic is attached to a point sensor, and the two-dimensional region is thus obtained by aggregating these "points."

Construction philosophies and techniques for automata vary considerably, and it is desirable to have some measure of system "size" or computational capability of learning automata. One of the more convenient and useful measures of automaton size s_a is the logarithm to the base two of the number of states N that the automaton can assume:

$$s_a = \log_2 N \tag{5}$$

For the special case of automata with n independent state variable elements that can assume either of two states, the size of the automaton reduces to n. In general, for automata with n independent state variable elements that can each assume m distinct values, the size is

$$s_a = \log_2 m^n = n \log_2 m \tag{6}$$

This measure of size is simply the amount of selective information required to specify the existing state of an automaton out of all the possible states. For most automata, this amount of information can be converted into an equivalent bandwidth in the frequency domain using the relationship

$$\frac{1}{2} WT = s_a \tag{7}$$

$$W = \frac{2s_a}{T} \tag{8}$$

where

W is the bandwidth

T is clock period (or, for asynchronous machines, the average time required for processing of inputs)

Using the above formulas, we can obtain a measure of the "size" and equivalent band pass of, for example, the human brain. One of the more commonly cited figures for the number of cells in the average human brain is 10^9.[5] Each nerve cell has branching dendrites (input lines) which connect to the axons (output lines) of anywhere from 1 to 1000 other cells, depending on the location of the cell in the brain. Using the figure of 100 as an average number of connections, and neglecting temporal summation, then, at any instant, each nerve cell can be in any of approximately 2^{100} states. For the entire brain, we thus obtain

$$s_a = 10^9 \log_2 2^{100} = 10^{11} \tag{9}$$

Using $T = 0.1$ sec (corresponding to the alpha frequency of the brain), we also obtain for equivalent bandwidth

$$W = \frac{2s_a}{T} = 2 \times 10^{12} \text{ cycles} \tag{10}$$

This figure is probably conservative due to neglecting temporal summation. By comparison, the size of a gain-switching adaptive controller (for example, one that can switch between two gain values) is 1, and, assuming a rise time of the controller of 0.001 sec, the equivalent band pass is 2×10^3 cycles.[6]

Mathematical Tools

There is, at this time, no universally accepted definition of automata, and the definitions we have given should be considered as working definitions that we have found to be useful. There is, likewise, no single mathematical approach to the subject of learning automata.

In the literature on automata theory, various mathematical disciplines have been used. These disciplines include the theory of Turing machines,[7-9] theory of finite state machines,[10,11] Boolean algebra and its extension, Boolean functionals,[12] probability and statistics,[13,14] decision theory,[15,16] and others.

It is not possible to give details on any of the mathematical tools of automata theory in this brief paper; however, some of the ideas behind the use of these tools will now be presented.

For the analysis of performance subsystems, we have used whenever possible in our own work a transfer function in the performance subsystem equation; i.e., we rewrite Eq. 1 in the form

$$y = T(s)f(x) \tag{11}$$

where $T(s)$ is a *transfer function* determined by the state s alone that operates on some function of the input. The transfer function is of utility in the first three types of performance subsystems mentioned earlier (those that provide algebraic transformations, compensation, or Boolean functions of the input) and is of little utility except in special cases for the last two types of performance (those that process digitally coded signals or those that generate signals coded in analog or digital form). In this paper we will generally confine our attention to the cases in which performance subsystem equations can be written in terms of a transfer function. Although much of the current literature on automata deals with systems that cannot be represented by a transfer function, a rather large and useful class can be so represented, and the problems of analysis and synthesis of performance subsystems are, in general, simplified by the transfer function approach.

While the transfer function approach is most familiar in servo system analysis, it can be applied to other systems not commonly identified with transfer functions such as logic networks. Many artificial nerve networks have been proposed using an artificial nerve building block that provides some class of logic functions of the inputs to the artificial nerve.[12,17-22] These building blocks, which are interconnected into networks with connectivity patterns that vary from highly regular to random, can also be analyzed using a transfer function technique.

Each artificial nerve in a net is usually such that it can perform any of a large set of functions on its input variables. The specific function provided at any given time by an artificial neuron depends upon its state, which is in turn controlled by the conditioning subsystem. As previously mentioned, the conditioning subsystem need not be separate from the artificial nerves that make up the performance system.

If the state-change rules are incorporated into the artificial nerve, then the information that leads to state changes must come from the local signal environment; two possible types of mechanisms have been proposed which could lead to a learning capability in such nets:

1. Each artificial nerve adjusts its state such that input and output energy are minimized (i.e., each nerve works on an extremal principle).[17]

2. Each cell changes state according to the statistical properties of the input signals (e.g., an artificial nerve that tends to have a greater output if it has had numerous inputs in the past).[22]

If the state-change rules are incorporated into a separate conditioning subsystem, then it is customary to have a fixed set of ways of changing state incorporated into each artificial nerve. Instructions as to which change rule to employ are sent out from the conditioning subsystem. To avoid the necessity of computing state changes for each artificial nerve in a network, however, only two types of conditioning information, positively reinforcing (sometimes called reward) and negative conditioning (sometimes called punishment), are sent out by the conditioning subsystem, and the state change in each artificial nerve is determined partly by the local signal and state conditions in each artificial nerve and partly by the conditioning signals.

Conditioning subsystems that are separate from performance subsystems are mechanizations of the score function and the conditioning algorithm;

their function is to select a new state or a change in state on the basis of current and past score function information. The problem of selecting a new state in a state space while attempting to satisfy the constraint of maximum score is equivalent to the so-called "hill-climbing" problem in optimization. Approaches to the solution of optimization problems range from experimental methods (which include many of the techniques used in automata) to deterministic techniques.[23,24]

Elements in the Design of Automata

The three major elements that must be considered in the design of automata to provide specific performance are the environment, the performance subsystem, and the conditioning subsystem.

AUTOMATON ENVIRONMENTS. The performance that we desire from an automaton can always be reduced to terms of bringing about or maintaining specified conditions in the environment. Consequently, automata are of necessity strongly coupled to the environment via their inputs and outputs and should not be considered in isolation from the environment.

Knowledge about an environment should be utilized to the extent that it is available to a designer, even though, somewhat paradoxically, learning automata are most useful for coping with environments about which we may have limited knowledge. The paradox is more apparent than real, however, because we often know that certain environmental variables are highly relevant to optimum processing of information, even though we may not know in advance what the values of those variables might be. In addition, a designer may know that certain environmental variables are functionally related in some way but may not know the nature of the relationship; i.e., he may not have a model of the environment. In both the case of parameter measurement and environmental modeling, learning automata can usually be constructed to ascertain or infer such information continuously.

Inferences about environmental conditions can either be explicit or implicit, and the choice of inferential technique to be employed usually depends upon the amount of information available and upon the extent to which system "tailoring" to specific circumstances is desired. The distinction between the explicit and implicit inference can be illustrated using a problem in sensing the rate of closure of two objects moving toward each other. If a rate measuring device, such as a Doppler radar, is used to measure the rate of closure, no inference is required and the rate information can be employed directly for control or other purposes. If a distance-measuring device is used (and if we ignore the possibility of using time differentiation of the distance signal), a suitably designed artificial nerve network can be taught to produce an output that is proportional to or equal to the time rate of change of the input signal; this output, which could be used just as the directly obtained rate information, could be termed the result of an *explicit inference*. Finally, if the output of a distance sensor is fed to an artificial nerve net that learns to provide a control signal output which would have required rate information for its proper computation, then the value of the rate must have been implicitly inferred by the net.

Similarly, learning automata can be trained to infer the properties or parameters of an image. From the properties of an image it is possible to classify the image, or automata can be trained to provide a direct classification of images without ever explicitly developing a property list.

SELECTION OF PERFORMANCE SUBSYSTEMS. In theory there are but two rules for the selection of performance subsystems:

1. They must be compatible with the system inputs and outputs and must provide transformations suitable for the desired performance.

2. They must be able to assume a sufficient number of states so as to provide a sufficient range of functions and thus cope with environmental uncertainties.

In practice, the transformational requirements imposed by the anticipated environment are seldom defined with sufficient precision to permit a straightforward application design. Most commonly, an existing artificial nerve network or performance subsystem is adapted to an application. To a large extent, this is a successful procedure in that most networks are capable of providing a very wide range of functions. However, all physically realizable function spaces are both finite and bounded, and disregard of such factors as adequate signal mixing (particularly in the case of many input nets) and sufficiency of degree of nonlinearity in the function space can lead to poor automaton performance.

SELECTION OF PERFORMANCE CRITERIA AND SCORE FUNCTIONS. The selection of performance criteria and score functions is dependent on the characteristics of the problem environment and on the speed with which learning is supposed to occur. The subject of criteria theory as it applies to learning automata is more of an art than a science, and only a few limited rules of criteria formulation exist. For dynamic, time-varying environments we have found that it is often desirable to add a predictor to the score function and utilize projected error values rather than present error values; the score function itself becomes some relatively simple function such as integral of predicted error squared. For static environments, such as those encountered in multiple trajectory prediction and multiple pattern recognition, it is sometimes useful to have a score function that is a weighted sum of the mean absolute error and the variance.

CONDITIONING ALGORITHMS AND LEARNING STRATEGIES. Each component of an automaton state vector can be treated as an independent dimension in a multidimensional search process. As we indicated earlier in this paper, optimum seeking methods range from experimental optimization procedures to deterministic methods. We have studied quite extensively two procedures that employ a random element. For environments about which we have no *a priori* information, there is always a finite probability that a random search will converge to the proper state, while the same is not always true of arbitrary deterministic search procedures.

The first of these methods called, for historical reasons, a *probability state variable* (PSV) search procedure associates a probability with each of the possible states that the performance system can assume or a probability with possible different sized changes about an arbitrarily selected reference point in state space.[12] This search procedure seems to be quite effective in bringing about convergence in learning in dynamic environments in which the location of the score function maximum may be shifting quite rapidly. However, the procedure does appear to be limited to state vectors with no more than five to ten components since learning time is proportional to some power of the number of dimensions to be searched.

The second method we have studied is termed, again for historical reasons, a *random state variable* (RSV) search procedure.[25] In the RSV strategy, selected components of the state vector are varied purely at random in a form of simultaneous search. The process is a modified search, however, in that the score associated with each trial is stored along with the coordinates of that point. On the second and all subsequent trials the two successive scores are compared, and the point corresponding to the higher score is used as the point about which the subsequent trial is made. This procedure, which might be termed a sequential sub-Martingale, works best in environments that have stationary score surfaces with respect to the state values, and is not particularly effective in dynamic environments. However, the RSV strategy provides a convergence in learning that is almost independent of the number of dimensions to be searched up to 360, which is as far as we have examined it.[25]

Neither the PSV nor the RSV strategy makes any great use of information accumulated during learning trials. For some applications, we can speculate that learning times for automata with either of these two strategies might be improved by using a correlation technique to bias the direction of new trials.

Applications to Information Processing Science

From the standpoint of information processing, the performance subsystem is of primary concern since it provides the actual information processing function. However, automata are used to process not only information in the form of mathematical variables but also information in the form of patterns.

Ultimately, we can predict that learning automata will find their greatest competitive advantage over more conventional information processing in two areas:

1. Where an on-line or real-time learning capability is a necessity (as in, for example, adaptive control).

2. Where the volume of data to be processed overtaxes computer technology (as, for example, might be the case in weather satellites that produce large volumes of optical image data).

The second of these two areas arises as much from the ability of learning automata to learn to recognize many different classes of patterns as from the fact that many automata are constructed to process information in parallel rather than sequentially. For image processing, in particular, this would constitute a fairly sizable advantage.

Present Devices

On the basis of available literature, we can summarize some of the more commonly encountered information processing devices or functions used or proposed for the construction of learning automata.

One-dimensional automata usually require devices of three types:

1. Conventional logic devices, such as gates, flip-flops, and storage registers.

2. Analog computation devices such as summers, multipliers, analog storage devices, and function generators.

3. Hybrid devices such as digital to analog and analog to digital converters and thresholds.

Quite frequently noise generators are employed to provide a random factor for search processes.

Two-dimensional automata (assuming spatial and temporal continuity in the images to be processed) require spatial and temporal differentiators, image storage devices (integrators) and active components, such as image intensifiers.

The functions of these devices have been obtained using conventional electronic circuitry and components, by unconventional devices, such as ferrielectrics[26] and optronics,[27] by devices that are electrochemical in nature such as the Memistor[28] and the peripheral access lattice,[29] and by devices that are combinations of all the above techniques and devices, such as the "Adaptive Sandwich."

It is almost axiomatic that any reasonable information processing function can be mechanized by existing technology, given sufficient time and money. However, the unit cost in obtaining, as examples, one-dimensional analog storage devices, weighted sums of analog signals, and noise generators, presently limits the complexity or "size" (as we defined it earlier) of learning automata. Many possible applications of learning automata must await the development of very inexpensive (and small) components and devices that will give us the functions required for automata.

Necessary Elements and Devices

As discussed earlier, there is a need for the development of a wide variety of inexpensive devices for application to automata. Present devices cannot be viewed as completely satisfactory because of the economic factor. Among the more pressing needs at the moment are the one- and two-dimensional storage devices and devices that provide weighted sums of many variables. Next in importance to these would appear to be spatial and temporal differentiators, which are presently obtained, in some cases, by combinations of photocells and light sources, together with their associated circuitry. Beyond this, smaller and less expensive waveform and function generators would probably materially contribute to the reduction of both the cost and bulk of learning automata.

The Role of Optical Modulation

In the construction of learning automata and similar information processing devices the optical modulator has played a relatively small role to date. There is every indication, however, that the unique properties of optical modulators will eventually lead to more compact and efficient devices and to widespread use.

The optical modulator has been used in both one- and two-dimensional information processing devices and has been employed in both volatile and nonvolatile devices. By a volatile device we mean one that has an output dependent on some input variable; the output of a volatile device always returns to some resting level upon termination of the input signal. A nonvolatile device is one that is proportional to or is a function of the time integral of the input signal. Nonvolatile, one-dimensional devices thus perform the function of analog signal storage, and nonvolatile, two-dimensional devices can perform image storage.

Every learning automaton utilizes an integrating device to provide the information storage function that is the key to every learning process. The one- and two-dimensional devices which are discussed in the remainder of this paper are integrating devices, although their speed of operation will permit them to be used in many applications where a volatile device would be indicated.

Automata that perceive (i.e., process patterns), but which do not necessarily learn, generally require devices that can provide spatial or temporal differentiation. This feature of perception is best exemplified by the physiological studies of frog vision and by the artificial frog retina that abstracts the four classes of properties: 1, edges; 2, moving convexities; 3, contrast changes; and 4, dimming.[30] It seems clear that all four of these properties can be accounted for by either spatial differentiation (single or double), by time differentiation, or by some combination of both.

Optical modulation configured to provide an information storage (integration) and to provide spatial or temporal differentiation thus appear to constitute basic building blocks that can be used in the construction of a wide variety of automata.

A One-Dimensional Device, NOVA STORD*†

General Configuration

In research and development provoked by basic componentry requirements for eventual implementation of "medium-sized" ($10^6 \leq n \leq 10^9$) and "large" ($n > 10^9$) automata, several basic elemental building blocks are under investigation. Of interest in this report is the fabrication of a NOnVolatile Analog STORage Device (NOVA STORD) attained by combination of a light source and photocell, modulated by an electrochemical storage cell. Pertinent elements and physical dimensions of the prototype device are presented in Figs. 2 and 3. In the former illustration, the element

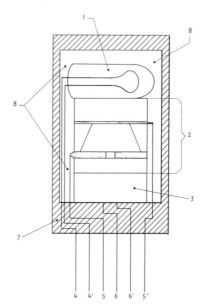

FIG. 2. Elemental designations for NOVA STORD.

labeled 1 is the light source with leads 4 and 4'; the storage cell is represented by 2 (with leads 5 and 5') and the photocell by 3 (with leads 6 and 6'). Labels 7 and 8 apply to the outer opaque casing and epoxy fillers (and heat-conductors when necessary), respectively. It is obvious that photocellular response is a function of both light source intensity, and the state

* Developed under corporate-sponsored research, Project 704.
† Patent in processing.

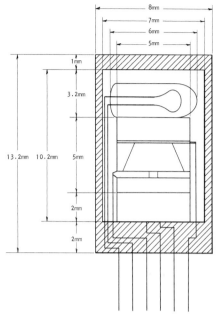

Fig. 3. Physical dimensions of NOVA STORD.

of the electrochemical cell, element 2 in Fig. 2. We now proceed to describe the latter factor in detail.

Electrochemical Cell

Figure 4 provides us with the salient features of the memory device; the labeling is as follows:

  2a: glass (Pyrex) or plastic substratum
  2b: thin film, *transparent*, inert conducting electrode
  2c: electrolyte (metallic cation) bath
  2d: metallic electrode with aperture
  2e: electrode aperture
  2f: plastic substratum
  2g: plastic collar and epoxy seal
5, 5′: electrode leads

Upon applied potential across the cell (after initial priming), one of the following modes of reactions occurs:

$$\text{Mode } P: \quad \text{anode, } 2d; \quad M^0 \rightarrow M^{+z} + Z\epsilon \tag{12}$$

$$\text{cathode, } 2b; \quad M^{+z} + Z\epsilon \rightarrow M^0 \tag{13}$$

$$\text{Mode } R: \quad \text{anode, } 2b; \quad M^{+z} + Z\epsilon \rightarrow M^0 \tag{14}$$

$$\text{cathode, } 2d; \quad M^0 \rightarrow M^{+z} + Z\epsilon \tag{15}$$

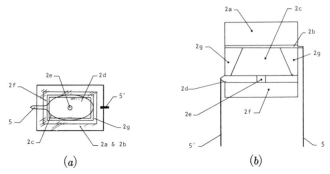

FIG. 4. Views of electrochemical cell. (a) Top view; (b) vertical cross section.

where

$$M = \text{metallic-electrode atoms}$$
$$Z = \text{electrochemical redox electrons per atom of } M$$
$$\epsilon = \text{the electron}$$

In its effect of optical modulation, Mode P amounts to plating of a metallic film of viable transmissivity on the transparent electrode while Mode R deplates from that electrode.

TRANSPARENT ELECTRODES.   Thin layers of zinc oxide or stannic oxide are in general use as transparent, inert electrodes; commercially available glasses (e.g., NESA glass) are satisfactory for application in NOVA STORD although it would be preferable to deposit the layer on plastics instead of glasses.

The two methods supplying the best results in stannic oxide deposition were solvent deposition of previously sintered oxides and a modification of the method of Gomer.[31] The former method consists of layering or spraying a suspension of treated stannic oxide (in elementary esters) on plastics; the latter technique directs an oxygen jet through a decomposition chamber containing hot stannic chloride and deposition of the resultant stannic oxide fumes on glass heated to 550 °C. Obviously, the method cannot be followed for plastics without modification.

Wyckoff[32] and Pauling[33] describe the crystal structure of cassiterite as rutile (i.e., each tin atom is surrounded by oxygen atoms at the corners of an octahedron; each octahedron shares two opposite edges with adjacent octahedra, forming long octahedral strings extending along the c axis of the crystal). Lattice dimensions are $a \neq b = c: 4.72 \text{ Å} \neq 3.16 \text{ Å} = 3.16 \text{ Å}$ with $c/a = 0.6695$, thereby classified in structural group $4P/\text{mnm}$ with two molecules per unit cell. Representative infrared spectra of our stannic oxide films deposited on plastics (modified Gomer technique on polystyrene), of slices of natural cassiterite,[34] and of pressed micropellets (with 10 per cent KBr) are presented in Fig. 5. In our measurements (Perkin-Elmer Model 221, with Prism Grating Interchange), the reference beam employed polystyrene or air as appropriate. From the figure, we note first the lack of homogeneity within large natural crystals as evidenced by these data from Kohnke;[34] our curves on thin film and micropellets share an absorbance peak at 3263 cm[-1] and a small peak at 3175 cm[-1] with the more typical of the Kohnke curves. Other rutile structures, e.g., TiO₂,[35] and quartz,[36] exhibit similar peaks and the group frequencies have been attributed to O—H stretching vibrations.[37] (Bellamy[38] finds an O—H deformation vibration

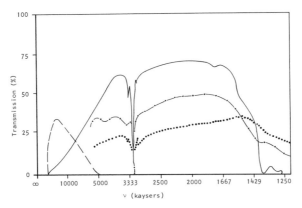

FIG. 5. Infrared spectra of various stannic oxides. ———— cassiterite sample 1. – – – cassiterite sample 2. – · – · stannic oxide (Gomer modification) on acrylic film. · · · · · stannic oxide (Gomer sintering in KBr micropellet).

range near 1459 cm[-1] which leads Kohnke to conclude the presence of planar orientation of O—H groups perpendicular to the crystal *c*-axis.)

The nature of this water incorporation is of interest as an insight to the method of layer deposition and to its correlation with conductivity considerations. Miloslavskii,[39] in using films deposited by stannic tetrachloride decomposition at elevated temperatures, finds increased absorption in the 5000 cm[-1] range; our curves find several broad bands in the 3200 to 3400 cm[-1] region, normally attributable to water of hydration. Studies are being undertaken to further elucidate the interaction mode, i.e., what combinations of water of constitution, coordinated water, lattice water, or zeolitic water are involved. With liquid electrochemical reactions, such information (and correlation with sintering procedure) is vital for maximizing operating life of the stannic oxide electrodes.

Difficulties are already being encountered in three areas: adherence of stannic oxide layer to plastic under operating conditions, action of moderate strength acids and bases on deterioration of the layer (possibly an electrode breakdown to β-stannic acid), and "popping" of the electrode at moderate voltages. Infrared spectrophotometric and polarization studies continue in this area.

ELECTROLYTIC SYSTEMS. Restricting our considerations in this report to liquid systems and concerning ourselves with optimizing readin time (or more generally, cycle time from full plate, i.e., 0 per cent transmission from the light source to photocell, to full deplate of the metallic layer on the transparent electrode), attention is next focused on time rate of opacity change. Some index of the function is obtained through inspection of electrochemical potentials, and thence through correlation of electrode surface charge density and optical density changes.

Changes in opacity are given by the well-known Lambert-Beer law which relates the intensity of a parallel beam of monochromatic radiation incident-normal (I_i) to a layer of absorbing medium, with the intensity (I_e) of the emergent beam:

$$I_e = I_i 10^{-\epsilon ch} \qquad (16)$$

The quantities ϵ, c, and h are the molar extinction coefficient (dependent on wave number ν, the temperature, and the solvent), the molar concentration, and the thickness of the absorbing layer, respectively. Equation 16 is often expressed in more useful forms:

$$\log_{10}\left(\frac{I_i}{I_e}\right) = \epsilon ch = D_0 \qquad (17)$$

$$I_e = I_i \exp(-Kh) \qquad (18)$$

The term D_0 in Eq. 17 is the optical density or absorbance; the absorption coefficient K in Eq. 18 is calculable:

$$K = 2.303\ \epsilon c \qquad (19)$$

$$K = 4\pi\eta K'\nu \qquad (20)$$

The new quantities involved are the index of refraction η and the index of absorption K'. We wish to relate absorbance to basic electrical circuit properties involved. Since ZF, where F is the faraday, represents the molar electron requirement,

$$\frac{Q}{ZF}M = Vd = A_c hd \qquad (21)$$

assuming full electrical efficiency. The quantities Q, M, V, d, and A_c are electrical charge (coulombs), atomic mass (amu), volume, density, and cross-sectional area, respectively. Rearrangement of Eq. 21 gives an approximation of surface charge density σ:

$$\frac{Q}{A_c} = \frac{hzFd}{M} \simeq \sigma = \frac{Q}{A_s} \qquad (22)$$

The approximation is significant for small h whence the surface area A_s approaches the cross-sectional area A_c. Relative ratios of absorbance to minimum charge density for various electrochemical thin-film depositions can be obtained from Eqs. 17, 19, 20, and 22:

$$D_0 = \epsilon ch = \left(\frac{K}{2.303}\right) h = \frac{4\pi\eta K'\nu}{2.303} \cdot \frac{\sigma M}{ZFd} \qquad (23)$$

TABLE 1 SELECTED OPACITY FACTORS FOR VARIOUS ELECTROCHEMICAL SYSTEMS

Element	d (g·$\overline{\text{cm}}^{-3}$)	Z	M	η	K'	ν (kayser*)	E_0^{25} (V†)	O_f ($\overline{\text{cm}}^2$ coul^{-1})
Sn	7.28	+2	118.7	1.48	3.55	16,980	+0.13	41.1
Ag	10.5	+1	107.9	0.18	20.6	16,980	−0.80	35.8
Cd	8.64	+2	112.4	1.13	4.44	16,980	+0.402	31.2
Au	19.3	+1	197.0	0.47	6.03	16,980	−1.5	27.7
Pt	21.5	+2	195.2	1.84	1.72	22,710	−0.2‡	18.5
I	4.93	−1	126.9	3.34	0.173	16,980	+0.535	14.3
Cr	7.2	+3	52.0	2.97	1.63	17,240	+0.557	11.4
Ag	10.5	+1	107.9	0.41	1.61	30,300	−0.80	11.4
Ni	8.90	+2	58.7	1.41	1.79	23,810	+0.22	11.3
Ni	8.90	+2	58.7	2.19	1.99	13,330	+0.22	10.7
Cu	8.92	+2	63.6	0.44	7.4	15,380	−0.346	10.2
Cu	8.92	+2	63.6	2.13	2.34	20,000	−0.346	9.4
Cu	8.92	+2	63.6	1.19	1.23	28,800	−0.346	8.2

* Kayser = rydberg = $\overline{\text{cm}}^{-1}$.
† Reductant → oxidant^z + Ze.
‡ In conjunction with chloride coordination.

$$\frac{D_0}{\sigma} = \left(\frac{4\pi}{2.303F}\right)\frac{M}{Zd} \cdot \eta K' \nu$$

$$\simeq 5.67 \times 10^{-5} \eta K' M \nu Z^{-1} d^{-1} = O_f \tag{24}$$

where O_f is defined as the opacity factor and has the dimensions $\overline{cm}^2$ $coul^{-1}$. Relative O_f values for selected elements are presented in Table 1. Optical values have significant disagreement in the literature and variation in deposition technique is given first-order blame;[40] further as seen from diffraction studies,[41,42] the optical constants begin to vary appreciably with thickness for $h < 20\ m\mu$; therefore, opacity factors must be treated as approximations until a more adequate treatment is developed for $K_i = f(h_i)$. In any case, some empirical results are available, particularly with silver cells.

Figures 6 and 7 present data[43,44] on transmission at given wave numbers

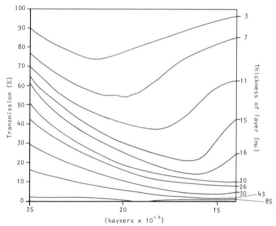

FIG. 6. Transmission curves of silver layers at various thicknesses.

for various thicknesses of silver layers. These data are not directly applicable since they were obtained from deposition on glass (as opposed to coated glass) substrata; however, the deposition rate (2 sec) is of the same magnitude. (See Table 2.) As can be seen from Fig. 7, NOVA STORD response, using silver electrochemical storage, can be specified by appropriate selection of wavelength and region of thickness through which cycling will occur. We have settled on silver-iodide cells since iodine accumulation can be easily controlled by the formation of the tri-iodide ion; although the yellow color of the complex ion presents potential problems, its conversion to iodate ion (colorless) at moderately high pH has been employed. (Unfortunately, the iodate reactions are rate determining and cyling time suffers.)

INTRODUCTION OF ELECTROLYTE AND SEALING OF CELL. The cell is fabricated by epoxy seal of the metallic (silver) electrode (2d, Fig. 4) to the plastic substratum (2f, Fig. 4) followed by joining collar 2g (Fig. 4). After curing of the epoxy, the electrolyte is introduced with a hypodermic needle, and the transparent electrode and substrate (2a and 2b, Fig. 4) attached (with epoxy) to form an airtight seal without entrapped air. (Any entrapped air or gas formation during operation will, of course, seriously interfere with performance.)

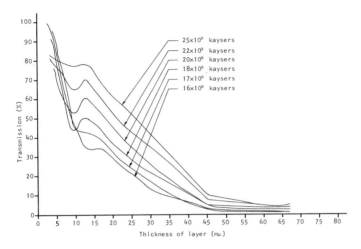

FIG. 7. Transmission of silver layers of varying thickness at constant wave number.

Much investigation of various "epoxy" compounds has been necessary to find a suitable nonconducting adhesive with the following properties:

a. moisture nonabsorbency;

b. acid-base resistivity;

c. glass-to-plastic bonding strength;

d. noninterreactivity with SnO_2 thin films;

e. coefficient of expansion (in the range 0 to 80 °C) amenable to that of plastics and, particularly, glass (Pyrex); and,

f. pressure resistivity to electrolyte expansion* under operating condition.

Only EPON RESIN 828 (Shell Chemical Company) appears to meet all criteria as adjudged by continuous cycling for 36 hours.

Plastics selected for use are narrowed to acrylates; although mediocre in several properties of interest, e.g., dc resistivity (30 °C, $\sim 10^{15}$ ohm-cm) and thermal conductivity ($\sim 5 \times 10^{-4}$ cal/sec cm °C), SnO_2-deposition technique was most successful with these plastics, and its water absorption and resistance to acid-base attack were preferable.

---

* Obviously a function of cycle time and thermal conductivity of the plastics and glasses employed. This restriction on cycle time is being theoretically investigated through opacity factors and ΔH for a given electrochemical system.

TABLE 2 CELL CHARACTERISTICS

Electrolyte*	Electrodes†	pH‡	$E_{impressed}$ (V)	ρ_1§ (ohm-cm)	ρ_2¶ (ohm-cm)	Electrode separation (mm)	t_{cycle}** (msec)
Ni(NO₃)₂	Ni, SnO₂	7.0	5	9.3×10^3	4.86×10^5	4.25	$\sim 6 \times 10^5$
		7.0	3	~ 1.6	123	1.25	$\sim 6 \times 10^4$
		6.5	4			2.0	$\sim 7 \times 10^4$
		5.9	5			2.0	$\sim 7 \times 10^4$
		4.0	5			2.0	
		2.0	5			2.0	
CuSO₄	Cu, SnO₂	7.0	6	9.4×10^1	3.3×10^2	2.0	$\sim 1 \times 10^6$
		5.1	5.9			2.0	$\sim 1 \times 10^6$
		4.3	5.9			2.0	$\sim 3 \times 10^6$
		2.5	6			2.0	$\sim 3 \times 10^6$
		1.0	6.1			2.0	$\sim 3 \times 10^6$
AgI	Ag, SnO₂	11.0	4.5	17	4.3×10^2	1.25	$\sim 1 \times 10^2$
		10.0	5.1	~ 19.2	$\sim 4.3 \times 10^2$	1.25	$\sim 1 \times 10^2$
		7.1	5.0	~ 19.2	$\sim 4.8 \times 10^2$	1.25	$\sim 1 \times 10^2$
		6.9	4.8	~ 19.2	$\sim 4.8 \times 10^2$	1.25	$\sim 1 \times 10^2$

* Moles l⁻¹ of electrolyte: Ni(NO₃)₂, 4.2 M; CuSO₄, 4.5 M; Ag⁺, 1 M, I⁻, 4.6 M.
† Oxide electrode is thin-film transparent, inert, and conducting.
‡ pH adjusted by acid of electrolyte-anion, or by NaOH.
§ Resistivity for cell with metallic electrode as cathode.
¶ Resistivity for cell with metallic electrode as anode.
** Photocellular criterion.

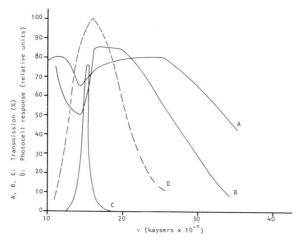

Fig. 8. Spectral response of NOVA STORD elements. (*A*) Electrochemical cell without electrolyte. (*B*) Electrochemical cell with silver iodide system (pH 10). (*C*) Commercial "red" acrylic (Plexiglas) film. (*D*) Photocell (Clairex 605L).

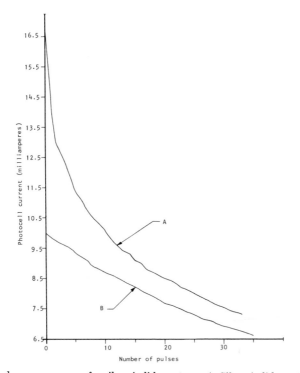

Fig. 9. Typical response curves for silver iodide systems. A. Silver-iodide system (pH 10) with clear acrylic (Plexiglas) cell wall. B. Silver-iodide system (pH 10) with commercial "red" acrylic (Plexiglas) cell wall. Pulse duration, 10 msec. Pulse height, 5 V (plating), 3.5 V (deplating). Photocell voltage, 10 V, dc. Light source, GE 680 bulb, 4 V.

DEVICE OPTIMIZATION.   Figure 8 presents spectral characteristics to be considered in maximizing response. The configuration is attuned to various spectral regions by substitution of commercially available colored plastics in the fabrication of the device. Figure 9 presents a typical response curve for a silver cell, and Fig. 10 indicates circuitry employed in the measure-

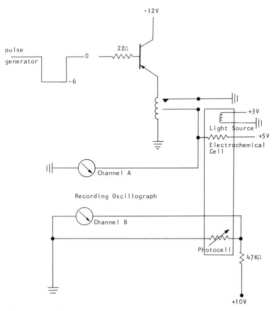

FIG. 10. Schematic for NOVA STORD measurements.

ments. Cell stability as a function of shelf life and continuous cycling (alternating 100 msec 5 V pulses), appears excellent; in the former criterion, we have observed no deterioration (several weeks has been our experimental limit) and, in the latter, none after 36 hrs of continual cycling. Present investigations are attempting to (a) decrease cycle time, (b) attain better reproducibility, and (c) implement solid-state modulation modes. Hysteresis is still present (maximum 5 per cent) and techniques are being devised to minimize same.

The "Adaptive Sandwich"*

Dimensionality

As discussed earlier, automaton dimensionality is viewed as input dimensionality +1, where the information processing is time-dependent, and as input dimensionality alone when information processing is independent of

* Patent application U.S. 229, 388.

time. Hence, NOVA STORD is applicable as a single element, to zero- or one-dimensional automata; of course, networks of the devices can be constructed to provide greater dimensionality, but our former comments on capability, efficiency, and compactness of componentry apply.

The "Adaptive Sandwich" has been designed to meet the needs of time-independent one- and two-dimensional automata, or time-dependent two- and three-dimensional automata.

System Function

Figure 11 supplies a conceptual view of the "Adaptive Sandwich" configuration exclusive of circuitry and leads.

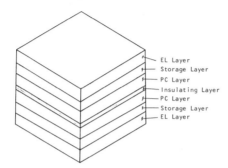

FIG. 11. Typical "Adaptive Sandwich" configuration.

The "Adaptive Sandwich" concept involves several layers of different materials that collectively adapt to environmental conditions by the formation of specific conducting paths, resistive and capacitive elements, and active elements within the layers. This is fundamentally a goal-directed process, and can be the basis of a particularly flexible type of machine learning, as will be seen.

A complete "Adaptive Sandwich" consists of thin layers of photoconductive (PC) and electroluminescent (EL) materials. In addition, layers of transparent conducting material and insulating layers are employed. Of particular importance to the concept is an analog storage layer that stores information in terms of optical transmissivity. It is in this storage layer that the action of a goal system is recorded, and it is therefore in this layer that learning occurs.

The "Adaptive Sandwich" typically consists of an outer layer of electroluminescent material (such as ZnS), followed by the storage layer, the photoconductive layer (CdS), the insulating layer, a second photoconductive layer, a second storage layer, and a second outer layer of electroluminescent material. External electrical connections are made to the edges of the storage layers and electroluminescent layers; the photoconductive layer connections are dependent on whether surface or volume conduction is preferable for a given application (as a function of automaton dimensionality). In the instances where electrical connections are made to two adjacent edges of a layer, selection of any given pair of orthogonal leads locates a given area of the involved layer (thereby activating the phosphor in a moderately resolvable area, or plating/deplating an area of the storage layer, or sensing photoconductor resistance). Variations on this scheme may, of course, be considered, and the "Sandwiches" may be stacked and interconnected in complex automata.

The photoconductive layers contain the principal information channels. In surface conduction application, these channels are formed *in the plane of the layers*, in patterns similar to the patterns of metal plating that remain on one side of a printed circuit board after etching. Their resistivity can be varied by optical means to produce multiple electrically insulated conducting paths within the layer. Switching can be accomplished by opening or closing the conducting paths within this layer. In addition, *areas* of conductivity can form in the plane of the layers. The information channels and areas in a photoconductive layer are dependent on the pattern of transparency or optical transmissivity in the storage layer. Volume conduction treats the photoconductive layer as a discrete array of variable resistances. The two modes differ in electrode configuration, and the latter is restricted by the bulk of this readout geometry.

The electroluminescent layers are prepared from commercially available phosphors and from our own activations. Among various phosphors employed were ZnO activated by Zn (0.1 per cent w/w) and Cu (0.005 per cent w/w) and two phosphors obtained from United Mineral and Chemical Corporation (EP/8a and EP/1). Results compare well with the literature.[45-47] In our activation, each of the phosphor mixtures is passed through a 100-mesh screen, and then heated for 90 min at 700 °C in a closed muffle furnace. The powder can then be slurried with a 15 per cent w/w solution of powdered acrylate (e.g., Lucite) in xylene and applied to SnO_2- or ZnO-coated glass or plastic. Such layers, still not reproducible to within 50 per cent, required 20 V, dc activation (carrier-injection luminescence) for brightness of 0.2 to 0.5 ft-L, which should be sufficient for our photoconductive requirements. Insufficient data are yet available on reproducibility of decay times and lifetime. Reproducibility at this stage is not of impressive import as is homogeneity of the layer. Wave number emission of the phosphor peaks in the green portion of the spectrum; impurity induced color shifts will be employed as well as colored plastics (for the storage layer walls) to maximize transmission of the photoconductor maximum sensitivity wavelength.

Photoconductive layers are being produced according to the procedures of Billups et al.,[48] using cadmium sulfide (with 4 per cent $CdCl_2$ and 0.1 per cent $CuCl_2$) in a layering technique between SnO_2 and Ag electrodes. Characteristics are in good agreement with those published by Billups, and experimentation is being completed on optimum coupling of electrolumi-nescent-photoconductor characteristics.[49]

The insulating layer is used to separate two photoconductive layers. Feed-through conductors in the layer allow a conductive path in one photo-conductive layer to cross another without interference, so that these con-ductors correspond to the eyelets in a printed circuit board. The patterns of conductivity in the two layers of photoconductive material on opposite sides of the insulating layer correspond to the metal channels on opposite sides of a printed circuit board.

The conductivity of channels or paths in a photoconductive layer can vary over a continuous scale depending upon the incident illumination. The incident illumination, in turn, is determined by the pattern of trans-parency or transmissivity in the storage layer and by the pattern of illumi-nation in the electroluminescent layer. Resistive elements can be formed by variation of the resistivity of a conducting path.

The Storage Layer

Figure 12 provides a view of the present storage layer fabrication; intent of the design is to allow resolution by photoconductive layers of four-by-

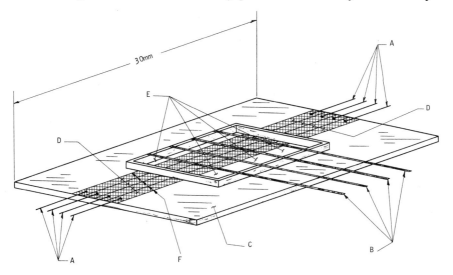

Fig. 12. Storage layer of the "Adaptive Sandwich."

four "cells" of variable optical transmissivity. The electrodes of the cell are four strips of thin layer stannic oxide (labeled D with leads A and separation F) and four metallic electrodes (labeled B in the sketch). The electrolytic bath, E, has a volume of *ca.* 0.1 ml; C is the substratum (plastic or glass) for the thin-film electrode and provides physical support. The "top" of the layer, not shown, is plastic (clear or colored as a function of given electroluminants and photoconductors) and is sealed (airtight) to the walls of the bath.

It is of interest to note that a difficulty encountered with stannic oxide films (see the foregoing) is utilized to achieve separation among the strips of these transparent electrodes. Since the films of SnO_2 "popped" at voltages above 35 V, dc, the layer of electrode is grounded and any desired pattern of SnO_2 completely removed (i.e., no conductivity across the pattern) by leading a point source of >35 V on the plate in the desired configuration.

For present prototype constructions, nickel electrolytes (see Table 2) are utilized since a cycle time of 1 sec has been postulated in requisite circuitry design.

Reward and Punishment in the "Sandwich"

Learning in the "Adaptive Sandwich" is accomplished by the effects of reward and punishment on the storage layers. For example, reward signals will cause an increase in transparency in the storage layer, and punishment signals cause a decrease in the transparency. If matters are progressing well for the machine as determined by machine goals, then the reward causes the storage layer to become *more* transparent in areas contiguous with the brightest areas of luminosity in the electroluminescent layer. If matters are not progressing well for the machine, then punishment causes the storage layer to become less transparent in areas contiguous with the brightest areas; this represents a slight oversimplification.[50]

As a result of this process, the pattern of transparency in the storage layer is a rough composite of the patterns of luminosity in the electroluminescent layer that resulted in reward and punishment. The selectivity of learning comes about because reward produces a *positive* imprint of the corresponding luminosity pattern, while punishment causes a *negative* imprint. The combined effect of an *even* luminosity across the entire electroluminescent layer and the pattern of transparency in the storage layer produces a pattern of luminosity on the photoconducting layer. This pattern images the composite of the past history of positive and negative imprints respectively due to reward and punishment.

Reward and punishment techniques allow a step-by-step process of autonomous adaptation and problem solving in complex environments, so that new functions can be produced without the destruction of old functions. However, old circuits can be broken up when no longer needed, and maximum use of a limited quantity of "Sandwich" material can be attained by re-using that released by the discarding of the old circuits.

In alternative approaches to system design, the change in transparency of the storage layer may be controlled either (1) by the color and brightness emitted by the electroluminescent layer or (2) by electrical means.

Spontaneity of behavior is obtained by means of a periodic insertion of random patterns, or *noise* signals, on the electroluminescent layer. At other times, this layer is uniformly luminous.

Because the formation of electrical conducting areas and pathways is governed by the total illumination on the photoconductive layer, and because the amount of illumination depends upon both the electroluminescent layer and the storage layer, the achievement of rudimentary switching functions and resistive circuits depends upon the interactions of these three layers. Capacitors could be formed by developing parallel conducting areas in the two photoconductive layers that are separated by the thin insulating layer which serves as the dielectric for the capacitor. In effect, the system should be able to "print" its own circuits and components by this process.

From the basic switching circuits and the RC-circuits thus obtained, more complex analog and digital functions can be built up. With the addition of active elements (such as transistors or diodes), a large number of functions can be produced. A particularly flexible type of machine learning results in this way, with connecting paths in the photoconductive layer being adaptive rather than fixed, and with functional elements arising as needed.

A number of advantages in the field of learning automata can be expected to emerge from this approach. First, the "Adaptive Sandwich" would not require the detailed fabrication and assembly of many different components, since it could form its own functional elements and continually refine them. This should bring about a decrease in the design time and manufacturing costs for automata. Second, the physical factors of size, weight, and complexity of automata should be improved, since the need for unused "standby" equipment would be reduced. Third, reliability should improve as a result of decreased complexity because of the flexibility of learning and the inherent capability of the "Sandwich" material to form parallel paths where feasible.

The System and Its Circuitry[1]

A five-valued value function has been selected for the four-by-four "Adaptive Sandwich." On a qualitative basis these five values could be said to correspond to

1. The score function has a very high value (high reward value).
2. The score function has a high value (reward value).
3. The score function has a value that is neither good nor bad (indifferent value).
4. The score function has a low value (punish value).
5. The score function has a very low value (high punish value).

On the basis of the value of the value function at any instant, the following modes of operation are used:

1. High reward value: the pattern then in existence on the EL layer is retained and no new patterns are tried; i.e., experimentation ceases.

2. Reward value: positive transfer of the EL layer pattern to storage takes place and new random patterns are also tested.

3. Indifferent value: no transfer of the EL layer to the storage layer takes place and new patterns are tested.

4. Punish value: a negative transfer of the EL layer pattern to the storage layer takes place and experimentation continues normally.

5. High punish value: all storage "cells"* are (partially) erased and random pattern experimentation continues normally.

The score functions that can be used with the type of five-valued value function described above depend ultimately on the characteristics of the environment. With the above five options for action sequences in the "Adaptive Sandwich," it seems likely that many different kinds of score functions could be adapted with a wide variety of conditioning algorithms to provide a fairly versatile learning system.

Design of the four-by-four "Adaptive Sandwich" includes provision for a score function generator that can be used with the five-valued value function. No specific problem environment has been selected to provide a vehicle for testing the "Adaptive Sandwich" as yet, however, and the detailed design of the score function generator cannot be made until the problem environment has been completely specified.

MODE REQUIREMENTS. The five possible modes of operation of the "Adaptive Sandwich" have three processes that must be controlled:

1. The selection and storage of a new pattern to be laid down on the EL layer (experimentation in pattern space).

2. The transfer of either a positive or negative version of the EL layer pattern to the storage layer (plating or deplating).

3. The cyclic readout of the EL layer pattern from storage to the EL layer (pattern readout).

Pattern readout must be performed for all "cells" in the EL layer within the decay time of the phosphor to maintain an essentially continuously illuminated pattern. Many common commercially available phosphors have decay times in the range of 10 to 30 msec, and the figure of 16 msec was selected as representative of a typical phosphor for purposes of analyzing timing requirements for the four-by-four "Adaptive Sandwich." No great loss in generality is incurred by the 16 msec decay time assumption, however, since the basic clock speed for driving the sandwich can be varied over the small range of 30 to 100 cps to match the chosen phosphor more precisely.

Over-all mode control is obtained by using a ten-stage binary counter.

* Cell in this context is defined as a resolvable element in any layer.

The counter is driven by a pulse source variable over a range to adjust for phosphor characteristics.

Since each "cell" of the four-by-four array in the "Adaptive Sandwich" must be illuminated once each 16 msec, then the scanning process must excite each "cell" for a 1-msec period. Hence, the clock that drives the ten-stage counter should run at a 1-kc rate. The slowest stage of the clock therefore has a period of 1.024 sec.

We are using a nickel storage "cell" that can be cycled from one extreme to the other in about 1 sec. By using 16 steps in the plating for any one cell, 16 more or less uniformly spaced gradations in storage "cell" opacity can be achieved.

Since each step corresponds to the amount that a given pattern is reinforced or torn down by reward or punishment, 16 steps appears to be as good as any for a starting point: more gradations (smaller reinforcement per pattern) would require more experiments in pattern space to find a good pattern, and fewer gradations (larger reinforcement per pattern) tend to assign a disproportionate weight to a pattern. It is likely that the exact number of gradations required is not critical, but the quantity can be adjusted in multiples of two by adding or deleting stages in the binary counter.

Using the 16 levels of storage, the last 4 stages of the binary clock can thus be used to control the plating cycle. Each cell in the storage layer is thus driven for about $\frac{1}{16}$ of a second and the entire storage layer is cycled in about 1 sec.

Applications

A few pertinent comments are called for anent the proximate application of "Adaptive Sandwiches" at the present state of the art in these laminar automata. (A four-by-four configuration is an automaton of extremely small size; the myriad of potential and challenging applications in the field of learning automata awaits development of medium and large networks.) Rather than list specific problems which lend themselves to solution with four-by-four "Sandwiches," it is more instructive to generalize functional properties.

Effectively, the "Sandwich" is a variable, distributed (as an array or planar paths and areas) resistance, with the possible interaction of active elements hung outside of the "Sandwich" proper. The system can be used as the ventral portion of a plastic neuron (n-input, 1-output device with variable attenuation of input signals); with the addition of threshold elements, external to the laminar structure, the device becomes a plastic neuron (1 output), a selector (any of n-inputs), or one of limited switching capability; various sensor thresholds can be set by a learning process, e.g., photocells. Since transformations are correlated, input data should be recognizable as correlative; this implies use in waveform analysis or sequence analysis, where sequence is correlated term by term for short distances on either side of a given term. Other areas of application suggest themselves in modification of the basic laminar relationships, e.g., storage layer-photoconductive layers could respond to optical images (instead of random electroluminescent layer patterns).

ACKNOWLEDGMENTS

The authors wish to express their appreciation to the Air Force Avionics Laboratory for their interest and/or sponsorship in these efforts. Except where noted, all investigations were sponsored under Contract No. AF 33(615)-1398 with the Air Force Avionics Laboratory, Research and Technology Division, Air Force Systems Command, United States Air Force, Wright-Patterson Air Force Base, Ohio.

The debt of the authors is extended to J. D. Roberts, and J. Q. Harrison of the Adaptronics, Inc., staff for their roles in pursuing the experiments, to D. L. Garrison for assistance in visual aids, to Miss J. B. Hauptli for editorial assistance, and to Miss P. W. Jenkins and Mrs. J. H. Fritts, Technical Typists.

REFERENCES

1. MODDES, R. E. J., AND L. O. GILSTRAP, JR., *Research of Adaptive Sandwiches and Learning Automata*, Adaptronics, Inc., Interim Engineering Report No. 1, Contract No. AF 33(615)-1398, Air Force Avionics Laboratory, Wright-Patterson Air Force Base, Ohio, May 1964.
2. GILSTRAP, L. O., JR., A. C. CHAULIAGON, H. J. KEMPA, AND R. E. J. MODDES, *Study of Neurotron Networks in Learning Automata, Vol. 1, Learning Automata and the Neurotron*, Adaptronics, Inc., Final Engineering Report, Contract No. AF 33(657)-10734, Air Force Avionics Laboratory, Wright-Patterson Air Force Base, Ohio, June 1964.
3. GILSTRAP, L. O., JR., AND M. J. PEDELTY, *The Epistemological Foundations of Machine Intelligence*, Adaptronics, Inc., Final Report under Contract No. AF 33(657)-9195, Technical Documentary Report No. ASD-TDR-63, Air Force Electronic Technology Laboratory, Wright-Patterson Air Force Base, Ohio, June 1963.
4. GILSTRAP, L. O., JR., R. L. BARRON, R. J. BROWN, R. E. J. MODDES, R. F. SNYDER, AND E. A. TORBETT, *Study of Neurotron Networks in Learning Automata*, Adaptronics, Inc., Interim Engineering Report No. 1, Contract No. AF 33(615)-1526, Air Force Avionics Laboratory, Wright-Patterson Air Force Base, Ohio, June 1964.
5. GEORGE, F. H., *The Brain as a Computer*, Pergamon Press, Ltd., London, 1962.
6. MODDES, R. E. J., L. O. GILSTRAP, JR., R. J. BROWN, AND R. F. SNYDER, *Study of Neurotron Networks in Learning Automata*, Adaptronics, Inc., Interim Engineering Report No. 2, Contract No. AF 33,(615)-1526, Air Force Avionics Laboratory, Wright-Patterson Air Force Base, Ohio, September 1964.
7. SHANNON, C. E., "A Universal Turing Machine with Two Internal States," in *Automata Studies*, C. E. Shannon and J. McCarthy, Eds., Princeton University Press, Princeton, N.J., 1956, pp. 157–165.
8. DAVIS, M. D., "A Note on Universal Turing Machines," in *Automata Studies, ibid.*, pp. 167–175.

9. McCarthy, J., "The Inversion of Functions Defined by Turing Machines," *ibid.*, pp. 177–181.

10. Minsky, M. L., "Some Universal Elements for Finite Automata," *ibid.*, pp. 117–128.

11. Moore, E. F., "Gedanken-Experiments on Sequential Machines," *ibid.*, pp. 129–153.

12. Gilstrap, L. O., Jr., R. F. Snyder, E. A. Torbett, R. J. Brown, and D. E. Kearney, *Theory of Probability State Variable Systems*, Adaptronics, Inc., Final Report under Contract No. AF 33(657)-7100, Technical Documentary Report No. AL-TDR-64-14, Electronic Technology Division, Air Force Avionics Laboratory, Wright-Patterson Air Force Base, Ohio, December 1963.

13. Steck, G. P., "Stochastic Model of the Browning-Bledsoe Pattern Recognition Scheme," *IRE Trans. Electron. Computers*, EC-11, No. 2, 174–282 (1962).

14. Kanal, L., "Evaluation of a Class of Pattern-Recognition Networks," in *Biological Prototypes and Synthetic Systems, Vol. 1*, E. E. Bernard and M. R. Kare, Eds., Plenum Press, Inc., New York, 1962, pp. 261–269.

15. Fu, K. S., "A Sequential Decision Model for Optimum Recognition," in *Biological Prototypes and Synthetic Systems, Vol. 1*, E. E. Bernard and M. R. Kare, Eds., Plenum Press, Inc., New York, 1962, pp. 270–277.

16. Wiesen, R. A., and E. H. Shuford, "Bayes Strategies as Adaptive Behavior," in *Biological Prototypes and Synthetic Systems, Vol. 1*, E. E. Bernard and M. R. Kare, Eds., Plenum Press, Inc., New York, 1962, pp. 303–310.

17. Griffith, V. V., "A Model of the Plastic Neuron," *IEEE Trans. Military Electron.*, MIL-7, Nos. 2 and 3, 243–253 (April–July 1963).

18. Dusheck, G. J., T. C. Hilinski, and F. L. Putzrath, "A Flexible Neural Logic Network," *IEEE Trans. Military Electron.*, MIL-7, Nos. 2 and 3, 208–213 (April–July 1963).

19. Guinn, D. F., "Large Artificial Nerve Net (LANNET)," *IEEE Trans. Military Electron.*, MIL-7, Nos. 2 and 3, 234–243 (April–July 1963).

20. Pedelty, M. J., *An Approach to Machine Intelligence*, Spartan Books, Inc., Baltimore, Md., 1963, pp. 42–80.

21. van Bergeijk, W. A., and L. D. Harman, "What Good Are Artificial Neurons?," *Bionics Symposium: Living Prototypes—The Key to New Technology*, WADD Technical Report 60-600, Wright Air Development Division, Wright-Patterson Air Force Base, Ohio, 1960, pp. 395–406.

22. Uttley, A. M., "Conditional Probability Machines and Conditioned Reflexes," in *Automata Studies*, C. E. Shannon and J. McCarthy, Eds., Princeton University Press, Princeton, N.J., 1956, pp. 253–275.

23. Wilde, D. J., *Optimum Seeking Methods*, Prentice-Hall, Inc., Englewood Cliffs, N.J., 1964.

24. Leitman, G., Ed., *Optimization Techniques*, Academic Press, Inc., New York, 1962.

25. Snyder, R. F., R. L. Barron, R. J. Brown, and E. A. Torbett, *Advanced Computer Concepts for Intercept Prediction, Volume 1: Conditioning of Parallel Networks for High-Speed Prediction of Re-entry Trajectories*, Technical Summary Report, Contract DA-36-034-AMC-0099Z, NIKE-X Project Office, U.S. Army Materiel Command, Redstone Arsenals, Ala., November 1964.

26. Pulvari, C. F., "Ferrielectrics and Their Application in Solid-State Devices as an Adaptive Control," *IEEE Trans. Military Electron.*, MIL-7, Nos. 2 and 3, 254–260 (April–July 1963).

27. Loebner, E. E., "Image Processing and Functional Retinal Synthesis," in *Human Factors in Technology*, Chapter 32, E. Bennett, J. Degan, and J. Spiegel, Eds., McGraw-Hill Book Co., Inc., New York, 1963, pp. 492–518.

28. WIDROW, B., *An Adaptive "Adaline" Neuron Using Chemical "Memistors,"* T. R. No. 1553-2, Stanford Electronics Laboratories, Stanford, Calif., October 17, 1960.

29. STEWART, R. M., "Theory of Structurally Homogeneous Logic Nets," in *Biological Prototypes and Synthetic Systems*, E. E. Bernard and M. R. Kare, Eds., Plenum Press, New York, 1962, pp. 370–380.

30. HERSCHER, M. B., AND T. P. KELLEY, "Functional Electronic Model of the Frog Retina," *IEEE Trans. Military Electron.*, *MIL-7*, Nos. 2 and 3, 98–103 (April–July, 1963).

31. GOMER, R., *Rev. Sci. Instr.*, *24*, 993 (1953).

32. WYCKOFF, R. W., *Crystal Structures*, Interscience Publishers, Inc., New York, 1951.

33. PAULING, L., *Nature of the Chemical Bond*, 3rd Edition, Cornell University Press, Ithaca, N.Y., 1960.

34. KOHNKE, E. E., *Electrical and Optical Properties of Natural Stannic Oxide Crystals*, Technical Report No. 1, Contract No. NONr. 2595(01), AD# 276 356, Oklahoma State University, Stillwater, Okla., May 1962.

35. SOFFER, B., *J. Chem. Phys.*, *35*, 940 (1961).

36. BRUNNER, G., H. WONDRATSCHEK, AND F. LOVES, *Naturwissenschaften*, *46*, 664 (1959).

37. WEST, W., Ed., *Chemical Applications of Spectroscopy, Technique of Organic Chemistry, Vol. IX*, Interscience Publishers, Inc., New York, 1956.

38. BELLAMY, L., *The Infrared Spectra of Complex Molecules*, John Wiley & Sons, Inc., New York, 1954.

39. MILOSLAVSKII, V., *Optics and Spectroscopy*, *7*, 154 (1959).

40. HEAVENS, O. S., *Optical Properties of Thin Solid Films*, Butterworth Scientific Publications, London, 1955.

41. ROUARD, P., *Ann. Phys.*, *7*, 346 (1937).

42. COTTON, P., AND P. ROUARD, *J. Phys. Radium*, *11*, 469 (1950).

43. CLEGG, P. L., *Proc. Phys. Soc. (London)*, *65B* (1962).

44. SENNETT, R. S., AND G. D. SCOTT, *J. Opt. Soc. Am.*, *40*, 4 (1950).

45. HENISCH, H. K., *Electroluminescence*, Pergamon Press, Ltd., London, 1962.

46. STEIN, I. H., *Electroluminescent Response to Pulse Excitation*, Technical Report No. 2452, AD# 601 049, Electronics Research and Development Laboratories, U.S. Army, Fort Monmouth, N.J., April 1964.

47. GROSSO, P. F., *Development of Phosphors Screens for High Resolution Display Devices*, Technical Documentary Report No. AL-TDR-64-94, AD# 600 724, Air Force Avionics Laboratory, Wright-Patterson Air Force Base, Ohio, May 1964.

48. BILLUPS, R. R., W. L. GARDNER, AND M. D. ZIMMERMAN, *Preparation and Performance of Sintered CdS Photoconductors*, Technical Report No. 200, M.I.T. Lincoln Laboratory, Lexington, Mass., March 1959.

49. ING, S., *Improved Photoconductors for Display Switching*, Technical Documentary Report No. RADC-TDR-63-554, AD# 433 671, Rome Air Development Center, Griffis Air Force Base, New York, February 1964.

50. MODDES, R. E. J., *Research of Adaptive Sandwiches and Learning Automata*, Adaptronics, Inc., Interim Engineering Report No. 2, Contract No. AF 33(615)-1398, Air Force Avionics Laboratory, Wright-Patterson Air Force Base, Ohio, August 1964.

CHAPTER 28

THIN-FILM MAGNETO-OPTICS
IN INFORMATION PROCESSING

Donald O. Smith

Lincoln Laboratory,* Massachusetts Institute of Technology, Lexington, Massachusetts

Introduction

It is the purpose of this paper to discuss theoretically the problem of optimizing the design of magneto-optical light switches using presently known magnetic materials and to discuss possible applications in memory and display.

General Magneto-Optical Considerations

A figure of magneto-optical merit f for switch design is given by the ratio of the Faraday rotation F to the absorption coefficient α; i.e., $f = F/\alpha$. Table 1 gives f for Fe, Ni, Permalloy, and YIG. Except for Permalloy the data are given for the wavelength at which f is maximum; this wavelength is not known for Permalloy but is probably near that for Ni. It is interesting to note that metallic Fe and "transparent" YIG have almost the same figure of merit in the same wavelength region, and that both are an order of magnitude better than Permalloy in this region.

In addition to a high figure of optical merit, a good switch material must be able to switch rapidly. The high-speed, low-energy, rotational switching of the magnetization **M** which is possible with thin films of Permalloy is well known,[7] and consequently considerable work has been done in attempting to use Permalloy films for light switches.[8] The ease of preparing metallic films compared to the probable difficulties which would be encountered with the complicated compound YIG and the high value of f for Fe near the visible suggest that Fe is the best known material

---

* Operated with support from the U.S. Air Force.

TABLE 1   Figure of Optical Merit $f = $ (Faraday Rotation)/(Absorption Coefficient) for Fe, Ni, Permalloy, and YIG

[Except for Permalloy, the data are given at the wavelength for which f is maximum. F and α for Fe, Ni, and Permalloy are calculated from $F = \pi|nq|/\lambda_0$ and $\alpha = 2\pi n''/\lambda_0$, where $n = n' + in''$ is the index of refraction and $q = q' + iq''$ is the gyroelectric constant defined in Eq. 1 (see Table 3)]

	λ_0	F	α	$f = \dfrac{F}{\alpha}$	Ref.
Fe	1.0μ	5.1×10^5 deg/cm	1.6×10^5 cm^{-1}	3.1 deg	1, 2
Ni	4.0	7.2×10^5	2.1×10^5	3.4	3
Permalloy	0.5	1.2×10^5	3.0×10^5	0.4	4
YIG	0.85	$\sim 10^3$	$\sim 4 \times 10^2$	~ 2.5	5, 6

with which to try to design a light switch. It is interesting to note further that not only is a thin film of magnetic material desirable for its switching properties, but also that the optical performance is found to be substantially improved (Eq. 4).

Magneto-optical effects are described at the level of Maxwell's equations by introducing a gyrotropic (skew symmetric) dielectric tensor $[\epsilon]$.[*9] To a good approximation, $[\epsilon]$ can be taken as

$$[\epsilon] \simeq \epsilon \begin{bmatrix} 1 & -iq & 0 \\ iq & 1 & 0 \\ 0 & 0 & 1 \end{bmatrix} \qquad (1)$$

with ϵ related to the complex index of refraction $n = n' + in''$ by $\epsilon = n^2/\mu_0 c^2$, and $q = q' + iq''$ the complex gyroelectric constant. Values of n and q for Fe and Permalloy are given in Table 2.

TABLE 2   Index of Refraction $n = n' + in''$ and Gyroelectric Constant $q = q' + iq''$ for Fe and Permalloy

	λ_0	n'	n''	q'	q''	Ref.
Fe	1.0μ	2.6	2.6	5.0×10^{-2}	-6.0×10^{-2}	1, 2
Permalloy	0.5	1.5	2.4	1.0×10^{-2}	-0.6×10^{-2}	4

* A gyrotropic permeability $[\mu]$ also gives magneto-optical effects. Measurements[9] show that in general, for the parameter p analogous to q, $|p| \approx 10^{-4}$, which is too small to be useful in switch design.

The problem of the reflection and transmission of light in plane parallel structures which do not contain gyrotropic media is characterized by two noninteracting polarization modes, namely modes with the optical electric vector **E** perpendicular ($\perp$) or parallel ($\parallel$) to the incidence plane, respectively. If a gyroelectric medium is present, two different types of interaction can occur: (1) if the magnetization **M** is perpendicular to the light propagation vector **s** (transverse effect), the $\mathbf{E}_{\parallel}$ mode will be amplitude modulated when **M** is reversed in direction, while the $\mathbf{E}_{\perp}$ mode will be unaffected; (2) for any other orientation of **M** mode interaction occurs with a transfer of energy from one mode to the other. In the first case the effect is one of impedance modulation, and the resulting light modulation can be optimized by adjusting the impedance mismatch between the incident wave and the magnetic material by means of dielectric layers. In the case of mode conversion the effect cannot in general be described by means of an impedance which is a constant of the magnetic material. However, in the presence of large isotropic optical absorption, mode conversion is maximized by impedance matching to the isotropic loss. It should be noted that matching to both polarization modes is necessary so that the problem is one of dual-mode impedance matching.[10]

In order to switch **M** with fields of a few oersteds, **M** must lie in the film plane, since any component $\Delta \mathbf{M}$ out of the plane must overcome a demagnetizing field $4\pi \, \Delta M$ ($4\pi M \sim 10^4$ in Permalloy). The longitudinal effect (**M** in the film plane, **s** at oblique incidence and coplanar with **M**; Fig. 1) and the transverse effect (**M** in the film plane and perpendicular

FIG. 1. The longitudinal magneto-optical effect.

(a)   (b)

to **s**; Fig. 2) are therefore of interest for possible use as a light switch. The polar effect (**M** perpendicular to the film plane) is not of practical interest.

(a)   (b)

$|E_{\parallel}^{r}|$ DEPENDS ON THE DIRECTION OF $\bar{M}$ $|E_{\perp}^{r}|$ DOES NOT DEPEND ON THE DIRECTION OF $\bar{M}$

FIG. 2. The transverse magneto-optical effect.

Optimizing the Longitudinal Effect

In the longitudinal effect incident light polarized with $\mathbf{E} \parallel$ or $\perp$ to the plane of incidence is reflected with a component in the opposite state of polarization (Fig. 1). The Kerr coefficient is defined as $k_{\perp,\parallel} = E^r_{\parallel,\perp}/E^i_{\perp,\parallel}$, and it is clear that the two cases are physically inequivalent so that in general $k_\perp \neq k_\parallel$. However, to first order in theory and experiment it is found that $k_\perp = k_\parallel$.

A simple classical picture of the origin of magneto-optical effects can be given in terms of the Hall effect. Thus a component of $\mathbf{E}$ perpendicular to $\mathbf{M}$ induces a current perpendicular to $\mathbf{M}$ which is then deflected around $\mathbf{M}$ with a consequent rotation of $\mathbf{E}$. With this picture in mind it is easy to see from Fig. 1 how the longitudinal effect can be optimized. Thus the components of the incident and reflected electric field $\mathbf{E}_\parallel{}^i$ and $\mathbf{E}_\parallel{}^r$ which are parallel to $\mathbf{M}$ do not contribute to mode conversion but only dissipate energy by optical absorption. Hence k will be maximized if a very thin magnetic film is placed in an optical standing wave at a position such that tangential $\mathbf{E}_\parallel = 0$ (very thin means $D = 2\pi\, d/\lambda_0 \leq 1/10$, where d is the film thickness and λ_0 the incident wavelength).

The condition tangential $\mathbf{E}_\parallel = 0$ suggests placing the magnetic film on the surface of a highly reflecting metal (a mirror) since then the total tangential $\mathbf{E} \simeq 0$. A surface with tangential $\mathbf{E} = 0$ will be called an electric mirror (E mirror). Calculation then shows that the maximum Kerr coefficient for a very thin film (VTF) is[10]

$$|k(\text{VTF})|_{\max} = \frac{\sqrt{3}|n|^2|q|}{4\,\text{Im}\,n^2} \tag{2}$$

A measure of the improvement can be obtained by considering $|k|_{\max}$ for a thick magnetic film or magnetic substrate (MS). For a MS[10]

$$|k(\text{MS})|_{\max} = \frac{\gamma_0|q|}{2n'} \tag{3}$$

where γ_0 is the direction cosine defined in Fig. 1. The ratio of the Kerr coefficients for the two structures is then

$$\frac{|k(\text{VTF})|_{\max}}{|k(\text{MS})|_{\max}} = \frac{\sqrt{3}|n|^2}{4\gamma_0 n''} \tag{4}$$

For $\gamma_0 = 0.87$, this ratio is 2.5 and 1.7 for Fe and Permalloy, respectively. Numerical values of $|k|_{\max}$ for Fe and Permalloy are given in Table 3 for both the VTF and the MS. Note that $|k|_{\max}$ for a very thin Fe film is $\sim$10 times greater than for a Permalloy substrate.

In order to realize these maximum values of $|k|$ it is necessary to match the incident wave to the gyrotropic properties of the magnetic material, i.e., to accomplish dual-mode impedance matching. For a VTF on an

TABLE 3 MAXIMUM KERR ROTATION $|k|_{max}$ FOR A MAGNETIC SUBSTRATE (FIG. 3a) AND A VERY THIN FILM (FIG. 3b)

		$|k|_{max}$
Very thin film on an E mirror	Fe	3.4×10^{-2}
	Permalloy	0.6×10^{-2}
Magnetic substrate ($\gamma_0 = 0.87$)	Fe	1.3×10^{-2}
	Permalloy	3.6×10^{-3}

E mirror, the real part of the film impedances for the two modes are

$$\mathrm{Re}\ z_\perp = \tfrac{1}{3}D^3\ \mathrm{Im}\ n^2$$

$$\mathrm{Re}\ z_{||} = D\gamma_0{}^2\ \frac{\mathrm{Im}\ n^2}{|n|^4} \tag{5}$$

where $D = 2\pi d/\lambda_0$, and d = film thickness. For small D ($\sim 2 \times 10^{-2}$ say) such as would be desired for high-density memory bits, $\mathrm{Re}\ z_\perp$ becomes extremely small, making matching difficult.

Dual-mode impedance matching can be made easier by noting that the use of an E mirror in effect reduces the basic Kerr interaction by making the magneto-optically active component $\mathbf{E}_\perp$ zero also. This suggests the use of a combination mirror for which tangential $\mathbf{E}_{||}$ and tangential $\mathbf{H}_{||} = 0$. A mirror with tangential $\mathbf{H} = 0$ will be called a magnetic mirror (H mirror) so that the required mirror will be called an $(EH)_{||}$ mirror. The film impedances are then

$$\mathrm{Re}\ z_\perp = \frac{1}{D\ \mathrm{Im}\ n^2}$$

$$\mathrm{Re}\ z_{||} = D\gamma_0{}^2\ \frac{\mathrm{Im}\ n^2}{|n|^4} \tag{6}$$

which are both first order in D.

The problem of generating an $(EH)_{||}$ mirror can be stated in terms of impedances: E and H mirrors have zero and infinite surface impedances, respectively. Thus at the mirror surface, the $\mathbf{E}_{||}$ mode is to have zero and the $\mathbf{E}_\perp$ mode infinite impedance. This condition can be met by using the phenomenon of total internal reflection.[10] Furthermore, the dual-mode impedance matching specified by Eqs. 6 can be accomplished to within $\sim$50 per cent of perfect match by the use of only one $\lambda/4$ dielectric film operating at less than but near the angle for total internal reflection into thin film.[10] A suggested structure is shown in Fig. 3.

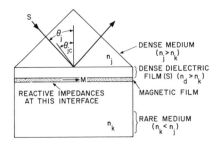

FIG. 3. Reactive mirror obtained by using the phenomena of total internal reflection. From Snell's law the surface impedance at the top boundary of the rare medium depends only on n_k, n_j, and θ_j and is not changed by the interposition of the magnetic and dielectric films between the rare medium and the dense incident medium. If desired, additional dielectric films can be placed between the magnetic film and the rare medium in order to adjust the impedance at the magnetic film.

Optimization of the Transverse Effect

In the transverse effect (Fig. 2) the impedance of the magnetic medium Z_M depends on the direction of **M**, so that in general

$$Z_M = Z \pm Z_q$$
$$= (R + iX) \pm (R_q + iX_q) \tag{8}$$

where Z and Z_q are the isotropic and gyroelectric components of Z_M, respectively. Then with the reflection coefficient $r = (Z_j - Z_M)/(Z_j + Z_M)$, where Z_j is the impedance looking toward the light source from the surface of the magnetic material, the change in reflection when **M** is reversed is

$$\Delta|r|^2 = \frac{4(\Delta R)R_q + 4(\Delta X)X_q}{(\Delta R + 2R)^2 + (\Delta X + 2X)^2} \tag{9}$$

where

$$\Delta R = R_j - R$$
$$\Delta X = X_j - X \tag{10}$$

Maximization of $\Delta|r|^2$ as a function of ΔR and ΔX is in general quite complicated. However, a useful simplification occurs when $R_q = X_q$; then by symmetry it is clear that the maximum in $\Delta|r|^2$ occurs with $\Delta R = \Delta X$, and setting $d\Delta|r|^2/d(\Delta R)^2 = 0$ leads to

$$(\Delta|r|^2)_{max} = \frac{2R_q}{|Z| + R + X} \tag{11}$$

For a magnetic substrate[10]

$$Z \simeq m_0\left(\mathrm{Re}\,\frac{1}{n} + i\,\mathrm{Im}\,\frac{1}{n}\right) \tag{12a}$$

$$Z_q = m_0\alpha_0\left(\operatorname{Im}\frac{q}{n^2} + i\operatorname{Re}\frac{q}{n^2}\right) \tag{12b}$$

where m_0 is the impedance of free space. From the values of n given in Table 2 for Fe and Permalloy, it is seen that the assumption $R_q = X_q$ is well satisfied. Then for Fe

$$(\Delta|r|^2)_{max} \sim 3\alpha_0 \times 10^{-2} \tag{13}$$

which is only slightly greater than the experimental value obtained by Krinchik[2] for an uncoated Fe surface. Thus the transverse effect from a magnetic substrate is very nearly optimum without the use of dielectric coatings to adjust the impedance.

Use of the transverse effect as described above suffers from lack of contrast since an analyzer cannot be used to block the unmodulated part of the beam. This difficulty can be overcome if the incident light is polarized out of the plane of polarization, as pointed out by Dove.[11] A simplified treatment is shown in Fig. 4, in which it is assumed that by a suitable

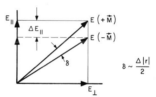

FIG. 4. Rotation of the plane of polarization using the transverse magneto-optical effect.

choice of incident components $\mathbf{E}_\perp{}^i$ and $\mathbf{E}_{||}{}^i$ (including phase adjustment), that nearly equal and in-phase reflected components are obtained. Then if the $\mathbf{E}_{||}$ component is magnetically modulated according to Eq. 9, a rotation of the plane of polarization by an angle $\delta \simeq \Delta|r|/2$ will occur.

Comparison between the longitudinal and transverse effect, both with respect to signal and contrast capability can now be made by comparing $|k|$ and δ: for Fe at 1 μ, $|k(MS)|_{max} \simeq 1.3 \times 10^{-2}$, $|k(VTF)|_{max} \simeq 3.4 \times 10^{-2}$, $\delta(MS)_{max} \simeq 15 \times 10^{-2}$. Thus the transverse effect from an MS is superior in both signal and contrast to the longitudinal effect from a VTF, while at the same time no matching dielectric structure is required with the MS transverse effect. Note, however, that it is possible to use the longitudinal effect in such a way that the effective $|k|$ is doubled (Fig. 7). For use in a memory a VTF may be desirable, and in this case the transverse effect is no longer competitive with the longitudinal effect. For the magnetic film placed on either an E or H mirror, it is found that $(\Delta|r|^2)_{max} \propto D$, and for $D \leq 1/10$ the reflectance modulation $\Delta|r|^2$ becomes a very small effect. The reason is that at the surface of an E mirror, the coupling to the gyroelectric $[\epsilon]$ (the gyroelectric impedance) goes as D^2, while the isotropic impedance goes as D; for an H mirror, the gyroelectric impedance is independent of D, but the isotropic impedance goes as $1/D$.

Random Access Memory

The use of the longitudinal magneto-optical effect for reading out random-access magnetic memories has been considered by a number of authors.[8,12] For the general configuration in which the transmission axes of the polarizer and analyzer are oriented out of the plane of incidence by angles ψ and $90 + \phi$, respectively (Fig. 5), the electric field incident on the detector is

$$E = r_{||} \cos \gamma \sin \phi + r_{\perp} \sin \gamma \cos \phi + k \cos (\gamma + \phi) \qquad (14)$$

where $r_{||,\perp} = E^r_{||,\perp}/E^i_{||,\perp}$ are the isotropic reflection coefficients. The inten-

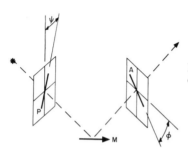

FIG. 5. Longitudinal effect with general orientation of the polarizer and analyzer (after Fan *et al.*[12]).

sity difference ΔI between the two state $\pm \mathbf{M}$, and the average intensity $\bar{I}$ are given by[12]

$$\Delta I \propto [(\operatorname{Re} r_{||}k^*)(\cos \psi \sin \phi) + (\operatorname{Re} r_{\perp}k^*)(\sin \psi \cos \phi)] \cos (\psi + \phi) \qquad (15)$$

$$\bar{I} \propto |r_{||}|^2 \cos \psi \sin \phi + |r_{\perp}|^2 \sin \psi \cos \phi + \tfrac{1}{2}(\operatorname{Re} r_{||}^* r_{\perp}) \cos 2\psi \sin 2\psi \qquad (16)$$

Optimization of the signal ($S \propto \Delta I$) to noise ($N \propto \sqrt{\bar{I}}$) ratio S/N as a function of ψ and ϕ is somewhat complicated, particularly for small k, and has been treated in detail in Reference 12 where signal terms proportional to $|k|^2 \sim 10^{-6}$ were neglected (thick Permalloy or Fe in the visible and imperfect conversion matching). However, for $|k| \sim 3 \times 10^{-2}$ (VTF of Fe) signals proportional to $|k|^2 \sim 10^{-3}$ are significant and a simplified treatment of the signal-to-noise ratio can be given.

Two methods of obtaining signals proportional to $|k|^2$ are shown in Figs. 6 and 7: both cases use incident light polarized $||$ (or $\perp$) to the plane

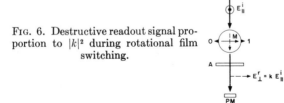

FIG. 6. Destructive readout signal proportion to $|k|^2$ during rotational film switching.

of incidence. In Fig. 6 the analyzer is crossed with the polarizer and when the film is in a 1 or 0 state, $\mathbf{M}$ is oriented as in the transverse effect; during

FIG. 7. Destructive or nondestructive readout signal proportional to $|2k|^2$.

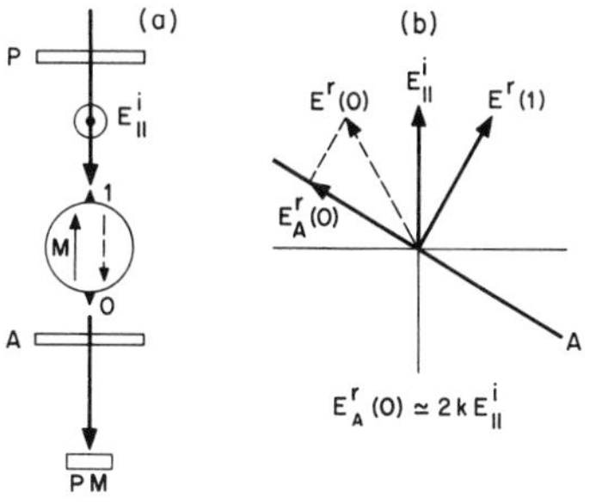

readout $\mathbf{M}$ is switched from say 1 to 0 which results, for a stored 1, in a transient light signal ΔI given by

$$\Delta I \simeq |k|^2 I_0 \tag{17}$$

In Fig. 7a $\mathbf{M}$ is oriented as in the longitudinal effect when the film is in the 1 or 0 state, and the analyzer is set to extinction for say the 1 state (Fig. 7b); when the film is rotationally switched to the 0 state (or the light turned on when in the 0 state), a steady light signal ΔI is generated where

$$\Delta I \simeq |2k|^2 I_0 \tag{18}$$

The corresponding electron currents S at the cathode of the photomultiplier are then

$$S = Q\Delta I \tag{19}$$

where Q is the quantum efficiency of the cathode. The electronic noise N at the photomultiplier cathode is[13]

$$N = (2\Delta f)^{1/2}(S + TQI_0)^{1/2} \tag{20a}$$

where Δf is the bandwidth and T the transmission coefficient of the crossed polarizer and analyzer. Now for $T \sim 10^{-4}$ or 10^{-6} for polaroid sheet or Nicol prisms, respectively, $TQI_0 \ll S$ and the noise becomes

$$N \simeq (2\Delta f S)^{1/2} \tag{20b}$$

Hence the signal to noise for the cell of Fig. 7 is

$$\frac{S}{N} = \left(\frac{S}{2\Delta f}\right)^{1/2}$$
$$= 2|k| \left(\frac{QI_0}{2\Delta f}\right)^{1/2} \tag{21}$$

which is actually the maximum possible which can be obtained even from the general case (Eqs. 14 and 15).[12] Of course the validity of Eq. 21 depends on the increase in $|k|$ from 10^{-3} to 3×10^{-2}.

Incorporation of the memory cells shown in Figs. 6 and 7 into memory systems is shown schematically in Figs. 8 and 9. The memory of Fig. 8 is derived from one of the most commonly used forms of magnetic film memory.[14] Word selection is by means of a unidirectional current pulse on a line which supplies a magnetic field transverse to the film easy axis,

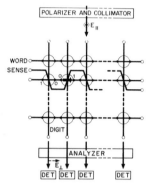

FIG. 8. Destructive optical readout of a word organized magnetic film memory.

while digit information is inserted by ± current on orthogonal lines which generate a magnetic field along the film easy axis. Conventional sensing is accomplished by pulsing a word line and observing the polarity of signal induced on the digit line. Magneto-optical sensing could be accomplished

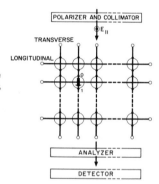

FIG. 9. Destructive or nondestructive optical readout of a bit from a digit plane.

by using the method of Fig. 6. When the sense line in Fig. 8 is pulsed, the magnetization in each digit is either rotationally switched by ∼180°, resulting in the maximum light-pulse output, or it is only rotated slightly, with a much smaller light-pulse output. If the sense line makes an angle of θ to the hard axis, the ratio of a 1 to 0 output is $\cos^2 \theta / \sin^2 \theta$; for $\theta = 20°$, the ratio 1 to 0 = 7. Note that the direction of a 1 or 0 alternates from digit to digit. Since the illumination is transverse to **M**, the background light reaching the digit detectors does not depend on the information content of the memory. Hence the number of words W which may be simultaneously illuminated will be approximately given by the ratio $|k|/T$ of the Kerr coefficient to the transmission coefficient of crossed polarizers.

For $|k| = 10^{-1}$, $T = 10^{-5}$, this gives $W \sim 10^4$. The problem of providing the required monochromatic, polarized illumination or the digit detectors will not be discussed here. Advances in laser technology will probably be required in order to make such a memory competitive.

A memory utilizing the readout method of Fig. 7 is shown in Fig. 9. In this case the memory is organized into digit planes, one of which is shown in Fig. 9. Information is inserted into a digit plane by the coincidence of half-select currents on orthogonal lines. Since the illumination is longitudinal to **M**, steady illumination will result in an average level of light passing through the analyzer which depends on the information content of the digit plane. This implies that the light or the detector must be scanned. At one extreme only one bit is illuminated at a time and one detector views all bits; at the other the illumination is complete and only one bit detector is turned on at a time. Between these extremes partial illumination and detection would probably be advantageous. Note that film switching could also be used to provide light-pulse output. For example, with steady illumination first pulse a transverse selection line with the detector off; then with the detector on pulse a longitudinal selection line, switching the bit at the intersection of the two lines and resulting in a light pulse; the ratio of 1 to 0 output depends on the square of the transverse field $H_\perp$ normalized to the anisotropy field H_K of the magnetic bit, i.e., the ratio 1 to $0 = (H_\perp/H_K)^2$, which reasonably might be $\sim 10^{-1}$.

Serial Access Memory

Magneto-optical readout of magnetic tape could use either the longitudinal or transverse effect. In present-day tapes the bit density is not high across the tape; i.e., track widths are of the order of tenths of an inch. Hence, the magnetic medium can be thick and the transverse effect could be used as described on pages 528 and 529.

If high track density were to be achieved, then it is probable that the magnetic medium would have to be a very thin film and use made of the longitudinal effect. Tape materials with simultaneously high anisotropy and high magneto-optical constant would probably need to be developed. The necessity of making a long tape coated with multilayer dielectric films would seem to present considerable further difficulty.

Display

The use of magneto-optics to accomplish large area display would appear to be a reasonable possibility. In the cell shown in Fig. 7, the contrast is nearly 1 (contrast $= \Delta I/\bar{I}$) and the maximum transmitted intensity is ~ 0.5 per cent (Fe with $\lambda_0 = 1\mu$). Better performance (~ 3 per cent) could be obtained from the transverse effect (Fig. 4). One difficulty is the necessity to operate at $\lambda_0 = 1\mu$ in order to achieve intensity levels in the few per cent range. Alloys could probably be developed with the peak in q occurring at visible wavelengths.

REFERENCES

1. LANDOLT-BÖRNSTEIN, H. H., *Optische Konstanten*, Vol. II, Pt. 8, 6th ed., Springer-Verlag, Berlin, 1962.
2. KRINCHIK, G. S., *Fiz. Metal. i Metalloved*, *5*, 694 (1959).
3. KRINCHIK, G. S., *Soviet Phys. JETP* (English Transl.), *36*, 724 (1959).
4. ROBINSON, C. C., *Longitudinal Kerr Magneto-Optic Effect in Ferromagnetic Thin Films*, Sc.D. Thesis, Massachusetts Institute of Technology, 1960.
5. DILLON, J. F., *J. Phys. Radium*, *20*, 374 (1959).
6. ANDERSON, L. K., *J. Appl. Phys.*, *34*, 1230 (1963).
7. SMITH, D. O., *Magnetism, a Treatise on Modern Theory and Materials*, H. Suhl and G. T. Rado, Eds., Academic Press, Inc., New York, 1963, Chap. 31.
8. LISSBERGER, P. H., *J. Opt. Soc. Am.*, *51*, 948 (1961); *51*, 957 (1961); *54*, 804 (1964).
9. KRINCHIK, G. S., *Zh. Eksperim. i Teor. Fiz.*, *47*, 778 (1964).
10. SMITH, D. O., *Opt. Acta* (to be published 1965).
11. DOVE, D. B., *J. Appl. Phys.*, *34*, 2067 (1963).
12. FAN, G., E. DONATH, E. S. BARREKETTE, AND A. WIRGIN, *IEEE PGEC*, 3 (February 1963).
13. ZWORYKIN, V. K., AND G. A. MORTON, *Television*, John Wiley & Sons, Inc., New York, 1940, p. 37.
14. RAFFEL, J. I., T. S. CROWTHER, A. H. ANDERSON, AND T. O. HERNDON, *Proc. IRE*, *49*, 155 (1961).

CHAPTER 29

AN OPTICALOGICAL
SELF-ORGANIZING RECOGNITION SYSTEM

George G. Lendaris and Gordon L. Stanley

GM Defense Research Laboratories
Mathematics and Evaluation Studies Department
Santa Barbara, California

I. Introduction

This paper discusses a pattern recognition system that incorporates an electro-optical preprocessor and a postprocessor which is an adaptive logic network.

As a starting point for our discussion, we state two well-known facts:

1. The Fraunhofer diffraction pattern of an aperture is the two-dimensional Fourier transform of the transmission function of that aperture.[1]
2. Except for a constant phase factor, the Fourier transform of any function is independent of a shifting of that function.[2]

During the last decade these facts have been used extensively in the development of spatial filtering techniques in coherent optical systems.[3–7] These filtering techniques have been applied, among other things, to the recognition problem.[8–10]

In this paper the point of view of sampling (for recognition), rather than filtering, is taken. Just as the servo engineer samples the frequency response characteristics of a "black box" to identify the box, we sample the frequency spectrum of a pattern to identify the pattern. The servo engineer learns to associate certain frequency responses with certain kinds of transfer functions (his characterization of a linear black box); in our case, we shall *teach* a network of adjustable binary logic elements (pupil) to associate given sets of frequency samples with certain binary codes (our characterization of a pattern). Having learned this, the pupil will later be able to identify a given pattern on the basis of the frequency samples it receives. As in the case of the servo engineer, we want the pupil to identify correctly a pattern similar to, but not exactly like, the ones encountered during training.

Implicit in the word *teach* is the necessity of a scheme for *teaching*. We call such a scheme a training algorithm. If the network contains many interacting adjustable elements, the most difficult problem facing a training algorithm is the preservation of good information within the pupil, once the pupil obtains it. For example, when the pupil gives the wrong output for a given input, which elements are at fault? To answer this and many other questions that arise, those properties of the network that are determined by the interconnection pattern (structure) of the elements should be investigated.

We have begun such an investigation and obtained several theoretical results dealing with the class of functions which a particular structure, called a LADICAN,* can realize.[11,12] One of the more important results of this investigation was the development of a training algorithm for two-element LADICANs which assures attainment of a solution in a finite number of iterations, if a solution exists.† This algorithm has been extended for training n-element LADICANs where the input set is unconstrained, and a limited extension has been made for the more usual case where the input set is constrained.‡

For reasons to be cited later, the authors used the universal logic element* as the basic adjustable element for these investigations. The number of stored variables required for an m-input universal element is 2^m. Therefore, as m becomes large, a single universal element becomes unfeasible, requiring in its stead a network of smaller universal elements. In addition, the more adjustable elements a network contains, the more difficult the training task. For these reasons, and for reasons of sheer economy, the number of inputs to a network of universal logic elements cannot be too large.

Although in many applications the number of inputs is large, in most of these situations not all possible configurations of these inputs are of interest—that is, the input environment is constrained—so that this large number of variables is not required for representing the input set. Hence, a preprocessor performing a many-to-few transformation may be employed. The major task of such a preprocessor in going to a smaller number of variables is to keep distinct members of the (constrained) input set distinct, or at least to keep members of distinct classes distinct. (One way to realize the many-to-few transformation of the preprocessor is to use sampling techniques.)

---

* Defined in Sec. III.

† To the authors' knowledge, this is the first such training algorithm for a network of more than one interacting adjustable binary logic element.

‡ These are, respectively, algorithms 1, 2, and 3 of Reference 12.

In addition to having the preprocessor's transformation be many-to-few, we may desire to have the transformation be invariant to certain properties of the input set. For example, in the realm of pattern recognition it could be of interest to have the transformation invariant under translation and, in some cases, invariant under rotation and/or scale change.

Whatever the operation of the preprocessor, its output must be a binary representation of the input pattern, which then serves as the input to the pupil. The pupil is trained to perform a further many-to-few transformation, whereupon each member of an input class is assigned the same output code, and each distinct class is given a distinct code (Fig. 1).

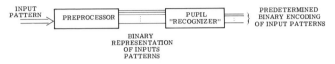

Fig. 1. Recognition system.

The primary reason for following the preprocessor with a (teachable) pupil is the pupil's potential ability to generalize well* over the patterns it does not "see" during training. In any realistic application, not all the possible pertinent patterns will be available during the design phase (or the training phase, in our case) of a recognition system. Thus it is important to have a device that is capable of giving a correct response for patterns that are not used in the design (training) phase.

In the sequel, an application of these techniques to a *character* recognition task is described: the preprocessor in Sec. II, the pupil in Sec. III,† and experimental results in Sec. IV.

The term "opticalogical" in the title refers to the optical nature of the preprocessor and the logic elements of the pupil.

II. Preprocessor

We assume that the pattern given for identification is in the form of a photographic transparency, and speak of the pattern as the amplitude transmission function of the transparency. Facts (1) and (2) of Sec. I tell us that the Fraunhofer diffraction pattern (FDP) of the given pattern will be independent of translation of that pattern (within the optical system's aperture). Therefore, if the FDP is sampled appropriately, a many-to-few transformation insensitive to translation can be performed.

An optical configuration for generating the FDP of an input pattern is shown in Fig. 2. As usual, the FDP is centered on the optical axis of the

* See Sec. III.

† A more complete treatment of the pupil and the training algorithm is given in Reference 12.

system. Since the Fourier transform preserves rotation, if the input pattern is rotated the FDP is rotated about the optical axis but remains otherwise unchanged.

In contrast to the electronic-communication-system analog, the optical image in the frequency plane has two degrees of freedom—that is, two

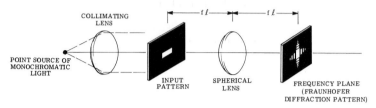

FIG. 2. Coherent Fourier analyzer.

dimensions instead of one. Because of this, the sampling we perform in the frequency plane can be done in a greater variety of ways than in the communication system.

As an example, we can determine the contributions of a particular frequency component, independent of direction, in the input pattern. This can be accomplished in the optical frequency plane by integrating the light amplitude along a circle of appropriate radius centered on the optical axis, and may be repeated for other frequency components by choosing appropriate radii. The resulting data will be independent of rotation.

In principle, such a sampling scheme is carried out by integrating over a (mathematical) line. In practice, of course, this cannot be done. But, because we want only a small number of samples and we want these samples to be insensitive to minute variations (e.g., for noise considerations), it is desirable to make the lines relatively wide to include a band of frequencies simultaneously. In this way, a certain amount of averaging is effected. If, say, m samples are desired, each line can be made $1/m$ units wide, where 1 is the normalized size of the interesting portion of the FDP. We call these lines sampling windows. Typical windows are shown in Fig. 3.

Currently, the integration mentioned above is performed optically and the result is converted to an electrical voltage. After these analog voltages representing the samples are obtained, the problem remains of digitally encoding them with a small number of bits—say one, two, or three bits. For the one-bit encoding, one threshold value has to be determined; for the two-bit encoding, three threshold values; and for the three-bit encoding, seven threshold values. There are many potential bases upon which such threshold determinations can be made—selection will depend upon many factors, including the application at hand.

We direct our attention to the application where the patterns to be recognized are the letters of the English alphabet. We generate and sample the FDP of each of the 26 letters of one type font, yielding $26m$ pieces of analog data, where m is the number of sampling windows. We construct a 26-by-m matrix of these data, where the rows correspond to the letters, and the columns to the sampling windows.

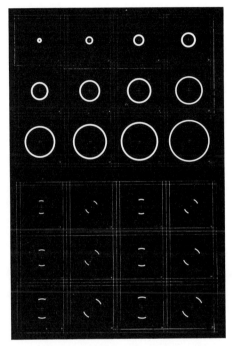

Fɪɢ. 3. Typical sampling windows.

One possibility for determining the encoding thresholds is to scan a row of this matrix to find the maximum and minimum values and establish thresholds to separate the resulting range into two, four, or eight equal parts. Then we assign the appropriate one-, two-, or three-bit code to each entry in the given row, repeating for all rows. Alternatively, the thresholds can be made to separate the members of the row into two, four, or eight equal population classes (e.g., median value for the one-bit case), again repeating for each row. Another method is to perform the above operations on the columns instead of the rows of the matrix. Or, these operations can be performed on the entire matrix, rather than on just rows or columns. The authors have experimentally investigated all six methods. Some of the results are cited in Sec. IV.

As an aid to understanding the over-all operation of the preprocessor, an annotated schematic diagram of the system used initially to determine the feasibility of this approach is shown in Fig. 4.

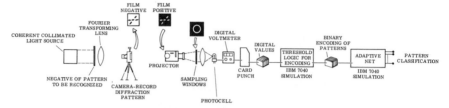

FIG. 4. Annotated schematic of recognition system.

III. Pupil

As mentioned in Sec. I, we have begun a program of investigating structure-dependent properties of networks of adaptive logic elements.[11,12] So that the properties thus obtained would reflect constraints imposed only by the structure and not by the elements, universal logic elements were used as the basic element in these investigations. A universal logic element is an element with m binary inputs and one binary output capable of performing all 2^{2^m} possible switching functions on its m binary inputs. Which of the 2^{2^m} functions the element performs is determined by internal parameter values (changed during training). An m-input universal element is designated by U_m.

The theoretical tool used in these investigations was the Ashenhurst-Curtis theory of decomposition of switching functions[13,14] (hereafter called AC theory). As a starting point, we decided to investigate a cascade type of network (because of the relative ease of applying the AC theory) and to begin with a disjunctive partitioning on the inputs (each external input goes to only one element within the net). This latter decision was based upon a conjecture put forth by Curtis that if a function can be realized disjunctively, then this realization is probably minimal.[14]

The network investigated is shown in Fig. 5. As indicated, the number of

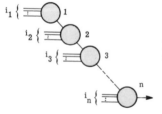

FIG. 5. Pupil: labeled disjunctive cascade network of n universal elements.

inputs to the jth element is given by i_j. A switching function realizable by such a network is called disjunctively decomposable—we therefore call this network a labeled disjunctive cascade network, where the word labeled means that a definite assignment is made for each external input. For notational convenience, we use the acronym LADICAN in place of labeled disjunctive cascade network.

The structure-dependent properties thus far determined for LADICANs are reported in References 11 and 12. Of interest here is the algorithm developed for training LADICANs. This algorithm assures that a solution will be reached in a finite number of iterations, if a solution exists. Basically, the training of the pupil proceeds as follows: An input is given to the pupil, and the resulting output is compared with what the output should be; if it is correct, a positive reinforcement is applied (to all the elements within the net); if it is incorrect, a negative reinforcement is applied. The present theorem of convergence[11] applies to the punish-only type of algorithm—a negative reinforcement is applied when the pupil gives an incorrect response to an input, but none when the response is correct; however, a reward-punish algorithm is being successfully used experimentally.

The LADICAN is used as the pupil in the present character recognition system. The primary reason for using such a device in a recognition system is its potential ability to generalize well. In Reference 12, we discuss the notion of generalization at some length and define a means of expressing generalization quantitatively. We will describe this notion briefly.

Referring to Fig. 6, let A be the set of all possible patterns of n binary variables. Let C be the collection of the patterns that we "care" about—for

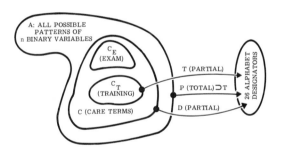

Fig. 6. Model for generalization discussion.

this discussion, we agree to "care" about a pattern if it (somehow) represents a typed letter of the English alphabet (e.g., output of the preprocessor). Let C_T be the collection of care-terms to be used for training the pupil.

At this point, we need the following definitions. Given a function $F(x_1, x_2, \cdots, x_n)$, if a value is assigned by F for each possible n-tuple $(x_1, x_2, \cdots, x_n)$, then F is said to be a *total function*. If there are some n-tuples for which F is undefined, F is called a *partial function*. Given two functions, F and G, with the same independent variables, if for every n-tuple for which F is defined G is also defined and assigns the same value as F, then G is an *extension* of F, denoted $G \supseteq F$. Alternatively, F is a *restriction* of G.

Let D be a partial function which assigns to each member of C an output indicating which letter of the alphabet it is; this function is known *a priori* by the teacher. Let T be a partial function, defined for only the members of C_T, which, like D, assigns to each of these (training) patterns an output indicating which letter it is.

Let the teacher train the pupil until the pupil issues a correct output for, say, each of the patterns in set C_T. Clearly, the pupil will issue *some* output for each input it receives, even for patterns not in C_T. Thus, a function, call it P, defining the input-output operation of the pupil is total. Since the pupil issues the correct output (as specified by T) for each pattern in C_T, P is an extension of T.

We now wish to compare the assignments of P with those of D for each of the care terms not in C_T (call this set C/C_T). Although the word "generalize" has been used to describe the case when all (or some) of these assignments are alike, this use of the word is not precise. The dictionary definition of "generalization" contains no assertion of "correctness." Therefore, any *extension* of a function is a *generalization* of that function. The problem is to compare this generalization with some other function, partial or total, to determine the degree of concurrence, or "correctness," over the set of care terms. No matter what the application, some standard must be used as the basis of an assertion of "correctness."

Assuming partial function D as our standard, we compare P and D for the terms in C/C_T. In practice, C will usually be a very large set. Thus, in general we will not be able to compare P and D for all the care-terms not in C_T. Therefore, any judgment of how well P and D compare in C/C_T will have to be made on the basis of an examination of some subset of these patterns. For this examination, we chose a subset C_E of C/C_T.

Any reasonably precise statement of generalization should include information regarding the size of C_T, the size of C_E, and the number of patterns in each for which P assigns the correct output. (It may turn out that even after training, the pupil will not assign the correct output for each term in C_T.)

Let the number of terms in set C_T be t, and in C_E be e. Let t_c be the number of patterns in C_T for which the pupil gives correct answers, and let e_c be the number of patterns in C_E for which the pupil gives correct answers. The total number of patterns presented to the pupil, then, is $t + e$, and the proportion used during training is $t/(t + e)$.

On this basis, we construct the following expression to express generalization quantitatively:

$$\frac{e_c}{e} \text{ generalization via } \frac{t_c}{t} \text{ training performance on } \frac{t}{t + e} \text{ exposure}$$

It is important to remember that this statement depends upon the exam set C_E. An *a priori* judgment has to be made that the set C_E is representative of the set C/C_T.

For comparing the generalization performance of one teacher-pupil* combination on a training and exam set with that of another combination on the same sets, or of one teacher-pupil combination on several training and exam sets for a constant $t/(t + e)$, we define a *Generalization Ratio*

$$\mathrm{GR} = \frac{e_c/e}{t_c/t}$$

When two Generalization Ratios are compared, it is assumed that either the sets C_T and C_E are held constant with variations occurring in the pupil and/or teacher, or that the pupil-teacher combination is fixed, with variations occurring in the selection of sets C_T and/or C_E for constant $t/(t + e)$. The first assumption is made for the generalization results cited in Sec. IV.

As an example, suppose pupil one has 0.8 generalization via 0.8 training performance on a given exposure, whereas pupil two has 0.8 generalization via 1.0 training performance on the same training exposure. Which pupil did "better" at generalizing? We assert that pupil one did, because it performed as well on the patterns to which it had never been exposed as it did on those of the training set. Pupil two, however, performed less well on the exam set than on the training set. For this illustration,

$$\mathrm{GR} \text{ (pupil one)} = 1.0$$
$$\mathrm{GR} \text{ (pupil two)} = 0.8$$

An examination of these ratios indicates that pupil one did better than pupil two at generalizing.

IV. Experimental Results

We cite a few experimental results to demonstrate the operation of this system.

A. Preprocessor

The first step in the preprocessor is the generation of the Fraunhofer diffraction patterns. The FDP's for the letters shown in Fig. 7 are shown in

FIG. 7. Type font used for FDP's of Fig. 8.

```
A  B   C   D   E   F   G  H  I
J  K   L   M   N   O   P   Q  R
S   T   U   V   W   X   Y  Z
```

Fig. 8. An encoding of these letters via the sampling windows of Fig. 9 is shown in Fig. 10. (There are five windows, each with a 3-bit encoding, yielding a 15-bit unique code for each of the 26 letters. Note that bits one

---

* The teacher, here, is the training algorithm.

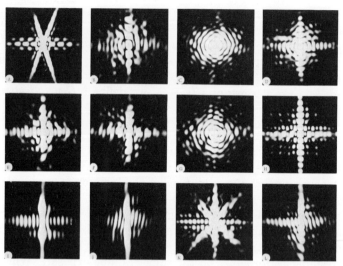

Fɪɢ. 8. (a) Fraunhofer diffraction patterns of letters shown in Fig. 7, letters A to L.

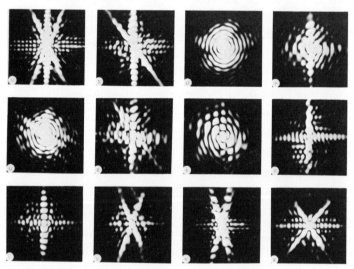

Fɪɢ. 8. (b) Fraunhofer diffraction patterns of letters shown in Fig. 7, letters M to X.

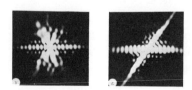

Fɪɢ. 8. (c) Fraunhofer diffraction patterns of letters shown in Fig. 7, letters Y and Z.

FIG. 9. Sampling windows used for encoding FDP's of Fig. 8.

and four, from the left, can be removed, and the resulting 13-bit codes will still be unique.)

A considerable amount of data has been taken on five different alphabet fonts. Eleven different sets of sampling windows were used, and all six methods of encoding were applied. The resulting codes ranged from 15 bits (Fig. 10) to 96 bits. As a rule, the longer codes had a wider Hamming separation.*

FIG. 10. A 15-bit encoding of the letters of Fig. 7 (and Fig. 8) via the sampling windows of Fig. 9.

WINDOW	1	2	3	4	5
A	1 1 0 1 0 1 1 0 1 0 0 1 0 0 1
B	1 1 0 1 0 1 1 0 1 1 0 1 0 1 0
C	1 0 1 1 0 1 1 0 0 0 1 1 1 0 0
D	1 1 0 1 0 1 1 1 1 1 0 1 1 0 0
E	1 0 1 1 0 1 1 0 1 0 1 0 0 0 0
F	1 1 0 1 1 0 1 1 0 1 0 1 1 1 0
G	1 1 0 1 0 1 1 0 1 0 1 1 1 0 0
H	1 0 1 1 1 0 1 1 0 0 1 0 0 1 1
I	1 0 1 1 0 0 1 0 0 1 0 1 0 1 1
J	1 0 0 1 0 0 1 0 0 0 1 1 0 0 1
K	1 1 0 1 1 0 1 1 0 1 0 0 0 1 1
L	1 1 0 1 1 0 1 1 0 1 0 0 0 1 0
M	1 0 0 1 0 1 1 0 1 1 0 0 0 1 0
N	1 1 0 1 1 0 1 0 0 0 1 1 1 0 0
O	1 0 1 1 0 0 0 1 1 0 1 1 1 0 0
P	1 1 0 1 1 1 1 1 1 1 0 1 0 1 1
Q	1 0 1 1 0 1 1 0 0 0 1 1 0 1 1
R	1 0 1 1 0 0 0 1 1 0 0 0 0 0 1
S	1 0 1 1 0 1 1 0 0 0 1 1 0 1 0
T	1 0 1 1 0 1 1 0 0 0 1 0 0 1 0
U	1 1 0 1 0 1 1 0 1 0 0 1 0 1 0
V	1 0 0 1 1 0 1 0 1 1 1 0 1 0 0
W	1 1 0 1 0 1 1 0 1 0 0 1 0 0 0
X	1 1 0 1 1 1 1 0 1 1 1 0 1 0 0
Y	1 0 1 1 0 1 1 0 1 1 0 0 0 1 0
Z	1 1 0 1 1 1 1 0 1 0 1 1 0 1 1

Several of the sampling-window/encoding combinations yielded a distinct code for each letter of a font; and when the five fonts were compared, no different letters had been given the same code. In the experimental work

* The Hamming distance between two codes is the number of bit position at which the codes differ.

to date, a different set of thresholds is computed for each font. In relation to the over-all system, this means that the preprocessor has to be "told" which font it is processing. With improvements that are to be made in the sampling process, and by processing all font data together, this problem should be overcome in future work.

B. Pupil

Various teacher-LADICAN combinations have been subjected to extensive experimentation with unconstrained environments, with the purpose of investigating the effects of various parameters on the relative efficiency of attaining a solution. (These results are given in Reference 11.)

Some experiments were performed to investigate the LADICAN's ability to generalize well. The authors have conjectured* that, for a given number of inputs, the longer the LADICAN used, the larger the generalization ratio will be.

Data for only five fonts were generated via the preprocessor. To give the LADICAN a larger sample over which to generalize, a different method of generating data was used for these experiments. A 4 × 4 grid (Fig. 11) was

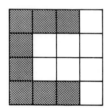

Fig. 11. The 4 × 4 grid used for generating generalization data.

used, and 41 different block C's and 41 different block T's were drawn on the grid in a black-on-white fashion. An encoding of these letters was effected by assigning a 1 to a dark square, and a 0 to a light square. The resulting 16-bit codes were used as inputs to the LADICAN in the generalization experiments.

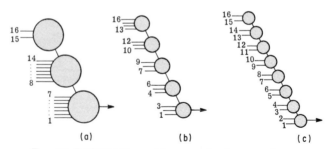

Fig. 12. LADICANs used in generalization experiment.

A training set of 58 patterns was arbitrarily chosen from the 82 patterns; the remaining 24 patterns were used for the exam set. Three networks were

* For reasons to be published later.

Structure	t_c/t	e_c/e	GR
a	1.0	0.834	0.834
b	0.983	0.875	0.890
c	0.776	0.750	0.967

FIG. 13. Results of generalization experiment.

tried (Fig. 12) via a version of algorithm 1 [12] and the results are tabulated in Fig. 13. These data support our conjecture. The 8-element network of Fig. 12c was then trained with another training algorithm (algorithm 3)[12] in an attempt to increase t_c/t, in the belief that GR would remain essentially

FIG. 14. Results of generalization experiment for structure C with higher t_c/t.

Structure C With Different Training Algorithm		
t_c/t	e_c/e	GR
0.948	0.918	0.967

the same. Results of this run are shown in Fig. 14. We note that GR is the same in both cases.

C. System

Finally, experiments were run with the entire system, including both the preprocessor and the postprocessor.

We know that $\log_2 26 = 4.82$. Therefore, at least five binary variables are required to represent the 26 letters of the English alphabet. As was shown in Fig. 5, a LADICAN has only one binary output. To obtain five outputs, we use five LADICANs in parallel where each net receives the same inputs. The outputs of the five nets taken together constitute the five-bit encoding for the letters.

The output code assignment is made *a priori*. It is an experimental fact that the choice of this coding can be important. Specifically, we found that with a consecutive counting-type assignment to the letters (i.e., $A = 00000$, $B = 00001$, $\cdots$, $Z = 11001$), the nets could not learn all five of the resulting functions. When an arbitrary assignment was made (by shuffling IBM cards), the nets learned all five of the functions. These facts serve to point out an area that will require further investigation.

We presented the letters of a given font to the system and trained it to issue the appropriate code (specified by us) for each letter. After training, the system successfully accomplished this task. We trained the pupil with each of the fonts separately, then with two at a time, three at a time, etc. Learning a single font perfectly required approximately 1300 iterations, and learning two fonts required approximately 2600 iterations. The LADICAN used was similar to that of Fig. 12a.

At the time of this writing, the above experiments had been carried out on only one set of data from the preprocessor and that set includes only four alphabet fonts. Unfortunately, in this data set the coding for the letter Y of font 1 (denoted Y_1) turned out to be the same as S_2, and the coding for S_3 the same as F_4.* These results are tabulated in Fig. 15. We list the t_c/t performance on the basis that the entire output codes are correct (i.e., all five LADICANs are correct simultaneously), and on the basis that the individual bits are correct (each LADICAN independently correct or not). An asterisk next to the run means that two distinct letters have the same input code, and hence the pupil cannot be "blamed" for making mistakes on these letters.

Run	Font	t_c/t 5 bits simultaneously	t_c/t Individual bits
1	1	1.00	1.00
2	2	1.00	1.00
3	3	1.00	1.00
4	4	1.00	1.00
5*	1,2	0.982	0.989
6	1,3	0.982	0.997
7	1,4	1.00	1.00
8	2.3	1.00	1.00
9	2,4	0.982	0.997
10*	3,4	0.962	0.997
11*	1,2,3	0.962	0.988
12*	1,2,4	0.936	0.983
13*	1,3,4	0.936	0.988
14*	2,3,4	0.936	0.985
15*	1,2,3,4	0.856	0.967

FIG. 15. Results of training system to recognize fonts of English alphabet.

The importance of the data in the last column of this table is that, since so few bits are wrong, perhaps some error-correcting scheme can be devised to improve the recognition. The attendant requirement of longer codes can be realized by adding a few more LADICANs in parallel. This process might also prove fruitful for generalization.

V. Conclusions

This paper has discussed one approach to the pattern recognition problem. Basically, the approach involves the use of an electro-optical preprocessor, and a postprocessor made up of binary logic elements. At this level of description, the approach is not new. Investigators at Stanford Research Institute are working on a recognition machine which is similarly structured.[15] It, too, incorporates an electro-optical preprocessor and an adaptive postprocessor. The differences lie in the realization of the two parts. Their preprocessor samples the original patterns, whereas ours samples the two-dimensional Fourier transform of the patterns. Their main

* This is unfortunate from the point of view of trying to use these data to have the pupil learn the font perfectly. However, if we consider this ambiguity as noise in the teacher-to-pupil channel, Fig. 15 shows us that the pupil's performance did not deteriorate beyond the ambiguity induced by this noise.

processor uses the threshold logic unit as the basic binary logic element; ours uses the universal logic element. The training of their main processor depends upon a basic one-element convergence theorem; ours depends on our two-element convergence theorem (extendable to n elements under suitable conditions).

Experimental results with our system, although meager, are encouraging. Present indications are that the type of sampling windows to use depend upon the given task and, perhaps, upon the characteristics of the data on which this task is to be performed. Further, attention will have to be given to the following questions:

1. In what order are the preprocessor outputs to be connected to the postprocessor?

2. How can the postprocessor output coding be selected to enhance the chances of obtaining a function realizable by the adaptive net and/or to enhance the generalization of the postprocessor?

REFERENCES

1. BORN, M., AND E. WOLF, *Principles of Optics*, Pergamon Press, New York, 1959.
2. PAPOULIS, A., *The Fourier Integral and Its Applications*, McGraw-Hill Book Co., Inc., New York, 1962.
3. ELIAS, P., D. GREY, AND D. ROBINSON, "The Fourier Treatment of Optical Processes," *J. Opt. Soc. Am.*, *42*, No. 2, 127–134 (February 1952).
4. CHEATHAM, T., AND A. KOHLENBERG, "Optical Filters, Their Equivalence to and Difference from Electrical Networks," *IRE Nat. Conv. Record*, *2*, Part 4, 6–12 (1954).
5. O'NEILL, E., "Spatial Filtering in Optics," *IRE Trans. Inform. Theory*, *IT-2*, 56–65 (June 1956).
6. AROYAN, G., "The Technique of Spatial Filtering," *Proc. IRE*, *47*, 1561–1568 (September 1959).
7. CUTRONA, L., E. LEITH, C. PALERMO, AND L. PORCELLO, "Optical Data Processing and Filtering Systems," *IRE Trans. Inform. Theory*, *IT-6*, 386–400 (June 1960).
8. HOROWITZ, L., AND G. SHELDON, "Pattern Recognition Using Auto-Correlation," *Proc. IRE*, *49*, 175–185 (January 1961).
9. VANDER LUGT, A., AND F. ROTZ, "Data Reduction by Coherent Optical Systems," *SPIE Proceedings*, Photo-Optical Data Reduction Seminar (March 1964).
10. VANDER LUGT, A., "Signal Detection by Complex Spatial Filtering," *IRE Trans. Inform. Theory*, *IT-10*, 139–145 (April 1964).
11. LENDARIS, G. G., AND G. L. STANLEY, *On the Structure-Dependent Properties of Adaptive Logic Networks*, GM Defense Research Laboratories Technical Report, TR63-219, July 1963 (this report is available by writing to the authors at GM DRL, Box T, Santa Barbara, California).
12. LENDARIS, G. G., AND G. L. STANLEY, "Self-Organization: Meaning and Means," *Information System Sciences: Proceedings of the Second Congress*, Spartan Books, Inc., Baltimore, Md., 1965.
13. ASHENHURST, R. L., "The Decomposition of Switching Functions," *Proceedings of an International Symposium on the Theory of Switching*, Harvard University Press, 1959.

14. CURTIS, H. A., *A New Approach to the Design of Switching Circuits*, D. Van Nostrand Co., Inc., Princeton, N.J., 1962.

15. ROSEN, C. A., *et al.*, *Graphical Data Processing Research Study and Experimental Investigations*, Stanford Research Institute, Reports 1–11, Menlo Park, Calif., 1960–1963.

CHAPTER 30

WIDEBAND READOUT OF THERMOPLASTIC RECORDINGS

K. F. Wallace

Ampex Corporation, Redwood City, California

Introduction

The rapid advance of modern technology has in recent years brought with it a great need for storing large quantities of information as rapidly as possible in the smallest possible space. One recording system utilizing an electron beam which offers promise of achieving great packing densities and also bandwidth is thermoplastic recording.[1] It has been shown that thermoplastic recording media have adequate sensitivity to allow information to be recorded by an electron beam at bandwidth approaching 50 Mc. It is, therefore, highly desirable to be able to regain the recorded information from a thermoplastic film into an electrical form at comparable bandwidth.

Electro-Optical Readout

A thermoplastic recording may be viewed with a relatively simple optical system such as a schlieren projector. This then suggests that well-known electro-optical readout methods such as flying spot scanners and camera tubes would lend themselves to reforming the recording into an electrical form. Camera tubes, however, are all basically optical integrators, and although bandwidths of 50 Mc can be achieved by their use, they do not lend themselves to the rapid scene changes which would be required for this application.

The flying spot scanner readout does lend itself to wide bandwidth but suffers from two fundamental limitations. The first limitation is that the phosphors presently available and used to generate a flying spot scan do not decay instantaneously to zero after the electron beam has moved to the next picture element. This, in practice, sets a limitation of some 10 to 15 Mc in bandwidth. The second and more fundamental limitation is that the optical efficiency is very poor. It must be realized that the signal-to-noise ratio (S/N) of any system is governed by the minimum number of particles per unit time or per unit area. In the case of photographic film, for example, the number of grains of silver that are deposited in a given area of the film determines S/N. In the case of the flying spot scanner, the amount of light that is obtained at the cathode-ray tube is limited by fundamental considerations of cathode brightness and image size in the cathode-ray tube. It is therefore very important to maintain the maximum possible brightness or number of photons per unit time throughout the system. Figure 1 illustrates why the optical efficiency of a flying spot scanner is very poor.

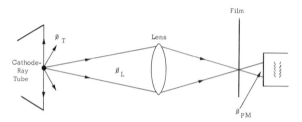

FIG. 1. Optical efficiency of flying spot scanner.

The over-all optical efficiency of the system may be calculated in the following manner. From fundamental lens laws we obtain

$$L = \frac{F(1 + M)}{M}$$

where

L = the object distance
F = the focal length of the lens
M = the magnification of the object at the image

Now

N = the lens number at infinity (f number)

$$N = \frac{F}{D},$$ where D is the diameter of the lens

$$D = \frac{F}{N}$$

The light gathered by the lens, ϕ_L, is expressed as a ratio of the total light available, ϕ_T.

$$\phi_L = \frac{\frac{\pi D^2}{4} \phi_T}{4\pi L^2}$$

$$= \frac{\pi \left(\dfrac{F}{N}\right)^2}{4.4\pi \left[\dfrac{F(1+M)}{M}\right]^2} \phi_T$$

$$= \left(\frac{M}{4N(1+M)}\right)^2 \phi_T$$

The flux that reaches the photomultiplier is further attenuated by the optical system:

$$\frac{\phi_{PM}}{\phi_T} = \left[\frac{M}{4N(1+M)}\right]^2 K_0$$

where

ϕ_{PM} = light flux reaching of the photomultiplier
K_0 = attenuation constant of the optical system

From this equation it can be seen that, for an average optical system (where $M = 1$, $N = 2.8$), approximately 0.1 per cent of the useful light reaches the photomultiplier. It should be noted in passing that this calculation is not the same as the calculation for brightness, since brightness does not enter the S/N value at the photocathode.

Secondary Emission Readout

Figure 2 indicates dimensions of the type of thermoplastic recording used for readout experiments. The slopes of the thermoplastic grooves are of adequate steepness to cause variations in secondary electron emission.

If an electron beam impinges on the surface of a solid material, electrons

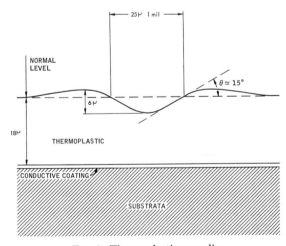

FIG. 2. Thermoplastic recording.

are emitted from its surface. The number of electrons emitted, and their energies, depends upon the manner of collision and the surface characteristics of the material. A small number of the primary electrons which collide with the material particles will be scattered and their direction changed by angles greater than 90°. They reappear as reflected electrons, which have energies very nearly equal to the primary energy. The majority of electrons that are emitted, however, are not at these high energies and are the true secondary electrons. For the purposes of this discussion, the complications of the various types of electrons, such as back-diffused electrons in elastically scattered primaries, etc., are ignored, and the total emission from the thermoplastic is assumed to consist of secondary electrons.

There are two possible ways of utilizing the characteristics of secondary emitted electrons for detecting the surface variations of the recording. The first method is similar to the technique used in scanning electron microscopes for examining specimens.[2] In this form of readout, all the secondary electrons would be collected, and the fact would be utilized that the secondary emission varies as the secant of the angle of incidence. Figures 3a and 3b illustrate this scheme. By placing the film at a large angle with

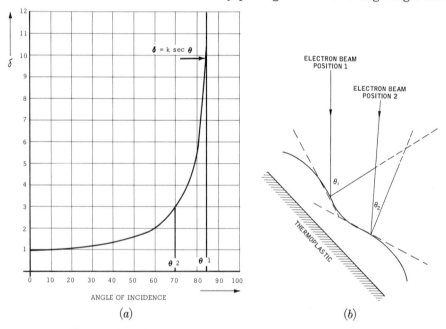

Fig. 3. (a) Angle of incidence readout. (b) Angle of incidence readout.

respect to the primary electron beam, the output current, which would be proportional to the secondary emission ratio δ, would correspond to the values shown as θ_1 and θ_2 with regard to the two beam positions, position 1 and position 2. Because the film has to be positioned at a rather large angle with regard to the primary electron beam, only a one-dimensional scan is practical. Furthermore, the practicalities of obtaining error signals so as to maintain the electron beam on the recorded track become extremely difficult.

The adopted method of readout relies on the distribution of the secondary electrons from the surface of the material rather than on the angle of incidence. Figure 4a shows the cosine distribution of the secondary elec-

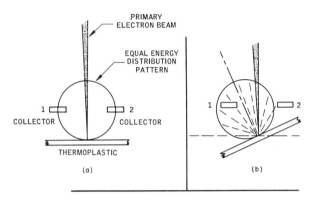

Fig. 4. (a) Cosine readout. (b) Cosine readout.

trons. The greatest number of electrons comes from the material at 90° with respect to the surface and as the angle is decreased, fewer electrons are obtained because of internal absorption of the secondary electrons within the material itself. If we now examine Fig. 4a and place two collectors in the stream of secondary electrons, then, when they are equally spaced from the material and no recording is present, an equal current will flow to collectors one and two. If, however, the side of the thermoplastic tract is bombarded by the primary electron beam (shown as the tilted film in Fig. 4b), then collector plate 1 receives more electrons than collector plate 2. Therefore, one has obtained a variation in secondary electron current as some function of the angle of the recorded film. Furthermore, if the beam is made wide enough to strike both sides of the recording at the same time, current collected by collector plates 1 and 2 will vary as the slopes of both sides of the thermoplastic recording are changed. This difference in current is used to servo the electron beam along the groove center.

The manner in which the output signal and servo signals can be processed is shown in the block diagram of Fig. 5. Here the difference signal $(A - B)$ is fed through an appropriate phase correction network to the deflection

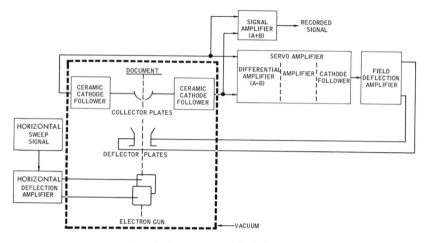

FIG. 5. Servo system block diagram.

plates which govern the scan in the plane parallel to the motion of the tape. In order to obtain a good packing density, the recording is made in a continuous raster fashion analogous to Videotape* recording.

Collector Design

In Fig. 6 the primary beam I_p strikes the document at the normal, and the document is then tilted by an angle θ. Let ϕ_1 and ϕ_2 be the extremities

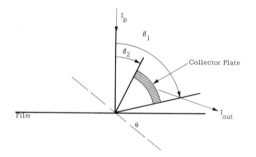

FIG. 6. Collector plate design.

of the collection area by which the secondary electrons are collected. In the general case, due to normal secondary emission,

$$I_{\text{out}} = I_p \delta \int \cos \phi \, d\phi$$

The output signal current I_s will be $I_s = I'_{\text{out}} - I_{\text{out}}$ where I'_{out} equals the collected current when the document is tilted by the angle θ. But when the

* Trademark of the Ampex Corporation.

document is tilted by θ, the factor δ will change to $\delta' = (\delta/\cos\theta)$. Therefore,

$$I_s = I_p\left\{\delta'\int_{\phi_2-\theta}^{\phi_1-\theta}\cos\phi\,d\phi - \delta\int_{\phi_2-}^{\phi_1-}\cos\phi\,d\phi\right\}$$

$$= I_p\delta\left\{\left[\frac{\sin(\phi_1-\theta)-\sin(\phi_2-\theta)}{\cos\theta}\right]-\left[\sin\phi_1-\sin\phi_2\right]\right\}$$

$$I_s = I_p\delta\tan\theta\{\cos\phi_2 - \cos\phi_1\} = \text{output signal}$$

This calculation shows that the linearity of the system is proportional to the tangent of the recorded angle. Note that no mention is made of the linearity of the recording relative to the initial signal. The concern here is merely the amount of distortion added to the system by the readout process.

Signal-to-Noise Ratio Considerations

The calculation of the best shape for the geometry of the collectors takes no account of the system S/N to be expected. If the amplifier which follows the collector plates generates a large amount of noise, then the best S/N is obtained when the output signal is greatest. If, however, the output amplifier generates very little noise, then it is not necessarily true that the maximum output signal is the one that gives the best S/N.

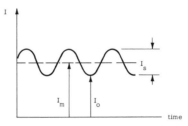

FIG. 7. Signal-to-noise ratio of collection.

In Fig. 7,

$$I_s = \text{peak-to-peak output signal}$$
$$I_0 = \text{standing current}$$
$$I_m = \text{mean current}$$

$$\text{rms signal} = \frac{I_s}{2\sqrt{2}}$$

and $(\text{noise current})^2 = 2eBI_m$

where B is the bandwidth and e the charge of an electron. Therefore,

$$\left(\frac{S}{N}\right)^2 = \frac{\left(\dfrac{I_s}{2\sqrt{2}}\right)^2}{2eBI_m}$$

but

$$I_m = I_0 + \frac{I_s}{2}$$

so that

$$\left(\frac{S}{N}\right)^2 = \frac{I_p\delta[\tan\theta(\cos\phi_2 - \cos\phi_1)]^2}{16eB\left\{\sin\phi_1 - \sin\phi_2 + \dfrac{\tan\theta(\cos\phi_2 - \cos\phi_1)}{2}\right\}}$$

$$\left(\frac{S}{N}\right)^2 = \frac{I_p\delta}{16eB}\left\{\frac{\tan^2\theta(\cos\phi_2 - \cos\phi_1)^2}{\sin\phi_1 - \sin\phi_2 + \dfrac{\tan\theta(\cos\phi_2 - \cos\phi_1)}{2}}\right\}$$

Hence, if the collecting area is extended to 90°, $\cos\phi_1 = 0$,

$$\left(\frac{S}{N}\right)^2 = \frac{I_p\delta}{16eB}\left\{\frac{\tan^2\theta\cos^2\phi_2}{1 - \sin\phi_2 + \dfrac{\tan\theta\cos\phi_2}{2}}\right\}$$

The result of this calculation of optimum collector plate design with regard to S/N is shown as a plot in Fig. 8. It is evident the condition at which the maximum output signal is obtained is not the optimum S/N condition.

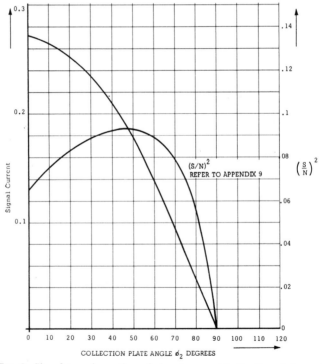

FIG. 8. Signal-to-noise ratio and signal current/collection plate angle.

Bandwidth Capability

Another point of concern with this secondary emission readout system is whether it is capable of providing adequate bandwidth. Here, the fundamental limitation is the transit time spread of the secondary electrons between the film and the collection system.

FIG. 9. Transit time of electrons in collection systems.

In Fig. 9, the transit time may be calculated in the following manner:

$$D = ut + \frac{1}{2} At^2$$

where

$u =$ the initial velocity in m/sec
$t =$ the transit time in seconds
$A =$ the acceleration
$D =$ the distance

$$D = \sqrt{\frac{2eV}{m}}\, t + \frac{1}{2} \cdot \frac{e}{m} \cdot E t^2$$

where

$e =$ charge of an electron $= 1.6 \times 10^{-19}$ C
$V =$ the potential in volts
$m =$ the mass of an electron in kg $= 9.1 \times 10^{-31}$
$E =$ the electric field strength in V/m

$$t = \frac{\sqrt{\frac{2e}{m} V} \sqrt{\frac{2e}{m} V + \frac{4}{2} \frac{e}{m} ED}}{\frac{e}{m} \cdot E}$$

$$t = \frac{1}{E} \sqrt{\frac{2m}{e} V} \left\{ \sqrt{1 + \frac{ED}{V}} - 1 \right\}$$

$$t = 3.38 \times 10^{-6} \sqrt{\frac{V}{E}} \left\{ \sqrt{1 + \frac{ED}{V}} - 1 \right\}$$

Figure 10 shows a plot of the transit time of various energy electrons as a function of a small accelerating potential placed between the collector plate and the film. The outline shows the transit time of the electrons which are emitted from the film with zero initial energy. The 5-kV-electron plot represents the reflected primaries. Thus, the total possible transit time spread is the difference between the zero energy and primary electron beam energies described between these two lines. It was estimated that most of the electrons coming from the surface were being liberated with about a 4-eV energy. This line has also been plotted.

Experiments showed that the maximum energy of the secondary electrons was 30 eV. This was shown by putting a negative potential on the

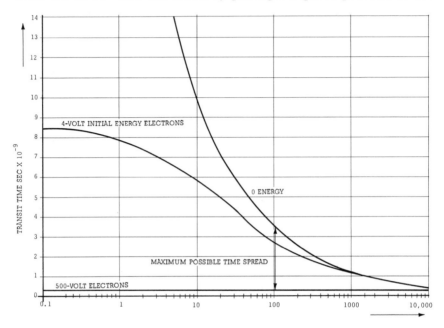

FIG. 10. Acceleration applied to collectors-volts.

accelerator and seeing when the current fell to zero. From these considerations of transit time, it can be seen that a 100-V accelerating potential will make the total transit time spread of the system approximately 3 nsec. This would be adequate for a 100-Mc response, and as such the theoretical limitations of the system could be extended beyond this bandwidth.

Signal Amplification

The need to amplify the extremely small currents (of the order of 10^{-7} A) at bandwidths of 50 Mc introduces a grave problem. The first approach to this problem was to make collector plates of extremely low capacity by placing a guard shield around them and feeding the output of a cathode follower to the guard shield. This technique reduces the total effect of the collector plate capacity to about 2 pF. However, even such low capacities still cause a serious limitation to the amplification and noise of the system. Calculations of the noise generated by the load resistor, which is placed in the amplifying system for optimum S/N, show that with the over-all system, a primary beam current of 1.2 μA is required for a 40 dB S/N at 50 Mc. This current is approximately 10 times greater than the current that would be required to generate a 40 dB S/N at 50 Mc with a noise-free amplifier when calculating the signal-to-noise ratio,

$$\frac{S}{N} = \sqrt{\frac{I}{2eB}}$$

A low-noise amplifier for detecting nanoampere currents was described for use on scanning electron microscopes.[3] This method of amplification was adopted. It consists of collecting secondary electrons, accelerating them to an energy of approximately 10 keV, and then making the electrons strike a plastic scintillator.[4] This plastic scintillator converts the electron energy to photon energy with a quantum efficiency greater than unity. The generated light is then transmitted to a photomultiplier. The outline scheme is shown in Fig. 11. The merit of this system lies in the short decay

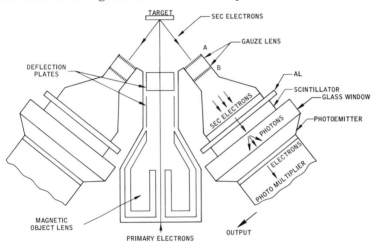

FIG. 11. Scintillator readout head in defocused form.

time of the plastic scintillators (about 3 nsec). Therefore, the bandwidth limitations of the system including the photomultipliers are well in excess of 50 Mc. Furthermore, the noise introduced in the system is extremely small, since the quantum efficiency of the scintillator and the quantum efficiency of the photocathode in the photomultiplier combination gives an effective gain of approximately unity. Thus, for every secondary electron reaching the entry port in the collector system, approximately one photo-electron is emitted from the photocathode of the photomultiplier. Thus, a noise factor of about 3 dB is achieved at a bandwidth in excess of 50 Mc.

Figure 12 shows one such system which was built; it is a direct adaptation of the scanning electron microscope technique. This system suffered one serious disadvantage in that the current density at the surface of the

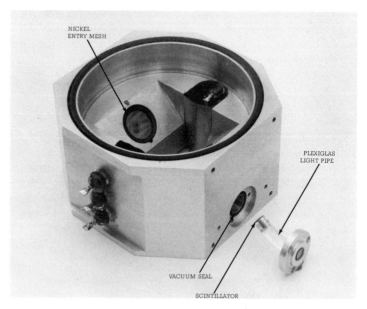

FIG. 12. Focused scintillator head.

scintillator was excessively high, and the life of the scintillator proved to be a matter of seconds. A redesign of the collection head was then undertaken, and the components are shown in Fig. 13. The new assembly was designed so as to diffuse the accelerated secondary electrons over a very

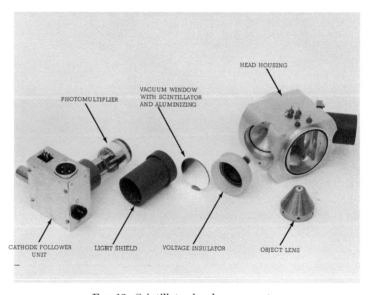

FIG. 13. Scintillator head components.

large area, thereby extending the life of the plastic scintillator to many hours. Experimental evidence showed that a current density of the order of 10^{15} electrons per centimeter squared would deteriorate the scintillator to approximately half light output.

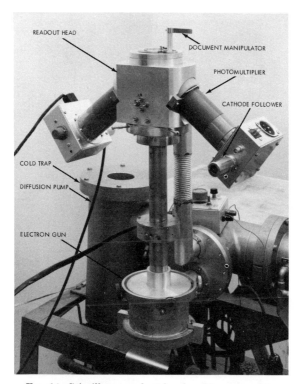

FIG. 14. Scintillator readout head and gun assembly.

Figure 14 shows the complete readout assembly. The electron source is at the lower end of the electron gun structure. The focus coil and readout head assembly are at the top of the structure; the photomultipliers are on both sides of the electron gun.

Results

Figure 15 shows the output of the servo channel. The electron beam was scanning a specially prepared test target which had the Y-scan made to represent errors in tape velocity. At the center of the photograph is the retrace of the electron beam, at which time the servo information is missing, causing the system to set to the initial position. In addition to the sine wave output there is a large sawtooth component which is the skew of the target relative to the mean position of the Y-deflection plates. The total error of the alignment of the beam relative to a straight line corresponds to some 15 spot diameters of deflection. In practice this amount of error would be excessive for a good tape transport. Figure 16 shows the frequency response of the system at 10, 25, and 50 Mc outputs corresponding

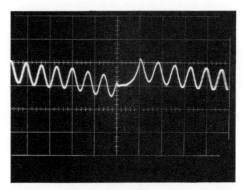

FIG. 15. Output of electron beam servo amplifier. *Y* modulation shown corresponds to 15 spot diameters. Interruption at center of picture caused by line retrace and skew document point.

to the top, middle, and bottom trace, respectively. The output is taken directly from the photomultiplier and has no frequency compensation. Subsequent work has shown that the photomultipliers used when operating in the specific conditions of low gain were causing the loss in amplitude at

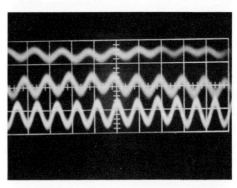

FIG. 16. Frequency response of an uncompensated system. Beam current 0.5 μA. 1-mil recording. Top trace: 10 Mc/cm. Middle trace: 25 Mc/cm. Bottom trace: 50 Mc/cm.

50 Mc. Figure 17 shows the output frequency of approximately 60 Mc with an *S/N* estimated to be better than 20 dB. The widening of the lines in the photograph is caused by the time base jitter. Several traces had to be taken, since an oscilloscope capable of single trace photography at these frequencies was not available.

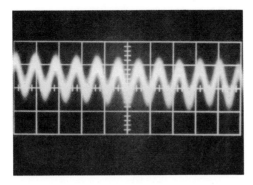

Fig. 17. 60-Mc output. Beam current 0.5 μA. Time base 20 nsec/cm.

Conclusions

A 50-Mc readout scheme of thermoplastic recording is feasible when relatively large beam diameters (of the order of 1 mil) are used. The signal amplification system is adequate for bandwidth in excess of 100 Mc. The fundamental recording system does, however, introduce a severe limitation in that the output signal with no recording present is still a large percentage of the maximum obtainable output signal and as such introduces considerable noise (i.e., the modulation index is low).

Acknowledgments

The work described in this paper was undertaken at the Ampex Research Laboratories in Redwood City, California. The program was sponsored by Air Research and Development Command, Rome Air Development Center, Griffiss Air Force Base, New York, under Air Force Contract AF30(602)2474, 27 March 1961. I am deeply indebted to J. Voss and J. Herbert, who undertook much of the painstaking work, and to E. Boblett and T. Everhart, without whose frequent consultations and whose original work, the program could not have been undertaken. I also wish to thank Mr. W. Moore and Mr. M. Bramer of Rome Air Development Center for sponsorship and encouragement of the work.

References

1. Glenn, W. E., "Thermoplastic Recording," *J. Soc. Motion Picture Television Engrs.*, *69*, No. 9, 577–580 (1960).
2. Zworykin *et al.*, *Electron Optics and the Electron Microscope*, Fourth Printing, John Wiley & Sons, Inc., New York, 1957, pp. 98–106.
3. Everhart, T. E., and R. F. M. Thornley, "Wideband Detector for Micro-Micro-ampere Low Energy Electron Detection," *J. Sci. Instr.*, *37*, 246–248 (1960).
4. Birks, J. B., *Scintillation Counters*, Pergamon Press, New York, 1960, pp. 102–103.

CHAPTER 31

PHOTOCHROMIC, HIGH-SPEED, LARGE CAPACITY, SEMIRANDOM ACCESS MEMORY

A. Reich

Military Systems Division, (LEC) Lockheed Electronics Co., Plainfield, New Jersey

and G. H. Dorion

American Cyanamid Company, Central Research Division, Stamford, Connecticut

Introduction to Photochromic Materials

The property of certain dyes and other chemical compounds to exhibit a *reversible* change in their absorption spectrum upon irradiation with specific wavelengths of light has been termed *phototropism*, or *photochromism*. The emphasis in this definition is on *reversibility*, because, upon removal of the activating radiation the systems must revert to their original states to be considered photochromic. Figure 1 describes the general equation for photochromic reactions and some performance definitions.

$$A \underset{h\nu_2}{\overset{h\nu_1}{\rightleftarrows}} B \quad \text{PLUS IRREVERSIBLE PRODUCTS}$$
$$\text{AND OR HEAT}$$

SENSITIVITY	(SWITCHING TIME), CHANGE IN OPTICAL DENSITY (LOG $\frac{T_0}{T}$) BY A GIVEN UNIT OF EXPOSURE (E = I x t).
PERSISTENCE	MEAN LIFETIME (T) OF B STATE IN THE DARK OR UNDER GIVEN VIEWING CONDITIONS.
STABILITY	OVER–ALL PHOTOCHROMIC STABILITY, USEFUL LIFETIME.

FIG. 1. Photochromic performance.

The use of photochromism in various data storage applications can be contemplated. For example, photochromic coatings can be applied to paper or clear film backings for use as image recording media. Plastic panels can also be fabricated, or glass panels can be coated with a thin photochromic layer. In all these devices, ultraviolet light will cause a color development

567

dependent on the incident light energy, which, as in normal photographic processes, is dependent on the intensity and time of exposure.

In these applications of the photochromic phenomenon, there would be no "grain" to the film since we have a molecular coating rather than, as in the case of silver halides, a grain dispersion in a gel. Thus, optical resolution should be much greater. On the other hand, the reversible nature of the phenomenon will give only a temporary image. This reversibility and the fact that the color development is a "dry" process might indicate many interesting uses where a quick positive or negative image is desired.

General Performance of Photochromic Materials

Each potential application, military or nonmilitary, has its own specific requirements as to quality of color change, rates of change in either direction, and over-all photochemical stability or resistance to fatigue. Photochromic compounds, therefore, must be carefully selected and tailored to suit their particular use. In attempting to select a suitable compound, one is confronted with a wide choice. Photochromism has been observed in organic and inorganic compounds, both in solution and in the solid state. But, although several hundred compounds have already been reported, the mechanisms of relatively few have been completely worked out. The better known types include photoinduced tautomerizations; heterolytic bond cleavage reactions; reduction oxidation reactions; *cis-trans* isomerizations.

In general, with the exception of *cis-trans* isomerizations, the spectral changes involve a bathochromic shift from the ultraviolet regions to the visible regions.

While it is apparent that a diverse variety of mechanisms can produce a photochromic effect, they do have a common basis in that they all involve bistable atoms or molecules. That is, there are atoms or molecules capable of "switching" between two distinct states A and B, which represent different atomic, molecular, or electronic configurations. It is the alterations to the electronic orbital structure which accompany these atomic or molecular changes that lead to the apparent spectral shifts within or between the ultraviolet and visible regions.

These shifts can be represented in a simplified form as is shown in Fig. 1 in which the frequency of light activating the A to B conversion is given by ν_1. Figure 2 shows the typical response of a photochromic compound to a pulse of activating light. Initially, a stationary condition exists in which the A state of the compound predominates. At time t_1 the activating energy is applied, producing an increase in the proportion of atoms or molecules in the B state. If, at time t_2, the activating energy source is removed, a spontaneous reversion to the initial condition will occur.

Photochromic behavior is kinetic. Taking A-to-B conversion process by itself, one finds that only certain wavelengths of light will activate it. To be active these wavelengths must meet two basic requirements. They must be absorbed by the A state of the photochromic chemical, and they must also be of sufficient energy to permit the photochromic species to pass over the most favorable minimum energy reaction path during conversion from the A state to the B state. For molecular rearrangements which involve the breaking of chemical bonds, the energy required would correspond to the photons of ultraviolet light absorbed.

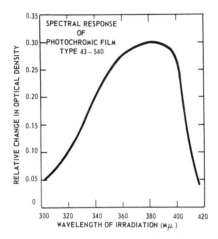

FIG. 2. Exposure characteristics of photochromic films.

According to Einstein's photoequivalence law, each absorbed photon activates one atom or molecule. In general, the rate of the A-to-B conversion process is governed by the rate at which active photons are absorbed. This, in turn, is a function of the flux density of the incident active radiation, the concentration and extinction coefficients of the photochromic species in the A state, the optical path, and the "blocking action" of other absorbing species which can compete for the active photons. But even in the absence of other competitive absorbing species, each active photon absorbed will, on the average, produce less than one A to B conversion. This is because only a certain percentage of the photoactivated species will be deactivated to the B state. Competing deactivation processes which tend to lower the yield of B include radiationless collisional deactivations back to the A state, irreversible chemical side reactions (fatigue), and in some instances fluorescent and phosphorescent deactivations (emission processes).

It is generally accepted that the reversion process, like any thermal process, proceeds via a "transition" state of higher energy than either the A or the B state. This means that a thermal energy barrier must be overcome when the B state reverts to the A state. It is this thermal energy barrier which gives rise to the temperature dependence of photochromic behavior. For example, should a photochromic compound be irradiated continuously at a sufficiently low temperature to suppress completely the thermal reversion process, all the atoms or molecules would eventually be trapped in the B state. They would remain trapped in that state indefinitely, even after the light source was removed.

Dependence of Performance on General Conditions of Exposure

The maximum optical density change at wavelength λ_{max}, $D_m(\lambda_m)$, of which a photochromic material is capable, is (aside from intrinsic properties of the active component) primarily governed by the position of the photochemical equilibrium between the colorless and colored form of the active component under excitation conditions. The position of the equilibrium will therefore depend on the intensity as well as the relative composition of the radiation reaching the photochromic material from the exciting uv source. As a result, the performance of a photochromic material will very markedly depend on the characteristics of the "switching" source. For optimum results, the output of this source should correspond to the spectral sensitivity of the photochromic film. Performance can be improved further if during exposure the temperature of the photochromic film is prevented from rising appreciably above room temperature. Under exposure, the position of the photochemical equilibrium, i.e., the maximum optical density toward which the photochromic layer tends, is depressed as the temperature increases. Furthermore, the rate of spontaneous reversal to the colorless condition after termination of the exposure will be enhanced by an increase in temperature as shown in Fig. 3 for two formulations.

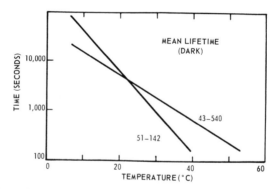

Fig. 3. Rate of spontaneous reversal to the colorless condition after termination of the exposure.

Accordingly, the lower the temperature, the more effective will be the response of the photochromic film.

Figure 4 shows the response characteristics of two photochromic formulations under stated exposure conditions. It also indicates the difference in response for identical formulations, differing in the concentration of photochromic dye.

Figure 5 shows the absorption spectra, before and after activation, of another photochromic material, Type 63-071. In this case the activating

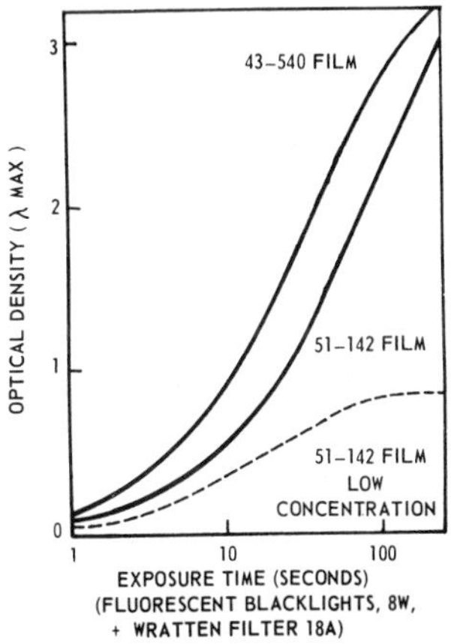

FIG. 4. Response characteristics of two photochromic formulations.

spectrum, shown by the dashed curve, is peaked in the blue visible at 4800 Å and falls off rapidly at the long wavelength end to substantially zero at 5700 Å. The irradiated B form has an absorption peak at 6000 Å, which in effect, denotes the peak change in optical density in this region.

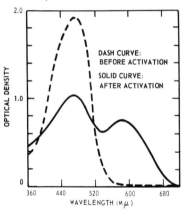

FIG. 5. Absorption spectra of blue-sensitive type photochromic film (room temperature).

To the eye, the material changes from a yellow-orange color to a blue-gray. This photochromic material will form the basis of the ensuing system discussions.

Advantages in Memory Systems

Photochromic materials can be considered for use in high-speed, large-capacity memories for a number of reasons.

1. The cost per bit can be extremely low.

2. After exposure of the photochromic system (to the writing beam) no development or fixing procedures are necessary to produce "switching" action.

3. Photochromic media can be employed for many write-erase-rewrite cycles and give almost nondestructive read.

4. Appropriate photochromic systems can retain stored data without power consumption. If necessary, the photochromic memory plane could be removed from the system with its data intact and another memory plane substituted. The memory can probably be designed to be stored for quite a long time.

5. The photochromic medium has extremely large storage capacity latently available in physically small dimensions. The basic photochromic switches are the molecules themselves. Each molecule can be in either of two states—absorbing or nonabsorbing (to the read beam), thus manifesting a binary character.

Molecular linear dimensions are generally in the 1 to 10 angstrom range. Therefore a monomolecular film of photochromic dye would contain on the order of 10^{14} molecules/cm^2 for an assumption of contiguous arrangement. If the system could be designed to uniquely write, read, and erase molecule by molecule and effect perfect registration, the latent capacity would be 10^{14} bits/cm^2 of surface. Obviously, with present technology this inherent capacity cannot be realized, or even approached. If the writing, reading, and erasing procedures are to be carried out by use of appropriate light beams, then the stated bit capacity shrinks markedly. The highest conservation of capacity requires the use of light beams of large energy density, such as focused laser beams. The beam can, at best (because of diffraction effects and speed of optics), be focused into a spot whose diameter is of the order of the wavelength of the light in the beam itself. The usual write beam is of ultraviolet or visible blue nature, the read beam is in the visible range, and the erase beam in the near infrared. The erase beam will then usually have the largest focused spot, and so control the maximum latent capacity. If this beam is assumed to operate at 1μ ($= 10^{-4}$ cm) then, at best, 10^8 spots can be focused side-by-side in a square centimeter of surface. A more realistic assessment, scaling down the linear figure by a factor of 10 so that spillover, halation, and registration restrictions would not be impossibly severe, still results in a contiguous bit density of 10^6/cm^2. For the near term a noncontiguous arrangement of 10^4 to 10^5/cm^2 would still constitute a good achievement.

6. The read-write-erase functions employed with the photochromic memory can probably be nonmechanical in nature, with no moving parts or vacuum techniques necessary.

7. The switching-speed of photochromic materials is inherently great.

As stated, the molecular switches can "flip" in times between 10^{-13} and 10^{-7} sec, depending upon the internal mechanism involved. The requirement for very large bit capacity brings along with it a concurrent limitation to extremely small bit size. The read system must then be devised to read the proper state as manifested by a comparatively small number of molecules. Fortunately, this moves the macroscopic switching speed constants toward values characteristic of the molecular level. The energy required to develop a given optical density change has been measured in specific dye systems and, where pertinent, will be indicated further on.

Acoustic Scanning of Light

The memory configurations to be presented make use of modulated laser beams of appropriate spectral content to perform the write and erase functions on a photochromic film plane. It will be necessary to scan the photochromic plane very quickly and accurately, with an extremely fine pinpoint of light. Lockheed Electronics has been exploring a method of rapidly deflecting a laser beam, nonmechanically, in two dimensions. The technique is based on refraction of the beam by acoustic energy.

Consider the configuration in Fig. 6. An acoustic wave can be generated

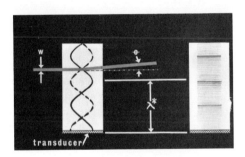

Fig. 6. Acoustic refraction of light.

by a suitable piezoelectric crystal at the frequency desired, and coupled into a propagating medium contained in a cell. Specifically a quartz transducer can be used at 1 Mc to launch the acoustic wave into water. The waves then proceed at the velocity of acoustic energy in the medium and are absorbed at the far end of the propagating cell by an impedance-matching absorber. The laser beam is directed through the glass acoustic cell parallel to the propagating acoustic wavefront. It is important that the laser beam cross section be small compared to the acoustic wavelength in the medium. Since the laser beam is stationary and the acoustic beam is moving, the conditions witnessed by the light beam change each instant. An acoustic disturbance in a transparent medium gives rise to a varying index of refraction in the medium. That is, if the direction of acoustic propagation is x, there will be a locally changing index of refraction dn/dx, where n is the index of the undisturbed medium.

The varying index causes the laser beam to bend. It will refract into the direction of greater index at each moment. The acoustic antinodes represent regions of greater acoustic pressure and of larger refractive index than the nodes. The beam will, therefore, bend toward the antinodes and away from the nodes, much as a light beam is refracted when it leaves a medium such as air and enters glass. If the acoustic disturbance is sinusoidal, the light beam deflection will be sinusoidal and bilateral with respect to the undeflected position.

For most purposes, two-dimensional scanning is required. This can be achieved as shown in Fig. 7. Two transducers, resonant at either identical

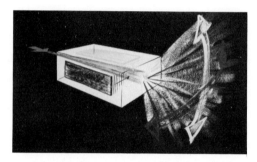

FIG. 7. Two-dimensional acoustic scanner.

or different frequencies, are mounted orthogonal to each other. The laser beam is positioned along the line of intersection of the two acoustic beams. Each acoustic beam will then exert its deflection effect independently.

We have constructed a scanner at Lockheed which operates at 1 Mc. It is shown in Fig. 8, along with an He-Ne laser, which bears beam-reducing optics. With this cell, powered by two independent 1 Mc supplies, we have

FIG. 8. Scanner operating at 1 Mc.

witnessed the expected Lissajous phenomena, when relative phase and amplitude are varied. We have achieved, using both silicone fluids and acetone as acoustic media, 4.5 deg in one-dimensional scan and 2 deg in two-dimensional scan with an acoustic path of 1 cm (transducer dimension). These are equivalent to 7.8 cm and 3.5 cm deflections at 1 m. The arrangement is still primitive, but we have measured about 100 linear resolution elements. To be useful in the system configurations to follow, improvement in this figure is necessary.

Photochromic Memory Systems

With this background we can look at representative memory systems which can be configured with photochromic materials. Figure 9 depicts a

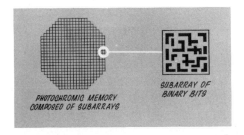

Fig. 9. Photochromic memory and subarray.

photochromic memory plane, which is made up of blocks of photochromic film material arranged as shown, separated by a nonphotochromic grid. This structure could be prepared on a glass or plastic substrate. The memory plane thus consists of many subarrays, each of which can be accessed individually.

The photochromic material which appears attractive for our purposes is Cyanamid Type 63-071. The sensitivity of this formulation is such that 1.5 joules per cm^2 (of radiation centered at 4800 Å) gives an optical density change of 1 at 6000 Å. (This is where the absorption band developed by "switching" peaks.) A density change of 0.2 in a bit of 10^{-6} cm^2 requires 3×10^{-7} joule.

Figure 10 shows one memory system configuration. The read function is here performed through CRT illumination of the photochromic memory matrix, with readout by means of an image dissector tube. The photochromic matrix is deposited on the flat side of a fly's-eye lens plate (made of glass or plastic). The fly's-eye lens[1] is composed of an array of very small, short focal length lenses, one for each photochromic subarray. The fly's-eye lens can be designed so that a relatively large object, disposed symmetrically with respect to the system optical axis, is imaged independently by each lenslet, with extremely good fidelity. Designs of over 1000 lenslets, each showing over 400 lines per mm axial resolution, have been fabricated, although the resolution drops somewhat at the edges of the unit cell. (We will consider the case of 100 bits per mm.) When the object is illuminated, a large array of very small images form in the image plane. This plane is designed to coincide with the back surface of the lens plate where the photochromic matrix is deposited.

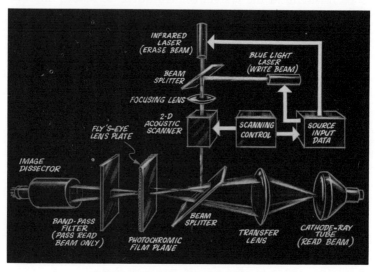

Fig. 10. Photochromic memory system.

Since the device is reciprocal, the fly's-eye principle can be used in reverse. The photochromic subarrays will be illuminated, only one at a time, by a narrow beam of light from the CRT, during the read operation. That is, the CRT deflection voltages and the Z-axis modulation voltage will address the CRT electron beam to only a small spot on the face of the tube. The light produced will be focused by the transfer lens on the photochromic matrix, illuminating the desired subarray only. This will cause an enlarged image of the illuminated subarray (consisting of many bits) to form. Regardless of which subarray is illuminated, the images will always form in the same position. The photocathode of the image dissector tube is positioned in this plane.

The dissector combines the principles of an image converter with scanning as in a camera tube. When the subarray is imaged on the photoemissive surface, an electron image is formed through electron emission. The emission density at any point of the photocathode is proportional to the illumination at that point. The electron image is spatially distributed and can be transferred, focused, and deflected by appropriate tube elements. The image is focused in the plane of a metal disk which shields this section of the tube from a following section. The disk bears a small aperture. The deflection system sweeps the electron image across the aperture in a pattern determined by the sweep voltages. The entire electron image is intercepted by the metal disk and annihilated, except the one small picture element just passing over the aperture. This signal is passed into the rear section, which consists of an electron multiplier. The signal is amplified in the multiplier. At any moment, the electrical output represents the illumination at a particular element (or bit) of the two-dimensional subarray. The sweep in the dissector can be electronically synchronized with the CRT and other appropriate electronic circuits to interrogate stored data. Present tubes can read out at a 5 to 10 Mc rate. The resolution is limited by disk aperture size and by electron-optical aberrations. With proper photocathode illumination, resolutions of 500 to 600 TV lines per linear dimension are possible. We can consider, therefore, memory subarrays of 200 by 200 bits (or 40,000 bits).

It will be recalled that the absorption curve of unactivated Type 63-071 photochromic film peaks at 4800 Å, and falls off on the long wavelength side to essentially zero at 5700 Å. The CRT phosphor is matched to the photochromic film response, so that it does not cause "switching," which peaks at 4800 Å. The phosphor persistence also must be considered in terms of the readout operation. Of the standard JEDEC phosphors, types P21, P25, and P27 appear suitable. With these phosphors, the unfiltered CRT beam can be permitted to scan the photochromic film for readout, without concurrently bringing about spurious write or erase action. However, where shortest persistence of the CRT spot is desired (to afford very high speed operation), the beam requires spectral filtering before striking the 63-071 photochromic film.

The write and erase (updating) operations are performed, as depicted in Fig. 10, by laser beams of appropriate spectral content, focused at the photochromic memory plane. (Thermal losses in the photochromic film must, of course, be considered in a practical implementation.) The focused spots can be scanned across the memory matrix by the 2-D acoustic scanner, as directed by the scan control. The source data cause amplitude modulation of the laser (write and erase) beams, as required.

The 63-071 film memory plane could also be held at an elevated temperature to cause erasure of the entire memory after a short period of time. The laser erase beam could then be eliminated, but the updated data would require regeneration on a scheduled basis.

Recently, an argon gas laser operating in both continuous and pulsed mode has become available. This laser is characterized by high average spectral power in very short configurations and narrow beam cross sections. One manufacturer has obtained a cw output of over 2 W from a tube 40 cm long, with a 2 mm beam diameter. Ninety per cent of this energy is equally divided bewteen the 4880 Å and the 5145 Å lines. Matched to the activation curve of Type 63-071 photochromic film, this is equivalent to about 1.5 W at peak absorption. If this beam were focused to irradiate an elementary bit of 10^{-6} cm, the time required to get a density change of 0.2 would be only 0.23 μsec.

Upon activation by the write beam, the 63-071 film would develop an absorption band peaking at 6000 Å. To provide a system with best signal-to-noise advantage, the CRT phosphor emission and the photodetector photocathode response should be maximized in this spectral region. Image dissector tubes of S-1 and S-11 response are generally available. At first sight, the S-1 surface with a relative response of 70 per cent of maximum at 6000 Å appears superior to the S-11 surface which has only 15 per cent relative sensitivity at this point. However, on an absolute basis, the S-11 photosurface is about 7 times as sensitive. A tube with this surface would be blind to residual erase radiation (since its response is essentially zero at 7000 Å), but would require shielding (by a spectral filter) from the residual write beam. On the other hand, the tube with S-1 response requires shielding from both write and erase beam components. Multilayer interference filters are prescribed today for many applications. However, they function by rejecting spectral energy outside the design passband. In this configuration, reflected write and/or erase components can once again strike the photochromic surface, decreasing the signal-to-noise. Hence, an absorption type filter may actually be more appropriate to this task.

A method of using the LEC 1 Mc scanner is being investigated. In the usual TV raster type of scan, the horizontal deflection is at a much greater frequency than the vertical deflection. To attempt this type of scan with the acoustic device leads to difficulties. The deflection angle of the light beam goes down as the operational frequency is lowered. Further, pressurized operation of the acoustic cell is required to prohibit cavitation of the medium. On the other hand, for frequencies much above 1 Mc, the light beam aperture is no longer small compared to the acoustic wavelength. Therefore it is not possible to implement a TV type of scan in the acoustic device.

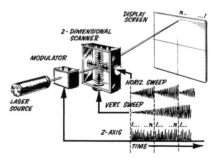

Fig. 11. Diagram of the LEC 1 Mc scanner.

In our scheme, the horizontal and vertical transducers are both excited in phase, at 1 Mc, and the voltages are individually amplitude modulated, as shown in Fig. 11. The laser beam is permitted to pass through the modulator only for a portion of the rf cycle around the positive peaks. In this manner it is possible to illuminate a continuum of spots in the upper right quadrant. The modulator (KDP quarter-wave retardation type) bandwidth requirements are much reduced by this scheme, although the laser beam is not being efficiently utilized. Further schemes are under study which permit utilization of the entire display plane.

To get an order of magnitude idea of the memory capacity, we will consider a memory plane of 2 in. square. The image dissector has been shown capable of resolving at least 200×200 bits, or 40 kilobits. At a bit density of 10^3 per cm, 200 bits occupy 2 mm. The photochromic subarray is then 4 mm^2. The areal magnification required of the fly's-eye arrangement is about 625. In a plane of 4 sq in., there will be approximately 645 subarrays. Consider that only one-half the memory plane is composed of active film. The memory would then contain almost 13 million bits.

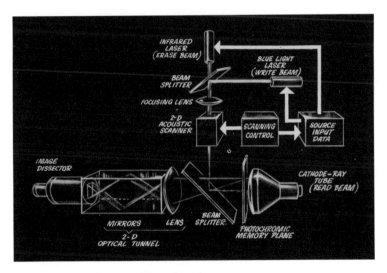

FIG. 12. Photochromic memory system.

Figure 12 shows another memory configuration, this time employing a two-dimensional optical tunnel[2] to achieve parallel processing capability.

ACKNOWLEDGMENTS

The contributions of Dr. L. Weissbein of American Cyanamid, and R. Lipnick of Lockheed Electronics are gratefully acknowledged.

REFERENCES

1. HARDING, W. E., W. E. MUTTER, AND W. E. RUDGE, "Fly's-Eye Lens Technique for Generating Semiconductor Device Fabrication Masks," *IBM J. Res. Develop. 7*, No. 2, 146 (April 1963).
2. KROLAK, L. J., AND D. J. PARKER, "The Optical Tunnel—A Versatile Electro Optical Tool," *Soc. Motion Picture Television Engrs., 72*, No. 3 (March 1963).

GENERAL REFERENCES

DORION, G. H., AND L. WEISSBEIN, "Photochromism," *Discovery* (January 1963).
LIPNICK, R., A. REICH, AND G. A. SCHOEN, "Nonmechanical Scanning of Light Using Acoustic Waves," *Proc. IEEE, 52*, No. 7, 853 (July 1964).
LIPNICK, R., A. REICH, AND G. A. SCHOEN, "Two-Dimensional Acoustic Light-Beam Scanner" (to be published).
REICH, A., AND S. S. VERNER, "Voice Modulation of an Electroacoustically Reflected Light Beam," *Proc. IEEE, 51*, No. 11, 1661 (November 1963).

CHAPTER 32

DIGITAL MICROTAPE RECORDER

*Ravendra Kumar Agarwal**

Fairchild Space and Defense Systems
A Division of Fairchild Camera and Instrument Corporation
Syosset, Long Island, New York

Introduction

The standard paper punch tape, available in the market today, has 7 or 8 bit binary-coded decimal characters across the tape. The new digital-tape reader and writer, to be discussed in this paper, is designed to use aluminum coated 35-mm Mylar-base tape with 49 digital bits across the tape. The reader and writer are two separate units. Photodiodes are used exclusively to read the bits, and an electric discharge through an air gap is used to write the bits.

Writing Technique

The technique in writing the bits is similar to the breakdown of gases between two metallic electrodes. A metallic wire 0.01 in. in diameter is used for the probes.

High-voltage pulses in the kilovolt range are applied to the probes, causing a spark over the gap. The current pulses, generated because of the ionization in the extremely localized high field around the air gap, are of microsecond duration and about 10 A in magnitude. A requirement of the coronalike discharge is to generate a source of negative ions. The metallic coating of the tape serves as this source. These current pulses generate heat over the tape surface directly under the probe being energized. Hence a small area is evaporated from the metallic coating, thus forming a transparent hole (bit) on the tape.

The hole size depends on a number of factors. The most important factors

* Present address: Sperry Rand Corporation, St. Paul, Minnesota.

are the amount of energy in the discharge pulse, the size of the airgap, and cleanliness of the tape surface and the writing probes. Investigation has shown that the spark could occur at a rate as high as 10 kc. It is of primary importance that the gap be very narrow in order to have discharge at each pulse.

In order to generate high voltage and current pulses, hydrogen thyratrons are used. This circuit for the thyratron is shown in Fig. 1. As men-

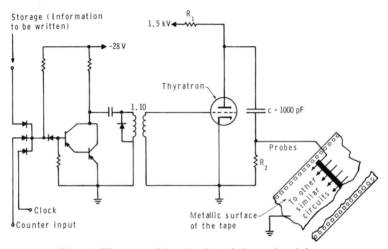

FIG. 1. Thyratron firing circuit and air-gap breakdown.

tioned above, the size of the hole depends on the energy in the discharge pulse, which is determined by the value of the thyratron anode voltage and the value of the capacitor C. Initially, the capacitor C is charged to the anode voltage. When the positive pulse appears on the grid of the thyratron, the thyratron appears as a short circuit and the capacitor C discharges through the thyratron and the resistor R_2. There is a voltage buildup during this time across the resistor R_2. When it reaches the breakdown voltage of the air gap, a spark appears across the gap, evaporating the aluminum from the tape and leaving an area of the transparent Mylar. Photographs of the pulses at the thyratron anode and at the probe are shown in Fig. 2. The size of the spark determines the size of the evaporated area, as mentioned earlier.

There is a maximum distance between the probes and the tape for a given anode voltage. If the probes are moved closer to the tape, the spark is brighter and broader. This results in evaporating a large area of the tape surface, thus increasing the hole size. However, there is a limit to the proximity of the probes to the tape surface, beyond which the sparks become weaker and there is a danger of the probes scratching the tape surface.

(The air gap being used at the present writing ranges from 0.02 in. to 0.08 in.)

Another way to increase the size of the holes is to increase the thyratron anode voltage, which in turn charges the capacitor C to a higher voltage generating higher current pulses through the air gap. Changing the value of capacitor C has the same effect as changing the anode voltage, but the selection of C effects the time constant $C(R_1 + R_2)$, which should be shorter

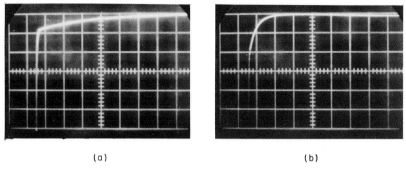

(a)   (b)

FIG. 2. Pulses at (a) thyratron plate and (b) a writing probe. 20 μsec/cm horizontal, 200 V/cm vertical.

than the time interval between the successive pulses at the thyratron grid. In other words, the capacitor should be allowed to charge to its full anode voltage before the next pulse appears at the thyratron grid. Therefore, the size of the bit can be controlled and ranges from 0.004 in. to 0.014 in.

The glow discharge forms ozone and nitrogen oxides in air. The amount and the rate at which oxidation occurs depend on the probe structure and the current through the gap.

Writing Head

The writing head consists of 49 tungsten wires 0.01 in. in diameter, mounted in a straight line in an insulated mold with their centers 0.02 in. apart, as shown in Fig. 3. This arrangement of the wires, as well as their adjacent separating distance, is quite critical. Each probe has a very sharp point and this end extends out from the mold surface by a maximum of $\frac{1}{4}$ in. The processes of sharpening the probes is by dipping them in a chemical solution and applying a 6 VAC between the probes and a copper electrode, as shown in Fig. 4. In this process, tungsten dissolves in the solution until the wires are above the surface of the solution, i.e., no current flows, thus leaving sharp points on the probe ends. (See Fig. 3.)

Each probe is capable of producing about one hundred million holes before deterioration is noticed (i.e., a cluster of aluminum oxide starts

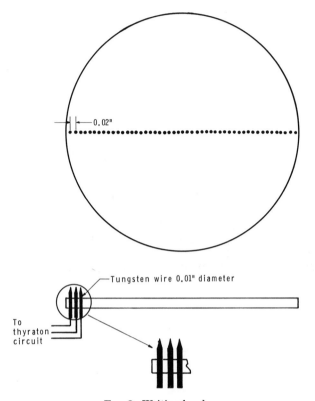

0.02"

Tungsten wire 0.01" diameter

To
thyraton
circuit

FIG. 3. Writing head.

forming around the tips). They can be cleaned and made ready to use again
by re-etching in the chemical solution.

The aluminized tape medium consists of 35-mm sprocketed Mylar, 0.003
inch thick, coated with a thin layer (500 Å) of aluminum. Coating is performed by means of a vacuum deposition. The writing process leaves the

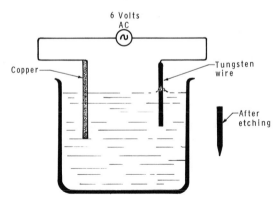

6 Volts
AC

Copper

Tungsten
wire

After
etching

FIG. 4. Etching process.

Mylar base material intact, hence the strength of the basic Mylar tape contributes excellent mechanical characteristics.

Any digital circuit can be used for writing control, such as a "ring counter" shown in Fig. 5. The counter should be able to give 50 digital

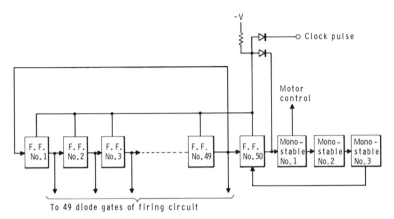

Fɪɢ. 5. A "ring counter."

pulses. Forty-nine of these pulses are connected to one of the three input "AND" gates, as shown in Fig. 1, one "AND" gate for each counter output. The second input to each of these forty-nine "AND" gates is connected together and goes to the clock. The third input to each of these gates is fed from a different data register, which transfers the data to be coded into the format of the microtape writer. The input to the register can be any data processing system, such as punch cards, magnetic tape, printer, typewriter, etc. This register gives a command pulse to fire the thyratrons, transferring information to the aluminized Mylar tape.

The last (fiftieth) pulse from the last flip-flop triggers a single-shot flip-flop, the output of which energizes an incremental motor control circuit and triggers a gate to inhibit the clock and the input to the data storage. The leading edge of the "single-shot" pulse is used to advance the motor while the trailing edge of the pulse stops it. The width of the pulse determines the amount of the tape to be advanced, which is set, in this case, to move the tape in steps of 0.02 in. The extra "single-shots" are present to give delay time to allow the tape to become stationary before it starts writing again. At the end of the delay time, the last "single-shot" triggers the last flip-flop in the ring counter. This allows the clock and data input to flow again.

The thyratrons are capable of coding at a rate of more than 10 kc, but there is a restriction due to the lack of availability of high-speed stepping motors. At present, the writer can step at the maximum rate of 500 steps/sec.

Reading Technique

The reading technique employs a photosensitive principle wherein the coded optical bits (holes) allow light to reach the junction of silicon planar photodiodes in an integrated array. The technology employed in fabricating the reading head is a direct outgrowth of the technique developed by Fairchild Semiconductor Division. The reading head consists of an array of forty-nine silicon photodiodes on 0.020 in. centers. This results in an array possessing the proven inherent high reliability of silicon planar devices. These photodiodes in the reading head are similar in characteristics to FSD 1N3734, except smaller in area, and result in "code" to "no code" (i.e., on to off) current ratio of 100:1 at 70 °C, with no temperature compensation. The active photodiodes are reverse biased and are essentially current generators whose output is a function of the light energy. The photodiode light versus current characteristic is linear to a certain amount of light, after which it starts saturating similar to common transistors or diodes. The amount of current in the linear portion of the photodiode curve is more than enough to trigger the micrologic circuits that follow the photodiode.

The actual aperture of the photodiode, in the present system, is a rectangle (0.016 in. × 0.02 in.). For this application, the window is modified by placing an accurate mask over the diode array, which reduces the aperture size to 0.012 in. × 0.012 in. The present fabrication technique is capable of arranging the photodiodes in an array as close as 2 mils from center to center. The frequency response of these photodiodes is above 2 Mc. The light source chosen for the reader consists of a bank of four miniature GE lamps rated for 5 V and 40,000 hr. In the present system, however, they are operated at lower than the rated voltage, to increase their life to 600,000 operating hours. Another advantage of the reduced voltage is that the circuit is designed to hold automatically the total illumination constant in the event of a single lamp failure. A simple cylindrical lens system is used to provide a line projection of uniform light across the coded word below the tape. The photodiode reading head is mounted over the top of the tape, and the light is under the tape; the aluminized surface of the tape faces the diode at a distance of a few mils. This cuts down the noise pickup in the diodes from outside light sources. A block diagram of the microtape reader is shown in Fig. 6.

A crosstalk measurement was made on the reader using oversized 14-mil holes on the tape. The experiment consisted of measuring the current of a diode under an opaque bit, with bits written on either side. The crosstalk current measured was less than 4 per cent of the value measured in the illuminated diode. This measurement acted as a figure of merit for the collimated light, the slight spread through the Mylar base, and in general, the validity of the light optical system. Under the most severe case, the ratio of "on-off" current is approximately 50:1 for the photodiodes themselves. It is observed that the threshold signal chosen to denote a "one" signal (a hole) can easily satisfy the 4 per cent crosstalk.

The photodiode current is detected and amplified by integrated circuits. Milliwatt micrological circuits are used to minimize the size of the reader. The microtape reader can be operated in different ways depending on the application to a particular system.

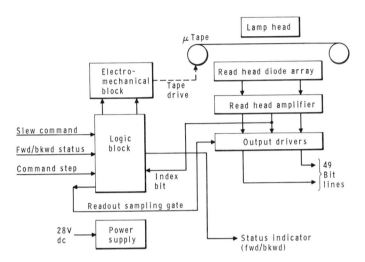

Fig. 6. Block diagram of the microtape reader.

The format of the digital tape word is such that the centrally located bit position is designed as the "index" or "sprocket" bit. This is written independently of the word structure that leaves 48 bits to carry the useful information. The "index" bit is used to trigger the tape braking system. The tape does not advance at fixed increments, but actually stops itself through the "index" bit. This type of arrangement makes row-to-row spacing noncritical, and it simplifies the writing procedure by eliminating tolerance buildup and data registration problems associated with long tape lengths. A command step (generated internally or externally, depending on the application) sets a motor drive mechanism to advance the tape. The receipt of an "index" bit through the trigger circuit energizes an electromagnetic brake which accurately and repetitively stops the tape in the optimum reading position. After the tape is in a stationary position under tension, a sampling pulse is generated which reads out the word (row) through the gating circuit. The transport at this point waits for the next "Step Command." It can perform either parallel or serial readout.

A choice of two reduction ratios is provided, one for normal step mode and one for slew mode. The slew mode yields a tape velocity of 200 in./sec in the present system. The slew mode is usually used to advance the tape forward or rewind it back to a particular word in the tape. It is important to note that the photodiode and the logic circuit can read the tape in the slew mode at a rate as high as 1000 in./sec and at the same time command

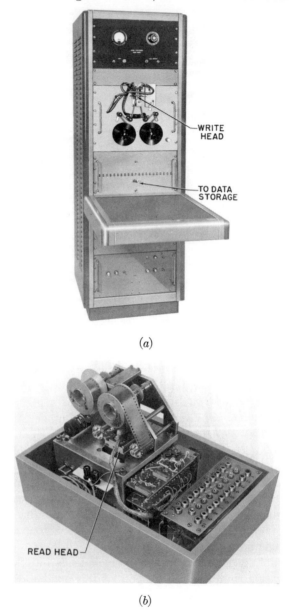

(a)

(b)

FIG. 7. (a) Prototype microtape writer. (b) Prototype microtape reader.

operation of the external unit. The primary factor limiting the reading rate mentioned above is in the drive system available at the present time.

Conclusion

The packing density of the aluminized digital tape is 2450 bits/in. of tape, which is the highest rating used among existing digital tape recorders. In addition to being economical, it can control five times more operations at single row reading than the paper tape. Since it is basically Mylar, it is more sturdy, it can be stored indefinitely, and programed tape can be run many times without damage to the tape. The complete prototype writer and reader are shown in Fig. 7.

Following are a few of many applications of the aluminized microtape recorder:

1. Block reader. By fabricating the photodiode array in more than a single row, the reader can read many words simultaneously. For example, if there were six rows of the photodiodes in the array, it would read six words (288 useful bits being read at one time).

2. Fixed memory programer. (To control any subsystem and event sequence.) Here the aluminized microtape reader offers several significant improvements in performance, capability, and reliability which are of great value in many subsystems. It can provide greatly improved accuracy of event timing to that achieved by current fixed memory programers; it can also provide control of many more events at no increase in size or weight.

3. Memory storage. This new microtape reader can provide memory storage to the digital computer or to any automatic control processes.

Because of its unique properties, the possible application for this type of recorder is governed by creativity and imagination of the potential user rather than by any limitations inherent in the operating principle of this system itself.

Granted that this type of electro-optical recorder does have its limitations when compared to other recording systems, some special properties, how-ever, endow it with characteristics which no other standard tape recorder could begin to equal. The scope of its future applications in military and commercial markets is large.

ACKNOWLEDGMENTS

This study was conducted during a program directed by Fairchild Space and Defense Systems devoted to generating new approaches in data storage and annotation. The author would like to express his gratitude to B. Pollick, I. Doyle, and L. Tregerman for their generous and enthusiastic support;

to I. Hirschberg and M. Vicars-Harris for many stimulating discussions; and to the Transducer Group of Fairchild Semiconductor for their valuable help and suggestions.

GENERAL REFERENCES

PENNY, G. W., AND S. CRAIG, *Trans. Am. Inst. Elec. Engrs., Pt. I, Communication and Electronics, 80,* 156 (1961).
Proc. Intern. Conf. Ionization Phenomena Gases, 4th, Uppsala, 17–21 August 1959.

CHAPTER 33

FIDAC: FILM INPUT TO DIGITAL AUTOMATIC COMPUTER AND ASSOCIATED SYNTAX-DIRECTED PATTERN-RECOGNITION PROGRAMING SYSTEM *

R. S. Ledley, L. S. Rotolo, T. J. Golab,
J. D. Jacobsen, M. D. Ginsberg, and J. B. Wilson
National Biomedical Research Foundation, Silver Spring, Maryland

The large-scale quantitative analysis of pictures cannot be approached by manual methods because of the tedium, manual precision, and extensive time that is necessarily involved. Hence we have embarked on a program designed to enable the automatic analysis of pictures by means of a digital computer, with particular emphasis on pictures of biomedical importance, such as photomicrographs, electron micrographs, x rays, and so forth. This capability of automatic quantitative analysis of pictures of biomedical importance promises to open up entirely new fields of investigation in biological and medical research which could not heretofore have been accomplished.

The task of quantitatively analyzing such pictures involved two steps: first, a scanning instrument called FIDAC was built which "reads" the picture into the high-speed memory of a digital computer; second, a computer programing system called FIDACSYS was written to recognize the object to be measured and to process the quantitative data as required by the particular biological or medical problem under consideration.

General Capabilities

The name FIDAC stands for Film Input to Digital Automatic Computer. The instrument is fundamentally an input device to a high-speed digital

* This work was supported by grants GM 10797, GM 10789, NB 04472, and GM 11201 from the National Institutes of Health to the National Biomedical Research Foundation.

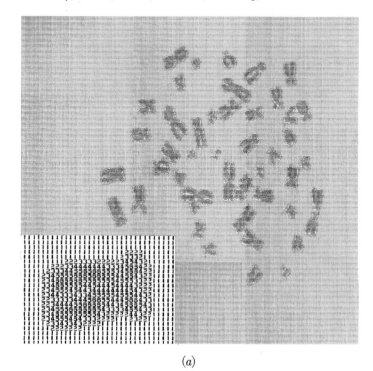

(a)

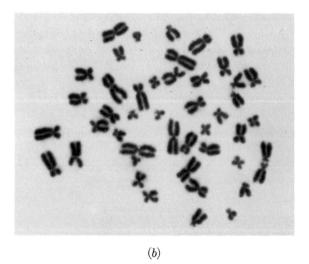

(b)

FIG. 1. Representation of chromosome photomicrograph in the computer memory. (a) Actual computer printout of picture (with detail inset) that has been put into the computer memory in 0.3 sec by FIDAC. (b) The original photomicrograph.

computer. It enables a roll of film to be brought to the computer for input to the high-speed memory, just as a magnetic tape reel can now be brought to the magnetic tape unit for direct input into the computer's memory. The FIDAC instrument puts the pictures directly into the computer's (IBM 7094) memory within 0.3 of a second, with about 800,000 points per picture (1000 × 800 point raster) being sampled in the black-and-white mode, using one memory bit per picture point, or 350,000 points per picture (700 × 500 point raster) are sampled in the eight-level gray mode, using three memory bits per point (see Fig. 1). The number of points that are sampled per picture is presently limited, not by the FIDAC, but rather by the large-scale high-speed computer being used (i.e., core memory size). The FIDAC can resolve more than 1500 points across the width of the picture. The new generation computers, with higher speeds and larger memories, will be able to take further advantage of the capabilities of the FIDAC instrument.

Figure 2 illustrates the main components of FIDAC. The film-transport unit positions the film for reading. Film movement in the unit is directed by output signals from the computer, which are properly gated and transformed into control signals for the film-movement circuits. The deflection and pin-cushion-correcting coils, the coil driver, the focus and intensity controls, and the high-voltage supplies are associated with the cathode-ray tube that produces the short-persistence 1.5-mil flying spot, with a maximum raster width of 10 cm. The fluorescence is focused by the optical system onto the film, which modulates the intensity of the light. The light then falls on the surface of the photomultiplier, which generates a video signal (the voltage divider and the power supplies are associated with the photocell). This video signal is amplified, sampled by the chopping signals, and sent through the level detectors. The resultant level signals are synchronized, and then are gated in the gray-level mode into the cyclic-encoding circuits to form a three-bit gray-level code for each sampled spot; in the binary black-and-white mode, only two gray levels are discriminated for a signal using only one bit per sampled spot. The sampled information is received by the parallel-serial shift register, which buffers 36 bits (one IBM 7094 computer word) for input to the computer. It can be connected either for twelve three-bit parallel stages or for thirty-six single-bit serial stages, depending on whether the gray or the binary black-and-white mode is being used. The signals are "matched" to the computer by the computer interface circuits. Synchronization is under the control of the master clock, clock-phase generators, and spot and word counters.

The amplified analog video signals from the photomultiplier are also fed to the monitor scope for visual display. The horizontal- and vertical-sweep signals are fed to both monitor and flying-spot scanner; and these are utilized as end-of-record and end-of-file signals (in the computer). Other control signals must be received from and sent to the computer for initiating

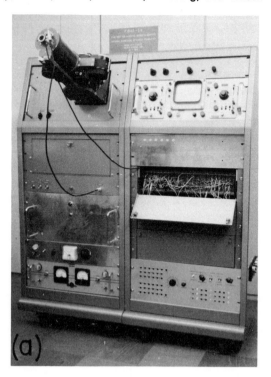

(a)

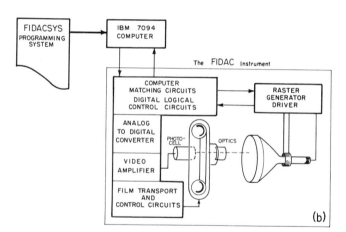

(b)

FIG. 2. (a) Photograph of FIDAC. (b) Block diagram of FIDAC system.

the operation of the FIDAC upon its selection by the computer and for synchronizing and gating the input information to the computer.

Summarizing then, the general capabilities of the FIDAC are those of a very-high-speed, high-resolution, on-line computer-input device, which can scan in real time with computer program feedback control. FIDAC was designed specifically for biomedical picture processing as follows: (1) for rapid processing of pictures for statistical analysis and screening purposes, it has a high-speed scan of less than 0.3 sec per frame; (2) for retaining all information when scanning photomicrographs, it has a high resolution (greater than that of the optical microscope) where for $1000\times$ magnification each 0.2μ of the specimen is sampled by more than three points;* (3) for presenting the capability of program control by the computer, i.e., to move automatically to the next film frame when the processing of one film frame has been completed, it has real-time operation; (4) for extreme flexibility, convenience, and economy of storage of data, it is a direct input to the computer.† As a comparison, FIDAC can load the computer's core memory 10 to 50 times faster than can conventional magnetic-tape input units.

More Detailed Discussion of the Engineering Design of the FIDAC

The discussion of the engineering design of the FIDAC will be presented under the following six subheadings: The High-Resolution Scanning CRT and Associated Circuits; The Optical System and Film-Transport Unit; The Photocell and Associated Circuitry; Analog-to-Digital Conversion; The Logic System; and Maintenance and Operation.

The High-Resolution Scanning CRT and Associated Circuits

The major units incorporated in the flying-spot scanner are shown in Fig. 2. The very fine spot (0.0015 in.) is produced by means of a high-resolution, rapid-decay, cathode-ray tube (CRT). The cathode-ray tube has a P16 screen phosphor, whose fluorescent-output peaks in the ultraviolet region and decays to 10 per cent of its initial brightness in $0.1\ \mu$sec. The present spot is small enough that variations in the grains of phosphor of the CRT may be seen at the output when it is viewed directly by a photomultiplier.

The horizontal sweep is synchronously triggered by a pulse from the logic circuit. On flyback it puts out a pulse which the control circuitry

---

* About a 50μ field diameter on the specimen is seen at a magnification of 1000. The 750 points across the field give about 15 points per micron on the specimen or three points near 0.2μ, where 0.2μ is the optical resolution of a microscope at 1000 power.

† The fact that FIDAC is on-line with the computer with no intermediate magnetic tape recording means that pictorial data on film can be used; a single 100-ft reel of 16-mm film which fits into a $3\frac{1}{2}$ in. diameter can contains 4000 frames and will record over 4 billion bits of information; this would require over 50 conventional digital magnetic-tape reels, making a stack of these reels over 4 ft high.

uses to indicate the end of a line sweep, and which is also used to blank the horizontal retrace sweep. Blanking between lines is considered essential to insure that the tube is dark when the scan of the next line begins. The retrace time (flyback or holdoff time) may be varied within the sweep-generator circuits. It is normally set to a minimum value of 40 μsec, which is the smallest allowed by the design of the drivers. However, in certain applications it is essential that this holdoff time be extended. For example, present programing requirements have necessitated an increase to 65 μsec. Thus in our system we have incorporated a variable holdoff time to accommodate the various needs that may arise. Of course, this holdoff time should be kept as small as is practicable in order to reduce the time required to read a picture into the computer.

The vertical sweep is synchronized to start with one of the horizontal sweeps, and it generates a signal which is utilized by the control system to indicate the beginning and the end of the frame. The vertical holdoff time has been fixed at 20 msec. This relatively long holdoff time does not really affect the speed of operation of the FIDAC system since in most applications a certain amount of time will be required to process the information which has just been read into the computer, and thus there is a considerable waiting period before the next complete scan should start. As noted, the sweep generators are also used to drive the sweep waveforms of a monitor display tube. However, the raster positioning controls for the monitor are independent of those of the flying-spot CRT. The scanner CRT raster control allows the height, vertical position, width, and horizontal position of the scanner raster to be adjusted independently of the positions of the monitor adjustments. Both signals are direct-coupled all the way from the sweep generator to the yoke. Thus even very slow sweep rates are possible.

In order to prevent burning of the phosphor of the high-resolution CRT, special protection features have been incorporated. The first protection circuit is one which cuts off the high voltages (+400, +5 kV, and +20 kV) unless the −100 V intensity-control voltage is available. A second circuit detects whether or not a varying current is passing through the horizontal yoke coil. If such a current is not present, the full −100 V will be applied to the control grid, blanking the CRT and preventing any phosphor burns. If only a line scan is desired, the vertical sweep is disabled and the positioning potentiometer is used to vary the horizontal line position.

The Optical System and Film-Transport Unit

This device is used to focus the fluorescent spot on the film, as well as to hold, move, and position the film under computer-program control. The light from the CRT is focused onto the film by means of a specially adapted wide-angle 5-mm lens enclosed in a light-tight tunnel. In addition, in order to insure that the CRT raster completely scans the film, mechanical adjustments have been included to allow for the accurate positioning and locking of the film holder to insure that focus is obtained as the entire film is being scanned. Additional features include the ability to vary the amount of light passing through the lens system.

In order to allow automatic control of a film by the computer, the system has been designed for the automatic movement of the film in a forward direction, at a rate of approximately 10 frames per second. This relatively slow speed of movement is a consequence of maintaining accuracy of film registration, which is absolutely essential. To insure that the scanning of the film does not begin until the film has been accurately positioned, the film-moving device puts out a control signal which is used to develop the triggering signal of the CRT scan. In our present FIDAC we have adapted standard 16-mm and 35-mm motion-picture film holders, as well as standard 35-mm slide–film holders, to perform these functions.

The Photocell and Associated Circuitry

The basic element of the light-sensing system is a high-gain photomultiplier. Many different types of photomultiplier tubes were tested to determine which particular tubes would best provide the characteristics which we considered essential. After many checks, the 3-in. EMI 9578U tube and the $\frac{3}{4}$-in. Westinghouse 7909 tube were selected, based on their very high amplification factor (2×10^6) and extremely fast response time. These tubes have additional special features, such as very low noise (dark current), and their light frequency response very closely matches the maximum light output of the CRT. To adapt these particular tubes to the FIDAC, it was necessary to design special voltage-divider networks to accommodate the type of signals which we encountered. It was noted that rotating the tube around its axis produced drastic changes in its output. Accordingly, each tube has to be specially tested to determine its best mounting position. This requirement necessitated a special mechanical design to allow the rotation of the photomultiplier after it has been installed in the system. It was further noted that by the addition of electronic focusing the output response curves of a photomultiplier could be altered. Accordingly, we have included in our system an electronic focusing adjustment. This adjustment has helped to compensate in part for some of the nonuniformities which exist in the optical system. Associated with the photomultiplier system is a 2000-V dc power supply, designed to give close regulation and extremely low ripple. These two features are considered essential in maintaining optimum performance from the photomultipliers.

The output of the photomultiplier is fed to a specially designed amplifier which incorporates both a gain and a bias control. These controls are needed to compensate for variations in film density. That is, if a film has a relatively low contrast, it will be possible with this system to amplify its narrow density range. Furthermore, if the useful information on the film is almost entirely in either the dark or the light areas, by shifting the bias control and then increasing the gain we are able to intensify the particular signal.

To insure uniform response from the entire optical system (that is, light source, lens, and photomultiplier), we have included shading generators in our light system, whose function is to compensate for any nonuniformities which exist in the optical system. This is accomplished by applying correcting voltages to the intensity control of the CRT; these correcting voltages are determined from tests of the optical system (with no film in the film plane) to determine the shape of the output response. The correcting voltage functions are designed so that completely flat response is obtained throughout the whole film plane.

Analog-to-Digital Conversion

The output of the photomultiplier tube is an analog signal which is a continuous measure of the opaqueness of the spots on the film. For this analog information to be put into a digital computer, it must be converted to digital form. The conversion of the analog signal to digital form is accomplished by a three-bit analog-to-digital converter. The analog signal is fed to the A-D converter, and at specified time intervals this signal is sampled by level-detector circuits, which discriminate among seven levels of signal amplitude. The outputs of the level-detector circuits are sent to a set of flip-flops which store the digitalized voltage level until the next sampling period. The outputs of the flip-flops are in turn fed to a logic network in which the coded digital representation of the analog signal for that particular sampling period is developed. The comparator is basically a tunnel-diode circuit. The comparator detects voltage levels from about -0.25 V to about -5.5 V. The tunnel diode has the advantage of extremely fast turn-on time. However, there is a lag in the turn-off voltage level. To overcome this shortcoming, a control signal is applied to the comparator circuits before the next sampling to force all the tunnel diodes into the nonconducting state. Each comparator circuit is provided with a level adjustment so that it may be set to turn on at any desired level (the relative settings of the levels are dependent on the response characteristics which the investigator is interested in obtaining, such as linear, or logarithmic, etc.). In our present system, we have used 6 comparator circuits, thus providing us with 7 distinct gray levels. The choice of the 7 gray levels was based in part on the fact that 7 gray levels can be represented by three binary bits; the eighth gray level that can be obtained with 3 bits is reserved for other purposes within the computer to facilitate the programing of picture analysis. In addition, it was felt that 7 gray levels would be sufficient for most biomedical applications we would encounter. (We have now discovered that for many applications additional gray levels are highly desirable.) At the present time, the level detectors are operating at a sampling frequency of 1 Mc. It is planned to increase this sampling frequency to at least 5 Mc in future systems. It should be mentioned, however, that the detector circuits have been tested at a 10-Mc frequency rate and appear to operate satisfactorily.

The output of the A-D converter is a 3-bit cyclic code. A cyclic output code was selected to avoid any chance of level jumping. The voltage comparator circuits have been designed in a package such that they can be readily removed from the FIDAC system, so that a desired video characteristic could be readily obtained by merely interchanging packages. Thus for the FIDAC system we provide several of these packages, each of which has a different response: for example, full-range linear response, full-range logarithm response, linear response over a portion of the output range, etc.

The Logic System

The FIDAC system uses so-called dynamic logic. This particular type of logic is employed because of its extreme versatility and high reliability. At the present time our logic system is operating with a 3-phase clock at a basic repetition rate of 1 Mc. The 3-phase clock is generated by means of a special master clock which operates at a frequency three times greater than the basic clock rate. This master clock consists of a very stable multivibrator and a flip-flop. The 3-phase clock, with a one-third overlap between clock pulses, is generated by an ingenious logic setup.

The logic system generates all of the necessary controls and also provides an intermediate storage (shift register) for the information which is to be read into the computer. The logic system has been designed for operation in three modes:

1. Octal gray: In this mode every spot on the film is converted to three binary bits which represent the density of a particular point.

2. Octal black-and-white: In this mode every spot on the film is represented by three binary bits, only one of which is significant. Thus in this mode we are distinguishing between black and white points. The two additional bits in the octal grouping are used internally to facilitate the programing.

3. Binary black-and-white: In this mode each spot on the film is represented by a single binary bit. Thus we are again distinguishing black and white points. Since only a single bit is used to represent the density of a point on the film, it is possible with this mode of operation to obtain higher resolutions (that is, the number of points per unit length can be greater than in the octal mode).

In order to accommodate these different modes of operation, it was necessary to design the shift register to act both serially or in parallel. That is, in the binary mode the shift register is utilized as a straight serial shift register, shifting one bit at a time. But in the octal modes of operation, since three bits are generated in parallel, it is necessary to have the shift register accept these three bits simultaneously and then to shift them serially in groups of three. Thus in effect we have three parallel-serial shift registers. The shift register is presently 36 bits long and can accommodate 36 black-and-white spots or 12 gray spots. The choice of a 36-bit shift register was based on the word length of the IBM 7094 computer, to which the FIDAC system is presently attached.

The control signals which are generated within the FIDAC system are basically timing control signals. For example, we generate control signals to indicate to the computer when we are at the end of a line scan, to inform the computer that a picture has been completely scanned, and to advise the computer that the intermediate storage device, the shift register, is completely loaded and that the information it contains is ready to be transferred into the memory. This latter control signal is formed from binary counters which count either to 12 for the octal modes or to 36 for the binary mode.

In order to observe the film which is being read into the computer, a monitor is provided. This monitor consists of a 5-in. cathode-ray display tube. In addition to providing a means of viewing the current film being read into the computer, the monitor provides a means of readily determining the suitability of the settings on the high-voltage supply of the photomultiplier and the intensity setting on the flying-spot CRT. Furthermore, it provides a means of adjusting the shading generators and the focus of the optical system.

In the event that a black-and-white readin is desired, switching arrangements have been provided which allow any one of the 7 gray levels to be displayed on the monitor. Thus this display may provide the criteria to determine the gray level to be selected for the black-and-white readin mode. Finally, the monitor can be used as a means of readily checking the registration of the film which is being scanned.

Maintenance and Operation

Throughout its development, the philosophy of designing the FIDAC system emphasized ease of operation and ease of maintenance. With these goals in mind, we have provided interlocking switching arrangements, first to provide protection of the system from improper operation, and second to simplify the operative procedure. In addition, great pains have been taken to provide monitoring lights which will indicate to the operator at a quick glance the present status of the FIDAC system.

In order to facilitate the testing and maintenance of the FIDAC, we have provided many other indicating devices and many readily accessible test points. With our present system it is possible for an individual to check the operation of the FIDAC system within a few minutes. If there is any malfunctioning in the system, these malfunctions can be readily determined by performing a few simple tests.

The FIDACSYS Programing System

Once the picture is recorded in the computer's core memory as a grid of points, each with one of seven gray-level values (see Fig. 1), the computer analysis proceeds. The programing system FIDACSYS is designed to perform such analyses. This system consists of a large number of basic computer programs that are integrated with each other in different ways for different problems, as a general pattern-recognition and -analysis language.

We shall now describe the ideas and concepts of our programing system FIDACSYS. To make the ideas concrete, the specific example of the analysis of chromosome photomicrographs will be used. This example represents an important application in its own right, and in addition, it presents a clear illustration of the general concepts involved in the FIDAC system design. Hence, before proceeding with the programing system discussion, let us first present a digression on the background to the chromosome-analysis problem.

The Chromosome Problem

Recently there has been much active interest in analyzing chromosomes in the metaphase stage of mitosis when they appear as structures split longitudinally into rod-shaped "chromatids" lying side by side and held to one another by a constricted area called the "centromere." The availability of good photomicrographs of this metaphase stage depends primarily on the recent improvement of the colchicine treatment of cells, which arrests cell division at the metaphase stage and results in the accumulation of large numbers of these cells in the culture. In the field of cytogenetics, investigation of such preparations is in its initial phases, but already abnormalities in the number and structure of chromosomes can be related to clinical conditions in animals and in man. For example, in man mongolism and the Klinefelter and Turner syndromes have been correlated with chromosome aberrations.

One of the problems that arises in the manual study of chromosomes is the long hours and great tedium involved in making enlarged prints from photomicrographs and in cutting out each chromosome from such a print so that it can be aligned with the others for classification into the so-called chromosome karyotype (see Fig. 3). With the use of the FIDAC system, the time required for analyzing, making measurements on, and classifying each chromosome, can be radically reduced to about $\frac{1}{2}$ sec per chromosome or about 20 sec for the full complement of human chromosomes. Here the computer is used to investigate large numbers of cells with respect to total chromosome complement counts, with respect to quantitative measurements of individual chromosome arm-length ratios, densities, areas, and other morphological characteristics, and so forth.

By processing large numbers of chromosome sets and statistically analyzing the data, it is possible to give very accurate descriptions of the standard complement of chromosomes and individual chromosome variability for

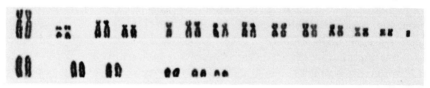

Fig. 3. A chromosome karyotype of an animal.

particular species. This statistical technique may be the only way to uncover small variations, which may prove important in relating chromosome karyotypes to diseases. For example, careful analysis of the chromosomes of individuals having myeloid leukemia, although performed previously to the availability of our automatic computer analysis, has shown that they characteristically lack a small portion of one arm of a small chromosome.

Processing a Roll of Film by FIDACSYS

Having described the biological problem, let us now consider a roll of photomicrographic film frames ready for processing. The film is placed in the film-transport unit of the FIDAC instrument, and the start button on the computer is pushed. Figure 4a illustrates the sequence of functions performed by the computer. After setting the frame count p to 1, the FIDACSYS (computer program) signals the FIDAC to scan the frame, and within 0.3 sec the picture is in the computer's memory.

Next a spectrum is computed for the picture, giving the number of points with gray value 1, gray value 2, $\cdots$, gray value 7. The eighth gray level is reserved for the erasing operation. From the spectrum the FIDACSYS can determine whether or not the picture is blank, i.e., either all black or all white (or at least 98 per cent black or 98 per cent white). If the picture is all black or all white, the program signals FIDAC to move to the next frame. In this way blank frames or leader frames can be skipped automatically. If the frame is not blank, then the spectrum information can be used for other purposes, such as determining the proper *cutoff gray-level* value that indicates those gray values that represent points inside the chromosomes. For example, it may be determined that the cutoff level L should be chosen as the gray level such that 10 per cent of the points have a gray value greater than L.

After every chromosome on the frame has been analyzed, the FIDACSYS program determines whether or not there is another frame on the film, and if there is, the FIDAC instrument is signaled to move to the next frame, and the process is repeated. If the predetermined number of frames has been processed, then the resulting information is statistically analyzed, such as giving the distribution of the number of chromosomes in each cell, the distribution of chromosome arm-length ratios by group, the distribution of relative positioning of homologous chromosomes, and so forth. Having completed the statistical analysis, the FIDAC system is now ready for another roll of film.

Processing the Objects of a Frame by FIDACSYS

In Fig. 4a, the heavy-outlined box represents the actual processing of the pictorial information on a frame. Figure 4b represents the details of this process. The object count i is set to 1 and the process starts by the FIDACSYS performing an interval scan on the picture image in the computer's high-speed core memory. This is accomplished in effect by moving a "bug" across successive horizontal rows of the raster of picture points, "searching" for points with gray level greater than the cutoff level. Such a point will be that of the next object to be processed.

If the search does indeed locate another object, then the object is processed by the FIDACSYS program. For our chromosome illustration, this processing consists of first making a determination of whether or not the object is truly a chromosome, and if it is, of determining the location, the length, the individual arms, the arm-length ratio, the over-all length, and the area of the chromosome. Having completed the processing of the object, the FIDACSYS then goes on to search for the next object in the frame.

Of course, eventually it will happen that all the objects have been processed, and no "next object" will be found. In such a case the "bug" will reach the end of the raster (i.e., the lower right-hand corner) indicating that all objects have been processed. Then the results of the measurements made on the objects of that frame are evaluated. The evaluation of these results consists of pairing homologous chromosomes by criteria of over-all length, of arm-length ratio, and of area; and then of placing each pair into one of seven groups or classes generally accepted for human chromosomes. A count of the chromosomes is also made; the total chromosome length for the frame is evaluated, and the fraction each chromosome contributes to this length is determined.

In Fig. 4b the heavy-outlined box represents the actual processing of the object. Figure 4c represents the details of this process. The first step in processing an object is to characterize the boundary of the object. This is accomplished by having the "bug" trace around the boundary by following a constant gray-level contour at a level just greater than the cutoff level. This contour or *boundary* is analyzed in terms of successive *segments*, and characterized by a *boundary list* of measurements from which the "curva-

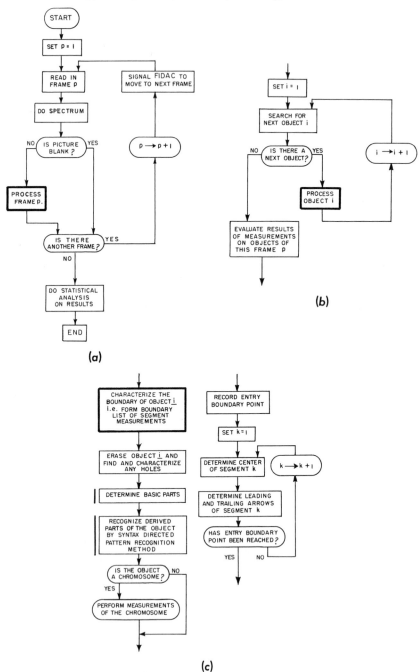

FIG. 4. (a) Processing a film roll. (b) Processing frame p. (c) Processing object i.
(d) Characterize the boundary of object i.

ture" and "direction" for each segment can be determined. Since in the analysis of the chromosome illustration the objects are considered conceptually as silhouettes, once the boundary list has been constructed the image of the object is no longer required. In order that the object not be counted or analyzed again, it is literally erased from the picture in the computer's memory.

From the boundary list, the so-called *basic parts* are determined, and then the *derived parts* are recognized to determine whether or not the object is indeed a chromosome. If it is a chromosome, then measurements on the object are made from the *derived-parts list*. We will now briefly describe this boundary-analysis approach to pattern recognition.

Boundary Analysis Approach

In Fig. 4c the heavy-outlined box represents the actual characterization of the boundary of an object. Figure 4d represents the details of this process. First the coordinates are recorded of the point at which the boundary of the object was entered, for this point marks the end as well as the start of tracing around the boundary. The boundary is traced in such a direction that the interior of the object is kept to the right of the "bug." The "next" boundary point is determined by looking clockwise around the "present" boundary point, starting from the "previous" boundary point (see Fig. 5).

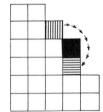

Fig. 5. The black box is the present boundary point; the vertically hatched is the previous boundary point, and the horizontally hatched is the next boundary point.

When a certain number N of boundary points (i.e., a certain boundary length) has been traversed, a *segment* is defined.

The segment is then characterized by (a) the coordinates of its *center point*, (b) the components of a *leading vector*, and (c) the components of a *trailing vector* (see Fig. 6). The length of a segment must be chosen small enough that the angle between the leading and trailing vectors becomes an approximation to the measure of the *curvature* of the segment. Then the vector sum of the leading and trailing vectors is approximately the tangent to the segment at its center point, and gives a measure of the *direction* of the segment. There are three parameters associated with a segment that are chosen to suit the particular problem under consideration: these are the segment length N, the arrow length A, and the distance D between centers of successive segments. Each boundary segment is analyzed successively, and a boundary *characterization list* is constructed until the original boundary entry point is reached again.

As each boundary point is traversed, its value is changed to the value "8" completely enclosing the object in the string of 8's. The erasing process becomes greatly simplified, for now only values on a row between 8's need to be erased. *Holes* in the object are discovered during the erasure procedure, and when found, their boundaries are characterized by segments.

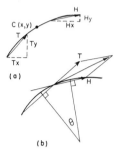

FIG. 6. (*a*) A segment illustrating the center of the segment $C(x, y)$, the trailing arrow components T_x and T_y, and the leading arrow, components H_x and H_y. (*b*) The tangent vector $\mathbf{T} + \mathbf{H}$ and the angle $\theta = L/K$, giving $K = L/\theta$, where K is the curvature and L is the segment length (and θ is in radians).

Hence erasing resolves two problems: it eliminates the possibility of analyzing an object more than once, and it locates any holes in the object. Islands within holes are found by filling in the holes, and holes within islands within holes are found by erasing, ad infinitum. However, only simple holes with no islands are found in chromosome applications.

Syntax-Directed Pattern Recognition

In Fig. 4c the two boxes with the heavy bar on the left side comprise the syntax-directed pattern-recognition portion of the FIDACSYS programing system. This approach to pattern recognition is based on some of R. S. Ledley's original work, and an introduction to the technique can be found in the references.[1,2] Here we will briefly describe the method as applied to the recognition of chromosomes.

Consider a characterization of the boundary of an object in terms of five types of curves: a clockwise curve, type A; a counterclockwise curve, type C; a relatively straight line, type B; a notch, type D; and a wide clockwise curve, type E (see Fig. 7a). Syntactical definition of the different kinds of chromosomes can be made in terms of such boundary-curve types. A boundary is first characterized as a list of such curve types, as shown in Fig. 7b, and then the syntactical definitions used to "build up" derived parts of a chromosome from combinations of these curve types. For example, Table 1 gives the syntax for a submedium chromosome and a telocentric chromosome (see Fig. 7). The recursive definition

$$\langle \text{arm} \rangle :: = B\langle \text{arm} \rangle | \langle \text{arm} \rangle B | A$$

means that the generic concept *arm* is defined as being a B type followed by an arm, or an arm followed by a B type or an A type. In this notation the angular brackets $\langle \ \rangle$ indicate that a generic name is enclosed, the ":: =" means "is defined as being," and the "|" means "or." The definition

TABLE 1 SAMPLE SYNTAX FOR SUBMEDIAN AND TELOCENTRIC CHROMOSOMES

$\langle$arm$\rangle$ :: = $B\,\langle$arm$\rangle$ | $\langle$arm$\rangle\,B\|A$	70 :: = $B,70\|70,B\|A$
$\langle$side$\rangle$ :: = $B\,\langle$side$\rangle$ | $\langle$side$\rangle\,B\|BD\|$	71 :: = $B,71\|71,B\|B\|D$
$\langle$bottom$\rangle$ :: = $B\,\langle$bottom$\rangle$ | $\langle$bottom$\rangle\,B\|E$	72 :: = $B,72\|72,B\|E$
$\left\langle\begin{array}{c}\text{right}\\\text{part}\end{array}\right\rangle$ :: = $C\,\langle$arm$\rangle$	73 :: = $C,70$
$\left\langle\begin{array}{c}\text{left}\\\text{part}\end{array}\right\rangle$ :: = $\langle$arm$\rangle\,C$	74 :: = $70,C$
$\left\langle\begin{array}{c}\text{arm}\\\text{pair}\end{array}\right\rangle$ :: = $\langle$side$\rangle\left\langle\begin{array}{c}\text{arm}\\\text{pair}\end{array}\right\rangle$ | $\left\langle\begin{array}{c}\text{arm}\\\text{pair}\end{array}\right\rangle\langle$side$\rangle$	75 :: = $71,75\|75,71$
$\qquad$ | $\langle$arm$\rangle\left\langle\begin{array}{c}\text{right}\\\text{part}\end{array}\right\rangle$ | $\left\langle\begin{array}{c}\text{left}\\\text{part}\end{array}\right\rangle\langle$arm$\rangle$	$\|70,73\|74,70$
$\left\langle\begin{array}{c}\text{submedian}\\\text{chromosome}\end{array}\right\rangle$ :: = $\left\langle\begin{array}{c}\text{arm}\\\text{pair}\end{array}\right\rangle\left\langle\begin{array}{c}\text{arm}\\\text{pair}\end{array}\right\rangle$	76 :: = $75,75$
$\left\langle\begin{array}{c}\text{telocentric}\\\text{chromosome}\end{array}\right\rangle$ :: = $\langle$bottom$\rangle\left\langle\begin{array}{c}\text{arm}\\\text{pair}\end{array}\right\rangle$	77 :: = $72,75$

is *recursive* in that it is used repeatedly. For example, consider Fig. 7c; our definition can be applied to the figure as illustrated diagrammatically in Fig. 8, where we first (1) identify the A type as an *arm*, and then build up the arm by repeated application of the definition to include (2) the

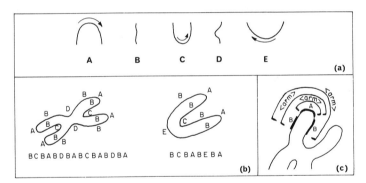

FIG. 7. (*a*) The basic types used in the illustration of the text. (*b*) Illustration of submedian and telocentric chromosomes. (*c*) Short example used in text.

B type on the left and (3) the B type on the right (see small numbers in brackets for the order of recognition). Further consideration of these concepts can be found in References 1 and 2. Figure 9 shows the building up of a submedian chromosome.

The process is, of course, systematic, and is carried out by a special program in the FIDACSYS system called the MOBILIZER (which is directly analogous to the "translator" of automatic-programing-language translation—see References 1 and 2). The mobilizer operates on a parts list for a particular object, and by using the generic syntactical description of various kinds of chromosomes "recognizes" the object as a chromosome or not a chromosome, and if a chromosome is recognized, as a particular kind of chromosome (see Fig. 10). Actually the mobilizer works with numbers: As shown in Table 1 the syntax can as well be written in terms

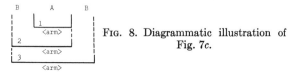

Fɪɢ. 8. Diagrammatic illustration of Fig. 7c.

of *level numbers*, where the numbers are assigned to the left-hand entities in the order in which they appear in the syntax. The basic parts, namely A, B, C, D, and E, are always considered to have number values less than any generic or "derived" part. Note that each syntax definition is given

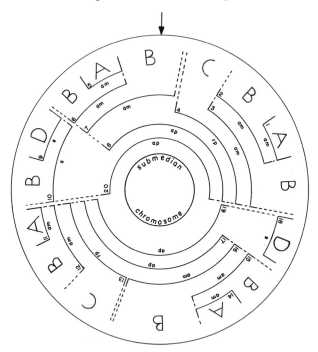

Fɪɢ. 9. Example of syntactical analysis or buildup process followed in a chromosome recognition. Here "am" stands for arm, "rp" for right part, "ap" for arm pair, and "s" for side.

as a list of *alternatives*, and each alternative is made up of one or two *components*. Thus in the definition of the arm, $B\langle\text{arm}\rangle$ is the first alternative, $\langle\text{arm}\rangle B$ the second alternative, and A the third alternative. In the alternative $B\langle\text{arm}\rangle$, B is the left component and $\langle\text{arm}\rangle$ is the right component.

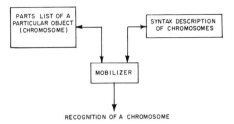

FIG. 10. Role of the mobilizer in recognizing a chromosome from a list of parts and a generic syntax description.

The mobilizer starts with the first part of the object (see the arrow in Fig. 9), and looks through the syntax list for a matching part; if, say, only the left component matches, then if the right component has a greater level number than the part of the object, an attempt is made to develop this part into the higher generic form. A simplified flow chart of the mobilizer is shown in Fig. 11, where the particular part being worked on is demarked by the *pointer*, and the syntactical alternative under consideration at any time is demarcated by the *locator*. A little reflection on the

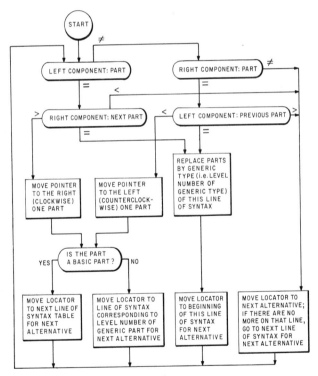

FIG. 11. Flow chart of the operations performed by the mobilizer. The *locator* normally moves from left to right, starting on a line with the leftmost alternative. The ":" represents "comparison" of *level numbers*, of course.

example of Fig. 9 in conjunction with Fig. 11 will make the details of this process clear.

Great Simplification of the Programing System

It should be pointed out that for the purposes of this paper the programing system FIDACSYS has been greatly simplified. Actually the system itself is vastly more complex than may appear from our discussions. On the other hand, while it is not appropriate to give a detailed treatment of the syntax and mobilizer in the present paper, further study of these concepts will reveal a rather simple but extremely powerful method for characterizing particular objects for recognition by the computer.

Some concept of the over-all programing system can be obtained from Table 2. Since the picture in the IBM 7094 memory takes up more than 25,000 words of the 32,000-word memory, the FIDACSYS programing system has to be broken into so-called *links*, where each link is executed separately in the memory. The initial link (Link 100,4) enables the user input parameters to be inserted into the program. Table 2 indicates the manner in which the parameter values are put into common storage. All of the subprograms that enter into the FIDACSYS system are listed in a manual, which specifies for each what user parameters are required and what values they may take on. By referring to this manual for the subprograms selected for any problem, the user-parameter list is compiled and the parameter values desired are chosen.

The second link (Link 1,4) is concerned with reading-in the picture and "compacting" the picture into the proper part of the memory in appropriate form. In Table 2, note that associated with Link 1,4 are the terms "specific READIN" and "specific COMPAK" enclosed in parentheses. This is to indicate that there are many options for the READIN subprogram, and a particular, or specific READIN subprogram must be selected and incorporated in the running deck for use by the Fortran statement "CALL READIN." Similar remarks hold for the subprogram COMPAK.

The next link (Link 2,4) will manipulate the picture, will move the film to the next frame if desired, and will print the picture as it appears in the memory if desired. Optional manipulations of the picture include masking, that is, widening the margins of the picture—reducing, that is, decreasing the density of spots of the picture as read into the computer—differentiating, that is, processing the picture to emphasize changes in gray level—and other related processes, as well as printing the picture. The statement "CALL WRITE" is used to write the picture out on magnetic tape temporarily so that two successive pictures may be processed at the same time. The subprogram SIMPOS will enable the picture on the magnetic tape to be read "on top of" a picture in the core memory, thereby enabling direct comparison of the two successive pictures. Utilizing the subprogram

TABLE 2   Over-all Linkage System of FIDACSYS

Link 100,4 Input parameter link	⌠ * FIDACSYS ⎪ * XEQ ⎪ * CHAIN (100,4) ⎨ COMMON ⟨parameter list⟩ ⎪ [⟨parameter name⟩ = ⟨parameter value⟩] ⎪ CALL CHAIN (1,4) ⌡ END
Link 1,4 Readin and compact link	⌠ * CHAIN (1,4) ⎪ CALL READIN ⎪ CALL COMPAK ⎨ CALL CHAIN (2,4) ⎪ END ⎪ (specific READIN) binary decks ⌡ (specific COMPAK)

Link 2,4
Manipulate and print
  picture, move film,
  etc.
	⌠ * CHAIN (2,4)
	⎪ CALL FILM
	⎪ CALL option for MASK, REDUCE
	⎪ CALL SPECT
	⎪ CALL CHECK
	⎪ [fortran for optional film movement]
	⎪ CALL option for DIFFER
	⎪ [CALL option for WRITE]
	⎨ CALL option for PRINT
	⎪ CALL CHAIN (3,4)
	⎪ END
	⎪ (FILM)
	⎪ (option specific MASK)
	⎪ (option specific REDUCE)
	⎪ (specific SPECT)
	⎪ (specific CHECK)
	⎪ (option specific DIFFER)
	⎪ (option specific PRINT)
	⌡ (special facility: WRITE and SIMPOS)

Link 3,4 Scan and process objects	⌠ * CHAIN (3,4) ⎪ CALL INPUT ⎪ 1000 CALL PHASE 1 ⎪ CALL ENDOFF ⎪ 1001 CALL PHASE 2 ⎪ CALL PHASE 3 ⎪ GO TO 1000 ⎨ 1002 CALL CHAIN (4,4) ⎪ END ⎪ (INPUT, REPLAZ) ⎪ (specific SEARCH and other decks) ⎪ (PHASE 1) ⎪ (specific BOUND and other decks) ⎪ (specific ERASE and other decks) ⎪ (BASIC and other decks) ⎪ (SYNTAX) ⎪ (TRANS and other decks) ⌡ (PHASE 3)
Link 4,4 Pair, classify, and do statistics	⌠ * CHAIN· (4,4) ⎪ CALL EVALUT ⎪ CALL PAIR ⎨ CALL STATIS ⎪ CALL CHAIN (1,4) ⎪ END ⎪ (specific EVALUT) ⎪ (specific PAIR) ⌡ (specific statistics)

FILM, a FORTRAN program can be written to enable any film-movement protocol desired.

The fourth link (Link 3,4) scans a picture and processes the objects as described previously. PHASE 1 concerns the locating, boundary tracing, boundary-list characterizing, and erasing of a chromosome. PHASE 2 is concerned with the syntax analysis leading to the identification of the parts of the chromosome. PHASE 3 is concerned with actually making the measurements on the chromosome. Again, as indicated in Table 2, associated with Link 3,4 there are many options for the user.

The fourth link (Link 4,4) accomplishes the pairing of homologous chromosomes for a frame and the over-all statistical processing.

Chromosome Measurements

The measurements made by the system can be summarized in three areas: (a) measurements on an individual chromosome, (b) measurements concerned with all the chromosomes of one cell, and (c) measurements (statistical results) of many cells from a single individual. For each chromosome, we can determine (1) the integrated density, (2) the area, (3) the individual arm lengths, (4) the over-all length, (5) the arm-length ratio, and (6) the perimeter length. For each cell, we can determine (1) the total chromosome-complement length, (2) the fraction of total chromosome length of each chromosome, (3) the pairing of homologues, (4) the classification of the chromosome complement into groups, (5) the location association of homologues and groups, and (6) the count within groups and total count. For the collection of cells from each individual person, we can determine (1) the distribution of ratios within groups, (2) the distribution of fractional lengths, (3) the percentages of the total counts and counts within groups if there is a variation, and (4) the location correlations.

Summary and Conclusions

The successful design and application of the FIDAC instrument and the FIDACSYS programing system can, we feel, present a new capability to the biomedical research scientist, opening new fields of investigation in the area of quantitative analysis of pictorial data of biomedical importance. The FIDAC is a high-resolution, high-speed, on-line, real-time scanner input to a digital computer, and the FIDACSYS programing system is an advanced and flexible pattern-recognition and measurement programing language for analyzing the pictures with a computer. Application to the analysis of chromosome photomicrographs was described. We feel that we cannot hope to predict the further applications to which the FIDAC system may be put in the future. The system represents an example of the important potential that modern technological advances may offer the biomedical research scientist.[3]

REFERENCES

1. LEDLEY, R. S., *Programming and Utilizing Digital Computers*, McGraw-Hill Book Company, Inc., New York, 1962, Chap. 8.
2. LEDLEY, R. S., AND J. B. WILSON, "Automatic-Programming Languages Translation Through Syntactical Analysis," *Comm. of the ACM, 5*, No. 3, 145–155 (March 1962).
3. LEDLEY, R. S., "Biomedical Electronics: Potentialities and Problems," *Science, 135*, No. 3499, 198–201 (19 January 1962).

CHAPTER 34

RELATIVE MOTION AND NONLINEAR PHOTOCELLS IN OPTICAL IMAGE PROCESSING *

J. C. Bliss and H. D. Crane

Stanford Research Institute, Menlo Park, California

Introduction

An interesting property of a parallel-plate photocell with nonlinear photo-conductive material is that its conductance is a function not only of the total incident light but of the light distribution as well. This can readily be demonstrated by considering a uniform photocell having one transparent electrode through which an image can fall on a thin photoconductive layer sandwiched between the transparent electrode and a back electrode. If we let $g(x, y)$ be the conductance per unit area of the photoconductive layer at point (x, y) in response to light intensity $I(x, y)$, then the total conductance of the cell, measured between the pair of plate electrodes, is expressed as

$$G = \int_A g(x, y) \, dx \, dy \tag{1}$$

where A is the area of the cell. If g depends linearly on the light intensity (e.g., a photocell model characterized by $g = kI$, where k is a constant), then Eq. 1 reduces simply to

$$G = kL_T \tag{2}$$

where L_T is the total incident light flux. With g a nonlinear function of intensity, however—e.g., the photocell model

$$g = kI^p \tag{3}$$

* This research was supported, in part, by a research grant from the Vocational Rehabilitation Agency, Department of Health, Education, and Welfare, Washington, D.C., and in part by Stanford Research Institute, Menlo Park, California.

where p is a constant—then G also depends on the particular distribution of light as well.

With certain relative motions in the optical system, the distribution of light can be made to vary with time even though the total light through the system may be invariant. By monitoring these variations with a nonlinear photocell, a considerable amount of information about the object space can be determined.

In this paper we discuss some methods for automatically tracking an object—both in range and angle—and for determining certain features of the object for the purpose of recognition. We think of these processing techniques as being relatively "simple" in the sense that we do not dissect the image and separately process the light intensity at each point, either by computer or individual circuitry. Rather, we process the signal obtained from a two-terminal photocell on which the entire field of view is imaged. In some cases, a set of photocells is used and their varying outputs are compared.

Determining Object Range

Point Source of Light

Consider a point source of light that ideally focuses to a point image, as in Fig. 1. A wide-area photocell perpendicular to the optic axis captures

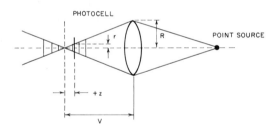

Fig. 1. Optical arrangement for calculating $G(z)$ for a point-source object.

all of the light from the lens, so that the total light falling on the cell is invariant with its axial position, though the light distribution continually changes. Let z be the distance of the photocell from the plane of focus. The light intensity I over the circular cross section of light is assumed to be uniform and given by

$$I = \frac{L_T}{\pi r^2} \tag{4}$$

for total intercepted light L_T, where

$$r = \frac{z}{2f^*} \tag{5}$$

and

$$f^* = \frac{V}{2R} \tag{6}$$

is the effective f number.

Using the photocell model of Eq. 3, we find for the point source that

$$G = k(L_T)^p \left(\frac{\pi}{4}\right)^{1-p} \left(\frac{z}{f^*}\right)^{2-2p} \tag{7}$$

or that G is proportional to $z^{(2-2p)}$. This implies that for $p > 1$ the conductance becomes infinite at the focus plane $z = 0$, and that for $p < 1$ the conductance goes to zero. The photocell model cannot hold over such a wide range of light intensity and, of course, these limits are never reached in practice. Nevertheless, we can expect a maximum or minimum in G at $z = 0$, depending on whether p is greater or less than unity, respectively. For example, with $p > 1$, we might expect a $G(z)$ curve like that of Fig. 2a, which is an even function of z, i.e., symmetric about $z = 0$.

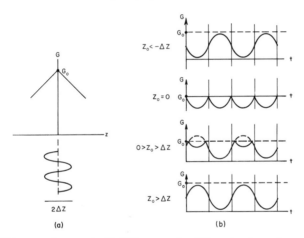

FIG. 2. (a) $G(z)$ curve for $p > 1$. (b) $G(t)$ curves for different values of z_0; peak-to-peak amplitude of photocell vibration of $2\Delta z$.

If we now vibrate the photocell along the optic axis, the variation in conductance depends critically on the average position—let us call it z_0— of the photocell. Assuming a peak-to-peak vibration amplitude $2\Delta z$, then G will vary with time, as shown in Fig. 2b. Whenever the photocell crosses the image plane, the conductance signal "folds over." Vibration exactly about the focus plane results in complete foldover.

With a constant voltage across the photocell, current flow is directly proportional to conductance. Thus, we can find the exact plane of focus by varying z_0 until we achieve maximum foldover in the photocell current, or alternately, for a fixed z_0 we can determine whether any objects are within the object range covered by the vibration amplitude. In the former mode, we have an automatic focus or distance-measuring device, and in the latter mode an object-detection device where the center of the range of search is varied by varying z_0, and the depth of range is determined by the amplitude of vibration. An object detection device of this type is discussed further in the article by Bliss and Crane.[1]

Let us make some further observations about this type of system that will be important for understanding some of the other types of configurations to be discussed.

Regarding the assumed photocell model of Eq. 3, an actual plot of total conductance G as a function of light intensity—for a uniformly illuminated experimental photocell—is shown in Fig. 3. Note that the actual photocell

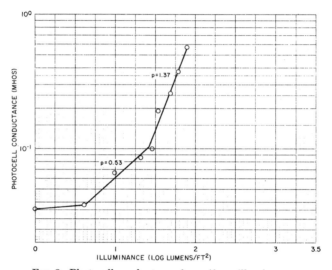

FIG. 3. Photocell conductance for uniform illuminance.

conductance can be reasonably modeled by the power function relation of Eq. 3 except that the value of p varies for different ranges of illumination. This particular photocell was relatively uniform, the conductance not varying by more than 4 per cent, as a test circle of light was successively swept over its surface.

Translation Independence

The size and intensity of the circular patch of light intercepted by the photocell of Fig. 1 are approximately invariant to the translational position of the point source within the range of the object plane in which vignetting is negligible, so that with a uniform photocell the $G(z)$ function of Eq. 7 is substantially independent of object translation. This leads to uniform results over a relatively large field of view, not limited merely to on-axis objects. This is true not only for a point source but for any object shape.

TABLE 1   Photocell Conductance as a Function of Axial Position
(α and β are geometric constants defined in Reference 1)

Form of Image in Focus	Assumed Lens Aperture	$G(z)$
Point	Square	$k \left[\dfrac{L_T}{(z/f^*)^2} \right]^p \left(\dfrac{z}{f^*} \right)^2$
Line of Length $2D$	Square	$k \left[\dfrac{L_T}{(z/f^*) \cdot 2D(1 - z/V)} \right]^p \left(\dfrac{z}{f^*} \right) \cdot 2D \left(1 - \alpha \dfrac{z}{V} \right)$
Circular Patch of Diameter X	Circular	$\approx k \left[\dfrac{L_T}{\pi X^2 (1 - z/V)^2} \right]^p \pi X^2 \left(1 - \beta \dfrac{z}{V} \right)^2$

Dependence on Object Shape

The $G(z)$ functions for ideal objects consisting of a one-dimensional line object of length $2D$, and for a two-dimensional circular patch of light, of diameter $2X$, are shown in Table 1. These results are taken from Refer-

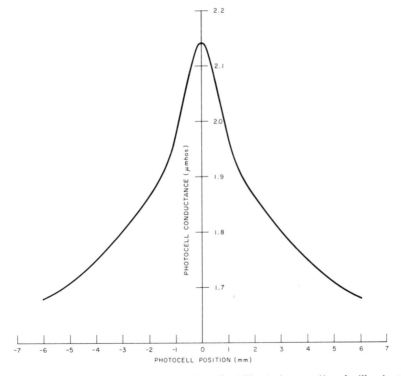

FIG. 4. Experimental $G(z)$ curve, using the cell of Fig. 3, for a uniformly illuminated annulus object having an outside radius of 3 cm, an inside radius of 2 cm, a luminance of 200 ft-L, and placed 78 cm from a 58-mm focal-length lens. (Image illuminance of 1.5 log lm/ft².)

ence 1. [Note that only for a point source of light and $p = \frac{1}{2}$ is the $G(z)$ curve actually linear away from the origin.] The determination of defocus patterns for $z \neq 0$ is the first step in the calculation of these $G(z)$ functions. This process can be greatly simplified by assuming different forms of lens apertures depending on the object being studied. For example, for a line object the calculation is greatly simplified by assuming a square lens of

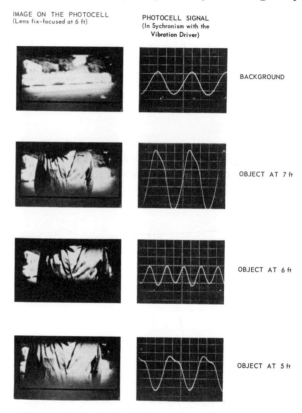

IMAGE ON THE PHOTOCELL
(Lens fix-focused at 6 ft)

PHOTOCELL SIGNAL
(In Sychronism with the Vibration Driver)

BACKGROUND

OBJECT AT 7 ft

OBJECT AT 6 ft

OBJECT AT 5 ft

FIG. 5. Photocell signals for various object distances.

side $2R$, whereas for the rotationally symmetric circular patch a circular lens is simpler. For a square lens Eq. 7 for a point source simplifies to that shown in the table.

In Fig. 4 is shown an actual $G(z)$ curve for the photocell of Fig. 3 and a uniformly illuminated annulus object. Although difficult to analyze, it seems apparent that a $G(z)$ plot for *any* two-dimensional object should have an extremum value at $z = 0$, and thus a strong foldover for vibration about focus. For example, in Fig. 5 is shown the variation in G for three positions of a real-life subject with a fixed background.* The photocell

---

* As explained in the Discussion section, Fig. 5 was taken with a different photocell geometry.

vibrated about a fixed position corresponding to an object distance of 6 ft. Note the strong foldover obtained in the photocell signal as the moving object passed through the 6-ft range, and the opposite phase of the signal on either side of focus.

The various signal components from a mixed field of objects—each at a different distance—sum together, the more "prominent" object in the field providing the dominant signal, as in the example of Fig. 5. To focus automatically on a particular object, that object must therefore be dominant in the field, or we must narrow the field of view until it is. If the object should happen to be near the edge of the field then we will have to find some way to "aim" at the selected object so that it remains in view as the field is reduced.

Determining Object Position: Aiming

Point Source of Light

For purposes of aiming, it is reasonable to consider a rotational mode of vibration about an axis orthogonal to the optic axis, as indicated in Fig. 6. Consider a point source object—displaced by angle θ from the optic axis—to be focused at point P. Let the axis of rotation of the photocell be displaced a distance z_0 from the focus plane. For $\theta \gg 0$, as the photocell vibrates through a total peak-to-peak swing of $2\alpha_{max}$, the patch of light on the photocell becomes alternately larger and smaller, with corresponding dimming and brightening of the intercepted image. From our previous analysis, we should expect that for $p > 1$, the cell conductance would increase with decrease in patch size, and decrease with increase in patch size. Thus, we can expect a substantially monotonic following of the cell conductance with the vibration, or no foldover in conductance signal for large θ. For $\theta = 0$, however, there is obviously complete foldover.

We can investigate the nature of the transition from signal foldover for small θ to no foldover for large θ by developing the general expression for G as a function of α and θ. From this derivation, which is given in the appendix, we can see that the $G(\theta)$ curve is different for each value of α. Sketches of three such $G(\theta)$ curves are shown in Fig. 7 for the cases $\alpha = 0$, and for the extreme values $\alpha = +\alpha_{max}$ and $\alpha = -\alpha_{max}$. There exists a value of θ for which $G(\alpha = +\alpha_{max}) = G(\alpha = 0)$. Let this value of θ be called θ_1. From the derivation of the appendix we find—for the easily calculated cases of $p = \frac{1}{2}$ or $p = \frac{3}{2}$—that the magnitude of θ_1 is

$$\theta_1 \approx \frac{z_0}{2V} \alpha \tag{8}$$

which is generally much smaller than α.

From Fig. 7 we see that for $\theta = 0$ we get complete foldover as we vibrate the photocell, the G value being the same for $\pm \alpha_{max}$. At $\theta = \theta_1$, we should

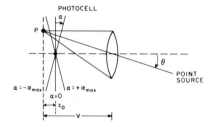

FIG. 6. Photocell vibrated about an axis removed a distance z_0 from focus.

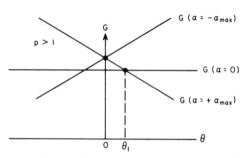

FIG. 7. Sketch of $G(\theta)$ for different angular orientations of the photocell.

expect a signal resembling a half-wave rectified sinusoid since $G(\alpha = 0)$ is the same as for $G(\alpha = +\alpha_{max})$. As θ increases, the G variation should become more like the α variation, i.e., proportional to α. To verify that these are indeed the types of results to be expected, a circular patch of light, 2.5 mm in diameter and 33 cm from a 58-mm focal length lens, was translated in its plane to obtain different θ values. The photographs of Fig. 8 are the result of varying the lateral position of the light source. Note in this case that θ_1 is just a little greater than one minute of arc. For these photographs the photocell vibrated through an angle of about ± 5 degrees. (Note the need for the photocell to be out of the focus plane, otherwise foldover signals would be derived—in the distance-ranging mode—from any image, regardless of its angular orientation.)

Object Position Tracking

Thus, simply from the phase of the conductance signal, we can tell in which direction a point source is off axis. This result is similar to that in distance tracking where the phase indicated the proper direction to move the photocell for purposes of focusing. For an object of known lumination distribution we could, in fact, get a measure of the angular displacement off axis by noting that the peak-to-peak swing in G is represented by the difference in $G(\alpha = +\alpha_{max})$ and $G(\alpha = -\alpha_{max})$ for the particular value of θ.

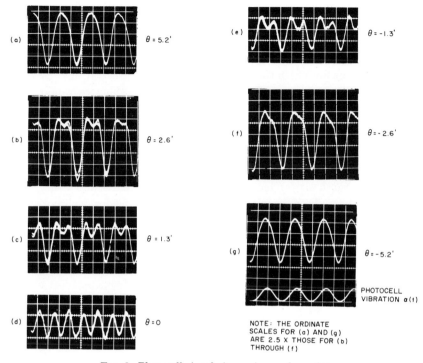

$\theta = 5.2'$

$\theta = 2.6'$

$\theta = 1.3'$

$\theta = 0$

$\theta = -1.3'$

$\theta = -2.6'$

$\theta = -5.2'$

PHOTOCELL
VIBRATION $\alpha(t)$

NOTE: THE ORDINATE
SCALES FOR (a) AND (g)
ARE 2.5 X THOSE FOR (b)
THROUGH (f)

FIG. 8. Photocell signals for various values of θ.

We see that this type of device, connected into a control loop, could be useful for purposes of automatic aiming, although with photocell vibration about only a single axis, we are sensitive only to object displacements orthogonal to this axis of rotation. However, by vibrating the photocell first about one axis and then about an orthogonal axis, or with two photocell systems vibrating about orthogonal axes, or with a tilted photocell rotating about the lens axis, it is clear that we can achieve sensitivity to angular displacement in any direction from the optic axis.

For an object at an arbitrary range as well as an arbitrary angular displacement, we could use the automatic focus technique to maintain a fixed value of z_0, or even z_0/V, independent of object range.

It is interesting that such high sensitivity can be achieved with such a simple system. Assuming we could resolve to within one part in five of θ_1, then we should be able to reproduce the position of an object to within one minute of arc. With care, even greater precision should be possible.

Nonideal Objects

Just as in the case of the range technique, which works for nonideal objects, so here too we should expect similar response for any object pattern, idealized or not. For example, with two identical point sources the same distance from the lens, maximum foldover will occur when the "center of light"—in analogy to "center of mass"—is aligned with the optical axis. For different intensities of the two sources, or with different distances from the lens, the results are more complex, but still there will exist some point for which there will be complete foldover. If, for any given shape, we know in advance just what the point is, then we would know that at maximum foldover the axis of the optical system is aimed directly at that point.

Image Scanning

Until now methods for locating objects without particular concern for their shape have been considered. Let us now consider techniques for identifying certain features of the object shape as well. We will see that relative motion and nonlinear photocells are again powerful tools. As a starting point, recall the earlier comment that in calculating defocus patterns for a given object there is often great simplification in the proper choice of lens or mask shape. In other words, the defocus patterns change with mask shape and rotation of a single mask shape results in changing defocus patterns. Thus, by using certain selected masks that are made to rotate, we should be able to extract significant information about the object with nonlinear photocells that are sensitive to the changing patterns of light distribution.

Defocus Patterns

Consider the case of a luminous line segment (lying anywhere in a plane perpendicular to the optic axis) and a narrow slit mask, which we rotate in front of the lens. The light passing through the lens from each source point has the cross-sectional shape of the mask—i.e., a narrow slit. In other words, the "cones" that come to focus in the image plane simply have the shape of the mask. In the in-focus image plane, the light reaching each point is emitted from the corresponding point of the object (neglecting diffraction effects) so that rotation of the mask has no effect on the light distribution. Only the orientation of each "cone" of light focusing on each point, not the total light within the "cone," is affected.

If the photocell is displaced slightly from focus, however, then the light reaching any point of the photocell is made up of contributions from overlapping cones. To visualize more readily the effect of the overlapping, assume that the line source is luminous at only a finite number of equally spaced point sources. If this line of dots and the slit mask are orthogonal, the defocused image is made up of the overlapping cones shown in Fig. 9a. With 45-degree relative displacement, the overlapping cones would appear as in Fig. 9b, and with perfect alignment of source and object the cones overlap in their long dimension, Fig. 9c.

Thus, the light patterns are sensitive to relative orientation of object and mask, the pattern being relatively thin and bright for complete alignment

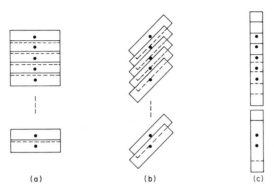

(a)   (b)   (c)

Fɪɢ. 9. Formation of defocus images of a line object with a line mask at three orientation angles.

and broader and dimmer for 90-degree displacement. The total light reaching the photocell, however, is independent of the relative orientation. With the line source uniformly luminated, instead of simply a series of bright dots, the light intensity is generally more uniform (i.e., no series of bright bars) but the over-all pattern of Fig. 9 is not changed.

We see then that with the slit mask and line source aligned a relatively bright, defocus image is formed. If we let θ measure the angle of rotation of the mask, then for a photocell with $p > 1$ we should find that the G vs. θ curve peaks at a value of θ equal to the angle of orientation of the line source. A sketch of such a $G(\theta)$ curve for a line source is shown in Fig. 10a. The result is independent of the position of the line—i.e., translation of the line—as long as its image falls on the photocell, and the photocell is uniform.

If the object were more complex than a single line, a correspondingly more complex $G(\theta)$ curve would result. The conductance would become relatively large whenever the mask became aligned with any line segment in the source. When rotating the line mask in front of a letter "E," for example, we should expect the $G(\theta)$ curve to have two relatively large peaks for each 180 degrees of rotation, the relative size of the peaks depending on the ratio of total vertical line segment to total horizontal segment. A typical $G(\theta)$ signal for a letter E is sketched in Fig. 10b.

By scanning characters consisting of different combinations of line segments with a slit mask, recognition of particular characters could be based on the position and magnitude of the various peaks in the $G(\theta)$ curve. An

alternate type of arrangement using the same idea is to compose each
character with lines having only a single direction, but with the direction
being different for each character. An example of such a character is shown
in Fig. 11a. The $G(\theta)$ curve for this object pattern would simply peak at a
value of θ equal to θ_0. For a capacity of ten characters, for example, the

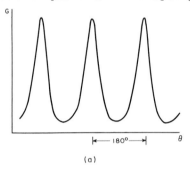

(a)

FIG. 10. (a) Sketch of a $G(\theta)$ signal for
a rotating slit scan of a luminous line
object. (b) Sketch of a typical $G(\theta)$ signal of a rotating slit scan of a letter E.

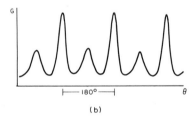

(b)

angular displacement from letter to letter could be arranged to be 180/10
or 18 degrees. For each character there would be but a single peak in the
$G(\theta)$ curve, with the peak displaced according to the angle of lines in the
character. With the mask rotating at a uniform velocity, letter identification would amount to identifying in which of ten possible time slots the
peak in the signal occurs.

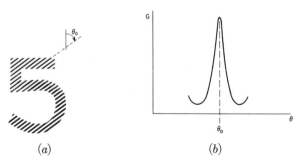

(a)   (b)

FIG. 11. (a) Character composed of a fine-line structure. (b) Sketch of $G(\theta)$ signal from
a rotating slit scan of the fine-line character.

Overlap Patterns

A line object scanned with a rotating slit mask results in a "smooth" $G(\theta)$ curve having a single peak and valley for each 180 degrees of rotation, as seen in Fig. 10a. With a series of n parallel lines that are just "slightly out of focus," we expect a similarly smooth $G(\theta)$ curve, with the G scale essentially n times larger than for the single line case. However, if we increase the amount of defocus so that at maximum line broadening—i.e., when the slit becomes orthogonal to the lines—neighboring patterns begin to overlap and relatively bright lines appear between each defocused line image, then we can expect new peaks to appear in the $G(\theta)$ curve. In other words, if a pattern is composed of simple elements, and their images do not overlap, then we obtain relatively simply composed $G(\theta)$ curves. With more complex patterns, or with overlap, the curves become more complex and, because of the photocell nonlinearity, can be difficult to analyze. It is necessary to appreciate this fact as we jump now into an arrangement that seems potentially powerful for pattern processing, but for which analysis is difficult and even intuition can often be but a weak crutch.

Cross-Correlation in the Focal Plane

With only a small amount of defocus, the light at any point of the image is contributed from only a relatively small local region of the object space. To search for larger features of a character—e.g., large arcs—we need a great deal more "overlap." For this purpose let us consider some special features of the focal plane.

From geometric optics, we recall that the interesting feature of the focal plane is that each point of the plane represents the point of focus for all rays approaching parallel to the line drawn between the center of the lens and the particular point of the focal plane. Or equivalently, it represents the point of focus of a plane wave approaching in the direction of this particular line. From this observation, it can readily be seen that the arrangement of object, mask, and lens shown in Fig. 12 can produce optical

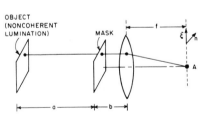

Fig. 12. Optical arrangement for obtaining cross-correlation functions.

cross-correlation functions. Thus, with a uniform noncoherent luminous object, the illumination I at any point (ζ, η) in the focal plane of the lens is given by

$$I(\zeta, \eta) = k \iint T_1(x, y) T_2\left(x + \frac{a\eta}{f}, y + \frac{a\zeta}{f}\right) dx\, dy \tag{9}$$

where x, y are the coordinates in the object and mask planes, T_1 and T_2 are the emission and transmission coefficients of the object and mask, respectively, and k is a constant. For example, the light falling at the point of intersection of the optical axis and the focal plane ($\eta = 0$, $\zeta = 0$) is the sum of those rays emitted from the source, parallel to the optic axis, each attenuated by the corresponding transmission coefficient of the mask. If the source and mask have identical pattern shapes and are axially aligned, the light intensity at this point is proportional to the zero translation value of the autocorrelation function. The whole focal plane pattern represents the two-dimensional autocorrelation function, i.e., the autocorrelation values with all possible translations of the object pattern with itself.

If the object translates in its own plane, the two-dimensional correlation function correspondingly translates but otherwise does not change form (except for the changes in light due to vignetting, which is small for relatively small angular displacements, say up to ±20 degrees). Note also that the cross-correlation function is merely changed in dimensional scale if the object film moves closer or farther from the lens, as can be seen from the way dimension a enters Eq. 9. Only for the focal plane do we achieve this translation independence of the shape of the cross-correlation function—i.e., the cross-correlation pattern translates but does not change form as the object translates—and simple linear scaling of the correlation pattern if the object moves closer or farther from the lens.

Pattern Matching

Suppose we have a set of objects and a corresponding set of masks. With a lens and photocell associated with each mask, cross-correlations of a given object with each mask would be formed simultaneously on the set of photocells. If the total emitted light is the same for each object, and if the total transmission is the same for each mask, then the total light reaching each photocell is independent of the particular object and mask. In this case, only the difference in light distributions will cause the conductances to vary from cell to cell. Using the photocell model of Eq. 3, we can consider a two-dimensional conductivity pattern corresponding to each cross-correlation pattern in that the light intensity at each point of the cross-correlation function is raised to the power p. The total photocell conductance is then proportional to the area under this conductivity function. For p sufficiently greater than 1, we might intuitively expect the autocorrelation function, with its bright central peak, to result in a conductance considerably higher than each of the other cross-correlation functions. In other words, the photocell conductance is a measure on the cross-correlation function that is particularly sensitive to distinguishing between a light distribution with a high peak and a light distribution composed of equal total light but lesser peaks. If, for any given object pattern, the set of conductances is such that the autocorrelation function can be uniquely identified, then we have the basis for a pattern detection scheme that is insensitive to a considerable shift (i.e., translation) of object position.

To study this possibility further, we simulated such a recognition scheme on a digital computer. For this purpose we used a set of black-and-white number patterns, shown in Fig. 13, each of which has exactly the same

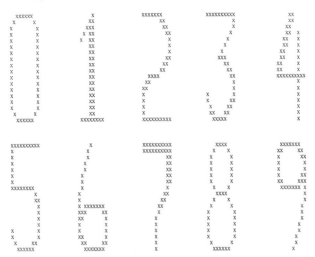

FIG. 13. Characters designed on a 10 × 18 matrix to have equal area.

area. This is reflected in the same total number of x's for each pattern. When a pattern is used as an object, the array of x's represents the distribution of emitted light. When used as a mask, the array of x's represents the region of transparency.

For each of the 55 different object-mask combinations using these 10 patterns, the computer formed the two-dimensional cross-correlation function

$$G = k \sum_{i,j} \{I_{i,j}\}^p \tag{10}$$

(where k is arbitrarily chosen to equal one, and i and j are integers that specify position on a 10 × 18 matrix), for different values of exponent p. The array of conductances for the case $p = 4$ is shown in Table 2. The array is, of course, symmetrical, so that only one-half of the array is shown. The worst discrimination ratios are shown to the right. For example, with a "0" object, autocorrelation leads to a G value of

$$G_{0,0} = 70.9 \times 10^5$$

The next lowest conductance is for the "1" mask; i.e.,

$$G_{0,1} = 20.6 \times 10^5$$

leading to a worst discrimination for the "0" of 3.4. For this arbitrary set

TABLE 2   Computer Simulated Photocell Conductances for
the Cross-Correlation Functions of the Characters of Fig. 13*

	0	1	2	3	4	5	6	7	8	9	Worst Ratio	
0	70.9	20.6	6.88	6.15	9.30	14.1	10.3	6.49	7.82	10.3	3.44	0, 1
1		154	7.5	10.9	23.4	8.40	14.5	20.8	9.24	15.1	6.6	1, 0
2			51.3	9.77	7.46	9.84	6.87	10.8	7.29	6.88	4.75	2, 5
3				47.1	7.37	15.3	6.36	10.5	7.55	8.13	3.08	3, 5
4					75.9	7.59	13.0	16.8	7.41	12.3	3.24	4, 7
5						50.9	9.18	9.48	6.75	10.8	3.32	5, 3
6							50.1	10.8	9.43	19.7	2.54	6, 9
7								76.5	6.48	16.3	3.68	7, 1
8									42.7	8.04	4.53	8, 6
9										50.1	2.54	9, 6

* Each entry is $\times 10^5$; $p = 4$.

of letters—for which there was no attempt whatever to optimize the design—the poorest discrimination ratio for $p = 4$ is 2.5 for the (6, 9) combination. The effect of different p values is to change this ratio from 1.0, to 1.4, to 2.5, to 5.0, to 9.6 for p values of 2, 3, 4, 5, and 6, respectively. The (1, 0) discrimination ratio changes from 1.9 for $p = 2$, to 34 for $p = 6$.

Of course, these results are highly idealized in the sense of the photocell model used. A more realistic model would at least include a constant term I_0; e.g.,

$$g = k(I + I_0)^p \tag{11}$$

which would tend to lower the discrimination ratios. On the other hand, the fact that the p value is different over different ranges of light intensity can be an advantage if it is arranged so that the highest p values occur for the highest light values. This would tend to lower considerably the more smeared out cross-correlation conductance values relative to the autocorrelation values.

An interesting result is that with this particular nonlinear measure on the cross-correlation function the conductance value is not necessarily monotonic with the degree of correlation, and that for $p > 1$, the conductance can actually be greater for a cross-correlation than an autocorrelation function. For example, with the previous letter set, $G_{4,6} > G_{6,6}$ for $p = 2$.

In other words, with a complex light pattern having many minor peaks the highest conductance is not determined simply by the pattern with the highest intensity peak. Of course with sufficiently high p, the highest peak can be made to dominate. It is interesting that, even with $p = 2$, we can have higher G values for cross-correlation than autocorrelation.

It is quite clear that a practical recognition scheme based on this approach would require considerable further study. Nevertheless it seems an interesting "existence proof" of the possibility of translation independent cross-correlation techniques based on the use of noncoherent light.

Scanning

Irrespective of the exact position of the photocell—from the focal plane to a slightly defocused plane—rotation of a lens aperture constitutes a scanning process just as does the more conventional optical or magnetic slit scan in which an object traverses a suitable reading head consisting of a slit which is effectively in the image plane. Let us make some comparisons between this more conventional scan and the rotational type of scan in which the slit is in the lens plane and the defocused images that we have been discussing are used. Let us refer to these schemes, which are shown in Figs. 14a and 14b, as the TS (translation scan) and RS (rotational scan) schemes, respectively.

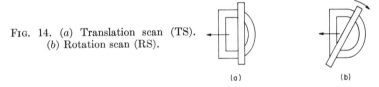

Fig. 14. (a) Translation scan (TS). (b) Rotation scan (RS).

(a)   (b)

Assume for the moment that in both schemes the signal from the reading head is matched against a set of stored signals, one for each possible character, and that a best fit is sought.

Skew

With the TS, the signal at any instant depends on the total area of the character appearing through the relatively narrow slit. Thus, the signal is sensitive to the angular skew of the letter with respect to the slit. With the RS, skew results only in a time shift but not a change in the wave shape of the signal.

Repetitive Reading

With the RS, each rotation of the head constitutes a complete scan of the character. Thus, the character can be reread with the same head for as long as the character remains in the field of view. To cope with serious skew problems, one could consider reading the character a number of times, while varying the instant at which the matched-filter signals are sampled. This is equivalent to introducing a different magnitude of compensating skew on each scan. The largest correlation function from the series of scans can be chosen.

Noise

Let us consider the effect of noise—such as stray ink spots—on the TS and RS schemes. Since in the TS scheme the mask is in the image plane, the signal from the noise spot adds only to a relatively small time sample of the character signal, but this can markedly change the shape of the waveform generated by the scan. In the RS scheme, however, the mask is in the lens plane and the signal from the noise spot adds more uniformly to the entire character signal, affecting each part much less. For example, for a circular ink spot and a photocell in a slightly defocused plane the waveform generated by the RS will suffer only a dc shift in level.

Shape of Scanning Aperture

In principle, an arbitrary shape of scanning aperture can be used in each type of scan. In the case of the TS, however, any mask shape other than linear would put a serious limitation on vertical registration. (With a linear slit the TS scheme is, of course, independent of vertical translation.) With the translational independence of the RS, however, any aperture shape can be used equally well without registration restriction.

Suppose, for example, that we had a character consisting simply of a half-arc of a circle. With an identical mask, and with the photocell in the focal plane so that the optical patterns correspond to cross-correlation functions, then we can expect a "smooth" $G(\theta)$ curve with an extremum value once per revolution occurring when the mask is exactly aligned with the object. We could identify then, if we wished, the angular orientation of the arc object, just as we could identify the orientation of a randomly placed line object with a slit mask.

Also, as with a line mask we could abstract information about patterns consisting of variously placed line segments, so with a curved mask, information can be obtained about patterns consisting of variously placed arcs. For example, if characters S and 3 are each composed simply of two identical arcs, as shown in Figs. 15a and 15b, then an idealized version of the corresponding $G(\theta)$ curves would exhibit two extrema per revolution in the case of the S, and one stronger extremum in the case of the 3.

Multiple Scanning

Because of the translation independence property, we could also arrange for simultaneous scanning with several different masks. Each of the scanning signals could be used for independently forming correlations with corresponding sets of stored signals, with a multiple "vote" subsequently

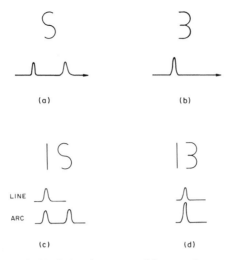

FIG. 15. Comparison of idealized signals generated by rotation scan of the characters S, 3, IS, and 13.

taken. Or, for sufficiently simple patterns, we could view the multiple scanning as a search for object features—lines, arcs, and so on. Relevant information is abstracted in this way by comparing the relative timing and strength of the various peaks in the $G(\theta)$ curves. For example, if a single-line stroke is added to the S and 3 patterns to form the patterns IS and 13, respectively, as in Figs. 15c and 15d, then the two new patterns could be distinguished from the original S and 3 patterns by noting a strong peak from a line scan signal, and distinguished from each other by again noting the single versus double peak from the arc scan. Because of the translation independence, the IS and 13 could not, however, on the basis of a simple line and arc scan, be distinguished from the patterns SI and 31, respectively.

Discussion

We have mentioned a number of relatively simple image processing techniques that are based on the use of wide-area nonlinear photocells used in an optical system in which relative motion of some of the parts causes the photocell signal to vary in certain predictable ways, permitting information to be abstracted about the object space. By "simple" it is meant that the optical image is not first dissected and the various pieces processed by computer program or individual circuitry. The signals from the systems described here derive from one or relatively few two-terminal photocells.

With the set of techniques discussed here we could, at least in principle, build a system having capability such that with an object pattern placed in a random position in the field, we could automatically focus on it (and therefore determine its distance), automatically aim at it (determine its angular orientation), as well as determine certain features present in the pattern, if not be able to identify the pattern uniquely.

The types of motion we have discussed are (1) photocell vibration along the optic axis for purposes of focusing, (2) rotational vibration of the photocell about an axis orthogonal to the optic axis, for purposes of aiming, and (3) rotation of various lens masks for purposes of pattern and feature recognition.

The photocells used in the experiments were primarily of the type in which a photoconductive layer of material is sandwiched between two conductive layers, one of which is transparent so that images can fall on the photoconductor. Cells of this type are not generally available because, for most photocell applications, it has been easier to manufacture cells with both electrodes interdigitated on the same side of the photoconductive material, in which case there is no possibility of short circuits from pinholes in the thin photoconductive layer. Some experiments made with such interdigitated structures show that they could find some use in the techniques discussed here, although not only is analysis much more difficult for such a geometry, but the performance is not actually independent of the exact positioning of the image on the cell.

Another interesting geometric arrangement involves the use of electrodes placed along two opposite edges of a square film of photoconductive material. With this geometry, the total resistance between the electrodes also depends on light distribution, even though the material itself may be linear. A cell of this type has been used in the most recent focusing experiments,[2] and the photographs of Fig. 5 were actually taken with such a cell, although similar signals would have appeared with a sandwich type of cell. Two advantages of the end-terminal configuration are (1) the cell is simpler to make, i.e., again there are no pinhole problems, and (2) the output signals are considerably higher. On the other hand, analysis is again very difficult for this configuration compared with the sandwich type.

Considerable study is required to determine from an over-all point of view just which types of photocell configuration may be best for these various applications. There is also a need to develop faster photoconductive materials. The frequency response from our present experimental cells does not permit a vibration frequency greater than about 200 cps. Considerably higher frequency response would be necessary for high-speed processing.

The distance-measuring technique discussed here has been subjected to considerable experimentation, and it is clear that it can readily be incorporated into practical engineering systems for detecting objects that fall within certain ranges of distance, or for automatic focusing. The aiming technique has had less experimental work, but it is clear that it too could be used in practical applications involving the detection of objects that fall within certain angular volumes of object space, or for automatic aiming.

As for practical application of these techniques in pattern-recognition systems, it is clear that there are a great many possibilities, but considerable additional study is required to determine where and just how these techniques might be best applied. The properties of a rotational scan, in comparison with the more familiar slit scan, will require a great deal of engineering evaluation to determine the relative merits of translation independence, and differently shaped "slits." For instance, the translation independence depends on the availability of relatively uniform cells. The ability to produce such cells in quantity is yet to be determined.

APPENDIX

Calculation of $G(\theta, \alpha)$ for the Rotational Vibration Mode of Fig. 6

The geometric arrangement is shown in detail in Fig. 16a for a point-source object. We wish to calculate the conductance G as both the object position, as measured by angle θ, and photocell orientation, as measured by angle α, vary independently.

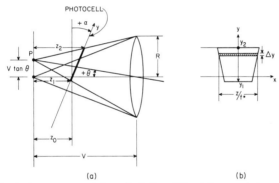

(a)   (b)

Fig. 16. Optical arrangement for calculating $G(\theta, \alpha)$ for a point-source object.

To determine $G(\theta, \alpha)$ it is convenient to consider a square lens shape of side $2R$. The cross-sectional shape of the intersection of the photocell and the square cone of light is trapezoidal as in Fig. 16b. Let z measure the distance from the focus plane to any particular point of the intercepted image. As in Eqs. 4–6 and neglecting vignetting, we can write the light intensity at that point as

$$I_z = \frac{L_T}{(z/f^*)^2} \tag{12}$$

Letting y measure distance along the photocell, and using the model of Eq. 3, we have

$$G = k \int_{y_1}^{y_2} \left[\frac{L_T}{\left(\frac{z_0 + y \sin \alpha}{f^*}\right)^2} \right]^p \left(\frac{z_0 + y \sin \alpha}{f^*} \right) dy \tag{13}$$

where z_0 is the distance from focus to the axis of rotation of the photocell. Converting the expression to one involving only z, by substituting

$$z = z_0 + y \sin \alpha \tag{14}$$

we find

$$G = \frac{kL_T{}^p}{(f^*)(1 - 2p)} \frac{z_2{}^{(2-2p)} - z_1{}^{(2-2p)}}{(2 - 2p) \sin \alpha} \tag{15}$$

where z_1 and z_2 are the extreme values for z for the intercepted figure. Substituting the proper geometric relations for z_1 and z_2—as functions of R, V, z_0, α, and θ—we finally obtain

$$G = \frac{kL_T{}^p(z_0 + V \tan \theta \tan \alpha)^{2-2p}}{(2 - 2p)(f^*)^{1-2p} \sin \alpha} \left\{ \left[1 + \tan \alpha \tan \theta - \frac{R}{V} \tan \alpha \right]^{2p-2} \right.$$
$$\left. - \left[1 + \tan \alpha \tan \theta + \frac{R}{V} \tan \alpha \right]^{2p-2} \right\} \tag{16}$$

Although Eq. 16 appears very cumbersome, it simplifies considerably for the values $p = \frac{1}{2}$ and $p = \frac{3}{2}$, in which case $(2 - 2p)$ has the value 1 and (-1), respectively. For these values of p let us first find the effect on G (for $\theta = 0$) as we rotate the photocell away from $\alpha = 0$. For $p = \frac{1}{2}$, we find

$$p = \frac{1}{2}; \quad G(\theta = 0) = G(\theta = 0, \alpha = 0) \frac{1}{\cos \alpha} \frac{1}{1 - [(R/V) \tan \alpha]^2} \tag{17}$$

For $p = \frac{3}{2}$, we find

$$p = \frac{3}{2}; \quad G(\theta = 0) = G(\theta = 0, \alpha = 0) \frac{1}{\cos \alpha} \tag{18}$$

A first interesting observation from Eqs. 16, 17, and 18 is that G increases as the photocell is rotated, for any value of $p \neq 1$. Thus we can expect a $G(\alpha, \theta)$ plot to be of the form shown earlier in Fig. 7 where it is assumed that the photocell vibrates between the values $\alpha = +\alpha_{max}$ and $\alpha = -\alpha_{max}$. For $\theta = 0$, G is higher for $|\alpha| > 0$ than for $\alpha = 0$. As θ increases we expect G to increase for one sign of α, and decrease for the other. For example, for $p > 1$ we expect G to decrease with $+\theta$, if $\alpha > 0$, since the image becomes dimmer and dimmer.

The value $\theta = \theta_1$, for which $G(\alpha = +\alpha_{max}) = G(\alpha = 0)$, is generally much smaller than α. Thus, starting with a small α, the term $(\tan \alpha \tan \theta)^2 \ll 1$ and can be neglected. With this approximation we find

$$\text{for } p = \frac{3}{2}; \quad \theta_1 \approx +\frac{z_0}{2V} \alpha \tag{19}$$

where we have also assumed $\tan \alpha \approx \alpha$ and $\tan \theta \approx \theta$. For $p = \frac{1}{2}$ we find exactly the same magnitude of θ_1, but opposite polarity, which of course is to be expected.

To get an estimate of the sensitivity of this angular displacement system let us assume that $z_0 = V/10$. For $\alpha = 2$ degrees, for example, we find

$$\theta_1 \approx 0.1° = 6 \text{ min} \tag{20}$$

REFERENCES

1. BLISS, J. C., AND H. D. CRANE, "An Optical Detector for Objects within an Adjustable Range," *J. Opt. Soc. Am.*, *54*, No. 10, 1261 (October 1964).

2. BLISS, J. C., H. D. CRANE, AND K. W. GARDINER, "An Ambient-Light Object Detector and Its Potential Extension to Convey Object Shape Information," paper presented at the Mobility Research Conference, Rotterdam, the Netherlands, 3–7 August 1964 (proceedings to be published by the American Foundation for the Blind, New York, N.Y., 1965).

CHAPTER 35

INFORMATION LIMITS OF SCANNING OPTICAL SYSTEMS *

Edward J. Farrell and C. Duane Zimmerman

Research Division, Control Data Corporation, Minneapolis, Minnesota

Introduction

Scanning optical systems for use in stellar navigation are of primary interest. The basic scanning system, illustrated in Fig. 1, consists of lens, slit, and photomultiplier. The entire system rotates and, consequently, the star images move across the slit. The basic problems are to (1) detect stars

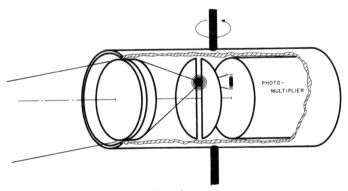

FIG. 1. Scanning system.

crossing the slit, (2) estimate their intensity, and (3) estimate the crossing times. These estimates, together with a star map, yield an estimate of the spin direction.† Also, there is background radiation and noise that enters

---

* This paper is based on a study sponsored by Control Data Corporation.

† This problem is discussed by R. L. Lillestrand and J. E. Carroll[1] and R. L. Kenimer and T. M. Walsh.[2]

the system and results in "false star detections." It is natural to characterize such a scanning system by four parameters:

1. Probability of detection.
2. Variance of the intensity estimate.
3. Variance of the crossing time estimate (angle accuracy).
4. Expected number of weak-star detections per scan.

Explicit formulas are derived for these four parameters in terms of slit width, star intensity, spin rate, diameter of the diffraction circle, etc. The objective is to develop the fundamental limits of optical scanning systems.

In the first section certain statistical models are postulated for the stellar radiation, background, and internal noise; see Table 1.† The photon arrivals

TABLE 1   Noise Sources

Source	Statistical Model	Relative Magnitude
Stellar radiation	Intensity fixed Photon arrivals—Poisson	1 (Fourth magnitude)
Background (Weak stars)	Random spatial distribution Photon arrivals—Poisson	$\frac{1}{10}$
Internal noise		
Dark current	Equivalent to homogeneous radiation	$\frac{1}{50}$
Electron emission of photomultiplier	Random—model based on empirical data	$\frac{1}{5} - \frac{1}{10}$
Thermal-electronic noise	Neglected	0

from the stars form a Poisson process. The background consists of "weak" stars with random spatial distributions.* Two sources of internal noise are considered, dark current and the random character of electron emission. Electronic noise is assumed to be negligible. The composite output of the photomultiplier is a sequence of pulses with random amplitudes and separation. Since the amplitude variations do not contain information about the stars, the output pulses of the multiplier are clamped to a fixed level when they exceed a threshold; see Fig. 2.

In Sec. II, the basic problems of detection and estimation are approached using statistical methods of hypothesis testing and estimation. A detection method is derived that maximizes the probability of detecting a star. Also absolute lower bounds are derived for the variance of the intensity estimate

* A similar problem has been studied for infrared detection by D. Z. Robinson[4] and H. G. Eldering.[5]

† D. C. Harrington has also investigated noise errors.[3]

and crossing time estimate. These results represent the "information limits" that may be achievable using the output of the threshold clamp.*

In general, one must compromise between ease of implementation and the desirable properties of the methods. A reasonable compromise is based on counting and threshold crossings. Namely, a holding filter counts the number of pulses in a sliding interval of fixed length. If the count exceeds

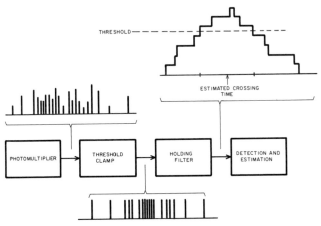

FIG. 2. Processing system.

a fixed threshold, a star is said to be "present" at the average of the first and second threshold crossing; see Fig. 2. In Sec. III, the probability of detection is evaluated for the threshold method of detection. Also, the expected number of weak-star detections per scan is determined. An intensity estimate is presented, and its variance is derived. To determine the variance of the crossing time estimate, it is assumed that the background and dark current are negligible compared to the star radiation, and that the diffraction circle is small compared to the slit width. An explicit formula is derived for the variance in terms of the system parameters.

In the final section, a specific scanning system is studied. The objective is to select the "best" slit width and scan period to satisfy certain design requirements.

I. Statistical Models

There are three sources of randomness or noise in a scanning system. The stellar radiation consists of photons whose arrival times are random. "Weak" stars appear as undesirable signals or noise; the stars are assumed to have random spatial distributions. The photomultiplier is the third noise source. Electronic noise is neglected.

* R. C. Jones has applied statistical information theory to the "detection problem."[6,7]

Star Radiation

The photons from a star are assumed to form a Poisson process with parameter λ_s; i.e., on the average λ_s photons are received per unit of time.* The photons have equal energy relative to the photomultiplier. The optical system produces a diffraction pattern that is two-dimensional Gaussian; the energy density in the focal plane is given by

$$\frac{\epsilon_0 \lambda_s}{2\pi\sigma^2} \exp\left[-\tfrac{1}{2}(x^2 + y^2)/\sigma^2\right] \tag{1}$$

where ϵ_0 denotes the optical efficiency. Let T_s be the time it takes the center of the star image to cross the slit. For convenience, time will be measured from the event of the star crossing the center of the slit. Hence, the photon arrivals at the photomultiplier form a nonstationary Poisson process with parameter $\lambda_s'(t) = \epsilon_0 \lambda_s G(t)$, where

$$G(t) = \Phi(t/\sigma + T_s/2\sigma) - \Phi(t/\sigma - T_s/2\sigma) \tag{2}$$

and

$$\Phi(t) = \frac{1}{\sqrt{2\pi}} \int_{-\infty}^{t} \exp\left(-\tfrac{1}{2}x^2\right) dx \tag{3}$$

Note that 80 per cent of the star radiation passes through the slit when $T_s/2 = 1.28\sigma$; i.e., $\lambda_s'(0) = 0.8\epsilon_0 \lambda_s$. The function $G(t)$ is graphed in Fig. 3.

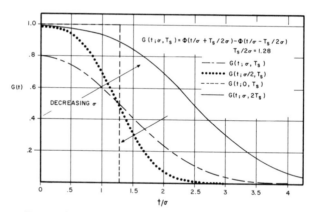

FIG. 3. Graph of $G(t)$, fraction of radiation passing slit.

Weak Stars

Assume stars with magnitudes M_0 and brighter are used for navigation and are included in the stored star map. One would like to obtain a detection method that discriminates against stars with magnitudes greater than M_0. If a weak star is detected, the system must recognize it as a weak star and delete it. This requires extra processing capability. Consequently, one would like a detection method that has a high probability (>0.9) of detect-

* Note that λ_s depends on the star magnitude and the aperture of the optical system.

ing a star of magnitude M_0 and that results in a few (two or three) weak-star detections in a scan period.

For a given scan direction, the photon arrivals at the photomultiplier (due to the background) form a nonstationary Poisson process with mean

$$\lambda_b'(t) = \epsilon_0 \sum_{M=M_0+1}^{\infty} \lambda(M) \sum_j G(t - t_j(M)) \tag{4}$$

where $\lambda(M)$ is the photon arrival rate for a star of magnitude M (for the specified optical aperture), and $t_j(M)$ is the time when the jth star of magnitude M is at the center of the slit. Since it is impractical to express $t_j(M)$ analytically as a function of the scan direction, they are assumed to be random variables. For each magnitude M, the $t_j(M)$'s are assumed to form a Poisson process with mean $\nu(M)$; parameter $\nu(M)$ is a measure of the average density of stars of magnitude M. The Poisson processes corresponding to different M's are assumed to be independent.

It is reasonable to assume the $t_j(M)$'s have a Poisson distribution. Let N be the total number of stars of magnitude M. Assuming the stars are uniformly distributed over the celestial sphere, the probability of n Mth magnitude stars in a specific solid angle γ is

$$\binom{N}{n} \left(\frac{\gamma}{4\pi}\right)^n \left(1 - \frac{\gamma}{4\pi}\right)^{N-n} \tag{5}$$

Since N is large and $\gamma \ll 4\pi$, the probability distribution of n can be approximated by

$$\frac{1}{n!} \left(\frac{N\gamma}{4\pi}\right)^n \exp\left(-\gamma N/4\pi\right) \tag{6}$$

with $\gamma =$ (slit length) $\times$ (sweep rate) $\times$ (time) and

$$\nu(M) = \frac{N \times \text{(slit length)} \times \text{(sweep rate)}}{4\pi} \tag{7}*$$

Therefore the $t_j(M)$'s form a Poisson process.

Internal Noise

There are three sources of randomness (or noise) generated by the photomultiplier: (1) the random character of the electron emission which modulates the amplitude of the output pulses, (2) internally generated noise or dark current, (3) the random time spread of electrons in a cascade. These effects are reduced by using a threshold clamp at the output of the photomultiplier. The output pulses below a fixed threshold are deleted; those above the threshold are clamped to a fixed level to form a "standard" pulse. This technique does not eliminate all of the dark current; high-energy pulses will exceed the threshold. These residual noise pulses are assumed

* A similar approach has been used by Bharucha-Reid to describe the distribution of stars and galaxies.[8]

to form a Poisson process with parameter λ_d. Also, the lower energy output pulses resulting from incident photons will be deleted. Let $1 - \alpha$ be the fraction of the pulses deleted.

The composite output of the threshold clamp is a sequence of pulses of fixed amplitude and random spacing, see Fig. 2. For a fixed background and an over-all quantum efficiency ϵ_q (pulses per photon), the output of the threshold clamp forms a Poisson process with intensity

$$\alpha\epsilon_q[\lambda_s'(t) + \lambda_b(t)] + \lambda_d \tag{8}$$

II. Information Limits

There are intrinsic limitations on the accuracy and reliability that can be achieved using the output of the threshold clamp. These limitations represent the "information limits" of the scanning optical system. In this section, the "information limits" will be developed using statistical methods of hypothesis testing and estimation. In the following section, a threshold method of detection and estimation is analyzed; the method has a relatively simple digital implementation.

The output of the threshold clamp is observed for a period $-T$ to T, with $2T$ much larger than the time required for the star to cross the slit; i.e., $T_s \ll 2T$. Assume one star crosses the slit in this period, at time t_0. Further, assume t_0 is not "near" the edges of the period; i.e., $|t_0| + T_s < T$. Let $\tau_1 < \tau_2 < \tau_3 < \cdots$ represent the times at which pulses are observed in the period. The joint density function of $(\tau_1, \tau_2, \cdots, \tau_n)$, conditional on observing n pulses, is*

$$f(\tau_1, \cdots, \tau_n | n, t_0, \lambda_s) = n! \prod_{j=1}^{n} \left\{ \frac{\alpha\epsilon_q\epsilon_0\lambda_s G(\tau_j - t_0) + \alpha\epsilon_q\lambda_b'(\tau_j) + \lambda_d}{\int_{-T}^{T} [\alpha\epsilon_q\epsilon_0\lambda_s G(t - t_0) + \alpha\epsilon_q\lambda_b'(t) + \lambda_d] \, dt} \right\} \tag{9}$$

In the following discussion, $\lambda_b'(t)$ is assumed to be constant, say $\epsilon_0\lambda_b$. The probability of obtaining n pulses in the period $(-T, T)$ is

$$P(n|t_0, \lambda_s) = \frac{\eta^n}{n!} e^{-\eta} \tag{10}$$

where

$$\eta = \int_{-T}^{T} [\alpha\epsilon_q\epsilon_0\lambda_s G(t - t_0) + \alpha\epsilon_q\epsilon_0\lambda_b + \lambda_d] \, dt \tag{11}$$

In Appendix A, it is shown that

$$\int_{-\infty}^{\infty} G(t) \, dt = T_s \tag{12}$$

Since t_0 is not "near" the ends of the period,

$$\eta = \alpha\epsilon_q\epsilon_0\lambda_s T_s + 2\alpha\epsilon_q\epsilon_0\lambda_b T + 2\lambda_d T \tag{13}$$

* E. Parzen[9] develops several basic relationships for Poisson processes.

and $P(n|t_0, \lambda_s)$ is independent of t_0. Further, the joint "probability" function of $(\tau_1, \cdots, \tau_n)$ and n is

$$f(\tau_1, \cdots, \tau_n|n, t_0, \lambda_s)P(n|\lambda_s) = \prod_{j=1}^{n} \{\alpha\epsilon_q\epsilon_0\lambda_s G(\tau_j - t_0) + \alpha\epsilon_q\epsilon_0\lambda_b + \lambda_d\}e^{-\eta}$$

$$(14)$$

This joint "probability" function is basic to the following discussion.

Detection

Detection is basically a statistical problem of testing the hypothesis that $\lambda_s = 0$ as opposed to $\lambda_s \geq \lambda(M_0)$. There are two types of errors: Type I, a star is "detected" when no star is present; Type II, a star is not detected when a star is present, see Fig. 4. In practice, most false star detections

FIG. 4. Detection errors.

		STATE OF NATURE	
		NO STAR PRESENT	STAR PRESENT
DECISION	NO STAR PRESENT		TYPE II ERROR
	STAR PRESENT	TYPE I ERROR	

can be eliminated by comparison to stored star charts. On the other hand, if a star is missed, the system accuracy is reduced; and it may be impossible to obtain the required attitude and position estimates. Hence, the goal is to select a detection method that minimizes the probability of a Type II for a fixed probability of a Type I error. The detection method which is developed in the following paragraphs meets this goal.

Assume the star which may occur in the period $(-T, T)$ has an intensity $\lambda_1 \geq \lambda(M_0)$. The optimum detection method is based on a likelihood ratio test statistic $\mathfrak{I}$, which depends on n and the τ_j's.* If $\mathfrak{I}$ is larger than a specified constant C_P, a star is said to be present. If $\mathfrak{I}$ is less than C_P, no star is detected. The constant C_P is selected so that the probability of a Type I error is P. The probability of a Type II error is minimized using this detection method for a star of intensity λ_1.

The test statistic is

$$\mathfrak{I}(\tau_1, \cdots, \tau_n; n) = \frac{\sup_{t_0} \{f(\tau_1, \cdots, \tau_n|n, t_0, \lambda_1)P(n|\lambda_1)\}}{f(\tau_1, \cdots, \tau_n|n, t_0, 0)P(n|0)}$$

$$= \sup_{t_0} \left\{\prod_{j=1}^{n} \left[\frac{\alpha\epsilon_q\epsilon_0\lambda_1 G(\tau_j - t_0) + \alpha\epsilon_q\epsilon_0\lambda_b + \lambda_d}{\alpha\epsilon_q\epsilon_0\lambda_b + \lambda_d}\right]\right\} \exp(-\alpha\epsilon_q\epsilon_0\lambda_1 T_s) \quad (15)$$

Note that $\mathfrak{I}$ is independent of the duration of the observation, $2T$. For convenience let

$$\rho = \frac{\alpha\epsilon_q\epsilon_0\lambda_1}{\alpha\epsilon_q\epsilon_0\lambda_b + \lambda_d} \quad (16)$$

---

* S. S. Wilks[10] discusses likelihood ratio tests.

which is the ratio of the star pulse rate to the "noise" pulse rate. The parameter ρ is like a signal-to-noise ratio. The detection method can be based equivalently on

$$\mathfrak{I}'(\tau_1, \cdots, \tau_n; n) = \sum_{j=1}^{n} \ln \left[\rho G(\tau_j - \hat{t}_0) + 1 \right] \tag{17}$$

where $\hat{t}_0$ is the value of t_0 that maximizes $f(\tau_1, \cdots, \tau_n | n, t_0, \lambda_1)$.

For many cases of interest, $G(t)$ can be approximated by an exponential function of the form

$$G(t) \approx G(0) \exp \left[-\tfrac{1}{2} (t/\sigma_1)^2 \right] \tag{18}$$

where σ_1 is a parameter selected to "minimize" the discrepancy between $G(t)$ and the approximation for $-T_s \leq t \leq T_s$. In general, the integral of the approximation is not equal to the integral of $G(t)$. From the mean value theorem,

$$G(t) = \Phi \left(\frac{t}{\sigma} + \frac{T_s}{2\sigma} \right) - \Phi \left(\frac{t}{\sigma} - \frac{T_s}{2\sigma} \right) = \phi(\xi) \frac{T_s}{\sigma} \tag{19}$$

where $t/\sigma - T_s/2\sigma \leq \xi \leq t/\sigma + T_s/2\sigma$ and

$$\phi(t) = \frac{1}{\sqrt{2\pi}} \exp \left(-t^2/2 \right) \tag{20}$$

As $T_s/2\sigma$ approaches zero, $G(t)/T_s$ approaches $\sigma^{-1}\phi(t/\sigma)$ uniformly on the real line. Note that the variance corresponding to the probability density function $G(t)/T_s$ is

$$\sigma^2 \left[1 + \frac{1}{3} \left(\frac{T_s}{2\sigma} \right)^2 \right] \tag{21}$$

In Fig. 5, $G(t)$ is graphed with an exponential approximation.

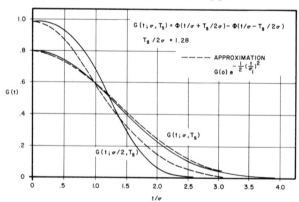

FIG. 5. Graph of $G(t)$ and Gaussian approximation.

Using this approximation to $G(t)$, one can determine $\hat{t}_0$. Setting the derivative of $\ln f(\tau_1, \tau_2, \cdots, \tau_n | n, t_0, \lambda_1)$ equal to zero, one obtains

$$\sum_{j=1}^{n} \left\{ \frac{\tau_j - t_0}{1 + [\rho G(\tau_j - t_0)]^{-1}} \right\} = 0 \qquad (22)$$

Assuming $\rho G(\tau_j - t_0) \gg 1$ for $j = 1, 2, \cdots n$, one has

$$\sum_{j=1}^{n} (\tau_j - t_0)\{1 - [\rho G(\tau_j - t_0)]^{-1} + [\rho G(\tau_j - t_0]^{-2} - \cdots\} = 0 \qquad (23)*$$

The first term is zero if

$$t_0 = \bar{\tau} \equiv \frac{1}{n} \sum_{j=1}^{n} \tau_j \qquad (24)$$

Since $G(t)$ is an even function, and since the τ_j are distributed about their average $\bar{\tau}$, the higher order terms will be small when $t_0 = \bar{\tau}$. Hence $\hat{t}_0$ can be approximated by $\bar{\tau}$. Note that $\bar{\tau}$ is an unbiased estimate of t_0. Also $\mathfrak{I}'$ has a simple approximation when $G(t)$ is approximated by an exponential function and when $\rho G(\tau_j - \bar{\tau}) \gg 1$. Namely,

$$\mathfrak{I}'(\tau_1, \tau_2, \cdots, \tau_n; n) \approx n \ln [\rho G(0)] - \frac{1}{2\sigma_1^2} \sum_{j=1}^{n} (\tau_j - \bar{\tau})^2 \qquad (25)$$

Hence the likelihood ratio test becomes

$$\begin{cases} \text{if } nL - \dfrac{1}{2\sigma_1^2} \displaystyle\sum_{j=1}^{n} (\tau_j - \bar{\tau})^2 > C_P' & \text{a star is present} \\[4mm] \text{if } nL - \dfrac{1}{2\sigma_1^2} \displaystyle\sum_{j=1}^{n} (\tau_j - \bar{\tau})^2 < C_P' & \text{no star is present} \end{cases}$$

where $L = \ln [\rho G(0)]$. In other words, a star is "present" if many closely spaced pulses are received. Using these approximations, one can estimate the probability of Type II and Type I errors.

First consider Type II errors. For $\rho \gg 1$, the unordered τ_j's have a density function $G(t - t_0)/T_s$. Further, if $T_s/2\sigma$ is "small," $G(t - t_0)/T_s$ can be approximated by a normal density function with mean t_0 and variance $\sigma^2 \approx \sigma_1^2$. Hence

$$\frac{1}{\sigma_1^2} \sum_{j=1}^{n} (\tau_j - \bar{\tau})^2 \qquad (26)$$

has a chi-square distribution with $n - 1$ degrees of freedom. For fixed n the probability of a Type II error is

$$P\{\text{Type II error}|n\} = P\{\chi_{n-1}^2 > 2(nL - C_P')\} \qquad (27)$$

Hence

$$P\{\text{Type II error}\} = \sum_{n=2}^{n} P(n|\tau_1) P\{\chi_{n-1}^2 > 2(nL - C_P')\} \qquad (28)$$

The probability of a Type II error is independent of t_0.

---

* The probability that $\rho G(\tau_j - t_0) > 1$ for all j approaches unity as ρ increases without bound.

Next consider Type I errors. In this case, the τ_j's have a uniform distribution over the interval $(-T, T)$. Since

$$\sum_{j=1}^{n} (\tau_j - \bar{\tau})^2 \tag{29}$$

does not have a simple distribution, it is convenient to approximate it by a chi-square random variable. The expected value of Expression 29 is $(n - 1)T^2/3$. Hence it is natural to assume

$$\sum_{j=1}^{n} \frac{(\tau_j - \bar{\tau})^2}{(T^2/3)} \tag{30}$$

has a chi-square distribution with $n - 1$ degrees of freedom. Then

$$P\{\text{Type I error}\} = \sum_{n=2}^{\infty} P(n|0)P\left\{\chi_{n-1}^2 < \frac{3\sigma_1^2}{T^2}(nL - C_{P'})\right\} \tag{31}$$

The parameter $C_{P'}$ is selected so that the probability of a Type I error is equal to P.

The detection method based on $\mathfrak{I}'$ has a relatively simple analogy implementation. The random process defined by

$$X(t) = \sum_{j=1}^{n} \ln\left[\rho G(\tau_j - t) + 1\right] \tag{32}$$

can be interpreted as "shot noise" corresponding to an impulse response function

$$W(t) = \ln\left[\rho G(t) + 1\right] \tag{33}$$

The process $X(t)$ can be generated by passing the output of the threshold clamp through a filter with an impulse response that approximates

$$\ln\left[\rho G(t) + 1\right] \tag{34}$$

The maximum value of $X(t)$ is $\mathfrak{I}'$. If output of the filter exceeds $C_{P'}$, a star is said to be present. Also the time $\hat{t}_0$ at which $X(t)$ achieves its maximum is a reasonable estimate of the time at which the star is in the center of the slit.

The impulse $W(t)$ is a positive, even function which converges to zero as $|t|$ increases without bound. If $\rho \gg 1$, the impulse function can be approximated by

$$W(t) \approx \ln\left[\rho G(0)\right] - \tfrac{1}{2}\left(\frac{t}{\sigma_1}\right)^2 \tag{35}$$

"near" the origin.

For a fixed value of t, the characteristic function of the probability density of $X(t)$ is given by

$$\log \phi_x(u) = \int_{-\infty}^{\infty} \{\exp\left[iuw(t)\right] - 1\}\left[\frac{\alpha\epsilon_q\epsilon_0\lambda_s G(t) + \alpha\epsilon_q\epsilon_0\lambda_b + \lambda_d}{\alpha\epsilon_q\epsilon_0\lambda_s T_s + 2\alpha\epsilon_q\epsilon_0\lambda_b T + 2\lambda_d T}\right] dt \tag{36}$$

Estimation

There are intrinsic limitations on the accuracy to which the star position t_0 and intensity λ_s can be estimated. In the following paragraphs, lower bounds are derived for the variance of estimators of t_0 and λ_s. Also maximum likelihood estimators are derived, and their variances compared to the bounds.

First consider estimation of t_0. For fixed observed values of $(\tau_1, \cdots, \tau_n)$ and n, the maximum likelihood estimate of t_0 is that value of t_0 which maximizes $f(\tau_1, \cdots, \tau_n | n, t_0, \lambda_s) P(n | \lambda_s)$, which is $\hat{t}_0$. Previously we have shown that $\hat{t}_0$ is approximately

$$\bar{\tau} \equiv \frac{1}{n} \sum_{j=1}^{n} \tau_j \tag{37}$$

With this approximation, clearly

$$\hat{t}_0 = \frac{1}{n} \sum_{j=1}^{n} t_j \tag{38}$$

where $(t_1, t_2, \cdots, t_n)$ is a random sample of size n with a density

$$\frac{1}{\eta} \left[\alpha \epsilon_q \epsilon_0 \lambda_s G(t - t_0) + 2\alpha \epsilon_q \epsilon_0 \lambda_b T + 2\lambda_d T \right] \tag{39}$$

The expected value of $\hat{t}_0$ given $n \geq 1$ can be shown to be

$$\mathcal{E}(\hat{t}_0 | n \geq 1) = t_0 \tag{40}$$

The variance of $\hat{t}_0$ given $n \geq 1$ can be shown to be

$$\mathrm{Var}(\hat{t}_0 | n \geq 1) = \mathcal{E}(1/n | n \geq 1) \, \mathrm{Var}(t) \tag{41}$$

with

$$\mathcal{E}(1/n | n \geq 1) = [e^{\eta} - 1]^{-1} \sum_{j=1}^{\infty} \frac{1}{k} \frac{\eta^k}{k!} \tag{42}$$

and

$$\mathrm{Var}(t) = \int_{-T}^{T} (x - t_0)^2 \frac{1}{\eta} \left[\alpha \epsilon_q \epsilon_0 \lambda_s G(x - t_0) + 2\alpha \epsilon_q \epsilon_0 \lambda_b T + 2\lambda_d T \right] dx \tag{43}$$

For

$$G(t) \approx T_s \phi(t/\sigma)/\sigma \tag{44}$$

$$\lambda_b / \lambda_s \ll 1 \tag{45}$$

$$\lambda_d / (\alpha \epsilon_q \epsilon_0 \lambda_s) \ll 1 \tag{46}$$

the variance of t is σ^2.

Using the Cramer-Rao[11] bound in this problem, one can determine a lower bound on the variance of unbiased estimators of t_0. The bound is the reciprocal of

$$\mathcal{E}\left[\frac{\partial}{\partial t_0} \ln \left[f(t_1, \cdots, t_n|n, t_0, \lambda_s)P(n|\lambda_s)\right]\right]^2$$

$$= \mathcal{E}\left[\sum_{j=1}^{n} \left(\frac{\alpha\epsilon_q\epsilon_0\lambda_s G'(t_j - t_0)}{\alpha\epsilon_q\epsilon_0\lambda_s G(t_j - t_0) + \alpha\epsilon_q\epsilon_0\lambda_b + \lambda_d}\right)^2\right]$$

$$= \eta\mathcal{E}_t\left[\frac{\alpha\epsilon_q\epsilon_0\lambda_s G'(t - t_0)}{\alpha\epsilon_q\epsilon_0\lambda_s G(t - t_0) + \alpha\epsilon_q\epsilon_0\lambda_b + \lambda_d}\right]^2 \quad (47)$$

Using Eqs. 44, 45, and 46, the bound becomes the reciprocal of

$$\frac{\alpha\epsilon_q\epsilon_0\lambda_s}{\sigma^2}\int_{-\infty}^{\infty}\frac{\left[\phi\left(\frac{x}{\sigma} + \frac{T_s}{2\sigma}\right) - \phi\left(\frac{x}{\sigma} - \frac{T_s}{2\sigma}\right)\right]^2}{\frac{T_s}{\sigma}\phi\left(\frac{x}{\sigma}\right)}\,dx = \frac{4\alpha\epsilon_q\epsilon_0\lambda_s}{T_s}\sinh\left(\frac{T_s}{2\sigma}\right)^2 \quad (48)$$

Hence for any unbiased estimator $g(\tau_1, \cdots, \tau_n, n)$ of t_0,

$$\mathrm{Var}\left[\frac{g(\tau_1, \cdots, \tau_n, n)}{T_s}\right] \geq \frac{1}{2}\left[\alpha\epsilon_q\epsilon_0\lambda_s T_s \sinh(T_s/2\sigma)^2\right]^{-1} \quad (49)$$

This bound and the variance of $\hat{t}_0$ are compared in Fig. 6.

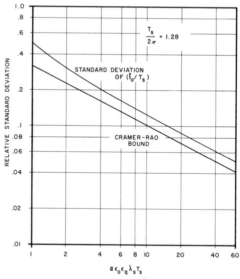

FIG. 6. Standard deviation of $\hat{t}_0/T_s$ and lower bound.

Next consider estimation of λ_s. The Cramer-Rao bound for unbiased estimators of λ_s is the reciprocal of

$$-\mathcal{E}\left\{\frac{\partial^2}{\partial\lambda_s^2}\ln\left[f(\tau_1, \cdots, \tau_n|n, t_0, \lambda_s)P(n|\lambda_s)\right]\right\}$$

$$= -\mathcal{E}\left\{\frac{\partial^2}{\partial\lambda_s^2}\ln\left[f(\tau_1, \cdots, \tau_n|n, t_0, \lambda_s)\right]\right\} - \mathcal{E}\left\{\frac{\partial^2}{\partial\lambda_s^2}\ln\left[P(n|\lambda_s)\right]\right\} \quad (50)$$

With use of approximations 45 and 46, the first term on the right of Eq. 50 can be neglected.

$$-\mathcal{E}\left\{\frac{\partial^2}{\partial\lambda_s^2}\ln\left[f(\tau_1, \cdots, \tau_n|n, t_0, \lambda_s)\right]\right\}$$

$$= \mathcal{E}\left\{\sum_{j=1}^{n}\left[\frac{\alpha\epsilon_q\epsilon_0 G(\tau_j - t_0)}{\alpha\epsilon_q\epsilon_0\lambda_s G(\tau_j - t_0) + \alpha\epsilon_q\epsilon_0\lambda_b + \lambda_d}\right]^2\right.$$

$$\left. - n\left[\frac{\alpha\epsilon_q\epsilon_0 T_s}{\alpha\epsilon_q\epsilon_0\lambda_s T_s + 2\alpha\epsilon_q\epsilon_0\lambda_b T + 2\lambda_d T}\right]^2\right\}$$

$$\approx \mathcal{E}\left\{\sum_{j=1}^{n}\frac{1}{\lambda_s} - \frac{n}{\lambda_s}\right\}$$

$$= 0 \tag{51}$$

The second term on the right of Eq. 50 is

$$-\mathcal{E}\left\{\frac{\partial^2}{\partial\lambda_s^2}\ln\left[P(n|\lambda_s)\right]\right\} = \frac{(\alpha\epsilon_q\epsilon_0 T_s)^2}{\eta} \tag{52}$$

Hence for any unbiased estimator $h(\tau_1, \cdots, \tau_n, n)$ of λ_s

$$\text{Var}\left[\frac{h(\tau_1, \cdots, \tau_n, n)}{\lambda_s}\right] \geq \frac{\eta}{(\alpha\epsilon_q\epsilon_0 T_s\lambda_s)^2} \tag{53}$$

if the background and dark current are small compared to the star signal. A natural estimator of λ_s is

$$\hat{\lambda}_s = \frac{n - 2T(\alpha\epsilon_0\epsilon_q\lambda_b + \lambda_d)}{\alpha\epsilon_q\epsilon_0 T_s} \tag{54}$$

The expectation of $\hat{\lambda}_s$ is λ_s. Also the variance of $\hat{\lambda}_s$ equals the lower bound, Eq. 53. Therefore, the estimator $\hat{\lambda}_s$ has minimum variance and is unbiased.

III. Threshold Methods of Detection and Estimation

In general one must compromise between ease of implementation and the desirable properties of the methods. A reasonable digital implementation is based on counting and threshold crossings. Namely, a holding filter is used to count the number of pulses in a sliding interval of fixed length. If the count exceeds a fixed threshold, a star is said to be "present" at the average of the first and second crossing; see Fig. 2. Let T_f represent the duration of the holding filter. The output of the filter $y(t)$ is a random step function. If the diffraction circle is small compared to slit width and the star is bright, $y(t)$ approaches a triangular pulse whose peak occurs at time $T_f/2$.

The conditional distribution of $y(t)$, given the $t_j(M)$'s, is Poisson with mean

$$\mu(t) = \alpha \epsilon_q \epsilon_0 \lambda_s H(t) + \alpha \epsilon_q \epsilon_0 \sum_{M=M_0+1}^{\infty} H(t - t_j(M)) + T_f \lambda_d \qquad (55)$$

where $H(t) = \int_{t-T_f}^{t} G(x)\, dx$. An explicit expression for $H(t)$ in terms of the standard normal distribution function is derived in Appendix A:

$$H(t) = (t + T_s/2)\Phi\left(\frac{t + T_s/2}{\sigma}\right) - (t - T_s/2)\Phi\left(\frac{t - T_s/2}{\sigma}\right)$$

$$- \left[(t - T_f + T_s/2)\Phi\left(\frac{t - T_f + T_s/2}{\sigma}\right) \right.$$

$$\left. - (t - T_f - T_s/2)\Phi\left(\frac{t - T_f - T_s/2}{\sigma}\right) \right]$$

$$+ \sigma\left[\phi\left(\frac{t + T_s/2}{\sigma}\right) - \phi\left(\frac{t - T_s/2}{\sigma}\right) \right]$$

$$- \sigma\left[\phi\left(\frac{t - T_f + T_s/2}{\sigma}\right) - \phi\left(\frac{t - T_f - T_s/2}{\sigma}\right) \right] \qquad (56)$$

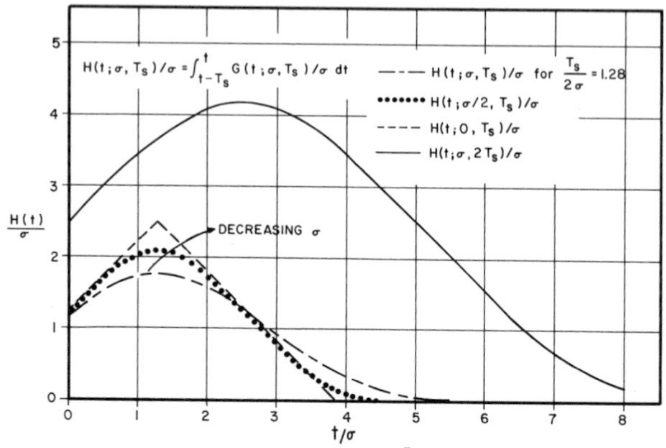

FIG. 7. Integral of $G(t)$, output of holding filter divided by λ_s.

The function $H(t)$ is graphed in Fig. 7 for $T_s = T_f$. Hence,

$$P\{y(t) = k | t_j(M)\} = \frac{[\mu(t)]^k}{k!} e^{-\mu(t)} \qquad (57)$$

Since the $t_j(M)$'s are random variables, $\mu(t)$ is a stochastic process. The unconditional probability distribution of $y(t)$ is

$$P\{y(t) = k\} = \int_0^{\infty} \frac{x^k}{k!} e^{-x} \psi_t(x)\, dx \qquad (58)$$

where $\psi_t(x)$ is the probability density function of $\mu(t)$. The summation

$$\alpha \epsilon_q \epsilon_0 \lambda(M) \sum_j H(t - t_j(M)) \qquad (59)$$

has well-known properties. Its mean and variance are

$$\alpha\epsilon_q\epsilon_0\nu(M)\int_{-\infty}^{\infty} H(t)\, dt \tag{60}$$

and

$$\alpha^2\epsilon_q^2\epsilon_0^2\nu(M)\lambda^2(M)\int_{-\infty}^{\infty} H^2(t)\, dt \tag{61}*$$

Hence, the mean and variance of $\mu(t)$ are

$$\mathcal{E}\mu(t) = \alpha\epsilon_q\epsilon_0\lambda_s H(t) + \alpha\epsilon_q\epsilon_0 \int_{-\infty}^{\infty} H(t)\, dt \sum_{M=M_0+1}^{\infty} \nu(M)\lambda(M) \tag{62}$$

and

$$\text{Var } \mu(t) = \alpha^2\epsilon_q^2\epsilon_0^2 \int_{-\infty}^{\infty} H^2(t)\, dt \sum_{M=M_0+1}^{\infty} \nu(M)\lambda^2(M) \tag{63}$$

In Appendix A, it is shown that

$$\int_{-\infty}^{\infty} H(t)\, dt = T_f T_s \tag{64}$$

$$T_f^2 T_s^2 < \int_{-\infty}^{\infty} H^2(t)\, dt < T_f^2 T_s \tag{65}$$

$$\int_{-\infty}^{\infty} H^k(t)\, dt < T_f^k T_s \tag{66}$$

In Appendix B, the summation

$$\sum_{M=M_0+1}^{\infty} \nu(M)\lambda^k(M) \qquad k = 1, 2, \cdots \tag{67}$$

is shown to be approximately

$$\frac{D^{2k}}{T_{sp}} \sin\left(\frac{\text{fov}}{2}\right) (5.06)^k (2.54 \times 10^{6k+2}) \cdot [1 - \Phi(0.173 M_0 + 5.32k - 7.12)] \tag{68}$$

where

$$D = \text{diameter of the optical aperture in inches}$$
$$T_{sp} = \text{scan period in seconds}$$
$$\text{fov} = \text{optical field of view}$$

This expression was developed for the optical system illustrated in Fig. 1.

The distribution of $\mu(t)$ is approximately normal for many cases of interest. The kth semi-invariant of the summation

$$\alpha\epsilon_q\epsilon_0\lambda(M)\sum_j H(t - t_j(M)) \tag{69}$$

is

$$\kappa_k = \sum_{M=M_0+1}^{\infty} \nu(M)\lambda^k(M)(\alpha\epsilon_q\epsilon_0)^k \int_{-\infty}^{\infty} H^k(t)\, dt \tag{70}$$

* A proof is given by S. O. Rice.[12]

If κ_k is small compared to κ_2, $\mu(t)$ is approximately normal. Using the above results one obtains

$$\frac{\kappa_k}{\kappa_2} < (\alpha\epsilon_q\epsilon_0)^{k-2} \frac{T_f^k T_s}{T_f^2 T_s^2} \frac{\sum \nu(M)\lambda^k(M)}{\sum \nu(M)\lambda^2(M)} \tag{71}$$

For the example presented in Sec. IV,

$$\frac{\kappa_3}{\kappa_2} < 1.08 \times 10^{-10}, \qquad \frac{\kappa_4}{\kappa_2} < 1.15 \times 10^{-34} \tag{72}$$

Assume $\psi\hat{\imath}(x)$ is a normal density with mean $m = \mathcal{E}\mu(t)$ and variance $v = \text{Var } \mu(t)$, and

$$P\{y(t) = k\} \approx \int_{-\infty}^{\infty} \frac{x^k}{k!} e^{-x}\psi\hat{\imath}(x) \, dx \tag{73}$$

Transform variables with

$$x = \sqrt{v}w - v + m \tag{74}$$

Then

$$P\{y(t) = k\} \approx \int_{-\infty}^{\infty} \sqrt{v}[\sqrt{v}w - v + m]^k \frac{1}{k!} e^{+v/2-m}\phi(w) \, dw \tag{75}$$

where ϕ is the standard normal density function. Further,

$$P\{y(t) = k\} \approx \frac{\sqrt{v}e^{+v/2-m}}{k!} \sum_{j=0}^{k} \binom{k}{j} v^{j/2}(-v + m)^{k-j} \int_{-\infty}^{\infty} w^j\phi(w) \, dw \tag{76}$$

and

$$\int_{-\infty}^{\infty} w^{2j}\phi(w) \, dw = \prod_{i=1}^{j} (2i - 1) \qquad j = 1, 2, \cdots \tag{77}$$

$$\int_{-\infty}^{\infty} w^{2j+1}\phi(w) \, dw = 0 \tag{78}$$

Note that $P\{y(t) = k\}$ is time-dependent through $\mathcal{E}\mu(t)$.

Star Detection

Detection is based on a threshold τ. Given $y(t)$ exceeds τ at time t' and remains greater than τ until t'', a *star detection* has occurred if a star is in the center of the slit between $t' - T_f/2$ and $t'' - T_f/2$. Hence, the probability of detecting a star (centered in the slit at time $t = 0$) is the probability that $y(T_f/2) > \tau$, which is

$$1 - \sum_{k=0}^{\tau} P\{y(T_f/2) = k\} \tag{79}$$

This sum can be evaluated using the foregoing results, assuming $\mu(t)$ is normally distributed. This detection method is similar to the optimum method (developed in the preceding section) in that a star is "present" if many closely spaced pulses are received.

Weak-Star Discrimination

A measure of the performance of a detection method is its ability to discriminate against undesirable signals, in this case weak stars. For example, if one is interested in fourth magnitude stars (and brighter), detection of fifth, sixth, and seventh magnitude stars is undesirable. One can show that the expected number of star detections for magnitudes greater than seven is negligible, even though the star density $\nu(M)$ is high.* Hence, it is reasonable to assume that the pulses resulting from different weak stars are widely spaced, and that the detections of the weak stars are independent.

Let $q_\tau(M)$ be the probability of detecting a star of magnitude M with threshold τ:

$$q_\tau(M) = \sum_{j=\tau+1}^{\infty} \frac{\beta^j}{j!} e^{-\beta} \tag{80}$$

where $\beta = \alpha \epsilon_q \epsilon_0 \lambda(M) H(T_f/2) + T_f \lambda_d$. Then the times of star detections (of magnitude M) form a Poisson process; and the number of Mth magnitude star detections in a scan period T_{sp} is a Poisson variable with mean $q_\tau(M)\nu(M)T_{\mathrm{sp}}$. Hence, the number of weak-star detections in a scan period is a Poisson random variable with mean

$$\sum_{M=M_0+1}^{\infty} q_\tau(M)\nu(M)T_{\mathrm{sp}} \tag{81}†$$

Angle Estimation

Given $y(t)$ exceeds τ at time t' and remains greater than τ until t'', a star is said to be at that center of the slit at time $t^* = (t' + t'')/2 - T_f/2$. Let $t_{\tau+1}$ be the arrival time of the $(\tau + 1)$th pulse, and $t'_{\tau+1}$ be the arrival time of the pulse which is τth from last. Then $t' = t_{\tau+1}$, $t'' = t'_{\tau+1} + T_f$, and $t^* = (t_{\tau+1} + t'_{\tau+1})/2$.‡ In the following paragraphs, we will derive the distribution of $t_{\tau+1}$, the distribution of $(t_{\tau+1}, t'_{\tau+1})$, the distribution of t^*, and the variance of t^*. In these derivations, it is assumed that the diffraction circle is "small" compared to the slit in width, that the background and dark current are negligible, and that $T_f = T_s$. The diffraction circle can be assumed to be "small" when $T_s/\sigma \geq 1.28$; see Fig. 7. Hence,

$$\lambda_s'(t) = \begin{cases} \epsilon_0 \lambda_s & \text{for } -T_s/2 < t < T_s/2 \\ 0 & \text{otherwise} \end{cases} \tag{82}$$

---

* D. Zimmerman demonstrates the relative sparsity of weak-star detections.[13]

† The problem of weak-star detection is very similar to the classical zero crossing problem; see the paper prepared by H. Levenbach.[14]

‡ The maximum likelihood estimate, Eq. 37, is an average of all the arrival times, not just the $(\tau + 1)$th and $(n - \tau)$th arrival times.

and

$$\mu(t) = \begin{cases} \alpha\epsilon_q\epsilon_0\lambda_s(t + T_s/2) & \text{for } -T_s/2 < t < T_s/2 \\ \alpha\epsilon_q\epsilon_0\lambda_s(-t + 3T_s/2) & \text{for } T_s/2 < t < 3T_s/2 \\ 0 & \text{otherwise} \end{cases} \qquad (83)$$

Let

$$p(n) = \frac{(\alpha\epsilon_q\epsilon_0\lambda_s T_s)^n}{n!} \exp\left(-\alpha\epsilon_q\epsilon_0\lambda_s T_s\right) \qquad (84)$$

$$P_\tau = \sum_{j=\tau+1}^{\infty} p(j) \qquad (85)$$

DISTRIBUTION OF $t_{\tau+1}$. The probability density of $t_{\tau+1}$ conditional on $y(T_s/2) > \tau$ is

$$f_{\tau+1}(t) = \frac{\alpha\epsilon_q\epsilon_0\lambda_s[\alpha\epsilon_q\epsilon_0\lambda_s(t + T_s/2)]^\tau}{\tau! P_\tau} \exp\left[-\alpha\epsilon_q\epsilon_0\lambda_s(t + T_s/2)\right] \qquad (86)$$

for $-T_s/2 < t < T_s/2$ and zero elsewhere. The expectation of $t_{\tau+1}$ is given by

$$\begin{aligned} \mathcal{E}[t_{\tau+1} + T_s/2] &= \int_{-T_s/2}^{T_s/2} \frac{(t + T_s/2)\alpha\epsilon_q\epsilon_0\lambda_s[\alpha\epsilon_q\epsilon_0\lambda_s(t + T_s/2)]^\tau}{\tau! P_\tau} \\ &\quad \cdot \exp\left[-\alpha\epsilon_q\epsilon_0\lambda_s(t + T_s/2)\right] dt \\ &= \frac{\tau + 1}{\alpha\epsilon_q\epsilon_0\lambda_s} \frac{P_{\tau+1}}{P_\tau} \end{aligned} \qquad (87)$$

Note that $\mathcal{E}[t_{\tau+1}/T_s]$ only depends on the product $\alpha\epsilon_q\epsilon_0\lambda_s T_s$ and τ. The second moment is

$$\begin{aligned} \mathcal{E}(t_{\tau+1} + T_s/2)^2 &= \int_{-T_s/2}^{T_s/2} \frac{[\alpha\epsilon_q\epsilon_0\lambda_s(t + T_s/2)]^{\tau+2}}{\alpha\epsilon_q\epsilon_0\lambda_s \tau! P_\tau} \exp\left[-\alpha\epsilon_q\epsilon_0\lambda_s(t + T_s/2)\right] dt \\ &= \frac{(\tau + 1)(\tau + 2)}{(\alpha\epsilon_q\epsilon_0\lambda_s)^2} \frac{P_{\tau+2}}{P_\tau} \end{aligned} \qquad (88)$$

Hence, the variance of $t_{\tau+1}$ is

$$\text{Var } t_{\tau+1} = \frac{(\tau + 1)(\tau + 2)}{(\alpha\epsilon_q\epsilon_0\lambda_s)^2} \frac{P_{\tau+2}}{P_\tau} - \frac{(\tau + 1)^2}{(\alpha\epsilon_q\epsilon_0\lambda_s)^2} \frac{P_{\tau+1}}{P_\tau} \qquad (89)$$

Note that $\text{Var}(t_{\tau+1}/T_s)$ depends only on $(\alpha\epsilon_q\epsilon_0\lambda_s T_s)$ and τ, and is graphed in Fig. 8.

DISTRIBUTION OF $(t_{\tau+1}, t'_{\tau+1})$. Let n be the number of pulses received from time $-T_s/2$ to $T_s/2$; i.e., $n = y(T_s/2)$. If $n > \tau$, then $y(t)$ crosses τ exactly twice (at t' and t''), and $-T_s/2 < t' \le T_s/2 \le t'' < 3/2T_s$ or $-T_s/2 < t_{\tau+1} < T_s/2$, $-T_s/2 < t'_{\tau+1} < T_s/2$. Let $g_n(a, a')\, da\, da'$ be the probability that n pulses are received, and that $a < t_{\tau+1} < a + da$ and $a' < t'_{\tau+1} < a' + da'$, given $n > \tau$. If $n > 2\tau + 1$, $g_n(a, a') = 0$ for $a' < a$. If $\tau < n < 2\tau + 1$, $g_n(a, a') = 0$ for $a' > a$. If $n = 2\tau + 1$, the density $g_n(a, a')$ is not defined.

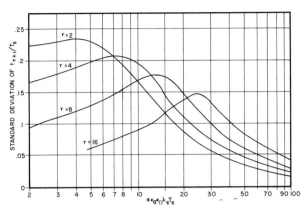

FIG. 8. Graph of the standard deviation of $t_{\tau+1}/T_s$ as a function of the expected number of pulses $\alpha \epsilon_q \epsilon_0 \lambda_s T_s$ for several thresholds τ.

For $\tau < n < 2\tau + 1$,

$$g_n(a, a')\, da\, da' = \left\{ \frac{[\alpha \epsilon_q \epsilon_0 \lambda_s (a' + T_s/2)]^{n-\tau-1}}{(n - \tau - 1)!} \right\} \exp\left[-\alpha \epsilon_q \epsilon_0 \lambda_s (a' + T_s/2)\right]$$

$$\cdot \alpha \epsilon_q \epsilon_0 \lambda_s\, da' \left\{ \frac{[\alpha \epsilon_q \epsilon_0 \lambda_s (a - a')]^{2\tau-n}}{(2\tau - n)!} \exp\left[-\alpha \epsilon_q \epsilon_0 \lambda_s (a - a')\right] \right\}$$

$$\cdot \alpha \epsilon_q \epsilon_0 \lambda_s\, da \left\{ \frac{[\alpha \epsilon_q \epsilon_0 \lambda_s (T_s/2 - a)]^{n-\tau-1}}{(n - \tau - 1)!} \exp\left[-\alpha \epsilon_q \epsilon_0 \lambda_s (T_s/2 - a)\right] \right\} (P_\tau)^{-1}$$

$$= \frac{p(n)}{P_\tau} \frac{n!}{(n - \tau - 1)!(2\tau - n)!(n - \tau - 1)!} \left[\frac{1}{2} + \frac{a'}{T_s}\right]^{n-\tau-1} \left[\frac{a - a'}{T_s}\right]^{2\tau-n}$$

$$\cdot \left[\frac{1}{2} - \frac{a}{T_s}\right]^{n-\tau-1} \frac{1}{T_s{}^2}\, da\, da'$$

$$= \frac{p(n)}{P_\tau} D\left(\frac{1}{2} + \frac{a'}{T_s}, \frac{1}{2} - \frac{a}{T_s}; n - \tau, n - \tau, 2\tau - n + 1\right) \frac{1}{T_s{}^2}\, da\, da' \quad (90)$$

where $D(-)$ represents the Dirichlet density function*

$$D(x_1, x_2; \nu_1, \nu_2, \nu_3) = \frac{\Gamma(\nu_1 + \nu_2 + \nu_3)}{\Gamma(\nu_1)\Gamma(\nu_2)\Gamma(\nu_3)} x_1{}^{\nu_1-1} x_2{}^{\nu_2-1}(1 - x_2 - x_1)^{\nu_3-1} \quad (91)$$

For $n = 2\tau + 1$

$$P\{t_{\tau+1} \leq a, t'_{\tau+1} \leq a', n = 2\tau + 1 \mid n > \tau\}$$

$$= (P_\tau)^{-1} \sum_{k=\tau+1}^{2\tau+1} \frac{[\alpha \epsilon_q \epsilon_0 \lambda_s (T_s/2 + a^*)]^k}{k!} \exp\left[-\alpha \epsilon_q \epsilon_0 \lambda_s (T_s/2 + a^*)\right]$$

$$\cdot \frac{[\alpha \epsilon_q \epsilon_0 \lambda_s (T_s/2 - a^*]^{2\tau+1-k}}{(2\tau + 1 - k)!} \exp\left[-\alpha \epsilon_q \epsilon_0 \lambda_s (T_s/2 - a^*)\right]$$

$$= \frac{p(2\tau + 1)}{P_\tau} \sum_{k=\tau+1}^{2\tau+1} \binom{2\tau + 1}{k} \left[\frac{1}{2} + \frac{a^*}{T_s}\right]^k \left[\frac{1}{2} - \frac{a^*}{T_s}\right]^{2\tau+1-k} \quad (92)$$

* The Dirichlet density is discussed by S. S. Wilks.[15]

where $a^* = \min(a, a')$. Note that $t_{\tau+1} \equiv t'_{\tau+1}$ for $n = 2\tau + 1$.

For $n > 2\tau + 1$

$$g_n(a, a')\, da\, da' = \left\{\frac{[\alpha\epsilon_q\epsilon_0\lambda_s(a + T_s/2)]^\tau}{\tau!}\exp\left[-\alpha\epsilon_q\epsilon_0\lambda_s(a + T_s/2)\right]\right\}$$

$$\cdot\, \alpha\epsilon_q\epsilon_0\lambda_s\left\{\frac{[\alpha\epsilon_q\epsilon_0\lambda_s(a' - a)]^{n-2\tau-2}}{(n - 2\tau - 2)!}\exp\left[-\alpha\epsilon_q\epsilon_0\lambda_s(a' - a)\right]\right\}$$

$$\cdot\, \alpha\epsilon_q\epsilon_0\lambda_s\, da'\left\{\frac{[\alpha\epsilon_q\epsilon_0\lambda_s(T_s/2 - a')]^\tau}{\tau!}\exp\left[-\alpha\epsilon_q\epsilon_0\lambda_s(T_s/2 - a')\right]\right\}(P_\tau)^{-1}$$

$$= \frac{p(n)}{P_\tau}\frac{n!}{\tau!(n - 2\tau - 2)!\tau!}\left[\frac{1}{2} + \frac{a}{T_s}\right]^\tau\left[\frac{a' - a}{T_s}\right]^{n-2\tau-2}\left[\frac{1}{2} - \frac{a'}{T_s}\right]^\tau$$

$$\cdot\, \frac{1}{T_s^2}\, da\, da'$$

$$= \frac{p(n)}{P_\tau} D\left(\frac{1}{2} + \frac{a}{T_s}, \frac{1}{2} - \frac{a'}{T_s}; \tau + 1, \tau + 1, n - 2\tau - 1\right)\frac{1}{T_s^2}\, da\, da' \quad (93)$$

DISTRIBUTION OF t^*. Since $t^* = (t_{\tau+1} + t'_{\tau+1})/2$, we will evaluate the distribution of $t_{\tau+1} + t'_{\tau+1}$. The probability density function of $t_{\tau+1} + t'_{\tau+1}$ can be derived from the following identity:

$$P\{b < t_{\tau+1} + t'_{\tau+1} \leq b + db \mid n > \tau\}$$

$$= P\{b < t_{\tau+1} + t'_{\tau+1} \leq b + db, \tau < n < 2\tau + 1 \mid n > \tau\}$$

$$+ P\{b < t_{\tau+1} + t'_{\tau+1} \leq b + db, n = 2\tau + 1 \mid n > \tau\}$$

$$+ P\{b < t_{\tau+1} + t'_{\tau+1} \leq b + db, n > 2\tau + 1 \mid n > \tau\} \quad (94)$$

Note that the density is symmetric in b about the origin. The first term is

$$\left[\sum_{n=\tau+1}^{2\tau}\int_{b/2}^{T_s/2} g_n(a, b - a)\, da\right] db \quad (95)$$

for $b > 0$.

The second term is

$$\left\{\frac{[\alpha\epsilon_q\epsilon_0\lambda_s(b/2 + T_s/2)]^\tau}{\tau!}\exp\left[-\alpha\epsilon_q\epsilon_0\lambda_s(b/2 + T_s/2)\right]\right\}\frac{\alpha\epsilon_q\epsilon_0\lambda_s}{2}\, db$$

$$\cdot\left\{\frac{[\alpha\epsilon_q\epsilon_0\lambda_s(T_s/2 - b/2)]^\tau}{\tau!}\exp\left[-\alpha\epsilon_q\epsilon_0\lambda_s(T_s/2 - b/2)\right]\right\}(P_\tau)^{-1}$$

$$= \frac{(2\tau + 1)!}{\tau!\tau!}\left[\frac{1}{2} + \frac{b}{2T_s}\right]^\tau\left[\frac{1}{2} - \frac{b}{2T_s}\right]^\tau\frac{(\alpha\epsilon_q\epsilon_0\lambda_s T_s)^{2\tau+1}}{(2\tau + 1)!}$$

$$\cdot\exp\left(-\alpha\epsilon_q\epsilon_0\lambda_s T_s\right)(P_\tau)^{-1}\frac{db}{2T_s}$$

$$= \frac{p(2\tau + 1)}{P_\tau} D\left(\frac{1}{2} + \frac{b}{2T_s}; \tau + 1, \tau + 1\right)\frac{db}{2T_s} \quad (96)$$

The third term is

$$\left[\sum_{n=2\tau+2}^{\infty} \int_{b/2}^{T_s/2} g_n(b - a', a) \, da' \right] db \tag{97}$$

for $b > 0$.

VARIANCE OF t^*.   Since $t^* = (t_{\tau+1} + t'_{\tau+1})/2$ and the mean of t^* is zero, the variance of t^* is

$$\tfrac{1}{4}\mathcal{E}(t_{\tau+1} + t'_{\tau+1})^2 = \tfrac{1}{4}\mathcal{E}[(t_{\tau+1} + T_s/2) - (T_s/2 - t'_{\tau+1})]^2$$

$$= \tfrac{1}{4}\mathcal{E}(t_{\tau+1} + T_s/2)^2 + \tfrac{1}{4}\mathcal{E}(T_s/2 - t'_{\tau+1})^2$$

$$- \tfrac{1}{2}\mathcal{E}[(t_{\tau+1} + T_s/2)(T_s/2 - t'_{\tau+1})] \tag{98}$$

Since $t_{\tau+1} + T_s/2$ and $T_s/2 - t'_{\tau+1}$ have the same distribution,

$$\mathcal{E}(t_{\tau+1} + T_s/2)^2 = \mathcal{E}(T_s/2 - t'_{\tau+1})^2 = \frac{(\tau + 1)(\tau + 2)}{(\alpha\epsilon_q\epsilon_0\lambda_s)^2} \frac{P_{\tau+2}}{P_\tau} \tag{99}$$

It is necessary to evaluate the last term in the variance with three steps: $\tau < n < 2\tau + 1$, $n = 2\tau + 1$, $n > 2\tau + 1$. For a *fixed* n *between* τ *and* $2\tau + 1$,

$$\mathcal{E}[(t_{\tau+1} + T_s/2)(T_s/2 - t'_{\tau+1})]$$

$$= \mathcal{E}[(T_s/2 - t_{\tau+1} - T_s)(t'_{\tau+1} + T_s/2 - T_s)]$$

$$= \mathcal{E}[(T_s/2 - t_{\tau+1})(t'_{\tau+1} + T_s/2)] - T_s\mathcal{E}[t'_{\tau+1} + T_s/2]$$

$$- T_s\mathcal{E}[T_s/2 - t_{\tau+1}] + T_s^2\frac{p(n)}{P_\tau}$$

$$= \mathcal{E}[(T_s/2 - t_{\tau+1})(t'_{\tau+1} + T_s/2)] + T_s\mathcal{E}(t_{\tau+1} - t'_{\tau+1}) \tag{100}$$

Since $\mathcal{E}(t_{\tau+1} + T_s/2) = \mathcal{E}(T_s/2 - t'_{\tau+1})$,

$$T_s\mathcal{E}(t_{\tau+1} - t'_{\tau+1}) = 2T_s\mathcal{E}(t_{\tau+1} + T_s/2) - T_s^2\frac{p(n)}{P_\tau}$$

$$= -2T_s\mathcal{E}(T_s/2 - t_{\tau+1}) + T_s^2\frac{p(n)}{P_\tau}$$

$$= -2T_s^2\frac{p(n)}{P_\tau}\frac{n - \tau}{n + 1} + T_s^2\frac{p(n)}{P_\tau}$$

$$= T_s^2\left[-2\frac{p(n)}{P_\tau}\left(1 - \frac{\tau + 1}{n + 1}\right) + \frac{p(n)}{P_\tau}\right]$$

$$= T_s^2\left[-\frac{p(n)}{P_\tau} + 2\frac{\tau + 1}{\alpha\epsilon_q\epsilon_0\lambda_s T_s}\frac{p(n + 1)}{P_\tau}\right] \tag{101}$$

Similarly,

$$\mathcal{E}[(T_s/2 - t_{\tau+1})(t'_{\tau+1} + T_s/2)]$$

$$= \frac{p(n)}{P_\tau} T_s^2 \frac{(n-\tau)!(n-\tau)!n!}{(n+2)!(n-\tau-1)!(n-\tau-1)!}$$

$$= \frac{p(n)}{P_\tau} T_s^2 \frac{(n-\tau)^2}{(n+2)(n+1)}$$

$$= \frac{p(n)}{P_\tau} T_s^2 \frac{[(n+2)-(\tau+2)][(n+1)-(\tau+1)]}{(n+2)(n+1)}$$

$$= \frac{p(n)}{P_\tau} T_s^2 \left[1 - \frac{\tau+1}{n+1} + \frac{(\tau+2)(\tau+1)}{(n+2)(n+1)} - \frac{(\tau+2)(n+2-1)}{(n+2)(n+1)}\right]$$

$$= \frac{p(n)}{P_\tau} T_s^2 \left[1 - \frac{\tau+1}{n+1} + \frac{(\tau+2)(\tau+1)}{(n+2)(n+1)} - \frac{\tau+2}{n+1} + \frac{\tau+2}{(n+2)(n+1)}\right]$$

$$= \frac{p(n)}{P_\tau} T_s^2 \left[1 - \frac{2\tau+3}{n+1} + \frac{(\tau+2)^2}{(n+1)(n+2)}\right]$$

$$= \frac{T_s^2}{P_\tau}\left[p(n) - \frac{2\tau+3}{\alpha\epsilon_q\epsilon_0\lambda_s T_s} p(n+1) + \frac{(\tau+2)^2}{(\alpha\epsilon_q\epsilon_0\lambda_s T_s)^2} p(n+2)\right] \quad (102)$$

Hence,

$$\mathcal{E}[(t_{\tau+1} + T_s/2)(T_s/2 - t'_{\tau+1})]$$

$$= \frac{T_s^2}{P_\tau}\left[p(n) - \frac{2\tau+3}{\alpha\epsilon_q\epsilon_0\lambda_s T_s} p(n+1) + \frac{(\tau+2)^2}{(\alpha\epsilon_q\epsilon_0\lambda_s T_s)^2} p(n+2)\right.$$

$$\left. -p(n) + \frac{2(\tau+1)}{\alpha\epsilon_q\epsilon_0\lambda_s T_s} p(n+1)\right]$$

$$= \frac{T_s^2}{P_\tau}\left[-\frac{p(n+1)}{\alpha\epsilon_q\epsilon_0\lambda_s T_s} + \frac{(\tau+2)^2}{(\alpha\epsilon_q\epsilon_0\lambda_s T_s)^2} p(n+2)\right] \quad (103)$$

For a *fixed* $n = 2\tau + 1$, the density of $t_{\tau+1}$ is

$$\frac{p(2\tau+1)}{P_\tau} D\left(\frac{a}{T_s} + \frac{1}{2}; \tau+1, \tau+1\right)\frac{da}{T_s} \quad (104)$$

and

$$\mathcal{E}[(T_s/2 + t_{\tau+1})(T_s/2 - t_{\tau+1})]$$

$$= \frac{p(2\tau+1)}{P_\tau} T_s^2 \frac{(2\tau+1)!}{\tau!\tau!} \frac{(\tau+1)!(\tau+1)!}{(2\tau+3)!}$$

$$= \frac{(\tau+1)^2}{(n+1)(n+2)} \frac{p(n)}{P_\tau} T_s^2 = \frac{(\tau+1)^2}{(\alpha\epsilon_q\epsilon_0\lambda_s)^2} \frac{p(n+2)}{P_\tau} \quad (105)$$

For a *fixed* n greater than $2\tau + 1$,

$$\mathcal{E}[(T_s/2 + t_{\tau+1})(T_s/2 - t'_{\tau+1})] = T_s^2 \frac{p(n)}{P_\tau} \frac{(\tau+1)!(\tau+1)!n!}{(n+2)!\tau!\tau!}$$

$$= \frac{(\tau+1)^2}{(\alpha\epsilon_q\epsilon_0\lambda_s)^2} \frac{p(n+2)}{P_\tau} \quad (106)$$

Therefore, twice the variance of t^* is

$$\frac{(\tau+1)(\tau+2)}{(\alpha\epsilon_q\epsilon_0\lambda_s)^2}\frac{P_{\tau+2}}{P_\tau} - \frac{T_s^2}{P_\tau}\left[-\frac{1}{\alpha\epsilon_q\epsilon_0\lambda_s T_s}\sum_{n=\tau+1}^{2\tau}p(n+1)\right.$$

$$+\frac{(\tau+2)^2}{(\alpha\epsilon_q\epsilon_0\lambda_s T_s)^2}\sum_{n=\tau+1}^{2\tau}p(n+2)\left.\right] - \frac{(\tau+1)^2}{(\alpha\epsilon_q\epsilon_0\lambda_s)^2}\frac{p(2\tau+3)}{P_\tau}$$

$$-\frac{(\tau+1)^2}{(\alpha\epsilon_q\epsilon_0\lambda_s)^2}\sum_{n=2\tau+2}^{\infty}p(n+2)/P_\tau$$

$$=\frac{(\tau+1)(\tau+2)}{(\alpha\epsilon_q\epsilon_0\lambda_s)^2}\frac{P_{\tau+2}}{P_\tau} - \frac{T_s^2}{P_\tau}\left[-\frac{P_{\tau+1}-P_{2\tau+1}}{\alpha\epsilon_q\epsilon_0\lambda_s T_s}\right.$$

$$+\frac{(\tau+2)^2}{(\alpha\epsilon_q\epsilon_0\lambda_s T_s)^2}(P_{\tau+2}-P_{2\tau+2})\left.\right] - \frac{(\tau+1)^2}{(\alpha\epsilon_q\epsilon_0\lambda_s)^2}\frac{P_{2\tau+2}}{P_\tau}$$

$$=\frac{(\tau+2)^2-(\tau+1)^2}{(\alpha\epsilon_q\epsilon_0\lambda_s)^2}\frac{P_{2\tau+2}}{P_\tau} + \frac{(\tau+1)(\tau+2)-(\tau+2)^2}{(\alpha\epsilon_q\epsilon_0\lambda_s)^2}\frac{P_{\tau+2}}{P_\tau}$$

$$+\frac{T_s^2}{P_\tau}\frac{P_{\tau+1}-P_{2\tau+1}}{\alpha\epsilon_q\epsilon_0\lambda_s T_s}$$

$$=\frac{2\tau+3}{(\alpha\epsilon_q\epsilon_0\lambda_s)^2}\frac{P_{2\tau+2}}{P_\tau} - \frac{\tau+2}{(\alpha\epsilon_q\epsilon_0\lambda_s)^2}\frac{P_{\tau+2}}{P_\tau} + \frac{T_s^2}{P_\tau}\frac{P_{\tau+1}-P_{2\tau+1}}{\alpha\epsilon_q\epsilon_0\lambda_s T_s} \quad (107)$$

and

$$2\,\mathrm{Var}(t^*/T_s) = \frac{2\tau+3}{(\alpha\epsilon_q\epsilon_0\lambda_s T_s)^2}\frac{P_{2\tau+2}}{P_\tau} - \frac{\tau+2}{(\alpha\epsilon_q\epsilon_0\lambda_s T_s)^2}\frac{P_{\tau+2}}{P_\tau}$$

$$+\frac{1}{\alpha\epsilon_q\epsilon_0\lambda_s T_s}\frac{P_{\tau+1}-P_{2\tau+1}}{P_\tau} \quad (108)$$

Note that $\mathrm{Var}\,(t^*/T_s) < \frac{1}{4}$.

The preceding variance estimate is a lower bound on the actual variance since background and dark current were neglected. The standard deviation of t^*/T_s is graphed in Fig. 9.

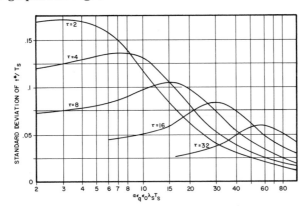

FIG. 9. Standard deviation of t^*/T_s as a function of expected number of pulses $\alpha\epsilon_q\epsilon_0\lambda_s T_s$.

A basic unsolved problem is to determine the variance of t^* when the diffraction circle is comparable to the slit in width. There are two approaches: (1) direct analytical approach, (2) indirect approach, using previous results. The analytical approach involves extending the foregoing results; the basic difficulty is the nonstationary character of $\lambda_s'(t)$ in $(-T_s/2, T_s/2)$. Note that $y(t)$ can be viewed as birth-death process with birth rate $\mu(t)$ and death rate $\mu(t - T_f)$. The indirect approach is based on previous results from radar applications, i.e., range estimation. In such applications, one must estimate the position of a pulse and determine the variance of the estimate.* As yet, neither of these approaches has yielded a solution to the basic problem.

Intensity Estimation

It is natural to use $y(t^* + T_f/2)$ to estimate the intensity of the star. From Fig. 7, we note that the mean of $y(t)$ (and consequently, its distribution) is a slowly changing function of t near $t = T_f/2$. If the variance of t^* is small compared to the slit width, the distribution of $y(t^* + T_f/2)$ is approximately Poisson with mean

$$\alpha \epsilon_q \epsilon_0 \lambda_s H(T_f/2) + \alpha \epsilon_q \epsilon_0 T_f T_s \sum_{M=M_0+1}^{\infty} \nu(M)\lambda(M) + T_f \lambda_d \qquad (109)$$

A natural estimate of λ_s is

$$\hat{\lambda}_s = \frac{y(t^* + T_f/2) - \alpha \epsilon_q \epsilon_0 T_f T_s \sum_{M=M_0+1}^{\infty} \nu(M)\lambda(M) - T_f \lambda_d}{\alpha \epsilon_q \epsilon_0 H(T_f/2)} \qquad (110)\dagger$$

which is unbiased. The standard deviation of $\hat{\lambda}_s/\lambda_s$ is

$$\frac{[\alpha \epsilon_q \epsilon_0 \lambda_s H(T_f/2) + \alpha \epsilon_q \epsilon_0 T_f T_s \sum_{M=M_0+1}^{\infty} \nu(M)\lambda(M) + T_f \lambda_d]^{1/2}}{\alpha \epsilon_q \epsilon_0 \lambda_s H(T_f/2)} \qquad (111)$$

IV. Example

The following example is presented to illustrate qualitative relationships between various system parameters, and their relative magnitudes for a reasonable scanning system. The following system parameters are fixed:

1. $M_0 = 3$
2. Diameter of optical aperture is 3 inches
3. $\sigma = 3.9$ seconds of arc
4. $\epsilon_0 = 0.5$
5. Field of view is 20 degrees

---

* This problem is discussed by Wainstein and Zubalsov.[16]
† This estimator has the same form as the minimum variance estimator, Eq. 54.

6. $\epsilon_q = 0.1$
7. $\alpha = 0.8$
8. $\lambda_d = 4 \times 10^3/\text{sec}$
9. $T_f = T_s$

The physical arrangement of the lenses, slit, and photomultiplier is illustrated in Fig. 10. The optical axis is inclined at 15° relative to the spin axis.

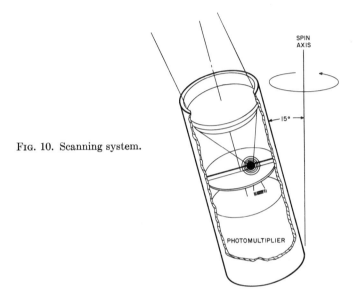

FIG. 10. Scanning system.

Hence, the over-all field of view is 50°, except for a 10° hole around the spin axis. The slit, spin axis, and optical axis lie in the same plane. The following calculations are based on a central ray.

The design objective is to select the "best" slit width maintaining the probability of detecting a third magnitude star at 0.8. To maintain the probability of detection, it is necessary to increase the detection threshold as the slit width is increased, for each scan period. Thresholds and probabilities of detection are presented in Table 2 for several scan periods and slit widths. For a specific slit width and scan period, the tabulated threshold is the largest value of τ such that the probability of detection is at least .8 for a third magnitude star. The angle accuracy is graphed in Fig. 11; intensity accuracy in Fig. 12; number of weak-star detections in Fig. 13. For a 4-second scan period and a slit width of 20 seconds of arc,

1. Standard deviation of the angle estimate is 1.6 seconds of arc.
2. Standard deviation of the intensity estimate divided by the true intensity is .2.
3. Probability of detecting a third magnitude star is .83.
4. Probability of at most one weak-star detection is not less than .9.

TABLE 2   THRESHOLDS AND DETECTION PROBABILITIES*

Slit Width (in sec)	Scan Period							
	1 sec		2 sec		4 sec		8 sec	
	τ	Prob.	τ	Prob.	τ	Prob.	τ	Prob.
5	—	—	—	—	1	0.80	3	0.85
10	0	0.90	2	0.84	6	0.80	14	0.82
15	1	0.91	5	0.81	12	0.81	27	0.80
20	3	0.80	7	0.85	17	0.83	38	0.81
25	4	0.84	11	0.82	24	0.81	51	0.82
30	6	0.84	14	0.80	30	0.82	64	0.82
35	7	0.82	16	0.83	36	0.84	77	0.81

* Based on third magnitude star.

From these graphs, one can select the best slit width. For example, it is necessary to distinguish stars whose intensities differ by one magnitude

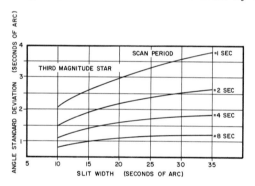

FIG. 11. Angle accuracy.

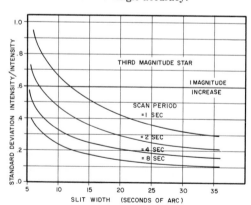

FIG. 12. Intensity accuracy.

with an angle accuracy of 2 seconds of arc. Also, the maximum scan period is 2 seconds. From Fig. 12, the slit width must be at least 7 seconds of arc. On the other hand, to achieve an angle accuracy of 2 seconds of arc, the slit width must be less than 16.5 seconds of arc. Since the number of weak-

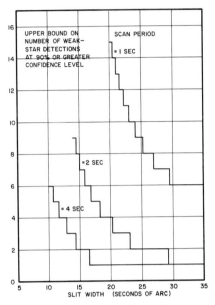

FIG. 13. Number of weak-star detections.

star detections is less with a wider slit, the best slit width is 16.5 seconds of arc.

APPENDIX A
Evaluation of *H(t)* and Its Integral

The function $H(t)$ is defined as

$$\int_{t-T_f}^{t} G(x)\, dx \tag{112}$$

where $G(x) = \Phi(x/\sigma + T_s/2\sigma) - \Phi(x/\sigma - T_s/2\sigma)$. For convenience, let $\alpha = t - T_f$ and $\beta = t$. Then

$$\int_{\alpha}^{\beta} \Phi(x/\sigma + T_s/2\sigma)\, dx = \int_{\alpha'}^{\beta'} \Phi(u)\sigma\, du \tag{113}$$

with $\alpha' = \alpha/\sigma + T_s/2\sigma$ and $\beta' = \beta/\sigma + T_s/2\sigma$.

$$\sigma \int_{\alpha'}^{\beta'} \Phi(u)\, du = \sigma\left[u\Phi(u)\right]_{\alpha'}^{\beta'} - \sigma \int_{\alpha'}^{\beta'} u\phi(u)\, du$$

$$= \sigma[\beta'\Phi(\beta') - \alpha'\Phi(\alpha')] + \sigma[\phi(\beta') - \phi(\alpha')] \tag{114}$$

where

$$\phi(u) = \frac{d}{du} \Phi(u)$$

Similarly

$$\int_\alpha^\beta \Phi(x/\sigma - T_s/2\sigma)\, dx = \int_{\alpha''}^{\beta''} \Phi(v)\sigma\, dv$$

$$= \sigma[\beta''\Phi(\beta'') - \alpha''\Phi(\alpha'')] + \sigma[\phi(\beta'') - \phi(\alpha'')] \quad (115)$$

with

$$\alpha'' = \alpha/\sigma - T_s/2\sigma \quad \text{and} \quad \beta'' = \beta/\sigma - T_s/2\sigma$$

Substituting α', β', α'', and β'', one obtains

$$H(t) = (t + T_s/2)\Phi\left(\frac{t + T_s/2}{\sigma}\right) - (t - T_s/2)\Phi\left(\frac{t - T_s/2}{\sigma}\right)$$

$$- \left[(t - T_f + T_s/2)\Phi\left(\frac{t - T_f + T_s/2}{\sigma}\right)\right.$$

$$\left. - (t - T_f - T_s/2)\Phi\left(\frac{t - T_f - T_s/2}{\sigma}\right)\right]$$

$$+ \sigma\left[\phi\left(\frac{t + T_s/2}{\sigma}\right) - \phi\left(\frac{t - T_s/2}{\sigma}\right)\right]$$

$$- \sigma\left[\phi\left(\frac{t - T_f + T_s/2}{\sigma}\right) - \phi\left(\frac{t - T_f - T_s/2}{\sigma}\right)\right] \quad (116)$$

The integral of $H(t)$ can be evaluated directly:

$$\int_{-\infty}^\infty H(t)\, dt = \int_{-\infty}^\infty \int_{t-T_f}^t G(x)\, dx\, dt = \int_{-\infty}^\infty \int_x^{x+T_f} G(x)\, dt\, dx$$

$$= T_f \int_{-\infty}^\infty G(x)\, dx \quad (117)$$

By direct integration, one can show that

$$\int_{-a}^a G(t)\, dt = (a + T_s/2)\Phi\left(\frac{a + T_s/2}{\sigma}\right)$$

$$- (-a + T_s/2)\Phi\left(\frac{-a + T_s/2}{\sigma}\right)$$

$$+ \sigma\phi\left(\frac{a + T_s/2}{\sigma}\right) - \sigma\phi\left(\frac{-a + T_s/2}{\sigma}\right)$$

$$- (a - T_s/2)\Phi\left(\frac{a - T_s/2}{\sigma}\right)$$

$$+ (-a - T_s/2)\Phi\left(\frac{-a - T_s/2}{\sigma}\right)$$

$$- \sigma\phi\left(\frac{a - T_s/2}{\sigma}\right) + \sigma\phi\left(\frac{-a - T_s/2}{\sigma}\right) \quad (118)$$

$$\int_{-\infty}^\infty G(t)\, dt = \lim_{a\to\infty} a\left[\Phi\left(\frac{a + T_s/2}{\sigma}\right) - \Phi\left(\frac{a - T_s/2}{\sigma}\right)\right]$$

$$+ \lim_{a\to\infty} a\left[\Phi\left(\frac{-a + T_s/2}{\sigma}\right) - \Phi\left(\frac{-a - T_s/2}{\sigma}\right)\right] + T_s \quad (119)$$

Since the first two terms vanish,

$$\int_{-\infty}^{\infty} H(t)\, dt = T_s T_f \tag{120}$$

It is easily shown that

$$H(t) \le H(T_f/2) < \lim_{\sigma \to 0} H(T_f/2) = T_f \tag{121}$$

Hence, $0 < \dfrac{H(t)}{T_f} < 1$ and

$$T_s = \int_{-\infty}^{\infty} \frac{H(t)}{T_f}\, dt > \int_{-\infty}^{\infty} \left[\frac{H(t)}{T_f}\right]^k dt \tag{122}$$

Further,

$$\int_{-\infty}^{\infty} \left[\frac{H(t)}{T_f}\right]^2 dt > \left[\int_{-\infty}^{\infty} \frac{H(t)}{T_f}\, dt\right]^2 = T_s^2 \tag{123}$$

Therefore,

$$T_s T_f^2 > \int_{-\infty}^{\infty} [H(t)]^2\, dt > T_s^2 T_f^2 \tag{124}$$

and

$$T_s T_f^k > \int_{-\infty}^{\infty} [H(t)]^k\, dt \tag{125}$$

APPENDIX B
Evaluation of Intensity Moments

To estimate $\sum\limits_{M_0+1}^{\infty} \nu(M)\lambda^k(M)$, we assume $\nu(M)$ is a continuous function which can be approximated by a Gaussian density. Hence

$$\sum_{M_0+1}^{\infty} \nu(M)\lambda^k(M) \approx \int_{M_0+1/2}^{\infty} \nu(M)\lambda^k(M)\, dM \tag{126}$$

Because of the nature of available data, we find constants a, b, c such that

$$N_M = a\Phi(bM + c) \tag{127}$$

where N_M is the number of stars per square degree brighter than photographic magnitude M, and where

$$\Phi(z) = \frac{1}{\sqrt{2\pi}} \int_{-\infty}^{z} e^{-t^2/2}\, dt \tag{128}$$

Let T_γ be the number of square degrees scanned per second by the optical device. Then

$$\nu(M) = T_\gamma \frac{d}{dM}(N_M) \tag{129}$$

Estimation of N_M

The basic problem is to determine a, b, c in Eq. 127 using three points (M_i, N_{Mi}) $i = 1, 2, 3$. The three points give three equations

$$N_{M_1} = a\Phi(bM_1 + c) \tag{130}$$

$$N_{M_2} = a\Phi(bM_2 + c) \tag{131}$$

$$N_{M_3} = a\Phi(bM_3 + c) \tag{132}$$

By taking ratios, we obtain

$$N_{M_1}\Phi(bM_2 + c) = N_{M_2}\Phi(bM_1 + c) \tag{133}$$

$$N_{M_2}\Phi(bM_3 + c) = N_{M_3}\Phi(bM_2 + c) \tag{134}$$

Differentiating with respect to c and taking natural logarithms of both sides gives

$$\ln N_{M_1} - \tfrac{1}{2}(bM_2 + c)^2 = \ln N_{M_2} - \tfrac{1}{2}(bM_1 + c)^2 \tag{135}$$

$$\ln N_{M_2} - \tfrac{1}{2}(bM_3 + c)^2 = \ln N_{M_3} - \tfrac{1}{2}(bM_2 + c)^2 \tag{136}$$

or

$$b[b(M_2 + M_1) + 2c] = -2K_{21} \tag{137}$$

$$b[b(M_3 + M_2) + 2c] = -2K_{32} \tag{138}$$

where $K_{ij} = \ln (N_{Mi}/N_{Mj})/(M_i - M_j)$. Taking ratios gives

$$\frac{b(M_2 + M_1) + 2c}{b(M_3 + M_2) + 2c} = \frac{K_{21}}{K_{32}} \tag{139}$$

which implies $c = -\tfrac{1}{2}\beta b$ where

$$\beta = \frac{K_{21}(M_3 + M_2) - K_{32}(M_2 + M_1)}{K_{21} - K_{32}} \tag{140}$$

Substituting into Eq. 137, we obtain

$$b[b(M_2 + M_1) - \beta b] = -2K_{21} \tag{141}$$

or

$$b = \left[\frac{2K_{21}}{\beta - (M_2 + M_1)}\right]^{1/2} \tag{142}$$

Using $M_1 = 2$, $M_2 = 12$, $M_3 = 21$, and using astrophysical data given by Allen[17] ($N_2 = 9.12 \times 10^{-4}$, $N_{12} = 5.89 \times 10^1$, $N_{21} = 2.51 \times 10^4$), we find that $\beta = 83.3$, which gives $b = 0.173$ and $c = -7.21$. Thus $N_M = a\Phi(0.173M - 7.21)$. Using $M = 12$, $a = [28.8/\Phi(-5.13)] = 1.99 \times 10^8$. Hence $N_M = (1.99 \times 10^8)\Phi(0.173M - 7.21)$. In Fig. 14 the per cent deviation $100 \times [a\Phi(bM + c) - N_M]/N_M$ is graphed as a function of M using data given by C. W. Allen.[17]

One of the uses for this formula is in estimating the starlight not accounted for by the stars of magnitude 21.5 or brighter. C. W. Allen lists this value as equivalent to 0.8 tenth magnitude stars. Using

$$\int_{21.5}^{\infty} \frac{d}{dM} (N_M)\lambda(M)\, dM$$

as an estimate of this residual starlight, we get a value of 2.07 tenth magnitude stars.

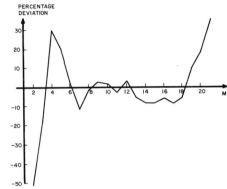

M	$a\Phi(bM+c)$	Tabulated Values (N_m)
2	3.96×10^{-4}	9.12×10^{-4}
3	2.05×10^{-3}	2.51×10^{-3}
4	10.05×10^{-3}	7.76×10^{-3}
5	2.80×10^{-2}	2.34×10^{-2}
6	7.42×10^{-2}	7.24×10^{-2}
7	1.79×10^{-1}	2.04×10^{-1}
8	5.57×10^{-1}	5.62×10^{-1}
9	1.59	1.55
10	4.24	4.17
11	1.09×10^{1}	1.12×10^{1}
12	2.98×10^{1}	2.88×10^{1}
13	7.00×10^{1}	7.41×10^{1}
14	1.66×10^{2}	1.82×10^{2}
15	3.82×10^{2}	4.17×10^{2}
16	8.95×10^{2}	9.55×10^{2}
17	1.95×10^{3}	2.14×10^{3}
18	4.12×10^{3}	4.36×10^{3}
19	8.80×10^{3}	7.94×10^{3}
20	1.76×10^{4}	1.48×10^{4}
21	3.42×10^{4}	2.51×10^{4}

FIG. 14. Cumulative star density. Note: The deviations are due to the accuracy of the available tables.

Evaluation of Intensity Moments

Now consider the calculation of

$$\int_k^\infty \frac{d}{dM}(N_M)\lambda^k(M)\,dM \tag{143}$$

where $\lambda(M) = a'e^{-b'M}$.

$$\int_k^\infty \frac{d}{dM}(N_M)\lambda^k(M)\,dM = \int_k^\infty \frac{d}{dM}[a\Phi(bM+c)]a'^k \exp(-kb'M)\,dM$$

$$= \frac{aba'^k}{\sqrt{2\pi}}\int_k^\infty \exp\left[-\frac{1}{2}(bM+c)^2 - kb'M\right]dM$$

$$= \frac{aba'^k}{\sqrt{2\pi}}\int_k^\infty \exp\left\{-\frac{1}{2}b^2\left[M + \frac{bc+kb'}{b^2}\right]^2 + \frac{1}{2}\left[\left(\frac{bc+b'k}{b}\right)^2 - c^2\right]\right\}dM \tag{144}$$

Letting $u = b[M + (bc+kb')/b^2]$ and $du = b\,dM$, we get

$$\frac{aba'^k}{\sqrt{2\pi}}\int_{b\left[k+\frac{bc+b'k}{b^2}\right]}^\infty \exp\left(-\frac{1}{2}u^2\right)\left\{\exp\frac{1}{2}\left[\left(\frac{bc+b'k}{b}\right)^2 - c^2\right]\right\}\frac{1}{b}\,du$$

$$= aa'^k \exp\left\{\frac{1}{2}\left[\left(\frac{bc+b'k}{b}\right)^2 - c^2\right]\right\}\left[1 - \Phi\left(bK + c + \frac{b'}{b}k\right)\right] \tag{145}$$

We assume

$$\lambda(M) = (5.06 \times 10^6)e^{-0.921M}D^2$$

= number of photons per second arriving from a star of Mth magnitude through an aperture of diameter D in inches.

Then

$$\left\{\begin{array}{l} k = M_0 + \frac{1}{2} \\[6pt] \nu(M) = T_\gamma \dfrac{d}{dM}[a\Phi(bM+c)] \\[6pt] \lambda^k(M) = a'^k e^{-b'kM} \end{array}\right\} \tag{146}$$

with $a = 1.99 \times 10^8$, $a' = D^2(5.06 \times 10^6)$, $b = 0.173$, $b' = 0.921$, and $c = -7.21$. Thus

$$\int_{M_0+1/2}^{\infty} \nu(M)\lambda^k(M) \, dM$$

$$= D^{2k}T_\gamma(6.17 \times 10^{-3})(5.06 \times 10^6)^k[1 - \Phi(0.173M_0 + 5.32k - 7.12)]$$

$$= \frac{D^{2k}}{T_{\text{sp}}} \sin \, (\text{fov}/2)(5.06)^k(2.54 \times 10^{6k+2})[1 - \Phi(0.173M_0 + 5.32k - 7.12)] \quad (147)$$

where fov is the field of view of the lens system in Fig. 1, and T_{sp} is the scan period in seconds.

Notation

The following is a list of symbols that have a consistent meaning throughout the paper. The number in the parentheses refers to the first equation in which the symbol is used.

λ_s = average number of photons received from a star per unit of time (1)

ϵ_0 = optical efficiency of lens system (1)

σ = dispersion of diffraction pattern on the focal plane (1)

T_s = time for star to cross slit (2)

$\lambda_s'(t)$ = average number of photons arriving at photomultiplier at time t (8)

$$\Phi(t) = \frac{1}{\sqrt{2\pi}} \int_{-\infty}^{t} \exp\left(-\frac{1}{2}x^2\right) dx \quad (3)$$

$$G(t) = \Phi\left(\frac{t}{\sigma} + \frac{T_s}{2\sigma}\right) - \Phi\left(\frac{t}{\sigma} - \frac{T_s}{2\sigma}\right) \quad (2)$$

M_0 = magnitude of the dimmest star we wish to detect (4)

$\lambda(M)$ = photon arrival rate for a star of magnitude M (4)

$\lambda_b'(t)$ = photon arrival rate at the photomultiplier for weak stars at time t (4)

$\nu(M)$ = average density of stars of magnitude M (7)

α = fraction of photoelectric pulses transmitted by threshold clamp (8)

ϵ_q = quantum efficiency of photomultiplier (8)

λ_d = number of noise pulses resulting from photomultiplier (8)

η = average number of pulses received in the interval $(-T, T)$ (10)

ρ = ratio of star pulse rate to "noise" pulse rate (16)

t_0 = time at which star crosses the center of the slit (9)

$\hat{t}_0$ = estimate of t_0 (17)

$\hat{\lambda}_s$ = estimate of λ_s (54)

T_f = time duration of holding filter (55)

$y(t)$ = number of pulses in holding filter at time t (57)

$\mu(t)$ = average number of pulses in holding filter at time t (55)

$$H(t) = \int_{t-T_f}^{t} G(x) \, dx \quad (56)$$

T_{sp} = scan period (68)

β = average number of pulses in holding filter when a star of magnitude M is at the center of the slit (80)

t' = time at which $y(t)$ exceeds τ

$t'' = $ time at which $y(t)$ drops below τ

$t^* = \frac{1}{2}(t' + t'') - T_{f/2} = $ estimation of the time that the star crosses the slit

$t_{\tau+1} = $ arrival time of the $(\tau + 1)$th pulse (92)

$t'_{\tau+1} = $ arrival time of the τth from last pulse (92)

$p(n) = $ probability of receiving n pulses from a star (84)

$P_\tau = $ probability of receiving more than τ pulses from a star (85)

$N_M = $ number of stars per square degree brighter than photographic magnitude M (126)

$T_\gamma = $ number of square degrees scanned by the optical device (129)

References

1. LILLESTRAND, R. L., AND J. E. CARROLL, *Self-Contained System for Interplanetary Navigation*, American Astronautical Society Meeting, August 1961.
2. KENIMER, R. L., AND T. M. WALSH, *A Star Field Mapping System for Determining the Attitude of a Spinning Probe*, Aerospace Electro-Technology Symposium of the International Conference and Exhibit on Aerospace Electro-Technology, April 1964.
3. HARRINGTON, D. C., *Noise Error Analysis of an Optical Star and Planet Scanner*, National Aerospace Electronics Conference, IEEE, May 1963.
4. ROBINSON, D. Z., "Methods of Background Description and Their Utility," *Proc. IRE*, *47*, 1554 (1959).
5. ELDERING, H. G., "Method for Complete Description of Infrared Sky Backgrounds," *J. Opt. Soc. Am.*, *51*, 1424 (1961).
6. JONES, R. C., "Energy Detectable by Radiation Detectors," *J. Opt. Soc. Am.*, *50*, 1883 (1960).
7. JONES, R. C., "Information Capacity of a Beam of Light," *J. Opt. Soc. Am.*, *52*, 493 (1962).
8. BHARUCHA-REID, A. T., *Elements of the Theory of Markov Processes and Their Applications*, McGraw-Hill Book Co., Inc., New York, 1960, Chap. 7.
9. PARZEN, E., *Stochastic Processes*, Holden-Day, Inc., San Francisco, 1962, p. 143.
10. WILKS, S. S., *Mathematical Statistics*, John Wiley & Sons, Inc., New York, 1962, p. 402.
11. CRAMER, H., *Mathematical Methods of Statistics*, Princeton University Press, Princeton, N.J., 1946, p. 477.
12. RICE, S. O., "Mathematical Analysis of Random Noise," *Bell System Tech. J.*, *23*, 282–332 (1944); *24*, 46–156 (1945).
13. ZIMMERMAN, C. D., *Comparison of Two Methods of Star Detection*, Memo. TM-141, Research Division, Control Data Corporation, Minneapolis, July 1964.
14. LEVENBACH, H., *The Zero-Crossing Problem*, Research Report No. 63-4, Department of Electrical Engineering, Queen's University, Kingston, Ontario, Canada, September 1963.
15. WILKS, S. S., *Mathematical Statistics*, John Wiley & Sons, Inc., New York, 1962, p. 177.
16. WAINSTEIN, L. A., AND V. D. ZUBALSOV, *Extraction of Signals from Noise*, Prentice-Hall, Inc., Englewood Cliffs, N.J., 1962, Chap. 8.
17. ALLEN, C. W., *Astrophysical Quantities*, Athlone Press, London, 1955, pp. 213–214.

CHAPTER 36

STATE OF THE ART OF THE OPTICAL LOGIC ELEMENT

T. E. Bray and G. B. Jacobs

General Electric Company, Electronics Laboratory, Syracuse, New York

I. Introduction

The primary purpose of this paper is to indicate the state of the art of an optical logic element for use in a digital data processor. To achieve this goal we not only must calculate the performance of several typical device configurations, but we also must not overlook any unusual combination of components that would permit much improved performance.

The first portion of this paper consists of a list of the requirements of a high-performance logic element, and a discussion of those particular requirements in which the optical element is most apt to excel. The next section describes the capabilities of the various components that might compose a useful logic element. The third section calculates the performance of three promising configurations.

A. Potential Advantages

1. UNIQUE PROPERTIES OF OPTICAL SIGNALS. The properties of optical signals which distinguish them from their counterparts in normal electronic computers are

   a. The lack of electrical charge of photons, leading to complete decoupling and isolation of signals, and very large fan-in.

   b. The two-dimensional wave nature of optical radiation at very short wavelengths which in turn involves

   1. Ease of propagation of many independent signals through simple channels without need for any conductors.

   2. Potentially, very small components, including the "waveguides," perhaps leading to smaller interlogic distances and hence, higher operating speeds.

3. Extremely high "carrier" frequencies—of the order of 10^{14} cps.

4. Propagation of two-dimensional signals, which may be viewed as parallel propagation of one-dimensional signals.

Of these characteristics, those mentioned most often (and, unfortunately, many times without understanding their origins) are "parallel," "isolation," and "small size." Interestingly, there are some who erroneously believe that optical computers will be faster, since signals propagate "at the velocity of light." This is true of all electrical signals, of course, if correction is made for the group velocity in the medium. However, the high frequency of optical radiation may, indeed, lead to faster operation.

The isolation property is known to be extremely useful in data processing, and ways in which it may be used are evident. The parallel nature of light, while apparently very desirable, is not as easy to utilize. Many have commented upon the desirability of a parallel computer, but implementing such a generalization requires further thought and insight. Some of this is discussed in the following sections.

2. SOME PROBLEMS. To formulate approaches to the development and construction of a general-purpose optical digital computer, problems associated with the optical approach should be delineated. One of the first is the question of a parallel computer. In this field much remains to be accomplished from a mathematical standpoint. However, it generally is agreed that if a number of computations need to be performed and the performance of each is independent of the other, then a saving of time can result by making those calculations simultaneously, or *in parallel*. Counterbalancing the increased speed is increased equipment, since the calculations are assumed to occur simultaneously and independently.

However, it is clear that some functions (e.g., relaxation of a finite network representing an N-dimensional partial differential equation) will often require sequential computation of some sort. Thus, *both parallel and sequential operations will need to be performed*.

A second problem arises from the tremendous capacity for the parallel (-sequential) processor to absorb input data. Large memories will provide some of this, while real-time inputs from many channels may provide another significant portion.

3. SYSTEM CONCEPT DEVELOPMENTS. As has been proved innumerable times in the past, the creation of new systems often stems directly from unique properties of new devices and techniques. Transistors, tunnel diodes, thin films, superconductors—all have led to new systems. The optical data processors will perhaps show the device-system interaction more fully than the others, because of a vast variety of related techniques awaiting use, and the wave nature of optical radiation.

4. FOUR PARTS OF AN OPTICAL COMPUTER. We may write down four generalized portions of an optical digital computer. The integration of all

portions will result in a relatively general optical computer. Most parts are essential, while one is highly desirable but not absolutely essential. The four areas are

   a. Optical logic—the elements and gates which operate upon and manipulate the information. (Necessary)

   b. Active optical memory—memory arrays into which information can be written, from which it can be erased and read. (Necessary)

   c. Permanent optical memory—techniques (such as photographic) which take advantage of the high-density recording possibilities, and which may help provide the large amount of input information an optical computer may eventually be expected to process. (Desirable)

   d. Logical organization or optical machine design—suitable means of assembling the devices and available techniques to provide a useful computer for certain classes of problems. (Necessary)

   Each of these is discussed in more detail in the next four sections.

   4.1 Optical Logic.   It is not enough simply to transmit signals or waveforms from one point to another in our hypothetical optical computer. Rather, there must be a "cross flow," or even feedback of the information, and it must be combined and operated upon (i.e., processed). To be useful, it is likely that the speed of operation (logic rate) should be above 10 Mc, preferably exceeding 100 Mc. In addition, high fan-in and fan-out will often reduce the number of gates required (and, thus, the expense), as well as the number of layers of logic (hence, decreasing the delay time, and increasing the logic rate).

   In the diagram of Fig. 1, note the use of fan-in and fan-out of the OR-gate, of which the output is Y_3. Gates whose fan-in is limited to 3 and output

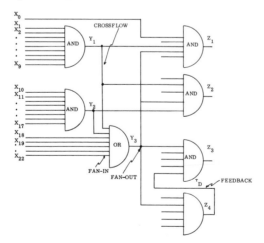

Fɪɢ. 1. Hypothetical logic illustrating high fan-in and fan-out, crossflow, and feedback.

to 2 would require at least one (and probably two) more layers of logic and two to four additional gates.

Hence, the extremely important area of optical logic, without which general optical digital data processing cannot be accomplished, holds forth promise of reducing the number of logic elements, while simultaneously increasing effective speed.

4.2 Active Optical Memory. Since logic elements and the memory function are closely related, we briefly allude to the area of active digital optical memories. It is very likely that large amounts of data, both externally and internally generated, will have to be stored, at least in the first generation optical computers. In fact, it may prove desirable to store even more information than we now do, to make full use of the central processor, and thus have a more nearly optimal system. The use of optical radiation for input and output of a memory is especially useful and inviting for two reasons:

a. The nondestructive parallel readout should provide a large increase in speed, since no recycling of the data is required.

b. Because of the isolation, write-erase and read modes do not have to be the same, or even synchronized—thus random access write and almost simultaneous associative search are possible.

Here, again, we see the advantage of optical techniques, this time applied to an active memory. Incidentally, it would be desirable to have write-erase and read times each less than a microsecond, and perhaps in the nanosecond region, in order that the memory be capable of communicating easily with the logic. Note that this type of optical memory could be most efficiently used with an optical logic system, since the interface problem is considerably reduced (e.g., the transducing of optical to electrical signals, if needed in the optical logic system, will provide the required gain. This may be a serious problem in coupling to high-speed electronic logic).

4.3 Permanent Memory. Two ideas, when coupled, demonstrate the utility of a "permanent" memory. The first is the availability of techniques by which large amounts of data can be stored, such as photographic and thermoplastic films, as well as perforated plates, cards, and tapes. The second is the probable ability of optical data computers to use large amounts of data. Thus, one is led to a permanent memory, such as a library or catalog file.

Note that such a technique would supplement, and not replace, the active memory, primarily because of the slow speed with which such data can be written (and, often, it cannot be changed).

4.4 Logical Organization and Machine Design. This important aspect includes the ability to define the capabilities and limitations of available techniques, and to combine them intelligently into an operable system. It is felt that a suitable approach would be to extrapolate from our present position in digital data processing, using the mathematics and logic design now available to design a machine with the new optical devices and circuits. During this initial design phase, realization of new approaches and systems will result in even further extrapolation. Though not required in this approach, one would expect "quantum jumps" in ideas pertaining to the design of an optical computer.

5. RELATED TOPICS. To pursue the thesis of this paper intelligently, it would be very unwise to ignore progress and programs in closely related areas. This section is not meant to be all-inclusive, but rather suggestive of interrelations which may develop.

It is interesting that in the optical region many separated technologies come together. Microwaves are used in radar and communications but not display or data recording. Electrical pulses are used for communications and data processing but not sensing. Optical signals, however, are being used or developed in all of these areas:

       a. Communication.
       b. Data recording.
       c. Sensors.
       d. Display.
       e. Radar and guidance.
       f. Analog correlation.

Thus, we certainly may expect a closer integration of the data processing function with each of the above. Again we see, dimly perhaps, but distinctly recognizable, some of the ways we might *obtain* the large amounts of data upon which an optical computer must operate; put another way, *we may be forced to develop optical data processing as the only sane way to handle the amount of data which will need processing!*

B. Requirements of Optical Logic Element

The primary requirements of any computer logic element are

      1. Competitive information processing rate.
      2. Gain.
      3. Threshold action.
      4. Amplitude limiting.
      5. Directionality.
      6. Isolation.
      7. Reclocking.

From a device having these characteristics, various logic functions (e.g., AND, OR) can be performed. Fan-in, fan-out, size, power consumption, reliability, cost, and many other factors also must be acceptable in order to provide a suitable logic element.

It is almost a truism that to become accepted a new technique must perform, in its initial undeveloped state, better than existing techniques that have the benefit of years of development. For this reason we have selected a minimum acceptable bit rate as being in the 10- to 100-Mc range and we consciously choose to ignore many otherwise extremely useful optical techniques and devices in the frequency range below 10 Mc.

It is no doubt fair to require flatly that over-all device gain must be greater than one, and if there is to be a useful fan-out, available gain* must be considerably higher.

Now although the remaining five requirements of a suitable logic element are all essential to some degree, it turns out that their magnitude is academic at this point. For example, it is generally conceded that optical systems have a high potential isolation, but until it is shown that even unity gain can be achieved, details of this isolation are not important. In this paper we will assume a requirement for 10–100 Mc and calculate the gain of three most promising configurations. Preparatory to this system synthesis we will briefly summarize the state of the art of potentially useful optical components.

II. Component Performance

A. Generalized Components of the Logic Element

A "black box" optical logic element could have any of four combinations of optical and electrical ports. We choose the optical-input, optical-output pair since it has, probably, the greatest potential for demonstrating the advantages of optical devices.† For example, a large number of devices in a matrix could be coupled with a single lens in the input and another in the output. Thus, the general block diagram, for purposes of this paper, is shown in Fig. 2. A logic element would consist of up to seven devices supplying conversion, coupling, gain, and/or the various desired nonlinearities.

This general block diagram, to the extent that an internal gain greater than unity and suitable nonlinearities are available, can provide any of the basic computer logic functions. For example, an AND gate would require transfer characteristics such that the output photon flux be negligible until the signal level of at least two standard optical signals is applied to the inputs. Consider briefly the meaning of the seven components in the generalized block diagram.

The only true optical-optical amplifiers (blocks 1 and 5) available are

* Current gain (or, more generally, quantum gain) is found to be the pertinent factor here.

† Optical radiation carries the information signals between gates (or logic elements) in this configuration. The electrical-input, electrical-output pair can be more efficiently designed for optical coupling (which occurs within the gate or logic element), but suffers from the problems of electrical transmission of information signals between gates.

those associated with the laser. Thus, amplification of the very coherent oxygen laser emission (0.84μ) by the GaAs forward-biased diode, or amplification of the less coherent sources of another GaAs laser offers a mechanism for very high theoretical gains. Further, the bandwidth of these devices is extremely high (kMc). The chief problems with these devices (which are small enough to be practical in computers) are the extreme difficulty in coupling signals into them and the very low temperatures presently required for high cw gain.

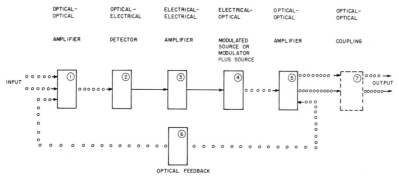

Fig. 2. General optical logic element block diagram.

The detector problem, block 2, is to achieve simultaneously sufficient gain and bandwidth, since nearly all can be made adequately small. Solid-state detectors have high quantum efficiency but until recently had no internal quantum gain in the 100 Mc and greater speed range. The vacuum detector (photoemitter) has a quantum efficiency considerably less than unity in the longer wavelength regions dominated by most useful lasers but has a so-called "coupling" advantage. Because the generated electrons are already in a vacuum, the output can be efficiently coupled to high-gain–bandwidth, high-impedance electrical amplifiers such as the electron multiplier, resulting in higher net gain.

The electrical amplifier, block 3, is the least desirable and at present most necessary component of the optical logic element. It is not desirable partially because if a better amplifier were available, it would already be in use in electrical logic elements and thus negate the need for an optical device in the first place (at least insofar as wide bandwidth for single channels is the advantage of optics). It is most necessary because no large gains are available yet in the other components. Probably the best amplifier for this service is the electron-multiplier amplifier. The usual equation for gain-bandwidth of electron multipliers (gain/transit time dispersion) is not applicable to computers where delay time is important. However, with gains of greater than 10^6 and transit times of less than 5×10^{-9}, the effective electron multiplier gain-bandwidth product is still quite high, 2×10^8 Mc.

Block 4, light source, can be of two important, basically different types. First, the light source can be directly modulated through its electrical input signal. An example of this is the injection electroluminescent diode. The second type consists of an optical modulator coupled to a fixed intensity light source. Since the signal gain of this latter configuration is dependent upon the ratio of light input to modulator power, the gain is limited only by available light power and/or modulator "sensitivity." More than any single event, the recent invention of the injection diode light source has spurred consideration of the optical computer concept. This light source, as a laser, is far more intense than the sun, can be modulated at near kMc rates directly and is more efficient at converting electrical power to light than any known source. Yet the numbers to be presented will show that the light source is still not entirely adequate.

Feedback, block 6, is useful primarily where the gain of the open-loop device is already quite high and an exchange is desirable to obtain more bandwidth. Feedback is also used as part of the process to convert a linear or monostable device into a bistable and/or logic device.

Coupling, block 7, is by no means minor in importance. Only by efficient optical coupling between devices can the rather meager available gains be utilized in an effective device. Since coupling, as an optical problem, is closely connected with the physical shape of the light source, this subject is covered chiefly under the heading of light source. In general, optical coupling efficiencies are between 1 and 50 per cent and the transit time is that of the velocity of light, about 1 nsec per foot, multiplied by the appropriate index of refraction.

One other factor necessary to obtain a useful logic element is the non-linearity usually supplied by threshold and limiting. Since several components discussed can provide this factor it will not be considered independently. In general, lasers and certain all-electrical components can supply both threshold and limiting. Most detectors and optical transmission devices, however, will not provide limiting without being damaged.

B. Optical Sources

1. INTRODUCTION.   Whether the optical source is used as a directly modulated source or in conjunction with a modulator, Fig. 3, it is most desirable that the device be capable of emission at high duty factor or cw. The requirements of the directly modulated source are low power and high efficiency, whereas for the modulator-plus-source configuration, the emphasis must be on high power and high intensity. Efficiency here is defined as optical output divided by electrical power input at the desired modulation rate. In the case of the directly modulated source, a desirable quality is "transformer action." If a number of units can be conveniently stacked, the output power would increase proportionately. Since most electrical sources in our case are constant current generators, and the most efficient

light sources are usually very low impedance devices, the system improvement can be quite significant.

For the directly modulated source configuration, it is desirable to use low light intensities to reduce the power dissipation requirements of both light sources and light detectors. Note that this can be carried only to the point where quantum noise becomes a problem, i.e., when the number of photons per pulse approaches unity. This means that at desired pulse rates and available detector efficiencies light sources cannot be modulated at much below a milliampere.

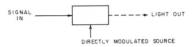

Fig. 3. Two light source configurations.

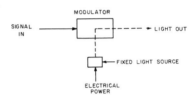

2. Injection Luminescent Diode. In the luminescent diode, electrons and holes are injected by forward bias from the *p*- and *n*-regions into the junction where they recombine resulting in light emission. The effective efficiency depends upon internal quantum efficiency (internal photons/electron), radiation efficiency (external photons/electron) and directionality. The two basic device categories are the noncoherent diode whose emission is primarily spontaneous and spread over hundreds of angstroms and the coherent (laser) diode whose emission is largely stimulated and confined to about 1 Å.

The noncoherent devices are less efficient but operate at very low currents. Shaping of the noncoherent injection luminescent diode improves the over-all efficiency by two effects. The first effect is to reduce the losses due to total internal reflection, and the second is to direct the emitted energy in a narrow beam toward the detector. Although the directionality can be partially achieved by an external lens (or optical fiber) system, it turns out that certain shapes can decrease both internal reflections and external beam widths. Figure 4 shows the efficiency or quantum transfer ratio of an injection electroluminescent diode shaped in a special way to improve its directional characteristics and made sufficiently small that this efficiency applies down to about 0.5 mA. The diameter of the diode spot size is about 0.02 in.

In the injection diode laser, the inverted population density of excited states is sufficient that the single pass internal gain by stimulated emission is sufficient to overcome all the single pass losses. These include diffraction around, and transmission through, the end mirrors and absorption and scattering along the active slab. At threshold, the beam becomes far narrower in angle, thus decreasing scattering, absorption, and internal reflection losses; the resulting reduced temperature rise further increases internal efficiency.

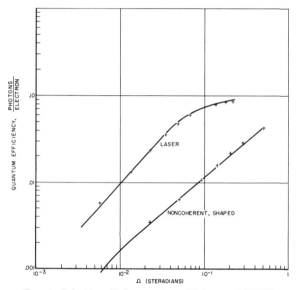

Fig. 4. Injection diode quantum efficiency at 77° K.

In the event the injection luminescent diode is used as an unmodulated optical source, the best present choice would be the GaAs cw laser which currently is capable of the order of 3 W continuous output at 20 °K. For low-current pulsed operation, devices are available with thresholds of about an ampere for 77 °K operation. These devices are capable of up to about 30 per cent duty factor.

Since some of the most useful detectors drop in quantum efficiency at rates of 100 dB per micron in the 0.9μ region, the exact wavelength of emission is of considerable importance. Although the GaAs diode emits only in the 0.85μ region, other wavelengths are available. GaAs-P diodes with emission down to 0.7μ are available but efficiency is about an order of magnitude less. New injection diode materials include indium arsenide[1] which has not only lased cw but nearly all the emission during lasing is stimulated.

Indium phosphide has been found to lase[2] at a wavelength of about 0.9 Å at 77 °K and cadmium telluride has been found to emit spontaneously at 0.85 Å at 77 °K at about 12 per cent efficiency.[3] Since neither of these materials is significantly better in any respect than the readily available GaAs, the latter will be used in illustrative computations.

Very recently, zinc and cadmium telluride have been found to give 4 per cent external quantum efficiency of spontaneous emission at about 7000 Å at 77 °K. This wavelength and efficiency is only, at best, equal to that of the gallium arsenide-phosphide devices.

One of the advantages of the laser over the spontaneous emission device is the so-called threshold gain. A 10 per cent increase in applied current may increase the output, in the laser direction, by 100 per cent,[4] but, of course, this is not applicable to the configuration using the separate modulator.

3. OTHER SOURCES.   The neodynium laser is a 4 level device and has been available in cw for some time at low power levels. Recently,[5] an improved host material, yttrium aluminum garnet, has been developed and 130 mW cw output achieved at room temperature with only a 600-W tungsten source for pump. Single devices with pump and reflector could be made about the size of a golf ball, but would most probably require water-cooling.

The gas laser has been considered briefly, chiefly because its extremely high coherence permits Fabry-Perot cavity Q's of millions. These cavities could then be used to increase the sensitivity of several modulator materials, such as KDP, and achieve, in effect, increased gain. A 1-W, cw, helium/neon gas laser has recently[6] been announced superseding the previous largest device of 150 mW. The earlier unit is 6 ft long and the newer unit 15 ft long. However, the gas laser is directly pumped by electrical power which saves considerable expense, size, and interference from the power supply.

The mercury arc is a powerful source of photons that might be useful in the separate modulator configuration. However, because it is a physically large, relatively low intensity light source, the amount of power that can be coupled into a small modulator is not significantly larger than that from a 3 A cw GaAs laser diode.

4. SUMMARY.   The decision of which light source is best must be made during a study of the over-all logic configuration, not by merely comparing light sources. Nevertheless, the injection diode is so small and efficient as to almost eliminate the other contenders immediately. Between the laser and the shaped diode, it must be noted that the laser costs about ten times as much to obtain about twice the efficiency into a large angle cone. Further, the noncoherent source can be made, so far at least, in lower current ranges.

C. Light Amplifier

1. INTRODUCTION.   One obvious way of making up the losses in light source, coupling, and detector of the optical logic element is by an optical

amplifier. (See Fig. 5.) For example, the single pass gain of the small-bore He/Ne laser operated at 3.4μ is over 40 dB per meter,[7] and the bandwidth is the spontaneous line width of about 0.5 kMc. By adding partially reflecting end mirrors to form a low Q (Fabry-Perot) cavity, the gain can be increased at the expense of bandwidth and gain stability. As high as this 40 dB/m gain appears, it is equivalent to only 4 dB in a device 10 cm long. A 10-cm dimension is too large and a 4-dB gain is far too small for a useful high-speed optical logic element.

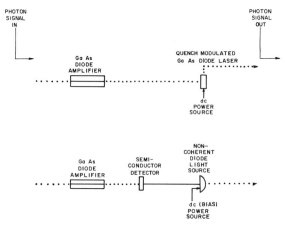

FIG. 5. Two typical optical amplifier configurations.

The GaAs laser, with the mirror effects of the diode ends removed, is also an amplifier. Figure 5 shows two basic configurations in which the device might be used. The first diagram shows an all-photon system which utilizes the capability of high-intensity light at the proper wavelength to quench the emission of a laser. Although Fowler[8] reports a quenching (gain) of only 7 per cent, he used no optical system to couple the diodes. The second utilizes a conventional detector. For the amplifier itself, Crowe and Craig[9] report a gain of over 1000 (at 77 °K) with better than 20 nsec response time in a GaAs diode with silicon oxide antireflection coatings. Konnerth and Lanza[10] report a laser modulation response of <0.2 nsec; thus, kMc bandwidths appear feasible.

2. THEORETICAL GAIN. The internal gain of the diode, once a photon has entered the active slab in the right direction at the right wavelength, is a difficult quantity to predict. One low temperature limit calculation indicates values that vary from 5000 to 10^{18}, depending upon the assumed active slab thickness of 10μ or 2μ, respectively. Since the former width is calculated from measured laser beam width and the latter from measured spot size, there is some question about the value of the calculation. A more sophisticated quantum-mechanical gain calculation gives gain values con-

siderably more accurate. For purpose of understanding those factors relating to gain, we show the elementary approach and quote the results of the more sophisticated work.

The diode laser consists of a forward-biased, heavily doped, p-n semiconductor diode junction with at least two parallel surfaces polished to serve as an optical cavity resonator. The injection current causes the electron-hole pair population to become inverted, i.e., greater than that of thermal equilibrium. In a "direct recombination" semiconductor, such as GaAs, the recombination results mostly in radiated photons. The recombination includes two terms, that due to spontaneous recombination and that "stimulated" by another photon (in the same mode). The stimulated emission is regenerative if the single pass absorption plus scattering plus diffraction loss (including the "mirrors") is less than the single pass gain, and lasing results. An amplifier results if reflection of the end surfaces is removed so that lasing will not occur, although superradiance at higher inversion levels will limit the maximum gain. Superradiance is spontaneous emission which, originating in one part of the active slab and proceeding down the slab, is amplified and reduces inversion density available to the incoming signal. Since superradiance is indicated by some subthreshold line width and beam-width reductions, its effect is measurable.

The gain coefficient g can be visualized as the quotient of the total number of excited hole-electron pairs available for stimulation during the time a (signal) photon passes by, divided by the number of possible different modes in which the stimulated emission may occur.[11] Thus,

$$g = \frac{R}{N} \tau \tag{1}$$

where

R = excited pairs available (per unit volume) per second
τ = photon transit time (per unit length)
N = number of modes, in the spontaneous line width (per unit volume).

If η is the quantum efficiency (hole-electron pairs produced per electron of exciting current),

$$R = \frac{J\eta}{ed} \tag{2}$$

where

J = current density
e = electron charge
d = thickness of active region

If n is the index of refraction, the time τ that a stimulating photon is available is n/c. This photon will stimulate a recombination only if they are both in the same mode (i.e., the same polarization, phase, direction, location, and frequency). The number of modes per unit volume per unit frequency is* $8\pi n^3/\lambda^2 c$, and the number of modes in the applicable band-width is thus

$$N = \frac{8\pi n^3 \, \Delta\nu}{\lambda^2 c} \tag{3}$$

where $\Delta\nu$ is the spontaneous line width, i.e., the range of energy of the transitions between the valence and conduction band. Thus,

$$g = \frac{J\eta}{ed} \frac{n}{c} \frac{\lambda^2 c}{8\pi n^3 \, \Delta\nu} = \frac{J\eta\lambda^2}{ed8\pi n^2 \, \Delta\nu} \tag{4}$$

The per pass gain G of a completed diode would be (neglecting absorption losses)

$$G = e^{g\zeta} \tag{5}$$

where

$$\zeta = \text{length between faces.}$$

For an order of magnitude calculation, consider the following numbers:

$$J = 1000 \text{ A/cm}^2$$
$$\eta = 0.5$$
$$\lambda = 0.85 \times 10^{-4} \text{ cm}$$
$$e = 1.6 \times 10^{-19}$$
$$\Delta\nu = 4 \times 10^{12} \text{ cps } (100 \text{ Å})$$
$$n = 3.6$$
$$\zeta = 5 \times 10^{-2} \text{ cm}$$

Substituting into Eq. 4, one obtains $g = 170 \text{ cm}^{-1}$ or 850 cm^{-1} for values of d equal to 10μ and 2μ, respectively. With use of Eq. 5 the over-all per pass gain will be 5000 or 10^{18}, depending upon which value of d is correct. The procedure is clearly inadequate.

A considerably more sophisticated calculation of g that, while it still ignores losses due to scattering and free carrier absorption, does take account of reduced gain due to temperature effects was made by Lasher and Stern.[12]

Using values of $d = 3\mu$ and $\eta = 0.5$, they computed the curves for gain coefficient shown in Fig. 6. At 4 °K, the gain at 1000 A/cm² is found to

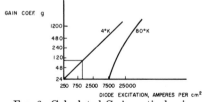

FIG. 6. Calculated GaAs optical gain.

* See any modern physics text such as C. Kittel, *Introduction to Solid State Physics*, John Wiley & Sons, Inc., New York, 1956, p. 127.

be about 100. The procedure is still not sufficiently precise to predict over-all laser gain G accurately. Thus, at 80 °K, the gain coefficient would be considerably less than 24, which for a 0.05-cm diode would give a per pass gain of $e^{0.1} \approx 1$. This would not even overcome mirror reflection losses (reflectivity = $(n - 1)^2/(n + 1)^2 = 0.3$ for GaAs), much less diffraction and scattering losses. Yet cw 77° lasing in GaAs has been achieved at 400 A/cm. This inaccuracy is, of course, accentuated by the extremely strong dependence of external gain on g. The computations do, however, predict fairly accurately the spontaneous line width and the shift of the laser emission line from the spontaneous emission peak. In the latter effect, the injection diode lases at a wavelength somewhat longer than that at the peak of the spontaneous emission line. Spontaneous line width is about 1 per cent.

Recent measurement, on one diode, at General Electric using the GaAs diode to amplify the emission from an oxygen laser indicates a total internal gain of about 50. In both gain studies, References 9, 13, and 14, gain measurements were possible only after considerable filtering of the spontaneous emission normally produced by the amplifier without input.

Thus, it appears that the state of the art of the laser amplifier is not well developed but offers possibilities of extremely high gain. The three basic problem areas are efficient coupling between the tiny active areas, cw operation (at temperature at least as high as 77 °K), and filtering the noise due to spontaneous emission.

D. Light Modulator

1. INTRODUCTION. The block diagram of Fig. 3 indicates how a light modulator could be used to provide an optical gain if the emission of a sufficiently high intensity, fixed light source were controllable with a sufficiently low power modulator. We will show later that presently obtainable gains (the ratio of photon rate output to electron flow input) are insufficient to overcome the losses of the detector and the coupling between stages. However, with higher intensity sources and lower power modulators being announced almost daily, the picture could change quickly. The following analysis shows those parameters most capable of improving the gain.

All modulators have an electro-optic constant that can be converted to V_m, which is the voltage required to provide full optical extinction. For most materials V_m is on the order of thousands of volts. Although the material is usually a dielectric of extremely low conductivity and dielectric loss, the electrostatic capacity of the device is sufficient that to obtain a wide (amplitude-modulated) bandwidth, a relatively high power must be dissipated in a resistive load connected somewhere in the electrical drive. It is this power loss that represents the chief circuit reduction of gain for the modulator. This is basically a material problem, i.e., finding a material requiring lower V_m. At frequencies below 100 Mc, particularly at the voltages appropriate to computer circuitry, problems due to heating by dielectric losses and conduction are, in general, negligible in these materials.

The next most important modulator parameter is source-detector coupling. Optimum modulator shape consists of large length to width ratio. Thus coupling losses between an uncollimated source and a very small detector may be larger than the switching gain of the modulator.

2. OPTICAL MODULATOR GAIN EQUATION.   A gain equation for a longitudinal field (E field in direction of light wave) electro-optic modulator using an injection diode light source can be used to indicate present performance. Assume, in Fig. 7, a light source emitting $i_D = \eta I_D(0.6 \times 10^{19})$

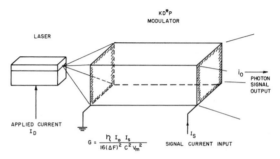

FIG. 7. Gain equation for unenhanced longitudinal modulator.

photons per second into a solid angle acceptable to the modulator, where η is the photon efficiency and I_D the input current at the source. If the modulator voltage is V, its minimum capacity C (usually determined by stray wiring capacity) and the bandwidth is ΔF, then the electrical signal input must be

$$V = \frac{I_s}{2\pi\Delta F C}$$

where

$$V = \text{signal voltage}$$
$$I_s = \text{signal current}$$

The output light signal of the modulator i_0 will usually depend upon the applied voltage V as

$$i_0 \approx = i_D \sin^2 \frac{\pi V}{2V_m}$$

and for the low percentages of modulation that will be necessary, since V_m is typically several thousand volts,

$$i_0 \approx i_D\left(\frac{\pi}{2}\frac{V}{V_m}\right)^2$$

where i_D is the input light to the modulator. Thus, the ratio of output photons to input electrons, or gain, is

$$\frac{i_0}{i_s} = \frac{\eta I_D}{I_s} \frac{0.6 \times 10^{19}(\pi/2)^2(V^2/V_m{}^2)}{0.6 \times 10^{19}} = \frac{\eta I_D I_s}{16(\Delta F)^2 C'^2 V_m{}^2}$$

Consider now some typical values. For deuterated KDP, V_m is about 3×10^3. Let η be, very optimistically, about 10^{-1} for a laser whose output is collimated to within the required 1 or 2 degrees of the modulator optical axis. For a cw laser cooled to liquid helium, I_D could be 3 A. If we make the modulator a few millimeters in dimensions, the electrostatic capacity C will be primarily that due to stray wiring capacity, say 5 pF. Our problem concerns a bandwidth of the order of 10^8 cps. If we assume initially that the available signal level will be about 1 A (final gain here must be determined by reiteration), then the initial gain would only be about 10^{-2}.

The equation shows that the best way to increase the modulator gain is to work on the modulator parameter V_m and that increasing light intensity I_D will be a process offering less returns. The calculation shows that without better material or some enhancement scheme, modulator-provided gain is inadequate.

3. MODULATOR MATERIALS. One of the earliest electro-optic materials was ADP, ammonium dihydrogen phosphate. At 0.9μ, the Pockels constant of this material is such that 13 kV is required for full extinction. The material is so hygroscopic and soft that optically flat surfaces are difficult to maintain. The relative dielectric constant is about 16 and the loss tangent about 10^{-3}. Except for dielectric heating which occurs at high voltages and frequencies, the frequency response is above 10 kMc.[15] The material is biaxial and thus requires a high degree of optical collimation ($\pm 1°$ for a $\frac{1}{2}$-in. length) to keep optical leakage below about 5 per cent.[16]

In this same category are KDP and KD*P which require about 7000 and 3000 V, respectively, for 100 per cent modulation. They have higher dielectric constants, about 20 and 40 respectively, but the resulting capacity in actual circuits is still due primarily to wiring. For example, a KD*P unit 1 mm $\times$ 1 mm $\times$ 1 mm would have a capacity of about 0.5 pF. The loss tangent is about 10^{-4}, and damaging dielectric heating does not occur even at full voltage until well above 100 Mc.[4]

KDP is biaxial, which means that when voltage is applied there are two optical axes, i.e., where waves of orthogonal polarization will see equal velocities. Cubic crystals such as cuprous chloride and hexamthylene tetramine (HMTA) are isotropic and become uniaxial with application of voltage. Since in the former, the angle between the two axes is only a few degrees, a high degree of collimation is required. In the cubic crystal, loss of modulation is not significant until angles of 10° or more are exceeded. Further, in the cubic materials, the voltage can be applied transversely to the optical propagation and the crystal will still conveniently provide the two slightly phase-shifted optical components needed for the interference effects of amplitude modulation. Since the phase shift is proportional to the gradient E, the cubic crystals can be made long for a large optical effect but narrow to reduce the voltage requirements. This "shape enhancement" is probably limited to length/width ratios of about 10 in good optical materials and is a major technique used to reduce the required modulation voltage.

Cuprous chloride has a V_m of about 5000 V and although it becomes oxidized in the presence of moist air, it is quite hard and its dielectric constant is only 8. HMTA requires about 7 kV and has a dielectric constant of 6 but is reportedly more immune to the atmosphere. Both materials are capable of modulation above 100 Mc and at voltages reduced 10:1 by length-to-width enhancement, have no problem with dielectric heating at this frequency. Unfortunately, both materials are extremely difficult to obtain in crystals of optical quality large enough (1 cm long) to demonstrate "shape" enhancement.

Many other materials have been investigated. KDP has a Curie point at about 123 °K at which temperature the Pockels constant increases by orders of magnitude. KD*P has a less extreme temperature requirement for enhancement. However, the changes occur in such a few degrees that the effect may be difficult to control, the dielectric constant increases by about the same amount that V_m is decreased and piezoelectrically generated shock waves may cause crystal damage at low temperature.

By modulating a high Q Fabry-Perot cavity, relatively small variations in optical dimensions can have large modulation effects. Since the technique requires very coherent light sources, precision alignment and some loss of bandwidth due to the cavity, no major improvement appears available here for computer application.

Several recent developments using field effects in semiconductors are interesting.[17,18] One technique,[17] for example, provides modulation by variation in the wavelength at which the semiconductor suddenly becomes transparent. However, for one reason or another, none of these presents a major improvement yet. For example, the system using the shift of the absorption edge is at the wrong wavelength for available light sources.

4. MODULATION ENHANCEMENT. Given the basic material, a number of enhancement techniques are available to increase the gain by, in effect, decreasing V_m. Some have already been mentioned earlier. These include laser cavity decoupling, transverse field, and Fabry-Perot resonance. Several involve traveling wave techniques to match the light and electrical velocities when the devices are long, and a large part of the technical literature is devoted to these when used with microwave carriers. Since a quarter-wave at 100 Mc, even taking into account the high dielectric constant of KDP, makes a large device inappropriate to computer elements,

these will not be discussed.[19,20] Other techniques designed to operate at a microwave center frequency and not extend to low frequencies at all would require the complexity of handling pulsed microwave carriers in the logic element.[4,21]

A simple technique to retain both the availability of KDP material and length to width enhancement is described by Wentz[22] and is the basis of a system calculation in Sec. III. In this concept, two KDP crystals are used in tandem to compensate each other. The voltage is applied as shown in Fig. 8. Note that the disparity of index between the Z and X-Y axes,

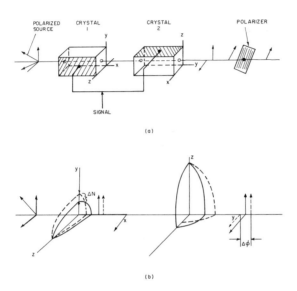

(a)

(b)

FIG. 8. A compensated KDP transverse modulator. (a) Physical diagram. (b) Index ellipsoid diagram.

which would otherwise produce only phase modulation, is compensated as long as the crystals are of equal length. Both crystals are fully as effective in producing the phase differences between components as in the longitudinal case. Thus, the total phase change is

$$\Delta\phi = \frac{n^4 \omega r_{63} \ell E_z}{c}$$

where

r_{63} is the Pockels constant

E_z is the applied field

ω is the optical frequency in rad/sec

c is the velocity of light

ℓ is the length of one crystal

The question of the maximum "length-to-width enhancement" possible depends primarily on diffraction and crystal collimation requirements. A 10:1 enhancement in a crystal 0.2 × 0.2 × 2 cm would be practical using a lens to collimate the emission of a diode laser. The problem of scattering is difficult to assess, but estimated to be on the order of 10 per cent in practical devices of these dimensions. Thus, unless the applied voltage was more than that required to give at least 10 or 20 per cent modulation efficiency, the device would be quite noisy.

5. SUMMARY. The use of KD*P is the most practical at the present. By using two crossed crystals, an effective 10:1 enhancement will be achieved but gain will still be only about unity.

E. Solid-State Light Detectors

1. INTRODUCTION. Two fundamental forms of solid-state detectors are the photoconductor and the p-n junction. In both, hole-electron pairs are produced in the semiconductor when entering photons have an energy greater than the band gap. The photoconductor carriers are either swept out by a bias potential or trapped, and a current persists until recombination takes place. Thus, the length of time this current persists (recombination time) is a factor in the gain (electrons/photon) of the device. In the p-n junction detector a reverse bias field generates a depletion region and recombination occurs as soon as the carriers cross the gap and the device normally has less than unity "current" gain. However, a recent development, the avalanche diode, apparently achieves gain by a process of collision similar to that in a plasma.

In their normal operation p-n junctions have external quantum gain on the order of 0.3. This is the result of nearly unity internal quantum efficiency and useful absorption of about 50 per cent. A wide variety of parameter combinations in this device are available with frequency response to several kMc and wavelength response out to several microns. The frequency response is related to active area and to obtain kMc response requires tiny, "difficult to focus," diameters on the order of mils. At 100-Mc response, effective areas as large as 0.1-in. diameter are available.

The p-n junction is least noisy at zero bias, but to reduce the junction capacity and increase the field for high bandwidths applications it is usually reverse biased at several tens of volts.

Figure 9 is an equivalent circuit of a typical p-n junction detector. The photon "current" of the device is i_p. If the load impedance is small or comparable to that of C, the over-all gain is not significantly reduced from that of the diode gain G. Unlike the communication situation, i_p can usually be held at such high levels such that KTB, quantum noise, and $1/f$ (detector) noise do not dominate. Since gain mechanisms to compensate for coupling losses and fan-out are essential to the system, the possibilities for detector gain are extremely important. The several gain mechanisms are now discussed.

2. AVALANCHE PIN DIODE DETECTOR.   The avalanche PIN diode detector has been demonstrated by several investigators. Anderson[23] reported gains of 1000 with response times on the order of kMc. Johnson[24] has measured avalanche current gain of ten although at a 1000-Mc signal

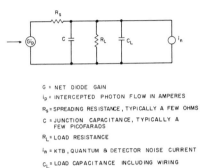

G = NET DIODE GAIN

i_p = INTERCEPTED PHOTON FLOW IN AMPERES

R_s = SPREADING RESISTANCE , TYPICALLY A FEW OHMS

C = JUNCTION CAPACITANCE, TYPICALLY A FEW PICOFARADS

R_L = LOAD RESISTANCE

i_n = KTB , QUANTUM & DETECTOR NOISE CURRENT

C_L = LOAD CAPACITANCE INCLUDING WIRING

FIG. 9. Equivalent circuit of diode detector and load.

frequency the noise increase was about a factor of 6. In some cases the diode is very heavily reverse biased, on the order of 2 kV, but by special material treatment the dark current is held to the submicroampere range. The device obtains its quantum gain by means of avalanche multiplication. A carrier that is liberated by the energy of an absorbed photon is accelerated by the high electric field within the depletion region; this carrier may then liberate other similar carriers by exchange of kinetic energy during collision with the lattice. Thus, for each photon absorbed within the depletion region, there will be several carriers contributing to the current. Some of the devices are silicon, have peak response in the 1μ region, and demonstrate gain and speed of response that is a function of light intensity. The devices are not generally available commercially, yet.

3. PHOTOCONDUCTOR.   In general the photoconductor is slower than the p-n junction device.[25] At the visible wavelengths and at speeds of response on the order of kc, gains of thousands are readily available. At the longer wavelengths and at the faster speeds of response, gains are considerably less, thus at about 1μ and about 1 Mc response the gain in available devices is considerably less than one. However the field is moving rapidly and much higher performance is predicted. Ing and Gerhart at General Electric Company have measured gain-bandwidth products on the order of 10 Mc in a silicon device.[26]

4. PHOTOTRANSISTOR.   The phototransistor combines the p-n junction with transistor gain in the one device. Optical absorption occurs in the base but because of the relatively slow diffusion velocity of carriers across

this region the speed of response is relatively low. Typical performance values are current gain of ten at frequencies of 1 Mc.[27]

5. SUMMARY. The problem of comparing photodetectors in general, considering all variables of noise, gain, apertures, frequency response, etc., is extremely complex. The problem of selecting a device for the optical logic element is relatively simple today. Only the reverse-biased p-n junction has available frequency response in the 10–100 Mc region and its gain is near unity. Coupling must provide for an effective area on the order of tens of mils. A number of potential areas for current gain are being studied, one of the most promising being the avalanche diode.

F. Vacuum Detector

1. INTRODUCTION. At 0.9μ the quantum efficiency of the vacuum detector (photoemitter) is less than 1 per cent and falling off at the rate of about 20 dB per 1000 Å. The device has the advantage however of direct, high-impedance coupling to the electron multiplier amplifier. The amplifier has no hot cathode, an extremely high-gain bandwidth product and potentially a very small volume. The chief advantage of the photoemitter detector is its access to the electron multiplier amplifier. The chief disadvantage of the photoemitter is its low quantum efficiency. The amplifier gain will compensate for the signal loss but cannot compensate for the decrease in signal to noise due to quantum noise.

Although the photoemitter is an "old" device and major new improvements will come slowly, there is reason to believe major improvements are possible, if only because the design goals are different.

2. QUANTUM EFFICIENCY. The very low quantum efficiency of an S-1 photocathode is caused partly by the inability of the photoelectrons to escape from the photocathode and partly by the poor absorption of the photons by the photocathode. The first situation is due to the loss of kinetic energy by the photoelectrons through collisions with atoms and ions of the photocathode; the second arises from the light transparency of the photocathode to the long wavelength photons. One can see that the basic problem is that the mean free path of the electrons is much shorter than that of the photons. Increasing the thickness of the photocathode will increase the photon absorption; however, it decreases the photoelectron escape probability. On the other hand, a thinner photocathode improves the photoelectron escape probability, but at the same time reduces the photon absorption of the photocathode. To improve the photocathode quantum efficiency, both the photon absorption and photoelectron escape probability must be increased. Among several concepts for photocathode quantum efficiency enhancement one[28] is shown in Fig. 10. By using multiple reflection techniques, much thinner photocathodes may be used without concern about low photon absorption.

3. TRANSIT TIME. For purposes of computer operation it makes no dif-

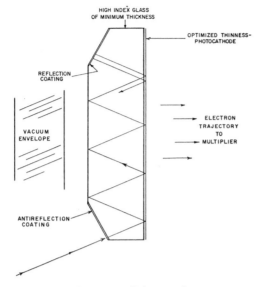

FIG. 10. Quantum efficiency enhancement.

ference that nearly 1 kMc bandwidths (1 nsec transit time dispersion) are available in commercial electron multipliers. Transit time is what determines the cycle time and thus the bit rate. Typical transit times are shown in Fig. 11 including a point for a small experimental RCA tube (the C70129)

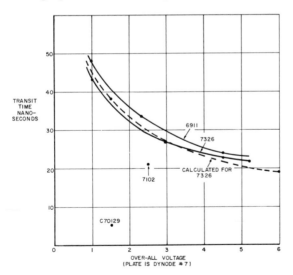

FIG. 11. Photomultiplier transit time, 6 dynodes.

which is basically a scaled down 1P21. Most of these tubes operate at about 100 V per dynode; thus, from Fig. 12 it is clear that, to the extent

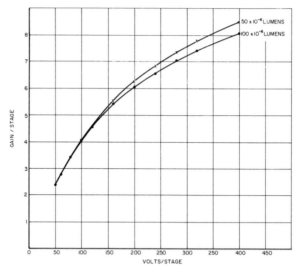

Fɪɢ. 12. Dynode gain versus voltage for photomultiplier 931-A.

allowed by internal arcover, much fewer than the usual 10 dynodes could be used without loss of gain. Then, both because fewer dynodes are used and a higher voltage per dynode is used, the transit time would be reduced and higher bit rates would be feasible.

Another electron multiplier concept based on a two-channel tube using the crossed-field multiplier is shown in Fig. 13.[30]

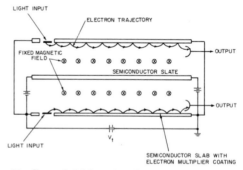

Fɪɢ. 13. Crossed-field semiconductor dynode multiplier.

Both the upper and lower slabs are made of semiconducting material. A voltage is applied across each slab to establish a horizontal electric field. The upper slab is further biased positive (V_t) with respect to the lower slab, thus providing a vertical electric field. In addition, there is a magnetic field normal to the two electric fields. Under such conditions, electrons originating from the lower slab, after executing a segment of a trochoidal motion, return to the lower slab and upon impact produce secondary electrons which would repeat the process down the slab. Because the multiplying stages are joined together into a continuous slab, the device is potentially capable of being made very small with an attendant shortening of transit time and transit time spread.

For design purposes, the required magnetic field B, the bias voltage V_t, and the transit time per stage τ, can be expressed as a function of the distance d in centimeters between the emission and impact point of an electron, measured along the semiconductor slab:

$$V_t = \frac{1.57 t V_i}{d}, \qquad B = \frac{6.3}{d} V_i, \qquad \text{and} \qquad \tau = \frac{2.82 \times 10^{-8}}{V_i^{1/2}} d$$

where V_i is the voltage corresponding to the impact energy desired, and d is the spacing between the top and bottom slabs in centimeters.

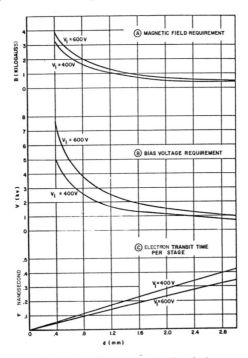

Fig. 14. Semiconductor photomultiplier design curves.

For a spacing of 3 mm, these equations are plotted in Fig. 14 for two values of impact voltage, V_i (400 V and 600 V). The transit time spread per stage may be estimated by the relation given previously. For a gain of 4 per impact, and to achieve a gain of 10^5, 7 multiplications are required, yielding a transit time of less than 3 nsec and a transit time spread of less than 0.3 nsec. It has been estimated that a multiple channel stack of these devices could be made with a density of about 4 channels per square centimeter.

4. SUMMARY. Although the quantum efficiency of present photoemitters is quite low, the enormous gain-bandwidth product of an associated electron multiplier makes it an attractive source of gain for the optical logic element. It should be noted that a very large optical fan-out is possible by using series injection diodes light sources in the output. Since the diode is a very low impedance device and the multiplier output is constant current up to tens of volts, no gain penalty is caused when adding the series diode fan-out.

III. Predicted Performance of Three Best Configurations

A. Introduction

Many devices fit the general block diagram shown in Fig. 2; however, most are not satisfactory because of frequency response and/or gain limitations. In this section, three promising configurations are analyzed and a demonstration experiment is described.

Without minimizing the importance of the many other logic element requirements, we can conveniently limit the field for the moment to three chief criteria:

1. Gain, which should have a value of at least 10 in order to provide fan-out.

2. Bandwidth or 1/transit time, whichever is the least, should approach 100 Mc.

3. Size, cost, and reliability must be competitive with transistors and integrated circuits.

The device configuration must also supply such nonlinearities as threshold and limiting if it is to be generally useful in various logic functions. The possibility of generating a radically new computer approach, such as some easily implemented parallel logic, also must be considered.

Significant losses in gain are encountered in practical configurations due to optical coupling. Even an $f/1$ lens, for example, collects only about 10 per cent of the energy from an isotropic source. One method of increasing this efficiency, other than resorting to fast lenses, reflectors, or optical fibers, is to build all of the devices in a single solid-state chip. For example, Ing and Jensen[31] coupled a GaAs diode light source and negative resistance diode light detector in a single tiny chip. No attempt has been made in the following examples to optimize construction techniques in this way and nominal optical coupling is assumed. For the configuration that has been finally selected, a multiple channel module for simple optical multiple channel coupling is discussed briefly.

B. *Configuration Based on Modulator Derived Gain*

Figure 15 indicates the basic elements of the separately modulated emitter configuration. The General Electric H2AI diode is capable of about

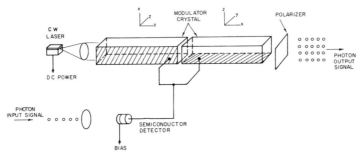

FIG. 15. Stationary emitter configuration.

$2\frac{1}{2}$ watt output, including collection and collimation optics, at about 20 °K. An L/D of 10:1 in the KD*P modulators, assuming, say, 50 V of detector signal, would provide an output light signal of

$$i_0 \left(\frac{\pi}{2} \frac{V \times L/D}{V_m} \right)^2 = \left(\frac{\pi \times 50 \times 10}{2 \times 3000} \right)^2 \times 2.5 \times 0.4 \times 10^{19}$$

$$= 0.7 \times 10^{18} \text{ photons/sec}$$

If a coupling efficiency to the next stage of 0.5 and a detector quantum efficiency of 0.4 is assumed, and if only 20 per cent of the output is used in each of several detectors to allow for fan-out capability, feedback, and/or nonlinear components, the detector output current will be

$$0.7 \times 10^{18} \times 0.2 \times 0.5 \times 0.4 \times 1.6 \times 10^{-19} = 4.5 \text{ mA}$$

If the detector plus modulator capacitance C could be reduced to 2 pF, the current required to bring the modulator to the assumed 50 V, ΔV, in a time ΔT, corresponding to 100 Mc or the order of 5 nsec, would be $i = c \, \Delta V/\Delta T$ or 20 mA, and thus the device lacks a factor of 4 in gain.

Although the effect of optical scattering in the modulator is unknown and the stray capacity selected is a little optimistic, this concept requires only a slightly better modulation Vm to be practical. Because of the low temperature and relatively high power requirements of the cw laser diode source, this technique may not be competitive. However, with all three major components, i.e., light source, modulator, and detector, improving rapidly in gain and thermal requirements, this concept may soon be useful.

C. *Configuration Based on Laser Amplifier Derived Gain*

Figure 16 shows a second promising configuration for optical logic. This concept is based primarily upon the work of Crowe and Craig,[9] who observed effective external gains of 1000 in GaAs laser diode oscillators used as amplifiers. The output of these devices, which are more or less linear, could be combined for logic purposes with the nonlinear GaAs "quenched laser" device reported by Fowler.[8] Although the output of the quenched laser was changed by an amount equal to only 7 per cent of the output of the signal source, there is reason to believe that this gain can be made much larger by better coupling. Even with the reported 7 per cent coupling and 1000 gain, this device offers a gross gain of 70 available for apportionment among coupling losses and fan-out. Since laser coupling

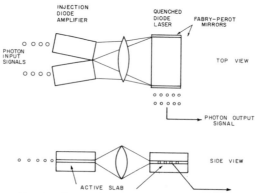

FIG. 16. Basic quenched laser configuration.

optics are more efficient than isotropic optics, a net available gain of 10 should be possible. The response of the amplifier plus the quenched laser is well above 100 Mc and the device could be made extremely small.

The primary difficulty is that cw laser operation is not available above about 20 °K and cw, high-gain amplifier performance is not probable above about 77 °K. Further the cw laser is still a rather high-power device. However, as shown in the amplifier gain calculations the potential is enormous; the device could become extremely useful in the foreseeable future.

D. Configuration Based on Electron-Multiplier Derived Gain

Figure 17 shows a directly modulated emitter configuration in which the quantum losses of both the light source and the photoemissive detector are overcome by the high current gain of the electron multiplier. It is this configuration that has been selected for demonstration and for examination of application.

The quantum efficiency of the low current (compatible with a small, low-current, electron multiplier), shaped, noncoherent diode is about 4 per cent in one steradian cone. The quantum efficiency of a standard 7102 photomultiplier S-1 surface is about 0.3 per cent. Thus, a current gain of about 4×10^4 is required in the photoelectron multiplier to obtain a net quantum gain of the order of 5. The electron multiplier should be operated at as high a voltage as possible in order to minimize the transit time (maximize the bit rate or "effective" bandwidth). At about 400 V per dynode, a gain of about 6 can be achieved for each dynode. Thus, where $6^n = 40,000$, a total number of n stages is required. This is 6 stages at a total dc voltage of 2800 V. Since only the last few stages are at full current the power requirements can be quite low.

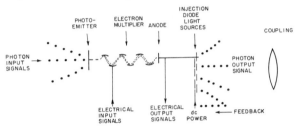

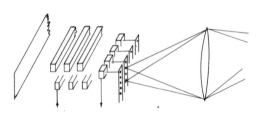

FIG. 17. Schematic and pictorial views of the basic "modulated emitter" configuration.

The transit time of a standard 7102 photomultiplier, modified for 6 dynodes, at this voltage is about 20 nsec; thus the bandwidth is about 50 Mc, if no other delays are introduced. Actually, the over-all gain can be increased by a factor of 100, by placing, say 100 diodes in series in the anode, since even with about 100 V across the load, the anode acts as a constant current source. Further, by designing the electron multiplier for shorter transit times (commercial tubes such as the 7102 are designed primarily for a minimum dispersion of the transit time), a much greater effective bandwidth can be achieved. As shown previously, a 3-nsec transit time can be built using the crossed field multiplier with a resulting 300-Mc data rate. Further, by building the compact dual channel form shown in Fig. 13, it is estimated that the frontal area of each channel could be as small as 0.25 cm^2.

Note that Fig. 17 shows long, common dynodes which, by suitable channel isolation, may allow even more compact operation. Because independent grids can be placed behind the emitter, electronic control of the logic element is quite easy. This flexibility is a main advantage of the photon/electron/photon concept compared to the photon/photon format.

Another promising variation of this configuration is to replace the anode (and some of the dynodes) by the avalanche diode.

E. Comparison of the Three Configurations

The first and second configurations require cw laser diodes which in turn require 20 °K operation. The first concept also requires a better modulator material, chiefly lower Vm. The third concept is made of readily available components, can operate at room temperature, and shows a growth capability. For the present at least, the third concept is the most feasible and is the subject of the demonstration discussed below.

F. A Demonstration

A demonstration of a free-running logical inverter has been made using the electron multiplier technique. Figure 18 shows the circuit. A Dumont

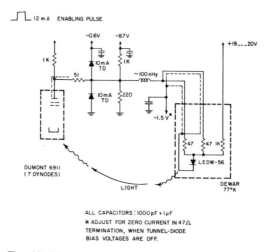

Fig. 18. Nor gate operating as free-running inverter.

6911 using only 7 dynodes but 600 V/dynode was connected to a small noncoherent source operating at 77 °K. Nonlinearity was provided by a pair of back to back tunnel diodes as an asynchronous nor gate. Figure 19 shows the output waveform which is equivalent to a 20-Mc bit rate. A 30-Mc bit rate was achieved using a faster tube, the 7102.

Since nearly an order of magnitude reduction in electron multiplier transit time can be achieved by going to special design, such as the crossed-field multiplier, it is believed that several hundred megacycles can be achieved with this electron multiplier concept.

Fan-out was not demonstrated in the present device, but adding more light diodes sources in series in the anode circuit would provide the increased light power without anode heating or degeneration of electron multiplier gain.

High fan-in requires, among other things, a wide dynamic range of the several series components. Since both the diode light source and the

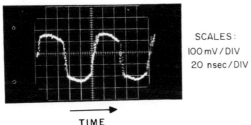

SCALES:
100 mV / DIV
20 nsec / DIV

TIME

FIG. 19. Tunnel-diode voltage of free-running inverter.

photomultiplier have many orders of magnitude of dynamic range separately, the problem is primarily one of stray light and dark current, and current ratings. It is believed that very large fan-in can be accommodated.

G. *Application*

One of the most useful immediate applications of the optical logic element is for the parallel transfer of information from the peripheral devices of a computer to the central data processing cabinets. In this application, the capability of a large element parallel array permits the rapid selection of words, in parallel, from various tapes, drums, card files, and input devices to delivery in parallel to the input-output control and/or the various logic, arithmetic, or memory units of the data processor. The advantage of this technique over that of usual coaxial cable is chiefly the elimination of the extremely bulky multiple coax connector. Elimination of the bulky coax

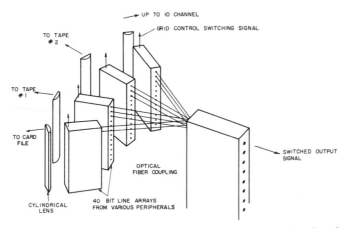

FIG. 20. Application of 40 × 1 to switching and communication function.

connector bundle reduces over-all size sufficiently to shorten internal wiring and materially increase the speed of data processing.

Figure 20 shows schematically the elements of the cable/connector/ switching function for handling ten 40 bit word peripherals.

IV. Summary

We have shown that the single most difficult problem of the optical logic element is quantum gain. The most immediately available gain mechanism is the electron multiplier with the laser amplifier, modulator gain, and avalanche detector gain offering large potential in the foreseeable future. The electron multiplier plus light diode technique offers bit rates and channel densities on the order of 100 Mc and 4 per cm² respectively.

Computer improvement is more than a matter of simple speed. Such problems as interconnection length and crosstalk are becoming dominant. The demonstrated configuration offers a major possibility here particularly in the form of parallel logic. Since parallel logic in machines is not yet well developed, the strongest asset of the optical logic device, high parallel channel capacity, is still difficult to use. One area of probably immediate advantage is the communication of and switching among computer functional elements such as peripheral equipment, memory, and arithmetic unit. In this application cables, cable connector mass, and switching circuitry are clearly reduced in size.

ACKNOWLEDGMENTS

The authors would like to thank G. Gerhard and S. Ing for data pertaining to semiconductor devices, J. Pua for vacuum detector studies, L. Trabinsky for system concepts, and H. Raillard for the circuit and testing of the demonstration device. We also thank J. Smith of the General Electric Semiconductor Products Department for the electroluminescent diodes tested on this program.

REFERENCES

1. MELNGALLIS, I., AND R. H. REDIKER, "Magnetically Tunable CW InAs Diode Maser," *Appl. Phys. Letters, 2,* 3, 202 (1 June 1963).
2. WEISER, K., AND R. S. LEVITT, "Stimulated Light Emission from Indium Phosphide," *Appl. Phys. Letters, 12,* 9, 178 (1 May 1963).
3. MANDLE, G., AND F. F. MOREHEAD, "Efficient Electroluminescence from *p-n* Junctions in CdTe at 77° K," *Appl. Phys. Letters, 4,* 8, 143 (15 April 1964).
4. BLUMENTHAL, R. H., *Proc. IEEE,* 452 (April 1962).
5. GEUSIC, J. E., MARCOS, H. M., AND L. G. VAN VITERT, "Laser Oscillations in Nd-Doped Yttrium Aluminum and Yttrium Gallium and Gadolinium Garnets," *Appl. Phys. Letters, 4,* 5, 182 (15 May 1964).

6. News Item, *Microwaves*, *3*, 8, 6 (August 1964).
7. BENNETT, W. R., JR., *Applied Optics, Vol. I, Supplement No. 1, Optical Masers*, 24 (1962).
8. FOWLER, A. B., "Quenching of Gallium Arsenide Injection Lasers," *Appl. Phys. Letters, 3*, 1, 1 (1 July 1963).
9. CROWE, J. W., AND R. M. CRAIG, JR., "Small Signal Amplification in GaAs Lasers," *Appl. Phys. Letters, 4*, 3, 57 (1 February 1964).
10. KONNERTH, K., AND C. LANZA, "Delay Between Current Pulse and Light Emission of a Gallium Arsenide Injection Laser," *Appl. Phys. Letters, 14*, 7, 120 (1 April 1964).
11. DOMKE, W. P., "Electromagnetic Mode Population in Light Emitting Diodes," *IBM J. Res. Develop., 7*, 1, 66 (January 1963).
12. LASHER, G., AND F. STERN, "Spontaneous and Stimulated Recombination Radiation in Semiconductors," *Phys. Rev., 133*, A553-A563 (20 January 1964).
13. KIM, C. S., *Solid State Device Research Conference*, Boulder, Colo. (July 1964).
14. Final Report of General Electric Study on *Semiconductor Laser Amplifier Techniques*, Contract No. AF 30(602)-3111.
15. BILLINGS, B., "The Electro-optic Effect in Crystals and Its Possible Application to Distance Measure," *Optics in Metrology*, Pol Mollet, Ed., Permagon Press, New York, 1960, p. 119.
16. STERZER, F., D. BLATTNER, H. JOHNSON, AND J. MINITER, "Cuprous Chloride Light Modulator," *International Solid State Circuits Conference*, 112 (February 1963).
17. FRAVA, A., AND P. HANDLER, "Shift of Optical Absorption Edge by an Electric Field in Germanium," *Appl. Phys. Letters, 5*, 11 (1 July 1964).
18. NELSON, D. F., AND F. K. REINHART, "Light Modulation by the Electro-optic Effect on Reverse-Biased GaA P-N Junctions," *Appl. Phys. Letters, 5*, 148 (1 October 1964).
19. RIGROD, W. W., AND I. P. KAMINOV, "Wideband Microwave Light Modulation," *Proc. IEEE, 51*, 137 (January 1963).
20. PETERS, C. J., "Gigacycle Bandwidth Coherent Light Travelling Wave Phase Modulator," *Proc. IEEE, 51*, 147 (January 1963).
21. ENDERBY, G. E., "Wideband Optical Modulator," *Proc. IEEE, 52*, 981 (August 1964).
22. WENTZ, J. L., "Novel Laser Q-Switching Mechanism," *Proc. IEEE, 52*, 716 (June 1964).
23. ANDERSON, *Solid State Device Research Conference*, Boulder, Colo. (July 1964).
24. JOHNSON, K. M., "Photodiode Signal Enhancement Effect at Avalanche Breakdown," *International Solid State Circuits Conference* (1964).
25. DIDOMENICO, M., AND L. K. ANDERSON, "Microwave Signal to Noise Performance of CdSe Bulk Photoconductor Detector," *Proc. IEEE, 52*, No. 7, 815 (July 1964).
26. ING, S., AND G. GERHARD, *Proc. IEEE* (to be published).
27. Hewlett-Packard Company, HPA Technical Bulletin Application Note No. 5.
28. RAMBO, B. E., "Improved Long Wavelength Response of Photoemissive Surfaces," ASD, ETD, project 4156 task 415605.
29. MAYER, H., *Z. Physik, 124*, 326 (February 1948).
30. WILEY, W., AND C. HENDER, "Electron Multipliers Utilizing Continuous Strip Surfaces," *IRE Trans. Nucl. Sci., NS-9*, No. 3, Bendix, 103–106 (June 1962).
31. ING, J., "Light-Coupled Negative-Resistance Device in GaAs," *Proc. IEEE, 51* 852 (May 1963).

CHAPTER 37

SILICON AVALANCHE LIGHT SOURCES
FOR PHOTOGRAPHIC DATA RECORDING

L. J. Kabell

Fairchild Semiconductor
A Division of Fairchild Camera and Instrument Corporation
Palo Alto, California

and C. J. Pecoraro

Fairchild Space and Defense Systems
A Division of Fairchild Camera and Instrument Corporation
Syosset, New York

Emission of visible light from avalanching silicon p-n junctions has been studied in some detail by many workers over the past decade. Chynoweth and McKay of Bell Telephone Laboratories have published descriptions[1] of the phenomenon and results of investigations into spectral distributions and efficiencies of light generation. Because of the relative inefficiency of this means of generating light, no practical applications of the phenomenon were made until 1960 when Fairchild Semiconductor began to market a silicon light pulser device for use in calibrating nuclear event detection systems. This application resulted from the extremely rapid turn-on and turn-off characteristic of the light pulser (less than 3 nsec) that made it possible to simulate scintillation pulses from nuclear event counters.

At the beginning of 1963 our work in exploring various possibilities of computer memories involving the recording of digital data on photographic film prompted additional investigation of the silicon avalanche light source. This work resulted in a device structure that improved the emission efficiency in the blue end of the spectrum by an order of magnitude, and made it possible to design an integrated circuit matrix array of light pulsers for recording digital data on photographic film.

The fundamental mechanism considered responsible for the emission of light from the avalanching junction is radiative transitions of "hot" charge carriers crossing the junction under the influence of the intense electric field on the order of 10^6 volts per centimeter existing in the depletion layer of the avalanching junction. These hot carriers have a broad distribution of energy and, therefore, the spectral distribution of the photons emitted on recombination is fairly broad. If transitions occur deep in the bulk of the silicon, most of the shortwave length photons are absorbed by the silicon, and the emitted light peaks sharply in the red and infrared portions of the spectrum. However, by designing a structure which forces the avalanche breakdown to occur close to the silicon surface, an appreciable amount of light can be generated in the blue-green region of the spectrum, and the emitted light will appear as a warm white to the eye. In the optimized structure developed for the photographic recording application, the spectral distribution of the emitted light over the visible region (as shown in Fig. 1) approximates the radiation from a blackbody having a color

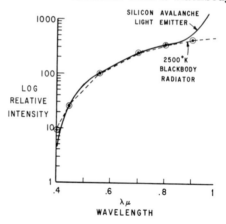

FIG. 1. Typical spectral distribution of avalanching junction light output.

temperature of 2500°K. This spectral distribution is achieved by fabricating a diffused structure that forces the avalanche breakdown to occur within a few tenths of a micron from the surface of the silicon (as illustrated in Fig. 2).

Microscopically, the light source appears as a line source having a brightness at maximum usable current density levels estimated to be in the range of 5000 ft-L. However, this high brightness value must not be confused with a high total light output because the emitting area is extremely small. The light is emitted from a line source and, in the matrix array, this line source is actually 6 mils in length and 0.3μ wide. Therefore, at a junction avalanche current of 100 mA, the total emitted light is 1.9×10^{10} visible photons per second and emission efficiency over the visible range is 3×10^{-8} photon per charge carrier crossing the junction. However, in spite of the low efficiency and low total output, sufficient light is emitted to expose moderate speed film to saturation density in times on the order of 1 msec.

Light emitted from the junction line source approximates a cosine distribution of intensity, because a uniform oxide protects the planar structure

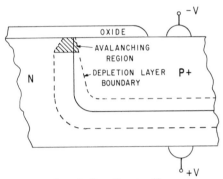

Fig. 2. Junction profile.

where the junction intersects the surface of the silicon. Light emitted from regions below the surface will be transmitted through the surface only over the angle permitted by the index of refraction of silicon relative to air. The extreme rays at the critical angle will be parallel to the surface of the silicon, and intensity will increase following a cosine law as the angle of emission approaches the normal to the silicon surface.

In the film recording of digital data, it is desirable that the data bit be recorded as a round dot having a density profile 8 mils in diameter at the 50 per cent transmission point and a flat top of approximately 5 mils diameter. Because the light is emitted from essentially a line source, a means of producing a round, uniformly dense dot of finite area from this source must be devised. The problem is solved by spacing a photographic emulsion at the proper distance from the source and shaping the source to approximate a circle so that the Lambertian distribution of light from each point in the source combines at the emulsion plane of the recording material to provide the desired density profile. An actual enlarged photograph of an active single data bit light source in the array is shown in Fig. 3. Figure 4 illustrates a series of constant illuminance contours for two spatially separated point sources, indicating how the desired density profile is achieved by spacing the recording emulsion at a given distance from the light source.

The data recording format consists of a block of dots arranged in a rectangular matrix with dots spaced on 18 mil centers. The block consists of 32 rows and 6 columns of dots. An enlarged photograph of an actual recording of a typical data pattern is shown in Fig. 5. Such a format precludes the use of individual devices without optical systems, and it was therefore necessary to integrate an array of 192 devices into a monolithic silicon chip. Technology has now been extended to produce a recording

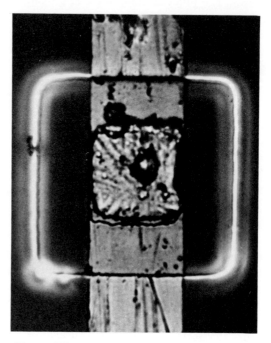

FIG. 3. Silicon junction emitting avalanche light.

matrix in a single integrated circuit chip containing over 500 active devices.

A recording light source chip consists of diffusion isolated p-n junctions (as shown in Fig. 6), fabricated in silicon by the planar technology and interconnected by standard metal-over-oxide techniques so that a single light pulser is energized by making electrical connections to the appropriate

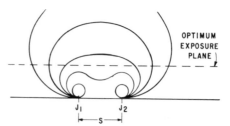

FIG. 4. Contours of constant illumination for parallel receiver.

row and column of the matrix array. Crossover of the interconnecting busses is accomplished by using the oxide-protected isolation diffusions as the interconnections between the metalized row interconnect bars shown in the figure.

An actual recording head utilizing the silicon light pulser array as packaged for installation in a recording system is illustrated in Fig. 7.

Applications requiring the photographic recording of data in dense dot formats have been studied, and indicated that the solid-state record technique has significant advantages to offer.

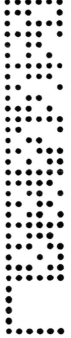

FIG. 5. Data pattern recorded with silicon light source.

Military applications require that the record system be rugged to sustain severe environments, small in size, light in weight, and reliable with a large mean time between failure.

The need for dense data recording systems is usually complemented with the need for a corresponding data reading system. The latter's feasibility and complexity is dependent on the geometric stability of the recorded data pattern and the degree of uniformity of the recorded dot characteristics, both within a single data format and between all generated data formats.

A comparison of the solid-state record system will be made on the foregoing parameters with a currently used technique wherein a miniaturized CRT is used.

The solid-state record head is extremely rugged since the construction

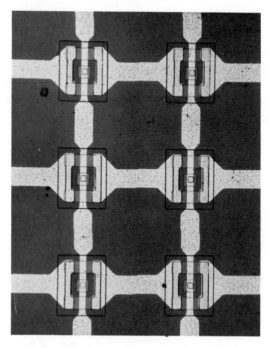

Fig. 6. Silicon light source array structure.

yields a compact cubical entity. There is no requirement to isolate this device from shock and vibration since the environments do not affect its operation any more than they affect the operation of planar integrated logic devices.

The CRT is a relatively fragile device. It contains a glass-enclosed vacuum cavity, and its gun elements and deflection system are very sus-

Fig. 7. Recording head utilizing the silicon light pulser array.

ceptible to vibration and shock. Without suitable provisions for isolation from these environments, the life of the tube should be greatly reduced.

The solid-state record head has the physical dimensions of 0.875-in. sq cross section with 0.875 in. height. The weight of this head including cable and connectors is 6 oz.

The CRT record head is approximately 4.5 in. long with 1.25 in. diameter and weighs approximately 1 lb. This value does not include weight of associated optics.

The solid-state record head, because of its small size, mounts directly through the cutout in the camera format plate and eliminates any need for an optical system. In several such installations, data patterns suitable for automatic reading were obtained.

The CRT, because of the sizable variation in the face thickness of the tube, cannot be used as a direct recording system but requires a high-resolution optical focusing system. In cases where there is insufficient room to mount the CRT and the lens directly behind the cutout in the camera format plate, a high-resolution optical transmission system would be required.

The solid-state record head offers extremely high reliability. All fabrication techniques used in the manufacture of the array have been previously used on the Fairchild integrated circuit production line.

Thirteen individual light pulsers have been subjected to a life test consisting of 1.2 billion cycles each. The devices were operated at 500 cps for a 4-week period at a 0.5 per cent duty cycle. The light output measurements indicated no variation of light output. No other light source known begins to approach this sort of life.

The CRT has the following aging problem. Light emission from the phosphor on the face of the CRT decreases as the accumulated exposure increases. Those data dots that are energized most frequently, such as index dots, will age fastest. Those data spots that are rarely energized will show little aging. Typical specifications allow peak dot variation of 30 per cent of the maximum over the data format. It is quite possible for this to occur within the half-life of the tube, which for small diameter tubes is 1000 hr.

The solid-state record head represents the ultimate in stability of the data format presented. Each data binary bit is represented by a unique 2-mil sq area. The dot to dot peak density variation is limited to less than 10 per cent by the uniformity of characteristics of all devices manufactured on the same chip. The dot to dot dimensional error is unvarying and is determined by the manufacturing process. Present techniques limit this error to 0.5 mil in the 18-mil dot pitch. All data formats from any record head will be exactly the same. Interdot space being inactive, the semiconductor never emits light.

The CRT record head represents the worst possible stability in the data format. The whole face of the tube is covered by the light-emitting phosphor. There is no direct physical correspondence between data bits and points on the tube face. The correspondence is established by means of gun emission of electrons and suitable deflections as the electrons traverse a path along the axis of the tube. In this technique a host of technical problems become extremely important: rigidity of gun and deflection structures under adverse environments, tight focus of an electron beam, deflection susceptibility to stray electric and magnetic fields, spreading of light emission within the phosphor, and light emission between the lighted dot areas due to stray electrons activating this phosphor.

Conclusion

The solid-state technique for digital data recording provides greater reliability, longer life, and ease of integration into recording equipment.

In addition to the advantages listed, this technique provides greater immunity from radio frequency interference and vibration effects encountered in military and other environments. It is in these areas that major advantages are possessed by this technique which may escape attention but which cause great difficulty in currently used approaches. The increased immunity to these effects provides indirect weight and cost savings in a photographic data recording system based upon the solid-state device which may not appear in a table of comparison.

Another indirect advantage is provided by the closer adherence of the recorded data to a specified geometrical arrangement than is possible with other recording methods. This improvement in recorded output quality improves the ability of machine reading equipment to provide error-free readout.

ACKNOWLEDGMENTS

The authors wish to acknowledge the contributions of Dr. R. H. Dyck and Mr. G. P. Weckler of Fairchild Semiconductor for their work in developing the optimized light pulser structure, and for many of the measurements and calculations in support of data presented in this paper.

The work was sponsored by Fairchild Camera and Instrument Corporation in a broad program to generate new approaches in data storage and readout. The authors would like to express their gratitude to Messrs. I. Doyle and L. Tregerman for their generous and enthusiastic support.

REFERENCE

1. CHYNOWETH, A. G., AND K. G. McKAY, *Phys. Rev.*, *102*, 369 (1956).

CHAPTER 38

ELECTRO-OPTICAL SIGNAL PROCESSORS FOR PHASED ARRAY ANTENNAS

Louis B. Lambert, Moses Arm, and Alexander Aimette

Columbia University
Electronics Research Laboratories
School of Engineering and Applied Science, New York, New York

I. Introduction

An optical configuration is a three-dimensional circuit in the sense that a complete description of the characteristics of the "circuit" involves the specification of the light amplitude, as a function of time, at each point in the object and image planes. This is different from a conventional two-port electric circuit which is a one-dimensional device and is completely specified by the temporal variations of the voltages at the input and output ports. An antenna aperture is also a three-dimensional circuit except that in conventional reflector antennas, a single feed point is used to illuminate the reflector surface with a time-varying signal so that the combination of feed and reflector reduces to a one-dimensional circuit. In a typical phased array, many separate elements are positioned in a plane and the terminal of each element is available for purposes of processing and observation as a function of time. Thus, an array antenna and an optical configuration are both three-dimensional circuits, and the use of optics to process the signals received by the elements of a phased array may have some advantages. This inference is made still more plausible when it is realized that the excitation of the elements of a phased array and the resulting radiation pattern form Fourier transform pairs, and that the image plane and object plane light amplitude distributions for an optical configuration also form Fourier transform pairs.

Techniques will be described for processing the signals obtained from the elements of a phased array by means of electro-optical devices. These techniques employ one optical device which simultaneously forms, as a continuum, all the beam patterns that a receiving array antenna is capable of forming. This differs significantly from the case of a conventional phased array beam processor where simultaneous beam formation is quantized since each beam must be formed in a separate electrical circuit. This basic difference is a direct consequence of the three-dimensional nature of optical devices as compared to the one-dimensional nature of electric circuits. The unique beam-forming capability inherent in certain electro-optical devices will be discussed.

On the assumption that electro-optical processing of phased array signals is possible, would it be of any practical value? In many array radar applications it has been found expedient to use separate arrays for transmission and reception. It is well known that in a search radar the product of transmitter average power and receiver area is fixed by the nature of the search problem. Therefore, without affecting radar performance, the transmitter array can consist of many low-power elements or few high-power elements. It is usually less expensive to build and maintain a few high-power transmitting elements than many low-power ones. However, if the transmitter array has fewer elements than the receiver array, it will have a broader beam pattern. If full use is to be made of the transmitted power, a number of receiver beams must be formed simultaneously in order to collect the energy from all parts of the transmitter beam. The additional cost and maintenance of the receiver beam forming networks and of their associated signal processing equipment usually offsets the potential saving in transmitter cost and maintenance that can be realized by the use of a small number of high-power elements.

Now, since one optical device can form all the beams of the receiver array simultaneously, it becomes possible to use transmitter arrays with smaller numbers of high-power elements without incurring additional receiver costs. It may also be practical to provide the electro-optical device with a time waveform processing capability so that, when the array transmits a suitable complex waveform, pulse compression can be simultaneously accomplished.

Furthermore, the beam-forming capability of the electro-optical signal processor is not adversely affected by the progressive envelope delay that is introduced at the receiving array. As a direct consequence of this inherent processor characteristic, the corresponding aperture-bandwidth constraint is relieved. The electro-optical signal processor does, however, introduce a constraint on the system bandwidth and the number of array elements that can be processed. Typically, it should be possible to process electro-optically 10,000 array elements with a system bandwidth in excess of 50 Mc.

II. Electro-Optical Fundamentals

A. *Past Results*

As was originally implied by Abbe[1] when he developed his theory of optical resolution for coherent illumination, optical systems are capable of processing information. Filter theoretic descriptions of optical systems are described in the text by Born and Wolf,[2] and in articles by Elias,[3] Rhodes,[4] Cheatham,[5] O'Neil,[6] and Cutrona.[7] In order to synthesize a spectrum analyzer which employs optical techniques, the input signal $v(t)$ must first be transformed to a signal $v(x)$ or $v^2(x)$, where x is a variable in physical space. This transformation may be accomplished by first converting $v(t)$ to a proportional time variation of light amplitude or intensity, and then employing a photographic process to obtain the spatial variation. Synthesis techniques of this general type are described by Howell[8] as applied to optical analog computers, and by Cutrona[7] as applied to data processing and filtering systems.

In order to circumvent the time delays, film transport problems, etc., that are associated with a photographic process, other spatial light modulation devices have been employed. An investigation of various instantaneous light modulation techniques was performed by Wilmotte.[9] Major successes have been achieved by employing the Debye-Sears effect[10,11] in a transparent ultrasonic delay line which is directly incorporated into an optical configuration. An instantaneous spatial light modulator of this type is analyzed in the following section.

The investigation of this class of electro-optical signal processors has been a part of the engineering research efforts at the Columbia University Electronics Research Laboratories (CUERL) since 1959. These studies have been sponsored by the Advanced Research Projects Agency, Department of Defense, Washington, D.C., and have included the theoretical analysis and the experimental demonstration of wideband instantaneous spectrum analyzers, two-dimensional autocorrelators and crosscorrelators, pulse compression systems, and phased array signal processors. A portion of this work has been reported in the unclassified literature (see references by Lambert *et al.*[12–19]). Laser light sources, diffraction limited optics, and liquid and solid type Debye-Sears light modulators have been developed and utilized during these studies.

As a result of all of the aforementioned studies, there exists a firm theoretical and experimental body of information which forms the foundation for the realization of coherent electro-optical signal processors.

B. *Coherent Optical Transfer Functions*

One of the most convenient descriptions for the light that propagates through a coherent optical system is that contained in electromagnetic wave theory especially when the traveling waves are written in complex form. Also, since we shall mainly be concerned with transfer functions, it will also prove to be convenient to normalize light amplitudes and power levels, realizing that absolute levels can always be obtained by applying the conservation of energy principle to the system. With this in mind, we shall now briefly review the basic characteristics of a coherent optical system.

1. MONOCHROMATIC, COLLIMATED LIGHT. Consider an electromagnetic (light) wave propagating in free space in the z direction. Let this wave be uniform, plane, and linearly polarized in the x direction. In this case, the only existing electric field vector is in the x direction, and it can be written as a real scalar quantity E_x. Using complex notation, this component of the traveling light wave can be written as

$$E_x \equiv E_x(t, z) = E_p \exp j(\omega_L t - k_L z + \phi_i) \qquad (1)$$

where E_p is the peak amplitude of the electric field in volts/meter, $\omega_L = 2\pi f_L$ is the radian frequency of the light carrier, f_L is light frequency in cps, $k_L = 2\pi/\lambda_L$ is the wave number, λ_L is the light wavelength so that the free space propagation speed is $c = \lambda_L f_L = 3 \times 10^8$ m/sec, and ϕ_0 is some initial phase of the wave at $t = z = 0$. In optical terminology, the traveling wave just defined is referred to as monochromatic, collimated light with a *plane* of polarization formed by the direction of propagation and the magnetic field vector, i.e., the y-z plane. The z axis is usually referred to as the optical axis.

The transfer characteristic of a coherent optical system is best defined in terms of the electric field distributions in two or more planes which are perpendicular to the optical axis (z axis). If we define the input plane at $z = 0$ and realize that the light frequency acts as a carrier, then the electric field vector can be written more simply. With the understanding that the carrier terms exist and must be introduced whenever necessary, the electric field for this uniform plane wave propagating in free space can be denoted by simply writing its peak amplitude E_p.

The light wave that is incident upon the x-y plane located at $z = 0$ could contain a variation in amplitude and phase which is a function of the (x, y) coordinates. For this general case, the electric field $E(x, y)$ can be denoted by writing its peak amplitude and relative phase in the complex form

$$E(x, y) = A(x, y) \exp j\phi(x, y) \qquad (2)$$

where $A(x, y)$ is the peak amplitude and $\phi(x, y)$ the relative phase of the electric field at $z = 0$.

2. TRANSFER FUNCTIONS FOR OBJECTS. Let monochromatic, collimated light be incident upon an object that is completely contained in the x-y plane so that the light emanating from the object is in the same plane. Theoretically, this object can modify the amplitude and phase of the

incident light E_p, producing a new wave of the form $E(x, y)$ as expressed by Eq. 2. The transfer function of the object can be defined as the ratio of the emanating light amplitude $E(x, y)$ to the monochromatic, collimated light amplitude E_p incident upon the object. This transfer function shall be called the complex transmission or complex transparency $T_c(x, y)$ of the object as given by

$$T_c(x, y) \equiv E(x, y)/E_p = T(x, y) \exp j\psi(x, y) \qquad (3)$$

where $T(x, y)$ is the relative amplitude or amplitude transparency of the object and $\psi(x, y)$ is the relative phase or phase transparency of the object. In this sense, we can refer to the object as having *spatially modulated* the incident light.

3. TRANSFER FUNCTION FOR AN IDEAL LENS. Derivations of the electric field distribution in the image plane of an ideal lens which results from a known incident distribution of electric field appear in the literature in various forms; see, for example, Born and Wolf,[2] Rhodes,[4] and Cutrona et al.[7] The results of these derivations will now be reviewed and presented in a form which will be convenient for future use.

Consider the optical configuration shown in Fig. 1 where $E_0(x, y)$ is the

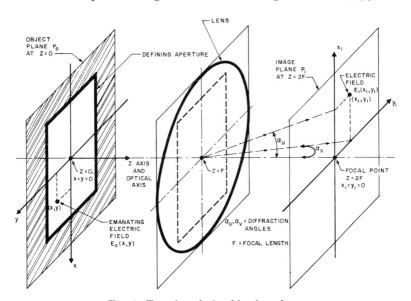

FIG. 1. Transfer relationships for a lens.

electric field emanating from the "object" plane P_0 located at $z = 0$, and $E_1(x_1, y_1)$ is the electric field in the "image" plane P_1 located at $z = 2F$. The lens is assumed to be ideal, and it is located at $z = F$ where F is its focal length. Subject to the usually fulfilled conditions that the diffraction angles (α_u and α_v) are small and that distance attenuation is negligible, it has been shown that, for the normalized image plane coordinates defined by

$$u \equiv \frac{\sin \alpha_u}{\lambda_L} \cong \frac{x_1}{\lambda_L F}$$

$$v \equiv \frac{\sin \alpha_v}{\lambda_L} \cong \frac{y_1}{\lambda_L F}$$

(4)

the electric field distribution in the image plane is given by

$$E_1(x_1, y_1) \equiv E(u, v) = K_1 \int\!\!\int_{-\infty}^{\infty} E_0(x, y) \exp\left[-j2\pi(ux + vy)\right] dx \, dy \quad (5)$$

Here, K_1 is a constant having a value which maintains the conservation of energy within the system, and λ_L is the wavelength of the light carrier.

It can be seen that the light distribution in the image plane is related to the light distribution in the object plane by a two-dimensional Fourier transform (Eq. 5) and this can also be recognized as the classical Fraunhofer or far field radiation pattern for a radiating aperture. Note that in order to force the exponential terms to appear with the conventional negative sign, the image plane axis must be reversed as shown in Fig. 1. Also note that since the lens has finite dimensions, the electric field emanating from the object must be bounded by some defining aperture. This aperture essentially insures the condition that the propagating wave $E_0(x, y)$ impinges upon the lens with a negligible loss in total energy.

C. Spectrum Analyzer Configuration

If the object plane P_0 in Fig. 1 is now considered as containing an object which presents a complex transmission function $T_c(x, y)$, and if this object is illuminated by an incident electric field which corresponds to a plane uniform wave E_p, then the electric field emanating from the object is

$$E_0(x, y) = E_p T_c(x, y) \quad (6)$$

Defining a new constant $K_2 \equiv K_1 E_p$, we can write the field distribution in the image plane as

$$E(u, v) = K_2 \int\!\!\int_{-\infty}^{\infty} T_c(x, y) \exp\left[-j2\pi(ux + vy)\right] dx \, dy \quad (7)$$

Here, $T_c(x, y)$ is visualized as the input signal and $E(u, v)$ as the output signal which is proportional to the two-dimensional Fourier transform of $T_c(x, y)$. Thus, the optical configuration produces the "spectrum" of the object's transmission function. However, a photodetector is energy (or power) sensitive, so that the resulting output signal will be proportional to $|E(u, v)|^2$. This corresponds to the power spectrum of $T_c(x, y)$.

In addition to providing a transfer function which is the two-dimensional spectrum of the object's complex transmission function, this optical configuration provides a third degree of freedom, namely, time. As time progresses, new sections of the signal can be automatically introduced into the object plane to modulate the light carrier, and the spectrum can be obtained as a continuous function of time. Finally, if the input signal contains only one independent variable, then the required integration need only be one-dimensional so that a cylindrical lens can be employed. The second optical dimension could then be used to multiplex (spatially) the spectrum analyzer so that it is capable of processing many independent channels simultaneously. A more detailed account of such devices can be found in the article by Cutrona[7] where the spatial light modulator (object) is photographic film and in the article by Lambert[13] where the light modulator consists of a spatially multiplexed Debye-Sears type delay line.

D. *Spectrum Analyzers Employing Debye-Sears Light Modulators*

As a simplified example of the Debye-Sears effect, consider the configuration shown in Fig. 2 where a transparent ultrasonic delay line is excited by an electrical signal and simultaneously illuminated with monochromatic, collimated light. The light modulator operates as follows: The input signal $v(t)$ excites the piezoelectric transducer which has been cut to vibrate in a longitudinal (compressional) mode. These mechanical vibrations cause a pressure wave to propagate in the delay medium with a characteristic speed S. For an aperture length of D, the signal duration which can just fill the aperture is $T = D/S$.

Now, consider the plane electromagnetic (light) wave which is incident upon the delay line as shown in Fig. 2. To a first approximation, a single electromagnetic "ray" experiences a uniform refractive index as it prop-

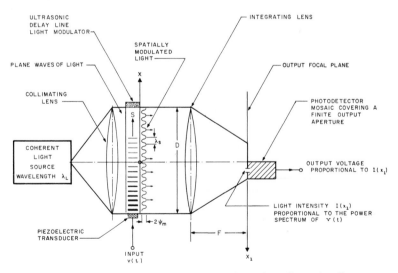

FIG. 2. Electro-optical spectrum analyzer (one-dimensional).

agates through the delay medium, but adjacent rays experience slightly different indices. For a piezoelectric crystal of length δ (along z), the phase of the electromagnetic wave can be shown to change by an amount

$$\psi(x) = \frac{2\pi\delta}{\lambda_L} n(x) \tag{8}$$

where λ_L is the wavelength of the electromagnetic wave and $n(x)$ is the index of refraction of the delay medium as a function of x (the aperture dimension). As has been shown by Raman and Nath,[20] Bhatia and Noble,[21] and Phariseau,[22] the change in the index of refraction is proportional to the input voltage. Thus, the light emanating from the delay line (at some time instant) is phase-modulated in space as a replica of the input voltage.

Quantitatively, if the input signal is

$$v(t) = V_m \cos (2\pi f_i t) \tag{9}$$

then the complex transmission function $T_c(x)$ for the Debye-Sears light modulator can be shown to be given by

$$T_c(x) = p_D(x) \exp \left[j\psi_m \cos (2\pi x/\lambda_s + \phi_0) \right] \tag{10}$$

The terms appearing in this equation are defined as follows: The finite aperture of length D limits the signal duration contained within the light modulator to $T = D/S$, and this is contained in the pulse function

$$p_D(x) \equiv \begin{cases} 1 & \text{for} & |x| < \tfrac{1}{2}D \\ 0 & \text{for} & |x| > \tfrac{1}{2}D \end{cases} \tag{11}$$

The peak phase deviation or modulation index ψ_m of the light carrier emanating from the delay line is given by $\psi_m = K_s V_m$ where K_s is a constant for a given piezoelectric crystal and V_m is the peak input voltage. Since the input signal has a frequency f_i and the ultrasonic wave propagates with a speed S, then the ultrasonic wavelength λ_s at any instant is $\lambda_s = S/f_i$. And finally, the term ϕ_0 is included to account for the phase of the modulation at $x = 0$ and at some particular instant in time.

The electric field distribution in the image plane (output focal plane of Fig. 2) is given by the one-dimensional Fourier transform

$$E(u) = K_3 \int_{-\infty}^{\infty} T_c(x) \exp \left[-j2\pi u x \right] dx \tag{12}$$

A direct comparison can be made with the usual Fourier transform notation for the input signal $v(t)$ by defining normalized input (object plane) and output (image plane) coordinates in the form

$$\left. \begin{array}{l} \tau \equiv x/S \\ f \equiv uS = x_1 S/\lambda_L F \end{array} \right\} \tag{13}$$

Now, the complex transmission function is given by

$$T_c(\tau) = p_T(\tau) \exp \left[j\psi_m \cos (2\pi f_i \tau + \phi_0) \right] \tag{14}$$

and the electric field distribution in the image plane is given by

$$E(f) = K_4 \int_{-\infty}^{\infty} T_c(\tau) \exp\left(-j2\pi f\tau\right) d\tau \qquad (15)$$

Note that τ is in units of time, f is in units of frequency, and that f is proportional to actual distance x_1 in the image plane. Also, the output photodetector mosaic actually detects light power so that the detected output signal in Fig. 2 is proportional to the light intensity which has a relative value given by $I(f) \equiv |E(f)|^2$ at any instant in time.

By combining Eqs. 14 and 15 and letting $K_4 = 1/T$, we obtain the output signal shown in Fig. 3, where $I(f)$ is plotted as a function of the

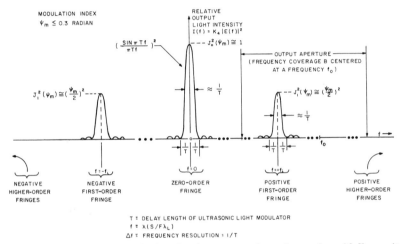

Fig. 3. Light intensity distribution in the output plane for a sinusoidally excited, ultrasonic delay line light modulator.

output frequency variable f. This output waveform is recognized as the power spectrum of the input signal when the modulation index ψ_m permits approximating the Bessel functions $J_n(\psi_m)$ with the terms shown. In fact, the condition that $\psi_m \leq 0.3$ rad is always met for large dynamic range systems so that the output signal $I(f)$ may be considered as being the power spectrum of the input signal.

Note that the spectrum is symmetrical about $f = 0$ and that no usable information is contained in the zero-order fringe which occurs at the focal point ($f = x_1 = 0$). We now see that it is necessary to detect only those output signals which fall within a frequency band B. This coverage band is shown in Fig. 3 as being centered at f_0, the nominal carrier frequency of the ultrasonic light modulator. In practice, the frequency coverage B is limited by the bandwidth of the light modulator. Special transducer matching techniques have been developed at CUERL which produce a 50 per cent linear phase bandwidth so that $B \cong 0.5f_0$. Details of such a design can be found in the articles by Lambert.[13,14]

Before proceeding with this analysis, it is worthwhile to note that since the modulation index ψ_m is usually maintained small ($\psi_m < 0.3$ rad), we can write the complex transmission function given in Eqs. 10 by using the first two terms for the power series expansion of the exponential term. Thus, for an input signal of the form $V_m \cos (2\pi f_i t)$, the complex transmission function can be approximated by

$$T_c(x) \cong p_D(x)[1 + j\psi_m \cos (2\pi x/\lambda_s + \phi_0)] \qquad (16)$$

Furthermore, if we are interested only in the light distribution in the vicinity of the first-order fringe (see Fig. 3) we need obtain only the Fourier transform of the portion of the complex transmission function given by

$$T_{c_1}(x) = p_D(x)\left[j \frac{\psi_m}{2} \exp j(2\pi x/\lambda_s + \phi_0)\right] \qquad (17)$$

This last expression can be obtained from Eq. 16 by expressing the cosine in terms of exponentials. The light amplitude (electric field) distribution in the vicinity of the first-order fringe is now given by

$$E_1(u) = K_3 \int_{-\infty}^{\infty} T_{c_1}(x) \exp (-j2\pi ux) \, dx \qquad (18)$$

III. Array Antenna Waveforms and Inherent Characteristics

The waveforms that are typically obtained at the elements of a radar receiving array will now be reviewed. Consider a reflecting target in space which is illuminated by a transmitted signal $v_T(t')$ having unit amplitude, a duration T, and a carrier (rf) frequency f_c so that

$$v_T(t') = p_T(t') \cos (2\pi f_c t') \qquad (19)$$

where

$$p_T(t') \equiv \begin{cases} 1 & \text{for} & |t'| < \frac{1}{2}T \\ 0 & \text{for} & |t'| > \frac{1}{2}T \end{cases}$$

The signal that is reflected by the target reaches the receiving antenna in the form of a traveling plane wave which is delayed by the round trip propagation time and shifted in frequency by the rate of change of this propagation path length. For simplicity, we first consider the linear, uniform array shown in Fig. 4.

The incident wavefront is not received simultaneously by all array elements for targets having a finite location angle θ_0. The signal received by the nth array element is delayed (relative to element zero in Fig. 4) by an amount given by

$$n\tau = n(d \sin \theta_0)/c \qquad (20)$$

where d is the spacing between array elements, $c = \lambda_c f_c$ is the speed of electromagnetic wave propagation, and λ_c is the carrier wavelength. The signals received by the N elements of the array therefore consist of an ensemble of pulsed carriers, all of duration T and carrier frequency f_c for each (stationary) target that reflects the transmitted signal and is within the volume covered by this receiving antenna.

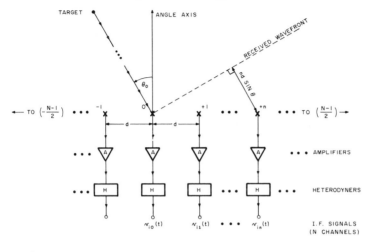

Fig. 4. Linear array antenna signals.

If the target is moving so that its range R is changing at a rate $\dot{R} \equiv dR/dt$, then the signal received at the nth element of the array will be of the form

$$v_n(t) = p_T(t - n\tau) \{\cos [2\pi f_R(t - n\tau)]\} \tag{21}$$

where

$$t = t' - \tau_R$$
$$\tau_R = \text{range delay} = 2R/c$$
$$f_R = \text{received frequency} = f_c + f_d$$
$$f_d = \text{Doppler frequency} = -2\dot{R}f_c/c$$
$$R = \text{target range for an essentially monostatic system}$$

This received signal is at a carrier frequency $(f_c + f_d)$, and the pulsed carrier contains a delay of $n\tau$. The incremental delay τ is given by

$$\tau = \left(\frac{d}{c}\right) \sin \theta_0 = \left(\frac{d}{\lambda_c}\right)\left(\frac{1}{f_c}\right) \sin \theta_0 \tag{22}$$

and this term contains the location angle θ_0 of the reflecting target.

An ideal phased array signal processor can be defined as a device which combines the N signals of form $v_n(t)$ to obtain an output signal of the form $v(\theta)$ such that at $\theta = \theta_0$ the signal-to-noise ratio is maximized and for all other values $\theta \neq \theta_0$, $v(\theta)$ varies in proportion to the antenna radiation pattern associated with this pulse mode of operation.

It can be shown that this is accomplished by (1) delaying each of the signals by an amount such that the nth signal is delayed by $n\tau$, (2) summing the resulting ensemble of N signals which are now of the same phase, and (3) coherently integrating the summed signal for its entire duration. However, since τ is unknown, the processor must perform the aforementioned operations for all values of τ of interest, i.e., for all values of the angle variable θ.

Usually, it is assumed that the pulse width T is large compared with the maximum envelope delay Nd/c that is contained in the ensemble of received signals. In this case, the output of the ideal processor corresponds to the continuous wave radiation pattern of the uniform antenna which is given by

$$|v(\theta)|^2 = K(\theta) \frac{\sin^2 \left[\pi N(d/\lambda_c)(\sin \theta - \sin \theta_0)\right]}{\sin^2 \left[\pi(d/\lambda_c)(\sin \theta - \sin \theta_0)\right]} \qquad (23)$$

Here, $K(\theta)$ is a function which represents the radiation pattern of an individual element in the array. Usually, $K(\theta)$ varies only slightly from unity for the values of θ of interest. Also, it can be shown that the half-power (3 dB) beam width $\Delta\theta$ of the radiation pattern, and of $|v(\theta)|^2$, is given by

$$\Delta\theta = \frac{0.886\lambda_c}{Nd \cos \theta_0}. \qquad (24)$$

Before proceeding with the electro-optical processor, we need to develop an additional expression for the ensemble of signals obtained from a linear array as was shown in Fig. 4. In many cases, it is necessary to preprocess the signals obtained from the array elements in order to increase their amplitudes and reduce their carrier frequency. Realizing that heterodyning to a frequency f_0 consists of first multiplying the received signal $v_n(t)$ by a coherent local oscillator signal of the form $\cos 2\pi(f_c - f_0)t$, and then taking the difference frequency component by filtering, it can be shown that the nth intermediate frequency channel contains a signal of the form

$$v_{in}(t - n\tau) = p_T(t - n\tau) \{\cos 2\pi(f_i t - n\tau f_r)\} \qquad (25)$$

Here,

$$f_i = \text{input frequency} = f_0 + f_d$$
$$f_0 = \text{intermediate frequency}$$
$$f_d = \text{Doppler frequency}$$
$$f_r = f_c + f_d$$
$$f_c = \text{carrier (radio) frequency}$$

When the pulse length T is large compared to the maximum delay $(n\tau)_{\max} = Nd/c \ll T$, we can neglect the envelope delay and write Eq. 25 in the *approximate* form

$$v_{in}(t) = p_T(t) \{\cos 2\pi(f_i t - n\alpha)\} \qquad (26)$$

with

$$\alpha \equiv \tau f_r = \left(\frac{d}{\lambda_c}\right)\left(1 + \frac{f_d}{f_c}\right)\sin\theta_0$$

If the envelope delay is not to be neglected, then it is convenient to write Eq. 25 in the form

$$v_{\text{in}}(t - n\tau) = p_T(t - n\tau)\,\{\cos 2\pi[f_i(t - n\tau) - n\beta]\} \tag{27}$$

with

$$\beta \equiv \tau(f_c - f_0) = \frac{d}{\lambda_c}\left[1 - \frac{f_0}{f_c}\right]\sin\theta_0$$

Note that if $f_c \gg f_d$ and $f_c \gg f_0$, then

$$\alpha \cong \beta \cong \frac{d}{\lambda_c}\sin\theta_0 \tag{28}$$

In practice, the ideal electronic processor can be realized only by quantizing the angle coverage. For a square, planar array consisting of N^2 elements, there are approximately N^2 delay lines or phase shifters needed for each angle of interest, and approximately N^4 delay lines if all angles of interest are to be processed simultaneously. Since modern arrays may consist of from $N^2 = 1000$ to 10,000 elements, the number of circuit components needed to process simultaneously just the quantized angles becomes prohibitive. The electro-optical processors discussed in the following sections provide a significant reduction in the number of electrical circuits needed and will also provide a simultaneous and continuous angle coverage for a multiple target environment.

IV. Spatial Multiplexing Technique for a Linear Array Antenna

The ensemble of waveforms obtained from the elements of a *linear* array can be processed by employing either one of the two electro-optical techniques to be described. As will be shown in Sec. VI, these two techniques can be advantageously combined in a single optical configuration to provide a unique processing capability for *planar* array antennas. In all cases, the inherent characteristics of the array antennas are realized directly as output signals from the processors.

The ultrasonic light modulator described in Sec. IID is essentially one-dimensional, since no spatial variations were introduced in the y dimension. This second dimension will now be exploited. The basic technique that appears particularly applicable to phased array processors consists of filling the y dimension of the object plane with separate and parallel ultrasonic channels as shown in Fig. 5. Each channel now consists of a piezoelectric transducer of width W which produces its own distinct ultrasonic traveling wave. The separation between adjacent channels is l and the optical aperture dimensions are L and D as shown. This spatially multiplexed, ultrasonic light modulator can be placed in an optical configuration similar to that shown in Fig. 1. This new configuration is a two-dimensional extension of the spectrum analyzer discussed previously.

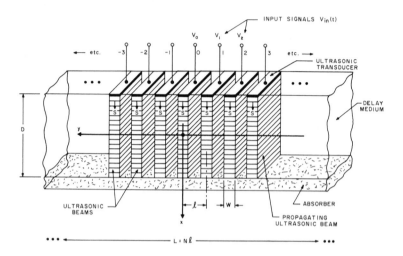

OPTICAL APERTURE: L x D
ULTRASONIC BEAMS: WIDTH W; SPACING ℓ; PROPAGATION SPEED S

FIG. 5. A spatially multiplexed light modulator.

Consider a target located at an angle θ_0 off the boresight axis; then the signal obtained at the nth intermediate frequency channel (Fig. 4) has been shown to be given by Eq. 26. This signal is now applied to the nth transducer of the spatially multiplexed light modulator. It produces its own distinct ultrasonic beam in the water delay medium as shown in Fig. 5. For simplicity in this analysis, we have neglected the envelope delay due to the angle of arrival of the signal, but we shall keep the proper phase term $(n\alpha)$ in each signal. This means that all signals arrive simultaneously (but with different phases) and at some instant of time they completely fill all the channels in the light modulator.

Now, by taking into account the proper location of each of the N channels in the light modulator, the complex transmission function which contributes to the first-order fringe of interest can be shown to be the two-dimensional extension of Eq. 17 so that

$$T_{c_1}(x, y) = \sum_{n=-(N-1)/2}^{+(N-1)/2}{}' \ [p_D(x)] \cdot [p_W(y - nl)]$$

$$\cdot \left\{ j \frac{\psi_m}{2} \exp\left[2\pi j(x/\lambda_s - n\alpha)\right] \right\} \tag{29}$$

In this equation, the spatial pulse function $p_D(x)$ defines the aperture length D along x, and the spatial pulse function $p_W(y - nl)$ defines the proper location and width for the nth channel along y. Note that the signal duration contained in the light modulator is $T = D/S$ and the number of phased array elements that are processed is $N = L/l$.

The relative light amplitude distribution in the vicinity of the first-order fringe $E_1(u, v)$ is given by the two-dimensional extension of Eq. 18. It can be shown that this Fourier transform gives (within a constant)

$$E_1(u, v) = \left[\operatorname{sinc} D \left(u - \frac{1}{\lambda_s} \right) \right] \cdot \left[\operatorname{sinc} vW \right] \cdot \left[\frac{\sin \pi N(vl + \alpha)}{\sin \pi (vl + \alpha)} \right] \quad (30)$$

where

$$\operatorname{sinc} Z \equiv \frac{\sin \pi Z}{\pi Z}$$

and the location angle θ_0 of the target is contained in the term (Eq. 28 for $f_c \gg f_d$)

$$\alpha \cong \frac{d}{\lambda_c} \sin \theta_0 \quad (31)$$

Note that the terms d and λ_c are design constants of the system and are, therefore, known quantities. As a result, α is proportional to the sine of the target location angle θ_0.

We can now convert the v dimension into one which is proportional to the space angle θ by letting

$$vl \equiv -\frac{d}{\lambda_c} \sin \theta \quad (32)$$

Substituting Eqs. 31 and 32 into Eq. 30 and evaluating the result along the line defined by $u = 1/\lambda_s$ in the image plane, we obtain the relative light intensity distribution in the form

$$\left| E_1 \left(u = 1/\lambda_s, v = -\frac{d}{\lambda_c l} \sin \theta \right) \right|^2 \equiv |E(\theta)|^2$$

$$= \operatorname{sinc}^2 \left[\frac{dW}{\lambda_c l} \sin \theta \right] \cdot \left[\frac{\sin^2 \left[\pi N(d/\lambda_c)(\sin \theta - \sin \theta_0) \right]}{\sin^2 \left[\pi (d/\lambda_c)(\sin \theta - \sin \theta_0) \right]} \right] \quad (33)$$

Now, the sinc^2 function is unity when $\theta_0 = 0$, and has a value for $\theta = 90$ degrees of sinc^2 $(dW/\lambda_c l)$. With $d = \frac{1}{2}\lambda_c$ and $W = \frac{1}{2}l$ as typical design parameters, we see that for $\theta = 90$ degrees, the sinc^2 weighting function has a value of $(2\sqrt{2}/\pi)^2 \cong 0.8$. This means that over all values of θ of interest (± 90 degrees), the sinc^2 weighting function varies smoothly from 1.0 to 0.8. It acts then as a slowly varying "constant," and all information is contained in the second term of Eq. 33. Thus, the light intensity distribution in the image plane $|E(\theta)|^2$ corresponds to the output signal obtained from an ideal phased array signal processor as was previously defined in Sec. III (see Eq. 23).

The light distribution in the focal plane can best be described in terms of normalized image plane parameters. For example, let us define an output "frequency" variable by $f \equiv Su$ and an output "angle" variable by $\phi \equiv vl$. Substituting these values into Eq. 30, we obtain

$$|E_1(f, \phi)|^2 = \text{sinc}^2[T(f - f_i)] \cdot \text{sinc}^2\left(\phi \frac{W}{l}\right) \cdot \frac{\sin^2[\pi N(\phi + \alpha)]}{\sin^2[\pi(\phi + \alpha)]} \quad (34)$$

Equation 34 describes the two-dimensional, relative light intensity distribution in the vicinity of the fringe of interest. The peak light intensity in this vicinity occurs at the coordinates (f, ϕ) given by

$$f = f_i = f_0 + f_d \quad (35)$$

$$\phi = -\alpha \cong -\frac{d}{\lambda_c} \sin \theta_0 \quad (36)$$

as shown in Fig. 6. Thus, the ϕ displacement of this light intensity peak corresponds to the location angle θ_0 of the target as given by Eq. 36, and

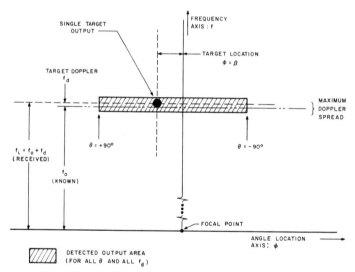

FIG. 6. Output from a spatially multiplexed processor.

the f displacement from the known intermediate frequency f_0 corresponds to the Doppler frequency shift f_d as given by Eq. 35.

Actually, the light intensity distribution contains sidelobes as does the microwave antenna beam pattern. Along the "angle" dimension ϕ, these sidelobes are described by the function $\sin^2[\pi N(\phi + \alpha)]/\sin^2[\pi(\phi + \alpha)]$ which is weighted by the function $\text{sinc}^2(\phi W/l)$. For example, the peak-to-null width of the main lobe is $1/N$ and the half-power beam width can be shown to be

$$\Delta\phi = 0.886/N \quad (37)$$

This can be directly related to the antenna beam width by differentiating Eq. 36 to obtain

$$\Delta\theta = \frac{0.886\lambda_c}{Nd \cos\theta_0} \tag{38}$$

which is identical to the half-power beam width of the antenna as given by Eq. 24.

It can be shown that for the case of multiple targets, the output response of the electro-optical processor will have a unique and distinct peak for each target location angle. Therefore, it can be said that this processor forms simultaneously, as a continuum, all the beams the receiving antenna is capable of forming; i.e., antenna beams are *not* formed in a quantized manner. Furthermore, targets with the same location angle will be separated in Doppler frequency if their range rates differ sufficiently and will be separated in time of occurrence if their ranges differ. The Doppler frequency separation is obtained in the f dimension of the image plane. Separation in range occurs due to the fact that targets at different ranges reflect signals which arrive at different times at the antenna and the proper light intensity fringe will not appear in the image plane until the signal fills the ultrasonic delay line light modulator.

The following conclusions can be formed from these derived results: (1) The target location angle θ_0 is obtained unambiguously for each and every target that can be resolved. (2) Target angle resolution is identical to the resolution inherent in the antenna array. (3) All antenna beam angles appear simultaneously as a continuum in a form which is identical to the beam forming capability and sidelobe response of the antenna array. (4) In addition to angle measurement, the second dimension provides Doppler frequency. (5) Doppler frequency is obtained unambiguously with a resolution which is identical to that obtained from an ideal coherent integrator. (6) Angle and Doppler appear at the output completely associated in orthogonal dimensions. (7) The time of occurrence of each output signal is proportional to the range of each target.

V. Time-Delay Multiplexing Technique for a Linear Array Antenna

The second electro-optical processing technique utilizes only one dimension of the light modulator. This is accomplished by forming a single waveform from the ensemble of waveforms obtained from a linear array as shown in Fig. 7.

Each of the signals of finite duration T obtained from an N element linear array is passed through a delay line and the delayed signals are then summed. The delay lines are designed to provide a constant incremental delay difference T_D between adjacent channels; i.e., $T_{n+1} - T_n \equiv T_D$. The incremental delay T_D is chosen so that the summed waveform $v_s(t)$ consists of a series of separated pulsed carriers, the nth pulse representing the delayed signal from the nth array element. This is accomplished when

$$T_D = T + |\tau|_{\max} = T + \left(\frac{d}{c}\right) |\sin \theta_0|_{\max} \tag{39}$$

Typically, for $|\theta| \leq 90$ degrees and $d/\lambda_c = \frac{1}{2}$, we have $T_D \cong T + \frac{1}{2}f_c \cong T$ since the radar carrier frequency f_c is usually much greater than the radar bandwidth $1/T$.

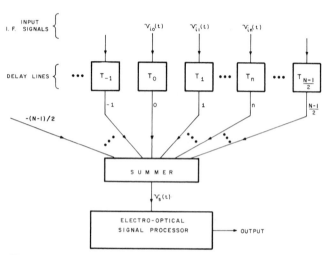

FIG. 7. Time-delay multiplexed electro-optical signal processor.

The summed waveform $v_s(t)$ now consists of N pulsed carriers, each of duration T and separation $T_s \equiv T_D + \tau$ so that the total signal duration is NT_s. The form of the nth signal is as shown in Eq. 27. After the indicated delay and summation is performed, the summed waveform can be written as

$$v_s(t) = \sum_{n=-(N-1)/2}^{(N-1)/2} p_T(t - nT_s) \{\cos 2\pi[f_i(t - nT_s) - n\beta]\} \tag{40}$$

where

$$T_s = T_D + \tau$$
$$f_i = f_0 + f_d$$
$$\beta = \tau(f_c - f_0) = \frac{d}{\lambda_c}\left(1 - \frac{f_0}{f_c}\right)\sin \theta_0$$

Note that t is here defined to include the range delay τ_R. This waveform now acts as the input signal to a single channel, ultrasonic light modulator and coherent optical configuration as was shown in Fig. 2.

When the signal $v_s(t)$ completely fills the (one-dimensional) aperture formed by the ultrasonic light modulator, the complex transmission function that corresponds to the positive first-order fringe of interest is

$$T_{c_1} = j\frac{\psi_m}{2}\sum_n p_a(x - na_s) \cdot \exp j2\pi\left(\frac{1}{\lambda_s}(x - na_s) - n\beta\right) \qquad (41)$$

where ψ_m = modulation index, $a = TS$, $a_s = T_sS$, and $\lambda_s = S/f_i$. The image plane light amplitude distribution in the vicinity of the positive first-order fringe is obtained from Eq. 18 as

$$E_1(u) = \text{sinc } a(u - 1/\lambda_s)\left[\frac{\sin \pi N(ua_s + \beta)}{\sin \pi(ua_s + \beta)}\right] \qquad (42)$$

Note the similarity between this result and Eq. 30 which was obtained for the spatially multiplexed processor.

In order to visualize this function, we shall again define the output "frequency" variable f by $f \equiv uS$. Equation 42 can then be written in the form

$$E_1(f) = [\text{sinc } T(f - f_i)]\left[\frac{\sin \pi N(fT_s + \beta)}{\sin \pi(fT_s + \beta)}\right] \qquad (43)$$

Note that the angle information is contained in the last bracketed term in Eq. 43. However, this factor is weighted by the sinc function which has a maximum at $f = f_i$. As a result, the principal maximum of interest must also be located in the vicinity of $f = f_i$. In general, the principal maxima occur when $(fT_s + \beta) = m$ with m being any integer. Hence the location of these principal maxima occur at $f = f_p$ where $f_p = (m - \beta)/T_s$. To obtain a useful output signal with maximum light intensity for a boresight signal, we let $m = f_0T_D$. This can be accomplished since both f_0 and T_D are design constants which are now chosen so that their product is an integer.

As a result, the principal maximum of interest is located at a "frequency" $f_p = (f_0T_D - \beta)/T_s$. The boresight signal occurs when $\theta_0 = 0$, $\tau = 0$, and $T_s = T_D$. The "frequency" of this boresight signal is given by $f_B \equiv f_p(\beta = 0) = f_0$. Note that the boresight location is independent of Doppler frequency. The frequency change from this boresight value for a target at any angle θ_0 is then

$$f_M \equiv f_B - f_p = f_0 - \frac{f_0T_D}{T_s} + \frac{\beta}{T_s} = \frac{\tau f_c}{T_D + \tau} \qquad (44)$$

Now, $\tau = (d \sin \theta_0)/c$ so that

$$\sin \theta_0 = \left(\frac{f_M}{1 - f_M}\right)\left(\frac{c}{d}T_D\right) \qquad (45)$$

Thus, the target location angle is obtained by measuring f_M in the image plane as is shown in Fig. 8 since c, d, and T_D are constants. Also, it can be shown that the resolution width Δf and the light intensity distribution in the vicinity of this first-order fringe are equivalent to the angle resolution $\Delta\theta$ and the antenna radiation pattern expressed by Eq. 23.

The following conclusions can be drawn from these derived results:

(1) Within the field of view required to include all possible location angles ($|\theta| \leq 90$ degrees), no ambiguities appear. (2) Within this field of view, all antenna beam angles appear simultaneously as a continuum in a form which is identical to the beam-forming capability of the antenna array.

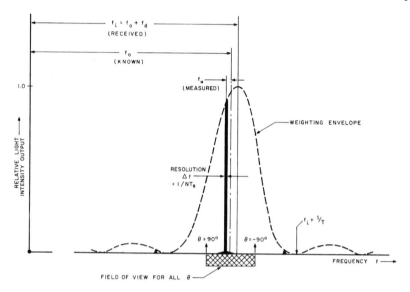

FIG. 8. Output from a time-delay multiplexed electro-optical signal processor.

(3) By measuring the location "frequency" f_M of the output signal, the physical location angle θ_0 of the target is obtained. (4) The output resolution width $\Delta f_M = 1/NT_s$ corresponds to an angle resolution $\Delta \theta$ which is the same as that obtained directly from the phased array. (5) All responses are weighted with an amplitude function centered at the frequency of the input signals ($f_i \equiv f_0 + f_d$). (6) The frequency location of the output signal is not a function of Doppler frequency.

VI. Electro-Optical Processors for Planar Phased Arrays

By combining the time-delay and the spatial multiplexing techniques in a single electro-optical device, two-dimensional angle information can be obtained. Typically, a planar array consisting of N columns and M rows is processed by employing an N channel light modulator which has each channel time-delay multiplexed M times. Such a configuration is shown schematically in Fig. 9.

Each element in the array has its signal amplified, heterodyned, and delayed. The resulting signals from each column are then summed (hence, time-multiplexed) in exactly the same manner as was previously discussed (see Fig. 7). The signal derived from the nth column of the array is fed to the nth ultrasonic transducer of the spatially multiplexed, electro-optical spectrum analyzer. The two-dimensional output response from this processor is similar to the output shown in Fig. 6, except that each ultrasonic channel is now time-multiplexed. As a result, it can be shown that the

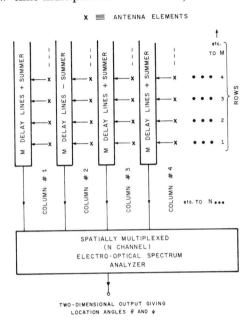

Fig. 9. Planar array processor.

output obtained in the f dimension is similar to that shown in Fig. 8. Thus, if the narrow beam dimension formed by the rows of elements in the phased array is called θ and the orthogonal angle is called ψ (formed by columns), then these angles appear at the output of the spectrum analyzer as measured values β and f_M as shown in Fig. 10. Note that since the complex transmission function is separable in x and y, we can obtain the two-dimensional light distribution by directly combining the results presented in Secs. IV and V.

As a direct consequence of the results presented in previous sections, we can conclude that: (1) All possible two-dimensional beam angles are obtained simultaneously as a continuum. (2) The angular resolution is identical to the resolution theoretically available from the antenna. (3) Multiple targets will produce multiple outputs with all angles properly associated. (4) The incremental delay between signals (τ) that is introduced by the phased array is processed so as not to result in an aperture-bandwidth constraint. (5) A two-dimensional matrix of delay lines or phase shifting networks is *not* required. (6) No ambiguities are contained within the output coverage region and the sidelobes of any output signal are identical to the sidelobes produced by the antenna. (7) Additional beam shaping

and sidelobe suppression can be directly introduced into the optical aperture in the form of shading masks and stops. (8) It can be shown that pulse
compression can be employed by transmitting a frequency-modulated
carrier and introducing variable pitch gratings into the optical subsystem

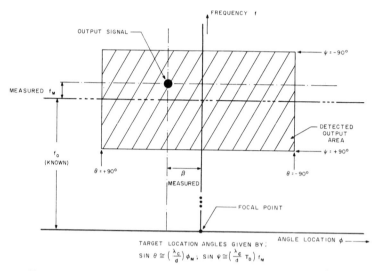

FIG. 10. Two-dimensional output from a planar array processor.

of the processor. This would, in general, require the addition of two more
lenses but would provide a time response consistent with the bandwidth of
the received signal.

VII. Experimental Results and Conclusions

A. Introduction and Past Results

In the preceding sections, a theory of operation was developed for the
electro-optical phased array processor based upon idealized system components. One of the objectives of the research program at the Columbia
University Electronics Research Laboratories has been to demonstrate the
engineering feasibility of realizing a planar array processor. These studies
have included the experimental investigation of (see References 12 to 19)
spectrum analyzers and correlators which employ coherent optics and
Debye-Sears light modulators. Results obtained from these studies have
been used to show that the time-multiplexed, *linear* array processor can
be realized in practice with a wide range of design parameters.

Typically, it can be shown that for a time-multiplexed system which
requires bandwidths of 10 Mc or less, water is the preferred delay medium
due to its low velocity of ultrasonic propagation. However, for signal band-

widths in excess of 10 Mc, amorphous quartz is the preferred delay medium due to its low acoustic attenuation at high frequencies. For example, if a square, planar array contains 10,000 elements, then 100 elements must be time-multiplexed. For a signal bandwidth of 2.0 Mc, a water delay medium can be shown to be optimum and the optical aperture must be 75 mm in order to contain the total time-multiplexed signal duration of 50 μsec. Similarly, for a bandwidth of 50 Mc, quartz is optimum and the optical aperture need be only 7.5 mm for the same 100 elements.

The problem area that will now be examined in more detail is that of obtaining a *spatially* multiplexed processor which does not degrade antenna performance. This involves the realization of a spatially multiplexed Debye-Sears light modulator which preserves the relative phase of applied signals while maintaining a bandwidth consistent with that of the received signal. Thus, we must be concerned with the characteristics of the laser light source and the optical configuration as well as the accuracy and stability of the light modulator.

B. Spatially Multiplexed Experimental System

In order to demonstrate the engineering feasibility of a spatially multiplexed configuration without incurring large equipment costs, it was necessary to compromise on the number of array elements N that were implemented into the experimental system. However, it was also important to include an experimental capability large enough to uncover clearly the major engineering problems and produce processor outputs comparable to actual phased array beam patterns. The processor capability that appeared to offer a reasonable compromise was 576 elements as produced by a 24 × 24 element square array. Also, in order to maintain an inherent capability for processing several thousand array elements, the optical configuration was designed with a 75-mm (3-in.) clear aperture.

A perspective drawing of the resulting experimental system is shown in Fig. 11 exclusive of the light source and readout mechanism. Each of these basic components will now be discussed further and typical measurements of their characteristics will be presented. Following this, we shall present some typical experimental measurements obtained with the configuration shown in Fig. 11 which demonstrate the basic properties and engineering feasibility of this electro-optical processor for phased array antennas.

1. COLLIMATION OF LASER LIGHT. The primary source of light for the experimental system was the Spectra-Physics Model 115 helium-neon gas laser which is shown schematically in Fig. 12 (left side). The laser was operated in a hemispherical resonator mode, and the resonator cavity was carefully adjusted so that only the lowest-order mode was dominant. The intensity distribution of the laser output beam was measured by scanning a 100μ slit across the beam and detecting the light with a photomultiplier. The resulting distribution is shown in Fig. 12. Also, the output power was

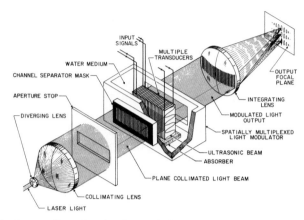

FIG. 11. System configuration for the spatially multiplexed phased array processor.

measured and found to be 4 mW at 6328 A°. To adapt this beam to the collimating lens, a 13-mm focal length negative lens was employed. This plano concave lens was located so that its focal point was coincident with the focal point of the collimating lens. As a result, the laser beam was caused to diverge and only the central region of the beam was utilized as shown in Fig. 12.

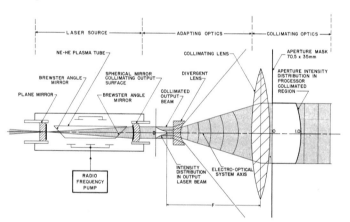

FIG. 12. Plane wave light source.

The collimating lens was a 150-mm aperture, $f/6.5$, air-spaced doublet which was restricted to a clear aperture of 70.5×35 mm by an aperture mask. As a result of restricting the aperture and employing a diverging laser beam, a more uniform intensity distribution was obtained in the collimated region as indicated on the right-hand side of Fig. 12. For the parameters just described, the phase distortion in the 70.5×35 mm collimated region was experimentally found to be due to the collimating lens rather than the laser beam.

2. Spatially Multiplexed Light Modulator. Typically, this Debye-Sears light modulator was constructed as depicted in Fig. 13. The light modulator cell consisted of a Teflon-coated rectangular aluminum container with glass windows of high optical quality on opposite ends. The transducer housing fitted into the cell as shown. This housing contained the piezoelectric crystal which was an X-cut synthetic quartz plate, ground to resonate at 20 Mc. Multiple channels were formed by plating gold sections in the form of stripes spaced 3 mm apart, each stripe being 1.5 mm wide and 10 mm long. For this experimental system, 24 channels were plated on the quartz plate and the sealed unit was immersed in distilled water contained in the cell. The base of the cell was provided with

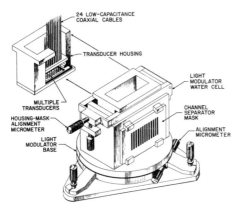

Fig. 13. Spatially multiplexed 24-channel delay-line light modulator.

micrometer adjustments to enable precise positioning of the ultrasonic beams relative to the optical axis of the light source subsystem described earlier.

By placing the cell in the region of collimated light and using a schlieren optical configuration it was possible to photograph the ultrasonic traveling waves obtained when the channels were excited with a 20-Mc sinusoidal voltage. A typical schlieren photograph for this system is shown in Fig. 14 with the multiplexed transducer and the acoustic absorber drawn in for clarity. From photographs of this type, it was possible to conclude that (*a*) separate ultrasonic beams are produced with negligible coupling between adjacent beams near the transducer surface, (*b*) the ultrasonic beams remain collimated so that over a 30-mm path length, most of the ultrasonic energy is contained in the form of a traveling plane wave, and (*c*) the striations which appear between channels are due to Fresnel diffraction and interference phenomena.

To minimize the effect of these interchannel striations on the optical transfer function, one window of the light modulator cell was modified to include the channel separator mask shown in Fig. 13. This mask consisted

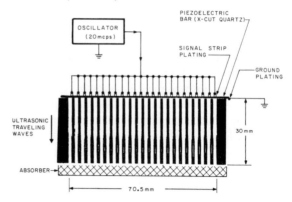

FIG. 14. Experimental schlieren photograph: the formation of 24 ultrasonic beams within the light modulator.

of the original flat glass plate which was plated and then ruled on a precision engine. An additional set of micrometer adjustments were mounted on the cell (Fig. 13) in order to permit the alignment of the transducer housing with the channel separator mask.

3. SIGNAL SIMULATOR.   The electrical signal source for this experimental system was designed to produce 24 separate sinusoidal waveforms, all coherent with each other but separately controlled in relative phase and amplitude. This was accomplished by employing the amplifier–delay-line configuration shown in Fig. 15. The signal generator was a 20-Mc oscillator which provided identical signals to each of the delay-line drivers. Each delay line was variable so that stable signals could be generated

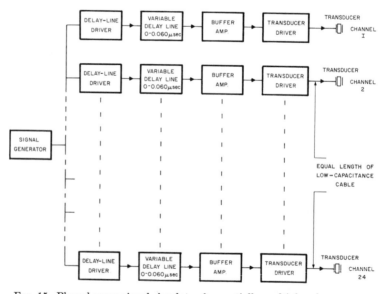

FIG. 15. Phased array signal simulator for spatially multiplexed processor.

which simulated any desired angle-of-arrival at the antenna. The buffer amplifiers and transducer driver amplifiers provided the desired gain control. Each channel maintained a 5-Mc bandwidth and could provide a 10-V rms signal across the transducer as needed for a (light) phase modulation index of 0.2 rad. The desired electrical phase of the signals at the transducers were measured with a precision phasemeter.

4. INTEGRATION AND THE IMAGE PLANE LIGHT DISTRIBUTION. For the electro-optical parameters already described, it can be shown that the area of interest in the output focal plane is centered at a point 8440μ vertically above the optical axis. This point corresponds to the 20-Mc carrier frequency of the input signals and to a target on the boresight axis of the antenna. The antenna coverage of ±90 degrees corresponds to a horizontal movement of this point by $\pm105\mu$. The half-power (3 dB) width of the fringe due to a boresight target is 7.8μ, and this corresponds to an antenna beam width of 4.2 degrees as formed by 24 array elements spaced at one-half wavelength.

Of course, additional primary maxima occur in the focal plane outside the area of interest; i.e., fringes appear at points which are $\pm210\mu$ (horizontally) removed from the boresight point and these correspond to the artificial back lobes of the antenna located at 180 degrees from boresight. There is a similar set of fringes horizontally displaced from the zero-order fringe which is always located on the optical axis.

5. READOUT SUBSYSTEM. For the experimental system, a mechanical scanner was employed in conjunction with a photomultiplier and logarithmic amplifier so that light level changes of 10,000:1 could be accurately recorded while maintaining a position error which was small compared to the 7.8μ resolution width of the fringe of interest. The readout subsystem is illustrated in Fig. 16.

A 1μ by 1-mm slit was mounted on a precision slide mechanism which,

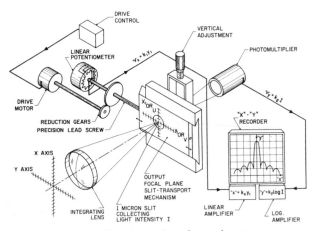

FIG. 16. Experimental readout subsystem.

in turn, was mounted on an orthogonal slide mount. The scan rate, scan width, and scan center point were all set electronically. Provision was also made for full manual control. The essential part of the slit transport mechanism was the micrometer slide which employed a lead screw with a 1-mm pitch. Attached to the lead screw was the shaft of an "infinite resolution" potentiometer with a linearity of better than 0.01 per cent. A constant voltage was applied to the fixed terminals of this potentiometer so that the wiper voltage was proportional to the position of the slit. This voltage was applied to the linear "x" amplifier of the recorder.

A photomultiplier was mounted directly behind the scanning slit, and this tube provided a 40 dB linear dynamic range. A dc amplifier inverted the polarity of the phototube output and matched the input impedance between the photomultiplier output circuit and the logarithmic amplifier. The output from the logarithmic amplifier was connected to the vertical channel (y) input of the x-y plotter. The log converter had a dynamic range of 80 dB with an accuracy of ±1 dB. This allowed the recording of light intensity over a dynamic range of 40 dB.

C. Results and Conclusions

In order to determine the basic fringe pattern produced by the light source and lens combination only, the light modulator was not excited

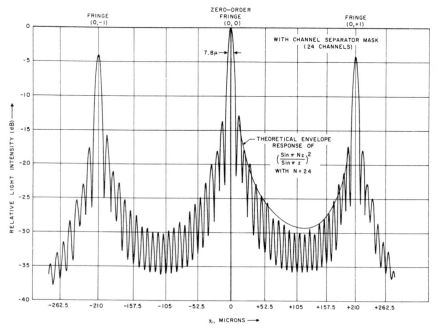

Fig. 17. Measured relative light intensity as a function of position in the vicinity of the optical axis.

and the scanning slit was set on the optical axis. By scanning horizontally along the y_1 axis (Fig. 16) the fringe pattern due to the 24-channel separator mask was obtained as shown in Fig. 17. The fine structure of the three fringes that were recorded here indicate that this portion of the system is essentially diffraction limited. The (3 dB) resolution width and the (peak) sidelobe levels are both very close to the theoretical values. However, the nulls in the vicinity of the primary maxima are not as deep as predicted by theory. A null pattern of the type shown in Fig. 17 would result if the optical system introduced a small quartic phase error across the aperture (a quadratic phase error is essentially removed by properly focusing the system). Additional experiments showed that this error was due to the lenses rather than the laser, and theoretical calculation showed that these results were essentially consistent with lens spherical aberration of the order of one-tenth of a wave.

Using the result shown in Fig. 17 as a standard for this particular optical system, the spatially multiplexed light modulator was excited and the scanning slit was shifted vertically 8440μ (along x_1 in Fig. 16) and scanned horizontally (parallel to y_1) to obtain the fine structure of the positive first-order fringe. A typical measured response pattern is shown in Fig. 18

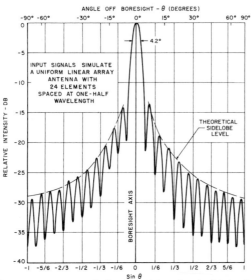

FIG. 18. Measured output response for a boresight signal obtained by exciting all transducers in parallel.

for the special case in which all 24 transducers were fed in parallel. Here, the electrical phase and amplitude of all electrical input signals are identical so that any significant phase or amplitude errors introduced by the light modulator would appear as changes in the fine structure of the first-order fringe pattern. Since this experimental result showed a mainlobe and side-lobe response which was essentially identical to the zero-order response, it was concluded that the light modulator does not additionally introduce significant amplitude or phase errors across the aperture.

Figure 19 shows the same fringe when the light modulator input signals were fed from the signal simulator. In this test, the input signals to each

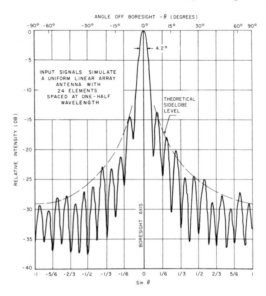

FIG. 19. Measured output response for a boresight signal obtained by exciting trans-ducers separately from the signal simulator.

channel were adjusted to be in phase and of equal amplitude so as to simulate the signal obtained from a linear array antenna for a target on the boresight axis. The resulting output response (shown in Fig. 19) was such that the 3-dB width of the mainlobe and the envelope of the sidelobes was essentially ideal. However, the sidelobes showed some irregularity in intensity which was indicative of small random type errors introduced in setting the phases and amplitudes of the input signals. Figure 20 shows the system response to a target located 19.5 degrees off the boresight axis. This result was obtained by setting appropriate phase shifts between adja-cent channels with the variable delay lines contained within the simulator. Note that here also a random phase error exists but the sidelobe peaks deviate only 1 or 2 dB from the theoretical sidelobe level. Additional results (not shown here) were obtained for signals simulating target locations over a range of ±90 degrees. These results indicated that a stable, nearly ideal, beam width and sidelobe response was obtained for this electro-optical processor.

Since modern phased array antennas employ some form of aperture weighting for sidelobe suppression, it is of interest to examine the spatially multiplexed system response under this condition. The electro-optical processor is capable of introducing amplitude weighting across the antenna aperture either by using a longer focal length for the diverging lens or by

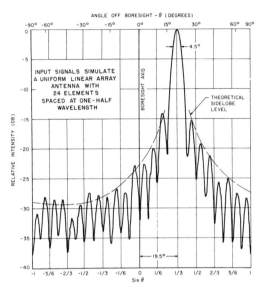

FIG. 20. Measured output response for a signal 19.5 degrees off boresight as set by the signal simulator.

setting the gain of each driver amplifier. Changing the focal length of the diverging lens results in the utilization of a greater portion of the laser beam. Unfortunately, for the laser employed here, this also introduced additional phase errors in the collimated region and the maximum sidelobe suppression obtained was only 20 dB.

An improved result was obtained by using the shorter focal length diverging lens and obtaining the desired amplitude weighting by setting the gain of each driver amplifier individually. The resulting light intensity distribution across the optical aperture is shown in Fig. 21. Here, the aperture was weighted in accordance with a Hamming type function having a pedestal intensity of 0.02. The measured results show the actual diffracted light intensity for each channel as set by properly adjusting the gain settings of the amplifiers used to drive the piezoelectric crystal strips. The results obtained by scanning the output focal plane in the vicinity of the first-order fringe is shown in Fig. 22 for a boresight signal. A peak sidelobe level of −25 dB was obtained which is 9 dB above the theoretically predicted value. It should be noted that this result is consistent with the depth of the second null shown in Fig. 17. Thus, the phase errors introduced by the lenses prevent complete sidelobe suppression. Furthermore, since

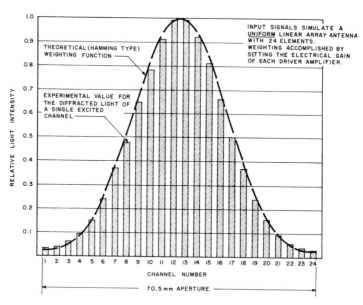

FIG. 21. Measured relative diffracted light intensity across the aperture for sidelobe suppression of signals obtained from a uniform array antenna.

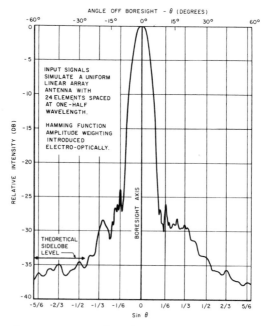

FIG. 22. Measured output response for a boresight signal from a uniform array with sidelobe suppression introduced within the processor.

these errors are fixed, it is possible to compensate their effect by introducing an opposing phase within the transducer driver amplifier. Such a technique is now being perfected and preliminary results indicate that the maximum sidelobes can be reduced to −30 dB below the peak. Of course, compensation of this type would not be necessary for a lens configuration with phase errors no greater than 1/20th of a wave.

From these results, it can be concluded that both the time-multiplexed and the spatially multiplexed processors for linear arrays are feasible. With improved lenses (1/20th wave), sidelobe suppression of at least 30 dB can be obtained so that the processor will not limit antenna resolution or discrimination capability. Also, signal bandwidths and the number of antenna elements that can be processed are consistent with modern system requirements. Engineering research efforts are continuing so as to demonstrate planar array processing using these basic techniques.

ACKNOWLEDGMENTS

This research is sponsored by the Advanced Research Projects Agency of the Department of Defense and is currently administered by the Air Force Office of Scientific Research under contract AF49(638)-1113. The authors would also like to acknowledge the help and advice given by Dean Lawrence H. O'Neil, Director of the Columbia University Electronics Research Laboratories and by Dr. Samuel Rabinowitz. For their assistance in designing and constructing many of the system components we thank Kurt Weil, David Brown, and Norman Wyman.

REFERENCES

1. ABBE, ERNST, *Arch. Mikroskop. Anat.*, *9*, 413 (1873).
2. BORN, M., AND E. WOLF, *Principles of Optics*, Pergamon Press, New York, 1959.
3. ELIAS, P., D. GREY, AND D. ROBINSON, "Fourier Treatment of Optical Processes," *J. Opt. Soc. Am.*, *42*, 127–134 (February 1952).
4. RHODES, J. E., JR., "Analysis and Synthesis of Optical Images," *Amer. J. Phys.*, *21*, 337–431 (May 1953).
5. CHEATHAM, T. P., AND A. KOHLENBERG, "Optical Filters—Their Equivalence to and Differences from Electrical Networks," *IRE Nat. Conv. Record*, 1954.
6. O'NEIL, E. L., "Spatial Filtering in Optics," *IRE Trans. Inform. Theory*, *IT-2*, 56–65 (June 1956).
7. CUTRONA, L. J., E. N. LEITH, C. J. PALERMO, AND L. J. PORCELLO, "Optical Data Processing and Filtering Systems," *IRE Trans. Inform. Theory*, *IT-6*, No. 3, 386–400 (1960).
8. HOWELL, B. J., "Optical Analog Computers," *J. Opt. Soc. Am.*, *49*, No. 10 (October 1959).
9. WILMOTTE, R. M., *Ultrasonic Spectrum Analyzer, Final Report: Summary and Recommendations*, Report 14, Raymond M. Wilmotte, Inc., AD 88698, 20 December 1955.

10. DEBYE, P., AND F. W. SEARS, "On the Scattering of Light by Supersonic Waves," *Proc. Natl. Acad. Sci., 18*, No. 6, Washington, D.C., (15 June 1932).

11. LUCAS, R., AND P. BIQUARD, "Nouvelles Proprietés Optiques des Liquides Soumis a des Ondes Ultra-sonores" (New Optical Properties of Liquids Excited by Ultrasonic Waves), in French, *Compt. Rend.*, 194 (1932).

12. LAMBERT, L., M. ARM, AND I. WEISSMAN, *Development of a Two-Dimensional Filter*, Technical Report P-2/153, Electronics Research Laboratories, School of Engineering and Applied Science, Columbia University, July 1959.

13. LAMBERT, L., "Wide-Band, Instantaneous Spectrum Analyzers Employing Delay-Line Light Modulators," *IRE Nat. Conv. Record, 10*, Part 6 (March 1962).

14. LAMBERT, L., AND M. ARM, "Electro-Optical Transfer Characteristics of Liquid Delay-Line Light Modulators," *IRE Intern. Conv. Record, 10*, Part 6 (March 1962).

15. LAMBERT, L., W. KONIG, AND M. ARM, "Electro-Optical Spectrum Analyzers and Correlators Employing Ultrasonic Delay Lines," *Institute of Radio Engineers Symposium of the Professional Group of Ultrasonic Engineers, Part A* (November 1962).

16. LAMBERT, L., "Electro-Optical Correlation Techniques," *Textbook of Modern Radar Techniques*, John Wiley & Sons, Inc., New York (in print).

17. LAMBERT, L., AND W. KONIG, *Research on Ultrasonic Delay Lines*, Progress Reports P-1/152, P-2/152, P-3/152, P-4/152, P-5/152, Electronics Research Laboratories, School of Engineering and Applied Science, Columbia University, 1959 through 1961.

18. LAMBERT, L., AND W. KONIG, "The Bandwidth, Insertion Loss and Reflection Coefficient of Ultrasonic Delay Lines," *IRE Intern. Conv. Record*, PGUE, New York (March 1961).

19. Lambert, L., and W. Konig, "The Effects of Bonding and Backing Materials on the Characteristics of Ultrasonic Delay Lines," *WESCON Conv. Record*, August 1961.

20. RAMAN, C. V., AND N. S. NATH, "The Diffraction of Light by High Frequency Sound Waves," *Proc. Ind. Acad. Sci.*, "Part I: Normal Incidence," Sec. A, *2*, 406 (1935); "Part II: Oblique Incidence," Sec. A, *2*, 413 (1935); "Part III: Time Variations," Sec. A, *3*, 75 (1936); "Part IV: General Periodic Wave," Sec. A, *3*, 119 (1936); "Part V: Oblique Incidence," Sec. A, *3*, 459 (1936); "Generalized Theory," Sec. A, *4*, 222 (1936).

21. BHATIA, A. B., AND W. J. NOBLE, "Diffraction of Light by Ultrasonic Waves, I: General Theory," *Proc. Roy. Soc. (London) A200*, 356–368 (8 December 1953); "II: Approximate Expressions for the Intensities and Comparison with Experiment," *A200*, 369–385 (8 December 1953).

22. PHARISEAU, P., "The Diffraction of Light by Ultrasonic Waves," *Simon Steven, 33*, No. 2, 72–78 (June 1959).

CHAPTER 39

THEORETICAL AND EXPERIMENTAL FOUNDATIONS OF OPTICAL HOLOGRAPHY (WAVEFRONT RECONSTRUCTION IMAGING)*

G. W. *Stroke*

The University of Michigan, Ann Arbor, Michigan

Introduction

Recent developments have generated a new interest in extensions of the wavefront reconstruction method first described by D. Gabor in 1948.[1,2]

It now appears possible to describe conditions under which an "x-ray microscope" might indeed be made to work so as to produce from x-ray holograms images which would be "true" well-resolved pictures of crystals, proteins, and molecules.

A great deal of work has been devoted to wavefront reconstruction since 1948.[1-22] Much progress has been made in developing methods for superposing the coherent background on the field scattered by the object, and for obtaining well-separated reconstructed "wavefronts" and "images." By and large, the optimism and foresight expressed by Gabor in his 33-page paper in the 1949 *Proceedings of the Royal Society* have appeared to be justified in the 15-odd years which have followed his work.[1-5]

It now appears that some of the principles required for new extensions of wavefront reconstruction methods may require additional clarification.

It is the purpose of this paper to discuss the theoretical and experimental principles of wavefront reconstruction imaging, as they now appear, in the light of new theoretical and experimental evidence. Four advances, two experimental and two theoretical, may be particularly singled out.

1. The successful reconstruction of wavefronts scattered from three-dimensional macroscopic scenes illuminated with 6328 Å laser light.

* This paper is the result of a collaborative effort with David G. Falconer.

2. The attainment by "lensless" wavefront reconstruction of greatly magnified ($\simeq$150 $\times$) microphotographs of biological samples, illuminated in 6328 Å laser light without the aid of any auxiliary lenses.

3. The new theoretical evidence, which we indicate, that considerably greater resolving can be obtained with x-ray holograms then had in the past been considered possible. Real rather than "empty" magnifications on the order of 1 million and more appear attainable, and should permit one to obtain the highly resolved x-ray pictures which have been sought.

4. The simple interpretation of the spatial and temporal coherence requirements, which led to the three-dimensional laser holograms, and which is necessary for the extensions of the method to such problems as x-ray microscopy.

It might be in order to recognize Gabor's unique role in introducing a new method of image formation in optics.[1-5] In analogy with photography, where lenses are used to form images, we suggest "holography" as the description for a process where holograms are used as aids in image formation.

I. Background and Experimental Foundations

The term "wavefront reconstruction" refers to a process in which the amplitude and phase of a scattered electromagnetic wavefront is recorded (usually photographically) together with a suitable coherent background in such a way that it is possible to produce at a later time a reproduction of the electromagnetic field distribution of the original wavefront. The coherent background is necessary for the separation of the "reconstructed" wavefront from the rest of the field scattered by the hologram. The various wavefront recording methods differ by the manner in which the coherent background is supplied, although the general idea of introducing a coherent background may be shown to be directly related to the methods introduced by Frits Zernike in 1934 with specific application to phase-contrast microscopy.[24-27]

Much similarity can be found between the manner in which the "phase" in the scattered field is recorded in a hologram, on one hand, and the manner in which the phase is being recorded in an ordinary two-beam interferogram, on the other (Fig. 1). This analogy is almost complete in the method which we use for illustration.

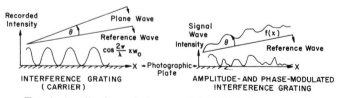

FIG. 1. Amplitude- and phase-modulated interference grating.

In fact, it can be readily shown[22] (Fig. 2 and Fig. 4) that an "interference grating" is formed on the photographic plate, both in the case of a two-beam interferogram (Fig. 2), and in the case of a hologram (Fig. 4) where the "background" or "reference" wave is made to fall at a suitable angle

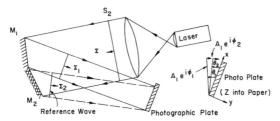

FIG. 2. Recording of hologram (modulated interference-fringe grating) for the case of a plane-wave generating object (M_1).

on the plate, with respect to the scattered wave. In the case of a plane scattered wave (such as that reflected by a mirror) and a plane background wave (Fig. 2), the "hologram" or "interferogram" is simply formed of a grating with sinusoidally varying, spatial straight-line interference fringes.

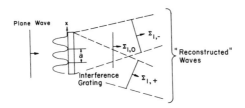

FIG. 3. Reconstruction of plane wave from hologram of Fig. 2.

When this "grating," forming the hologram, is illuminated by a "plane" wave (Fig. 3), it will produce by diffraction a set of plane diffracted waves, which are readily seen to be the "reconstructions" of the originally plane "scattered" wave.

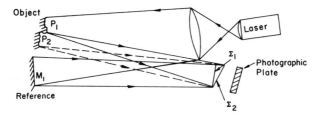

FIG. 4. Recording of hologram in case of a three-dimensional object.

In the case of a scattered wave containing both amplitude and phase variations, the fringes in the "hologram" will still form a "grating" in the general sense (Fig. 4). The fringes in the grating will be suitably modulated in position and in intensity, according to the distribution of the electromagnetic field in the scattered wave near the photographic plate. When the "modulated interference-fringe grating" is now illuminated by a plane wave, it will reproduce, in two *distinct* sets of diffracted waves, precisely the phase and amplitude modulations which were present in the original scattered wave at the plate. An observer "looking" at one of the diffracted waves would "see" the same object which he would have seen by looking at the waves scattered by the original object. The other wave has the property of actually forming a real image of the object without the aid of any auxiliary lenses.

Interference and diffraction principles of gratings are not only basic, but sufficient to explain the physical aspects of wavefront reconstruction.[22,23] It may frequently appear convenient to visualize the generalized holograms as "modulated interference gratings," or as "diffractograms."

The Fresnel-zone plate interpretation of some aspects of holography was already recognized by Gabor,[1,2] and later clarified by several authors, among whom are Rogers[6] and El-Sum.[14]

For the purposes of clarity we shall briefly review those elements in the theory which are required for the further development of the theory which we present.

II. Theoretical Foundations

Strictly speaking, rigorous electromagnetic theory of scattering, diffraction and polarization is required for an exact treatment of holography. Under the conditions discussed elsewhere,[23] the "physical optics" approximations used in this paper are generally found to be sufficient.

Let Σ_2 be a wavefront, such as that scattered by an illuminated object (Fig. 4). Then the complex amplitude of an electromagnetic wavefront may be decomposed into two parts: its magnitude $A(x)$ and its phase $\phi(x)$, each of which is essential to the structure of the wavefront. In order to be able to reconstruct this wavefront at a later time, care must be taken to lose neither the magnitude nor the phase of the scattered amplitude during the recording process. The magnitude, or rather some power of it, can be captured by simply photographing the wavefront; however, the phase is invariably lost in such a process, since photographic emulsions are sensitive only to the absolute value of the scattered amplitude. Fortunately, there exist several methods for recording the phase as well as the magnitude of a scattered wavefront.

Perhaps the best-known methods for recording the phase in a wavefront are the methods of *two-beam interferometry*. For instance, it is possible to photograph the phase distribution in a wavefront diffracted by a ruled optical grating (Fig. 5) by means of the interferometer shown in (Fig. 6). The spatial displacements of the interference fringes in the interferogram

FIG. 5. Diffracted wavefront interferogram of a 200 groove/inch echelle grating, according to Stroke [*J. Opt. Soc. Am.*, *45*, 30 (1955)]. Note characteristic Fresnel-diffraction images produced by the individual grating grooves (the grooves are orthogonal to the interference fringes shown). The phase increases by 600 × 2π from groove to groove here, plus or minus the small phase differences resulting from irregularities in the positioning of the grooves. Holograms are basically similar to diffracted wavefront interferograms.

are linearly related to the phase distribution in the diffracted wavefront one fringe spacing corresponding to 2π. Using this interferogram, it is possible to reconstruct the diffraction pattern, either empirically, or by Fourier-transform computation (Fig. 7). Many other two-beam interferometer systems are known to permit similar recordings of the phase in a wavefront. It may suffice to recall the Lloyd mirror, the Fizeau interferometer, the Michelson, Twyman-Green interferometer, and so on. Heterodyning methods, using lasers, also have many points in common with two-beam interferometry.[22]

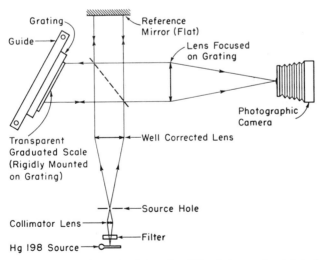

FIG. 6. Interferometer used in obtaining the diffracted wavefront interferogram of Fig. 5.

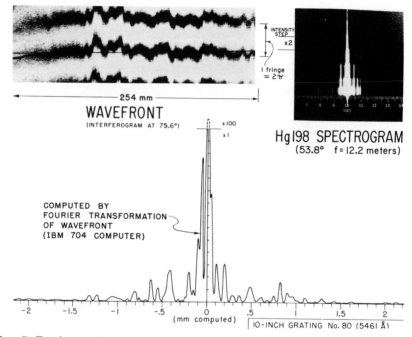

FIG. 7. Fourier-transform computation of point-source image (diffraction pattern) corresponding to diffracted wavefront interferogram of a 300 groove/mm grating shown. The spectrogram of the green line (5461 Å) of Hg 198 is shown. See G. W. Stroke, *J. Opt. Soc. Am.*, *51*, 1321 (1961).

An important method of recording both the amplitude and the phase distribution in scattered wavefronts was introduced by Frits Zernike in 1934 in connection with microscopy.[24–27] Zernike's method of phase-contrast microscopy is based on bringing a suitably phased and attenuated background to interfere with the wavefront scattered by the object, the interference taking place before the recording. The coherent background originates in the object itself, and is in fact nothing but the "undiffracted" portion of the field scattered by the object (Fig. 8). The coherent background is superposed on the widely scattered field, produced by small-size object regions in the object. The superposition as it occurs in the Fourier

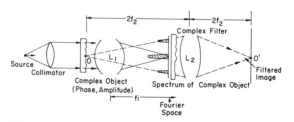

FIG. 8. Phase-contrast imaging according to Zernike.

space before the second imaging by the lens L_2, is shown in Fig. 8. The entire process then amounts to a *one-step* imaging process. The role of the complex filter in the Fourier space is to suitably shift the phase and to attenuate the generally strong coherent background with respect to the field scattered by the small object regions under study. Principles similar to those illustrated in Fig. 8 are basic to the methods of spatial filtering, originated by Maréchal in 1953,[28] and developed by many authors.[29-31]

In a general sense, the two-step hologram imaging process introduced by Gabor was already noted by him to have some significant basic similarities with Zernike's phase contrast microscopy.[2] As in Zernike's method, the coherent background is introduced by means of scattering from the object itself. The important difference between the two methods results from Gabor's successful prediction and demonstration that the "diffractogram" or "interferogram" obtained by interference between the background and the scattered light can in fact be first photographed and subsequently used to form an image by a second diffraction, rather than proceeding directly from the "diffractogram" to the image, as in the method by Zernike.

Unfortunately, the in line or forward introduction of the coherent background in Gabor's method has proven to be a basic limitation in some applications of optical holography, in that radiation from the "twin image" interferes with the reconstructed wavefront, and hence reduces its fidelity with respect to the original wavefront. This is a very serious problem when actual image formation is desired, for instance in photography and microphotography. A method for eliminating the difficulties associated with the twin images was hinted at by Gabor in the conclusion of his original (1949) paper,[2] and was subsequently developed by Lohmann[18] in 1956 in direct reference to wavefront reconstruction work as well as by Cutrona *et al.*[31] in 1960. Additional theoretical and experimental work, and various spectacular verifications were reported by Leith and Upatnieks[20,21] in 1963 and 1964. The method can best be described as the "interferometric wavefront reconstruction method." [22] Its physical principles as given above can be described without elaborate mathematical formulation. The various aspects of this method will be further developed in our discussion of the theoretical foundations of optical holography.

A. *The Recording Process*

The magnitude and the phase of a scattered wavefront can be recorded photographically by superposing a coherent "reference beam" or background-wave on the field striking the photographic plate. Perhaps the simplest technique for carrying out this superposition is the one illustrated in Figs. 4 and 9, wherein a plane wave illuminates a region containing a scattering object and a plane mirror[22] or simple triangular prism[20] respectively. The object, of course, diffracts the incident radiation to generate a

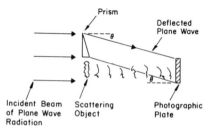

Prism

Deflected
Plane Wave

Incident Beam   Scattering   Photographic
of Plane Wave   Object   Plate
Radiation

Fig. 9. Arrangement illustrating recording of holograms (see also Figs. 2 and 4).

field with some magnitude $A(x)$ and some phase $\phi(x)$ at the photographic plate, while the prism simply turns the incident plane wave through an angle θ to contribute a field with a uniform magnitude A_0 and a linear phase variation αx, where α is a constant relating the angle θ and the wavelength λ according to

$$\alpha\lambda = 2\pi\theta \tag{1}$$

Thus the total amplitude striking the plate is

$$A_0 e^{-i\alpha x} + A(x)e^{i\phi(x)} \tag{2}$$

Hence, the intensity, i.e., the quantity to which the emulsion is sensitive, is

$$I(x) = A_0^2 + A(x)^2 - 2A_0 A(x)\cos(\alpha x + \phi(x)). \tag{3}$$

It will be noted that the phase $\phi(x)$ of the scattered wavefront has not been lost in computing the intensity, as it would be if the reference beam were not present.

The emulsion, of course, records some power of the intensity; that is, the *amplitude* transmittance $T(x)$ of the resulting photographic plate, providing one works in the linear range of the *H-D* curve, is proportional to $T(x) \propto [I(x)]^{-\gamma/2}$

$$\begin{aligned}
&= [A_0^2 + A(x)^2 - 2A_0 A(x)\cos(\alpha x + \phi(x))]^{-\gamma/2} \\
&\simeq A_0^{-\gamma-2}[A_0^2 - \tfrac{1}{2}\gamma A(x)^2 + \gamma A_0 A(x)\cos(\alpha x + \phi(x))] \\
&\propto 2A_0^2 - \gamma A(x)^2 + 2\gamma A_0 A(x)\cos(\alpha x + \phi(x)) \\
&= 2A_0^2 - \gamma A(x)^2 + \gamma A_0 A(x)e^{i\phi(x)+i\alpha x} + \gamma A_0 A(x)e^{-i\phi(x)-i\alpha x}
\end{aligned} \tag{4}$$

where γ is the slope of the *H-D* curve. It has been assumed that the intensity of the reference beam greatly exceeds that of the radiation scattered by the object, so that the approximation made in dropping the higher orders terms of the binomial expansion is justified. The photograph described by Eq. 4 is called a *hologram* after Gabor.[1,2]

There are two aspects of Eq. 4 that should be pointed out. The first involves the role of γ: Contrary to the requirements of many similar processes, neither the sign nor the exact magnitude of γ is of any consequence in the recording process; that is, making a contact print of the hologram, which is equivalent to changing the sign of γ, serves only to shift the phase of the nonconstant portion of the transmittance of an inconsequential 180°, while changing slightly the magnitude of γ serves only to enhance or to suppress the magnitude of this same portion of the transmittance. The second facet involves the relationship between $A(x)$ and $\phi(x)$: it will be noted that the magnitude $A(x)$ and the phase $\phi(x)$ of the scattered wave appear in the natural way, i.e., as $A(x) \exp[i\phi(x)]$, in the third term of Eq. 4, and with the sign of the phase reversed in the fourth term. The fact that each of these terms has been multiplied by $\exp[\pm i\alpha x]$ is a consequence of the presence of the coherent reference beam, which solves the otherwise vexing problem of the "twin" or "virtual" image.

B. *The Reconstruction Process*

With the hologram of Eq. 4 the reconstruction process is simple, involving no lens systems, schlieren disks, half-plane filters and the like. In fact, to reconstruct the original wavefront it is only necessary to illuminate the hologram with a plane wave of radiation, as illustrated in Fig. 10. As the

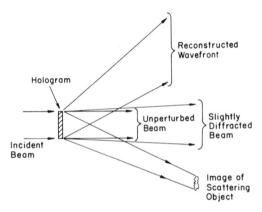

FIG. 10. Wavefront reconstruction and image formation from a hologram in case of plane-wave illumination.

plane wave passes through the photographic plate it is multiplied by the transmittance $T(x)$, producing thusly, four distinct components of radiation corresponding to four terms of Eq. 4. The first term, being a constant, attenuates the parallel beam uniformly, but otherwise does not alter it. The second term also attenuates the beam, but not uniformly, so that the plane wave suffers some diffraction as it passes through the photograph.

The patterns produced by the third and fourth terms are more complicated. To understand how they affect the incident plane wave, it is necessary to recall that a common triangular prism shifts the phase of an incident ray by an amount proportional to its thickness at the point of incidence (Fig. 11), a positive phase shift deflecting the ray upward and a negative one deflecting it downward. Thus, the third term of Eq. 4 may be interpreted as the product of the amplitude of the scattered wavefront and a positive prismatic phase shift; similarly, the fourth term of Eq. 4 may be viewed as a composite of the complex conjugate of the amplitude of the original wavefront and a negative prismatic phase shift.

By virtue of these prismatic phase shifts the third and fourth terms of Eq. 4 deflect the incident beam respectively upward and downward through

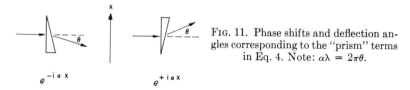

FIG. 11. Phase shifts and deflection angles corresponding to the "prism" terms in Eq. 4. Note: $\alpha\lambda = 2\pi\theta$.

an angle θ, as defined through Eq. 1. Moreover, in the case of the third term the upward deflected beam is also multiplied by the scattered amplitude $A(x) \exp[i\phi(x)]$, and hence reconstructs a copy of this wavefront. On the other hand, the fourth term multiplies the downward beam by the complex conjugate of the scattered amplitude, and hence constructs a copy of the scattered wavefront, except that it travels backward in time and consequently constructs a three-dimensional image of the scattering object. (The physical principles underlying this process are explained in the next section.)

C. *Physics of the Method*

The physical principles of the process described above can be illustrated by tracing the history of a vanishing small object through the recording and reconstruction process. This method was originally introduced by Gabor[2] and later clarified by Rogers[6–9] and El-Sum.[14]

Our approach is similar to theirs in that we suppose that the object used in the recording process is an opaque plate with a very small hole in it. When this aperture is illuminated with a plane wave it will act as a simple spherical radiator according to "Huygen's principle." Thus, the amplitude striking the photographic plate will be of the form

$$A_0 e^{-i\alpha x} + A \exp\left(i\,\frac{\pi}{\lambda f}\,x^2\right) \qquad (5)$$

where A is now some constant, λ is the wavelength of the radiation, and where f is defined in (Fig. 12). Hence according to formula 4 the trans-

FIG. 12. Hologram of a point object (pinhole aperture). Arrangement used in discussion of magnification in Sec. IID, in the discussion of Eq. 6, and in the discussion regarding Figs. 13 and 14.

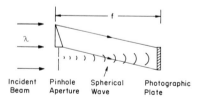

Incident Beam | Pinhole Aperture | Spherical Wave | Photographic Plate

mittance of the hologram corresponding to this elementary source will be
of the form

$$T(x) \propto 2A_0{}^2 - \gamma A^2$$

$$+ \gamma A_0 A \exp\left(i\frac{\pi}{\lambda f}x^2 + i\alpha x\right) \qquad (6)$$

$$+ \gamma A_0 A \exp\left(-i\frac{\pi}{\lambda f}x^2 - i\alpha x\right)$$

The relative simplicity of this formula together with that of the diffracting object permits one to discover the mechanism of the reconstruction
process in the following way. When the hologram described by Eq. 6 is
placed in a parallel beam three distinct components of radiation are generated, as shown in Fig. 13. The first component arises from the first two

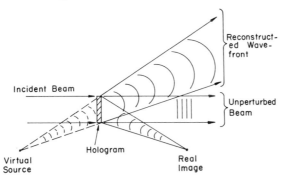

FIG. 13. Wavefront reconstruction and image formation from hologram of a point
scatterer (see Fig. 12).

terms of Eq. 6, which, being constants, uniformly attenuate the incident
waves producing another parallel beam to the right of the hologram. The
third and fourth terms produce two additional components by deflecting
the incident waves upward and downward, respectively, by virtue of the
linear phase shift in their exponents.

To understand how the quadratic phase shifts in the terms

$$\left[+\gamma A_0 A \exp\left(i\frac{\pi}{\lambda f}x^2 + i\alpha x\right)\right] \quad \text{and} \quad \left[+\gamma A_0 A \exp\left(i\frac{\pi}{\lambda f}x^2 - i\alpha x\right)\right]$$

in Eq. 6 act on the incident radiation one simply recalls that a thin spherical
lens shifts the phase of an impinging ray by an amount proportional to the
square of the distance between the optic axis and the point of incidence,
a positive phase shift describing the action of a negative lens, and a negative
phase shift describing the action of a positive lens Fig. 14. Thus, the third
term of Eq. 6 acts not only as an upward deflecting prism, but also as a
negative lens on incident radiation; i.e., an incident plane wave will be
deflected upward and given a convex spherical wavefront, and this spherical

wavefront will in fact be identical to the one which exposed the hologram. Similarly, the fourth term of Eq. 6 acts not only as a downward deflecting prism, but also as a positive lens on incident radiation; i.e., an incident beam will be deflected downward and given a concave spherical wavefront, and this spherical wavefront will in the normal way come to focus at a

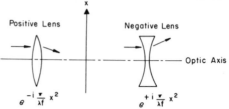

FIG. 14. Lenslike effects and phase shifts associated with terms of Eq. 6.

distance f from the hologram. Thus, in illuminating the hologram with a *plane wave* one not only reconstructs the scattered wavefront, but also obtains as a "bonus" an image of the object, which in this case was a point source. The image formation with *point-source* illumination of holograms, and the associated very considerable magnification characteristics inherent in holography are discussed in Sec. IID.

D. Magnification

A surprisingly large magnification is attainable with wavefront reconstruction systems especially if one uses a longer wavelength radiation in the reconstruction process than in the recording process. To obtain a formula for the degree of magnification we suppose that the object is again an opaque plate, but now with two identical and vanishingly small holes in it which are separated by a distance 2δ. Then, since each of the holes will act as a simple spherical radiator according to Huygen's principle, the amplitude of the wavefront at the photographic plate will be

$$A_0 \exp\left(-i\alpha x\right) + A \exp\left[i\frac{\pi}{\lambda f}(x-\delta)^2\right] + A \exp\left[i\frac{\pi}{\lambda f}(x+\delta)^2\right] \quad (7)$$

Hence, according to Eq. 4 the corresponding hologram will have a transmittance of the form

$$T(x) \propto 2A_0^2 - 2\gamma A^2\left[1 - \cos\left(\frac{4\pi}{\lambda f}\delta x\right)\right]$$

$$+ \gamma A_0 A \left\{\exp\left[i\frac{\pi}{\lambda f}(x-\delta)^2\right] + \exp\left[i\frac{\pi}{\lambda f}(x+\delta)^2\right]\right\} \exp\left(i\alpha x\right) \quad (8)$$

$$+ \gamma A_0 A \left\{\exp\left[-i\frac{\pi}{\lambda f}(x-\delta)^2\right] + \exp\left[-i\frac{\pi}{\lambda f}(x+\delta)^2\right]\right\} \exp\left(-i\alpha x\right)$$

At this point we depart from the usual method of reconstruction and use instead the system shown in Fig. 15. Here a *point source* of wavelength λ'

is used to illuminate the hologram, rather than a plane wave of wavelength λ. The fourth term of Eq. 8 still focuses the radiation from the point source according to the lens plus prism interpretation introduced in Sec. IIC.

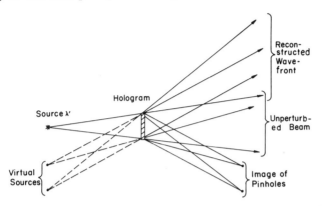

FIG. 15. Wavefront reconstruction and image formation with point-source illumination of hologram, in the case of an object formed by two point scatterers. (See also Fig. 16.)

However, since we have changed the wavelength used in the reconstruction the focal length of the "lens" will no longer be f but f', where

$$\lambda'f' = \lambda f \qquad (9)$$

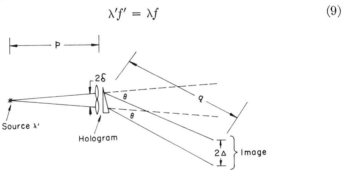

FIG. 16. Magnification property inherent in holograms. In comparing the geometry shown with Fig. 15, it should be noted that the hologram of Fig. 15 has been replaced by its equivalent lens-prism arrangement. (The central and upper beam components have been omitted for clarity.)

Of course (see Fig. 16), the object distance p will be related to the image distance q according to the classical formula, namely,

$$\frac{1}{f'} = \frac{1}{p} + \frac{1}{q} = \frac{\lambda'}{\lambda f} \qquad (10)$$

Moreover, the linear magnification M attained with this method of reconstruction will obviously be Fig. 16

$$M = \frac{2\Delta}{2\delta} \qquad (11)$$

In order to reduce this formula to one involving known parameters we observe from Fig. 16 that

$$\frac{2\Delta}{2\delta} = \frac{p+q}{p} \tag{12}$$

because of the similar triangles involved. (The prism deflects the two rays through an equal angle θ and thus does not affect the similar triangles argument.) Hence, we immediately obtain the following formula for the linear magnification:

$$M = \frac{\lambda'}{\lambda} \frac{q}{f} \tag{13}$$

In this equation, f is the distance of the original object from the hologram (Fig. 12), when photographed in the wavelength λ, and q is the distance of the hologram from the final image plane (Fig. 16), when the wavelength used in the reconstruction is λ'. This number could exceed 10^6 in applications to x-ray microscopy.

E. Resolution

It is well known that magnification alone is "empty" unless it is accompanied by a corresponding degree of resolution. As a number of writers, notably Baez[12,13] and El-Sum,[14] have pointed out a resolution capability of *conventional* projection holography[1-21] is limited ultimately by (1) to that of the photographic plate used to make the hologram and by (2) the diameter of the source used in the recording process. Since holographic recording systems are fundamentally interferometers, the source diameter and emulsion limitations enter into holography as they do into interferometry in general (see references in Fig. 6). The intensity which strikes the photographic plate in recording the hologram for a single point with a plane-wave reference beam is

$$I(x) = A_0^2 + A^2 - 2A_0A \cos\left(\alpha x + \frac{\pi x^2}{\lambda f}\right) \tag{14}$$

Now, the frequency ν of the term of interest, i.e., the third term, is a function of x since by definition

$$\nu(x) = \frac{1}{2\pi} \frac{d}{dx}\left(\alpha x + \frac{\pi x^2}{\lambda f}\right)$$
$$= \frac{\alpha}{2\pi} + \frac{x}{\lambda f} \tag{15}$$

Thus, if the emulsion used in the recording process has a resolution of N lines per unit length, the only frequencies which will register on the plate will be those which satisfy

$$|\nu(x)| = \left|\frac{\alpha}{2\pi} + \frac{x}{\lambda f}\right| \leq N \tag{16}$$

In other words, an oscillating pattern will be recorded only if x falls in the range defined by

$$-N - \frac{\alpha}{2\pi} \leq \frac{x}{\lambda f} \leq N - \frac{\alpha}{2\pi} \qquad (17)$$

where the length d of this range is obviously

$$d = 2N\lambda f \qquad (18)$$

Physically, the finiteness of this range means that the positive "lens" which brings the incident plane wave to focus in Fig. 13 has a finite diameter d. Moreover, as is well known from classical diffraction theory, the the diameter ϵ of the spot produced by a lens of focal length f and diameter d when illuminated by a plane wave is

$$\frac{\lambda}{d} = \frac{\epsilon}{f} \qquad (19)$$

Thus, in light of Eq. 18, we see that

$$\epsilon = \frac{1}{2N} \qquad (20)$$

Equation 20 applies also to the more general case where an off-axis spherical wavefront is used as a reference beam, and where the source diameter d exceeds the resolution limit $(1/N)$ of the emulsion. Indeed, with presently available pinhole sources and photographic emulsions d is of the order of $(1/N)$. Consequently, the ultimate resolution of the conventional projection wavefront reconstruction technique is seen to be approximately one-half that of the recording media. Since the best emulsions, e.g., Kodak spectroscopic plate 649 F, have a resolution of about one-half micron, the conventional projection wavefront reconstruction technique is limited to resolutions to the order of somewhat above one micron independently of the wavelength used in the recording process. However, our recent theoretical investigations[32] have revealed that considerably higher real resolutions may be attainable in certain cases where resolution-preserving methods of recording are employed.[32] Attainment of high resolutions in holography is discussed in our Reference 32.

F. Temporal Coherence Requirements

Simple interferometric considerations[22] readily show that a primary coherence requirement in holography is that the source be a steady-state source over the range of extreme path differences between the object and background. In fact, the term "coherent" background implies this condition. The degree of temporal coherence required to carry out the recording of the hologram may be determined by a simple argument. In order that the interference pattern produced by the superposition of the reference beam and the scattered waves not be destroyed, it is necessary to arrange the prism, object, and photographic plate in such a way that the maximum

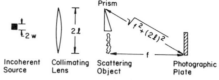

Incoherent   Collimating   Scattering   Photographic
Source   Lens   Object   Plate

FIG. 17. Geometry used in discussion of spatial and temporal coherence requirements in holography.

path difference between any two interfering waves will be less than, say, a quarter of the coherence length of the radiation. Now, according to Fig. 17 the maximum path difference in this arrangement is approximately

$$f - \sqrt{f^2 + (2l)^2} \sim \frac{2l^2}{f} \tag{21}$$

where l is a measure of the dimensions of the object. Thus, since the coherence length is equal to $\lambda^2/4\pi \, \Delta\lambda$, where $\Delta\lambda$ is the rms bandwidth about the central wavelength λ, we obtain the condition

$$\frac{2l^2}{f} < \frac{1}{4} \cdot \frac{\lambda^2}{4\pi \, \Delta\lambda}$$

or

$$32\pi l^2 \, \Delta\lambda < f\lambda^2 \tag{22}$$

G. *Steady-State Coherence Requirements*

The "coherence" requirements just discussed must exist between the coherent background on one hand, and each object point (i.e., re-radiator point) on the other. Unlike some arguments which have been made to this effect, the relative phase difference between the various object points calls for no special requirements. Accordingly, one can, for instance, illuminate the "object" through a stationary or moving diffusing glass or other diffusor, if desirable, provided only that the reference background is indeed a continuous wave (for example, plane or spherical) as shown above. The three-dimensional holograms (Figs. 19 and 20) made following these and other relevant considerations[22] have indeed permitted the successful verification of the various holography principles which we discuss in this paper.

III. Summary and Results

The theoretical and experimental foundations of holography are implicit in the discussions of the previous sections. We recall here for clarity the principles involved, notably:

1. Interferometry.
2. Diffraction gratings.
3. Phase-contrast methods using coherent background.
4. Coherence requirements.

 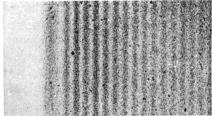

Fɪɢ. 18. Interference fringes at x-ray wavelengths (*b*) illustrating likelihood of success of x-ray holographic microscopy. Interference fringes produced with Lloyd's mirror. Figures 18 *a* and *b* according to F. A. Jenkins and H. E. White, *Fundamentals of Optics*, McGraw-Hill Book Company, New York (1957). (*a*) Taken with visible light λ = 4358 Å (after White). (*b*) Taken with x rays, λ = 8.33 Å (after Kellström[34]).

In view of extensions, such as the x-ray domain, it is important to note that the interferometric criteria permit an *a priori* evaluation of the likelihood of success of a holography method, provided that suitable experimental evidence is available.

In Fig. 18 we show, according to Kellström,[34] interference fringes produced with λ = 8.33 Å x rays, by means of a Lloyd's mirror system. Such

Fɪɢ. 19*a*. Images of three-dimensional scene reconstructed from a hologram according to Leith and Upatnieks[21] and Stroke.[22] All four images were photographed by means of a camera looking through the hologram, and so focused and inclined to reveal the three-dimensional nature of the reconstruction. (*a*) and (*b*) are photographs with small camera aperture, at two angles to show parallax. (*c*) and (*d*) are photographs with a large camera aperture, at the same angle with respect to the hologram, to three-dimensional field depth. (Holograms and reconstructions in 6328 Å laser light.)

evidence can be taken as an indication of the orders of magnitude of attainable coherence, and therefore of the attainable holograms, according to the principles discussed in the preceding section, and notably in Figs. 1 to 4.

Reconstructions of three-dimensional scenes illuminated according to the

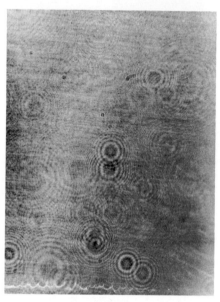

FIG. 19*b*. Hologram used in reconstruction of three-dimensional scenes, such as that of Fig. 19, according to Leith and Upatnieks[21] and Stroke.[22]

principles which we describe[21,22,32,33] are shown in Figs. 19 and 20. Holograms corresponding to the three-dimensional scenes are also shown (hologram and reconstruction in 6328 Å laser light).

A photomicrograph of a fly's wing (magnification $\cong 120 \times$) obtained by holography, entirely without lenses, according to the principles discussed in Sec. IID is shown in Fig. 20. The distance F from the source to the object was about 45 mm in this case, and the distance f from the object to the hologram about 35 mm (see Fig. 17). Exposure times used were on the order order of 5 sec, both for the hologram (649 F Kodak plate) and on the magnified reconstruction (on positive Polaroid ASA 3000 film).

IV. Electron Microscopy and X-Ray Hologram Microscopy

Some remarks may be in order concerning the possible applications of hologram microscopy, in the light of the remarkable results obtained with modern electron microscopes.

Modern electron microscopes appear to readily provide resolving powers on the order of the Angstrom (10^{-10} meter). Even the most optimistic present estimate makes it unlikely that these values would be exceeded

FIG. 20. Photomicrograph of fly's wing, obtained by holographic wavefront reconstruction imaging in 6328 Å laser light, entirely without lenses. Magnification about 120×, corresponding here to only the q/f factor in Eq. 13, giving $M = [(\lambda'/\lambda)/(q/f)]$. An additional magnification of 6328× should result when the hologram is taken say in a $\lambda = 1$ Å x-ray wavelength, and the reconstruction imaging is carried out in $\lambda' \equiv$ 6328 Å laser light. Note very remarkable resolution attained.[32]

by an x-ray hologram microscope, or for that matter by any x-ray microscope, using the wavelengths of the x rays contemplated. On the other hand, it is not at all unlikely that even these remarkable resolutions will be exceeded by future electron microscopes, and that sample-heating problems will be satisfactorily eliminated.

There are, however, several aspects in which an x-ray hologram microscope, if developed, would fill a role which cannot at the moment be filled by electron microscopes. Considerably greater penetrations without heating of the sample can be obtained with x rays than even with very-high-energy electron beams. This would be of a particular interest in areas such as metallurgy, and especially biophysics, in particular perhaps with "live" tissues and so on. It is also of interest to note that an x-ray microscope would not necessarily require a vacuum, which is a necessity in the electron microscopes. Considerably greater resolutions could be attained if the hologram technique could be extended to gamma rays.

Conclusion

In addition to the material given above, we should like to refer the reader to our Reference 32.

ACKNOWLEDGMENTS

We are greatly indebted to a number of colleagues and associates who have given us inspiration and helped us with many fruitful discussions and work, in particular Professors L. J. Oncley, S. Krimm, C. R. Worthington, Dr. H. M. A. El-Sum, as well as E. N. Leith, J. Upatnieks, and J. Winthrop. We wish to also thank Douglas Brumm and Arthur Funkhouser for continued kind assistance in the experimental aspects of this work. Figures 19 and 20 were obtained as a part of a collaborative effort between one of us (G. W. Stroke) and E. N. Leith. Finally, we should like to thank Professors W. C. Bigelow, L. J. Oncley, and Frank Denton for very fruitful discussions on the subject of electron microscopy.

REFERENCES

1. GABOR, D., "A New Microscopic Principle," *Nature, 161*, 777 (1948).
2. GABOR, D., "Microscopy by Reconstructed Wavefronts I," *Proc. Roy. Soc. (London), A197*, 454 (1949).
3. GABOR, D., *Proc. Roy. Soc. (London)*, "Microscopy by Reconstructed Wavefronts II," *B64*, 449 (1951).
4. GABOR, D., *Research, 4*, 107 (1951).
5. GABOR, D., "Generalized Schemes of Diffraction Microscopy," *Proc. Congrès de Microscopie Électronique* (1952).
6. ROGERS, G., "Gabor Diffraction Microscopy: the Hologram as a Generalized Zone-Plate," *Nature, 166*, 237 (1950).
7. ROGERS, G., *Proc. Roy. Soc. (Edinburgh)*, "Experiments in Diffraction Microscopy," *A58*, 193 (1950–1951).
8. ROGERS, G., *Proc. Roy. Soc. (Edinburgh)*, "Artificial Hologram and Astigmatism," *A63*, 193 (1952).
9. BRAGG, W., AND G. ROGERS, "Elimination of the Unwanted Image in Diffraction Microscopy," *Nature, 167*, 190 (1951).
10. HAINE, M., AND J. DYSON, "A Modification to Gabor's Diffraction Microscope," *Nature, 166*, 315 (1950).
11. HAINE, M., AND MULVY, "The Formation of the Diffraction Image with Electrons in the Gabor Diffraction Microscope," *J. Opt. Soc. Am., 42*, 763 (1952).
12. BAEZ, A. V., "A Study in Diffraction Microscopy with Special Reference to X-Rays," *J. Opt. Soc. Am., 42*, 756 (1952).

13. BAEZ, A. V., AND H. M. A. EL-SUM, "Effects of Finite Source Size Radiation Band-width and Object Transmission in Microscopy by Reconstructed Wavefronts," in *X-ray Microscopy and Microradiography*, Academic Press, Inc., New York, 1957, pp. 347–366.

14. EL-SUM, H. M. A., *Reconstructed Wave-Front Microscopy*, Ph.D. Thesis, Stanford University, November 1952; available from University Microfilms, Inc., Ann Arbor (Dissertation Abstracts 4663, 1953).

15. KIRKPATRICK, P., AND H. EL-SUM, "Image Formation by Reconstructed Wave-fronts," *J. Opt. Soc. Am.*, *46*, 825 (1956).

16. U.S. Patent No. 3,083,615, Granted 2 April 1963 (Filed 16 May 1960 by H. M. A. El-Sum, assignor to Lockheed Aircraft Corp.), *Optical Apparatus for Making and Reconstructing Holograms.*

17. EL-SUM, H. M. A., "Information Retrieval from Phase Modulating Media," in *Optical Processing of Information*, Donald K. Pollock, Charles J. Koester, and James T. Tippett, Eds., Spartan Books, Inc., Baltimore, Md., 1963, pp. 85–97.

18. LOHMANN, A., "Optische Eiseitenbandudertragung angewandt auf das Gabor-Mikroskop," *Opt. Acta*, 3, 97–99 (1956).

19. LEITH, E., AND J. UPATNIEKS, "Reconstructed Wavefronts and Communication Theory," *J. Opt. Soc. Am.*, *52*, 1123 (1962).

20. LEITH, E., AND J. UPATNIEKS, "Wavefront Reconstruction with Continuous-Tone-Objects," *J. Opt. Soc. Am.*, *53*, 1377 (1963).

21. LEITH, E., AND J. UPATNIEKS, "Wavefront Reconstruction with Diffused Illumination and Three-Dimensional Objects," *J. Opt. Soc. Am.*, *54*, 1295 (1964).

22. STROKE, G. W., *An Introduction to Optics of Coherent and Non-Coherent Electromagnetic Radiations*, Engineering Summer Conferences Text, The University of Michigan, Ann Arbor, Michigan, May 1964, 77 pages.

23. STROKE, G. W., "Diffraction Gratings," in *Handbuch der Physik*, Vol. 29, S. Flügge, Ed., Springer Verlag, Berlin and Heidelberg (in print).

24. ZERNIKE, F., "Begungstheorie des Schneidenverfahrens und seiner verbesserten Form, der Phasen Kontrast Methode," *Physica, Haag*, *1*, 43 (1934).

25. ZERNIKE, F., *Z. Tech. Phys.*, *16*, 454 (1935).

26. ZERNIKE, F., "Das Phasenkontrastverfahren bei der mikroskopischen Beobachtung," *Physik Z.*, *36*, 848 (1935).

27. WOLTER, H., "Schlieren-, Phasenkontrast- und Lichtschnittverfahren," in *Handbuch der Physik*, *24*, S. Flügge, Ed., Springer Verlag, Berlin, 1956, pp. 555–645.

28. MARÉCHAL, A., ET P. CROCE, "Un filtre de fréquences spatiales pour l'amélioration du contraste des images optiques," *Compt. Rend.*, *237*, 607 (1953).

29. ELIAS, P., "Optics and Communication Theory," *J. Opt. Soc. Am.*, *43*, 229–232 (1953).

30. O'NEILL, E. L., "Selected Topics in Optics and Communication Theory," Optical Research Laboratory, Boston University, Technical Note 133, October 1957.

31. CUTRONA, L. J., E. N. LEITH, C. J. PALERMO, AND L. J. PORCELLO, "Optical Data Processing and Filtering Systems," *IRE Trans. Inform. Theory, IT-6*, No. 3, 386–400 (June 1960).

32. STROKE, G. W., AND D. G. FALCONER, "Attainment of High Resolutions in Wavefront-Reconstruction Imaging," *Phys. Letters*, *13*, 306 (1964).

33. STROKE, G. W., Private Communications to E. N. Leith and Associates, August 1963 to November 1964.

34. KELLSTRÖM, G., "Experimentelle unterschungen über interferenz- und beugungserscheinungen bei langwelligen röntgenstrahlen," *Nov. Act. Reg. Soc. Sci. Uppsaliensis*, *8*, No. 5, (1932).

35. BRAGG, W. L., *Nature*, "A New Type of X-Ray Microscope," *149*, 470 (1942).

CHAPTER 40

CRITIQUE OF SYMPOSIUM ON OPTICAL AND ELECTRO-OPTICAL INFORMATION PROCESSING TECHNOLOGY

W. V. Smith

Thomas J. Watson Research Center, International Business Machines Corporation
Yorktown Heights, New York

I have found this a most interesting conference, and one in which I learned of new advances in some areas with which I had previously been relatively unfamiliar. It has been most worthwhile.

I shall address this critique to seeing what answers this symposium has given us to two questions: (1) Can optical devices and interconnections replace existing magnetic and electric devices and interconnections in conventionally organized computers? Are they (*a*) faster? (*b*) more compact? (*c*) cheaper? Do they consume less power, etc.? and (2) Are there particular types of data processing activities for which optical techniques are more suited than other techniques? If so, what are they and how important are they? Most important, do any of these areas have the potential for use in drastically reorganized computer designs, possibly capable of displacing conventional computers?

In considering question (1)—conventional computers—neither the results presented at this conference, nor my independent considerations of the physics involved, suggest obvious simple reasons why light is advantageous. Its speed of propagation is essentially the same as that of electrical signals on transmission lines. Also, though the concepts of optical fibers and the high resolution of photographic images suggest the possibility of compact optical systems, the ultimate resolution of the wavelength of light is actually much larger than the corresponding limit for the wavelength of electrons. We may remember that electron microscopes resolve images to a few angstroms. Indeed, Mr. Wallace's paper on electron beam readout of thermoplastic recordings served to remind us of the advances being made in this competitive technology. (I will not try to make specific comparisons —I only note that here as in other areas optical techniques must be compared realistically with other approaches to doing the same job.) Finally, the advantage of trading interconnection problems of wires or deposited metal strips for those of optical fibers is far from obvious. Indeed, we remember that Mr. Cooke-Yarborough, after analyzing an opto-electronic system that seemed potentially competitive with conventional systems from power–time constant considerations, felt that a major difficulty remaining was to achieve an optical fiber equivalent of the back panel wiring maze in conventional computers. This is not to say that optical fibers do not have important applications—only that wiring computers may not be one of them. On a more positive note, however, we were reminded by Mr. Jacobs that a single lens can serve to connect arrays of diode light emitters on a fixed one-to-one relation to arrays of detectors.

One must next proceed from generalities to specific numbers. Perhaps on detailed examination some of the specific optical devices examined may prove superior to their specific electrical counterparts. Furthermore, to be fair in the analysis, one must be prepared to allow marriages between electronic and optical devices, using the best features of each where advantages seem possible. Certainly many examples of such opto-electronic marriages have been examined in this conference. Fortunately, numerical comparisons have been included in several cases. I find Mr. Ruegg's comparisons between opto-electronic and all-electronic logic circuits particularly useful, and his conclusion that for the same time per logical decision the power required by solid-state opto-electronic circuits seems to be about two orders of magnitude greater than that required by all-electronic circuits is a sobering one. Indeed, the only examples where opto-electronic circuits were potentially competitive in this respect with all-electronic circuits were ones that utilized high power-gain stages in which electrons were accelerated in vacuum by high voltages (E. H. Cooke-Yarborough, G. B. Jacobs). Thus opto-electronic devices seem suited only to those parts of conventional computers that require optical effects, such as visible display, and we have had some interesting papers dealing with that and other input-output applications. Indeed, we may use these to compare some electro-optic and electronic approaches to similar problems by noting the attention here given to the deflection of light. It is obvious that the deflection of electron beams is far easier—an electric or magnetic field acts directly on a moving charge but only indirectly, through its effect on the polarization of a dielectric, on a light beam. It is only because one is interested in applications requiring *intense light* that one even considers deflecting beams of photons instead of beams of electrons.

Next let us consider the approach of all-optical, fairly conventional (i.e., serial) logic. Several papers have been devoted to this subject. I include the neuristor because it too is serial and can be implemented in nonoptical components. Here too, I feel that the numbers, although not presented as quantitatively at this symposium as in the case of opto-electronic logic, are unfavorable. One notes for example that those optical nonlinearities that arise from nonlinear susceptibilities—harmonic generation and frequency mixing, for example—are generally associated with giant laser pulses (megawatts). This is another example of the indirect way in which light beams interact with each other. One sometimes advances the optical isolation between two crossing light beams passing through lenses as an advantage of optical interconnections, and indeed we have already cited this example. Such weak interactions cannot simultaneously be an advantage when one tries to utilize nonlinear optical phenomena. Of course, one selects different materials for lenses than for harmonic generators. Nonetheless, the basic problem remains. Thus I question the projection of optical parametric amplification as a useful logic device.

The optical fields required to saturate optical transitions or to quench lasers are not as phenomenal as those required for parametric amplification. Nonetheless, as Mr. Kosonocky pointed out, general relations exist between the time constants of the processes involved and the fields, and these are hardly comforting if we are interested in fast devices. I agree with Mr. Kosonocky that these relations are more favorable for GaAs lasers than for neodymium glass lasers by three or four orders of magnitude, essentially because of the larger optical cross sections of the allowed optical transitions involved in the latter case. Even so, it would require considerable miniaturization to get the power per logical decision, in the nanosecond time constant range, below one watt, still far from the required goal of a few milliwatts. And there are still the problems of low-temperature operation and optical interconnections remaining. Indeed, as one of my colleagues has remarked, if we had been able to achieve an all-optical serial computer before achieving one electronically, we would very likely be grateful if someone then invented transistors, copper wire, printed circuits, etc.

Well, this is the negative side of the picture. I will now turn to the more positive aspect of considering those types of data processing for which optical techniques are more suited than other techniques. Clearly we have seen examples of such applications in several of the papers presented here. I have already mentioned the obvious categories where either input or output data are required by some particular problem to be optical in nature. I will pass on to the question of how much progress has been made in using optics as an approach to parallel organized computers, and to the somewhat related problem of using holograms and coherent light for image processing. Now I am rather inexperienced both in the fields of computer organization and hologram optical Fourier transforms. Consequently it is with considerable restraint that I refrain from a long discourse on all my recently acquired understanding of these subjects. Nonetheless, I shall analyze briefly the general problem as I see it. Masses of data, in batches, are to be sorted for relevant information. The size of the batch may be fairly small—as a single alphanumeric character—or large—as an aerial photograph. A printed page is, however, a sequence of batches for most purposes, though one could be interested merely in selecting one page from many, in which case it would be a batch. One may make the general thesis that the larger the batch, and the simpler the selection criteria (the fewer the alternatives), the more appropriate the problem is for *Fourier transform* (hologram) analysis. Also, for hologram analysis the *space location* of the unknown in the batch is neither known nor desired. If, however, one were sorting aerial photographs of a ship at sea as a target, to see how well centered they were on target, one obviously would compare pictures directly rather than as holograms. Holograms are diffraction patterns, hence, just as with familiar x-ray diffraction patterns, they reveal regularities in small-scale structure at the expense of losing large-scale structure. We remember the striking aerial photographs of parked cars in regular patterns and the hologram picture revealing the regular parking structure. If we had been interested in locating a winding road going through the parking lot, it would be lost in the hologram.

Examples were given of image processing, by parallel (coherent light) techniques or by sampling and digital analysis of the samples. The discussion following Dr. Ledley's description of digitally processing and recognizing chromosome photomicrographs emphasized the flexibility of the latter approach when the recognition criteria were difficult and requiring modification as a result of experience. Thus it seems difficult to generalize on the pros and cons of parallel versus serial image processing. It seems that both approaches have their areas of applications—parallel, essentially analog computer type processing where the recognition criteria are clear and simple, and only small amounts of data are to be retrieved from a large background of unused data, and serial processing where large amounts of complex data are to be retrieved and perhaps re-examined under changing rules of analysis. We have seen that the laser has contributed substantially to the progress achieved in coherent light image processing—and certainly the three-dimensional hologram reproductions of Leith and Upatnieks are most impressive. I project a growing future for these techniques, but not one that will seriously impact digital computer applications. I feel it is too early to comment on the possible extension of these techniques to the x-ray region as suggested by G. W. Stroke. This would be an exciting development, if feasible.

Finally, I found the discussions of adaptive learning machines interesting, but I consider them a separate subject, not restricted to the field of optical devices, and not likely to affect greatly the applications of optical and electro-optical phenomena.

In closing let me say again that I found the symposium quite worthwhile, and I wish to thank Mr. Tippett for inviting me to give this critique.

INDEX